History

of the

World Christian Movement

History
of the
World Christian Movement

Volume I: Earliest Christianity to 1453

DALE T. IRVIN
SCOTT W. SUNQUIST

ORBIS BOOKS

Maryknoll, New York 10545

Twenty-First Printing, November 2022

Founded in 1970, Orbis Books endeavors to publish works that enlighten the mind, nourish the spirit, and challenge the conscience. The publishing arm of the Maryknoll Fathers and Brothers, Orbis seeks to explore the global dimensions of the Christian faith and mission, to invite dialogue with diverse cultures and religious traditions, and to serve the cause of reconciliation and peace. The books published reflect the views of their authors and do not represent the official position of the Society. To learn more about Maryknoll and Orbis Books, please visit our website at www.maryknoll.com.

Library of Congress Cataloging-in-Publication Data

Irvin, Dale T. 1955–
    History of the world Christian movement / Dale T. Irvin, Scott W. Sunquist.
      p. cm.
    Includes bibliographical references and indexes.
    Contents: v. 1. Earliest Christianity to 1453.
    ISBN 1-57075-396-2 (pbk.)
     1. Church history. I. Sunquist, Scott, 1953– II. Title.

BR145.3 .I78 2001
270—dc21

2001041424

Contents

Foreword   vii
List of Maps   xiii
List of Illustrations   xv

PART I
INTO ALL THE WORLD
Beginnings of the World Christian Movement   **1**

1. The Civilizations and Cultures of the World   3
2. Judaism at the Time of Jesus   11
3. Christian Beginnings
   The Jesus Movement   22

PART II
DIVERSE TRAJECTORIES
OF THE EARLY CHRISTIAN MOVEMENT   **47**

4. Apostolic Memory in Several Gospels   50
5. The Early Christian Movement in Syria and Mesopotamia   57
6. The Early Christian Movement in Greece and Asia Minor   66
7. The Early Christian Movement in the Western Mediterranean   74
8. The Early Christian Movement in Alexandria and Egypt   86
9. "Every Foreign Land"   92

PART III
THE GREAT CHURCH TAKES SHAPE   **99**

10. The Great Church Emerges   102
11. Gnostics, Catholics, and Manichaeans   115
12. Christians, Jews, and Israel's Heritage of Monotheism   129
13. Spiritual Currents and Social Life across Cultures   137

PART IV
THE AGE OF THE IMPERIAL CHURCH
Affirmations and Dissent (c.300 to c.600)   **155**

14. The Conversion of Constantine and the Making
    of an Imperial Church   160

15. Donatists and Catholics
    A Struggle over Holiness and Unity in Roman North Africa   166
16. The Arian-Nicene Controversy and the Making of Orthodoxy   173
17. The Road to Chalcedon and Christological Diversity   184
18. The Christian Movement in the East
    Syria and the Emergence of a Persian National Church   195
19. Christianity in Egypt and Ethiopia   209
20. Rome and the Latin Churches in the West   220
21. The Age of Justinian and Theodora in the Eastern Roman Empire   240

PART V
NEW CHALLENGES, NEW BEGINNINGS
600 to 1000   257

22. The Land of Arabia, the Prophet Muhammad, and the Rise of Islam   260
23. The Christian Movement and the Islamic Caliphate
    Syria and Persia   271
24. The Christian Movement in Africa and Spain   289
25. Expansion of the Christian Movement in India, Central Asia,
    and China   305
26. The Making of Christendom in the West   323
27. Monasticism in the West   343
28. Christianity in the East Roman Empire   354
29. Christian Expansion Northward   372

PART VI
NEW POLITICAL HORIZONS
1000 to 1453   383

30. Controversy and Crisis in Christendom   387
31. Christendom on Crusade in the Twelfth and Thirteenth Centuries   395
32. Spiritual Renewal in Western Christendom 1100-1300   406
33. Intellectual Renewal in Western Christendom 1100-1300   423
34. Byzantium in the Thirteenth Century   440
35. Christianity in Asia under the Mongols   450
36. Egypt, Nubia, and Ethiopia   470
37. Western Christendom 1300-1450   476
38. The Christian Movement in the East until 1453   492

Index to Names of Persons and Deities   507
Index to Subjects   514

Foreword

How this book was written

The Christian movement has always been greater than any individual or local church community has imagined it to be. Its history reflects an enormous diversity of beliefs and practices over the past two millennia. Few would agree with everything that has been said or done in the name of Christianity, and indeed the history of the movement itself teems with contentions. Narrating a faithful history of the movement requires an accounting of such diversity, of the differences that have often separated various parties from one another, without reducing their common story to the perspective of one. We are compelled to bring together in a common history individuals and communities who in life often struggled to distance themselves from each another, and whose ecclesiastical descendants often remain at odds with one another today. Many of these differences arose as a result of the Christian faith crossing historical borders of language, culture, and identity. Time itself has introduced further changes in meaning, expression, and practice. The Christian movement is one that has continuously diversified itself through its expansions, all the while claiming to remain the same.

All of these factors add up to convince us that representing the history of the world Christian movement through its first two millennia must be a collaborative affair. Writing the history of this movement from a global perspective requires the insights of more than any one individual or community. With that realization in mind, the authors set about to shape these two volumes from their inception in close collaboration with a wider body of consulting scholars. The members of the consultation are listed below. They have come from Asia, Africa, Latin America, North America, and Europe; belong to Protestant, Roman Catholic, Pentecostal, and Orthodox communions; and represent the disciplines of history, missiology, theology, and sociology. Twice a year, beginning in October 1998, members of the consultation have gathered to shape the outline, review the text, and suggest revisions for the next stage. Our discussions have often moved page by page, examining the work for both its adequacy and its accuracy of representation. On points where we found disagreements in the history and in the text, the authors have endeavored to represent the various concerns and commitments voiced in the consultation process. A number of members of the consultation have provided critical resources and specific insights from their own areas of expertise and research. Several have even suggested specific wording for a paragraph or so that we have incorporated into the final text of the book. The consultation itself over the course of the past several years has taken on something of a life of its own as members have worked together and have expanded on each others' areas of interest and concern. Throughout the process we have stated that we do not expect everyone to agree with everything that is said in the final text of these two volumes. We are nevertheless extraordinarily grateful to each individual for the work that this body has undertaken as we endeavor to tell in a new way the history of the world Christian movement.

In addition to those who attended meetings, several individuals who were unable to be a part of the consultation read portions of the text and provided critical comments that proved helpful. They are identified below with an asterisk by their name. We wish to thank the Luce Foundation for its financial support of the project, through a major grant to the World Mission Initiative at Pittsburgh Theological Seminary. We also wish to thank Anne Hale Johnson and Robert B. Birge for the contributions they made to Orbis Books early in the project that made the first phase of the consultation possible. Susan Ramsey has served as the project coordinator at Pittsburgh Theological Seminary and has earned our accolades for making things work well. Our editor at Orbis Books, William R. Burrows, has played a critical role from the project's inception. It was Bill who initially brought the two authors together and helped us conceptualize the consultation process. He has participated in each of the meetings, adding his insights to those of the group and helping find the way from consultation discussions to the written page. To Bill and the other members of this consultation, we extend the thanks of ourselves and the many readers who will benefit from your having made this a much better text than we could ever have accomplished on our own.

Consultation participants

Akintunde E. Akinade
Assistant Professor of World Religions
High Point University
High Point, NC USA

Charles Amjad-Ali
The Martin Luther King Jr. Professor
    of Justice and Christian Community
Luther Seminary
St. Paul, MN USA

Ana María Bidegain
Professor of Latin American Church History
National University of Colombia
Sante Fé de Bogotá, Colombia

David Bundy
Librarian and Associate Professor
    of Church History
Christian Theological Seminary
Indianapolis, IN USA

William R. Burrows
Managing Editor
Orbis Books
Maryknoll, NY USA

Gonzalo Castillo-Cárdenas
Professor of Church and Society
Pittsburgh Theological Seminary
Pittsburgh, PA USA

John Coakley
L. Russell Feakes Memorial Professor
    of Church History
New Brunswick Theological Seminary
New Brunswick, NJ USA

David D. Daniels
Associate Professor of Church
    History
McCormick Theological Seminary
Chicago, IL USA

Donald W. Dayton
Professor of Historical Theology and
    Church History
Drew University
Madison, NJ USA

Pablo A. Deiros
Professor of History of Mission
Fuller Theological Seminary
Pasadena, CA USA
Professor of History of Christianity
International Baptist Seminary
Buenos Aires, Argentina

Frederick S. Downs
Professor of the History of Christianity
    (retired)
United Theological College
Bangalore, India

Lilian Dube Chirairo
Lecturer of African and Political
    Theology
Religious Studies, Classics and
    Philosophy Department
University of Zimbabwe
Harare, Zimbabwe

John Erickson
Professor of Canon Law and Associate
    Dean
St. Vladimirs Orthodox Seminary
Crestwood, NY USA

Victoria L. Erickson
Associate Professor of the Sociology of
    Religion & University Chaplain
Drew University
Madison, NJ USA

Douglas Jacobsen
Professor of Church History and
    Theology
Messiah College
Grantham, PA USA

Jeffrey Jones
Union Theological Seminary
New York, NY USA

Michelle Lim Jones
Drew University
Madison, NJ USA

Ogbu U. Kalu
Professor of Church History
University of Nigeria
Nsukka, Nigeria

John Kaserow, M.M.
Professor of Mission Studies
Catholic Theological Union
Chicago, IL USA

Karla Ann Koll
Professor of History, Missions and
    Religions
Latin American Biblical University
San Jose, Costa Rica, and Quetzaltenango,
    Guatemala

Klaus Koschorke
Evangelisch-Theologische Fakultät
Institut für Kirchengeschichte
Universität München
München, Germany

Sunja Kwok
Drew University
Madison, NJ USA

*Wing-hung Lam
Research Professor, Church History and
    Chinese Studies
Tyndale College and Seminary
North York, Ontario Canada

Ka Lun Leung
Professor of Church History
Alliance Biblical Seminary
Hong Kong, China

Alderi Souza de Matos
Professor of Church History
Centro Presbiteriano de Pós-Graduação
    Andrew Jumper
São Paulo, Brasil

William D. McCarthy, M.M.
Senior Researcher
Center for Mission Research and Study at
    Maryknoll
Maryknoll, NY USA

*John A. McGuckin
Professor of Early Church History
Union Theological Seminary
New York, NY USA

Melanie A. May
Vice President for Academic Life and
    Dean of the Faculty
Professor of Theology
Colgate Rochester Divinity School
Rochester, NY USA

Samuel Hugh Moffett
Henry Luce Professor of Ecumenics and
    Missions, Emeritus
Princeton Theological Seminary
Princeton, NJ USA

A. Mathias Mundadan, CMI
St. Antony's Monastery
Aluva, Kerala, India

Lawrence Nemer, SVD
President and Professor of Church
    History
Missionary Institute London
London, UK

Peter Tze Ming Ng
Associate Professor, Department of
    Religion
Chung Chi College, The Chinese
    University of Hong Kong
Hong Kong, China

Frederick W. Norris
Dean E. Walker Professor of Church
    History & Professor of World Mission
    and Evangelism
Emmanuel School of Religion
Johnson City, TN USA

J. Steven O'Malley
John T. Seamands Professor of Methodist
    Holiness History
Asbury Theological Seminary
Wilmore, KY USA

Peter C. Phan
The Warren-Blanding Professor of
    Religion and Culture
Department of Religion and Religious
    Education
The Catholic University of America
Washington, DC USA

Susan Ramsey
Pittsburgh Theological Seminary
Pittsburgh, PA USA

Luis N. Rivera-Pagán
Professor of Humanities
University of Puerto Rico
Río Piedras, Puerto Rico

Roger Schroeder, SVD
Assistant Professor of Cross-Cultural
    Ministry
Catholic Theological Union
Chicago, IL USA

Andrea Sterk
Adjunct Assistant Professor of History
University of Notre Dame
Notre Dame, IN USA

David Kwang-sun Suh
Professor of Theology, Emeritus
Ewha Women's University
Seoul, Korea

*Maureen A. Tilley
Associate Professor of Religious
    Studies
University of Dayton
Dayton, OH USA

Frans J. Verstraelen
Professor of Religious Studies
    (retired)
University of Zimbabwe
Harare, Zimbabwe

Andrew F. Walls
Honorary Professor and Curator of
    Collections
Centre for the Study of Christianity in the
    Non-Western World
University of Edinburgh,
Edinburgh, Scotland

Jean-Paul Wiest
Senior Researcher
Center for Mission Research and Study at
    Maryknoll
Maryknoll, NY USA

A note on dating conventions

Throughout this text we will be using a system of dating that was first developed by a Christian author named Dionysius Exigus around the year 530. Chroniclers of the Christian movement prior to his time had typically dated events according to the reign of various emperors and kings. Longer spans of time had been measured by adding up the reigns of these rulers sequentially, while accounts that crossed cultural or political boundaries required correlating regimes that were contemporary with one another. Dionysius suggested instead a universal system of dating that counted from the year he calculated to be the birth of Jesus Christ.

Dionysius's initial proposal was theological in nature, an assertion of the universal meaning of the incarnation in history. The idea was not quick to catch on among Christian historians. One of the first to use it was an English monk known as the Venerable Bede, whose *Ecclesiastical History of the English People* was written in 731. In time, the system became common throughout western Europe, where events were dated "in the year of our Lord" (*anno Domini*, abbreviated AD in Latin). The years before Christ (BC) were dated in reverse order so that all human history appeared to lead toward the year Dionysius calculated as being the birth of Jesus Christ, or AD 1 (there was no year 0). Ironically, many modern scholars now believe that Dionysius was off by four years in his calculations, meaning that Jesus himself might have been born around 4 BC.

The influence of western culture and scholarship upon the rest of the world in turn led to this system of dating becoming the most widely used one across the globe today. Many scholars in historical and religious studies in the West in recent years have sought to lessen the explicitly Christian meaning of this system without abandoning the usefulness of a single, common, global form of dating. For this reason the terms *common era* and *before the common era*, abbreviated as CE and BCE, have grown in popularity as designations. The terms are meant, in deference to non-Christians, to soften the explicit theological claims made by the older Latin terminology, while at the same time providing continuity with earlier generations of mostly western Christian historical research. Others have noted, however, that it remains an implicitly Christian system for dating world history.

The text that follows is an explicitly Christian history. At the same time the authors acknowledge current scholarly practice. For this reason we will use where necessary in volume one the abbreviations "CE" and "BCE." We would like to suggest, however, that these abbreviations stand for "Christian era" and "before the Christian era."

A note on references

Early in the consultation process, we made a decision to keep notes to a minimum. The reader will find them only to cite the sources of direct quotations. We have sought in these cases to use standard published English translations of primary works, although we have resorted to our own translation from time to time when we found published translations inadequate.

Members of the consultation decided, given the enormous amount of material that was being covered, and the amount of secondary material being drawn upon by all who were involved, that attempting to document every primary or secondary source of information would overburden the book and readers alike. A number of participants read all or part of the text at various stages of its writing and production. They offered a phrase here, a sentence there, or a correction in detail in another place. They also noted that the ideas of one or another historian whom we had not used were more relevant on a particular page. It would be impossible to document everything in this dynamic process. The consultation members themselves, in the course of our three years of conversation together, became the critical apparatus for the book, checking facts, forging interpretive insights, and debating the positions of various schools of thought.

The process explains our procedure in listing only a few bibliographical references for each part of this volume. We have not attempted to provide a comprehensive listing of the secondary sources that were consulted in our research, or drawn upon in the course of the consultation meetings, or sent to us between consultations. This kind of bibliography would have to be annotated with comments on how and why our interpretations differ from or add to standard sources, and such a bibliographical listing would itself become volume length.

We do provide an introductory list of works at the end of each major part for further reference as an aid to the reader who would like to go on. We have attempted to list works that are readily available and in English. We look forward to the contributions others will make in their research and writing in other languages and from other parts of the globe. For now, we offer our resources and insights as a small contribution to the project of remembering the global past of the world Christian movement.

List of Maps

The chief cities of the world near the beginning of Christianity   6-7

The world where Christianity arose—Asia Minor, Israel, and Syria   31

The boundaries and chief jurisdictions of the Roman empire
    in the year 300   104

Principle cities and regions of Christianity by the beginning
    of the seventh century   157

Arabic-Islamic empire and the Christian world circa 900   256

Central Asia, China, and India   306

Centers of European Christendom, circa 600-1000   325

Approximate areas of predominant world religions,
    circa 1450   468-69

List of Illustrations

Jesus the Good Shepherd, Catacomb of Callista, Rome, 3rd century.　　27

Reconstruction of the baptistry in the church at Dura Europos
　　in Syria, ca. 240 C.E.　　59

Jesus as Philosopher, Catacomb of Domitilla, Rome, 3rd century.　　119

Constantine the Great, bust from Constantinople, 4th century.　　161

Crescentia, a 5th century child from Tabarka, North Africa.　　170

Crucifixion and the Women at the Tomb, illustration from the
　　Rabula Syriac Gospels, from Zagba on the Euphrates, ca. 586.　　205

Ansate Cross, from Coptic Acts of the Apostles, Middle Egypt,
　　5th century.　　211

Christ Enthroned with Madonna and Child and Saints. Fresco
　　from church in Baduit, Egypt, 6th century.　　211

Mosaics of Justinian and Theodora, early 6th century.
　　San Vitale Church, Ravenna, Italy.　　242

Mar Saba monastery in the Kidron Valley east of Bethlehem,
　　as it appears today.　　275

Copper plate charter for Christians in Kerala, South India.　　308

Scene from mural of church at Kocho, near Turfan oasis.　　309

Stone monument at Xi'an with inscription recording Christianity
　　in T'ang dynasty, China.　　316

Crowning of Charlemagne, illumination from the manuscript
　　"History of the Emperor."　　335

Abbey of Cluny monastery and tower as they appear today.　　352

The Giralda tower in Seville.　　399

The Cathedral of Notre Dame de Paris as it appeared in the 16th century.　　429

Self-portrait of Hildegard of Bingen inspired by divine fire,
from the pages of *Scivias*.   438

Icon of St. Sava, first Serbian archbishop, from the Serbian monastery
on Mount Athos.   446

Church of St. George, one of the churches at Lalibela in Ethiopia
hewn from living rock, 13th century.   472

Photograph of 14th century edition of John Wycliffe's English translation
of the Bible.   487

Hagia Sophia as it appears today.   497

Part I

INTO ALL THE WORLD

Beginnings of the World Christian Movement

T wo thousand years ago in the land of Israel in western Asia, a man named Jesus of Nazareth began to gather around him a small group of followers. For a short time (perhaps only a year or two) he carried on an itinerant ministry of healing, exorcism, and preaching in the region around the Sea of Galilee and in the vicinity of the city of Jerusalem. His message was directed primarily to the outsiders of his society, including the poor and the disabled. They were to be first in the coming age when God would rule over all the earth, he said. At least some among those who heard him and became his disciples saw in him the fulfillment of their national hopes for Israel. They identified Jesus as the Messiah (Hebrew for "anointed one," later translated into Greek as "Christ") whom they expected to come and set the people free. A demonstration he staged against the Temple in Jerusalem during the season of Passover led to Jesus' arrest by the authorities in the city. Like others around whom messianic expectations had swirled, Jesus was judged to be not only a religious deviant, but a political threat. He was crucified on the order of the Roman governor of Judea, Pontius Pilate, around the year 30 CE.

Pilate's execution did not bring about an end to the movement. Soon after Jesus' death, his disciples began to proclaim that he had appeared to them in person. Through the power of the Spirit, they said, God had raised him from the dead, vindicating both the person and message of Jesus. A new messianic age had thus begun, accompanied by signs and wonders of the Spirit of God. It was an age in which the crucified Jesus was now regarded as Lord and Savior over all, for in his resurrection he was seen to transcend human limitations of geography and culture. Members of the band were soon able to put this belief into practice. Dispersed from Jerusalem by persecution, a number took refuge in other cities of the region where they continued to spread the message of the risen Messiah. The movement grew, attracting not just other Jews but non-Jews, or Gentiles, as well. The Gentiles brought with them new expectations and understandings, expanding the meaning of the risen Christ beyond the definition given to him by his original followers in Israel.

1

The book of Acts provided the early Christian movement with a compelling symbol of its expanding cultural and linguistic boundaries. According to Acts 2, the disciples had gathered in Jerusalem shortly after Jesus' resurrection. It was the day of Pentecost, or the Jewish festival of Shauvot, when pilgrims from distant lands had come to the city to worship in the Temple. Suddenly, with a surge of wind and dancing tongues of fire, the disciples began to speak in other languages. Drawn by the commotion, visitors who had come to the city from distant lands east, north, south, and west gathered to listen. Each one miraculously heard and understood the message being spoken in his or her own language. One of the disciples, Peter, explained that this was the work of the Spirit of God, being poured out upon all humanity by the crucified and risen Christ.

The pilgrims whom Acts describes in Jerusalem listening to the message of Jesus' disciples on the day of Pentecost would have come by way of the trade routes of the ancient world. In the years that followed, the disciples of Jesus traveled along these same trade routes to take that message to other cities. In new urban locations they shared the story of Jesus Christ and began to organize communities in his name. Those first followers of Jesus had little idea what they were getting themselves into as they journeyed with their message to new places. They trusted that the risen Christ did, however, and they were willing to follow him wherever they believed his Spirit was leading them. The disciples claimed that the Spirit of God had been sent upon them to cultivate their expectations and equip them with gifts for ministry. With an extraordinary burst of energy they set off to find their new religious identity in new urban locations. The ultimate horizon of the movement was nothing less than "the ends of the earth" (Acts 1:8).

From our historical vantage point we can see far beyond what any individual living in western Asia in the first century could possibly have seen or known about the world at that time. The diversity of languages, religions, and cultures was much greater than any of the early disciples of Jesus could have imagined. Yet over the course of generations and centuries, the message of Jesus has continued to cross the boundaries of human habitation and culture, reaching eventually to the ends of the earth as those first disciples believed that it would. Along the way, as we shall see, the history of the Christian movement has continued to give rise to new articulations of belief, new forms of worship, new institutional strategies, and new practices of faith. Telling the story of the background and emergence of the early Christian movement is the task of this first section.

1

The Civilizations and Cultures of the World

A network of urban civilizations

Israel was a nation at the crossroads of empires and civilizations in the first century. The eastern Mediterranean was part of a much wider network of cities and civilizations that stretched like a girdle across a wide expanse of the ancient world. This urban network connected several broad, overlapping cultural regions on three continents in a continuous flow of politics and trade that reached from the Atlantic to the Pacific oceans. On the western end was the Mediterranean basin, a civilization that had incorporated a multitude of ancient cultural traditions including Egyptian, Ethiopian, Greek, Jewish, Mesopotamian, Persian, and Latin. Usually referred to by scholars today as Greco-Roman civilization, by the time of Jesus it had become unified by the diffusion of a common Greek language and culture, under the imperial rule of the city of Rome.

East of the Mediterranean basin, ancient political dynasties had succeeded in uniting the various lands and peoples from the Euphrates River to the Himalaya Mountains into a more or less unified civilization. Centered politically in the region today known as Iran, the Persian empire likewise incorporated a multitude of cultures and traditions, including Greek, Jewish, Mesopotamian, Iranian, and Indian. The dominant religion of the Persian world was Zoroastrianism, but other faiths (including Judaism) were found among the population as well. Like the Greco-Roman world, the Persian world was dominated by cities and was tied together by commerce and trade as much as by the military power of its various imperial regimes. At the time of Jesus it was under the rule of a Parthian dynasty from northern Iran.

A third cultural field extended east and south of Persia, encompassing the Indian subcontinent and sections of southeast Asia beyond it. This was the civilization of India, home of the religious traditions that found expression through the ancient sacred writings known as the Vedas. India's languages, religions, and cultures had been formed through the creative interaction of descendants of ancient invaders from Iran and the vast array of indigenous people in the land. Some

3

260 years before Christ, a single military ruler named Ashoka had succeeded in consolidating most of India into one empire before converting to the religious faith of Buddhism and renouncing all violence and warfare. Ashoka's political domains included most of the Indian subcontinent. His cultural legacy was to extend the unifying vision of Buddhism as a missionary movement beyond the land of its origin.

At the eastern end of this urban belt of civilization, across the Himalaya Mountains and Tibetan plateau, was China, the fourth great cultural complex in this network. For many centuries China was a civilization in which small kingdoms or warring states had struggled for control over one another. A common written language and a common heritage of ancient texts provided the basis for a unifying cultural identity, however. In 206 BCE a unified government emerged from the successful rebellion of a peasant movement under a leader known as Liu Bang. He was given the title Han Gao Zu, and the dynasty he founded became known as the Han. Although the Han rulers were not propelled by the same imperial visions that drove Greek and Roman emperors eastward, the influence of Chinese civilization nevertheless spread under them, westward into central Asia and eastward into Korea. During this period Confucianism began to be followed by the ruling classes throughout the country for the first time. It provided a coherent political-religious ideology that coincided with the common language and culture of the Chinese people and helped unify the empire.

Scattered across these ancient civilizations were numerous cities that concentrated high numbers of people, material wealth, and political power in relatively small geographical areas of space. Cities were home to the ruling elite of the ancient world, but they also housed significant numbers of merchants, artisans, workers, slaves, and those considered simply the riffraff. Outside the cities' walls the vast majority of people in the ancient world lived in small villages or in the countryside. Their lives were dominated by agriculture and herding, supported by various forms of light production (pottery, weaving, carpentry, and some metal working). The urban elite extracted both food and other resources from the countryside, either in the form of direct land ownership or through tribute and taxes. Precious metals in the form of coinage (gold, silver, or copper) were the preferred media of exchange in the cities, allowing the elite to purchase goods from artisans and merchants near and far.

Cities were often clustered close together in particular regions of the world. The regions themselves were in turn often separated from one another by expanses of mountains, deserts, and seas. Such natural barriers helped preserve the distinctive identities of cultures and civilizations by separating them from one another. War and trade, on the other hand, were two common pursuits that brought people from different regions into contact with each other across the barriers of both geography and culture in the ancient world. The armies of emperors often crossed vast terrains to conquer distant lands and extend their rulers' domains. Often these armies included soldiers from other parts of the world who were paid or pressed to fight for a particular king. Kings and emperors sometimes moved whole populations of people or sponsored colonization in order to further their ends in another part of the world. Soldiers returning from a military campaign and prisoners of war taken as slaves brought new cultural practices or beliefs with them in a reverse flow of influences into a local city.

Over the centuries a number of city-based empires rose and fell in these civilizations. Each empire in its own way sought to extend political control over lands and peoples under the rule of a small elite. Power was concentrated in the hands of a few, usually headed by a single male military leader whose authority rested upon his army. The most common pattern that had emerged for political succession by the first century was for rule to be handed on from fathers to sons in a dynasty. (An exception emerged among the Romans, where emperors came to be chosen by the army and were not always descended from the previous emperor.) Almost all warriors and military leaders in the ancient world were men, and most imperial civilizations were male-dominated or patriarchal. The extensive militarization of empires and rulers was reflected in the language of the ancient world's sovereigns who were lords and kings. The rulers of the earth held their titles by means of the violence that they exercised.

Even more important than warfare for sustaining trans-regional contacts and cross-cultural influences were the merchants who went before and after the generals. They were the ones who established the most enduring contacts between cultures and peoples. Among the most significant trade routes of the ancient world was the Silk Road, which stretched westward from the Great Wall of China into India, and to the Mediterranean coast. Passing through numerous central Asian kingdoms through the Persian empire and into Armenia and Syria, it brought people of various languages and cultures into contact with one another regularly as goods passed back and forth along it. Chinese merchants also traded with peoples to their east, extending their language and cultural influences in that direction as well.

On the other end of the Silk Road in Syria and Arabia, caravans regularly crossed the deserts to carry goods between cities and to the seacoasts. Ships navigated the Mediterranean Sea, Red Sea, Arabian Sea, Indian Ocean, and parts of the Pacific to bring goods from India or China to markets in the cities of Alexandria, Carthage, or Rome. An extensive system of Roman-built roads helped link the various urban centers of the Mediterranean world into an efficient economic network by the first century. Goods from the Roman world were traded all the way north into Scandinavia. Roman coins have been found as far south as the modern African nation of Uganda. In India, Roman-built harbors and numerous Roman coins testify to high levels of trade being conducted. Ancient legends even suggest that Phoenicians, Egyptians, or others might have arrived on the shores of South America several centuries prior to the birth of Christ.

Although the goods that were produced and transported were most often reserved for the use of the few in the upper classes, the process of making, moving, and trading them brought about wider social contacts among people. A wealthy citizen of Alexandria could purchase silk from China and ivory from Ethiopia while watching the ships loaded with Egyptian grain pulling out of the harbor and heading toward Ephesus. A craftsman such as Paul of Tarsus could travel from city to city, finding work in districts where tentmakers and tanners labored in small shops. Not only could he count on finding a place to practice his craft,

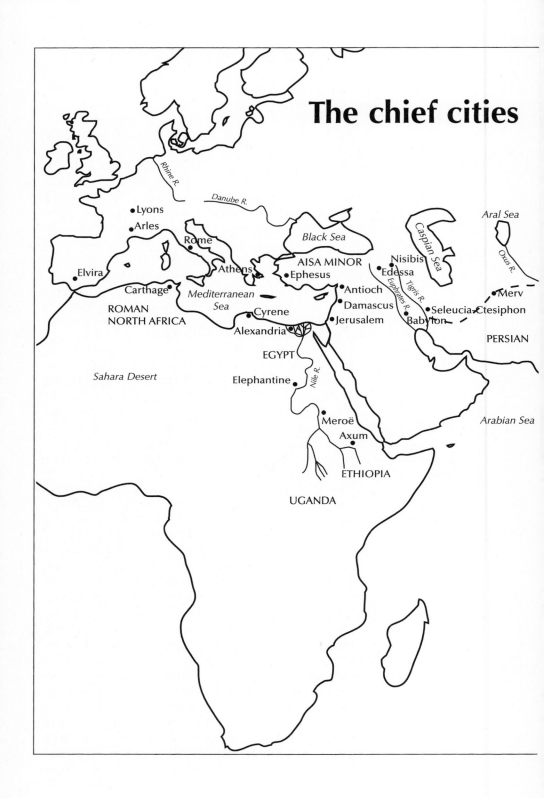

The chief cities

Rhine R.

Danube R.

Black Sea

Caspian Sea

Aral Sea

Oxus R.

● Lyons

● Arles

● Rome

Athens

Elvira ●

Carthage ●

ROMAN
NORTH AFRICA

Mediterranean
Sea

AISA MINOR

● Ephesus

Nisibis
● Edessa

● Antioch

● Damascus

Tigris R.

Euphrates R.

● Merv

● Seleucia Ctesiphon

Babylon

PERSIAN

Cyrene ●

Alexandria ●

● Jerusalem

EGYPT

Sahara Desert

Elephantine ●

Nile R.

Arabian Sea

● Meroë

Axum
●

ETHIOPIA

UGANDA

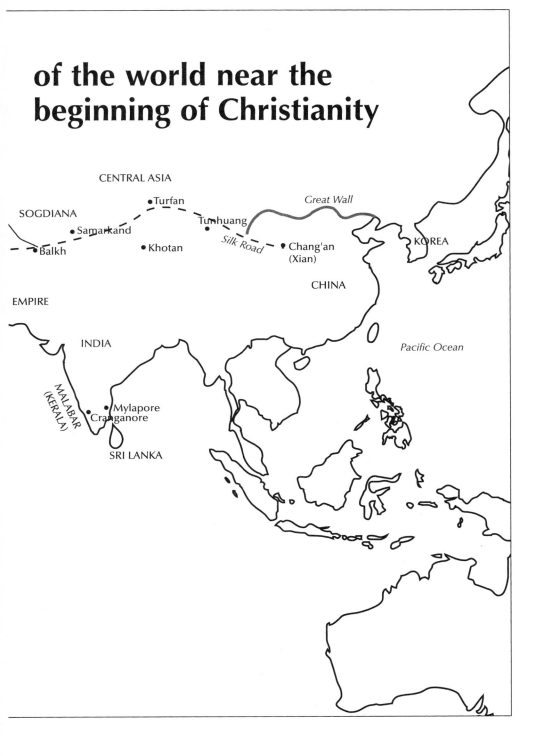

of the world near the
beginning of Christianity

CENTRAL ASIA

SOGDIANA

• Turfan

Great Wall

• Samarkand

Tunhuang

Silk Road

• Balkh

• Khotan

• Chang'an
(Xian)

KOREA

CHINA

EMPIRE

INDIA

Pacific Ocean

MALABAR
(KERALA)

• Mylapore
Cranganore

SRI LANKA

but he could communicate with others in *koine* Greek, a common form of the language that was spoken and understood from the Pyrenees to the Himalaya Mountains.

The Mediterranean, Persian, Indian, and Chinese civilizations were all ones in which cities were central. They were also civilizations that had developed writing. By the first century each of them could lay claim to an extensive literary tradition. Sacred writings in particular passed on the heritage of religious faiths through hymns, priestly writings, philosophical (or wisdom) treatises, and sacred stories. During the millennia before the birth of Christ, these civilizations had witnessed the rise of a number of especially important or inspired teachers whose writings transformed the religious and philosophical character of humankind. The works of these teachers still inform the project of human civilization today. Kung-fu-tzu (Confucius in Latin), Lao-Tzu, the Buddha, the writers of the Upanishads, Zoroaster, the prophets of Israel, and the philosophers of Greece all belonged to a revolution in human consciousness that had significantly shaped the world into which the disciples of Jesus first moved.

The wider network of world civilizations and cultures

To the north of this string of urban civilizations in the first century lived an extensive number of nomadic tribal peoples, scattered from Siberia across central Asia into modern Russia and northwestern Europe. A shared linguistic and religious heritage linked various tribes together into several major families of Celtic, Germanic, Slavic, Turkish, and Mongol cultural identity. By the first century many were on the move in waves of migrations that eventually had a lasting effect upon the urban civilization of the Mediterranean world.

South of the Mediterranean on the continent of Africa were numerous tribes and peoples, some of whom had also begun to engage the urban world to their north and east by the first century. Once again the major forms of relating were those of warfare and trade. The Nile River was the major artery leading south of Egypt, with the ancient city-kingdom of Meroë (in Northern Sudan), the dominant political entity in the first century. To the west of the Nile River, the Sahara desert proved to be too formidable a barrier for extensive trade to develop with the north, leaving significant contact with the urban civilization of the Mediterranean world for a later date. Several major currents of migration began to take place further south around the first century of the Christian era. The largest was that of the Bantu-speaking people, which eventually made them the dominant linguistic group south of the Congo River.

From Asia, and possibly northern Europe or even Africa, tribal people had crossed the seas to the Americas many millennia earlier, leading to the inhabitation of these two continents as well. In North America the cultural patterns of hunting and gathering, with minimal development of towns and virtually no true urban centers, lasted a thousand years beyond what was the case on the other side of the globe. By the first century of the Christian era, on the other hand, urban empires in Central America and Mexico were emerging along parallel but separate pathways. The ancient city of Teotihuacán (in Mexico) may have had a population of as many as 200,000 people at one time.

Over the same time period as the migration of people to the Americas was taking place, there were a series of migrations by sea from southeast Asia into present day Oceania. The first major wave of settlers established hunter and gatherer societies in Australia, Tasmania, and New Guinea, possibly as long as fifty thousand years ago. Later, perhaps as long as ten thousand years ago, agriculturalist peoples migrated into other areas of the western Pacific into what is today known as Melanesia and Micronesia. Eventually some moved by boat to settle among the wide expanse of islands in the eastern Pacific that make up Polynesia. The scattered nature of these island societies, and the fact that travel was possible only by sea, limited the amount of contact they had with other cultures and civilizations of the world prior to the modern era.

The history of Israel amid nations and empires

At the time of Jesus' birth, Israel had become integrated into the Roman political system. The Gospel of Luke names Caesar Augustus as the emperor in whose reign Jesus was born, and the procurator Pontius Pilate as the Roman governor under whom he died. Prior to that, the land had been ruled by the Greeks, who in the centuries following the conquests of Alexander the Great had succeeded in introducing their language and culture (called Hellenism) extensively across the ancient world. Greek was understood and used among the upper classes from India to Spain, and from the Black Sea to Ethiopia. The language thus provided a vehicle for communication that could reach across numerous national boundaries.

Before the Greeks it had been the Persians, and before them the Babylonians and the Egyptians, who had dominated Israel's life as a people. Except for brief periods of limited national sovereignty, Israel had long been a small nation caught up in the swirl of events of a wider international history. Waves of successive empires and colonial incursions provide the background against which the first followers of Jesus emerged from their center in Jerusalem. These first disciples were Jews, and like all Jews they drew their primary religious identity from the Torah, that body of divine Law or Teachings that had first been revealed to Moses at Mount Sinai. The Torah provided the terms of a covenant God had made with Israel as a people. The first followers of Jesus understood their movement to be a reformulation of that covenant that extended its embrace to those who were being left out or excluded.

The history of Israel's covenant was the story of salvation. But Israel's calling, according to its scriptures, was also to be a nation of priests set amid the nations of the world. The diversity of the world was traced in the Hebrew scriptures in the genealogy of nations in Genesis 10, which told the story of the dispersion of the children of Noah after the flood. Its own distinctive faith identity Israel drew from the patriarch Abraham, who left his home in the city of Ur in Mesopotamia and journeyed to the land of Canaan. Abraham trusted God and in return was promised that his descendants would be as numerous as the stars, a covenant that would embrace a multitude of nations. The early Christians recalled this tradition as being a promise that had been fulfilled in Jesus.

For several hundred years after Abraham and Sarah, his wife, their descendants had sojourned in Egypt, where they were eventually forced into slavery by a pharaoh. Then under the leadership of Moses, God brought them out of Egypt in the great event of the Exodus, and led them on to Mount Sinai to worship God. There at that sacred mountain, the people of Israel recalled, the Lord God had made a covenant with them that set them apart from other nations. The terms of this covenant provided the contents of Torah: Israel was to worship the Lord God only; to refrain from making any images of the divine; to keep the Sabbath holy; to maintain moral purity; and to act toward one another in ways that were just and compassionate. Such covenant-making was again rehearsed, and extended, in the life of the early Christian movement.

For several centuries following the Exodus, the people of Israel had maintained various degrees of independence in Canaan. An earlier tribal confederacy under charismatic judges was succeeded by a monarchy. The height of Israel's political influence came in the reign of King David and his son Solomon, whose rule stretched from the Philistine cities on the Mediterranean seacoast to the city of Dan in the north and the Negev desert in the south. It was under Solomon that the first Temple of Israel was built in Jerusalem as well. This temple was destroyed by the Babylonians after they captured the city in 586 BCE and took many of the inhabitants off into exile. It was subsequently rebuilt under the Persians, extended under Herod the Great, and then destroyed a second and final time by the Romans in 70 CE. The story of the Temple's fate at the hands of foreign powers stands as a metaphor for the experience of Israel at the hands of the ruling nations and empires that surrounded it.

The first Christians emerged from this crucible. They shared the history and experiences of being Jewish in a world that was foreign, and sometimes hostile, to their faith. As members of the people of Israel, they shared the memories of exodus and exile that were being remolded in the context of their own first century. As a missionary community, the early Christian movement sought at the same time to relate its understanding of the covenant to the nations and cultures beyond Israel's own boundaries. The early history of Christianity is one of continuous reformulations and reappropriations of this ancient covenantal faith in new and varying political-cultural contexts. The story thus unfolds in the interaction between Israel's national covenant and a series of widening international horizons.

2

Judaism at the Time of Jesus

The land of Israel

The land in which Jesus was born was one that had been scarred by the ravages of armies and empires for centuries. Each had been driven by an imperial vision of a unified world under one ruler. In the course of this history, successive waves of foreign cultural influence had swept through the region, creating a complex religious landscape with multiple layers of influence. Egyptian, Babylonian, Persian, Hellenistic, Roman, and Parthian traces were all found to some degree within Judaism in the first century. Yet through it all, the people of Israel (called Judeans after the return from exile, from which the term *Jews* is derived) had remained committed to their strictly monotheistic religious faith. They worshiped the one true God who, they believed, had revealed the Torah through Moses on Mount Sinai, and who had instructed Solomon to build the Temple in Jerusalem. Israel's life as a people in the first century revolved around the twin pillars of Temple and Torah.

All of Judaism recognized the historical significance of the land of Israel, stretching from Galilee in the north to the desert of Judea. It was only here that one could fulfill the whole of Torah, and only here that one could worship in the Temple. Yet the Judaism that was practiced in Israel was far from being a unified religious system at the time of Jesus, so much so that some have spoken of there being "Judaisms." Although all the parties were strictly monotheistic, competing schools of interpretation and the various influences of other cultures from outside of Israel combined to make for a diversity of religious practices.

Politically, the land of Israel had been continuously carved into different jurisdictions over the course of the two centuries between the Maccabean revolt of 167-164 BCE, when limited national sovereignty was regained, and the end of the war against the Romans in 70 CE when Jerusalem and the Temple were destroyed. The Maccabeans established a new line of kings, known as the Hasmonean dynasty. The heart of their kingdom was the city of Jerusalem and the surrounding districts of Judea and Perea (on the west and east banks of the Jordan River, respectively). To the north was a third district called Galilee, which was the home of Jesus.

11

Separating Galilee from Judea was Samaria, whose inhabitants claimed to descend from those who were left after the Assyrian conquest of the northern kingdom of Israel in the eighth century BCE. Samaritans had a version of Torah and a Temple that was built on Mount Gerizim. The latter was destroyed by the Hasmonean king John Hyrcanus in 128 BCE when he conquered them. This same king conquered and forced the conversion of the Idumeans, an Arab people to the immediate south of Judea who claimed to have descended from the ancient biblical Edomites.

The Mediterranean seacoast during the Hasmonean period remained dominated by Hellenistic cities. Jews resided there but often felt the pull of cultural assimilation more strongly than their co-religionists in Jerusalem. After the Romans appeared around 60 BCE, other Jews began to look for ways to cooperate with them. One of the political collaborators in this regard was an Idumean named Antipater. In 37 BCE with the help of Rome's backing, Antipater's son, Herod the Great, was placed on the throne as king of the Judeans.

Parties in Israel

Much of our knowledge of this period in Israel's history comes from a Jewish historian named Flavius Josephus, who ended his days in Rome. Josephus tells us that within Israel itself during the first centuries before and after the birth of Christ, there were several schools or parties (he used the Greek term *hairesis*, the source of the English word "heresy") with competing interpretations of Torah. Readers of the New Testament are familiar with two of these in particular, the Sadducees and the Pharisees, who are represented in the Christian scriptures as being opposed to Jesus and his followers in Galilee and Jerusalem.

Of the two parties, the Sadducees were the more conservative. They were closely identified with the aristocracy in Jerusalem and the high priesthood in the Temple (although not all priests were members of this party). They sustained their influence through several successive regimes: during the rule of the Hasmoneans who descended from the Maccabeans; under Herod the Great, who ruled as king with Rome's backing from 37 to 4 BCE; and finally under Roman governors. During the life of Jesus, their influence appears to have been strong in the ruling body of religious elders in Jerusalem known as the Sanhedrin, although after 60 CE it appears to have waned. For the most part, they succeeded in accommodating Roman governance, accepting a limited degree of autonomy in place of national independence.

The Sadducees recognized only the written Torah found in the five books of Moses as authoritative scripture, rejecting for instance the books of the prophets that others in Israel considered canonical. They did not believe in the resurrection of the dead or in the existence of angelic spirits. In the pages of the New Testament one meets them in confrontations with Jesus in the vicinity of Jerusalem, and again in Acts 23 when Paul, a former Pharisee who became a Christian, engaged with them in disputation before the Sanhedrin.

Little is known of the Pharisees prior to the period of Herod the Great other than that they arose as a reform movement under the Hasmoneans. Pharisees were mostly represented among the middle social classes of artisans and scribes within Jewish society. For a brief time under Hasmonean rule they exercised some political influence, although this had waned by the time of Jesus. The maxim of one of their ancient teachers recorded in the Talmud describes well their position regarding social-political life: "Love labor, shun power, and do not become close with the ruling authorities" (*Avot* 1:10). Above all, the Pharisees were known for their diligence and interpretation of Torah. The legacy was institutionalized by several important teachers during the period of Herod the Great. Among the greatest of these were Hillel (originally from Babylon) and Shammai.

In the first century CE, the Pharisees were quite close to Christians in both their beliefs and practices, despite the perception to the contrary many have from the New Testament. The gospels often present Jesus in conflict with the Pharisees. Yet they also record the use of the title "rabbi" by his disciples, a term commonly used for Pharisee teachers. On a number of points the two groups were in agreement. With the followers of Jesus, for instance, Pharisees believed in the resurrection of the dead and an afterlife. In several places, the gospels tell of Jesus having table fellowship with the Pharisees. The Gospel of John gives us the name of one in particular, Nicodemus, who was a secret follower of Jesus. The apostle Paul himself claimed to have been a Pharisee prior to his conversion.

The conflict between Jesus and the Pharisees seems to have centered on the latter party's teachings on tithing, purity, Sabbath observance, table fellowship, and other issues of day-to-day piety. In Matthew's gospel, Jesus acknowledged their authority by telling his followers that the Pharisees sat on the seat of Moses, but that they taught one thing and did another (Matt. 23:1-4). Pharisees drew upon a body of tradition that they believed had been handed down orally from previous generations reaching back to Moses himself, and was authoritative for them in interpreting the written Torah. Both written and oral Torah provided the basis for *halakhah* (Hebrew for "holy way of life")—the hallmark of Judaism after the first century as shaped by the rabbis who were the Pharisees' successors. It was the authority of the oral tradition on matters such as Sabbath observance and purity that Jesus appears to have directly challenged.

The Pharisees were emerging as the dominant interpreters of Torah in the period when the gospels were being written. They were the only party of Judaism recognized by Rome after the destruction of the Temple in Jerusalem in 70 CE. In the process Pharisees and Nazarenes (as the followers of Jesus were called by some in Israel; see Acts 24:5) became increasingly hostile to one another, in a way only siblings can. One cannot help but see in the pages of the New Testament a reflection of the polemics the followers of Jesus were directing toward their chief rivals to the claim of being Judaism's rightful heirs. By the end of the first century, the rabbis had begun to codify the teachings of their intellectual predecessors, showing the way to keep Torah in the absence of the Temple and its sacrifices. Through study, prayer, and observance of all aspects of the oral and written Torah, they provided the means for reconstituting the religious life of

Israel. Jews were thereby able to experience the sanctification of life that had previously been offered to them through the Temple and its priesthood in Jerusalem. The teachings and interpretations of Torah that the rabbis preserved were eventually collected into what is known as the Talmud.

A third party or group within Judaism at the time of Jesus, according to Josephus, were known as the Essenes. They rigorously rejected what they considered the corruptions of their contemporary religionists, especially among the Hasmonean priesthood in Jerusalem. Conversion was required of all who would enter into the New Covenant, they believed, and the community administered regular ritual washings for cleansing of sins. While many lived in cities and towns in small bands or communities, including in Jerusalem, others withdrew to the desert to live individually or in separate communities. Some formed monastic communities and followed ascetic discipline awaiting God's eschatological intervention in the affairs of Israel, which, they believed, would surely come to reestablish the true priesthood in the Temple.

The term *Essene* is not used in the New Testament. In the book of Acts, however, there are several references to Jews in Jerusalem whom Luke calls "pious" (see Acts 8:2, for example); these might have been Essenes. John the Baptist also appears to be one who was influenced by the teachings of the Essenes, if he was not actually a member of the movement. John called for repentance and instituted baptism for forgiveness of sins in the Jordan River as an alternative to offerings of sacrifice in the Temple. The leader of the early Christian community in Jerusalem, James the brother of Jesus, who was also known as James the Righteous, has been thought by some to have possibly once been an Essene.

One of the communities often associated with the Essenes is a group whose writings were discovered in the caves of Qumran near the Dead Sea in 1947. The Qumran scrolls speak of one who was known as the Teacher of Righteousness, whose teachings on Torah the group followed in opposition to those of the Pharisees. The Qumran community also taught that the Temple priesthood had become morally and religiously corrupted. Several of the scrolls depict apocalyptic beliefs in the imminent end of the present historical era and God's triumphant reign over evil. They looked forward to the day when God would miraculously intervene to purify the Temple and restore the true faith of Israel.

Similar ideas were found in a number of other esoteric texts known as "apocalypses" (from the Greek word meaning "to reveal"). Composed and circulated throughout the Jewish world during the centuries before and after the birth of Jesus, they were usually anonymous works written under the names of patriarchs or sages from the distant past (the Assumption of Moses and the Epistle of Enoch, for example). They usually purported to reveal events of the *eschaton* (Greek for "end-time") through fantastic symbols, otherworldly journeys, and personalities of mythical or cosmic proportions. Apart from Qumran and the early Christian communities that held apocalyptic expectations, we have little evidence of the kinds of groups that might have received or read these visionary writings. The anonymity of the authors and the esoteric nature of the writings themselves served to cloak both authors and communities with a shroud of mystery. Nevertheless, the popularity of these texts is attested to by the numbers of them that were produced and the general influence they had at that time.

Apocalyptic texts offered prophecies under the names of figures from the distant past, claiming to foresee events in the future. Through this literary device their authors were able to depict more immediate events that they expected to be resolved in the near future. The texts often contained veiled or symbolic references to contemporary persons and events. Their message was intended to encourage faithful (if passive) resistance against forces of evil (Jewish and Gentile). The secret they revealed in myriad ways was that God would soon intervene in history either directly or through heavenly intermediaries to restore righteousness and end the reign of evil on earth. Many apocalypses recounted Israel's long history of redemption, but then posed a sharp contrast between the present historical age and the future age that is to come. In vivid scenarios involving heavenly beings, they revealed a coming transformation or transition in human history. Almost always the books portrayed a belief in the transcendence of human history in an afterlife, with judgment against the wicked being exercised by God and the righteous being raised on the other side of historical death to an everlasting world of rest. This last theme, usually depicted in apocalyptic writings by the symbol of the coming "kingdom of God" or the building of a "New Jerusalem," was echoed in early Christian writings.

Essenes and apocalyptic writers alike appear to have advocated nonviolent forms of resistance against the ruling establishment and its corruptions. This was not the case with other Jewish resistance groups from the period. Sources tell of numerous popular uprisings, often led by local resistance leaders who were viewed as bandits by the political rulers. While not all bandits operating in the countryside were resistance fighters at the time of Jesus, political resistors were most often accused as being bandits. Some were drawn from the educated classes, but most were peasant based and emerged from among the common people, who were overwhelmingly illiterate. One such group, known as *Sicarii* (Latin for "knife"), engaged in acts of urban terrorism by carrying out political assassinations. Another group that emerged at the time of the revolt against Rome in 66 CE were called the Zealots.

Movements of social unrest, at least at the popular level, were linked to increased taxation and worsening economic conditions under Hasmonean and Roman rule. There were also nationalist religious dimensions to resistance, stemming from the program of increased Hellenization of the cities that took place under successive foreign regimes. Resistance movements in the countryside sometimes found national religious expression in the form of their expectations for an anointed (or messianic) royal leader who, like David, was expected to deliver the people from foreign oppression. The knowledge that some of the resistance leaders hid out in the hill country near Galilee would not have been lost on the people who came out to the same hills to hear Jesus preach as he did in the story of the Sermon on the Mount in Matthew 5. A number of messianic movements emerged during the period of Roman rule, not just among the followers of Jesus of Nazareth but also within Judaism during the revolt of 66-70 CE, and again in 132-135 CE under a popular Jewish leader named Simeon bar Kochba. Jesus himself and his early followers appear to have neither advocated nor engaged in armed resistance. Nevertheless he and they appropriated the messianic symbolism of popular royal kingship within Israel, reflected in the title "King of the Jews" that Pilate had written in three languages and hung on the cross on which Jesus was crucified.

Few among the common people could read and write. Fewer still could read and write Hebrew, the language of Israel's scriptures, which only the educated religious leaders continued to study. For the most part, the common people heard and remembered the stories of Israel's sacred scriptures through oral versions that were rough translations (or paraphrases) in Aramaic, the common language of Israel and Syria, which was closely related to Hebrew. In the synagogues, a common person might have heard the scriptures read in Hebrew, followed by some form of exposition in Aramaic delivered by a Pharisaic teacher. On important ceremonial dates during the life of a family or village, and on high festival occasions, the educated and common people alike from Galilee, Perea, Judea, and Idumea would journey to Jerusalem to worship in the Temple. There they would be joined by Jews from elsewhere in the world for whom the Temple was the center of religious identity.

Judaism in the diaspora

The latter were Jews of the *diaspora* ("scattering"), who lived throughout the cities of both the Persian and Greco-Roman worlds. In the east they were descendants of the Jews forcibly removed in captivity by the Assyrians and Babylonians but who had not returned to Jerusalem or Israel following the Persian edict that granted such permission in the sixth century BCE. At the time of Jesus the number of Jews living in the Persian world, mostly in or near Babylon, may have approached one million. Sizable Jewish communities could be found in other cities, such as Edessa in Mesopotamia and Nisibis in Persia. Aramaic was their common language, although Greek remained important among the upper classes. Many common Jews lost the ability to speak Hebrew, and Aramaic paraphrases and commentaries on scripture provided them their only access to the Torah.

Under Parthian rule (which began around 240 BCE), Jewish life in Babylon and elsewhere in the east was relatively unmolested. The Parthians, who were officially Zoroastrian, supported the conversion to Judaism of the royal house of the small border state of Adiabene around 35 CE, although the reason for doing so had much to do with having an anti-Roman client on the Parthian-Roman border. Jews were mostly merchants and administrators. They regularly crossed the Roman-Parthian border to worship at the Temple and study Torah in Jerusalem. Some who were engaged in trade traveled across Asia. Others became scribes and scholars, laying the foundation for generations of Babylonian Jewish interpretation of the scriptures. The Pharisee teacher Hillel, we have noted, was from Babylon before he resettled in Jerusalem. Although it is not known what form of education he might have had in his home city, it is safe to assume that he was already recognized as a scholar before coming to Jerusalem.

While many Jews had been taken off to Babylon in the sixth century BCE, others had resettled in Egypt. Eventually Judaism was being practiced as far south as southern Egypt and across the Red Sea in Arabia. A military outpost founded during the Persian period in the southern Egyptian city of Elephantine (near the modern Aswan dam) included a sizable Jewish garrison and even had a Jewish temple. With the coming of Alexander the Great, and the Greek dynasties of the Seleucids and Ptolemies that followed in his wake, the dispersion of Jews in both Syria and Egypt increased. A large number settled in the city of Alexandria, which under the Ptolemies became the leading center of education and learning in the Mediterranean world. By the first century of the Christian era, the Jewish community was scattered across several districts and might have numbered as much as one-third of the estimated 300,000 inhabitants of the city. There were a number of synagogues in Alexandria, and Jews had their own administrative ruler and exercised a considerable degree of autonomy regarding their affairs. This is not to say that life for Jews in Alexandria was always peaceful. Severe riots in the year 37, for instance, were directed against them and resulted in tens of thousands being killed. Nevertheless, Jews for the most part found life tolerable there and were even open to accommodating Hellenistic cultural ways. A number of Jews in Alexandria were able to gain Greek citizenship, and some even gave up their own religion entirely in order to assimilate into the dominant Hellenistic world.

During the reign of Ptolemy II, Jewish scholars in Egypt produced a Greek translation of the scriptures that came to be known as the *Septuagint* (Latin for "70," derived from the tradition that there were seventy translators). The work was sanctioned by Ptolemy II to provide him with access to the sacred books of the Jews who were under his rule. It was supported by the Jews themselves as well, for many no longer read Hebrew. According to Jewish tradition, the seventy translators were appointed by the high priest in Jerusalem, giving the work even greater credibility among those living in the diaspora. The Septuagint soon proved to be both a symbol and a vehicle of a wider religious transformation taking place in Hellenistic Judaism. Those who read its words found new meaning to their faith through translation. The process of cultural adaptation in turn allowed them to question aspects of obedience to Torah and the necessity for periodic return to Jerusalem to worship in the Temple. Hellenistic Jews who had access to their scriptures through the Septuagint were involved in a process of cultural translation that prefigured the arrival of Christianity in the Hellenistic world.

The rich legacy of Hellenistic Judaism was expressed in a number of books of wisdom that were written in Greek in the centuries before Jesus, such as the Wisdom of Solomon. Many of the apocalyptic books also bore evidence of Hellenistic influences in their ideas. All the books of the Christian New Testament were originally written in Greek, a fact that is especially significant in light of the likelihood that Jesus and his first disciples from Galilee spoke Aramaic as their day-to-day language. The gospels themselves are to be numbered among the books of Hellenistic Jewish literature from the era. They also are among the first efforts to translate the words of Jesus into another language, giving them a wider circle of comprehension.

Hellenized Judaism in Alexandria eventually found its greatest teacher in the person of Philo Judeus (c.20 BCE–c.50 CE). Philo was a philosopher who sought to render Jewish thought intelligible to educated Greeks of his day by interpreting the biblical message in ways that were consonant with Greek philosophical concepts. The stories in the Hebrew scriptures were to be understood as allegories, he explained. They represented in symbolic or spiritual form the truths that Greek philosophy grasped through reason. Philo used the Greek concept of the *logos* ("reason" or "word") to link the creative work of the God of Israel with the Greek concept of divine reason. In his *Timeus*, the Greek philosopher Plato had described the logos as a divine principle or pattern found throughout the world. Philo identified this with the word of God that was found in the Hebrew scriptures, thereby building a bridge between Greek philosophy and Jewish thought. It was a bridge that many generations of Christian theologians later walked as well, borrowing Philo's allegorical method as well to interpret the meaning of scriptures.

Jews also represented a sizable portion of Antioch, another city in the eastern Mediterranean region whose rise was related to the Hellenistic dynasties. Founded in 300 BCE by the Seleucids, Antioch's population is estimated to have been as high as 200,000 at its peak in the ancient era, with a density that rivals that of modern Calcutta. Situated at the western end of the Silk Road, Antioch was a vital link in international commerce. The presence of Chinese pottery found among the ruins of the city testifies to the international flavor of the place. There was also considerable ethnic diversity during this period as waves of immigrants came to live within (or just outside) its walls. The capital of the province of West Syria, Antioch was considered by Rome to be a vital strategic outpost in its military struggles with the Parthian empire to the east. It was also militarily strategic for controlling the smaller kingdoms of Armenia to the north and Arabia to the south.

The Jewish community in Antioch could trace its descent back to the time of the founding of the city itself under the Seleucids. During the first century CE Antiochene Jews numbered in the tens of thousands, and lived not in any single quarter but throughout the city. During the reign of the Roman emperor Gaius Caligula, around 40 CE, a riot against the Jews broke out, resulting in a high number of casualties and the destruction of several synagogues. Anti-Jewish sentiment in Antioch might have been connected with similar riots occurring in Alexandria during this period and resulted in a confrontation with the priesthood in Judea that led to Roman intervention. For the most part it appears, however, that Jews retained the right to live according to their own religious laws. No doubt some Jews in Antioch had even been granted Roman citizenship without being forced to abandon their Jewish religious identities, as Paul, who was from Tarsus, was able to claim.

The initial political rapprochement between the Hasmonean rulers and Rome opened the door to Jews resettling in cities throughout the regions under Roman domination. Rome extended official recognition to Judaism, allowing for the practice of Jewish religion even in the capital city itself. A sizable Jewish population was found there by the time Roman armies under Cassius and Pompey were wreaking havoc in the lands of Israel, providing a local base for redeeming many Jewish prisoners of war carried off to Rome as slaves. Recognition of Judaism reflected a wider Roman practice that encouraged every community, as far as possible, to maintain its national customs, even in the empire's capital.

Rome tolerated a great deal of diversity in religious customs and beliefs, providing a favorable climate for both the dispersion of ideas and the profusion of new religious practices within the imperial borders. In time its emperors required peoples living under its rule to observe aspects of the Roman imperial cult, namely, worship of the Roman state gods, and later, the emperor himself as divine. The requirement was relaxed for Jews in deference to their religious prohibition against worshiping other gods. In the cities of the Roman and Hellenistic world, opposition to Judaism was expressed on cultural grounds rather than on imperial political grounds. Jews were common targets of satires in the theaters as actors mocked their Sabbath observance or their refusal to eat unclean meats. Their separate identity often exposed them to intense local persecution that from time to time exploded into full-scale riots.

At the same time there were Jews who had relaxed some of the cultural prohibitions found in the Torah in order to participate in the religious and cultural world around them. Jews attended the amphitheater in many cities, for instance, a practice that most religious leaders in Israel condemned. In the Greco-Roman world males participated in athletic events in the nude. Jewish men were thus easily identified by the mark of circumcision (the removal of the foreskin that according to Jewish scriptures was originally commanded of Abraham by God as a sign of the covenant). In some cases Jewish men tried to reverse the telltale mark of their circumcision, a practice also condemned by most religious leaders.

Jewish women had no such mark on their bodies that identified them as Jewish, but their lives were no less set apart from their neighbors by the rituals of home and family. Among the most important of these regulating rituals were those associated with menstruation. Jewish biblical law considered women ritually unclean during their menses. Menstruating women were expected to remain apart from men and were not allowed to participate in religious activities. Women in Judaism in general had little public religious function. Like others in the ancient world, Jewish women were also restricted in the level of education they were allowed to attain. For the most part they were not allowed to study Torah (there were exceptions, and some women have even been identified as heads of synagogues). None were allowed to serve as priests in the Temple in Jerusalem. Jewish women were not even allowed to view the sacrifices that male priests performed in the Temple in Jerusalem. These restrictions were in contrast with the role of women in other religious communities in the Greco-Roman world, where priestesses often served at shrines of local gods.

We have seen how some Jewish thinkers such as Philo had sought to reconcile the religion of Judaism with the philosophy of the Greeks. The numerous books of Jewish wisdom written in Greek, and reflecting Hellenistic influences from around the time of the early Christian movement, indicate that Philo was not alone in his quest. But the influences went both ways. Many in the cities around the Mediterranean and across the Syrian and Persian worlds were attracted by the doctrine of monotheism, the moral teachings of Torah, the stories of Israel's scriptures, and the community way of life that Judaism offered. Monotheism was attractive in the Hellenistic world, where the teachings of such people as Plato and Aristotle, and of philosophical schools such as Stoicism, pointed away from the many gods of Greek and Roman mythology and toward the unifying presence of a supreme being. The Stoic philosophers in particular emphasized human ethical responsibility and the need for individuals to restrain the exercise of their passions in order to achieve the good life. They believed that the active principle in the world, the logos or divine reason, was like an animating spark of fire that could be found in every individual. Each of these Greek schools of philosophy had come to emphasize the universal nature of truth and the unifying character of divine reality by the time of Jesus.

Similar emphases could be found in the monotheistic faith of the Zoroastrian religion in Persia in the east. Zoroaster (or Zarathustra) was a prophet who lived in eastern Iran sometime before 600 BCE. He taught his followers to worship one God, whose name was Ahura Mazda. Zoroastrianism held that there were twin spiritual forces that emanated from Ahura Mazda, one good and one evil, and that they pervaded the entire creation. The evil force, known as Angra Mainyu (or Ahriman), was evil by choice. All human beings are presented with the ethical responsibility of choosing between good and evil. All will face judgment at the end of life, Zoroastrianism taught, with the followers of good being invited in to eternal paradise while those who pursue evil are destroyed by fire.

Zoroastrianism shared a number of features with the religious traditions of India that had been shaped by the ancient hymns of the Rig Veda, which in turn gave rise to the various schools of philosophy known collectively as Vedanta. In India the search for the unifying force or presence within the diversity of divinities and experiences in creation had been one of the major themes of the writings of the Upanishads. Many scholars of world religions term the Indian traditions "monistic" rather than "monotheistic," however, for the unifying principle was not necessarily conceived to be a personal deity but an impersonal principle (usually termed Brahman). This was in contrast to Judaism, which insisted that the unifying One had a personal name and history. Judaism taught that this personal God, whose name was so holy it was not to be pronounced, had entered into a covenant with his people. The covenant called upon the people of Israel to exercise a degree of separation from their various Hellenistic and Persian religious neighbors.

By the first century there was a small but symbolically significant class of proselytes to Judaism from among the Gentiles in the Greco-Roman and the Persian worlds. Within the Hellenistic world, there were many who were simply called by Jews "God-fearers." They attended synagogue services but did not undergo full conversion to Judaism. The most significant barrier was the practice of circumcision. Hellenistic culture harbored strong prohibitions against marking the male body in such a way, prohibitions not found among other Semitic cultures. The apostle Paul made the relaxation of the requirement of circumcision central to his proclamation of the gospel and thus a key element in the adaptation of the Christian movement to Greek culture.

Throughout the diaspora, Jews built synagogues in cities where they lived that served as both prayer houses and community centers. Jews all over the world were also expected to contribute funds for the support of the Temple in Jerusalem, the central religious institution of their faith. On high festival days such as Passover or Shauvot (Pentecost), Jews traveled from across the world to worship in this sacred location. Gentiles were forbidden to enter its inner sanctuary upon the pain of death. In the streets of Jerusalem and in the outer courtyard of the Temple, Jews from all across the world mingled freely and joined in celebrating their faith. Those who were in attendance in the city during one Passover season in particular, probably in the year 30 CE, might have witnessed a disturbance in the city swirling around a young Galilean teacher named Jesus of Nazareth.

3

Christian Beginnings

The Jesus Movement

Nazareth was a village of fewer than two hundred people during the years when Jesus was growing up there. He was the son of Mary, a woman who was married to Joseph, but who would be long remembered in Christian tradition as being still a virgin when she conceived her firstborn son, Jesus. The gospels identify Joseph only as a carpenter. He appears to have died before Jesus reached adulthood. Luke's gospel tells of the presentation of the child at the Temple, and later of his visiting there with his family at age twelve. The portrait it paints of a faithful Jewish family provides important background against which Christian self-understanding emerged. Whatever else it may be, Christian identity is rooted in the prophetic promise of salvation found in Israel's life and faith.

From his childhood Jesus was exposed to influences that originated from beyond the immediate circle of Israel's particular faith tradition. Galilee had long felt the impact of the Hellenistic cities in its neighboring regions. Although the people normally spoke Aramaic in their day-to-day life, Greek would not have been unknown among the artisan and ruling classes in the larger towns. During the time when Jesus was growing up, there was an increasing Roman military presence in the Galilean countryside. Familiarity with Roman military practices is reflected in several parables or teachings of Jesus recounted in the gospels (see Mark 5:9 and Matt. 5:41, for example).

Both Matthew and Luke weave the threads of foreign culture into birth and infancy narratives of Jesus to demonstrate his universal significance. According to Luke he was born under the reign of Caesar Augustus at a time when the emperor had decreed that "all the world" should be enrolled in a census (Luke 2:1). According to Matthew 2, magi, or members of the Zoroastrian priestly class, came looking for the one whose birth they believed had been heralded by a star that they had seen. The implication of the story is that creation itself bore witness to the birth of the Christ in the form of a sign that these sages from the East had been able to interpret through astrological practices. Matthew reports that Herod conspired to kill the child, but that the life of the young Jesus was preserved by his family taking refuge in Egypt, that is, in Africa. This gospel's theological prologue provides a genealogy of Jesus Christ that includes four women: Tamar, Rahab, Ruth, and Bathsheba. According to Jewish tradition all were Canaanites, and all had a degree of social stigma attached to them.

At some point around his thirtieth year, Jesus responded to the call of John the Baptist (to whom, according to the gospels, he was related through his mother, Mary) and underwent John's baptism in the Jordan River. Almost immediately Jesus began an itinerant ministry of his own in the area of Capernaum, calling around him a group of disciples. Word spread quickly of his reputation as a healer and exorcist, as well as of his abilities as a preacher. People from a variety of classes responded to his message, including rural workers, artisans, and social outcasts. Among his closest disciples were several fishermen, at least one former tax collector, and several women. Jesus identified his mission as being primarily to reach the marginal people of Galilean society, those whom he called the "lost sheep of the house of Israel" (Matt. 10:6), but whom others called simply "sinners." He did not confine his message to them alone, however, for the gospels recall a number of encounters and positive relationships with members of the upper classes as well. While his travels took him primarily among Jews in Galilee and Judea, on several occasions he journeyed into regions beyond Israel. The gospels recall several favorable encounters with Samaritans, and one journey into the Decapolis, a region of federated Hellenistic cities to the east of the Jordan River.

One of the aspects of his ministry that has generated lasting debate concerns his relationship to women. Jesus is depicted in a number of gospel stories showing an unusual openness to women in ways that challenged traditional cultural roles. The gospels identify women among the circle of followers whom he taught; this contrasts to other schools of Judaism of his day, which forbid teaching the Torah to women. Several women even supported him with funds. The books of the New Testament contain the names of a surprisingly large number of women who were disciples or who joined the early Christian movement after Jesus' death: Mary the mother of Jesus, Mary Magdalene, Mary the mother of John Mark, Lydia, Prisca, and Phoebe, just to name a few. These women all exercised some form of leadership in the movement in its early years.

Jesus challenged many of the ritual practices of his day that separated women and men in society. In one of the stories from the gospels, he allowed himself to be touched by a woman with a menstrual flow of blood, thereby violating the laws of ritual purity that set her apart. Throughout his teaching ministry he invited women and men alike to begin to live in a new family pattern that was nonpatriarchal, doing so according to the values of the coming reign of God. The pattern continued after his death. The first witnesses to the resurrection were women. Mary Magdalene in particular was remembered by later ages as being "the apostle to the apostles." Women were likewise present among the community on the day of Pentecost, when the Spirit fell. Throughout the early years of the Christian movement they remained a considerable force behind the spread of its message.

In Galilee, Jesus had begun to send out followers on itinerant ministries of their own. He sent them two by two (some think as women and men traveling together), instructing them to extend his own work of healing the sick, exorcising demons, and bringing words of hope to the poor. Jesus also began in Galilee the practice of having table fellowship with persons of various social classes and conditions of ritual impurity, including those regarded as sinners by other teachers of Torah. This practice of table fellowship challenged in a concrete manner the religious boundaries that separated people from one another in society. On the other hand, it tended to set Jesus and his own followers apart from others in society who did not share their convictions or their willingness to break social boundaries.

The gospels also recall several open-air fellowship meals where large numbers of people were fed by Jesus in the hill country of Galilee. On these occasions, after Jesus had given thanks to God and broken bread before them, he distributed food that proved to be sufficient for them all to eat. These meals were later remembered by his disciples in eschatological terms as foretastes of a messianic banquet that they believed was yet to come. Jesus himself was remembered as saying in Matthew 8:11 that "many will come from east and west and will eat with Abraham and Isaac and Jacob in the kingdom of heaven." Those who followed him continued after his resurrection the practice of sharing meals and giving thanks in expectation of God's universal reign.

Some among his disciples in Galilee began to see in Jesus the fulfillment of their messianic hopes for the restoration of Israel. It was an identity he did not discourage but on the contrary seemed to embrace. Turning his attention toward Jerusalem, he set off for the city one last time, arriving at the season of Passover. A symbolic demonstration of cleansing in the Temple resulted in a confrontation with the priesthood. Several testified later that he had threatened to tear the building down and rebuild it in three days, a charge that played a crucial role in the decision to put him to death. According to the gospel tradition, on the eve of the Passover, after he had eaten a last supper with his closest male followers, he was arrested by the religious authorities of the city with the help of one of his disciples named Judas. The charges they brought against him included threatening the Temple and blasphemy (the latter stemming from his public claim to forgive sins). The Roman administrator, Pilate, ordered him crucified on the charge of claiming to be the king of the Jews. With his arrest many of his followers scattered.

That most likely would have been the end of the movement had not those same disciples in the days and weeks after his death begun to claim that he had appeared to them. Several women from among his followers had gone to anoint his body shortly after his death and claimed to have found only an empty tomb. Reports soon began to circulate of sudden and unexpected appearances in both Galilee and Jerusalem. The effect was electrifying. God had raised the crucified Jesus from the dead, his disciples proclaimed, thereby vindicating not only his message but his very person. Direct appearances of the resurrected Lord ended a short time later for the most part. But the memory of them, combined with the powerful testimony of the women concerning the empty tomb, provided the content of their new messianic message and identity as a movement.

A group of these followers regathered in Jerusalem, where they met regularly in anticipation of Jesus' final return. Others appear to have continued to meet in Galilee. In the period following the resurrection, the disciples of Jesus experienced his presence in their midst as they gathered for fellowship and to share the common meal in his name. At the same time, they experienced his presence as the risen Lord reaching beyond them in identity and mission. In his resurrection, they believed, the crucified Jesus was now the universal Lord, destined by God to reign not only over Jerusalem but throughout all the earth. The events narrated as taking place on the day of Pentecost set this expanding vision of mission in motion. The impetus was summarized in the closing words of Matthew's gospel: "Go therefore and make disciples of all nations."

From Jerusalem to Damascus and Antioch

The book of Acts says that the group of disciples in Jerusalem began to take in new members. Some of these were Greek-speaking, Hellenistic Jews. The group soon found itself dealing with the increasing complexity of being a community of Greek- and Hebrew-speaking Jews. We see an indication here of the context in which the message about Jesus was first translated from Aramaic (the language that Jesus himself had most likely spoken in his day-to-day interactions) to Greek (the language of the Hellenists in which the New Testament was eventually written). The book of Acts reports that some of the group, namely Peter, James, and John continued to worship on a regular basis in the Temple, while others who belonged to the Hellenistic synagogue (some were proselytes to Judaism) carried on public preaching at this latter location. Meanwhile an Essene-like discipline was established by the whole community, with believers selling their properties to give to the poor and sharing their goods in common.

This new experiment was not without its own internal dissension and conflict. A controversy arose, according to Acts 6, when the Hellenists complained of unequal distribution of food to the widows among the Greek- and Hebrew-speaking parties in the community. The result was the selection of a special group of ministers called deacons to oversee distribution among the Hellenists who were in need. Among the leaders of this Greek-speaking group was one named Stephen, who had been engaging in disputation with the other Hellenistic Jews in the city. Acts says the controversy was taking place in the Jerusalem synagogue of the freedmen, where former slaves from Rome and other cities of the diaspora gathered. According to the account, Stephen rejected the need for the Temple and its sacrifice, criticizing the notion that salvation came through a central place of worship. His preaching led to a public confrontation with the authorities in Jerusalem that ended with his death by stoning. This in turn, says Acts, led to the scattering of the other Hellenist followers of Jesus in the Jerusalem group. Some of them went to the cities of Samaria, some to the seacoast, some to Damascus, and some even to Antioch.

In each of these cities the followers of Jesus appear first to have visited the synagogues where the Jewish community gathered. Their message of the crucified and risen Jesus was not well received, however, and before long they left the synagogues (whether voluntarily or by coercion is not always clear) to gather instead in private homes. From the book of Acts it appears that a number of these homes belonged to women. Since women in both Jewish and Greco-Roman society exercised a significant degree of influence over affairs of their households in general, we can imagine that this move on the part of the early Christian communities would have strengthened the role women played within the movement overall. The number of people who gathered in each home was also relatively small. It is not insignificant that the historical Jesus was remembered in the Gospel of Matthew as saying that where only two or three were gathered in his name, there he would be in their midst.

It is also of no small importance that it was persecution of the group in Jerusalem that led to their scattering to other cities beyond Israel, opening up a new chapter in the spread of the movement. Only in Jerusalem did Jewish religious rulers have the authority to persecute a dissident group. Among the cities of the diaspora, the Jewish leadership might have been able to exclude members of the Jesus party from speaking in their synagogues, to denounce them before the local civil magistrates, or to administer some form of punishment such as a public whipping as testified to by Paul. Other than this, however, persecution of the Jesus movement outside the land of Israel was in the hands of civil authorities of the Gentiles. After the first century CE there is little historical evidence of Jews persecuting Christians again, while the record of Christians persecuting Jews is long and bloody.

Eventually Christians would march under imperial banners to conquer new cities and nations in the name of Christ. But the earliest Christian missionaries from Jerusalem went out as refugees and victims of persecution, an experience that offers a sharp contrast to the imperial armies that brought the message of other universal lords and emperors to these same cities before and after them. These first Christians had expansionist tendencies without worldly power. That legacy would eventually be eclipsed, but it could never be entirely forgotten by the wider Christian movement.

Paul and the gospel to the Gentiles

One of those who joined in the stoning of Stephen, according to the book of Acts, was a Hellenistic Jew named Saul. Originally from the city of Tarsus, he had come to Jerusalem to study, and by his own admission was one who was zealous for Torah. The teachings of this new sect of Nazarenes were for him an affront to the Torah, and Saul's response was, again by his own admission, to engage in vigorous persecution (Phil. 3:6). The book of Acts recounts that Saul not only approved the stoning of Stephen, but then set out with the consent of the religious authorities in Jerusalem to pursue the new movement in Damascus, where most likely some of those who scattered had gone.

Jesus the Good Shepherd, Catacomb of Callista, Rome, 3rd century. The earliest known depiction of Jesus in art. Reproduced with permission of Pontifical Commission for Sacred Archeology, Rome.

Damascus, a Hellenistic city in the Roman province of Syria, was surrounded by a countryside whose culture was Semitic. Inside the walls of the city dwelt a sizable Jewish community whose life centered around the synagogue. Synagogues in Damascus, as they were in other first-century cities of the Hellenistic world, were attracting an increasing number of God-fearers, Gentiles who were drawn to Jewish monotheistic teaching but did not choose to undergo circumcision. Saul appears to have initially planned to visit such synagogues to help them organize against the Nazarenes. However, according to the book of Acts again, on the road outside Damascus he experienced an appearance of the risen Lord that led to his conversion to the movement he previously had been persecuting. After three days in Damascus he was baptized by another believer who was already there. Years later, in a letter to Christians in a different urban context, Paul (as he was known following his conversion) listed this experience on the way to Damascus as the last of several appearances of Jesus as the risen Lord. He saw in it the authorization of his own apostolic vocation to bring the message to the Gentiles.

Immediately this new apostle of the Nazarene party set off on his first missionary journey into Gentile territory, in the country of Nabatea (modern Jordan) to the southeast of Israel. An independent Arab nation under Roman political influence, the Nabateans were a semi-nomadic people whose cities provided an important route for caravans traveling through the desert from Damascus to the

Red Sea. Like their cultural neighbors in Israel, the Nabateans were Semitic people, speaking a language close to Hebrew and accepting the practice of circumcision. Like many other Arab peoples of the time, however, they recognized a diversity of local tribal gods and practices, an experience that contrasted sharply with the monotheism of Israel. While we do not have any significant information on this first missionary journey of Paul other than the fact that he stirred up the opposition of King Aretas IV (II Cor. 11:32), we can assume that he was already following the method of preaching the message of Jesus Christ to the Jews first and then to the Gentiles.

After a number of years Paul returned by way of Damascus to Jerusalem where, according to his own account in Galatians, he visited with the "pillars" of the church, namely James, Peter, and John. He says in Galatians 1:18 that he stayed with Peter for fifteen days, perhaps the first time the two met. Paul then traveled to his home city of Tarsus and continued his missionary work in the surrounding district of Cilicia. It was in Tarsus that Acts says Barnabas, a Jew from Cyprus who had joined the Nazarene movement in Jerusalem before being sent to Antioch to help lead that community, sought Paul out to come and work with him.

From the beginning of their activities in Antioch, the followers of Jesus appear to have formed themselves into communities that met apart from the synagogues of the city. The first believers who came from Jerusalem certainly would have visited at least some of the synagogues upon their arrival in the city, for these were the places Jews customarily gathered for sharing news and events. But in Antioch at least some of the Nazarenes shared their story with Gentiles who became believers and were accepted as members of the community without undergoing circumcision. The mixing of Jews and Gentiles in Antioch is all the more significant given the history of persecution, riots, and near-pogroms directed against the Jews by their neighbors there. Jewish and Gentile believers in Jesus gathered together in houses belonging to members of their group, not in the synagogues. This perhaps is also why it was at Antioch that the movement was given its distinctive name as "Christian," indicating that they were clearly setting themselves apart from the synagogue in their new community. Barnabas exercised a leadership role by virtue of his connection with Jerusalem. In addition, the book of Acts names a group of prophets and teachers in Antioch, suggesting at least the beginnings of an organizational structure that permits one to speak of there being a single church in the city.

Across the city Jews and Gentiles not only worshiped together as members of a common Christian community, but they ate together as well, a practice that was alien to the synagogues and became a source of conflict with other Christians from Jerusalem. For these newly named Christians in Antioch, the boundary between Jew and Greek was no longer at the edge of either community. That boundary was now incorporated into the life of their community when they gathered together to eat. Their new identity was literally found on the table, as Jews and Greeks in a common household. The practice of common table fellowship took on new significance for early Christian life and worship in a context of Jews and Gentiles joining together.

By all accounts these early fellowship gatherings were full-fledged community meals in which members shared with one another their daily sustenance. In addition to these larger fellowship meals, at which even non-baptized persons appear to have partaken, followers of Jesus from the earliest days of the movement in Jerusalem gathered regularly for a special meal known as a *eucharist* ("thanksgiving"). The elements at this meal were simply bread and wine. With them, believers remembered and proclaimed the death and resurrection of Jesus Christ. In a letter written to the Christians at Corinth some years later, Paul reminded the Corinthians of the tradition that he had received and passed on to them regarding this special act of worship,

> that the Lord Jesus on the night when he was betrayed took a loaf of bread, and when he had given thanks, he broke it and said, "This is my body that is for you. Do this in remembrance of me." In the same way he took the cup also, after supper, saying, "This cup is the new covenant in my blood. Do this, as often as you drink it, in remembrance of me." (I Cor. 11:23b-25, NRSV)

The tradition handed on to Paul identified the bread and cup with the body and blood of Jesus Christ. Paul in turn linked the common loaf with the commonality the Corinthians shared in community. The eucharistic meal in Corinth and in Antioch thus became the Christian alternative to the sacrifices offered to the other gods in these Hellenistic cities.

The early believers in Antioch also gathered for public worship that included hymns, reading of scripture, teaching, and ecstatic speech or prophecies. Such early Christian gatherings resembled synagogue services, although they appear to have been held in private homes. In his letter to the Corinthians, Paul admonished them concerning the tone of such meetings, for it was these, he indicated, to which outsiders were invited. Piecing together the evidence scattered across the letters of Paul, we can reconstruct something of the worshiping life of Christians in the various cities: regular weekly gathering for prayer, Bible study, admonition, and expression of prophetic or charismatic gifts; common meals and sharing of one another's resources, including with those who were poor; and a special celebration of eucharist, consisting of bread and wine, for baptized Christians only. These elements provided for Christians the counterpart to the temple worship their neighbors attended in various local shrines in these cities.

Scattered and small in number, these first Christians nevertheless understood themselves to be connected to one another in a larger movement. The Antiochene community's connection with Jerusalem was expressed in a concrete manner through financial support. Jerusalem was symbolically significant as the source from which the movement emerged. It was also the eschatological city to which Jesus would one day return, they believed. Antioch might have served as the base from which the mission of Paul and Barnabas into Cyprus and Asia Minor was launched, but it was to Jerusalem that they traveled to decide in council with the other apostles the question of the status of Gentile converts to the Christian movement.

At that council, convened some time around the year 48 CE, the decision was made that the Gentile converts would not be required to undergo circumcision. Gentiles would also not be bound to keep all the injunctions of the Torah, the council decided. Non-Jews were only enjoined to abstain from eating meat that had been sacrificed to idols or had been improperly slaughtered, and from engaging in fornication. Here the major breakthrough of Antioch was ratified by Jerusalem: male Gentiles would be admitted into the Christian movement without undergoing circumcision, as proselytes in Judaism were required to do.

The decision was not without dissent, however. In his letter to the Galatians, Paul recalls that when Jewish Christians from Jerusalem came up to Antioch, there was a dispute between himself and the other leaders over whether to suspend their common table fellowship for the sake of the Jerusalem group's concerns. Paul subsequently took off for the first of several missionary journeys to Asia Minor and Greece. He supported himself by his tent-making trade, while visiting the synagogues and speaking in the public squares about Jesus Christ.

In Corinth Paul met a Jewish couple, Aquila and Priscilla, who were also in the tent-making trade. Apparently they had been among a group who had recently been exiled from Rome by the emperor Claudius. The Roman historian Suetonius tells us that around the year 50 CE the emperor had "expelled the Jews from Rome because they, incited by Chrestus, were constantly creating an uproar."[1] Priscilla and Aquila appear already to have been Christians when they met Paul, and Acts says that they traveled on together to Ephesus. There, according to Acts 18:24, Priscilla and Aquila met Apollos, an Alexandrian Jew who knew of the "way of the Lord." After a time of further instruction from Priscilla and Aquila, Apollos himself went on to Corinth, where he in turn served as a teacher. His time in Corinth resulted in factions emerging among the community that Paul addressed in the opening pages of his letter to them.

We can see in the pages of the New Testament a crisscrossing network of itinerant teachers, prophets, and apostles. Paul's list of greetings in Romans 16 gives a glimpse at this network in action. Through them the Christian message was being spread from city to city. The original followers of Jesus who had gathered in Jerusalem following his resurrection were symbolically significant in connecting the movement with Jerusalem and Galilee. But a wider group of evangelists, prophets, teachers, and apostles played a major role in spreading the message in its first years. How else can one explain the opening of I Peter, which is addressed to Christians in Pontus, Galatia, Cappadocia, Asia, and Bithynia? Some of these are regions in which Paul founded churches, but others are not.

No one can say for sure how the Christian message first came to Rome. By the time Paul wrote to introduce himself prior to a personal visit, the community was already established. The letter Paul sent is now the book of Romans in the New

---

[1] Suetonius, *Claudius* 25.4. This translation is from Hans Conzelmann, *History of Primitive Christianity*, trans. John E. Steely (Nashville, Tenn.: Abingdon Press, 1973), 163. We can assume that Suetonius refers to the same event, although it was followers of "Chrestus" and not Christ himself who were creating the disturbance in the Jewish community in Rome.

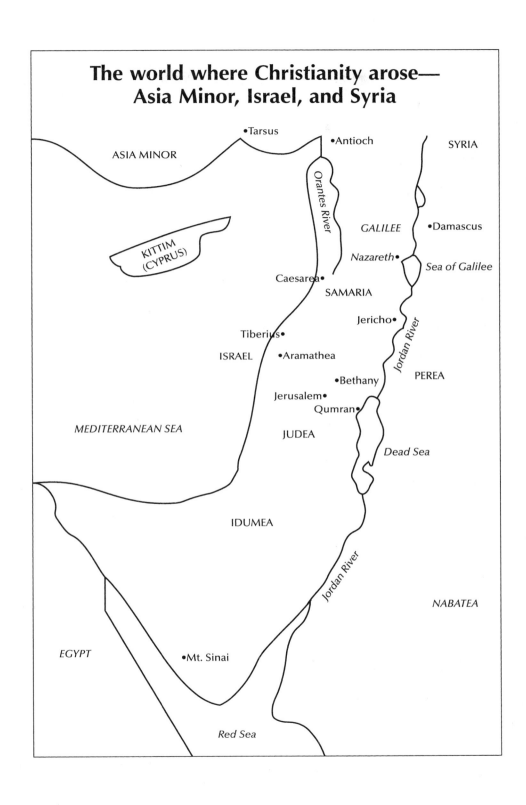

The world where Christianity arose—
Asia Minor, Israel, and Syria

•Tarsus

•Antioch

SYRIA

ASIA MINOR

Orantes River

KITTIM
(CYPRUS)

GALILEE

•Damascus

Nazareth•

Sea of Galilee

Caesarea•

SAMARIA

Jericho•

Jordan River

Tiberius•

•Aramathea

ISRAEL

PEREA

•Bethany

Jerusalem•
Qumran•

MEDITERRANEAN SEA

JUDEA

Dead Sea

IDUMEA

Jordan River

NABATEA

EGYPT

•Mt. Sinai

Red Sea

Testament. In it he told the Roman Christians that he hoped to visit them on his way to Spain, where he planned to continue spreading the faith. He was going to make a trip first to Jerusalem to deliver to the community there a fund he had collected from among the churches of the Gentiles. The trip to Jerusalem resulted in his arrest, however, for like Jesus he caused a disturbance in the Temple. Charged with having brought Gentiles into its inner sanctuary and thereby having desecrated the place, Paul was placed under house arrest. Acts reports that Paul eventually exercised his right as a Roman citizen to appeal to the emperor himself, thereby taking his case in Rome. The appeal took him on his last voyage, this time as a prisoner to Rome, where tradition says he was executed under Nero sometime around 64.

Why did Gentiles first join the Christian movement?

Paul left for us a rich legacy in the letters that he sent to various churches he had founded and that are now part of the canon of the Christian New Testament. Reading these letters one gets a glimpse of the earliest Christian communities in the cities that the apostle worked among and an indication of why Gentiles joined the movement. From their pages, other books of the New Testament, and other first-century records, we can perceive something of the understanding that Gentiles brought with them.

When the earliest generation of Christian evangelists traveled to new cities, the first places they usually visited were the local synagogues, where they sought to spread their message. Greeted by hostility or indifference, however, they soon moved out of the synagogues and into private homes. A careful reading of the New Testament suggests that the synagogue was not the primary place for Christian missionary activities, although it often was the place where contact with other Jews was first made. Christian evangelists met others out on the streets, in the marketplace, in workshops, and around public buildings. The main form of communication in ancient cities was word of mouth. The Christian message spread through people sharing news and gossip, through curious visitors stopping by open doorways to see what a group was doing inside a home, through family members and neighbors being invited to listen to a speaker, and through stories spreading of someone being healed by an itinerant apostle.

Part of the attraction of the Christian message lay in its inclusive message. Christians spoke of Jesus Christ as a universal person who offered hope for overcoming the divisions of the world around them. The Mediterranean world was one of great social mobility. Cities had become quite heterogeneous in their cultural composition. Yet for many this mobility had brought with it a sense of cultural dislocation. In the words of I Peter, they were aliens and exiles (2:11). Many among the first converts were Gentiles who had been God-fearers frequenting the synagogue. From what we know through various sources, the attraction they found in Judaism was precisely the hope of a single, universal God who was over the entire world. Joining the Christian community allowed them to realize their monotheistic faith and its ethical implications.

Jewish members of the early Christian communities appear to have been free to continue to attend synagogue services and to participate in Jewish worship, at least until the time when they were expelled from the synagogues (it is not clear historically if or how often this happened). On the other hand, there is no evidence in the book of Acts or other writings of the New Testament that Gentile members of early Christian communities were permitted to continue to practice their previous religion. On the contrary, virtually all associations with Gentile religious practices were rejected, suggesting that Christians did not intend to separate themselves from the heritage and promises of Israel. Clearly it was the God of Israel whom they understood themselves to be worshiping, whether they were Jews or Gentiles. It was the Messiah or Christ of Israel who was the agent of salvation to all the nations.

People worshiped a diversity of gods in temples and shrines throughout cities in the ancient world, usually with the support of city magistrates. Religion was an integral part of the overall economy of the cities, both politically and financially. People were expected to pray to their various gods for the well-being of the city. As the story in Acts 19 portrays concerning the silversmiths in Ephesus and the temple of Artemis, any challenge to the legitimacy of the various gods of the ancient world carried serious political and financial implications. Nevertheless, among the people themselves a significant degree of dissatisfaction with the various gods and their cults was taking root. The Christian message offered a universal alternative to the religious divisions of the ancient Mediterranean world.

The fact that Paul wrote to members of the Christian community in Corinth to flee from worshiping these idols suggests that a considerable number were formerly worshipers in the other temples of that city (I Cor. 10:14-22; 12:2). Christian leaders claimed that these others were false gods, positing an exclusivist claim that was not congruent with the general consensus of Greco-Roman religious life. Others might have claimed the superiority of one particular deity over another, but they did not challenge whether those other gods in fact existed. Christians did, claiming that these other gods were lesser spirits or even demons, in what one historian has called a "campaign of demotion."[2]

Elsewhere—namely, in the philosophical circles of Hellenistic society—such a campaign was already well under way by the first century, but it was mainly being conducted by the intellectual elite. Christians took this campaign to the masses. They shared Judaism's critique of other gods being idols or demons, that is, things that are not divine but are part of creation (I Cor. 10:19-20; Gal. 4:8). Christians, however, sought more aggressively than their Jewish counterparts to win converts away from these other religions and to the worship of the one true God of Israel. Christians criticized those aspects of Judaism that separated Jews from other people, namely, circumcision and the purity codes surrounding table fellowship. The campaign they undertook was thus double-sided: the gods of the Roman, Greek, and Semitic cultural worlds were being demoted, and the exclusive cultural identity of Judaism was being denied.

---

[2] Ramsay MacMullen, *Christianizing the Roman Empire (A.D. 100-400)* (New Haven, Conn.: Yale University Press, 1984), 18.

This double-conversionist practice drew the resentment and hostility not only of local Jewish leaders but of others, including local civil authorities in the cities where Christianity first spread. Christians were considered atheists by their opponents because they decried the divinity of all except their own God. Once the civil authorities understood that these Christians were not regarded by other Jews as being legitimate members of the household of Israel, Christians were denied legal status. Rome recognized the legitimacy of religions within its empire on the basis of their national origin. Christians, however, were people without a homeland. The shift in opposition was decisive for Christian self-understanding in the Roman political world: followers of Jesus Christ went from being merely disruptive to being politically subversive and anti-state as the status of their religious identity shifted from being regarded as that of a troublesome party within Judaism to being a separate, and homeless, religion.

Christians claimed that the Jesus whom they worshiped as Lord and savior had once lived among them in the flesh. The image of a suffering savior must have arrested many who first heard it. By its very contradiction it appealed to those who experienced suffering or social dislocation, or were among the lower classes in society. Christian teaching about the resurrection might have appeared foolish to the philosophers of the age, but to those who found hope in it, it carried the promise of redemption for their suffering. The emphasis upon the bodily existence of Jesus, the stories of his own healings, and the experiences of healings accompanying early Christian evangelism all gave profound emphasis to the importance of bodies to those whose bodies often did not matter to the world. Christian outreach practices included ministering to those who were ill among their own membership (James 5:14). Paradoxically, such emphasis was coupled with teachings about self-denial that sought to temper the excesses of bodily desires through discipline. The concept of discipline offered a way to find meaning in certain forms of suffering, while its practice appears to have improved the overall quality of relationships within the community.

Social life and early Christian evangelism

Those who joined the Christian movement were generally members of the middle and lower classes: artisans, workers, and even slaves. The presence of the latter class is attested to among the letters of Paul; on several occasions he notes the inclusion of both slave and free in the Christian community. Toward the end of his life, while he was under house arrest (most likely in Rome), Paul was visited by a runaway slave owned by a Christian named Philemon in Colossae. Under the apostle's influence the slave, whose name was Onesimus, became a Christian. Paul then proceeded to send the servant back to his master, with a letter asking that he be taken back and forgiven. In the letter Paul hints that their relationship is no longer to be that of master and slave but now Christian brothers. "I write to you, knowing that you will do even more than I say," implores the imprisoned apostle, hinting perhaps at manumission (Philemon v. 21).

Paul's position here reflected the general attitude he and other New Testament writers held toward slavery. Christians did not advocate freedom from social slavery but freedom within it. In the first century slavery was a well-established social and economic institution in almost every culture. The degree of severity with which it was practiced varied from place to place, and most had either laws or social customs that offered at least some restraint against excesses in violence. Elsewhere Paul advised those who were slaves in the community not to seek their freedom but to remain in the state in which they were called. If the opportunity arose to secure freedom, slaves should avail themselves of it, he said. On the other hand, those who were themselves free ought to consider themselves slaves of Christ (I Cor. 7:17-24). A gradual modification of social attitudes was the realistic prescription early Christian writers offered for the inequalities of social slavery.

A similarly ambiguous attitude attends the inequalities of women and men within early Christian writings. Once again, the New Testament letters of Paul and other leaders from the first generations reflect many of the assumptions and practices of the cultures around them. In the Mediterranean world upper-class women often lived secluded lives, while lower-class women (including women slaves) had much more contact with men in public places. Roman law accorded women far greater legal status than other cultures of the day. Roman women were allowed to own property and run their own financial affairs, for instance, and Roman law required a woman's consent for marriage to be legal. Greek, Egyptian, and Persian practices were far less supportive of women's legal equality or access to social power. Among Jewish women, those who lived in the diaspora (in both the Greco-Roman and Persian worlds) generally faced fewer restrictions than women did in Israel. None of these cultures, however, sought social equality for women and men.

Against this background the presence of women in the early Christian movement offers something of a contrast. Many women rose to positions of leadership in these early communities. Since they were organized as house churches, and in many cultures women exercised major authority over the affairs within a household, women were able to exert considerable authority within the community. A quick glance through the pages of Acts reveals the names of many women in whose homes the church was meeting, and who thus presumably were presiding at the community's table fellowship. The name of Priscilla (or Prisca) is featured prominently before that of her husband as an early Christian teacher. As the Christian movement grew in subsequent years, the influence of women would be significant within its ranks. By the end of the century, there was even a report that the emperor Domitian's niece, Flavia Domitilla, had joined the Christian community, reflecting an early pattern of Christian inroads into the upper classes of Roman society through the conversion of women.

This is not to say that the early Christian movement was entirely egalitarian or free of gender discrimination, for it was not. Here again Christian practice often reflected aspects of its surrounding world. The pages of the New Testament offers several versions of Christian household codes that are quite restrictive of the role of women. Within them one can read a subtle encouragement of mutual submission and accommodation to one another in family relationships, but the overall framework maintains patriarchal rule. Women did exercise an important degree of authority within homes, but few women traveled, and almost never alone. The lack of opportunity to travel favored men as the traveling evangelists in the first generation. Moreover, even though some women learned to read and write (usually so they could teach their male children), they were not permitted to work as scribes. Writing and copying texts, including the gospels, was a male privilege.

Jesus himself, we have seen, demonstrated a noticeable openness to women in his ministry. But even he (at least according to the New Testament traditions) chose only men for the twelve disciples who represented the leadership of the new community as a whole. The ambiguous character of gender divisions within the early Jesus movement is manifest starkly in the narratives of his death and resurrection: only men celebrate with Jesus the last supper, which became the basis for the eucharist, while women were the first witnesses to the resurrection and the empty tomb, the basis of Christian proclamation.

Among the social institutions that Christian teaching addressed, none was more affected than that of marriage. All of the urban-based civilizations of the first century were characterized by strong patriarchal domination of the institutions of marriage and family, and most embraced polygyny. Roman custom and law made monogamy the norm, but even the Romans accepted concubinage and prostitution as common practices. Judaism at the time of Jesus had followed Greco-Roman culture and made monogamy the norm for married life. Jesus' teaching regarding marriage and divorce reinforced the pattern of lifelong monogamous relationships between men and women. At least one time in the gospel tradition Jesus is recalled as having taught that marriage and sexual relations were not the state after which his followers ought to seek (Matt. 19:10-12). It was a position that was left to the apostle Paul to explicate.

Paul's most complete teaching on marriage is found in I Corinthians 7. There he restates the principle of monogamy. But then he goes on to say that, in his view, it is better to remain single. Paul regarded marriage as a concession to inordinate passions and sexual desires. He recommended asceticism as the preferred mode of Christian life, although marriage, he was quick to point out, was not a sin (I Cor. 7:36). The apostle expected the imminent return of Christ, which would bring with it the end of practices of marriage and traditional family life. Other New Testament texts share this imminent expectation of the end of the age, joined with an intense personal discipline that serves as a means of preparation.

One of the outcomes of the Christian embrace of an ascetic lifestyle was to free women from the expectations of marriage. The state of being single for a woman was generally not considered a positive lifestyle option in first-century urban cultures, east or west. Among the Christians, single women, on the other hand, were regarded as free to be workers in the church, to give themselves entirely to its ministry, and even to be supported by the community as a whole for their public endeavors. The Christian movement enabled a number of women to step into leadership roles in public life as an alternative to their traditional confinement within patriarchal marriage.

Just how extensive that ministry was in the first century remains another issue of debate among historians and biblical scholars today. A number of New Testament texts appear to forbid women playing any significant leadership role in worship or teaching in the community. Several of these texts are found in letters said to come from Paul himself. Yet Paul cites several women in leadership in various Christian communities. To the church at Corinth, a city where women priests performed rituals addressed to other gods with ecstatic abandon, Paul instructs the Christian women to cover their heads while prophesying. The fact that he does so indicates that he recognized their ministry alongside that of men in the church. The early Christian movement provided a space for women to exercise leadership in worship and work in the community. In some places they may have led eucharistic celebrations (the evidence for this remains sketchy and intensely debated). Such opportunities, however limited they might have been, attracted women to the movement as a whole.

Paul's summary of Christian baptismal identity in Galatians 3:28 testified to the Christian ideals regarding unity and equality: "There is neither Jew nor Greek, there is neither slave nor free, there is neither male nor female; for you are all one in Christ Jesus." It was an ideal, however, and not always a reality. Even Paul himself backed away from the assertion that there were no gender differences in Christ (I Cor. 12:13; see also Col. 3:11). The Christian movement had been born from a radical eschatological experience of resurrection and Spirit. As it grew, it came to live in the tension between its initial radical expectations and the reality of existing social institutions in the world around it. Part of the attraction to the movement was precisely its ability to generate hope and change by living in the midst of the tension.

Closely related to the egalitarian values that the Christian gospel affirmed was the moral character Christians demonstrated in their lives. In the first century many believed a moral life was something only one who practiced philosophy could attain. Despite the diversity of systems and beliefs, one thing the great teachers of the ancient world agreed upon was that reasoning shaped the soul. The way of reason, however, required a discipline of mind and body that only an elite class was considered capable of practicing. In his letter to the Galatians, Paul provided a list of moral virtues that he wrote were the fruit of the Spirit. Those whose lives were guided by the Spirit were therefore expected to manifest "love, joy, peace, patience, kindness, goodness, faithfulness, gentleness, self-control" (Gal. 5:22). Especially effective in terms of evangelistic witness was the courage Christians often showed in the face of severe persecution or even death. Several generations after Paul, Christian apologists continued to make the point that unlettered Christians demonstrated in their lives the virtues, especially courage, considered the sign of a true philosophy.

All of these features played a role in attracting Gentiles to the Christian movement. Judging from the Christian writings themselves, none was more important or effective than the demonstrations of signs and wonders that were regularly reported in early Christian life. Stories of the miraculous abound in the first-century world, and not just among Christians. The Christian movement, how-ever, tended to democratize the miraculous. The first followers of Jesus believed they were living in a new age of the Spirit, who had endowed them with special spiritual gifts. Early Christian worship was often ecstatic. Members spoke in languages they did not previously know, received prophecies regarding the fu-ture, exorcised evil spirits, and practiced physical healings. Throughout its long history across many centuries and in many different cultures, such signs and wonders would prove time and again to be the most effective means of drawing new members into the communion of Christian faith.

Unity and diversity in the earliest Christian movement

According to the New Testament, Paul was not the first to take the message of the gospel to Gentiles beyond the household of Israel. The gospels portray Jesus himself engaging several Samaritans, a Syro-Phoenician woman, and even a Roman centurion in a positive manner. Acts 8:26-40 recounts a story of the con-version and baptism of a government official from the African kingdom of Meroë south of Egypt. Two chapters later in Acts, Peter receives a vision instructing him to take the good news of Jesus Christ to a Roman centurion named Cornelius, of the Italian cohort stationed in Caesarea. In the midst of Peter's sermon, the story continues, the Spirit of God suddenly fell upon Cornelius and his household, being manifested through a charismatic experience of speaking in tongues as had happened on the day of Pentecost. Peter proceeded immediately to baptize Cornelius in the name of Jesus Christ. These apostolic experiences in the gospels and Acts form an emerging theological paradigm of inclusion. It was Paul's con-tribution to carry the project further and to articulate its theological basis.

Paul began within a Jewish framework that regarded the covenant with God to be salvific. For most parties of Judaism, Gentiles were by definition people out-side the covenant, and thus unrighteous. The terms *Gentile* and *sinner* could be used interchangeably in Judaism. Jesus was remembered by the early Christian movement as having challenged these categorizations by having gone among the sinners while challenging the righteous. The early Christian mission to the Gen-tiles was then an extension of his practice. Nevertheless, the problem of the theo-logical status of Gentiles within the covenant called for clarification.

Paul's argument was that neither circumcision nor observance of Torah made one righteous before God. Instead, righteousness came through Jesus Christ alone, who had been himself pronounced "cursed" under the terms of Torah. Because Jesus, who was righteous or without sin, had been counted among the sinners, those who were sinners could now be counted among the righteous who had entered into the covenant with God. For Paul, justification before God resulted not from one's behavior as measured by the Law but by the grace of God freely given. All human beings had sinned, Paul asserted, and had thus fallen short of the righteousness of God. Those who had been given the Torah and those who had not were seen equally in the eyes of God to be sinners, and thus they were equally in need of being accepted.

The promise of divine grace, of forgiveness and acceptance by God, Paul argued, was first given to Abraham and now realized fully in the person of Jesus Christ. Hence the door was opened for Jews and Gentiles to enter into a new relationship. This was also the opening chapter of God's new creation, an apocalyptic concept that Paul put to good theological use. Freedom from the old creation of sin and death was achieved through a baptismal experience of identification with Christ. At the same time it was a freedom for a new relationship through what Paul elsewhere called the "law of Christ," that is, the unconditional love of God. The notion that the Gentiles were held accountable by God to a more general law was a common one among Paul's rabbinic contemporaries. What Paul perceived to be uniquely achieved in Jesus Christ was a new form of communion in which Jews and Gentiles engaged one another under the same law of love. He sought not the eradication of Jewish and Gentile identities but their inclusion in a new form of community in Christ that embraced these differences.

This is not to say that the new Christian community was to be without moral boundaries or ethical definition of its own. While he argued against binding Gentile converts to all the stipulations of Jewish law, Paul was not antinomian. A large portion of his writings were in fact taken up with moral considerations and ethical instruction concerning day-to-day living. Paul sought to shape the lives of the believers so that they would become more congruent with the life of Christ. He instructed his readers in Galatia to behave in specific ways in order to "fulfill the law of Christ" (Gal. 6:2), which he summarized as the law of love. He counseled the Corinthians on a number of matters concerning their community life, including an explicit instruction to banish someone for immoral sexual behavior. The Thessalonians were urged on to holiness and purity of love through the power of the Holy Spirit. What Paul condemned was any separation of Jews from Gentiles in the Christian community, especially in its table fellowship, on the basis of Judaism's purity codes. He did not intend this to mean an end to a distinctive Jewish identity within the Christian community, which he expected would be carried on in a new form in Christ.

Paul provided a powerful theological argument for a trans-cultural experience that was emerging in the movement. Early Christian communities embraced several cultural identities within their ranks. Gentiles and Jews alike brought much of their past with them when they joined the Christian movement. Some elements, such as rituals directed toward other gods or spiritual practices explicitly identified with savior figures other than Jesus Christ, they were strictly instructed to give up. Others they began to modify, including personal behaviors, sexual moral norms, patterns of family life, economic activities, and forms of worship. At a deeper level a significant degree of cultural continuity with multiple pasts was maintained through the diversity of languages spoken in the various communities. Here the story of the day of Pentecost narrated in Acts 2 was paradigmatic. Translating the message of Jesus Christ into new languages entailed as much a conversion of the gospel to new and diverse cultures as it did the conversion of people from different cultures to faith in Jesus Christ.

Christian life and Christian worship thus began to look different in different locations. At the same time, a lively sense of trans-regional connection emerged among the churches. Paul himself spent a significant portion of his time organizing a collection among the Gentile churches that he could take to the church in Jerusalem. This collection was to be a concrete demonstration of the Gentiles' connection through thankfulness for the gospel that had come to them from Jerusalem (see II Cor. 8-9). The funds that they gave were for Paul a spiritual gift and an act of grace. In this sense his understanding of the connection among churches separated by cultural and geographical distances can be said to have been charismatic. The material sharing of goods across geographical distances encouraged a sense of belonging to one another in the movement and ultimately served the spiritual unity of the church as a whole.

Paul's sense of connectedness was also apostolic. He recognized the priority of those whom he called the "pillars" of the church, namely Peter, James, and John (Gal. 2:9). Like others, Paul recognized the authority of charismatic prophets through whom the risen Christ spoke. But the authority and teachings of these prophets were judged in light of the critical memory of the remembered words of Jesus himself. Those who knew Jesus in the flesh, or to whom the risen Lord had appeared, were hence accorded a privileged position as apostles among the leadership. By according them the privilege of reviewing his own position on the gospel, Paul not only gained credibility for his teachings; he helped to maintain the cohesion of the movement as a whole.

As the Christian movement expanded in the first century, the authority of those who knew Jesus in the flesh grew in significance. Their connection to Jesus, and to one another, provided a critical component for the institutional foundations of a trans-regional church. The collective apostolic memory was the ground out of which a common church emerged. The first written gospels were all composed and circulated under the authority of apostles. Most of them had, according to tradition, journeyed to different parts of the world where they had died. Following the destruction of the city of Jerusalem in 70 CE by the Romans, and the physical death of the first generations of Christians, the role of apostolic memory in the churches became even more important. The connectedness the apostles had with one another through their common experience with Jesus in Galilee and Jerusalem was understood to continue in the communities they had founded in various parts of the world, even after the church in Jerusalem effectively ceased to exist.

In an important sense this form of apostolic connection embodied what they believed to be Jesus' own trans-regional presence through the Spirit. The early Christian proclamation of the empty tomb meant Jesus' historical body and identity were not necessary for believers to have access to him. This was the message of the angel at the tomb who told the women in the Gospel of Mark that "he is not here . . . he goes before you in Galilee." In the resurrection, writes a recent New Testament scholar, "The kingdom of God was getting around the borders and leaking through the cracks of civil, social, psychological, and physical impediments."[3]

The city of Jerusalem had served as an eschatological center for the movement in the first days following the resurrection. But then the dispersion and eventual elimination of Christians from that city had the same impact as the empty tomb. The Christian movement was in effect denied its center. It could only live beyond itself because it remained connected not to Galilee or Jerusalem, but to the apostolic memory of one who was going before them. Paradoxically, retaining such a memory enabled the movement to move to new peripheries of its own history. The dispersion of the apostles to regions beyond Jerusalem did not lead to the breakup of the movement. Their unity, they believed, was found in the person of Jesus, who beckoned them from the edges of history.

The original twelve, according to later traditions, went to different regions of the world. Historical tradition remembers Thomas as having traveled to Edessa and India to the east, while Mark is remembered as evangelizing in Alexandria, and Matthew in Ethiopia. John most likely spent his last days in Asia Minor, while Peter and Paul were held by ancient tradition to have been executed in Rome. In each place where these apostles were said to have gone, early traditions identify bishops (or overseers) as their successors, maintaining a sense of connection with the original apostles.

At the beginning of the second century, Ignatius, bishop of Antioch, used the term *catholic* (*kat'holos* in Greek, "according to the whole") to describe this embodied sense of connectedness. Writing to the Christians of Smyrna on his way to Rome to face his own execution, Ignatius counseled his readers to shun divisions by following their bishop as Jesus Christ followed the Father. "Wherever the bishop appears, there let the people be; as wherever Jesus Christ is, there is the catholic church," he told them.[4] Churches in various locations were connected with others by sharing their resources, by traveling itinerant ministers, and by common memories they held of Jesus. The connection was manifest as well through the relationships among leaders of churches, the overseers or bishops. Centuries later the concept of catholicity would be defined in stronger doctrinal terms; but in the days of the early Christian movement, concrete connections through persons and memories were more important than intellectual formulations of the faith.

Diversity amid unity: Confessing that Jesus is Lord

We have seen that the expanding Christian community and its initial translation beyond the boundaries of Palestinian Judaism set the conditions for a diversified,

[3] Marianne Sawicki, *Seeing the Lord: Resurrection and Early Christian Practice* (Minneapolis, Minn.: Fortress Press, 1994), 264-265.

[4] Ignatius of Antioch, *Letter to the Smyrnaeans*, in *The Apostolic Fathers*, trans. Francis X. Glimm, Joseph M.-F. Marique, S.J., and Gerald G. Walsh, S.J. (Washington D.C.: The Catholic University of America Press, 1969), 121.

and diversifying, faith. As it moved beyond an initial small group of disciples from Galilee, the Christian movement encountered new languages, religions, and philosophies. As it did so, it sought to make them its own. Sometimes the engagement was explicit. The book of Acts recalls Paul at the Areopagus in Athens as having quoted the Greek Stoic philosopher Aratus, who said that we are all God's offspring. Other times the engagement appears to have taken place at a deeper, implicitly conceptual level. The book of Hebrews offered an allegorical exegesis that resembled the Jewish-Platonism of Philo of Alexandria, without stating as much directly.

Nowhere was the diversity in early Christian understanding more evident than in the central meanings given to the terms used to identify the risen Jesus. "Son of God" and "Son of humanity" for instance could mean different things in different contexts as Christian proclamation moved across the borders of language and culture. The translation of the Hebrew term *Messiah* ("anointed one") into the Greek term *Christ* is another example. None is more emblematic of the process than the diversity of meanings of the term *Lord*, which emerged by the end of the first century of the Christian movement.

Early Christians referred to Jesus as Lord. While the New Testament was written in Greek, it contains several Aramaic expressions that most likely were remembered because of their close association with Jesus and his disciples in Galilee. One of these Aramaic expressions addressed toward Jesus is the phrase *maranatha*, used by Paul in I Corinthians 16:22 and translated either as "come Lord" or as "the Lord has come." The Aramaic word, *maran*, could be a term of respectful address, a designation of a ruler, or a designation for a god. No doubt it was used by some in referring to Jesus in his lifetime.

A comparable Hebrew term had by the second century BCE come to be used in Judaism in place of pronouncing the sacred name of God. When reading the Hebrew scriptures, Jews used the Hebrew word *adonai* ("Lord") instead of pronouncing the Tetragrammaton, YHWH. The Septuagint reflected this practice by substituting the Greek word *kurios* ("Lord") for the divine name. While the term *kurios* had a similar range of meanings as *maran*, its use in the New Testament for Jesus, in light of the usage in the Septuagint, indicates more clearly a divine designation. Throughout the pages of the New Testament, the term *kurios* is used as a designation for Jesus, the one Jesus himself called the Father and the Spirit. Hearers of the early Christian message who were familiar with the Septuagint could not help but hear the attribution of divine status to Jesus Christ.

Other early Christians in Antioch and elsewhere in the Hellenistic world who were not familiar with Jewish practice or the Septuagint could also have heard divine attribution in the use of the term *kurios*. The Greek term *christos* did not carry the same meaning for a Gentile. Without its Jewish background and Davidic connotations, it might simply have meant "ointment" to someone in Antioch. The word *kurios* on the other hand was commonly used to refer to human rulers, but also in shrines and temples to speak of the deities of the Hellenistic world. Jews and Gentiles alike observed sacrifices to various invisible (or spiritual) Lords being performed each day. Thus when Christians used *kurios* in worship, they were imparting divine attributes to Jesus. The confession that Paul states in

I Corinthians 12:3 to be the work of the Holy Spirit, namely, that "Jesus is Lord," is especially significant when posed in this context.

The message that Jesus was Lord was a challenge to the non-Jewish hearer insofar as this Jesus was a human being who had suffered in the flesh. Moreover, he had suffered the ignominious death of being executed by a Roman governor, no small matter for Christians living in Antioch or Corinth under Roman rule. The message was that this Lord valued human bodies, having himself come in the flesh. He valued those who suffered, having been himself subjected to the suffering of the cross. God had raised him up to glory, promising to do the same for those who followed him as disciples.

Before the end of the first century there was a marked tendency within the Hellenistic cultural context for the proclamation of Jesus as Lord to be absorbed into the more general pantheon of gods. The response of the writer of I John was to draw a boundary of acceptable belief on the issue of the embodiment of Jesus in the flesh. I John 4:2 calls upon readers to test every spirit by means of the critical confessional principle "that Jesus Christ has come in the flesh." One or two generations later Polycarp, bishop of Smyrna, and Ignatius, bishop of Antioch, were still writing against those who claimed that Jesus was only a phantom, or that he only appeared to come in the flesh, a belief that became more generally known as *docetism* (from the Greek word *dokein*, "to appear").

Polycarp and Ignatius sought to draw a boundary to acceptable Christian diversity regarding the reality of the flesh and blood of Jesus. One of the most influential early church historians, Eusebius, whose *Ecclesiastical History* was written in the fourth century, identified another group on the fringes of the early Christian movement. Eusebius called them Ebionites and identified them as a party who held a lower view of Jesus' person (hence the possible reason for their name, which means "poor ones" in Hebrew). They believed Jesus was a prophet, but they denied that he was preexistent in the form of the eternal Word, as the Gospel of John stated. They believed he was born of the virgin Mary, but that it was his virtue that set him apart, not a divine nature. Ebionites kept the Jewish law, including the Sabbath, but they also celebrated the resurrection on Sunday with other Christians, Eusebius said. Other early Christian authors reported that they only accepted Matthew's gospel, and that they used the Hebrew language. They represented a way of being obedient to Jesus that was still Jewish.

These early Christian bishops and teachers struggled to define the boundaries of acceptable interpretations of Jesus within shifting cultural contexts. They faced the problems of translating the meaning of their confession of Jesus as Lord in situations of cultural pluralism and cultural boundary crossings. One place where they united in their confession, however, was in their opposition to the imperial cult of the Roman world, which confessed the emperor to be divine. Christian criticism of other lords, and their worship, could only be in direct confrontation with the Roman imperial cult.

After Augustus the Roman Senate had decreed several emperors upon their deaths to be divine and included their images among the Roman gods who were to be worshiped. Augustus had permitted veneration of his person while alive, but it was Gaius Caligula (37-41 CE) who first proclaimed his own divinity during his rule. The emperor Nero likewise encouraged such adoration while he was alive. The great crisis came at the end of the century, however, when Domitian (81-96 CE) began to be called *dominus et deus* ("Lord and God"). Nero and Domitian are both candidates for being the great beast in chapter 13 of the book of Revelation, while the imperial city of Rome itself is most likely the Babylon the Great whose destruction is prophesied.

Revelation portrays the Christian confrontation with emperor worship in apocalyptic terms, calling upon Christians to witness against the image of the imperial anti-Christ to the point of death. Through this they are promised a share in the triumph of the true Lord, Jesus Christ, the Lamb who was slain by Roman imperial power. Paul had provided a milder form of criticism of the emperor in his letter to the Romans, written half a century or so earlier. Romans 13 is often read out of context as a blind statement of support for the imperial state. But read in a situation in which the emperors were worshiped as divine, Paul's argument can be seen as a subtle act of resistance. There is no authority except from God, who has instituted worldly authorities. Rulers are God's servants, he asserted; he therefore implied that they are not themselves divine.

Widespread imperial persecutions in the Roman empire did not come under Domitian, as the writer of Revelation seemed to expect. There would be no systematic campaign against Christians in the Roman world for another century. In the Parthian world and in Arabia, official persecutions were even further away. But the groundwork was already in place in the early days of the movement for a confrontation between Christ and Caesar (the Roman emperor) or the shah of shahs (king of kings, the Persian emperor). Christians confessed Jesus Christ, who had died on a Roman cross. The point of their witness was that the confrontation had already taken place, and that Christ had been victorious. The resurrection was already God's triumph in human history over the forces of domination and death. Taking that message into the various worlds around them was the compelling mission of the first Christian believers.

Recommended reading

Those wishing to read further in the history of the world Christian movement have a number of options. Three popular introductory texts that tell the story of the history of Christianity in the West are Williston Walker, *A History of the Christian Church*, 3d ed. rev. Robert T. Handy (New York: Charles Scribner's Sons, 1970); Justo L. González, *The Story of Christianity*, 2 vols. (New York: Harper & Row, 1983); and Kenneth Scott Latourette, *A History of Christianity*, rev. ed., 2 vols. (New York: Harper & Row, 1975). Gonález begins the transition to telling the story of Christianity as a world religion, the theme around which this volume organizes itself. Latourette is well known for his seven-volume history of mission entitled *A History of the Expansion of Christianity* (New York and London: Harper and Brothers, 1937-45). Hubert Jedin and John Dolan, eds., *History of the Church*, 5 vols. (New York: Herder and Herder, 1965-81) provide an extensive overview of western church history with great attention to Roman Catholic institutional identity and less to World Christianity as a trans-denominational reality.

W. H. C. Frend, *The Rise of Christianity* (Philadelphia: Fortress Press, 1984), examines in considerable detail the first six centuries of Christianity in the Roman imperial world. The story of how early Christianity presented itself through visual forms is told by Robin Margaret Jensen, *Understanding Early Christian Art* (New York and London: Routledge, 2000). Peter R. L. Brown, *The Rise of Western Christendom: Triumph and Diversity* (Oxford: Blackwell, 1996) narrates the history of the first millennia, with attention to cultural diversity and an increasing amount of attention paid to what became northern Europe. An accessible overview of the historical formation of Eastern Orthodox tradition is found in Alexander Schmemann, *The Historical Road of Eastern Orthodoxy* (Crestwood, N.Y.: St. Vladimir's Seminary Press, 1992). Mary T. Malone, *Women and Christianity*, vol. 1, *The First Thousand Years* (Maryknoll, N.Y.: Orbis Books, 2001), is an excellent study of the contributions women have made to western church history.

Two books that trace the history of Christianity east of Jerusalem are Samuel H. Moffett, *A History of Christianity in Asia,* vol. 1, *Beginnings to 1500* (Maryknoll, N.Y.: Orbis Books, 1998); and Ian Gillman and Hans-Joachim Klimkeit, *Christians in Asia Before 1500* (Ann Arbor, Mich.: University of Michigan Press, 1999). Concern for the history of Christianity east of Jerusalem as well as in Egypt also occupies Aziz Suryal Atiya, *A History of Eastern Christianity*, rev. ed. (Millwood, N.Y.: Kraus Reprint, 1980). An important contribution to Asian church history is that of A. M. Mundadan et al., *History of Christianity in India*, 6 vols. (Bangalore: Church History Association of India, 1989).

Beginning and advanced students alike are likely to find several encyclopedias useful, including Everett Ferguson, ed., *Encyclopedia of Early Christianity*, 2d ed. (New York and London: Garland Publishing, 1997); Aziz Suryal Atiya, *The Coptic Encyclopedia*, 8 vols. (New York: Maxwell Macmillan International; Toronto: Collier Macmillan Canada, 1991); and George Menachery, *The St. Thomas Christian Encyclopaedia of India* (Trichur: St. Thomas Christian Encyclopaedia of India, 1973). While not an encyclopedia, the Paulist Press series Classics of Western Spirituality is encyclopedic in scope. This series now includes over 130 works in English translations from Jewish, Christian, and Muslim authors spanning the last two millennia. The Christian texts that are represented include works of writers from Orthodox, Catholic, and Protestant traditions. Also helpful to students is *A Dictionary of Asian Christianity*, ed. Scott W. Sunquist (Grand Rapids, Mich.: Wm B. Eerdmans Publishing Co., 2001).

The best introduction to the background of the history of the civilizations of the world discussed in Part I is to be found in the thirteen volumes of *The Cambridge History of China*, ed. Denis Twitchett and John K. Fairbank (Cambridge and New York: Cambridge University Press, 1978); the five volumes of *The Cambridge History of Iran* by various authors (Cambridge and New York: Cambridge University Press, 1968); the eight volumes of *The Cambridge History of Africa*, ed. J. D. Fage and Roland Oliver (Cambridge and New York: Cambridge University Press, 1970-86); or the two volumes of *The Cambridge History of the Native*

Peoples of the Americas, ed. Richard E. Adams and Wilcomb E. Washburn (Cambridge and New York: Cambridge University Press, 2000). Background on the history of various religions across the world can be found in John R. Hinnells, ed., *A Handbook of Living Religions* (Harmondsworth, UK: Penguin Books, 1984); and Willard G. Oxtoby, ed., *World Religions,* vol. 1, *Western Traditions,* and vol. 2, *Eastern Traditions* (New York: Oxford University Press, 1996).

Among the introductions to the New Testament, Raymond E. Brown, *An Introduction to the New Testament* (New York: Doubleday and Co., 1997), and Bart D. Ehrman, *The New Testament: A Historical Introduction to the Early Christian Writings,* 2d ed. (New York: Oxford University Press, 2000), are highly respected. Ehrman has collected primary texts of Christianity from the first century into *The New Testament and Other Early Christian Writings: A Reader* (New York: Oxford University Press, 1998). Not included in this work, but of increasing interest to scholars of early Christianity, are *The Dead Sea Scrolls: A New Translation,* trans. Michael Wise, Martin Abegg Jr., and Edward Cook (San Francisco: HarperSanFrancisco, 1996). Helmut Koestler, *History and Literature of Early Christianity,* 2d ed., vol. 1, *History, Culture, and Religion of the Hellenistic Age,* and vol. 2, *History and Literature of Early Christianity* (New York and Berlin: Walter De Gruyter, 2000), provides a fairly comprehensive examination of Hellenistic and Roman influences from the time of Jesus as they affected the early Christian movement. Much of what we know of Israel (or Palestine) from the first century comes to us from the works of Flavius Josephus, whose works *Antiquities* and *The Wars of the Jews* are included in a collected volume of *Works* (Grand Rapids, Mich.: Baker Books, 1995).

The list of recent works on the historical Jesus is vast enough and the controversy that surrounds the quest heated enough to prevent us from recommending any single text. A popular introduction to the discussion is Marcus J. Borg and N. T. Wright, *The Meaning of Jesus: Two Visions* (San Francisco: HarperSanFrancisco, 2000). Dale C. Allison, *Jesus of Nazareth: Millenarian Prophet* (Minneapolis, Minn.: Fortress Press, 1998), explores many of the methodological issues involved in the historical study of Jesus, while Ben Wirtherington, *The Jesus Quest: The Third Search for the Jew of Nazareth* (Downers Grove, Ill.: InterVarsity Press, 1999), looks at a number of the more important theorists working in the English language. Those interested in gaining a better understanding of the religious context of first-century Israel will find help in Frederick J. Murphy, *The Religious World of Jesus: An Introduction to Second Temple Palestinian Judaism* (Nashville, Tenn.: Abingdon Press, 1991). Alan F. Segal, *Rebecca's Children: Judaism and Christianity in the Roman World* (Cambridge, Mass.: Harvard University Press, 1986), explores the manner in which these two faiths emerged from the crucible of first-century Israel. Finally, a ground-breaking work in feminist biblical studies and a major contribution to understanding the place of women in the New Testament is Elisabeth Schüssler Fiorenza, *In Memory of Her: A Feminist Theological Reconstruction of Christian Origins* (New York: Crossroad, 1983).

Part II

DIVERSE TRAJECTORIES
OF THE EARLY CHRISTIAN MOVEMENT

Christianity entered a world that was inhabited by a host of other religions and gods. A second-century author named Maximus of Tyre estimated that there were some thirty thousand deities being worshiped around the Mediterranean alone. It was a world of great cultural diversity as well. Languages, customs, and practices varied from region to region, and even from street to street in the cities. Those who first heard the message of the apostles were not blank slates upon which the gospel could be written. People brought their own ideas about life, religion, and salvation with them when they joined the new movement. The households of faith that early Christians formed reflected many of the social and cultural realities of their environment. In time the meaning of those ideas and the patterns of social and cultural life changed without being entirely abandoned. The new Christians continued to use old languages. They borrowed from existing social structures to build their new communities, making use of much that was at hand. However much the message of the Christian gospel called upon its listeners to break with their past in a radical act of conversion, its practice was to make contact with the world around it in its linguistic and cultural depths. To understand the history of the early Christian churches, we must then attend to the diversity of social and cultural locations into which the movement spread.

The apostolic message crossed a number of political, cultural, geographical, and linguistic borders in its first decades. The reasons why people in various regions joined the movement, and what they understood themselves to be doing as they did, were diverse. Unfortunately for the historian, they are also difficult to document. Relatively few firsthand narratives of conversion to the Christian movement from the first century exist. Most joined anonymously, leaving little in the way of a historical record that reveals their reasoning. We can generalize from the sources that we do have, of course. Among the most prominent features in early Christian narratives are stories of miracles performed by the followers of Jesus in his name. We can assume that the impact of such signs and wonders was a significant factor.

Another factor at work drawing people into the ranks of the churches was the social inversion the movement proclaimed. The world into which Christian evangelists first traveled was often one where honor was reserved to the few. Only the elite had access to privilege and power. The story of a powerless Jesus who was dishonored in his own land but was raised up by God resonated with people who faced similar challenges and conflicts in their own lives. A number of early Christian sermons make the point that Jesus was a person whom the powerful of the world rejected, but whom God had glorified. The regularity with which the theme shows up in early Christian preaching is an indication of its effectiveness in reaching people.

Closely related to this last point was the appeal of the gospel message to those longing for greater inclusion of women in community. Many of the stories about Jesus gave a key role to women. Several were counted among his students or disciples, including Mary Magdalene, and the sisters Mary and Martha. Women, including his own mother, played a visible role in the expanding Christian movement after the resurrection. The measure of freedom they found in it was an important factor in the movement's appeal. Often this freedom was manifested in a woman's decision to embrace a celibate life, thereby removing herself from the domination of a husband, brother, or father in patriarchal culture.

A second-century apocryphal text known as the *Acts of Thecla* (which is part of a collection of texts called the *Acts of Paul*) illustrates this attraction well. Thecla was a young woman from Iconium who was engaged to be married when she heard Paul preach on the virtues of virginity. The words of the apostle brought her a great sense of joy, leading her to embrace celibacy and join the Christian movement. Her family brought her before the governor of the city on charges of abandoning marriage, and she was condemned to death. But when they tried to burn her on a pile of wood and straw, a rainstorm put out the fire. Next she was thrown to wild beasts in an arena, yet according to the story the animals refused to harm her. Finally, according to the *Acts* she was released, whereupon she became a teacher of the word at Paul's instruction. The story of Thecla might well have been a legend, but its appeal was certainly a historical reality.

We will see in subsequent chapters that the fire of these early Christian commitments in time began to cool, without the embers ever entirely dying out. The message that the poor were to be first in the reign of God was not always prominent as the movement attracted members from upper classes. The social egalitarianism found in Paul's message of men and women being one in Christ was partially eclipsed by the influences of the patriarchal cultures around them. Christian life came to reflect many of the inequalities that characterized day-to-day life in the ancient world. Yet long after churches had accommodated themselves to the dominant patterns of social relations, the fires of social change could still flare up and the call to greater equality in the body of Christ still be heard.

The expansion of the Christian movement in its first decades took the message of Jesus into several cultural and geographical regions beyond Palestine. Jesus himself is remembered in the gospels as having extended his mission beyond the household of Israel only tentatively. The larger task of extending the Christian community beyond the borders of Israel and Judaism fell to the disciples, who in doing so became known as apostles. Compelled by the risen Lord, they sought to reach beyond the boundaries of Israel to bring the message of

God's universal reign through Christ to what the New Testament called "the ends of the earth." One or two generations after the original spread of the apostolic movement from Israel, its memory of Jesus and his first followers was committed to writing in several missionary texts known as gospels. These helped to fix the authority and identity of the initial band of Jesus, while facilitating the wider communication of the message in other parts of the world. By the end of the first century, roughly three generations after the apostles and Jesus, churches had formed in several different cultural locations with diverse memories of their various apostolic founders but committed to a common faith in Jesus Christ.

We will look at the initial expansion of the Christian movement in the pages that follow, tracing the story through the first two centuries into several different regions of the world. In most cases, the initial expansion was into cities, followed by the spread of the movement later into the surrounding countryside. The main institutional form the movement took in each place was a particular kind of community called the church. Becoming a Christian usually entailed a decision to enter the church through the rite of initiation known as baptism. In most places Christians remained in the minority and did not exercise much political or social power for the first several centuries. Where they began to gain significant numbers, there was often organized opposition from among those who saw in the Christian movement a direct threat to the existing order of society. For their part Christians often turned such opposition into an occasion that called for greater sacrifice and commitment, providing an incentive for further missionary activity.

The movement was not without internal conflicts and differences. Nor was it entirely contained by the structures of church and apostolic traditions. By the end of the second century there was a general consensus among most of those who called themselves Christian that the major institutional structure of the movement was found in churches led by bishops, elders, and deacons, and that these churches stood in historical continuity with the original apostles of Jesus. This was the position of the Catholic wing or party of the movement. The message of Jesus, however, overflowed the boundaries of these ecclesiastical structures. The history of such excesses also belongs to the wider history of the Christian movement, but to tell it we must often return to the texts of Catholic faith, which also transmitted them. Hence we are led back to the structures that transmitted the message of Jesus, and from them to the apostolic memory itself, beginning with the shape it took in scriptures.

4

Apostolic Memory in Several Gospels

The years 66-70 CE were a major turning point in both Christian and Jewish histories. A general uprising by Jews in Israel against Roman rule broke out in 66 CE. The results were catastrophic. In 70 CE the Roman general and future emperor Titus destroyed Jerusalem and razed the Temple. Only the west wall of this great edifice was left standing; it remains today as a reminder of the destruction. Following the destruction of the Temple, religious leadership in Judaism worldwide shifted decisively from the priesthood to the rabbis. Synagogues became more important as centers of Jewish worship. The land of Israel itself became known by its Roman name, Palestine.

By 66 CE most of the followers of Jesus had been dispersed from Jerusalem. The leader of the community there, James, had been executed several years earlier by order of the Sadducee leaders. After that, the remaining members of the group appear to have migrated away. Later church traditions gave theological meaning to the dispersion of the church from Jerusalem by assigning to each of the original twelve whom Jesus had gathered (except Judas, of course) a different part of the world as his evangelistic domain. Historical traditions of various reliability followed most of these original apostles to their persecution and martyrdom as well. By the end of the first century, a new generation of church leadership was emerging from these apostolic forebears. A variety of ministerial offices were known to Christian communities, but three had emerged as the most common: deacons *(diakonos)*, elders *(presbyteros)*, and bishops *(episcopos)*. To the new generation of leaders fell the major portion of the task of remembering, interpreting, and handing on the memory of Jesus.

Multiple gospel traditions

Crucial for the transmission of this memory was the composition of books we call gospels. They were the work of early Christian scribes who sought both to fix and to pass on the apostolic memory. We know of as many as thirty such texts from the first three centuries of the Christian era, many of them surviving today only in fragments or in quotation in other works. Four of them were eventually recognized as canonical, or authoritative, by the majority of Christian churches:

Matthew, Mark, Luke, and John. Others, such as the *Proto-Gospel of James*, continue to be read and treasured by various communities within the Christian movement without attaining the wider acceptance that the first four received. Still others, such as the *Gospel of Mary* and the *Gospel of Thomas*, were lost for many centuries but have either been partially or completely discovered in the last one hundred years. Finally there are works such as the *Gospel of the Hebrews* and the *Gospel of the Egyptians,* which were read among some early Christians but have been lost.

Many biblical scholars today believe that the Gospel of Mark was written just prior to or during the crisis of 66-70 CE, and that it reflects the situation of the Galilean countryside. Such indicators in the text as the demons' name, "legion" (the term for a Roman military unit) in Mark 5:9, and the message of the young man to the women at tomb that Jesus is going ahead of them to Galilee seem to point to this time and location. Early tradition identified its author as a student of Peter, giving the book an apostolic genealogy necessary for its eventual acceptance into the Christian canon. Early tradition also held that the book was written in Rome. This need not be in contradiction to there being a Galilean tradition behind Mark, of course, for it is conceivable that the writer in Rome was making use of reports originally derived from Galileans.

In Palestine the Pharisees emerged following the destruction of the Temple to begin the process of reconstructing Judaism on the other side of the crisis. Increasing conflict with the Nazarene party led to a final break between Jews and Christians in Palestine before the year 100. Matthew, often called the most Jewish of the four gospels, reflects such a bitter struggle with the Pharisees over the meaning of Torah, the authority of tradition, and the heritage of Israel. Matthew's gospel is concerned to show how Jesus Christ fulfills all the prophecies and requirements of Israel's scriptures regarding the Messiah. By the time it was being written, however, the Pharisee party was on the ascendancy in Galilee. There is evidence that Christians were being excluded from synagogues. Some believe Matthew was originally the book of a small community that went into exile outside Galilee. Many scholars believe that it was written in Syria, with Antioch often mentioned in this regard.

The two-volume work of Luke-Acts was written around the same time as Matthew. Tradition says the author was a converted Gentile who traveled with the apostle Paul for a time. Luke was concerned to show the worldwide horizon of the Christian message from the beginning of Jesus' life and ministry. The universal claims of Rome posed the counterpoint for Luke to the universal reign of Christ. Hence the Gospel of Luke (volume one) opens in the days of Caesar Augustus sending out a decree into all the world, while the book of Acts (volume two) ends with Paul in Rome, proclaiming the gospel of Jesus Christ.

Matthew and Luke are generally believed today to have incorporated earlier sources that they shared in common. Many, although not all, biblical scholars believe Mark was one of these common sources for the other two gospels, and that there was another, lost source (the so-called "Q" hypothesis). Hypothetical reconstructions of "Q" portray it as a collection of sayings of Jesus, similar in many ways to the collection known as the *Gospel of Thomas*. The teachings of

Jesus, especially concerning last things, occupy most of this collection. Even if one disagrees with the hypothesis regarding "Q," enough commonalities in style and actual wording exist to suggest that the writers of the Matthew and Luke were drawing from common literary sources, if not from one another.

Whether the writer of the Gospel of John knew of the other gospels or not is a more difficult question to answer. A number of scholars believe that the final version of the Fourth Gospel may have been written as late as 100 CE. Early Christian tradition held that the apostle John, the "beloved disciple" upon whose testimony the book is based (John 21:24) eventually settled in Ephesus, in Asia Minor. The Gospel of John also appears to be the work of a circle of disciples that gathered around the beloved disciple. There are enough theological points of contact with the three epistles of John and the Revelation of John to argue for a wider circle of influence for this community or school. The opening pages of the book of Revelation attest to the Asia Minor location. Yet the fact that the Gospel of John contains material that reflects detailed knowledge of Judea and Jerusalem, is sympathetic to Samaritan concerns, and is conversant with Hellenistic Judaism (especially the logos doctrine of Philo) makes it difficult to identify any particular geographical location as the site of the gospel's final composition.

By the end of the second century these four gospels had gained a wide reading as authentic stories of Jesus. By the end of the third century they were regarded by the great majority of churches and leaders as canonical, or authoritative. One reason was their reputation for being the work of the first generation of apostles (or the work of those close to them). A second criterion for canonicity was that their contents were congruent with the message that was handed on through the bishops. The variations among them concerning the sayings and events that they narrated were recognized as a legitimate diversity in the authoritative memory of Jesus.

In addition to these four, as was noted earlier, there were many other early Christian gospels that did not win such widespread acceptance. Some were considered semi-canonical; that is, they were accepted as useful for teaching but were not considered fully authoritative. Most of these other gospels were intentionally suppressed by later generations of church leaders who considered their contents to be doctrinally aberrant and without apostolic authority. Those that survived did so because they were hidden away or lost amid collections of other writings.

Among the texts that had semi-canonical status among some churches, and one eventually included in several apocryphal collections, was the *Proto-Gospel of James*. It circulated in the second century under the authority of James and told of Jesus' family background and birth; one reads of Mary's parents, Anna and Joachim, and of Mary's own childhood. Joseph, the *Proto-Gospel of James* informs us, was an older widower with grown sons. Jesus was born in a cave where, immediately after his birth, Salome and a midwife "tested" Mary's condition to verify that she was a virgin (19:3—20:2). The *Infancy Gospel of Thomas* also dates from the second century, but unlike the *Proto-Gospel of James* was largely repressed or forgotten by later generations. Announcing itself in its opening verse to be the work of Thomas, an Israelite, its pages portray a childhood

Jesus who performs miracles for good and ill. The young Jesus is said to have struck another child dead for having run into him in the village one day, for instance. When people in the town complained to his family about his behavior, Jesus blinded them. One of the more whimsical stories from the *Infancy Gospel of Thomas* tells of Jesus on a Sabbath forming twelve sparrows out of clay and then making them fly off as living birds.

Several other gospels that also date from the second century but came to be suppressed were the *Gospel of Peter*, the *Gospel of Mary Magdalene*, and the *Gospel of Thomas*. Fragments alone have survived of the first two, while the third has been found in its entirety. The portion of the *Gospel of Peter* that has survived tells of the passion and resurrection of Jesus. According to it, a crowd gathered outside the tomb following the Sabbath to see what would happen to Jesus. Suddenly the stone was rolled away, and three men came out of the grave. Two of them were angels, with their feet on the ground and their heads touching clouds. The head of the third, the risen Christ, stretched above the heavens. Following Christ out of his tomb was the cross, which miraculously spoke to the crowd.

The sizable portion of the second-century *Gospel of Mary Magdalene* that was discovered in Cairo in the 1890s also tells of post-resurrection events. Here it is a series of dialogues that supposedly took place between Jesus and his disciples. After Jesus' departure Mary Magdalene emerges in this gospel to become the leader of the band. She reveals to the rest of the group the spiritual meaning of Jesus' words and tells them of secret teachings Jesus had entrusted only to her. Peter objects that Jesus would not favor Mary above the men, but Levi defends Mary's leadership role in the community. The *Gospel of Mary Magdalene* suggests that women were spiritually qualified to be apostles and teachers in the early church, a stance that was challenged by many others.

In 1945 a large jar containing portions of thirteen ancient books was uncovered near the Egyptian town of Nag Hammadi. Buried in the fourth century, most likely by monks but for reasons that remain unclear, the collection included a copy of the long-lost *Gospel of Thomas*. The text of the book claims it was written by Thomas, although most scholars date it to the early second century. It is a collection of 114 sayings of Jesus, many of them similar to those of the canonical gospels. The *Gospel of Thomas* is without any narrative framework and does not mention the death or resurrection of Jesus. Like the *Gospel of Mary Magdalene*, it recognizes Mary Magdalene as having played an important leadership role among the disciples, and speaks of secret teachings that Jesus shared only with the closest followers.

Most of these non-canonical gospels are dated by historians from the second century or later. Like other texts written during these years such as the *Acts of John*, the *Acts of Thomas*, the *Acts of Peter*, and the already-mentioned *Acts of Paul*, they purport to have apostolic authorship. One of the reasons church leaders moved to define the canonical boundaries of the apostolic writings was precisely because of the expanding list of claimants to apostolic authorship. Diverging memories of Jesus in and of themselves were not in question; the four canonical gospels provided abundant examples of those. The problem had to do with determining the mode of authoritative transmission (whether through institutional structures or secret teachings) and the content of teachings about Jesus. Divergence in tradition was not outright rejected, but neither was it left unchallenged.

Diversification was facilitated even more by another early Christian practice, one that likewise grew in the second and third centuries. Here we are referring to the translation of Christian scriptures. The four gospels, like the rest of the books of the New Testament, were originally written in Greek. An early Christian bishop named Irenaeus (c.115-c.202), writing around the end of the second century, noted that he had heard from an earlier teacher named Papias that Matthew had "issued a written gospel among the Hebrews in their own dialect," presumably Aramaic or Syriac.[1] The possibility of such a gospel cannot be entirely discounted, especially given the early date of the tradition (Papias would have been around 130 CE). Unfortunately, there is no firm literary evidence to support it. Most biblical scholars today agree that the version we have of Matthew, like the other three canonical gospels, was composed in Greek.

By the year 300, Christian scriptures had been translated into several languages. In Roman North Africa portions of the Bible were translated into Latin, while in Syria the *Peshitta* (a "simple" Bible) rendered most of the Old Testament and portions of the New in Syriac. The mobility of its texts across linguistic boundaries greatly facilitated the expansion of the Christian movement across political and geographical borders during this period. Translocation and translation went hand in hand. In the process meanings often shifted and changed in subtle yet decisive ways. The double dimension of pluralization, of the four gospels recounting the one life of Jesus, and by the end of the second century their being rendered into new languages through translation, extended greatly the range of acceptable interpretations and meaning that could be found in churches of the world.

Diversity in understanding

An illustration of the diversity of interpretations and understandings accepted across a wide range of churches can be found in the various portrayals of the meaning of salvation that have come down to us from early Christian communities. In the ruins of Dura-Europos, a Roman garrison city in Mesopotamia that was destroyed by the Persians in 256, archeologists have found the remains of the earliest known building to be used explicitly as a Christian house of worship. The building was a converted house, with a large meeting room and a second smaller room holding a baptistery. The walls of the baptistery offer mural depictions of Jesus the good shepherd, Jesus performing miracles, and the women at the tomb. These scenes, most likely intended to illustrate the meaning of the

[1] Irenaeus, *Against Heresies* 3.1, in *The Ante-Nicene Fathers: Translations of the Fathers down to A.D. 325*, vol. 1, *The Apostolic Fathers, Justin Martyr, Irenaeus*, ed. Alexander Roberts and James Donaldson (Grand Rapids, Mich.: Wm. B. Eerdmans Publishing Co., 1981), 415.

salvation into which candidates were being baptized, reflect themes of deliverance and miraculous transformation.

A somewhat different way of depicting salvation can be found in the philosophical treatises of a second-century Christian teacher in Rome named Justin Martyr (d. c.165). Justin had been trained as a philosopher in the Greek tradition. Several of his books were addressed (at least ostensibly) to the Roman emperor Marcus Aurelius, who was himself a philosopher of some repute in the Stoic school. Justin's work sought to persuade the emperor to legalize the Christian religion. He argued that in Jesus Christ the divine Logos known to the great philosophers had become incarnate. Followers of Jesus were thus true philosophers. The truth of their teachings was made evident by the moral lives Christians now led. For Justin, the moral dimensions of salvation brought to humanity by Jesus Christ through his teachings dominated the theological landscape in his understanding of salvation.

A third way of understanding the biblical story of salvation is given to us in the writings of a North African theologian named Tertullian (c.160–c.215). Converted in Carthage around 195, he was the first theologian we know of to write in Latin. Although this was the dominant language in Roman North Africa, the region was culturally still quite diverse. Remnants of ancient Punic and indigenous Libyan cultures dwelt side by side with the dominant Latin culture of the Roman ruling classes in the second century. By the year 200 the Punic language was in decline, and Latin was necessary if one wanted a career in the cities. The ancient Syro-Phoenician gods Baal and Tanit were still being worshiped in the temples of Carthage during Tertullian's day; however, in many places Baal had taken on the Roman name of Saturn. Blood sacrifices offered to these gods in order to satisfy or appease them were still common, as they were elsewhere in the world. Tertullian drew upon the theme of blood sacrifice being necessary to appease the wrath of God as a means of interpreting the death of Jesus. Jesus Christ was sent by God to die as a sacrificial victim. Because he died free from sin, he is able to take our sins away. Such ideas are not foreign to the Bible, of course; in Roman North Africa, however, they found a particular resonance through Tertullian with the world around him.

All three of these interpretations of the meaning of salvation found a hearing by Christians in various parts of the world. The one who was depicted on the walls of a church in Dura-Europos as the shepherd, and by Justin Martyr in Rome as the teacher of true philosophy, in North Africa was depicted as also being the Lamb who was sacrificed to provide satisfaction for sin. All three of them were biblical images, and all offered a way of interpreting the New Testament story in ways that made sense to believers. The different focus of each reflected in part differences in cultural and social contexts (the house transformed into a public church building in Dura-Europos, the philosopher's teaching hall in Rome, the priest's sacrificial altar in Carthage). This is not to say that such interpretations were unique to each context, for they were not. Tertullian also knew of philosophical debates in Carthage, and Rome certainly had its share of house churches as well as religious altars. Various interpretations or teachings were not confined to any particular location, as the Christian movement was far too mobile for that.

Nevertheless, one can begin to see and hear subtle differences in theological tone, reflecting various cultures and locations that facilitated mutual enrichment among churches in various parts of the world without reducing their sense of a common identity.

Aided by their written texts, their networks of mobile leaders, and their options for different interpretations, Christian communities spread from city to city across the Mediterranean and western Asian worlds. Leaders were often bicultural, and in some places church members spoke two or even three languages or dialects. The linguistic pluralism of the early church leadership greatly facilitated translation. It also facilitated multiple levels of interpretation of meaning, drawing upon various literary methods and discursive styles. A sizable number of the early Christian leaders ended up living in places far beyond their homelands, adding to the complexity of the movement and its teachings. Christian churches sprang up in these places where cultural traditions met and mixed.

In the chapters that follow, we will explore the expansion of the Christian movement into urban centers in several regions of the ancient world where existing networks of social relationships were used to spread the Christian message. Local communities remained connected to one another across geographical distances by means of a relatively mobile network of leadership that represented churches to one another in distant places. These networks were made concrete through the common beliefs and practices that various Christian communities shared among themselves. To the degree that commonalities and agreements did indeed exist (the experience was not uniform), the groundwork out of which emerged a wider sense of catholicity or universality was laid.

Antioch, Edessa, Ephesus, Smyrna, Rome, Carthage, Alexandria, Meroë, and Mylapore will be some of the cities that help us locate several initial regional trajectories of the Christian movement. We will find that often the line between what is history and what is tradition is hard to discern. Did Thomas ever arrive in India to preach the good news of Jesus Christ there? Did Peter suffer crucifixion upside down after serving as the first bishop of Rome? Did Matthew preach and die in Ethiopia? In each of these cases we lack the kind of external confirmation that counts today as solid historical evidence. Yet in each case we encounter an ecclesiastical memory that later generations of churches and Christians looked back upon as authentic sources for identity. These diverse memories of traditions and histories enabled churches both to be grounded in particular locations and to maintain a trans-locational (universal) faith. The tension between particularity and universality is as much evident in the history of the early Christian movement as it is today.

5

The Early Christian Movement
in Syria and Mesopotamia

When the followers of Jesus were first forced to leave Jerusalem, one of the places to which they scattered was the Roman province of Syria, located to the north and east of Israel (or Palestine, as we will henceforth call it). Its three major cities, Antioch, Damascus, and Edessa, figure prominently in early Christian history. Indeed, one could almost say that Christianity was born in Syria, because it was in Antioch that the new name was first used for the Nazarene party of Jews. Paul was traveling to Damascus to carry on his efforts against Christians when he was converted, an indication that the Nazarene's teachings had already spread to that city. In addition to its cities Syria provided a home for Christians in its small villages and sparsely populated desert regions. One or more groups, possibly from Galilee in the north of Palestine, might have relocated in these rural areas after 70 CE (if not before). Semitic-speaking people from the Syrian region might well have been among the first Gentiles to come into the Christian movement (see the story of the Syro-Phoenician woman in Mark 7:24-30). We have already noted the possibility that Matthew was written there. A number of post-apostolic early Christian writings are also given a Syrian location for their composition, pointing to the continuing growth of the movement there. The *Odes of Solomon* and the *Didache (Teachings) of the Twelve Apostles*, both dating from as early as the end of the first or beginning of the second century; the *Gospel of Thomas* from perhaps the middle of the second century; and the *Didascalia Apostolorum* from the middle of the third century all testify to the vitality of the churches.

A number of texts from this region were either originally composed or translated into Syriac, a dialect of Aramaic that was closely related to Hebrew and originally spoken in the vicinity of Edessa. Because it was related to Aramaic but distinct enough to allow for a new literary tradition to emerge that was identifiably Christian, Syriac became the language of choice among Christians in eastern Syria, Mesopotamia, Persia, and eventually India, Mongolia, and China. Late in the first or early in the second century, a Syriac version of Old Testament texts began to appear in the form of a rough translation or paraphrase known as the Peshitta. No one knows who was responsible for these "simple" translations, or in what order the books appeared. What we do know is that by the end of the second century, Christians had access to Old Testament books in the Syriac tongue. By the end of the fourth, they had the New Testament as well in the form of the Peshitta.

The most influential version of the gospels in Syriac during the first several centuries was a harmony that circulated throughout the region. Around the year 170 an Assyrian convert named Tatian returned from studying in Rome to establish a school of his own. Tatian had been a student of Justin Martyr but appears to have left following the death of his teacher. The exact location in which he finally settled in the East is not known, and few of his writings have survived to help provide a clue. Some scholars have placed him in Mesopotamia, while others have argued he might have made his home in the city of Arbela, east of the Tigris River. Tatian's most lasting contribution to the Christian movement came not through his school, however, but in the form of this harmony of the gospels in Syriac (whether it was originally composed in Syriac, or in Greek and then translated to Syriac remains debated).

Known as the *Diatessaron* (Greek for "From Four"), it was for at least two hundred years the preferred edition for many Syrian churches and theologians. Tatian's project sought to present the message of Jesus in Syriac, not Greek, to its readers. Something of his reason for doing so can be found in the only other major work of his that survived, an apology for Christianity known as the *Oration Addressed to the Greeks*. In fine Hellenistic rhetorical style the treatise argued for the greater antiquity, and thus the superiority, of "barbarian" philosophy over that of the Greeks. The greater antiquity of Moses over Plato, he said, likewise proved Christianity to be superior to the dominant philosophical schools of Hellenism. Tatian's *Oration* has been called by a contemporary African scholar "the vindication of the Barbarians against the Greeks."[2] His *Diatessaron* similarly sought to free readers and hearers from the Greek language in order to discover the story of Jesus in their own tongue.

Antioch and Edessa

The capital of the Roman province of Syria was Antioch. We have already noted the importance of this city, the third largest in the Mediterranean world, located on the Orontes River. At the other end of the region was the city called Orhay in Syriac, but better known by its Greek name, Edessa. Situated east of the Euphrates in what was in fact northern Mesopotamia, Edessa was a city built by trade. Through it passed the western extension of the Silk Road that ran between China and the Mediterranean world. The major trade route connecting Arabia and Armenia ran north and south.

As was the case in most of the cities of the province of Syria (including Antioch), Edessa was a place of cultural mixing. Among the upper class of the

---

[2] Kwame Bediako, *Theology and Identity: The Impact of Culture upon Christian Thought in the Second Century and Modern Africa* (Oxford: Regnum Books, 1992), 64.

Reconstruction of the baptistry in the church at Dura Europos in Syria, ca. 240 C.E. Yale University Art Gallery. Reproduced by permission of Yale University.

city the Hellenistic influences were strong, but elsewhere in the city and surrounding countryside Aramaic cultural traditions were dominant. As we have already noted, the dialect known as Syriac was the first language of the city and surrounding countryside. Greek was spoken only among the urban upper class. Some in Edessa had studied the Greek philosophers, while others turned eastward to study astrology from Persia. Many who were learned in the city did both, mixing Persian and Hellenistic philosophical and religious concepts freely. In a similar manner there were numerous gods worshiped throughout the city, including the Babylonian deities Nebo and Bel, several Hellenistic deities, and the deities of Arab tribes from the south. A sizable Jewish community resided in the city, adding to its religious and cultural diversity.

Edessa had been renamed by the Seleucids around 300 BCE. After the Parthians defeated the Seleucids, Edessa became the capital of a semi-independent kingdom known as Osrhoene, which was under an Arabian king. During the first century of the Christian era it remained within the Parthian sphere of influence. In 116 CE Roman armies sacked the city as part of their Persian campaign, and then in 165 the king cast his lot, and that of Osrhoene, with the Romans. In 214 Osrhoene become a Roman *colonia*. Hence its independence as a kingdom came to an end just prior to the fall of the Parthians to a new Persian power known as the Sassanids in 225 CE.

The Christian message came to Edessa through the city's Jewish community and its connections with Jerusalem. No one can say with historical certainty when or how that happened, but one of the more intriguing legends that has come down from early Christian tradition concerns the role of an original disciple of Jesus named Addai (Thaddeus in Greek). The story is found at the end of book one of Eusebius's *Ecclesiastical History*, reproduced from what he says are documents he found in the public archive in Edessa and translated from Syriac. According to Eusebius, the king of Edessa during the lifetime of Jesus, named Abgar, was afflicted with a disease. Hearing of the miracles Jesus was performing, Abgar sent a letter asking him to come and perform a cure. Jesus returned a message by Abgar's courier, promising to send a disciple after he had been received by God. After the ascension, the story continues, the apostle Thomas sent Addai, one of the seventy mentioned in Luke 10:1, to Edessa. Addai stayed at the house of a Jew in the city named Tobias. When word came to Abgar of the miracles Addai was performing, he sent for the disciple and upon meeting him received a vision confirming this was the one Jesus had promised. The king was both healed and converted to the Christian faith, according to Eusebius, and along with him many in Edessa. While the story of the exchange of letters is legendary, the possibility that behind it is an authentic tradition of Addai cannot be entirely discounted.

The next report of the conversion of a king in Edessa comes from around the year 200, when Bardaisan (c.154-222), a Christian theologian and philosopher from Edessa, noted that Abgar VIII had "come to the faith."[3] While there is no historical evidence that this particular king, also known as Abgar the Great, was baptized, it does appear that Christians were able to exercise their faith free from political persecution during this period. The earliest historical notice of a public church building is found in a report of damage caused by a flood in Edessa in 201. Taken with various other bits of evidences of growth in Christian numbers in the region, it suggests that the city was a relatively hospitable place for Christians.

The tradition of Addai reflects a self-understanding among the churches of this region that they were linked directly with the movement around Jesus. The tradition suggested that the message of the gospel came directly to Edessa from Jerusalem, and not by way of Antioch or another church from the west. Eusebius records that Palut of Edessa eventually went to Antioch to receive ordination from Serapion, bishop of Antioch from 180 to 221. It would not be surprising to see the churches of Edessa and Antioch together in their theological conversations, given the language and cultural affinities shared across Syria. But the apostolic tradition of Addai and Thomas linked the churches of Edessa directly with Jesus. Thomas especially was an important figure to Christians throughout the East, revered by churches from Armenia to India as their founding apostle. The *Acts of Thomas*, an early third-century apocryphal book that reports on Thomas's journey as a missionary to India, was actually written in Syriac and first circulated in the region of Edessa before being translated and taken into other regions of the world. Many believed that the bones of Thomas were eventually carried back from India to Edessa, an indication of the latter's importance as a center as well as crossroads for the Christian movement.

---

[3] Bardaisan of Edessa, *The Book of the Laws of Countries: Dialogue on Fate of Bardaisan of Edessa*, trans. H. J. W. Drijvers (Assen, The Netherlands: Van Gorcum and Co., 1964), 59.

One noticeable feature of the early stories of Christians in Edessa and eastern Syria is the relative absence of persecution of the Christian movement. The Parthian rulers who fell in 225 exercised a significant degree of tolerance toward the various religions of their realm. The east Syrian region was a safer place for Christians under the "Parthian Peace" than the Roman world. Although the number of Christians in Syrian and Persian cities was never very large, they appear for the most part to have carried on their community life unmolested. In Edessa relations between Jews and Christians were relatively friendly, to the point where the two communities appear to have cooperated in such matters as Bible study and dealing with the city's rulers.

The same openness was not true for Antioch and the regions under Roman control in West Syria. The Roman emperor Nero in 64 had instituted a local campaign against Christians in the empire's capital city. Domitian, as we saw in the last chapter, had raised for the author of the Apocalypse at least the specter of martyrdom by the end of the first century. Beginning with the early years of the second century, Rome began to make persecution of Christians its official policy, although at first it was only local and sporadically enforced. One of the better known figures of Christian history from the beginning of the second century is Ignatius, bishop of Antioch, who was arrested and sent to Rome, where he was martyred. On his way to Rome to be thrown to the wild beasts in the arena, Ignatius wrote several letters to churches and individuals in Asia Minor. The letters do not provide a great deal of information regarding conditions in Antioch. Reading them, however, one gets a sense of the general climate of the churches, at least from the perspective of one who identified himself as bishop of Syria.

Church leadership

We have already noted Ignatius's high regard for the episcopal office. Elsewhere the notion of apostolic succession was taking shape within churches, but this does not appear to have been a significant concern for Ignatius. In several places he indicated the importance of both Peter and Paul having been to his city, providing Antioch with an impressive apostolic genealogy alongside that of Rome. The Gospel of Matthew, which had a strong Antiochene connection, stated that it was Peter on whom Christ said he would build his church, thereby establishing his primacy among the apostles. The authority of Peter is reflected as well in the Syrian *Gospel of Peter,* which appeared in the second century. Paul, it will be remembered from the New Testament, had been sent out as a missionary from that church.

For Ignatius, the bishop had an almost mystical role representing Christ at the eucharist. The eucharist was also presented as a central liturgical practice in a book known as the *Didache of the Twelve Apostles.* This manual for church leaders compiled sometime near the beginning of the second century does not assign the bishop nearly as prominent a role in the church as Ignatius does, however. The *Didache* reflects a social location more rural than urban. It advises that baptisms be performed in running streams, for instance, and recalls the Galilean tradition of Jesus' open air meals in the countryside ("As this broken bread was scattered over the hills and then, when gathered, became one mass, so may thy church be gathered from the ends of the earth into thy kingdom," 9.4).[4] Leadership is more charismatic and egalitarian in the *Didache*. The ministry of wandering prophets is still recognized and affirmed, although it warns that those who seek any form of payment for such ministry are false ones. The visiting prophets are to be allowed to give thanks as much as they desire, it states (10.7), suggesting that they were celebrating the eucharist along with (or perhaps even apart from) the bishop. The bishop is hardly mentioned at all in the document.

By the end of the second century, Ignatius's monarchical episcopal conception of the church had won out over the more egalitarian and charismatic forms of leadership reflected in the *Didache*. The results can be seen in the mid-third-century Syrian book of church order, the *Didascalia Apostolorum*. Originally written in Greek, the *Didascalia* describes orders of deacons and deaconesses (the latter to assist with anointing by oil of women candidates for baptism), presbyters, and bishops. The bishop is described as one who sits on an ecclesiastical throne, clearly at the head of the gathered community of faith. It was an image with which Ignatius might have agreed.

Another type of church leader that appeared early in Syria was the teacher of hidden mysteries, who followed in the apostolic footsteps as well. One of the apostolic traditions that passed through Syria, as we have already noted, concerned Thomas. The *Gospel of Thomas*, written sometime in the second century and most likely in Greek, was often associated with Syrian Christianity. Some even accepted it as canonical during the first centuries. In verse 12 of the book Jesus is depicted establishing the leadership of James the Just over the rest of the disciples. To Thomas, on the other hand, he taught certain mysteries of the faith to which the others were not privy. The prominence that these mysteries received in the gospel (without being actually revealed) lent the book an air that soon identified it with Christian Gnosticism, a movement that emerged in the second century and will be discussed in more depth in the following chapter. Here it is sufficient to note that both bishops and mystery teachers alike were important for Christians in the early Syrian context.

Bishops, prophets, and mystery teachers were not the only ones who exercised spiritual authority among the early Syrian churches. Early in the Christian movement a type of extreme asceticism appeared in the Syrian deserts. These ascetics were women or men who renounced all worldly associations, practiced strict celibacy, ate no meat, and drank only water. A number of early Christian writers attributed the origin of these *Encratites* (Greek for "self-denial") to Tatian. The evidence suggests that there were already people pursuing such a life of extreme self-denial in the Syrian desert before Tatian's time, but he gave the practice an important theological voice. The Encratites taught that all forms of sexual relations, including marriage, were adultery. Among the Syrian churches

---

[4] The *Didache*, in *Ancient Christian Writers: The Works of the Fathers in Translation*, ed. Johannes Quasten and Joseph C. Plumpe, vol. 6, trans. James A. Kleist, S.J. (Westminster, Md.: The Newman Press; London: Longmans, Green and Co., 1961), 20.

some believed that baptism could be administered only to those who were celibate. The third-century *Didascalia* acknowledged the legitimacy of ascetic practices but warned against those who taught that Christians were not to marry. The fact that it found it necessary to condemn such teaching explicitly indicates the strength of this position in Syria.

Theological characteristics

The Semitic cultural flavor of early Syrian church traditions is quite noticeable. Early Christian hymns that came from the region resemble psalms from the Hebrew scriptures, for instance. Sometimes this has been mistaken for a tendency toward Jewish Christianity. Jewish-Christian groups were certainly known during the first several centuries in the region, but the majority of early Syrian churches shared a common Semitic culture, not the Jewish faith. The *Didache* offers instruction in moral behavior that are the commandments of the Lord similar to those found in Judaism, but it teaches different fast days than those observed by the "hypocrites," by which the author no doubt meant those associated with the Pharisees. An even stronger rejection of Jewish law is found in the *Didascalia* a century and a half later. The fact that Christians and Jews in Syria were closely related culturally might have caused Christians to seek ways of distinguishing themselves more clearly from their Jewish neighbors.

The story of the healing of the king of Edessa that we read about above echoes the New Testament traditions of early Christian miracles. It also points toward the practical side of early Syrian Christianity. In general, the early Syriac literature preferred hymnody and liturgy over philosophical treatises. The emphasis upon the humanity of Jesus was prominent, as seen in Ignatius's rejection of the teaching that Jesus did not have a real body. At the same time the Syrian tradition often spoke of a Spirit christology in place of the Logos christology articulated in the Gospel of John. Most churches remembered that Jesus had healed and spoken through the power of the Spirit and that the same charismatic power was to be found in their midst as well. The Syrian churches celebrated this more intensely and with a fuller theological understanding of the incarnational character of the Spirit. The rich descriptions of the Spirit in relation to Christ are one of the more enduring contributions the early Syriac churches have made to Christian history.

Another distinctive feature in Syriac Christian literature concerns the positive use of feminine images in liturgy and theology. Often Syriac writers employed images of the Spirit as woman, reflecting a theological inclusiveness in gender that has contributed to contemporary discussions of trinitarian language. An early Syriac eucharistic liturgy calls upon God as both Father and Mother to descend upon the elements being shared. The Syrian tradition sometimes provided strong feminine imagery for both Christ and the Holy Spirit. It was not uncommon in the early Christian movement for newly baptized persons to be fed milk and honey as a sign of their crossing the Jordan River. *The Odes of Solomon*, a collection of Christian hymns from the end of the first or very early second century, extends that image in a strongly feminine direction to encompass all three divine figures in Christian worship. The Son is a cup of sweet milk, the book tells us, while the Father is he who was milked, and the Holy Spirit she who milked him. In another place the *Odes* contain a hymn of Christ that suggests Christ is the one who feeds us. Christ says:

> I fashioned their members
> And my own breasts I prepared for them,
> That they might drink my holy milk and live by it.[5]

By the end of the second century we find in Syria a vibrant Christian movement shaped by diverse theological reflections and pastoral practices. Culturally the Christians appear to have shared much with their Jewish neighbors, but theologically they sought to distinguish themselves. The city of Antioch had become home to a particular form of episcopal leadership and was quickly gaining a reputation for its distinctive theological reflection. Among the most influential of these early Antiochene theological expositors was its bishop, Theophilus, who assumed the position around the year 170. He is sometimes seen as the first in a distinctive line or school of Christian thought that came to be associated with the city of Antioch. For Theophilus, the Jewish scriptures were of supreme authority and an important source of wisdom for Christians. In them alone the revelation of God was manifest. He argued the superiority of Christian knowledge over "Egyptian or Chaldean prophets," as well as Greek poets and sages (a position articulated earlier by Tatian as well).[6] Theophilus offered the historical events of the Hebrew scriptures as the source of truth, prefiguring what in the course of one or two more centuries would become recognizable as a distinct Antiochene school of exegesis and theology.

From the days of the earliest followers of Jesus crossing into Syria through the end of the second or beginning of the third century, this diverse Christian community grew in the cities, villages, and desert lands. The strong Semitic cultural influences in the region gave to the worship and spiritual life of Christians a particular flavor that was closely related to Judaism, yet distinct. The churches were not uniform in their organization and practices in the region. Some, especially in the major city of Antioch, favored strong episcopal hierarchy, while others, especially in the rural regions, it appears, favored more egalitarian and charismatic structures of the church. A significant number of ascetics abandoned all forms of community life to move into the wilderness, living off wild grasses and water. As late as the third century some in Syria were still teaching that all baptized Christians were expected to be celibate.

---

[5] *The Odes of Solomon*, trans. James H. Charlesworth (Oxford: Clarendon Press, 1973), 42.

[6] *Theophilus to Autolycus* 2.33 and 3.6, in *The Ante-Nicene Fathers: Translations of the Fathers down to A.D. 325*, vol. 2, *Fathers of the Second Century*, ed. Alexander Roberts and James Donaldson (Grand Rapids, Mich.: Wm. B. Eerdmans Publishing Co., 1981), 107 and 112.

At the eastern end of this region was the major city of Edessa. Located at the border between the Roman and Persian empires, it was a strategic center for international commerce and trade. Here Christians appear to have experienced fairly good relations with their neighbors. The first public building specifically identified as a church appears as early as 200, suggesting a publicly visible role. As strong as the Christian community in Edessa appears to have been, however, it was the community in Antioch that played the major role in shaping Christian practice in the region. From Antioch emerged not only the impetus for a strong monarchical episcopacy, but eventually a tradition of theological reflection that would reach far beyond the province itself. Before the beginning of the third century the first articulations of what would eventually become known as the Antiochene school were making their way into print in the writings of Theophilus. Few of Antioch's church leaders in the late second century could have imagined the storms that eventually engulfed their successors.

6

The Early Christian Movement
in Greece and Asia Minor

Most of the letters that Ignatius wrote on his way to face the wild beasts in the arena in Rome were addressed to churches in cities of Asia Minor. From the amount of surviving historical evidence, it appears that the Christian movement grew rapidly in its first years in this part of the world. The names of the cities are familiar to readers of the New Testament: Corinth, Ephesus, Smyrna, Philadelphia, and others. Paul had worked among them; later his co-workers Timothy and Titus, both located in the region by the pastoral epistles bearing their name, continued to build upon his work. Other apostolic agents appear to have crossed through the region as well. The letter of I Peter is addressed to churches located in the northern section of Asia Minor, while from Paul's letter to the Galatians we have an indication that agents from Jerusalem associated with James had visited churches in the province. According to later church traditions, John and Philip eventually settled in the region near Ephesus, lending their apostolic authority to the churches there.

Much of our knowledge of the early life and growth of the churches in this region comes from letters that were sent and circulated among the churches. The first were the letters of Paul, addressed to specific churches and later gathered into an early Christian canon. After Paul's death his followers continued to circulate and read them. The institutional structures and interpersonal networks reflected in these letters, in the pastoral epistles, and even in the Revelation of John were the foundations for an enduring movement. By the second century these structures and networks were firmly in place in the churches around the Aegean Sea and across Asia Minor.

The continuity of the apostolic tradition

In each city where the message of Jesus found a hearing, followers, both Jews and Gentiles, gathered in what the New Testament called the *ekklesia*, a Greek word meaning "those called out" or "assembly." These gatherings took place in local households, connected to one another through their leadership networks

66

to form city-wide communities. From texts such as Eusebius's *Ecclesiastical History*, one gets a sense that the network of episcopal leadership that emerged early in the movement was quite effective in sustaining its growth. As death caused a tear in the fabric, the church as a whole could mend it through the selection and then consecration of new bishops. Bishops were consecrated, or endowed with spiritual authority, through the prayers and laying on of hands of other bishops from nearby churches. Letters were exchanged back and forth among them, building their connections with one another. At both a symbolic and an actual level, these bishops provided a sense of historical connection with the memory of the first followers of Jesus. So we find Papias, the bishop of Hierapolis in the district of Phrygia, writing in a book now lost to us (but cited by the historian Eusebius) that he carefully gathered information from elders of the church who reported what they in turn believed to have stemmed from the Lord. Papias himself had never met any of the original apostles, but he listened for words of those who knew them. "I simply took for granted that book knowledge would not help me so much as a living or still surviving voice," he said.[7]

Among those Papias spoke about was John the apostle, whose tomb Eusebius reported was in Ephesus. The tradition that John had left Jerusalem after the crisis of the 60s and had resettled in Ephesus where he lived to an old age was well-attested among the early churches. Irenaeus, who was originally from Asia Minor but had become bishop of Lyons in Gaul, recalled around the year 180 a story concerning the apostle John that had been related to him years earlier by Polycarp (d. c.156), bishop of Smyrna and Irenaeus's own instructor in the faith. Going into the public bath at Ephesus John met a certain man named Cerinthus who also claimed to be a Christian teacher in the city. Seeing Cerinthus, John turned and ran without taking his bath, saying, "Let us fly, lest even the bathhouse fall down, because Cerinthus, the enemy of truth, is within."[8] Irenaeus said that Polycarp also had told him of encounters with others who had seen the Lord in person. According to Eusebius, among the early leaders who had ended their days in Asia Minor was Philip, whose two daughters were prophets in the church there.

Human kings exercised their rule through representatives who were of a lower order. So the bishops stood in a representative relationship to Christ, it was asserted. The model of institutional leadership clearly reflected cultural practices and patterns in the world. Although it was not stated explicitly, it was assumed by most Christians that bishops were to be male. The name of no female bishop has come down to us from among the dominant parties of the ancient churches in any region of the world after the first century.

Despite the fact that such models of kingship and power were being drawn upon, what ultimately held the church together, Ignatius, Polycarp, and others insisted, was love. Christians exercised a solidarity of love that was not of national origin or culture. They took care of one another, tending to those who were

---

[7] "Fragments of Papias," in *Ancient Christian Writers*, 6:116.
[8] Irenaeus, *Against Heresies* 3.3.4., in *The Ante-Nicene Fathers*, 1:416.

sick and enrolling widows who were in need of support, for instance. In this regard bishops were expected to act more like shepherds than kings and rulers of the world, tending to the needs of their flocks rather than dominating the wills of their subjects. The empires of the world were held together by violence and the threat of violence. The unity of the church rested on the diligence of its members in seeking to live at peace with each other and in agreement with one another in matters of identity and practice—or faith and order. The model of authority that episcopal leadership sometimes drew upon reflected the context of the patriarchs and kings who exercised violence, but the true power that joined people together in churches was that of love and faithfulness.

The fact is that bishops had few resources other than the power of persuasion with which to exercise authority and enforce ecclesiastical discipline in the first centuries. If those whose writings we still possess are any indication, they used the power of persuasion with skill and hyperbolic zest. One encounters an array of rhetorical strategies enjoining the faithful to avoid false teachers and their doctrines. The language was often quite strident. "Therefore let us leave untouched the senseless speculations of the masses and the false doctrines, and turn to the teaching delivered to us in the beginning," implored Polycarp.[9] Seldom were opponents in the faith simply wrong; they were wicked and insane. Opinions with which one did not agree were derided as false doctrines meant to lead the people to perdition. We need to see such strategies for the rhetorical devices that they were, however. Those who wrote them were without any significant means of enforcement, other than that of excluding persons from their fellowship ("excommunication"). These bishops had no access to civil or political power that could enforce their injunctions. Ironically, they could often be equally strident in enjoining one other to avoid divisions and to refrain from acting in such a way as to break the unity of fellowship that was expressed in love. Maintaining the unity of the community and maintaining true teaching regarding Jesus Christ could be at odds with one another.

Later centuries would find people of good faith agreeing that the churches needed to be a connected community, without agreeing on specific issues concerning doctrine or practice. Eventually the apparatus of the state was drawn upon in the Roman world to enforce the majority party's decisions concerning such matters. Catholicity came in time to be synonymous with conformity in matters of liturgy and belief. But this was not yet the case in the second and third centuries. Catholicity was an organic concept, achieved not through adherence to precise formulation of ideas but through relationships in and among various communities. Those elected to episcopal leadership within the churches (after the first century it was the general practice for congregations to elect a new bishop from among their own number) were expected to maintain good relations with other bishops. A lively sense of catholicity fostered the conception that, although they were scattered throughout many different cities, Christians belonged to a common movement. It was held together by a common apostolic memory embodied in

---

[9] Polycarp, *Epistles to the Philippians*, in *Ancient Christian Writers*, 6:79.

the current generation of leadership. This was the sense in which Ignatius and others after him could speak of the church being catholic, that is, universal.

Christians as strangers and martyrs

One of the reasons that these structures of internal solidarity and unity were so important for Christians was precisely their lack of common blood or land. Unlike other communities in the ancient Mediterranean world (including the Jews), Christians had no homeland, no place of national origin that they could say they came from. It was the homeland that typically gave people their name, their culture, their religion, and their identity. Christians followed Jesus, who had been rejected by many of his own people and executed by Rome. In a world where religion, culture, and identity were found in the land of origins, Christians looked forward to a land that was their destiny. It is a striking admission, made over and over in their early writings, that wherever they found themselves, Christians considered themselves *paroikoi*—strangers, sojourners, or displaced people without a home.

So Polycarp opened his letter to the Philippians, "To the church of God which resides as a stranger at Philippi." Likewise an epistle from Clement of Rome to the Corinthians written at the beginning of the second century was addressed to the strangers or sojourners at Corinth. The report of the martyrdom of Polycarp was sent "from the church of God which resides as a stranger at Smyrna to the church of God residing at Philomelium and to all the communities of the holy and catholic church residing in any place."[10] Because they were strangers, aliens, or a people without a nation, their religion was illegal and their identity illegitimate in the eyes of the Roman authorities.

Very few residents of the Roman empire (the Jews, as noted, being an exception) found any difficulties acknowledging the gods of the city of Rome while they continued to worship their own national deities. Such inclusiveness did not present worshipers of Isis, Artemis, or Baal with problems of conscience in the ancient world. One could acknowledge other deities without violating an allegiance to one's own. But Christians refused to offer sacrifices to any other gods, including those of imperial Rome. Christians persistently claimed that these gods and their statues were idols made of stone and wood, or even worse, that they were demons and thus antithetical to Christ. Rejection of all other gods apart from the One made manifest in Jesus made Christians, in the eyes of many, guilty of the crime of atheism.

One of the earliest references to Christians in the ancient world found outside the pages of the New Testament is in an exchange of letters from the year 112 between Pliny the Younger and the Roman emperor Trajan. Pliny had been appointed governor of Bithynia, a province in the north of Asia Minor. He was seeking direction on the proper way to proceed against Christians, about whom

---

[10] *The Martyrdom of St. Polycarp*, in *Ancient Christian Writers*, 6:90.

he knew little other than that their religion was illegal. The general practice at the time was that Christians were not to be sought out, but if someone reported them they were to be required to sacrifice to Rome's gods in order to demonstrate their loyalty. Some Christians had been turned in by former believers, and so Pliny had acted.

His letter described what he had learned from several former members who had now abandoned the religion, as well as from two slave women who were ministers and whom he had tortured to extract information. All in all, he concluded, the movement seemed rather harmless:

> They met regularly before dawn on a certain day, when they sang an anthem to Christ as to a god, and bound themselves by a solemn oath *(sacramento)* not to commit any wicked deeds, nor to practice fraud, theft and adultery, nor to break their word, nor to deny a deposit when called upon to honor it. After this it was their custom to separate, and then to meet again to partake of food, but food of an ordinary and innocent kind.[11]

Nevertheless, there was reason to be concerned. For one thing the growth of Christians seemed to have a negative effect on the economy of the region. Noting the success of his attempts to stamp out the movement, Pliny wrote toward the end of his letter:

> It is not only the cities, but villages and rural districts which are infected through contact with this wretched superstition. I think though that it is still possible for it to be checked and rooted out. At any rate, it is certain that the temples, which were almost deserted, are drawing crowds again. The sacrifices that were neglected are being offered again. The meat of the sacrificial animals, for which until recently a buyer could hardly be found, is on sale everywhere.[12]

For the sake of the good order of the empire, then, Pliny acted to stop the spread of Christian belief under his rule. Those who were turned in were ordered to repeat a sacred formula invoking the Roman gods, to offer wine and incense to a statue of Trajan and images of the other gods, and to curse Christ. Since he had heard that no true Christian could do these things, to do so proved the innocence of an accused. Those who would not recant were put to death, as "their stubbornness and obstinacy" deserved punishment.

A similar story is told from the Christian point of view by one who witnessed Polycarp's martyrdom in 156 in Smyrna. Public opposition had turned to mob violence. The local Roman authority was forced to bring Polycarp to trial. Respectful of the bishop's reputation, the official tried to get him to swear by Caesar and reject his atheism. Polycarp refused. The mob then responded: "This is

---

[11] Pliny the Younger, letter XCVI to Trajan, in *Letters and Panegyricus*, vol. 2, ed. and trans. Betty Radice (Cambridge, Mass.: Harvard University Press, 1969), 285-289.
[12] Ibid.

the teacher of Asia, the father of the Christians, the destroyer of our gods! He teaches many not to sacrifice and not to worship!"[13] Threatened with fire, Polycarp responded to the official that such is better than the eternal fire he would face if he were to be unfaithful to Christ. His execution was ordered, and Polycarp was put to death by the knife. His body was then burned for good measure. His followers gathered up the remains and buried them; the narrative concludes that they continued to honor him at the site of his burial on the annual date of his martyrdom.

For all the attention that they were given in Christian literature, the actual number of martyrdoms was quite small during the first centuries. When persecution did come, it was in intense outbursts followed by periods of relative calm. But Christians lived with a consciousness of being under constant threat. They lived with an equally vivid consciousness of impending, apocalyptic promise. Martyrdom and apocalyptic glory were thus commonly joined in popular Christian thought, and both in turn were linked to charismatic forms of prophecy. Apocalyptic seers were another form of prophets, as is illustrated by the Apocalypse of John. In Asia Minor the prophetic and apocalyptic impulses persisted long after they had subsided elsewhere among Christians in the world. Images of apocalyptic destruction and millennial hope continued to erupt in the churches, but not without reason. Christians were from time to time being called upon to give the ultimate witness (martyria) for their faith. Those who did so provided powerful inspiration to others through their courage.

Martyrdom had an egalitarian edge as far as the place of women was concerned. Women who suffered for their faith did so like men. Whatever inequalities might be attributed to gender disappeared inside the arena. Martyrdom was one of the few public roles women could play. The lives of those who underwent it were ironically invested with a meaning and authority that their subjects could never enjoy while they were yet breathing. The courage Christian women showed in the face of persecution was often considerable, and many were remembered for it long after their suffering was done.

In Christian discourse apocalyptic expectations and the threat of martyrdom were often joined to strong moral injunctions. Remain sober, keep watch, and be ready, the teachers of the churches instructed their people. Live godly lives so that when the day of judgment comes at the end of time, you not be found guilty of any fault. Christians were to be people free from sin (see Heb. 6:4-6). Many believed that sins committed after baptism could not be forgiven. Bishops and elders were to be ever watchful over the flocks that they tended. Christians were to display such virtues as patience, kindness, courage, and humility to those around them. Everyone was charged to see that the name of Christ not become an occasion for slander.

Controversies over beliefs

With most schools of ancient philosophy, Christians agreed that moral virtue and philosophical truth were inextricably connected. Philosophical truth was in

---

[13] *The Martyrdom of St. Polycarp*, in *Ancient Christian Writers*, 6:96.

fact a necessary condition for virtue, many held, while one who lived a virtuous life demonstrated truth in action. This was one reason why Christians were often so concerned with cultivating proper beliefs regarding Jesus Christ. False doctrine was a moral concern. The crucible of persecution could heighten the moral dimensions of proper doctrine for those living through it. Some Christians in Asia Minor, called Docetists by their opponents, believed Jesus did not have a real human body of flesh, but that he only appeared to have a body. The teachings were gaining a foothold in Asia Minor early in the second century. In the letters that he wrote en route to his death in Rome, Ignatius argued that those who believed this were minimizing his own suffering in the flesh that was about to take place. Polycarp later pointed in the same direction by making a connection between the confession that Jesus Christ came in the flesh and the testimony of the cross. The event of Jesus' suffering in the flesh provided moral direction for Christian faith. The message of Jesus being Lord in the flesh took on new meanings in the face of the pain and suffering inflicted upon the flesh of his followers in Asia Minor and Rome.

The letters of Ignatius and Polycarp show that in the middle of the second century there were others who claimed to be within the Christian movement but were challenging their understanding of the apostles' teachings. In some cases such challenges were made on the basis of alternative apostolic traditions. Others were the result of different interpretations of the same texts and traditions that Polycarp, Ignatius, and others knew. Teachers such as Marcion (d. c.155), whose ideas we will explore in greater depth in the next section, were also part of the movement. Marcion was the son of a bishop from Asia Minor; he gained a reputation as an influential teacher of the faith after moving to Rome around 140. At one point he was almost elected a bishop of the church in Rome, but then began organizing new churches apart from the Catholic party, some of them eventually spreading as far as Persia. By the end of the second century it was clear that Marcion's teachings were far from those the majority party considered to be true and that his network of communities constituted a new and different church.

One of Polycarp's disciples, Irenaeus, in his capacity as bishop of Lyons in the last decades of the second century, entered the fray against Marcion and several other teachers like him. Irenaeus argued that the traditions of the majority party went back to the apostles from whom they had been handed on to bishops in the churches. Collectively they represented the catholic, or orthodox, point of view. This is not to say that there was always unanimity among the leaders of the Catholic party. For Irenaeus, various ideas were to be tested against apostolic teachings and accountable to the authority of those who were the apostles' successors in the churches, the bishops. Others were heretics, persons who had left the true faith. What Irenaeus and his fellow bishops sought to encourage by such a distinction was fidelity to Jesus Christ and a sense of solidarity with those who handed on the teachings of the apostles.

The Christian movement was gaining numbers in the cities of Asia Minor and Greece, possibly the region of greatest Christian growth at the time. But growth did not come without opposition. As early as 112 CE Christians had become the victims of imperial persecution. The new religion was perceived to be potentially disruptive of local economic life and a challenge to the imperial order. Christians refused to acknowledge the gods who guided Roman fortunes and even the divine nature of the Roman emperors. They embraced an oppositional stance, expressing it in the form of apocalyptic expectations and in actual martyrdoms.

What held the Christian communities together was not their common homeland, for they had none. Heightened expectations of life in the coming kingdom of God show up repeatedly in Christian letters and accounts from this period. Such end-time expectations played a major role in imparting a sense of hope in the face of local persecution and impending death. Actual martyrdoms were relatively few, but those who did go to their death inspired others to face the hostility of their neighbors. Imperial opposition was not the only difficulty they faced, of course. Christians lived in close proximity to a host of other gods whose temples and cults decorated the cities of Greece and Asia Minor. Overwhelmingly the Christians rejected these competing gods and goddesses but not the philosophical ideals of Greco-Roman life. Christian virtue was an important part of Christian witness.

One common theme we encounter in the second-century letters and treatises written by leaders of the churches concerns the immediate threat perceived to be made by false teachers in the region. The network of leadership among churches was strong. The bishops knew one another's names, wrote to one another, and analyzed one another's interpretation of apostolic traditions. The network they formed across the region as successors of the apostles provided the churches with a sense of both community and continuity. By the same token, however, as groups of bishops determined that one or another church leader was wrong, or heretical, in his teachings, they did not hesitate to name names and expose the errors. The rhetoric was often strong, for Christian truth was considered a matter of utmost moral and spiritual concern. Many of these disputes spread across great geographical expanses and involved the churches in continuous controversy over generations. We will follow them in more detail in the next chapter.

7

The Early Christian Movement in the Western Mediterranean

The Christian movement in the Mediterranean world grew in the shadows of Roman power. Churches could not help but feel the effects of imperial culture. They responded by mirroring the Roman imperium, reshaping it in the image of Christ. Christians might have been small in number and considered marginal in the eyes of the state, but for Irenaeus, Polycarp, Ignatius, and others, they were colonies of a new civic order over which Christ alone was ruler. The book of Revelation provided veiled representations of Rome's power and wealth in the images of a terrifying beast and a seducing harlot. Over against the imperial city on earth the seer foresaw a coming city from heaven, the New Jerusalem, from which Christ would reign for a thousand years.

As an urban center Rome deserved the awe and respect that Christians begrudgingly accorded to it. The city on the Tiber was most likely the largest and wealthiest on earth at the time. The capital of an extensive empire, it dominated the material and cultural life of the entire western Mediterranean region. The city's language was spoken in day-to-day life across Italy, southern France, and the Iberian peninsula, as well as in the urban areas of North Africa. No one living in any city or town in these regions failed to feel the effects of Rome's presence.

Toward the end of the second century, Irenaeus of Lyons made the case for the authority of what he considered to be the true apostolic tradition, in opposition to certain ideas that other Christian teachers were advancing. This apostolic tradition, Irenaeus said, had been handed down to him in Asia Minor from a teacher who in turn had received it from others in a succession that went back to some who first knew Jesus in the flesh. Standing in the wake of this line of succession, he was assured of the fidelity of his own doctrines to the teachings of the apostles. In another context, however, Irenaeus wrote that since it would be tedious to identify the entire succession of churches across the world, he will take "that tradition derived from the apostles, of the very great, the very ancient, and universally known Church founded and organized at Rome by the two most glorious apostles, Peter and Paul . . . which comes down to our time by the successions of

74

the bishops" as being his standard for determining the faithfulness to the truth of a particular doctrine or teaching.[14]

The shift from Asia Minor to Rome as the historical context for the apostolic tradition reflected, of course, a shift in Irenaeus's own historical location. Brought up in the Greek-speaking world, by the 180s he was serving a church located in Gaul, in modern France. Lyons was a Roman city located along the Rhone River in what was predominantly Celtic territory. His small congregation most likely had been started by merchants who were also from Asia Minor, and its members spoke both Latin and Greek. Other inhabitants of the city were Celts, and Irenaeus says that he had preached to them (although we do not know for sure what language he used to do so). From his vantage point in this northern city of the western Roman world, Irenaeus perceived the imperial capital to play the most important role in grounding apostolic tradition in the West. Christians further east looked toward several cities where churches claimed to have had original apostolic connections. But in the West only Rome could make such a claim. Although neither Peter nor Paul can be said historically to have planted the church in Rome (as Irenaeus seemed to imply), the tradition that both ended their apostolic careers there has enough historical support to bolster Irenaeus's argument.

We cannot say with any certainty who started the first church or churches in Rome, or how the Christian movement first arrived in the western end of the Mediterranean region. We know that by the year 50 CE there were followers of Jesus numbered among the large Jewish community in Rome (some estimates of this Jewish community number as high as fifty thousand). When the apostle Paul wrote his letter to the Christians in Rome sometime around the mid-50s CE, he noted that for some time he had wanted to visit them. By implication, he must have known of their existence for several years, if not more, by then. The letter also stated that he planned to stop and visit them on his way further west to Spain, where he planned to open a new mission. Scattered throughout its pages are several references that indicate Paul had at least a general knowledge of the situation of Christians in Rome. It is not surprising that the city drew the attention of Paul. The size and prestige of Rome could hardly have been ignored by a movement that sought to reach all the world.

Rome is not alone in its obscurity concerning Christian origins. Throughout the entire western Mediterranean world the historical record of the initial spread of the Christian message remains little more than conjecture, without much even in the way of legend or tradition. We know that Christian communities emerged in the regions of Italy, Spain, and even Gaul prior to the end of the second century, but how they made their way there is not clear. A possible reference to Christians in Italy other than in Rome can be found at the end of the New Testament book of Hebrews, which sends greetings from "those from Italy" (13:24). Outside of archeological evidences from burial inscriptions, the record in Spain is even more silent until the middle of the third century, when several bishops are noted as being martyred. Documents of Spanish Christianity survive only from

---

[14] Irenaeus, *Against Heresies* 3.3.2., in *The Ante-Nicene Fathers*, 1:415.

the beginning of the fourth century and the proceedings of a church council held at Elvira.

The spread of Christianity to the provinces of Roman North Africa (the region of Africa north of the Sahara, from Libya westward to the Atlantic) is likewise still virtually unknown. The gospels record the name of a visitor to Jerusalem named Simon from Cyrene (a city in North Africa, halfway between Alexandria and Carthage), who was forced to carry the cross of Jesus. The book of Acts also mentions this particular city as the home for several Christian converts. But further to the west in the Roman provinces of Africa, Numidia, and Mauretania, any record of Christianity prior to the end of the second century has yet to be discovered. Historians are unsure how the Christian message first came to Carthage, and whether its initial spread was among the sizable Jewish community in that North African metropolis or among Gentiles. By the year 200, however, it had a significant Christian community.

Christians in Rome

Rome not only dominated the western Mediterranean world but drew to its neighborhoods a myriad of residents from across the world, including many Jews. Christianity first spread among the Jewish population of the city, but Paul's letter to the Christians there appears to be addressed to a community composed of Jews and Gentiles alike. From what we can tell, no clear organizational structure was yet in place uniting the various local house churches that were scattered across the city. Nevertheless, Paul could assume there to be enough communication among believers that his letter would be circulated among them. He closed his letter with a series of greetings that suggest something of a recognized leadership group in the city. Their names and locations indicate that most, if not all, had originally come from another part of the world.

The early churches in Rome were made up of members who were almost entirely from the lower and foreign classes in the city. The latter point shouldn't surprise us; by the first century of the Christian era, the majority of Rome's population was foreign born. A large number were slaves or descendants of slaves who had been taken there as captives from the many wars Rome had fought across the world. A large number of them were employed in some capacity within the imperial household, which is to say in the vast bureaucracy that actually ran the empire in Rome. Slaves could attain high degrees of education and some exercised considerable power within the bureaucracy. Since slaves of Roman citizens could be granted Roman citizenship upon being freed, some were able even to advance in social class.

The predominantly foreign identity of the first Roman Christians is reflected in the fact that they were a *koine* Greek–speaking community in a city where the ruling language was Latin. Using Greek (even its *koine* form) in Edessa might identify someone as belonging to an upper class, but in Rome it identified someone as a member of a lower class or a foreigner. Christians did not start using Latin in Rome until the latter part of the second century, suggesting that they remained a community of lower and foreign classes. The use of Latin first appeared in the Roman churches only when Victor, a native of North Africa, became bishop of Rome late in the second century. The churches were still bilingual there well into the third.

In 64 CE fire destroyed much of the city of Rome. The emperor Nero, seeking to divert public anger, accused the Christians of having started the inferno and launched a wave of persecution against them. Hundreds appear to have been executed during this episode, including both Peter and Paul, according to the later letter of *I Clement*. After that there is little evidence of Christians having trouble with the state until the end of the century, when the emperor Domitian banished his niece, Flavia Domitilla, and executed her husband. Although the deed was more than likely a result of Domitian perceiving a threat to his throne, the official charge made against them was that they had shown Jewish leanings. Domitilla is remembered by Christian tradition in Rome as having been a follower of Jesus. Assuming this to be the case, her conversion was a harbinger of future Christian growth among upper-class women in Rome.

Around the year 95 CE Rabbi Gamaliel II, head of the Jewish academy that had been formed at Yavneh (Jamnia) in Israel, visited the emperor in Rome to solidify the relationship between Rome and the Jews. We don't know if the question of Christian legitimacy came up in their meeting, but we do know that by this time the rabbis had turned against the followers of the Nazarene. Given the project of reconstructing Judaism on the other side of the destruction of the Temple, the rabbis' opposition to Christians is understandable. How could one claim to be inheritors of the promises of Israel but fail to observe the Law on matters as fundamental as circumcision and dietary practices? How could Christians maintain that Jesus was divine and not violate the basic tenet of monotheism? For the Christians in Rome, such Jewish opposition could only spell further trouble. Already they were suspect in the eyes of the city's authorities. Opposition from other Jews could only worsen the Christians' situation as an outlawed religion.

The final chapter of Jews and Christians being co-religionists in the Mediterranean world was being written at the end of the first century. Soon many synagogue services included a curse on the Nazarene party that was meant to drive them out. For their part, Christians intensified their demonization of Judaism and claimed to be the sole and rightful inheritors of the faith tradition of Israel. A slice of Christian attitudes toward Judaism is preserved for us in the *Dialogue with Trypho*, a book written by Justin Martyr in Rome sometime toward the middle of the second century. There were a few Christians still practicing Jewish religious traditions, Justin informs us, but as far as he was concerned the two faiths were separate. Christians were now the true spiritual inheritors of the promises given in Israel's scriptures. Jews who were the inheritors of the physical promises had been cut off. Since Christ had fulfilled the Law, only those who followed Christ could claim the Mosaic tradition as their own.

Through the first decades the organizational structure of the Christian movement in Rome remained loosely defined. Foreigners in the city were permitted to organize *collegia* that were recognized by Roman law and allowed members to assemble undisturbed. Such voluntary associations were formed on the basis of ethnic, religious, or professional identity. Many had a specific purpose, such as a funeral society that provided for its members' burials. This appears to be the vehicle Christians utilized to secure permission to gather apart from synagogues in Rome. The basic structure of Christian community continued to be the house church, as we can see in Acts 28:30, where Paul's rented quarters served such a purpose.

Noticeably absent from our information about the church in the first decades in the city are references to a centralized episcopal structure. In a letter sent ahead to Rome on his way to his martyrdom there, Ignatius of Antioch around the year 110 made no mention of the office. In the other letters that he sent to churches along his way, he had emphasized the importance of a monarchical bishop in the church. The absence of a greeting in Ignatius's letter to Rome suggests that there was no such single head of the church there to greet. This did not mean that the church was without bishops. One of the persons we know of who bore this title, for instance, was Clement, an educated ex-slave with social connections that took him among members of the upper class. Clement's influence reached even beyond Rome, as shown by a letter that he sent to the Corinthian church *(I Clement)* around the year 100, addressing an internal dispute that was disrupting its communion.

The church in Corinth had recently removed several leaders from office. Expressing his concern about that action, Clement made the point that the apostles themselves had appointed their successors to carry on their work. The succession of leadership ought to continue in an orderly fashion through bishops and deacons who were appointed with the consent of the people, he said. From the letter it is clear that Clement recognized the importance of these offices of leadership in the church. At the same time Clement's description had a collegial ring to it. A contemporary of his in Rome who was known as Hermas, and who recorded a series of charismatic visions he received around this same period, mentioned Clement in the capacity of a corresponding secretary for the churches in Rome without specifically referring to any episcopal office. A half-century later Justin Martyr could still write about Christian practices and beliefs in Rome without any reference to a strong episcopal office or a single bishop over all the churches of the city.

Justin had come to Rome sometime around the year 135 and had gathered around him a small group of students. In his *First Apology*, a book that he addressed to the emperor as a defense of the faith, Justin sought to refute the charge that Christians were subversives. Describing a Christian eucharist, Justin identified the one who gives thanks over the bread and wine in the eucharist simply as the president of the brethren. Deacons then distributed the food and took it to those who were absent, he said. Justin regarded the bread and wine as the flesh and blood of Jesus. The presiding person occupied a priestly office in his description. But the meetings he described appear still to have been those of house churches, not organized under the authority of a single bishop.

This description may well have been penned on the eve of change in the pattern of Christian leadership in the city. From Eusebius we know of a bishop named Anicetus who came to office in 154 CE. Eusebius reproduced a line of succession from Peter to Anicetus for bishops who were reportedly the head of the church in Rome. From Anicetus it was a short step to Victor, whose pastoral term began in 189. After Victor we can see a pronounced pattern of leadership under a single bishop in the city.

A major controversy regarding the dating of Easter erupted in Rome in the latter half of the second century. The dispute revealed not only something of the factions that existed among the Christians there but the growing power of a senior bishop that was emerging as well. Early in his episcopacy, according to Eusebius, Anicetus had received a visit from Polycarp, the bishop of Smyrna in Asia Minor. Among the issues they discussed were their differences on the dating of Easter. Christians in Asia Minor celebrated on the 14th of Nisan, the Jewish festival of Passover, even though it often fell on a weekday. It was a tradition that they claimed originated with the apostle John. Most other Christians celebrated Easter on the Sunday following the 14th of Nisan, to coincide with the day of resurrection. In Rome, Christians who had originally come from Asia Minor were celebrating Easter on one date, while others were celebrating it on another date. In the words of one observer, some were feasting while others were fasting, hardly a strong case for them being one people. The issue wasn't resolved at this time. According to Eusebius, Anicetus and Polycarp agreed to maintain their separate practices without breaking their fellowship.

Several decades later the controversy flared up again. Whether it started in Rome and spread to other parts of the Christian world, or started elsewhere and then spread to Rome is not clear from Eusebius. In any case Victor, the North African who became bishop of Rome in 189, was soon at the center of the dispute. He called for a conference of local bishops to gather in his own city, and sent letters to bishops in other parts of the world, asking them to take up the issue in similar gatherings. Eusebius says that bishops from churches in such places as Osrhoene, Gaul, Pontus, and Palestine all held councils among themselves to consider the matter. We have no indication that they saw themselves as setting a precedent in calling such gatherings to settle the dispute, although later generations of church historians would do so. All we know is that the various bishops were subsequently supposed to have circulated letters among themselves, reporting on their decisions. Most of them sided with Rome.

Not surprisingly, however, the churches in Asia Minor refused to abandon their tradition. One of their bishops, Polycrates of Ephesus, wrote to Victor defending the practice. Polycrates pointed to a distinguished list of church leaders who had celebrated this date in his part of the world. Victor was not impressed and wrote back announcing that he had excommunicated those who kept the 14th of Nisan for Easter. A response then came from Irenaeus of Lyons, advising the bishop of Rome to allow for diversity in liturgical practices in the church. Such need not be an occasion for breaking the peace and unity of the whole. Irenaeus sent similar pleas to other leaders in various places, arguing for tolerance of different traditions. We don't know what the immediate outcome in Rome was regarding Victor's excommunication and Irenaeus's plea of tolerance. The issue was still being disputed well into the third century in Rome; it finally was resolved only by a great council at Nicaea in the fourth.

The Easter dating dispute was an important issue dividing churches that held different apostolic traditions. More important in Rome itself was the way Victor handled the situation. For the first time we see the pattern of a single episcopal leader assuming oversight of all the churches in the city. Even if not all the Christians there accepted his authority (we don't have any evidence that those who were celebrating the 14th of Nisan immediately ceased to do so, for instance), the pattern was in place. A single bishop exercising authority within the church provided a degree of administrative and theological unity that the movement had previously lacked there. External factors weighed in on the side of the increased institutional strength that was gained by having a single Christian leader of the city. A new round of persecution had broken out, for one thing. Around the year 165 Justin had charges brought against him by one of the Cynic philosophers in the city. The Christian teacher was brought before the civil magistrate and ordered to offer a sacrifice to the gods. Refusing to do so, Justin and several of his associates were then executed, adding their names to the list of martyrs for the faith. Shortly after that Justin's student Tatian left for the East. In Rome further violence at the hands of the state loomed on the horizon. In the face of such opposition, the disciplinary structure of a single leader seemed at least to some to be vital for sustaining church life.

A second reason for the development of a stronger institutional church in Rome was in response to the growing body of ideas and options being offered in the name of Christ. By the middle of the second century, Rome was becoming a "who's who" of renowned teachers from across the empire. As new arrivals set up shop in the capital, they began preaching their various versions of the Christian message to the faithful and winning a following. Justin was one of these. So was Marcion, the wealthy son of a bishop from the province of Pontus in Asia Minor, who was introduced in the previous chapter. Marcion preached that the God who created the world was not the one Jesus called Father but an evil God named YHWH. This native of Pontus began organizing his followers in Rome into a church of their own. Eventually his movement spread to other, more distant regions of the world. A third teacher of renown among the Christians was Valentinus, originally from Alexandria. He brought a message of secret mysteries or knowledge (Gnosticism) that supposedly had been communicated by Christ to his original disciples. Valentinus did not go on to develop a church of his own, but his teaching was for a time given a hearing by many in Rome. There were others as well. Added to the already diverse cultural life of the Roman community, one can see why a central Christian leadership structure gained support.

Deciding which of these teachers could be trusted as faithful to the way of the apostles, and which could not, called for greater institutional oversight within the church overall. Irenaeus, bishop of Lyons, and Tertullian, a presbyter from Carthage, both favored a strong episcopal structure for guiding the churches on matters of faithful teaching. In each city there was to be one church that was united through its bishop, presbyters, and deacons. Presbyters and deacons were accountable to the bishop, and bishops were accountable both to the people and to each other.

Early in the third century in Rome, a teacher by the name of Hippolytus wrote down what he asserted were the practices handed on from the earliest days of the movement. The treatise is known as the *Apostolic Tradition*. Its pages provide, among other things, guidelines for ordaining deacons, presbyters, and bishops, and liturgical instructions for conducting worship. "Let the bishop be ordained after he has been chosen by all the people," it states. After that presbyters and other bishops were to lay their hands on him, the other bishops praying aloud and the presbyters praying in silence (2:1-3). "Imitate Christ always," the *Apostolic Tradition* elsewhere instructs, "by signing your forehead sincerely; for this is the sign of his passion, manifest and approved against the devil" (36:15).

The second century, as we have seen, found the bishop of Rome beginning to be seen by others in the western Mediterranean as playing an important symbolic role in the region. In part the reason was the prestige of the city of Rome itself. The treasury of Rome's churches was stronger than that of other cities, due to the number of its members who were employed in the imperial bureaucracy. The tradition that both Peter and Paul were martyred there gave it a special status as both recipient and defender of the apostolic memory. Of course bishops and traditions were not all that sustained the churches' faith. In his *First Apology* Justin noted that Christians made use of what he called "the memoirs of the apostles" that had been collected.

We have already come across the name Marcion. Around the middle of the second century this teacher from Asia Minor arrived in Rome and began gathering a following among the churches. Marcion argued that the God of the Old Testament was not the one Jesus called Father. The material world was evil in its very nature, and thus the one who had created the heavens and earth was of necessity an evil god. Jesus Christ came to set us free from the material world. Thus Marcion severed the connection between Judaism and Christianity, as well as the Old Testament from Jesus. This meant that he also had to reject a number of the teachings of the apostles who had been with Jesus, for they were Jewish. From Marcion's point of view, they misunderstood what Jesus had taught. Only the writings of Paul and a modified version of Luke were on his approved reading list. A number of historians have suggested that Marcion was the first to publish such an authoritative list or canon for a New Testament, which he circulated as part of his new movement.

If that is indeed the case, then Christians might well have been responding to Marcion when they began drawing up their own authoritative lists of books to be included in a canon. By the second half of the second century the four gospels that are now part of the New Testament were regularly consulted in Rome, as they were elsewhere, for trustworthy information regarding Jesus. Along with these the writings of Paul and several other letters that carried an apostle's name (or were associated with an apostle) were being read as authoritative by Christians. The earliest list of Catholic books that has been found is known as the Muratorian Canon. Named for the scholar who discovered it almost two hundred years ago in a library in Milan, the list appears to come from the middle of the second century. The fact that it is written in Latin strongly suggests a location in

Italy, if not Rome itself. A total of twenty-four books are identified as authoritative by the list, including the *Wisdom of Solomon* and the *Apocalypse of Peter*. Two epistles that the Marcionites claimed were written by Paul to the Laodiceans and Alexandrians were rejected, as were the writings of several others who were considered Gnostics (who will be considered in the next section). Catholic Christians also accepted the Jewish scriptures, joining the two Testaments into one Bible.

Elsewhere in the western Mediterranean world: Origins in persecution

Our knowledge of the Christian movement elsewhere in the western Mediterranean world in the first two centuries remains sketchy at best. The first word we have of churches usually comes in the form of a report of persecution and martyrdom. The history of the Christian movement is one that is often inaugurated through suffering and blood. Such was the case, for example, for the church in Lyons. The first historical report is of a local persecution that began in 177, when members of the community were charged publicly before the governor of the region. The emperor, Marcus Aurelius, under whom Justin had been executed, was consulted and confirmed that those who refused to recant their Christian commitments were to be executed. Some fifty martyrs lost their lives, among them a slave woman named Blandina and her mistress, both Christians, and a fifteen-year-old boy named Ponticus. Irenaeus survived this persecution and shortly thereafter was elected bishop.

Equally severe was the situation that marks the irruption of the Christian movement in our historical knowledge of Roman North Africa. The first word of Christians we have in the region comes with the story of the martyrdom of several believers from a town just outside Carthage in 180. Carthage had been founded many centuries earlier by Phoenician traders whose assimilation into the surrounding African environment had given rise to the region's Punic culture. The city had been destroyed by Roman forces in 146 BCE and refounded as a Latin colony. It had soon become a major center for trade, and by the time Christians arrived it was a teeming, multicultural city. One could hear indigenous African, Punic, Latin, and *koine* Greek languages spoken in its streets. There were numerous local shrines and places of worship dedicated to gods from Palestine, Egypt, Italy, and North Africa. Holding it all together was the official cult of the Roman state, in which Christians defiantly refused to participate.

Local Roman authorities encountered little public resistance to their initial measures against the Christians. Persecution was sporadic, however, and the overall number of martyrs usually relatively small. In North Africa it was sometimes even carried out reluctantly by local officials. Nevertheless, martyrdom played an enormous role in shaping Christian self-understanding. Once it occurred, it tended to shift public perception in the Christians' favor. The faithfulness and courage that martyrs showed in the face of death served to strengthen and encourage the commitment of other believers and drew new people into the community. Thus it was that a period of rapid growth set in following the first waves of persecution and martyrdom in 180 in North Africa. Fifty years later, at a council held around the year 230, some seventy bishops were in attendance from the region. As the North African theologian Tertullian wrote toward the end of the second century, "the blood of Christians is seed."[15]

One of the most compelling testimonies of martyrdom and courage from the early church is that of Perpetua and Felicitas, two women who were executed in Carthage during the persecution that broke out in 203 under the emperor Septimius Severus. Severus had ordered that violence be directed against new converts to try to dissuade people from joining the movement. Perpetua was one such new believer, a young mother with a nursing infant. Felicitas was her attendant slave, herself eight months pregnant at the time of her arrest. They came from a relatively well-to-do household, which made their decision to join the Christian family even more subversive in the eyes of the Roman authorities because by challenging the authority of her father, Perpetua challenged Roman society at its very core. After a trial before the local magistrate, both women were condemned to face the beasts in the arena on the birth date of the emperor's son.

While in prison awaiting death, Perpetua received a series of prophetic visions that she recorded in a diary that was circulated after her death. These visions had an apocalyptic character, and they comforted and guided her on her way to martyrdom. Felicitas received a sign as well. Concerned that she would not be allowed to meet death with her fellow martyrs due to her pregnancy but would be executed later with common criminals, she and the others prayed for divine help. Two days before their scheduled martyrdom, God allowed her to deliver her child early and so be ready to enter the arena on the appointed day.

On the day of their martyrdom Perpetua refused to put on the gown of a priestess of the goddess Ceres as her executioners demanded. Victims in the Roman arenas were often presented as human sacrifices to the gods; Perpetua understood herself instead to be preparing to be the bride of Christ. Their male companions were led out and mauled by various animals. Perpetua and Felicitas were set before a mad heifer that tossed them but did not kill them. Finally the martyrs were led out to the arena, where they were ritually put to death by the sword of a gladiator in a manner thick with sacrificial overtones. Perpetua herself guided the young man's blade to her throat. The account of their martyrdom was anonymously circulated after their death. Its compelling mix of prophecy and passion became a powerful vehicle for further Christian growth in the region.

The early history of North African Christianity was decisively shaped by these and other experiences of martyrdom. Historians have also often noted the rigorous moral tones that reverberated in the churches there as well. Tertullian's writings, for instance, touch on numerous matters concerning dress and behavior. Some have seen affinities with Judaism in what amount to Christian holiness

---

[15] Tertullian, *Apology*, 50, in *The Ante-Nicene Fathers: Translations of the Fathers down to A.D. 325*, vol. 3, *Latin Christianity: Its Founder, Tertullian*, ed. Alexander Roberts and James Donaldson (Grand Rapids, Mich.: Wm. B. Eerdmans Publishing Co., 1981), 55.

codes or have even speculated that the primary source of new members in churches was the Jews. The strong Semitic influences of North African Punic culture, however, could also account for the affinity between the Christians and Jews in the region. There seems to have been little conflict between the two communities as late as the early third century, a situation one would not expect if Christians were drawing many members from among the Jewish community. While the Christian message might well first have been heard among the Jewish neighborhoods in the region, it quickly became a predominantly Gentile movement in Roman North Africa. The cultural background upon which Tertullian and others drew was that of the region's various religions and Greco-Roman philosophy, suggesting as well the community they were targeting for conversion.

Looking back over the history of the Christian movement in the western Mediterranean world, we see churches emerging first in Rome itself, only a decade or so after Jesus' death. Sketchy reports suggest that churches had formed in a few other urban locations. It is possible that Christians might have visited some areas of Spain (the place Paul intended to go after Rome). In Rome the church was formed before any apostle actually reached there. The tradition that both Peter and Paul eventually did so, however, gave it illustrious apostolic credentials lacking elsewhere in the western Roman world. The authority the church had was symbolically important for later generations of bishops, who looked to the imperial city as a source and standard of tradition.

The actual situation in Rome was far from illustrious. For the better part of its first one hundred years, there was not so much a single church as a scattering of house churches organized by various leaders. Some appear to have been worshiping communities similar to those in other cities, while others appear to have been philosophical clubs or even small academies. Christians spoke mostly *koine* Greek, an indication of their foreign-born and lower-class status in the city. More than a century passed before we can say with certainty that there was a single bishop over all the churches that were part of the Catholic party in the city. When the institution of a strong episcopal office did emerge, it was in a context of controversy and dissension. Meanwhile, Christians did not escape imperial opposition. City officials watched carefully over religious affairs and outlawed any they considered at odds with the well-being of the empire. Worshiping a messianic claimant to Israel's throne was certainly not seen as a harmless religion by the authorities in Rome. Justin Martyr sought to present a case for the moral benefits of Christianity to the empire, but his efforts cost him his life around 165.

Yet the community survived. It faced its first major persecution in 64 CE, possibly a second episode around 96, and increased imperial opposition in the middle of the second century. Early in the second century at least one of its leaders, named Clement, was recognized elsewhere as an important church figure. By the middle of the century the institution of central episcopal leadership was beginning to emerge. This is not to say every Christian in Rome agreed with the development. We see too many independent teachers and enough controversy (such as that over the date for celebrating Easter) to reach such a conclusion. Controversy and development of a centralized church structure seem to have gone hand in hand. The church was negotiating its way between uniformity and diversity.

Elsewhere in the western region persecution and martyrdom were the occasions for our first solid historical evidence of churches. In Lyons, Gaul, in 177, and then in Carthage, Roman North Africa, in 180, small but intense imperial persecutions were carried out against Christian believers. Those who went to their deaths, women as well as men, were remembered by other Christians in ways that gave the movement new power. In Roman North Africa the women who were martyred were remembered as prophets as well, adding a charismatic dimension to their martyrdom. The story of Perpetua and Felicitas gave testimony to the continued immediacy of the presence of the Spirit, at least among those who were facing the ultimate test of faith.

8

The Early Christian Movement in Alexandria and Egypt

Alexandria was the preeminent intellectual city in the Mediterranean world in the first century of the Christian era. To it came some of the finest minds of the ancient world, and from it emanated intellectual influences far and wide. A city estimated by some to have had a population of 300,000 persons, it boasted one of the finest libraries the world has ever known. Egyptian, Greek, Roman, Persian, and even Indian influences were found among its teachers and traditions. A late second-century Christian theologian, Clement of Alexandria (c.160-215), was among the first persons in the Roman empire to identify correctly the Buddha by name, writing, "Some, too, of the Indians obey the Buddha whom, on account of his extraordinary sanctity, they have raised to divine honors."[16] If any city in the Mediterranean world could claim to be cosmopolitan, it was this one.

As was the case concerning other places in the ancient world, exactly how Christianity came to Alexandria in the middle of the first century remains shrouded in mystery. Jerusalem is the best candidate for the source of the initial mission to this city on the delta of the Nile. Acts 2 mentions Egypt among the locations represented in the crowd gathered on the day of Pentecost, but Luke might not necessarily have understood them to be Alexandrians. Another possible connection for an early mission is the Greek-speaking synagogue in Jerusalem, but this remains speculation. In Acts 18:24-25, Apollos is identified as an Alexandrian Jew who was already a follower of the Christian way, although he had only been baptized into John the Baptist's movement. An early variant New Testament textual tradition adds that Apollos learned of the way of Jesus in Alexandria, suggesting that the Christian message had been heard there within a decade or two after the first Easter.

If Apollos had indeed first learned of the way of Jesus while he was still in Alexandria, it would no doubt have been within the Jewish community. Jews were numerous in the city, by some estimates more than a quarter of the population. They were officially recognized as a separate people with their own political leadership and special rights granted by the emperor. For all their demographic

---

[16] Clement of Alexandria, *Miscellanies* 1.25, in *The Ante-Nicene Fathers*, 2:316.

strength in the city, or perhaps because of it, however, the Jewish community was often the target of violence there. At times these were full-scale pogroms, the most devastating occurring in 117 CE under the emperor Trajan. Even during peaceful times, Jews appear to have been the target of significant levels of hostility from their neighbors.

These tensions were no doubt felt among the first followers of Jesus in Alexandria. Christian mission efforts were directed to both Jews and Gentiles but appear to have been carried out separately, at least at first. Two non-canonical books, the *Gospel of Hebrews* and the *Gospel of Egyptians*, were known to have circulated in the city in the early days of the movement. Several scholars have advanced the notion that they were originally two different missionary documents compiled for evangelizing the two different communities in the city.

The Jewish community in Alexandria provided the first Christian converts, as we see in the case of Apollos. It also imparted to the Alexandrian church, and through it to others, its distinctive method of allegorical biblical interpretation. Alexandria was home to the Jewish philosopher Philo, who, it will be recalled, had sought to show the harmony between Plato and Moses. To do this Philo interpreted scriptures allegorically, seeking spiritual or philosophical truths that were hidden beneath the surface of historical events and narratives in scriptures. In the New Testament the book of Hebrews employed a similar allegorical method to speak about heavenly realities. One of the themes that was expressed in Hebrews and became predominant in Alexandrian theology was that of Jesus as a divine teacher of salvation. Another early Christian document that many believed came from Alexandria was the *Epistle of Barnabas*. Written near the beginning of the second century, it employed a similar method of interpretation to disclose the meaning of Jewish scriptures for Christianity. The manner in which both books assume the authority of the Jewish scriptures suggests both were directed toward a Jewish or Jewish-Christian audience.

Early Christian tradition credits Mark with being the apostle who first preached the gospel in Alexandria. While the tradition cannot be historically confirmed, the discovery in 1958 by Morton Smith of a long-lost letter believed to be from Clement of Alexandria from the end of the second century adds an interesting twist. According to Clement's letter, Mark originally wrote his gospel in Rome during Peter's residency there. After Peter was martyred, Mark came to Alexandria, where he composed a longer version of his gospel, using information he had received from Peter. The longer version included mysteries that Jesus had taught his disciples, according to Clement. However, the letter continues, the disciples of a teacher named Carpocrates in Alexandria were misusing this expanded version for their own purposes, leading Clement and others from the Catholic party to suppress it.

Clement's comments about a secret Gospel of Mark and the mysteries it imparted resonate well with the tenor of the Alexandrian intellectual world of the second century. The notion that Jesus had passed on a secret body of teaching to his closest disciples was one that had wide currency in the city. Alexandria had long provided a home for the mystery religions. Before Christianity arrived, the city's syncretistic atmosphere had proved conducive to wedding Egyptian with

Greek, Jewish, and even Persian philosophical and religious elements. At the turn of the first century there were already teachers along the edges of the Jewish community who were busy appropriating its religious ideas in Egypt and Palestine. The Jewish scriptures with their story of creation and of the ineffable name of God proved to be especially fertile ground for those seeking mysterious spiritual truths. In Egypt, teachers of magic had long appropriated an Egyptian form of the Hebrew name of God—IAO—for their magical purposes. The Christian message about Jesus, with its sacred name, healing miracles, and story of death and resurrection, offered itself in the first and second centuries as an even more powerful expression along these lines.

By the middle of the second century a number of new schools of Christian thought were flourishing in this environment. Generally referred to as Gnostics (from the Greek term for "one who knows"), these believers pursued salvation through secret teachings about God and creation. Fuller consideration of Gnostic teachings must await the next chapter. Here it will suffice to say that they sought to re-articulate the apostles' message about Jesus in a creative synthesis of Hellenistic, Egyptian, and Jewish philosophy. The first Gnostic leaders might have come from Palestine or Syria, but from Alexandria came the greatest Gnostic teachers. As its influence spread across the Mediterranean and Persian worlds, Gnosticism continued to bear evidence of a strong Egyptian Christian ancestry.

Among the best known Gnostic teachers in Alexandria were Basilides, who first appeared around the year 130, and Valentinus, who immigrated to Rome around 140. Valentinus was originally received as a teacher within Catholic circles in Rome, although by the time of Justin and Irenaeus this was not so. Most leaders in the Catholic wing of the Christian movement condemned the Gnostic teachers in the harshest possible terms. Irenaeus, for instance, denounced them for their secret teachings, asserting among other things that the true apostolic movement had to be public and open in its offering of salvation to all. Like other Catholic writers in the second century, Irenaeus traced the Gnostics back to the teachings of Simon Magus, the magician of Samaria spoken of in Acts 8. When it came to describing their errors, he attributed these to their dependency on Hellenistic teachings. The virulence of his criticism left no doubt as to how Irenaeus felt about what he considered the speculations of Gnostic teachings that he had encountered in Gaul.

For their part, many who considered themselves to be part of the Gnostic movement seem to have rejected the arguments of Irenaeus and others who identified themselves as the Catholic party without rejecting the name of being Christian. Christian Gnostics claimed as much to be inheritors of the apostolic tradition as did their Catholic opponents, although the names of Thomas, Matthew, and Philip stand equal to or above those of Peter, James, and John. Gnostic teachers were not adverse to claiming as their own the same apostolic authors treasured by the Catholic party. They only interpreted them through lenses that they believed uncovered their true meaning. In addition, Gnostics valued the names of several of the women disciples such as Mary Magdalene and Salome more than did the Catholic writers.

Over the centuries many have denied that the Gnostics can properly be described as Christian. Their own leaders certainly rejected the teachings of Catholic Christianity. Nevertheless, Gnostics always claimed to be followers of the Christ. They often considered themselves outside, or above, the Catholic wing of the Christian movement. Gnostic teachings sought to open their adherents to those higher spiritual realms that exist beyond the material world. Their truths were not for the uninitiated and the common people but were reserved for the intellectuals and the elite. Set against the background of Alexandrian intellectual and spiritual life in the second century, as exemplified by a thinker such as Clement, the Gnostics do not look like entire strangers to the Christian way, only seekers after a mystical higher life.

Gnostics differed with Catholics over various ideas each side attributed to the apostles. They also disagreed over institutional structures that were emerging on the Catholic party's side. The *Apocalypse of Peter*, an early third-century Gnostic text found among the library that was buried in the Egyptian desert near Nag Hammadi, sums up at least one visionary's hostility to the Catholic party's leadership. The *Apocalypse* represents Christ as saying:

> And there shall be others of those who are outside our number who name themselves bishops and also deacons, as if they have received their authority from God. They bend themselves under the judgment of the leaders. Those people are dry canals.[17]

One also does not need to look too hard to find a candidate for the bishop being described in the text. Demetrius, bishop of Alexandria from 189 to 232, offers himself readily for this role. Hailing from the countryside, Demetrius was not only married but reportedly illiterate. He might have had strong support among the common people from the lower classes of the city, but he would most certainly have confirmed the worst fears about the Catholic party for the educated teachers of Christian Gnosticism.

Demetrius himself recognized this dichotomy and moved to overcome it by opening up a catechetical school near his church. In doing so he opened the door in Alexandria for a merging of the two streams of Christian tradition that had grown up together there—the Catholic and the Gnostic. The catechetical school of Alexandria played a significant role in the successful integration of philosophical reflection and Catholic faith. Its first three teachers, Pantaenus (dates unknown), Clement (c.160-215), and Origen (c.185-c.250), represent one of the most formidable intellectual successions ever witnessed within the world Christian movement. They reworked the intellectual heritage of Hellenism into a fully biblical Christian form, opening up new insights for Christian theology and worship. We will return to the contributions of the Alexandrian school in the next section.

---

[17] *Apocalypse of Peter*, trans. James Brashler and Roger A. Bullard, in *The Nag Hammadi Library in English*, ed. James M. Robinson, 3d ed. (San Francisco: Harper & Row, 1988), 376.

The formation of the catechetical school in Alexandria went a long way toward answering the attraction of a separate Gnostic movement, more so in the long run perhaps than did the literary attacks of authors such as Irenaeus and Tertullian, who both wrote against what they perceived to be the errors of various other Christian groups of their day. Irenaeus and Tertullian contributed immensely to the formation of what became known as Orthodox Christian identity by drawing sharp distinctions between ideas they regarded as orthodox and those they called heretical. The Alexandrians were just as concerned with representing the truth, and just as concerned to rebut what they perceived to be errors. But they sought to do so open to the possibility of evangelizing Hellenistic intellectual culture. There were a number of reasons why the Gnostics eventually declined, but one of them was the openness of the Catholic party to Christian intellectual life.

Theologians such as Clement and Origen sought to remain faithful to both the faith expressed in the Catholic church and to the intellectual heritage of Hellenism. Origen in particular is often credited with having helped open up a new phase in that wider philosophical world, being one of the first exponents of the doctrines of what is called Middle-Platonism, a broader philosophical school of thought that emerged in the third century CE. Ironically perhaps, all three of the first teachers of this school of Alexandria ended up departing from the city before they concluded their productive years of education and teaching. According to tradition Pantaenus, as we will see shortly, went to India to missionize. Clement fled during the persecution that followed the Roman emperor Septimius Severus's visit in 202. Origen went into exile in Caesarea in Palestine after a dispute with Demetrius, the same bishop mentioned above, over Origen's irregular ordination as a presbyter.

As for the Gnostic party, by the third century its numbers proportionally had dwindled. The causes for this were more than simply the opposition expressed by the Catholic party. Despite the vehement character of the Catholic writers' attacks, we have little evidence that books alone caused the Gnostic movement to diminish. Catholic leaders had no power other than that of persuasion to employ against the Gnostics or any other party that they considered to be unacceptably deviant in the second and third centuries. Gnosticism died down not because the Catholic party suppressed it—although that did come later, in the fourth century—but because the Catholic party simply swallowed it up with its numbers. The increase in members in Catholic Christianity in Alexandria and elsewhere eventually proved to be too great.

The Catholic church opened the doors of salvation to the common people. In Alexandria these people eventually proved to be its greatest strength. With their bishops, the people of the city might not even be able to read or write well, but this did not exclude them from participating in the mysteries of baptism, eucharist, and other rites of Christian life. As the numbers of common people becoming Christian grew, Alexandria's visibility as a center for Christian learning increased as well.

The Christian movement was strong in Alexandria, but by no means was it confined there. By the end of the second century there were communities formed along the seacoast to the west and south down the Nile. Outside Alexandria the Egyptian cultural influences were stronger and began to appear more pronounced. By the third century, the Egyptian language was being employed for both liturgical and theological purposes throughout the land. The memory of Egypt's philosophical and in some cases religious heritage from before Christianity was kept alive even among some Christians. The Nag Hammadi collection, for instance, contains a passage from *Asclepius*, one of the Hermetic books. In it the God Trismegistus says:

> Or are you ignorant, Asclepius, that Egypt is (the) image of heaven? Moreover, it is the dwelling place of heaven and all the forces that are in heaven.[18]

The day will come, Trismegistus continues, when Egypt will be ruled by foreign people and foreign religions. Then the true Egyptians and gods will flee up to heaven, and Egypt will be left a desert. One can only wonder how a Christian monk, even one with Gnostic leanings, interpreted such words in the Egyptian desert in the fourth century.

---

[18] *Asclepius 21-29*, trans. James Brashler, Peter A. Dirkse, and Douglass M. Parrott, *Nag Hammadi Library*, 334.

9

"Every Foreign Land"

A missionary identity

The preceding chapters have examined Christian churches and communities formed in several regions of the ancient world. A quick glance at a map shows them radiating out from Jerusalem across urban trade routes east and west. The apostolic impulse led people to travel to new regions of the world, where they began telling the story of Jesus and organizing new house-church communities in his name. Christians worshiped together regularly, served others in their city, shared their faith with family and neighbors, and communicated with believers in other places. We have witnessed their movement crossing political, cultural, and linguistic boundaries. As their message took root, new expressions of faith emerged in the languages and cultures of the regions they were in.

These early Christian communities were possessed by what can best be called a missionary identity. Inviting others to join in their movement was of utmost concern. Closely related to this identity was the ascetic impulse to purge oneself of excess worldly obligations in order to be free to follow Christ entirely. When persecution arose, these twin impulses combined to enable women and men alike to embrace their impending deaths as an opportunity for public proclamation or witness, free from the shackles of material ("this world's") expectations. The actual number of martyrs were few, but their memory far exceeded their own immediate history. In the early Christian cult of the martyrs we encounter the missionary and ascetic impulses coinciding in extremely effective ways.

Our historical sources from the first two centuries tell us enough about the churches around the Mediterranean and as far east as Edessa to allow us to speak with relative confidence about the kinds of communities that were formed there. But what about regions beyond them? What about the history of missions beyond these first communities? Here our historical sources become much more sketchy. Christians are reported by Clement in the second century to be in Ethiopia, although how he knew it, he did not say. In Edessa, Bardaisan wrote that Christians could be found as far east as modern Pakistan, but he did not cite any names by which we could identify them. Irenaeus of Lyons said Christianity had reached the Germans on the other side of the Roman border and that he had himself preached to Celts who were in his own city. He did not indicate anything more about either case. We know that after leaving Rome in the late second century, Tatian settled further east. Most historians assume it was in Mesopotamia, but quite possibly it was as far east as the city of Arbela in the country of Adiabene, east of the Tigris River. Wherever he ended his career, we can assume he continued to speak about Jesus.

Thomas and the mission to India

Among the most important traditions of early Christian missions are those of the journey of the gospel into India. A majority of these traditions identify the apostle Thomas as being the first missionary to that part of the world, although some name Bartholomew as the apostle. The frequency of early reports that Thomas preached in India is significant in itself. There is enough historical evidence to support at least the possibility that the apostle did indeed travel to that Asian land. Even if he did not, however, the tradition is worthy of historical note as a commentary on Christian self-understanding as a global church in the first centuries of the movement.

To determine the possibility of the Thomas tradition and India, we need to see the wider historical picture of the age. Around the first century the Mediterranean world was experiencing something of a surge in its fascination with things Indian. The interest was fueled by the new commercial ties that were bringing Indian goods and people through Egypt while taking Greco-Roman goods and people into India. About the time St. Paul was setting off for his first missionary voyage across the Mediterranean Sea, an Egyptian pilot of a Roman ship discovered the secret of the monsoon winds that blow across the Arabian Sea. What had previously been an Arab and Persian shipping secret was now exploited by the Romans to open wide their trade with India.

According to the apocryphal *Acts of Thomas* (a book most likely composed in Edessa in the third or fourth century), an agent of an Indian king named Gudnaphar had come to Jerusalem seeking artisans to build a new palace back home. Thomas, a carpenter like Jesus, heard the offer and took on the job. With his Indian host he traveled to northern India, where he was given necessary money to begin the construction. Instead of building a palace, however, Thomas gave the money to the poor and set about performing miracles in the land as he shared the message of Christ. After being jailed and then freed, the *Acts of Thomas* says the apostle traveled to other parts of India, reaching at last the region of modern Madras. There he was martyred by an angry king whose queen Thomas had converted to his radical ascetic doctrine. Tradition locates the site of his burial at a shrine in the southeastern city of Mylapore, where his tomb is still said to stand.

Among the Indian churches a number of oral traditions and folk songs trace the origins of Christianity back to St. Thomas. The Indian oral traditions say Thomas first landed in 52 CE in South India along the Malabar coast, not in the North. There he preached to the people and won many converts to the Christian faith. Some who converted were Brahmins, while others were from various other castes. His preaching angered the Brahmin leaders, who ordered him to worship the goddess Kali. Thomas refused and was executed with a lance through his side. July 3 is still celebrated by the Indian churches as the anniversary of this martyrdom.

The *Acts of Thomas* are best described as legends, and oral traditions can hardly be cited as being beyond question. Yet there is historical evidence that supports the Thomas narrative's main lines. A king named Gudnaphar did exist in northern India in the first century. Coins minted under his reign have been discovered in Afghanistan. The possibility of Thomas traveling by ship to India is fully credible as well. More than a hundred Roman vessels each year journeyed from the Egyptian ports along the Red Sea to India and back for trade. The sizable number of Roman coins that have been found in India from this period testify to a high degree of commerce. Workers such as carpenters are included among historical records of those who made the journey. Certainly there is ample reason to believe he *could* have made the trip.

Providing an adequate historical assessment of these traditions is difficult. The sheer weight of their abundance in several variant streams commands our respect. An enormous body of legendary materials concerning Thomas accrued in the early centuries of the Christian church. Surprisingly, none disagrees that Thomas journeyed to the east; where and how far he went are what are in question. In the end we are left with a fascinating body of tradition, found in apocryphal sources, abundant later accounts, and a rich body of oral traditions and folk songs. The safest historical stance that we can take is to say that the evidence is compelling without yet being historically decisive.

Another ancient Christian tradition says that Pantaenus, the first teacher of Alexandria's famed catechetical school, went to India as a missionary at the end of the second century. Both Eusebius and a later Latin author named Jerome preserve this tradition for us. According to these sources Pantaenus was an eminent Stoic teacher who was converted to the Christian faith. Sometime around 190, several Indian visitors to Alexandria (merchants, we would guess) met Pantaenus. Impressed by his erudition, they invited him to visit India. Pantaenus accepted the offer and with the approval of Bishop Demetrius left Alexandria to travel east. According to Eusebius he reached India where he found the apostle Bartholomew had already been, and where he discovered a copy of Matthew's gospel in Aramaic. Unfortunately, we have no other historical evidence for such a visit. It is possible that his sources used "India" to refer to another place, such as Arabia. While we cannot simply discount this tradition out of hand any more than we can the stories of Thomas, it remains little more than an intriguing historical possibility.

On the other hand, even if we grant the historical possibility of these traditions of Thomas, Pantaenus, and even Bartholomew, another historical question arises, one that is closer to the concerns of this book. In these first chapters we have been exploring the history of the early formation of Christian communities and examining the incarnational shape that the Christian movement took in them. One of the most significant factors concerning these stories of missions to India is the lack of evidence of a Christian community formed in India before the fourth century. We have evidence of foreign visitors to India, but none that indicates a sustained Christian presence. We have no early Christian documents written in an Indian script, although there is a rich body of oral tradition that was passed down within the churches that remember Thomas. When Christian communities do finally emerge in the historical record from India in the fourth century, they are primarily foreign in character and made up of merchants who have traveled there. It is not always clear if there were Indians joining these communities.

In this sense Thomas, Bartholomew, and Pantaenus might be identified as the first Christian missionary evangelists to India; but they do not represent yet the history of the Christian movement in India. The mission of Thomas and Pantaenus (if either did actually journey to India) represents a part of Christian missionary history that did not result at the time in a new incarnation of the Christian movement. The very possibility that Thomas once set foot on land in India is sufficient for grounding a later identity in many Indian churches whose history will be considered below. Later generations in this way help fulfill the original vision of the apostolic movement.

The shape of the world Christian movement at the end of its first two centuries

Where we do have evidence of the movement taking institutional shape, we find a number of common factors emerging. Political challenges dominated the lives of Christians in many areas of the Mediterranean world, where churches lived in the shadow of imperial Rome. To the Syrian east the political challenges were not so severe, except for Antioch, which was an important Roman city in the East. In Edessa, we have seen, Christians lived relatively open lives by the year 200. In other places in the Syrian deserts they followed a rigorous asceticism but were relatively unmolested by the state. In Alexandria the challenges Christians faced in the first two centuries were not so much political as they were philosophical and intellectual. Alexandrian Christian churches suffered a degree of political persecution, but the dominant concerns were those raised by philosophical speculations.

In each of the regions where the Christian movement first spread, churches had their own sense of history, their own line of tradition that linked them back to the story of the apostles of Jesus. Yet in each location they also had a sense of belonging to something that was greater than themselves. Christians continued to look beyond themselves in their local situations, toward other Christians and churches in places that they knew of, and beyond into new regions of the world in mission.

A peculiar double-consciousness came to characterize these Christians who belonged but didn't belong. Never more than a troublesome minority in most places where their churches grew, they were gripped by a sense of belonging to a world-transforming movement. This consciousness is expressed well in an anonymous letter written in the second or third century to a recipient identified only as Diognetus. Its author, a Christian, was offering an apology or defense of the

Christian movement by explaining what Christians believe and why they act the way they do:

> For the Christians are distinguished from other people neither by land, nor language, nor customs; for they do not inhabit cities of their own, nor use a particular language, nor lead a life that is unusual. . . . But inhabiting Greek as well as barbarian cities, according to each person's lot . . . they display to us their wonderful and admittedly paradoxical way of life. They inhabit their homelands, but as strangers. . . . Every foreign land is their homeland, and every homeland a foreign land.[19]

Despite the admittedly hyperbolic assertion about "every foreign land," the letter articulates well the paradoxical sense of early Christian life. Becoming a part of the movement made one a stranger and gave one a home, both at the same time. The next chapter will explore some of the common themes of Christian life in the second and third centuries, looking at the cross-cultural and trans-regional connections that emerged among churches of the world.

Recommended reading

Readers wishing to follow historical trajectories from the New Testament into early Christian texts can consult Bart D. Ehrman, *After the New Testament: A Reader in Early Christianity* (New York: Oxford University Press, 1999). One of the more popular introductions to the urban life of early Christianity, viewed through the lens of social science, is Wayne A. Meeks, *The First Urban Christians: The Social World of the Apostle Paul* (New Haven, Conn.: Yale University Press, 1983). Those who are interested in reading the major early Christian writers will find many of them in multi-volume sets such as *Ancient Christian Writers: The Works of the Fathers in Translation*, ed. Johannes Quasten and Joseph C. Plumpe (Westminster, Md.: The Newman Press; London: Longmans, Green and Co., 1961) or *The Ante-Nicene Fathers: Translations of the Writings of the Fathers down to A.D. 325*, ed. Alexander Roberts and James Donaldson (Grand Rapids, Mich.: Wm. B. Eerdmans Publishing Co., 1981).

Detailed studies of the emergence of Christianity in the various regions described in this book abound. One of the more widely respected names in eastern church history is Hans J. W. Drijvers, *East of Antioch: Studies in Early Syriac Christianity* (London: Variorum Reprints, 1984). Wilfred C. Griggs, *Early Egyptian Christianity: From Its Origins to 451 C.E.* (New York: E. J. Brill, 1990), analyzes in considerable detail the literary record of early Christianity in Alexandria and Egypt. Cecil M. Robeck, *Prophecy in Carthage: Perpetua, Tertullian, and Cyprian* (Cleveland: Pilgrim Press, 1992), not only provides a look at the background of Christianity in Roman North Africa but does so with an eye toward

---

[19] This is our original translation of the text. See *Epistle to Diognetus 5, Ancient Christian Writers*, 6:139.

modern Pentecostal and charismatic concerns. A collection of essays edited by Karl P. Donfried and Peter Richardson, *Judaism and Christianity in First-Century Rome* (Grand Rapids, Mich.: Wm. B. Eerdmans Publishing Co., 1998), provides a wealth of social historical and archeological information on the emergence of Christian communities in Rome. Finally, the story of Morton Smith's discovery of a secret version of Mark is told in his book *Clement of Alexandria and a Secret Gospel of Mark* (Cambridge, Mass.: Harvard University Press, 1973).

Part III

THE GREAT CHURCH TAKES SHAPE

The Christian movement was spreading through two major empires and a host of smaller kingdoms by the beginning of the third century. Its members were found mostly in cities and towns. Christians were landowners, artisans, rural workers, and slaves. Some were in the Roman military, while others were merchants trading in the city of Nisibis in the Persian empire. Most were members of churches that still gathered in people's houses, although by the third century separate church buildings were beginning to appear. Christians met to hear the words of scripture, preach the message of Jesus Christ to newcomers in their midst, exhort one another to pious living, and share a common eucharist meal open to those who had been baptized. Many regarded this meal as a sacrificial event that took the place of what their neighbors performed in temples with live animals. The bishops and presbyters who led these services were seen as priests.

Through their social relief activities Christians had gained a reputation that reached beyond their immediate numbers. Churches cared for the sick and dying during the periodic plagues that swept through the urban regions, for instance. They raised funds to ransom prisoners and slaves, gathered foods to provide for the hungry, and assisted sailors who had been shipwrecked. Such efforts did much to boost the Christian ranks, as much as the other evangelistic activities that churches undertook.

Having spread so rapidly and across such great distances in geography, the movement inevitably faced questions of identity amid its differences. From the earliest days Christians in different cultural settings had been actively translating the message of the apostles into their own various languages and ways of understanding the world. A variety of new teachers arose within the movement, with a corresponding variety of interpretations of the apostolic memory. Even when Christians lived right next door to one another and spoke the same language, they often had differences in their understanding of who Jesus was or what salvation meant. Such differences pressed for a solution in a movement that valued unity in community on a universal scale.

Added to this were new intellectual questions raised in the course of Christian teaching that cried out for clarification. During this period Christians began

99

developing arguments that addressed the charges being made against them by hostile neighbors and regimes. These multiple tasks of articulating the truth of the apostolic memory and addressing new questions raised by those around them were taken up by a select group of teachers in the dominant Catholic party who collectively have become known as the apologists.

There were others who claimed to be followers of Christ but did not claim to be a part of the Catholic majority of the Christian movement. The most important of these in the first three centuries were those who were part of the alternative Christian movement we have already identified as Gnosticism. Gnostics usually met in secret and shared mystery teachings that imparted a deeper wisdom. Their teachers looked back to the person of Jesus as being their savior, but they generally made use of other gospels that they considered to be more authoritative. Gnostics for the most part drew a hostile response from the educated leadership within the Catholic party. In this section we will examine the work of Gnostic teachers in the second and third centuries, doing so with an eye toward perceiving the boundaries of identity that were emerging for Christians.

One of the more important figures in the history of world religions arose in the third century as a quasi-Christian teacher in the Persian empire. His name was Mani, and he taught a blend of Christian, Zoroastrian, and other doctrines. Mani was brutally executed in 277 by the Persian authorities, but the churches he organized continued to grow. Manichaeism, as the movement is called, was severely persecuted in both the Persian and Roman empires. Yet its followers eventually spread not just across the Roman empire but north into central Asia as well.

The question of identity was felt within the Christian movement in a poignantly painful way in its relationship with Judaism. This was becoming especially so between the emerging rabbinic movement in Judaism in the second and third centuries and the Christian movement. Christians generally agreed that Judaism as it was emerging after 70 C.E. was wrong in its interpretations of its scriptures, especially those concerning the Christ or Messiah. But were Jews to be considered siblings of Christians, a parent who was now abandoned by God, or something else that was altogether evil? The question of the Christian movement's relationship to living Judaism was not resolved in the second and third centuries. Just as important was the question of Christianity's fidelity to its monotheistic heritage, an issue that was problematic in light of the distinctive Christian practice of worshiping God as Father, Son, and Spirit. Chapter 12 will examine these twin issues.

Christians lived in widely divergent cultural locations, but some general patterns of spirituality were shared by many. The last chapter of this section will examine some of the practices that were common to churches in the third century scattered throughout a variety of locations in the world. Asceticism would not be organized into a full-fledged community movement, nor would it be integrated more fully into the life of the churches until the fourth and fifth centuries. Its early expressions in the second and third centuries were still highly idiosyncratic and individualistic. Nevertheless, its early emergence is important in light of the role monasticism eventually would play. In this same chapter we will look at responses Christians made to several social structures and institutions in some of the places where the movement spread. The growing sense that the churches were places of sacred gathering, that their eucharistic meals were sacrificial events, and that Christian churches belonged to the categories of altars and temples was giving a decisive shape to the majority of the movement as well. Throughout this entire section we are looking to discern the boundaries of diversity and the contours of something that has often been called "the great Church."

10

The Great Church Emerges

Toward the end of the second century a caustic critic of Christianity named Celsus penned a full-scale attack against the new religion. We know little about the author of this work. The treatise, entitled *True Doctrine*, is lost in its original form. Fortunately, a leading Christian intellectual in Alexandria named Origen who responded to Celsus's challenge quoted extensively from the work in order to refute it. Origen's *Against Celsus* preserves a significant amount of the original text of *True Doctrine,* enough not only to show us what some of the intellectual arguments being raised against Christians were but also to provide us with a description of the Christian movement in the last decades of the second century that was written from the perspective of a hostile outsider.

Celsus was well-read in the Christians' own literature. He had unearthed some scandalous stories about Jesus and his family in Palestine, and he knew of the various factions or parties who were competing with one another at the time. Referring to the divisions among the Christians he wrote:

> Some of them will agree that they have the same God as the Jews, while some think there is another God to whom the former is opposed, and that the Son came from the latter. . . . A third kind exists, and they call some natural and others spiritual. . . . There are some too who profess to be Gnostics . . . some also accept Jesus . . . although they still want to live according to the law of the Jews like the multitude of the Jews. . . . And these . . . slander one another with dreadful and unspeakable words of abuse. And they would not make even the least concession to reach agreement; for they utterly detest one another.[1]

Despite these divisions and the slander they tended to produce, however, most Christians at the time did not perceive themselves as belonging to a party or faction. The majority (Celsus referred to them as the "multitude") were simply members of churches that in turn were related with one another through networks of fellowship and pastoral leadership. The effect in essence created a majority

---

[1] Origen, *Contra Celsum* (5, 61-62), trans. Henry Chadwick (Cambridge: Cambridge University Press, 1965), 311-331 (italicization removed).

party within the movement whose leaders identified themselves as Catholic, or, by the fourth century, Orthodox. Earlier in his book Celsus referred to this majority to which the multitude belonged as "the great Church."[2]

The shape of the great Church

What did this great Church look like at the beginning of the third century? First, it was scattered across a broad geographical expanse of the world. Most of its members lived in cities, although they were beginning to show up in rural areas as well. Overall its numbers were growing, but the increase was by no means uniform across the various parts of the world. According to the sixth-century *Chronicle of Arbela*, there were some twenty bishops in all of Persia around the year 225. Cornelius, bishop of Rome, on the other hand, easily gathered some sixty bishops from the neighboring districts in Italy alone for a council in the middle of the third century. In some areas, notably Asia Minor and Roman North Africa, conversions were so great that Christians might have made up a majority of the population by the end of the third century. The conversion of the ruling family of the kingdom of Armenia, east of the Roman empire and north of Mesopotamia, at the beginning of the fourth century gave Christianity a considerable boost in that nation. Most Christians, however, remained members of a minority religious movement in a world that was hostile to their message.

As the movement had spread, it had begun to take on aspects of the local cultures around it. Christians worshiped the same God but did so in different languages. By the third century prayers were being offered in Syriac, Greek, Latin, Egyptian, and other tongues. Believers confessed the same Jesus Christ, but they did so through a variety of images, ideas, and expressions of faith. New elements were being absorbed by the movement as Christians sought to relate the story of Jesus to their own local contexts.

Most Christians who were part of the great Church exercised their faith as members of local gathered communities or churches. Bishops oversaw the appointment and training of presbyters (or priests) and deacons, ordaining them into service by laying on of hands. Presbyters and deacons assisted bishops in leadership in worship, although only presbyters could preside along with bishop over the "mysteries" or "sacraments," as the rites of baptism and eucharist were often called. New bishops were selected by the people of the particular churches in which they were to serve but were consecrated to their positions by other bishops from surrounding towns and cities through a ceremony of laying on of hands. Bishops and presbyters were for the most part offices reserved entirely for men by the beginning of the third century (below we shall see one notable exception among the New Prophecy or Montanists). Deacons were both male and female, however, for among their assignments they assisted those undergoing baptism, which involved candidates stripping and being anointed with oil.

---

[2] Origen, *Contra Celsum* (5, 59), in Chadwick 310 (italicized in original).

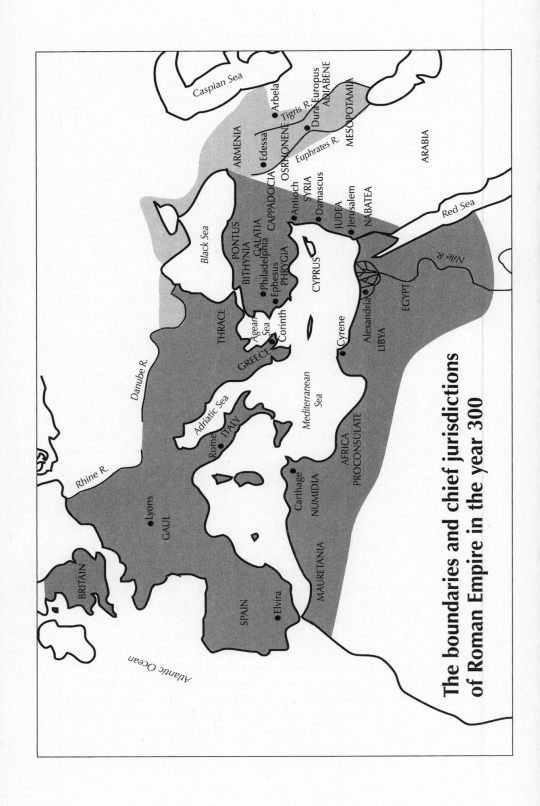

The boundaries and chief jurisdictions of Roman Empire in the year 300

Church leaders prepared new believers by teaching them the essential doctrines of the faith, a process that was known as catechism. Short formulations of the essential elements of the faith, called creeds, were used to guide the preparation of candidates. Upon completion of catechism, the new believers would undergo a rite of baptism, performed by immersing them in a pool of water in some places or pouring water over the head in others. This was accompanied by an anointing of oil, signifying the anointing of the Spirit. Clement of Alexandria described the first eucharist following baptism as including milk and honey, symbolizing the new believer's first food of the gospel.

Many church members were still first-generation converts in the third century, but a sizable number were now persons raised since childhood in Christian communities. Children generally underwent the same preparation and baptism as new converts, although there is evidence that a number of church leaders allowed infants of Christian parents to be baptized in situations where it appeared the infant might not survive. In all cases it was clear that the children of Christian parents were considered part of the church community from birth.

On a regular weekly basis church leaders presided over the worship services of the communities. Generally these included prayers, hymns, reading and interpretation of scriptures, and the eucharistic meal. The first generation of Jesus' followers had been Jews. Their worship services were spirited affairs, more akin to a synagogue setting than that of a temple. As Christianity gained a greater Gentile following, it also moved into neighborhoods and cities where temple sacrifices were the dominant religious practices. By the third century church leaders had assumed for their own communities many of the functions of the priests of other religions. Cyprian, bishop of Carthage in Roman North Africa in the middle of the third century assumed that the eucharist was not only a fellowship meal, it was the Christians' sacrificial practice as well.

The sacrificial association of Christ's death with the forgiveness of sins was found in the biblical sources to which Cyprian and others turned. Biblical passages that linked the last supper of Jesus with his sacrifice were particularly important in this regard. From there it was only a short step for Cyprian and others to see the Christians' eucharistic table as taking the place of the altars found in other temples in their neighborhoods. There was a growing sense of the mystery of the eucharist, of its sacredness, that set it apart from other parts of church life. Celebrating the eucharist together joined the Christians into one, but at the same time it set them apart from others who were not Christian. The tension between the uniting and dividing functions of the eucharist continues to be the subject of interchurch discussions today.

Not everyone agreed that the eucharist was best understood in such a sacrificial manner. At the beginning of the third century in Roman North Africa, Tertullian tended to regard it as a fellowship meal that the church shared. He also knew of Christian ascetics who refused to touch meat or wine because of the non-Christian sacrificial associations in the wider world that these foods carried. Some ascetic groups chose to forego the use of wine altogether in the eucharistic meal, using only bread and water. While the position of these ascetics was not that of the majority of those who were part of the Catholic churches, they were not entirely dismissed by Catholic leaders as being outside the boundaries of the faith.

Members of these Catholic churches were conscious of being connected with one another across the cities and regions of the world as part of a wider movement. A testimony to this is found on the tombstone of a Christian named Avircius Marcellus in Hieropolis (in modern Turkey) from the end of the second century. In his life he had traveled to Rome to meet the emperor and empress, and to the plains of Syria all the way to the city of Nisibis, east of the Euphrates. Wherever he went, his epitaph read, he had found persons with whom he could converse (most likely in *koine* Greek). Everywhere he went the faith had preceded him, and he found other Christians who set before him "the fish" (an acronym for Jesus Christ in Greek) from "a holy virgin" (Mary), accompanied by bread and wine.[3]

In a similar manner a converted Jew named Hegesippus was reported by Eusebius in the late second century to have visited bishops and collected reports on churches from Jerusalem to Corinth and Rome. In each place, he claimed, he found bishops and deacons who were in agreement in their teachings. "In every succession, however, and in every city, the doctrine prevails according to what is declared by the law and the prophets and the Lord."[4] "What shall we say of the new people of us Christians, that the Messiah has caused to arise in every place and in all climates by his coming?" asked the Christian apologist Bardaisan in Edessa around the year 225. "For behold, we all, wherever we may be, are called Christians after the one name of the Messiah."[5]

This is not to say that there was absolute unanimity among them regarding matters of doctrine and practice. Hegesippus, for instance, noted that a number of new teachers had arisen who had begun to introduce ideas of their own inspiration. They had deviated enough from the way of the apostles that they could not even be called Christian, as far as he was concerned. The creative energy unleashed by the stories of Jesus overflowed the boundaries of the original apostolic message. Prophetic inspiration often combined with creative interpretation to give rise to a range of new insights and ideas about who Christ was or what it meant to be his follower. Expansion took place not only in the movement's doctrines but in its institutional forms as well. By the end of the third century a number of splits already had occurred in the Christian movement, in some cases resulting in the organization of new church bodies.

The great Church of the third century cannot be described as a monolithic entity. Institutionally it was a network of local churches stitched together across several cultural zones by lines of communication and personal relationships. There

---

[3] The inscription can be found in William M. Ramsay, *The Cities and Bishoprics of Phrygia*, vol. I, part II (Oxford: Clarendon Press, 1897), 722-723.

[4] Eusebius, *The History of the Church from Christ to Constantine*, 4.22, trans. G. A. Williamson (New York: Barnes and Noble, 1965), 181.

[5] Bardaisan, *The Book of the Laws of Countries: Dialogue on Fate of Bardaisan of Edessa*, trans. H. J. W. Drijvers (Assen, The Netherlands: Van Gorcum and Co., 1964), 60-61.

was no single administrative head over the great Church, although the senior bishop of Rome was deemed to possess an especially important spiritual role in the Mediterranean world. No structure was in place to impose upon Christians a uniform doctrine or liturgy other than the structures of mutual love and fellowship. No single creed guided converts entering the faith in Edessa, Alexandria, or Rome. The churches did not even have a unified list of canonical books, although a general consensus was emerging concerning which gospels and epistles were to be included alongside Israel's scriptures.

Key to the network that made up the great Church were the bishops. By the third century each city typically had one recognized episcopal leader or senior bishop. There were instances where someone was challenged, or where episcopal governance itself was questioned, but they were not the majority experience. In some cases individual groups broke away to form their own new episcopal structures. We saw this earlier in the case of Marcion, and we will see it below with the New Prophecy movement and the Novatianists. The boundary lines of who was within and who was outside the great Church were sometimes unclear. A particular group might be accepted by some bishops and rejected by others, for instance. Sometimes disagreements among groups led to churches breaking fellowship, with other churches then called upon to take sides. Sometimes bishops or teachers challenged particular doctrines as being outside the acceptable range of Christian belief, what Justin Martyr termed heresies. These were often the occasion for the most acerbic forms of Christian writing.

Some individuals even moved back and forth across the lines between orthodox and heretical faith, which were not as rigidly fixed in the third century as they would become in the fourth and fifth. One of the most important theologians of the period was Tertullian of Carthage. A lawyer prior to his conversion, he was well educated in the philosophical schools of his day. After becoming a Christian he put his considerable intellectual abilities to work on behalf of the Christian cause. Tertullian applied legal principles to scriptures, interpreting them in a rigorous manner as a guide to Christian life. In matters of church order he advocated a non-hierarchical structure in order to guard against the church succumbing to elitism. His contributions in the area of doctrine were extensive. He was the first person, as far as we know, to use the term *trinitas* in Latin to name God's existence, which he explained was three persons and one substance. A number of Latin theological terms appear to have been first coined by him, shaping the western tradition in decisive ways.

Toward the end of his life Tertullian associated with a party known as the New Prophecy (or Montanists) in North Africa, drawn by their discipline and their openness to charismatic experiences. Meanwhile the New Prophecy was being charged as heretical in Rome. We do not know if Tertullian actually left the Catholic church in Roman North Africa while he was associated with the New Prophecy group, or even if he didn't go on to organize his own independent congregation at the end of his life. The question of whether one characterizes Tertullian as catholic or heretic is still debated today.

Another early Christian teacher whose orthodoxy remains debated is Origen of Alexandria. Many have called him the first systematic theologian of Christianity.

Born into a devout Christian family toward the end of the second century, he was by his early twenties being recognized as a teacher of the church. By some accounts Origen was the most prolific writer the ancient world ever knew, having dictated nearly two thousand separate works over the life of his career. Yet several centuries after his death a number of his more distinctive ideas were deemed heretical by church councils, and his works were systematically destroyed by the orthodox leaders of the day. As a result only a handful of his works survive today.

At times there were breaks or disruptions in the network of the great Church brought about by differences in pastoral practice among churches that otherwise recognized one another's teachings as faithful to the apostles. Disagreement between churches regarding the dating of Easter, as we have seen, was the focus of a controversy in the second century that continued through the third. Differences in pastoral practice in the third century emerged around the issues of the readmission of lapsed believers to communion following times of persecution, the validity of baptism administered by one who was outside the great Church, and the level of ascetic self-denial a baptized Christian was required to practice in life.

Despite these occasional breaks in communion, the web of networking that made up the great Church was nevertheless sufficient to enable a general consensus to emerge among those within it to consider themselves part of one movement. In this regard the bishops and teachers were successful in guiding the great Church forward in interpreting the gospel in new contexts and situations. Teachers often knew of one another's works. Bishops were exposed to ideas and practices from various regions. Sometimes these ideas and practices didn't translate easily or made less sense outside their original contexts. More often they had a positive impact in spurring a church on to new insights into its own situations.

Along these lines Origen provided a guiding rule for theological interpretation in a treatise that many have called the first Christian systematic theology, *On First Principles*. There he wrote:

> [Many] who profess to believe in Christ, hold conflicting opinions not only on small and trivial questions but also on some that are great and important; on the nature, for instance, of God or of the Lord Jesus Christ or of the Holy Spirit, and in addition on the natures of those created beings, the dominions and the holy powers. In view of this it seems necessary first to lay down a definite line and unmistakable rule in regard to each of these.

That rule was straightforward: "We maintain that that only is to be believed as the truth which in no way conflicts with the tradition of the church and the apostles."[6]

Origen argued that the apostles delivered those teachings essential to the Christian faith for salvation. Yet the ground of those doctrines the apostles left to be

---

[6] Origen, *On First Principles*, trans. G. W. Butterworth (New York: Harper & Row, Publishers, 1966), 1-2.

investigated by others who would receive the gifts of wisdom and language from the Holy Spirit. Furthermore, he went on, the apostles left some things unsaid "as to how or why; their intention undoubtedly being to supply the more diligent of those who came after them, such as should be lovers of wisdom, with an exercise on which to display the fruit of their ability."[7]

Filling in the unfinished understanding with the wisdom and languages unknown to the apostles was a major missionary task of the great Church in the second and third centuries. Not only did Christians continue to expand into new areas of the world, and not only did they continue to increase their numbers from conversions among their neighbors in each city or region they inhabited; but they also took on the task of bringing into the church the fruits of wisdom from among the other cultures, philosophies, and even religions that were around them. Justin, Origen, and Bardaisan set about not only to convert their hearers and readers to the way of Christian belief, but to incarnate Christian belief in the idiom of their own particular cultural locations. We will return to their work in the following chapter.

The great Church amid empires and kingdoms of the world

Rome

Christian churches grew in the second and third centuries primarily within the context of two major empires, the Roman and the Persian. The Roman empire reached its peak of power in the second century, stretching from Hadrian's wall in Britain in the west, to Edessa and Dura-Europos on the Euphrates River in Mesopotamia in the east. By the beginning of the third century Roman rule was showing signs of internal political decline. An overgrown bureaucracy added to the problems. Attempts by various emperors to reform Rome's administrative structures only increased the economic burdens of those under their rule, particularly in the regions of Egypt and North Africa. External pressures from the north were felt as tribes living beyond Rome's administrative boundaries began crossing into its territories to settle, drawn there in part by the lure of Rome's wealth and culture. The first waves of military incursions by these tribes were felt during the third century in the cities. Added to the nearly constant warfare with Persia to the east, they stretched Roman military resources thin.

Despite its increasing administrative and military problems, Roman rule continued to support a high degree of travel and trade among the cities of its empire. Christians made use of the peace Rome had secured to travel and extend their churches. At the same time imperial attacks upon Christians and their leadership heightened as the Roman emperors sought to instill greater loyalty among their people. The result was four major waves of persecution. The first of these took place under the rule of Septimius Severus at the beginning of the third century. It was this wave of persecution that took the lives of the martyrs Perpetua and

---

[7] Ibid., 2.

Felicitas in North Africa in 203. The intensity of the violence in Alexandria sent Clement into flight to Caesarea in Palestine. The same wave of persecution in Alexandria brought about the execution of the father of Origen, Clement's immediate successor in Alexandria's catechetical school. It would have brought an end to Origen's life as well had his mother not prevented him from turning himself in to the authorities by hiding his clothes.

After a decade of sporadic persecution in the Roman world, Christians enjoyed almost a full generation of peace. Then, under the reign of Decius, persecution began again in the year 250. Determined to secure the allegiance of the entire empire, Decius issued an edict that required every resident within the Roman world to offer sacrifices to the Roman gods and to receive a certificate to that effect. This proved to be one of the more decisive waves of persecution, especially for the churches of Carthage and the surrounding region in North Africa. Although it only lasted a year (Decius was killed in battle in 251), the persecution claimed a large number of Christian victims, including Fabian, bishop of Rome, and Origen, who had moved to Caesarea in Palestine and who died from the wounds he received from torture.

Perhaps even more important, the persecutions revealed new tensions within the Christian community concerning the degree of commitment among its members. During the nearly forty years of peace prior to the reign of Decius, the numbers of Christians had increased dramatically throughout the Roman world, including many whose faith did not withstand the fires of persecution. When called before the imperial magistrates, they had given in to the demand to offer sacrifices or pour libations. Others found ways of illegally securing the certificates that proved they had done so. When the persecution was then relaxed, many of these same people sought to rejoin the Christian community and to be readmitted to the eucharist. The question of their repentance, and of the conditions under which they might be readmitted, caused serious divisions among churches in both Italy and North Africa.

The emperor Valerian in 258 renewed persecution of Christians after only a few years of peace. It was during this third wave that Cyprian, bishop of Carthage, was executed after having been in hiding for several years. Sixtus II, bishop of Rome, was executed as well the same year. Two years later Valerian was captured by Shapur I, emperor of the Sassanid dynasty, which had come to power in Persia earlier in the century. Valerian's son, Gallienus, became emperor in Rome, ending the persecutions and restoring confiscated Christian properties. Once again Christians knew an extended period of peace in the Roman world during which their numbers dramatically increased.

The final wave of imperial persecution of Christians came at the end of the third century during the reign of Diocletian. Facing both increased bureaucratic administrative burdens and increased pressures on the imperial borders, Diocletian divided the empire into four regions, with four rulers (a "tetrarchy"). He maintained the title of augustus in the eastern region of the empire and appointed one named Maximian the augustus of the western region. Two subordinates were appointed as caesars under them, Galerius in the east and Constantius in the west. The new system did not stop the economic decline caused by dwindling taxes. In response the imperial government increased the pressure on regions that provided the bulk of resources for the empire, leading to further rebellion, especially in North Africa.

In 303 a decade of severe persecution opened up under Galerius and Diocletian. An edict to destroy all church buildings in the empire was issued (separate buildings had begun to appear in the half-century of peace), and burning of all Christian books was ordered. Further edicts were directed against the Christian clergy. So great were the numbers of persons arrested that Rome decided to commute the death sentence to hard labor in the mines for those who refused to sacrifice to its gods. The story of the end of this final wave of imperial persecution in the Roman world must await the next chapter. Suffice it to say that it brought the Roman empire to the edge of its internal religious crisis and then took it beyond.

Persecution diminished the ranks of the Christians in the short run but aided Christian growth in the long run. This was especially so in the African regions of Mauretania, Numidia, and Egypt. In Numidia and Mauretania not only was the courage Christians showed in the face of violence an incentive for new members after persecution had subsided, but the movement's status as an illegal religion was a positive asset as it came to be increasingly identified with resistance to imperial power. A distinctive tradition of theology and church practice emerged from the crucible of Roman North Africa in the third century, bequeathing to the world Christian movement the names of Perpetua, Felicitas, Tertullian, Cyprian, and Donatus. Their legacies have become the inheritance of the entire Christian world.

In Egypt persecution helped spread Christian faith into the rural areas as believers from Alexandria sought refuge outside the city. Growth in the towns and villages in the countryside spread the movement further beyond the urban centers of Latin and Greek culture. The growth of Egyptian-speaking churches fostered identification of Christianity with Egyptian nationalism. By the middle of the third century Christian communities were growing in the villages further up the Nile River, and by the end of the century a full-fledged spiritual retreat into the wilderness regions of the upper Nile was under way. We will return to the wilderness of Egypt below, considering its connection with the asceticism practiced in the Syrian desert as well as its importance for groups on the margins of orthodoxy.

Persia

The third century witnessed a passage of another kind in the Persian empire in the East. In 224-226 the Parthian rulers fell to a coalition force made up of southern Persians and Medes who had the collaboration of the kingdom of Adiabene. The ruler of the new dynasty that came to power, Ardashir, claimed to be a descendant of the ancient Achaemenids through his father, Sasan. Hence the new regime became known as the Sassanid dynasty. Ardashir assumed for himself the title shah of shahs and vigorously sought to extend the Zoroastrian faith throughout the empire. He ordered that new sacred fires be started (the central rites of the Zoroastrian faith called for perpetual fires in the names of the emperor) and appointed a priest named Tansar to be *mobad*, a combined office of high priest and royal advisor. Tansar undertook a new recension of the Zoroastrian sacred scriptures, the *Avesta*. His successor under Ardashir's son, Shapur I, was the mobad Kartir, who proved to be an even more enthusiastic missionary for Zoroastrianism. Together they laid the groundwork for an imperial revival of the Zoroastrian faith among the Sassanids that eventually brought about brutal persecution of Christians in the Persian empire.

The first one hundred years of Sassanid rule left Christians relatively unmolested. The Sassanids directed their persecutions against the Buddhists in the eastern end of their empire and moderate parties within their own household of faith. Toward the end of the third century there were indications that the situation was beginning to shift.

The Syrian *Acts of the Martyrs* tells of an incident that can be roughly dated in the last decade of the century. The story is of a wife of Shah Varahran II, a woman who was the daughter of Roman captives. According to the *Acts of the Martyrs* she had been made a wife of the emperor and offered a place as a queen on account of her great beauty. Yet she was also a Christian, and she refused to abandon her faith. Consequently Varahran is said to have had her tortured and publicly paraded naked through the city before having her executed. Whether or not the story is historically true (and much of the narrative appears to be apocryphal), it reflects a growing consciousness among Christians in the Persian world both of the rise of their numbers and the threat that loomed on their horizon. Large-scale persecutions of Christians in the Persian empire finally came in the reign of Shapur II in the fourth century, and then it was in response to a Roman emperor's recognition of Christianity as the legal religion of the Roman world.

Throughout the third century the border zone between the Romans and the Sassanids remained a region of conflict. Cities passed back and forth between the two powers, affecting the churches that were within them. The Sassanids held the upper hand throughout much of the century, taking back the cities of Nisibis and Edessa from Rome around 250 (Rome would recapture them by 298), and reaching Antioch in 260. They inflicted a humiliating defeat upon Rome in 260 when Shapur I took Valerian prisoner and executed him in the capital, Seleucia-Ctesiphon. A monument commemorating Shapur's triumphant victory over Roman imperial power can still be found in the huge rock carving at Bishapur, near the ancient city of Persepolis. The Persians did not remain in control of Antioch and West Syria for long, although they did take many Christians captive and resettled them in Khuzistan. The Romans soon regained imperial control of the region, but the warfare with the Sassanids continued for centuries.

One result was a shift in the theological center of Syrian Christianity eastward, toward the city of Nisibis. The language of the church in the Persian imperial world remained Syriac, for this was understood wherever Aramaic was used in Syria, Mesopotamia, and Persia. Historically the Parthians had used Aramaic to write their own language, as their own Pahlavi alphabet was not as widely known among those they ruled. The revitalization of Zoroastrianism under the Sassanid rulers brought with it a revitalization of the Pahlavi language of the Persians as well. The Christian church's status as an opposition movement thus facilitated their continued use of Syriac for liturgy and theology. In the end, Syriac was identified as the official language of the churches of Persia, even when they sent missionaries into other regions, such as China and India, in much the same way that Latin became identified as the official language of the churches of the western Mediterranean world, even when they sent missionaries to the north among the Germanic tribes.

Armenia

Both the Roman and Persian imperial governments remained officially opposed to the Christian religion through the third century. There is some evidence that Abgar of Edessa, ruler of the small kingdom of Osrhoene, might have converted to Christianity at the beginning of the third century, but that nation was eventually swallowed up by Rome and disappeared as an independent kingdom. The first documented conversion to the Christian faith of both a royal household and a kingdom comes at the end of the third century, with the conversion of Armenia.

The story of the conversion of this semi-independent kingdom north of Mesopotamia is cloaked in a rich tradition that is treasured still by the Armenian church. Christians had visited Armenia probably as early as the first part of the second century. Eusebius reported that Dionysius, bishop of Alexandria, sometime near the middle of the third century sent a letter to the Armenians where one named Meruzanes was bishop. According to its national tradition, however, the missionary of Armenia was Gregory the Illuminator, who brought Christianity to the land during the time of King Tiridates III. The child of Parthian parents settled in Armenia, Gregory became a Christian in Cappadocia after leaving Armenia in the late second century. Around the year 300 he returned to his home country, where he was imprisoned in a pit for thirteen years due to his refusal to sacrifice to the Armenian goddess. According to the tradition, however, the king became sick, and Gregory was brought from his pit to pray for healing. Tiridates III was healed and he converted, submitting to baptism at the hands of Gregory. In 314 Gregory was ordained a bishop and proceeded to establish the church in Armenia. Within a relatively short time the scriptures were translated into the Armenian language, using a new script that was reportedly invented for this specific purpose. Christianity soon became deeply intertwined with the Armenian national cultural identity.

India

By the end of the third century the churches of Persia were looking further to the east in missions as well. In 200 Bardaisan had referred to Christians living in Bactria (modern Afghanistan), writing about "our sisters" there who did not go along with certain sexual practices accepted among the people. Unfortunately, little else is known of these communities: how they were founded, how they were organized, or what particular beliefs they thought were important. We have seen above the traditions of Thomas and Bartholomew bringing the gospel to

India, but as we noted these can be dated no earlier than the third century, and much about them is legendary. The traditions concerning Thomas in particular consistently make a connection between the Syrian and Indian churches. This association has more than a kernel of truth to it.

An eighth-century Syriac text known as *The Chronicle of Seert* offers us a glimpse at what might have been one source of this connection in the last half of the third century. According to the *Chronicle*, David, bishop of Basra on the Persian Gulf (in modern southern Iraq), left his episcopal see to begin mission work in India. It is not implausible that the trade routes from Mesopotamia to India would have taken this bishop to the eastern country. The Indian community among which he worked could well have been a colony of Syrian or Persian traders among whom there were Christians. Evidence supporting this possibility is found in the fact that when we again encounter reports of a church in India, it is under the authority of the Persian church. The record of bishops attending the fourth-century Council of Nicaea includes one named John, who signed on behalf of the churches of Persia and all India.

Joining a Christian community in the second or third century in India, Persia, Armenia, Egypt, or Italy still meant joining a religion that had no historical homeland. Christianity was an illicit religion in the Roman empire, and Christians were subject to periodic persecution. Under Persian rule Christians began to feel the pressure brought about by a revival of Zoroastrianism as the national religion, although outright persecution or martyrdom remained a rare occurrence through the third century. In both empires Christians were considered aliens. The mobility of Christian faith across both geographic and linguistic boundaries was facilitated by the practice of translating its message and reflected in the mobility of its sacraments (baptism could be practiced anywhere, not just in Israel; the eucharist could be celebrated everywhere, using local foods). Both were an impetus for missionary expansion and theological inculturation throughout the movement.

11

Gnostics, Catholics, and Manichaeans

Gnosticism and the challenge of philosophical contextualization

The first generations of Christians had gained a reputation for denouncing the other gods of the cities in which they lived. At the same time they borrowed from the storehouses of indigenous languages, cultures, religions, and ideas that they found around them. The results were new and sometimes creative expressions of faith that reflected the living nature of the Christ whom they worshiped. Efforts to recast the Christian message in new contexts also raised questions concerning the limits of Christian beliefs. How far could one go without losing the truth about the living Christ?

The movement that raised these questions most forcefully for early Christians was Gnosticism. The Gnostics drew their ideas from a variety of sources, including Judaism, other religions, the canonical and non-canonical gospels, and at times special revelations delivered to their teachers. For many Gnostics (those with whom we are most concerned here) the figure of Christ was at the heart of their teachings. Essentially these Christian Gnostics recast the story of Jesus and the disciples in a manner that better synthesized the figure of Christ with the dominant Hellenistic religious and philosophical world of the day. Their teachings emerged early, stemming according to their Catholic opponents (and much of what we know about Gnosticism is found in Catholic writers who described them in order to refute them) from Simon Magus, the Samaritan magician of Acts 8. Justin Martyr, a second-century Catholic teacher in Rome, reported that Simon had constructed an elaborate system of doctrine that incorporated Christ into a framework of Hellenistic religion. Simon eventually journeyed to Rome, said Justin, where he met the apostle Peter but established himself with a following of his own. Whether that was historically true or not, it pointed toward the close relationship Gnosticism had to other apostolic Christian traditions.

Hippolytus, who was also from Rome, reported that Simon was the teacher of one named Valentinus. Originally from Alexandria, Valentinus came to Rome around the year 140 and quickly gained acceptance as a popular teacher and church leader. According to some accounts he was nearly elected bishop in Rome. Without a doubt he was among the greatest Gnostic minds, skillfully blending his own speculative insights with biblical stories and Platonic philosophical doctrine to create a comprehensive system of salvation. Valentinus taught that God is a threefold mystery from whom emanates some thirty orders or Aeons of heavenly worlds. These Aeons represented divine attributes in male and female form. The last of them included the Mother figure, Sophia ("Wisdom"). God the Forefather and these Aeons (including Sophia) constituted the spiritual universe that Valentinus called the Pleroma ("Fullness").

According to this great Gnostic teacher, at some point in the past Sophia had been seized by an inordinate desire to fathom the mystery of the Forefather, leading her to disrupt the Pleroma. The birth of a demiurge who was ignorant of the spiritual universe was the result. This demiurge, or lesser god, in turn created the material world and humanity, breathing souls into them. Unbeknown to him, however, his mother, Sophia, breathed in spirit as well. Freeing those spirits from the ignorance into which they were created and returning them to the heavenly order was the work of a further Aeon named Christ. Christ came to the lower world of material creation in what appeared to be a body in order to save all who would receive his perfect knowledge. Those who followed his teaching were thus set free from their imprisonment in material creation, as they ascend through the heavenly orders in salvation.

This basic system of salvation was found among almost all the Gnostics, each teacher giving his (and possibly her) own version of it. Basilides, for instance, who was first reported to be active in Alexandria around the year 130, also taught a cosmological schema of descending orders of virtues and angelic beings emanating from God. Like Marcion and Valentinus, Basilides identified the God of the Jewish scriptures as a lesser being who had created the material world in which spirits were imprisoned. Ignorance led this deity to believe he alone was creator. The basic cause of sin and suffering in the world among human beings was their ignorance of their true spiritual nature, which could only be overcome through the revelation of knowledge.

Along with Marcion, Valentinus, and others, Basilides conceived the creation itself to be a prison of spirit and thus fundamentally evil. The agent of material creation was a lesser and even demented God. Often he was named Ialdobaoth, a name that was a play upon the Hebrew name for God. The serpent in the garden who seduced Adam and Eve to transgress the law of this creator deity was believed by many Gnostics to be an agent of Sophia. Others held that those who were Gnostics were really children of Adam's son Seth, not Abel, who was the father of the Jews.

Integral to all the Gnostic systems was the belief that the material body with its passions and corruptions was part of a world essentially alien to spirit. Some Gnostics went so far as to teach that salvation could be found by engaging in activities that ritually violated the body, or transgressed moral prohibitions surrounding it. This appears to have been the position of an Alexandrian Christian named Carpocrates, for instance, whose followers were accused of licentiousness. Gnosticism made use of the story of Christ to provide a new articulation of Hellenistic mythical-philosophical religion. In doing so, however, it left unchallenged a fundamental definition of divine ultimacy as perfectly self-contained and thus incapable of being directly related to a changing and corruptible creation.

Gnostics denied the assertion that in Jesus the divine was directly incarnated in human form. They preferred instead to believe that a series of emanations from the highest realm of the divine mediated salvation. These emanations upon emanations promised the eventual release of humanity's spirits from their captivity to a material creation while preserving the doctrine of divine immutability. A God who would be directly implicated in the act of creating a material world was, for Gnosticism, by definition less than ultimate. The Gnostic solution was to hold that the god who created the heavens and the earth was a lesser force who imprisoned sparks of pure light (spirit) in material creation. The Christ was an emanation from the unknown mystery of God beyond this lesser god, and he freed people from their bondage to material creation. Christ only appeared to be of a material nature like ours. Among the Gnostics, women and men found redemption through knowledge that released them from their bondage to bodily existence upon death, a tradition that resonated with the Egyptian mysteries of Isis and the Greek philosophical tradition of Plato.

The Gnostics taught a salvation that promised release from the suffering and confinement of material bodily existence. On this point they proved to be particularly capable of addressing issues affecting women, whose lives were often shaped by cultural norms that defined them primarily in terms of childbearing. Women were seen as being of a lesser nature than men due to their reproductive functions and were relegated to subordinate social and political roles accordingly. The Gnostic promise of release from material bodily existence carried with it the promise of transcending gendered existence by elevating women to the more spiritual status of men. The closing words of the *Gospel of Thomas* expressed the Gnostic conception of gender equality well:

> Simon Peter said to them, "Mary should leave us, for females are not worthy of life."
>
> Jesus said, "Look, I shall guide her to make her male, so that she too may become a living spirit resembling you males. For every female who makes herself male will enter heaven's kingdom."[8]

Those in the Catholic party were offering no such egalitarian vision during the second and third centuries. Although some have argued that there is evidence of women serving liturgical offices in the Catholic churches of the second and possibly the third centuries, it was far from being a normal practice. For the most part, regarding matters of priestly leadership, among Catholics the office was reserved to men. Gnostics, on the other hand, proved to be more willing to assign women a place of leadership in worship. Irenaeus wrote of one Gnostic group in his region in Gaul in which the head of the community, a man named Marcus, led rituals in which women were invited to say words of consecration over a chalice they then drank from. Irenaeus appeared annoyed in part because Marcus had gained the patronage of several of the wealthier women, which the Catholic writer

---

[8] Logion 114, quoted from *The Gospel of Thomas: The Hidden Sayings of Jesus*, trans. Marvin Meyer (San Francisco: HarperCollins, 1992), 65.

could only explain as the result of the Gnostic teacher having seduced them. The same author reported that the Gnostics also baptized "into the name of the unknown Father of the universe—into truth, the mother of all things—into Him who descended on Jesus—into union, and redemption, and communion with the powers."[9] The words of the liturgy suggest a more gender-inclusive understanding of God.

Catholic writers such as Irenaeus, Clement, and others rejected the fundamental tenets of Gnosticism's understanding of the creation and thus its understanding of salvation. They sought to refute Gnostic doctrines on these points to prevent others from joining their gatherings. Gnosticism was more than a set of ideas, however. Its followers laid claim to the same biblical and apostolic heritage that Catholic leaders cited as their authority. Gnostics often cited alternative or secret lines of tradition that were different from the ones the Catholic bishops claimed as their authority but were no less a means of communicating stories about Christ. The Gnostics might have read scriptures that Catholics considered to be without authority, but they were still a scriptural community. Some of these Gnostic scriptures survived later Catholic attempts to destroy them. The most notable are those that were included in the buried collection at Nag Hammadi in Egypt, which was referred to in chapter 4 above. Gnostic writers also provided abundant commentaries on biblical books that the Catholics accepted, thereby forcing Catholic writers to respond with commentaries of their own.

For the most part the great wave of Gnostic teachers crested after the second century and dwindled through the third. The combination of increased numbers and united opposition on the Catholic side weighed heavily against Gnostic communities. The fact that their primary appeal was always to an intellectual elite helped to bring about the demise of their party. Much of Gnosticism's insights, if not its communities, were eventually absorbed by other movements that arose after the second century. The most important of these was a new religion known as Manichaeism, which we shall examine at the end of this chapter.

Some separate Gnostic communities continued to exist beyond the third century, primarily in the regions of Syria, Mesopotamia, and Persia, where there was less political and social pressure to conform to Catholic teaching after the fourth century. In many cases the spiritual impulses of Gnosticism continued to permeate Catholic Christian teaching in Syria and Egypt enough to cause some who did not identify themselves as Gnostics to be later charged with such associations by Catholic defenders of orthodoxy.

The Catholic apologists

Catholics and Gnostics alike were under the reproach of the Roman state in the second and third centuries. The secretive nature of Gnosticism gave its members

---

[9] Irenaeus, *Against Heresies* 3.1, in *The Ante-Nicene Fathers: Translations of the Fathers down to A.D. 325*, vol. 1, *The Apostolic Fathers, Justin Martyr, Irenaeus*, ed. Alexander Roberts and James Donaldson (Grand Rapids, Mich.: Wm. B. Eerdmans Publishing Co., 1981), 346.

Jesus as Philosopher, Catacomb of Domitilla, Rome, 3rd century. Reproduced with permission of Pontifical Commission for Sacred Archeology, Rome.

the advantage of being less visible as targets of public persecution. As far as we can tell historically, most Gnostics were willing to offer sacrifices to the imperial gods when called to do so before the civil magistrates. Gnostic teaching required its adherents to keep their faith hidden and thus allowed them to perform the sacrifices in order not to reveal their secret beliefs. The cult of public martyrdom, on the other hand, gave Catholics the edge in attracting new members. The most effective response the Catholic party mounted against the challenge of Gnosticism came in the form that was directed not against the Gnostics at all but against the imperial state.

As for their efforts to refute Gnostic heresies, Catholic authors offered arguments based on scripture, apostolic tradition, and reason. Often they drew upon the same intellectual sources as the Gnostics did, but reached different conclusions. Ironically, the most lasting effect of these apologetic works was not to stem the growth of Gnosticism (other factors helped more to accomplish that) so much as to shape Catholic Christian identity within the Hellenistic philosophical context.

Several books of the New Testament had partially engaged that Hellenistic worldview, but they addressed it from a perspective that remained fundamentally Jewish. The first generations of church leaders and bishops after them had opened up a campaign of criticism directed against the gods and religions of the various cities in which they came in mission. The question of how Christians could positively engage and appropriate cultural and philosophical traditions at a deeper level, or whether they should even do so, was left unanswered. But these were precisely the questions Gnosticism successfully addressed and a major reason why it exercised attraction. Eventually those who identified with the Catholic party found they too had to address Jesus Christ in terms that were comprehensible within the philosophical framework of the world into which the movement was spreading.

Justin Martyr

Among the earliest Catholic authors to engage in such a task regarding Hellenism was a converted student of Greek philosophy named Justin. The child of Greek colonists in Samaria, Justin had embraced Christian belief around the year 135. He had settled in Rome after a stay in Athens, opening up a small academy in the capital that was modeled along the lines of the more famous one in Athens. Justin identified himself as one who had journeyed to the Christian faith by way of various schools of philosophy, ending with Platonism. In Rome he penned several works, among them a treatise against Judaism and two apologies.

In his *Dialogue with Trypho* Justin tried to convince his Jewish interlocutor of the truth of the Christian belief that Jesus had fulfilled the messianic prophecies found in the Jewish scriptures. Christians were the true inheritors of the religious heritage of Israel, he argued. On the other hand was his conversation with Greek philosophy. A longer work, known as the *First Apology,* was addressed to the Roman emperor, Marcus Aurelius; while a shorter work, called the *Second Apology,* was addressed to the Roman Senate. Both sought to convince the imperial officials that Christian teaching embodied the best of the Hellenistic philosophical traditions. The emperor had nothing to fear from Christians, for not only did Christians lead virtuous lives, which contributed to the well-being of the empire, but theirs was the true philosophy, Justin argued.

Central to his apology regarding Greek philosophy was the concept of the Logos. For Justin, the Logos was partially known by the great philosophers such as Socrates and Plato. What they knew partially was incarnated fully in the person of Jesus Christ. Through him virtuous living was now made possible even for the common people. Justin appropriated the Stoic conception of logos as a divine fire, which they believed to be the soul of the universe. This same logos, he argued, Plato had recognized to be the principle or pattern by which the world was created. The universal Logos was made incarnate in Jesus and communicated to his followers through both his teachings (found in the memoirs of the apostles, who showed forth its greatness by their commonality and illiteracy) and in the sacraments the Christians celebrated in their worship.

Justin acknowledged that other religions came close to the teachings of the incarnation. They did so, he said, because evil demons who foresaw God's plan revealed in the scriptures fabricated myths that resembled the Christian message. When Plato was in Egypt, he noted, he might have read Moses and possibly Jeremiah, thereby accounting for the similarities between Plato and the teachings of Moses. But the decisive point in Justin's argument revolved around the work of the Logos itself, whose reflections or seeds were to be found throughout the world. The Logos was related to God, he argued, as a fire derived from a fire that does not reduce the original fire but stands alongside and is of the same essence; or as a word that is spoken as the perfect manifestation of a word that is thought and thus unmanifest. Hence the Logos was divine. At the same time Justin argued that the eternal Logos could be found throughout creation. Hearing the message of Jesus Christ, who was the incarnation of the Logos, thus fulfilled what was already given to humanity in its initial creation. The doctrines of the Christians made complete what was already partially known and available in the best of human teaching and understanding.

Irenaeus of Lyons

Justin sought to make contact with the philosophies of the Greeks. His near-contemporary, Irenaeus, bishop of Lyons, was more concerned with articulating these ideas through a stronger biblical lens. Irenaeus had originally come from Smyrna, where he had been a student of Polycarp. He had moved to Lyons around 165 where, he said, he was "resident among the Celts."[10] At the time of the persecution in 177, he had been sent to Rome with a letter to the church there, returning after the martyrdoms to be elected bishop the following year. Nearly a decade later he took up his pen to address the challenge he saw coming from Gnostic teachers both in Rome and in his own region.

For Irenaeus, the doctrines that the Gnostics taught were essentially vain speculations of their own invention. Over against them he held that the body of teachings that had been handed down from the apostles in the Catholic church alone could secure true faith. Moreover, not only did he believe that this tradition had been handed down intact to him, but that it was the same among all the churches who followed the teachings of the apostles throughout the world. Thus he wrote:

> The Church, though dispersed throughout the whole world, even to the ends of the earth, has received from the apostles and their disciples this faith. . . . For the faith being ever one and the same, neither does one who is able at great length to discourse regarding it, make any addition to it, nor does one, who can say but little, diminish it.[11]

For the bishop of Lyons the fundamental unity of the church mirrored the unity of God. God is the ultimate and immediate source of all creation, thereby assuring the goodness and completeness of creation. The apostasy of angels and disobedience of humanity accounted for the wickedness in the world. Yet God who is the ultimate power behind creation is responsible for its salvation, as the one who swings the axe is responsible for the cutting of the tree and not the axe. The Gnostic separation of the unknown Father from creation was thus categorically rejected. Instead, Irenaeus argued that Jesus Christ, the Son of God, and the Holy Spirit were eternally with God as Word and Wisdom. Christ and Spirit are the two hands of God's direct divine activity in creation and human history.

Against the Gnostic teaching that the Christ descended as a spirit on the human person Jesus, Irenaeus argued that Jesus Christ is at once fully divine and

---

[10] Ibid., 1.Intro, in *The Ante-Nicene Fathers*, 1:316 (spelling of "Celts" modified).

[11] Ibid., 1.10, in *The Ante-Nicene Fathers,* 1:330-331.

fully human. As Son of God he was from eternity fully God; as Son of humanity he was fully human and born of Mary. The role of Mary was important for Irenaeus, for it meant salvation extended to women and men alike. As Jesus was parallel to Adam, so Mary, the virgin who obeyed God, was parallel to Eve, the virgin who disobeyed. In the incarnation, Irenaeus argued, God recapitulated in the divine self the full span of human existence from birth to old age. This was done in order to destroy sin and death and give new life to humanity in every respect. Jesus lived through every period of human life, thereby sanctifying every period: infancy, childhood, youth, and old age (Irenaeus believed Jesus was around fifty years of age when crucified).

The concept of salvation that Irenaeus posed over against Gnostic teachings was not that of a release of spirit from the corruptions of material existence, but rather the coming of God in material form in order to transform mortality into immortality. The incorruptible had to first become corruptible so that the corruptible could become incorruptible. Those who are adopted into Christ thus become partakers of his incorruptibility. Irenaeus believed salvation to be essentially a process of divinization. Christ became human so that humanity might become divine. Or, as he argued in sacramental terms, as a grain of wheat planted in the earth first decomposes to be raised by the Spirit to life, and then through the Word of God becomes the eucharistic food of immortality, so our bodies when placed in the earth decompose but will be raised to immortal life by the same Word of God.

In place of the Gnostic dualism of spirit and material creation, then, Irenaeus argued that salvation comes through material form. Jesus could have made wine independent of the existing material substance, water, but he did not; he transformed water into wine. The same was true with the loaves and fishes. According to Irenaeus the invisible works through the visible, the incomprehensible through the comprehensible—not against it, or apart from it. On this point the Gnostics were overdependent on the philosophers and poets of the Greeks, he believed, and were not adhering closely enough to the revelation of God through Jesus Christ that was found in scriptures. Irenaeus accepted the two testaments to be fully authoritative but understood a progressive unfolding of revelation to have taken place through their writing. Nevertheless, there are no hidden mysteries from the apostles, no secrets that are reserved for the perfected, since all in the church are called to be perfect. Asserting the priority of love over knowledge in the plan of God's redemption, he argued that faith among the "barbarians" is found as a truth that is written on their hearts, not with paper and ink but by the Spirit. These barbarians do not speak Greek and thus are not regarded as wise by the standards of Hellenism (to which he has accused the Gnostics of adhering too closely), but they are nonetheless considered wise by Irenaeus on account of their possession of the truth of faith.

Clement of Alexandria

Like Justin, Irenaeus thus turned to the living witness of the members of the church as an answer to the philosophical question of truth. In the end Irenaeus discounted the standards of Hellenistic philosophy as an adequate measure of truth. Justin, on the other hand, sought to articulate an understanding of the Logos that was at once faithful to the biblical and apostolic witness and at the same time coherent within the intellectual framework of Greek philosophy. The degree to which Justin succeeded in doing justice to both sides of the coin is open to debate. But his efforts mark a turning point in the missionary attempt to incarnate the gospel anew in a foreign idiom and culture. In Alexandria, Clement echoed these ideas and extended them to engage an even wider circle of philosophy.

According to Clement, all philosophies (he knew of the Brahmans, Buddhists, Chaldeans, and Egyptians besides the Greeks) can be useful in preparing people for understanding the gospel. Any wisdom or philosophy that teaches righteousness can be understood as having come from God, although this is no guarantee that those upon whom divine wisdom has been bestowed have made adequate use of it. Faith alone is sufficient for salvation, Clement argued, but faith combined with knowledge brings an added benefit of maturity. "Philosophy, therefore, was a preparation, paving the way for him who is perfected in Christ. . . . The way of truth is therefore one. But into it, as into a perennial river, streams flow from all sides."[12]

Gnosticism was unequivocally condemned by Irenaeus, writing in Lyons. In Alexandria his contemporary, Clement, was more sympathetic toward those who sought a Gnostic pathway to salvation. Clement declared no less than Irenaeus his adherence to the apostolic tradition, and he argued that those who rejected the unity of the church were engaging in heresy. He counseled those Gnostics who would cause others to stumble to cover their wells and protect the mysteries that they would teach. Their teaching was advanced meat for the mature, not milk for spiritual infants. For Clement, the knowledge of the gospel was made known to all through apostolic proclamation, but to only a few were the advanced mysteries revealed. It was for these true Gnostics who remained in the church that Clement wrote. He was not even adverse to quoting others, such as Valentinus and Isidore, son of Basilides, when they provided support for his own position.

Clement believed that these mysteries of God were available through the Bible and Jesus' teachings. Hence he continued to think along the lines of the Alexandrian tradition of interpreting scriptures through an allegorical method. For him, Jesus was above all else the Word who was the instructor in the ways of divine life. The Word was a priest who put off his old robes and put on new robes when performing sacred duties: "The Lord puts off and puts on by descending into the region of sense," he wrote of the incarnation.[13] The believer then does the same in becoming consecrated. At times this Alexandrian teacher came close to embracing the docetic christology that many of his gnostic contemporaries relished. Jesus ate only to be able to relate to those around him but in fact did not

---

[12] Clement of Alexandria, *Miscellanies* 1.5, in *The Ante-Nicene Fathers: Translations of the Fathers down to A.D. 325*, vol. 2, *Fathers of the Second Century*, ed. Alexander Roberts and James Donaldson (Grand Rapids, Mich.: Wm. B. Eerdmans Publishing Co., 1981), 305.

[13] Clement of Alexandria, *Miscellanies* 5.6, in *The Ante-Nicene Fathers*, 2:454.

require material nourishment, he argued at one point; Jesus was entirely impassible *(apathes)*. The apostles became the same through Jesus's teaching, Clement went on. Those who follow in the way of salvation likewise ascend to such a spiritual state. The end of salvation for Clement, as for Irenaeus, was found in communion with God. "I seek after God, not the works of God," he asserted.[14] Yet the works of God in one's life still mattered. A true Gnostic was known by his or her pious living.

Clement sought in the end a universal philosophical framework in which the articulation of the mystery of Christian faith could be understood by those who were truly wise. He argued on the one hand against the reigning Hellenistic philosophies of his day that failed to recognize the wisdom of the gospel by asserting their inferiority. After all, he went to great lengths to try to show, the Greeks had taken their wisdom from virtually everyone else in the world. They had plagiarized the Egyptians, Chaldeans, Indians, and a host of others. Clement's point was not to detract from the Greeks' achievements but rather to gain a hearing for Christian truth. He put Christian dogma in the camp of other world philosophies and wisdom traditions, thereby legitimating its claims. At the same time he followed Justin's lead in locating within the Greek thinkers themselves points of contact with Christian wisdom. For instance, he found the notion of God's threefold nature in Plato's philosophy. Clement's student and successor as head of the Alexandrian school, Origen, would go even further in this direction.

Origen

In many ways Origen set the standard by which later Christian theology would be judged in both its range and its level of philosophical engagement. He was one of the most important Platonists of his day, standing alongside the philosopher Plotinus as an interpreter of that ancient Greek teacher. Origen's biblical exegesis was extensive and his method influential long after his star burned out among later imperial defenders of Christian orthodoxy. According to Origen the Bible has three levels of meaning: the literal, the moral, and the allegorical. With other Alexandrians he held that the third of these levels is the one that is most spiritual and most important. Historical events are the outer covering to inner, secret truths. Events narrated in the text of scripture are fleshly, but the inner truths are the eternal truths of the soul. The inner truth of Jesus was found in the Logos that was incarnate in him. According to Origen, Jesus taught his followers the divine truth of Logos and thus acts as the intermediary between humanity and God. It was not so much his suffering in the flesh as it was the Logos that he taught that was redemptive. In short, the way of Jesus was the way of wisdom.

The silence of the apostles on a number of themes seemed to Origen to be an invitation to later generations to take them up and consider such questions. For his own part he sought to advance a number of speculative suggestions concerning the relationship between spiritual and material realms of existence to answer

---

[14] Clement of Alexandria, *Exhortation to the Heathen* 6, in *The Ante-Nicene Fathers*, 2:191.

the age-old Platonic dilemma of the relationship of the realm of changing, historical existence to the unchanging, eternal realm of the good. Origen speculated that in Genesis 1 we have the story of the creation of the spiritual universe, while in Genesis 2 we have the story of the creation of the material world. The souls of human beings have fallen into the material world where Christ finds them to teach them the way back to their true spiritual selves.

Origen accepted the doctrine of the incarnation of Jesus, who was the Logos made flesh, but his understanding of the relation of the Logos to God left room for it being understood as of a lesser divine nature, at least in the eyes of some of his later interpreters. Another area of speculation that earned for him the label of heresy several hundred years after his death concerned his theories on the preexistence and transmigration of the soul. Origen himself was not as committed to these theories as some of his later critics accused him of being. Unfortunately, however, the condemnations led to the widespread destruction of his work.

Perhaps the greatest tragedy was that later generations did not always share the Alexandrian teacher's willingness to accept the invitation to expand upon the truth of Jesus Christ. Origen perceived that scripture was open to different interpretations. The meaning of any particular passage could not be reduced to a single interpretation. This opened the door for him for engaging in new theological reflection, always guided by the rule of faith. He was not afraid of drawing from other philosophies the valuable wisdom and insights they had to offer. At the same time he understood that these other philosophies contributed to the overall meaning of the gospel by expanding it in new directions. Such a notion of an expanding body of theological work was essentially a missionary practice for Origen, for it was part of bringing the whole world into engagement with Christ.

Bardaisan

Origen was not the only apologist among the early Catholic party to be later charged as a heretic. The Aramaic philosopher from Edessa, Bardaisan, would suffer the same fate, being variously charged by later generations as both a Gnostic and a teacher of Mani, founder of Manichaeism. Bardaisan was born around 155 of parents who were Persians in exile in Edessa. Converted in 179 by Hystaspes, bishop of Edessa, he was an early opponent of Marcionism in Syria. According to Bardaisan, God was one, not two. At the same time he held to what would later be recognized as an orthodox trinitarian understanding of the divine persons. His most controversial ideas were found in his acceptance of certain traits from the Chaldean or Zoroastrian philosophical traditions of the East, namely those associated with belief in Fate. Human beings were created in the image of God, equal with the angels, and had free will. They had been commanded by God to do good and not evil, and they could exercise moral choice. No commandment was too hard for anyone to follow, he believed.

The limits of the choices are established by the conditions into which human beings were born. These conditions are governed by Fate, a force that lies in between God and the world. Fate disturbs the purity of the basic elements of the material order, although God is over Fate. Whenever nature is deflected from its true course, Fate is responsible, he argued. Nature, Fate, and free will together structure the course of history. Yet only the coming of Christ, the Logos or First Thought, was able to restore order and overcome the disruptions of Fate. Hence Christ corrected but did not displace the laws of the various nations or their particular histories. In this way, for Bardaisan, the twin notions of Logos and Fate could be reconciled. Christians lived by the laws of each place in which they dwelt and were bound by the limitations of Fate by the configurations of the stars (he accepted the concept of the zodiac and the work of the astrologers). Where these laws were judged immoral, however, Christians dissented, thereby showing the way toward their correction and fulfillment.

It was his positive attitude toward the philosophies and laws of the countries of the world as much as his acceptance of the concept of Fate that earned him the scorn of later theologians. Bardaisan was condemned by Ephraem of Syria in the fourth century as a heretic, and his writings were banned by later bishops. Suspicions that he was a Gnostic sent his work into obscurity. Yet in many ways Bardaisan was one of the most Catholic thinkers of the early third century. Living in Edessa at a time when the city and region were being taken over by Rome, he looked further eastward than did some of his contemporaries and had a knowledge of world cultures. Bardaisan wrote of the ways of the Chinese, Indians, Persians, Arabs, Greeks, Germans, and Britons. He saw the means by which Jesus Christ, the First Thought of God, could bring about the redemption of all without the displacement of their various laws and cultures, given to them by Fate. He foresaw a time when a new world will be created and all possibility of harm will cease. On that day peace will reign as the gift of the Lord, he believed.

Manichaeism

That Bardaisan was accused by later theologians as being the teacher of Mani and himself a Gnostic is not entirely surprising. There were important points of contact in their ideas, but these may reflect as much their shared religious, cultural, and intellectual climates as they do the dependence of one upon the other. Both Bardaisan and Mani formed their ideas in the rich context of the Mesopotamian-Persian intellectual world. They knew of the faith of the magi, and of other eastern religions. They formed their systems in dialogue not just with Hellenists but with these eastern religions and philosophies as well. But where Bardaisan remained an apologist for the Christian movement, Mani became the organizer of a new church. By the end of his life Mani had provided the basis for a new movement that became a world religion in its own right. Manichaeism absorbed insights from a number of world religious streams, but its resonance with Gnostic Christianity is especially noteworthy.

Mani was born in 216 in Babylon. His mother was Persian, his father a member of the Elkesaites, a baptist group that had blended Christian and Persian teachings. Mani was brought up in the group but eventually rejected the ablutions they were required to perform. His concerns echoed those of the Zoroastrian magi, that Christians polluted water by baptizing within it. At the age of twelve he received the first of many visions, this one telling him that he was the Seal of the Prophets who was being called to gather all religions on earth together into one. Mani identified himself in the succession of Zoroaster, Buddha, and Jesus. With them he proclaimed that the present world is one of conflict between the principles of light and darkness. In terms that echoed Zoroaster, Mani taught that these two principles were opposites, manifest in all material things. Evil is eternal, so salvation can only come through total separation from it. Since creation is currently under the rule of darkness, the goal of salvation is liberation from creation's darkness, he explained. This is gained by knowledge that leads to the separation of darkness from light. Those who are saved can then choose to live according to the light, awake to both the despair of this material creation and the ethical responsibility of those who live in the light.

The prophet proved to be a competent religious organizer as well. Soon after his visions, Mani began preaching and gathering followers into new churches over which he presided. Believers were organized into two levels: the elect and hearers. The elect were those who strove to attain the fullness of salvation through knowledge of Mani's teachings. Strict ascetics, they ate no meat and drank no wine. They were the clergy within the church, living together in monasteries that were modeled after those of Buddhist monks. Their number included twelve apostles assisted by various teachers, ministers, deacons, and stewards. The laity of Mani's church (the hearers) were not required to maintain as strict an ascetic life. Hearers adhered to ten moral laws (one of which was monogamy), observed purity rites, prayed four times a day, confessed their sins once a week, and fasted one day each week and one month each year. Over this entire structure was a single leader who guided the universal church.

Mani himself was the most effective missionary of the faith. He traveled widely as an apostle throughout Persia and into India. (One can only speculate as to whether there might have been some relation to the story of Thomas traveling to India to preach.) Other missionaries were sent out, some toward China and others still to the Roman world. The major focus of Mani's own missionary efforts was the Persian empire. Here the prophet's message received a positive hearing at first from the new Sassanid rulers, who had come to power in 225. Mani was given permission to preach throughout the empire. But the Sassanid revival of Zoroastrianism soon turned the state against the new prophet. In 277 Mani was arrested and brutally executed by order of the shah. His mutilated body was hung on the gates of the capital, Seleucia-Ctesiphon.

Almost immediately the shah ordered the persecution of Mani's followers to begin. Countless numbers of them were slaughtered throughout Persia. Many escaped north into Sogdiana along the Silk Road that passed all the way to China. Others went into hiding in Persia, while still others went west toward the Roman empire. By the fourth century Manichaean churches could be found scattered across the Mediterranean world. The Romans were as brutal as the Persians in their efforts to eliminate Manichaean teachings. Persecution of Mani's followers in the West continued long after it was relaxed against Christianity.

Manichaeans and Christians suffered side by side but also journeyed side by side along the same missionary routes of the ancient world. Centuries later in central Asia the two movements grew to become so close that it is difficult at times today to tell their texts apart. To an outside observer in the third century, it would not be apparent which one was destined to grow and which was destined to diminish.

The Manichaeans understood themselves to be a new religion, members of a universal church of which Mani was the founder. Salvation came for them through following Mani's teachings. Gnostics, we have seen above, understood themselves to be followers of the apostles of Christ. They understood salvation to be through Christ, who had descended into the lower realms in order to teach them the way into the upper echelons of truth. Hence the Gnostics remained within the wider Christian family, however much some Catholic writers condemned them.

In this chapter we have explored the intellectual challenges that the Gnostic teachers posed to the entire Christian movement in the second and third centuries. We have also examined the response of several Catholic writers often known as the apologists. However much one might decry the tone of their polemic or criticize the philosophical contents of their argument, there can be no doubt that they left a lasting mark upon the shape of Christian thinking. Later generations of Catholic writers continued to address the shortcomings they perceived in various parties or factions that arose within the movement. Many of the later debates continued to follow lines of reasoning first articulated by Irenaeus, Justin, Clement, Origen, and others. If Origen was correct, that the apostles didn't say all that was to be said regarding Christian truth in order to leave room for later generations to bring their own resources to the task, then the apologists were as much engaged in a missionary task as were the original apostles. In their own way Gnostics, Catholics, and even Manichaeans gave expression to this ongoing missionary task of engaging philosophy and culture.

12

Christians, Jews, and Israel's Heritage of Monotheism

The Christian movement struggled to define the degree of accommodation it could make to other philosophies and religions without abandoning its fundamental commitment to the revelation of the God of Israel it found in Jesus Christ. At the same time it struggled to define itself over and against Judaism, which did not cease to exist as a religious community. Christians actively vied with their Jewish neighbors over the question of which community was the legitimate heir to the faith of Abraham and Moses. Judaism had weathered several major crises in the first and second centuries, and by the beginning of the third was well on the way toward reconstruction.

The destruction of the Temple in Jerusalem in 70 CE had marked a major turning point in Jewish history. In 132-135 another war of rebellion took place in Palestine under a self-proclaimed messiah named Simon Bar Kochba. The Romans crushed this rebellion as they had the former revolt in 66-70. To make sure there was not a third, they exiled Jerusalem's Jewish inhabitants, forbidding Jews from even entering its precincts. The result was a shift of Judaism's center from Jerusalem and the Temple to Torah and synagogue, a shift similar to the one the Christian movement had previously taken. Jews in the diaspora were already moving away from the sacrifice in the Temple being a significant part of their religious life. Following the events of 70 and then 135, they increasingly looked to the oral traditions of the rabbis and to the presence of Torah in their midst as their guides for renewing Judaism on the other side of crisis.

One crucial difference separating Christians and Jews within the Roman imperial world was that Jews had legal status as members of a subjugated nation. This remained so despite a period of suppression following the revolt in 135. Christians, on the other hand, were extended no such legal status by the Roman government. Apologists such as Justin argued for legal recognition to little avail. While not ethnically descended from the nation of Israel, Justin said, Christians were nevertheless the legitimate heirs to its religious tradition. The Jews had rejected God's chosen messiah, Jesus, and hence had forfeited their birthright, he argued. The implications were that Christians ought to enjoy the same rights Rome extended to the Jews.

Many Christians believed that the Jews were collaborators, if not the primary agents, in the execution of Jesus. Some Christian apologists went so far as to charge that all Jews had blood on their hands for the role that the high priest in Jerusalem had played in the crucifixion. Christians of Jewish and Gentile backgrounds alike argued that Judaism was incapable of realizing the universal prophecies offered in the scriptures of Israel, which the followers of Jesus, Israel's true messiah, had fulfilled. The particular injunctions of the Torah, they argued, had been given to the people of Israel only due to their lack of faithfulness. The universal messiah of Israel, Jesus Christ, was given to the whole human race.

For their part Jews simply found the Christian's arguments incomprehensible if not blasphemous. Jews rejected the claims of the Nazarene party that Jesus had fulfilled the requirements of being Israel's messiah. Celsus's unflattering charge that the story of the virgin birth was invented to cover the truth that Mary was made pregnant by a Roman soldier named Panthera and driven away from her home by her husband, Joseph, might even have come from Jewish opponents in Palestine. The rabbis found in the oral tradition handed on from Moses at Mount Sinai the means for interpreting Torah in a coherent and constructive way. Christians refused to recognize its validity. For a Jewish believer who did not accept the Pauline perspective regarding the end of the Law, Jews who became Christian and failed to maintain the strictures of the Torah were living impure lives. Hence Jews were not attacking Christians so much as they were seeking to preserve the integrity of Judaism. The leadership of the synagogues was especially concerned about stemming conversions of Jews to Christianity in the diaspora. Christians were creating confusion among Jews regarding their heritage of faith. Admission to the covenant of Israel apart from circumcision was simply impossible, according to the rabbis.

The two sides of the polemic were by the third century being sharply drawn. Even so, there continued to be places where the two communities met and influenced one another. For one thing Christians still sought access to Jewish scriptures. While most Christian teachers read their Old Testament in the Greek Septuagint version, some sought to learn Hebrew in order to read the original work on their own. Among them was the great theologian Origen, who sought out a Jewish teacher in Caesarea. Eusebius reported that in the second century Melito, bishop of Sardis, journeyed to Palestine in part to ascertain an accurate listing of the books that were to be included in the Old Testament. In the third century Christian understanding, especially of morality and the Law, was still being shaped in some places by Jewish influences. From Antioch come reports that Christians were even given refuge in the synagogues during periods of persecution.

Catholics for the most part rejected the tenets of the Torah that would set them apart from the Gentile world. There were still those in the second and third centuries in the Christian movement, however, who held that Christians were to keep the full Jewish Law. We noted in an earlier chapter the widespread rejection among Catholic writers of a group called the Ebionites. Another group known primarily from the criticisms of Catholic writers were the Elkesaites, whom we have already mentioned as the community to which the father of the prophet

Mani belonged. Little is known about them other than they were a Jewish-Christian group that originated in Parthian territory, practiced repeated baptisms, and were ascetics. They appear to have taught the transmigration of souls and that Christ and the Spirit represented male and female principles, the latter a doctrine that was known among the Gnostics as well.

Christian monotheism

Although the majority had come from religious and ethnic backgrounds other than Jewish, Christians in the third century still claimed to belong to the heritage of Israel. The Jewish inheritance was often drawn upon for polemical purposes against Hellenism. For many in the ancient world the antiquity of an idea was a measure of its value. Catholic apologists appealed to Abraham and Moses, who were more ancient than Plato or the other Greek philosophers. Their opponents no doubt countered that its Jewish origins made Christianity a "barbarian" tradition. At this point Catholic apologists might have been tempted to abandon their Jewish inheritance in order to argue, as Marcion and the Gnostics did, that the God of Jesus had nothing to do with the God of the Jewish Old Testament. The apologists opted instead, however, to argue for the superiority of barbarian philosophies, situating Greek philosophy as being more limited in its scope. The classification of Christianity with its Jewish origins among the traditions of the barbarians was a point in its favor according to Justin, Tatian, Clement, Theophilus of Antioch, and others. It pointed toward the fact that Christian doctrines were more truly universal than Hellenistic philosophies.

Bardaisan or Clement of Alexandria could have easily made the last point by arguing for Chaldean or Indian roots for Christian doctrine. Judaism's "outsider" status in the Hellenistic philosophical world gave the Catholic apologists a perspective that they at least considered more universal. But this was not the only reason for their defense. The Catholic writers were convinced that the God revealed in the Old Testament was the one to whom Jesus spoke. Christians remained firmly committed to the Jewish doctrines of monotheism and creation, and the concomitant ethical injunction to worship no other gods. Although their Jewish opponents considered Christian worship of Jesus Christ to violate the commandment to worship no other gods, Christians insisted that it was the one true God of Israel who was revealed to the world in the person of Jesus Christ. Christians worshiped Jesus Christ as the Son of God.

The Christian position was likewise often at odds with many non-Jewish intellectual currents of the day. A number of schools of thought believed that the divine was by nature incorruptible and unchanging. Human existence was in contrast one of corruption and change. Various philosophies posed some sort of mediated, indirect relationship between the unchanging nature of God and the changing, corruptible nature of human existence as a way of relating the two distinct realities. Catholic writers instead asserted that God has an immediate and direct relationship to creation and humanity. Creation was indeed other than God. The sun and the stars were not divine beings or astrological forces but part of the created order that is ultimately ruled by God. In the human person Jesus Christ, on the other hand, the divine person of God was made present and manifest through the flesh. The ultimate hope of humanity and the entire cosmos was not escape from the conditions of bodily existence but the transformation of bodily existence in the resurrection of the dead.

For many Catholic Christian thinkers the close relationship between God and creation or God and humanity was expressed most fully and radically in the incarnation of Jesus Christ. *That* the divine and the human were mutually related and implicated with one another in Israel's life and then in Jesus, who was Israel's messiah, was taken as a cardinal point of Christian faith. *How* the divine and the human were brought together in Jesus Christ was a matter of great controversy, however. For some, the implications that God would be directly implicated in Jesus while still remaining God seemed to contradict both the biblical doctrine of God's transcendence and the biblical depiction of Jesus as a human being upon whom the Spirit of God descended. The divine Logos was a distinctive person or presence that rested upon the man named Jesus, suggested Theophilus, bishop of Antioch late in the second century.

Theophilus practiced a method of biblical exegesis that shared much in common with that of Irenaeus. Both writers avoided allegorical interpretation of the Old Testament in favor of a stronger historical understanding. In a series of apologetic treatises addressed to someone named Autolycus, Theophilus coupled this commitment with a willingness to embrace the Logos doctrine we have already read about in other Catholic writers. We cannot directly know the ineffable nature of God, who transcends all creation, Theophilus argued, but the invisible God is known through visible creation. God's being is God's own place and thus is in need of nothing. Internal within the divine self God begat the Logos, through which God created the world and humankind. Thus the world and humankind stand in an external, dependent relationship to God, while the Logos is internal within God. The Logos is the Spirit for Theophilus, the origin, wisdom, and power of all things. It came down upon prophets, inspiring them in their work. It descended in a final and unique way upon Jesus. Salvation comes by faith, or trusting God, who will one day raise up to immortality through the resurrection those who believe.

Theophilus of Antioch displayed something of his debt to Judaism in his extended exegesis of the biblical texts on the six days of creation. The Christian life for him was one that was a life of righteousness and holiness, recognizing our dependent relation as part of the creation. The concern especially for the full humanity of Jesus Christ and his being anointed by the Logos or Spirit can be seen in another, far more controversial bishop of Antioch who became the head of the church around the year 260. Paul of Samosata was his name, and his episcopacy coincided with a period of political turmoil in the region. There is a strong possibility that he was a Roman administrator in the city prior to assuming the episcopal office. In 260 the Persians marched against Roman Syria and sacked Antioch, carrying off many inhabitants (including Christians) into exile. The Persians soon withdrew, without Rome's army immediately returning to the area. Complicating the political picture was the presence of Queen Zenobia, ruler of the small city-state of Palmyra. By 268 her military had extended her influence across Syria into sections of Asia Minor and Egypt. The extent to which she affected the political circumstances in the Roman city of Antioch, or whether she in fact even did so at all, remains debated by historians. Samosata was, however, a city that had come under her domain, and Paul has been depicted by some as having had her support.

Eusebius informs us that Paul had established himself politically as the Roman official in the city and had used the office of bishop for personal financial gain. He was accused of keeping company with several women in a scandalous fashion as well, all of which Eusebius reports was exposed by a presbyter in the city who opposed him. The original charges made against him were of administrative abuse and personal immorality, but Paul of Samosata soon earned the scorn of other Catholic bishops because of his doctrine concerning Jesus Christ. According to Eusebius (and here we must be alert to the possibility of later distortions of his teaching), Paul refused to confess "that the Son of God descended from heaven." Instead, he asserted that "Jesus is from below."[15] Mary did not give birth to the Logos, for she is not older than the Word. Jesus was anointed at his birth by the Logos through the Spirit, just as the prophets of Israel had been anointed. The anointing of Jesus by the Logos was total, so that Jesus experienced complete inspiration. At his baptism the Spirit took up abode in Jesus as in a Temple. For Paul, the Logos appears to have been conceptualized not so much as a distinct self-manifestation of the person of God as an endowment of the Spirit. Jesus was one who was endowed with this power by God.

Several regional councils composed of other bishops from Syria and Asia Minor were convened in Antioch to hear the charges against Paul. Finally, in 268 a synod condemned him and declared him deposed. Letters were sent around to other heads of churches, including the bishops of both Alexandria and Rome, informing them of the decision. There was little at the time that they could do to remove Paul from office in Antioch. But in 272 the situation changed. Zenobia was defeated by the Roman emperor, Aurelius, who restored Roman imperial rule throughout the region. Soon the synod's petition was brought before the emperor with the request that he act upon it. Christianity was still officially an illegal religion in the Roman empire. Nevertheless, the emperor decided to hear the case. In one of the first hints of the growing acceptance of Christian churches in the Roman world, as well as an indication of the importance of the church of Rome, Aurelius turned over the decision to the church, agreeing to support whatever the bishop of Rome decided on the matter. The incident is an indication of the unofficial recognition the church of Rome had gained as a corporate body in the city, as well as the authority the church of Rome commanded by virtue of its proximity to the imperial household.

As for Paul of Samosata, his teachings were eventually rejected by the broader stream of the Catholic tradition as heretical. But the Antiochene emphasis upon the humanity of Jesus and the mode of divine indwelling that was conceived as the Logos descending upon him persisted. Such a christology resonated more

---

[15] Eusebius, *The History of the Church* 7.30, in Williamson, 317.

comfortably with the monotheistic concerns of Judaism, and Christians and Jews in Antioch generally enjoyed good relations. The exegetical method and christological commitments of Theophilus, and to a lesser degree Paul of Samosata, continued to be elaborated in the work of others who followed in the Antiochene school. Among them would be Theodore of Mopsuestia, whose biblical exegesis and theological reflections would become the standards of orthodoxy for the churches in Persia in succeeding centuries.

Emphasizing the manner in which the Logos or Spirit descended on the human person, Jesus, appeared to the Antiochenes to be both biblically sound and theologically correct. It preserved the transcendence of God in relation to creation while affirming the manner in which God's presence indwelt Jesus Christ. The Antiochene theologians accepted the concept of the divine Logos, which had first been expressed in the Gospel of John and then developed by Justin and the Alexandrian theologians. Implicit in the Logos doctrine of Justin, Clement, Theophilus, and others was the notion of a distinction between God and the Logos. Such a distinction allowed them to affirm what Gnostic and other Hellenistic opponents were concerned about philosophically—preserving the notion of the immutability of God—and at the same time enabled them to assert a direct relationship between God and creation.

To others within the ranks of the Christian movement, however, such an affirmation appeared to jeopardize the fundamental doctrine of monotheism regarding the oneness of God. For many, it made more sense to teach that the one true God was directly incarnate in the human person, Jesus of Nazareth, even if it meant accepting the implications that God suffered in the flesh and that God was subjected to the vicissitudes of human historical existence. Such was the paradoxical assertion of Melito, bishop of Sardis in the second century. Melito claimed that in Jesus Christ the impassible suffered and the immortal died. He interpreted Christ as the paschal Lamb, reflecting in part the tradition of Asia Minor in the second century that celebrated Easter on the date of Passover. But his high christological affirmation also led him to charge Jews with deicide, killing God, a polemical charge that Christians would continue to make against Jews for centuries to come.

Melito's position came close to being a radical assertion of simple identity: Jesus Christ was God in the flesh. Other Christian teachers went even further. Sabellius was one of these. Originally from Libya, he had settled in Rome around 220. He argued that the one God related to creation in three successive modes or aspects: as Father in creating, Son in redeeming, and Spirit in sanctifying or prophesying. Hence the strict monarchy of the Father was preserved in his eyes, while accounting for the different modes of his appearing in human history. Noetus, who was from Smyrna in Asia Minor and had come to Rome several decades before Sabellius, taught an even more straightforward monotheism. The Father himself had become incarnate in Jesus Christ and had thus suffered on the cross, a position that came to be known as Patripassianism.

One of Noetus's disciples, Praxeas, gained the dubious honor of being the object of Tertullian's major treatise on the doctrine of the Trinity, thereby having his name permanently listed among the heretics by subsequent Catholic generations. According to Tertullian, his opponent "put the Paraclete to flight and crucified the Father."[16] In the same treatise Tertullian first employed several of the terms and categories that would eventually come to be accepted as orthodox by most Christians of the world. He argued in Latin that God was of one substance, existing in three persons. Such language echoed the works of Irenaeus, Theophilus, and others before him, but went further in naming God as Trinity. It would take several centuries of theological debate to work through all the implications of Tertullian's assertion, but when it was done the essential contours of the Christian doctrine of the Trinity that he provided would be secured.

Neither Paul of Samosata nor Sabellius have fared well in the telling of the history of the Christian movement over the centuries. Yet for both of them, what was at stake (theologically at least) was the integrity of the biblical revelation concerning God. The Antiochenes were concerned about righteousness. To them there was an impiety lurking in the denial that Jesus was a human being, as the prophets were before him, and just like us; such a denial was tantamount to a denial of his flesh. It also appeared to contradict the clear biblical teaching that he was born of Mary, suffered, and died. The Logos cannot suffer and die.

Those like Melito of Sardis, who preferred simply to say that in Jesus Christ God suffered, or like Sabellius, who were willing to go further and say that the Father himself suffered, were concerned to maintain the essential unity of God. Asserting the plurality of God seemed to them to be a greater impiety. Both Melito and Sabellius affirmed with the Catholic party an essential understanding of God's direct and immediate engagement in the human predicament, and both were strongly committed to the biblical revelation of God as creator, savior, and continuing presence.

As we have seen, Christian relations with Jews in the first several centuries were complex. In some places there was outright hostility on the part of Christian teachers toward Judaism. In other places relations appear to have been more amicable. Jews in Antioch are reported to have offered refuge to Christians during times of imperial persecution. And in Edessa, Christian teachers and Jewish rabbis in the fourth century were still arguing about theological ideas (which means they were in regular conversation with each other). Such factors present a complicated picture of Jewish-Christian relations in the third century.

Christians continued to relate to Jews through their common inheritance of faith in the God who was revealed through the Old Testament. On this count Christians struggled in particular to articulate their understanding of monotheism and divine transcendence in relation to their claims regarding Jesus Christ. A distinct way of answering this problem was heard in Antioch, where Jesus was depicted as a prophetic figure upon whom the Logos of God rested in a unique way. Theophilus of Antioch sought to maintain the historical meaning of the Old

---

[16] Tertullian, *Against Praxeas*, 1, in *The Ante-Nicene Fathers: Translations of the Fathers down to A.D. 325*, vol. 3, *Latin Christianity: Its Founder, Tertullian*, ed. Alexander Roberts and James Donaldson (Grand Rapids, Mich.: Wm. B. Eerdmans Publishing Co., 1981), 597.

Testament as well, exemplifying an exegetical concern that would continue to resonate with others who followed him.

Theophilus maintained the transcendence of God by positing what some have described as an external relationship between the Logos and Jesus. Others in the Christian world, such as Melito of Sardis and Sabellius, took an alternative track and argued that in Jesus the divine actually suffered or became passible, that is, open to historical change. Sabellius went so far as to say that the one God, who is the Father, became incarnate in Jesus the Son and suffered, a position that the majority of Catholic writers eventually condemned. Melito of Sardis did not go so far, although he did affirm that God the Logos suffered on the cross. Melito is sometimes given the infamous distinction of being the first to charge the whole Jewish community with deicide on account of the role the Temple authorities played in the execution of Jesus, a charge that has continued to echo through world Christianity down through the ages. The hostility Christians such as Melito of Sardis expressed against Judaism was without much effect as long as Christians were without political standing. That would quickly change in the fourth century.

13

Spiritual Currents
and Social Life across Cultures

In the preceding chapters we have looked at several of the major theological currents that came into focus in the second and third centuries for Christians across the ancient world. From Celsus, a vehement critic of the movement, we heard of the formation of what he called "the great Church." Yet that same critic told us that there were several factions and parties competing with one another over claims of Christian identity during this period. The major struggles in the second century between the Gnostic and Catholic parties, we have seen, eventually gave rise to a series of apologetic writings that helped define Christian identity on a philosophical level. In their relations with Jewish neighbors, Christians defined themselves as a distinct religious community. All of this took place while Christians remained subject to periodic outbreaks of persecution. In the final chapter of this section, we will look at several aspects of the movement that cut across its various cultural locations.

Confessing the faith in the midst of persecution: The martyrs

Everywhere we turn in the history of the early Christian movement, we encounter the memory and presence of martyrs. The experience of those who witnessed to Christ by suffering for the faith is pervasive. The actual number of those who suffered martyrdom in the first three centuries was actually relatively low. In the Persian empire before 225 the Parthian rulers were rather tolerant of religious diversity, and we hear of no martyrdoms among Christians there. Even in the Roman empire most church members were never actually called before the authorities and ordered to offer imperial sacrifices. When times of persecution did occur, many church members consented to the imperial decrees. In Carthage it was reported that the number of Christians lining up to obey the imperial edict in the middle of the second century was so great at one point that people were asked to go home for the day, to come back on the morrow. The total number of Christians who died under the Romans was most likely under ten thousand—this in an empire that numbered as many as fifty million persons at its peak.

It was not their numbers but their example that gave the martyrs their power within the Christian imagination. They were considered extraordinarily holy figures. The dates of their deaths were remembered and celebrated annually, the places of their suffering identified by later shrines and churches. Martyrs were believed to be especially close to God after their death, and thus people turned to them with requests for intercession. The courage they showed was recounted time and again as the goal of Christian life. The willingness to abandon all for Christ, including life itself, became a metaphor for self-denial that was easily transposed into more general moral categories. By the fourth century martyrdom and asceticism had merged in Christian life at a general level, shaping the spiritual life of churches throughout the world for centuries to come.

Many early Christians considered the martyrs to be the best argument for the faith. Such was the position of both Justin and Tertullian, for instance. Martyrdom could in some cases restore the memory of one whose works had been questioned. Tertullian's contemporary in Rome, Hippolytus, has often been called schismatic for his bitter dispute with the elected Catholic bishop of the city, Callistus. But both Callistus and Hippolytus are numbered among the Catholic martyrs of the church of Rome. Exhortations to martyrdom often circulated among churches along with accounts of the trials of those who had died for their faith. Those called upon to pay the ultimate cost for confessing their faith were seen as having received a special blessing by the Holy Spirit in making their witness before the authorities.

During the first two centuries of Christian history, persecution leading to martyrdoms was generally scattered and local in character. Things changed, however, with the period of persecution that opened in the year 250 under the Roman Emperor Decius. Now for the first time there was an empire-wide attempt to force Christians to submit to the imperial code of religion. Concerned about the loyalty of its subjects, Decius ordered everyone in the Roman empire to offer sacrifices to the imperial gods and obtain certificates proving they had done so. The punishment for failure to do so was death or exile to forced labor and confiscation of all property. Throughout the Roman empire for more than a year chaos reigned in Christian churches. Many suffered martyrdom, while others committed apostasy by offering the proscribed sacrifices, doing so either immediately or after a period of torture. Some found ways to secure the certificates without offering sacrifice, while still others, including Cyprian, bishop of Carthage, and Dionysius, bishop of Alexandria, went into hiding.

The storms of persecution soon subsided, leaving the churches with the question of what to do about the sin of those who had lapsed into apostasy. Everywhere bishops agreed that offering sacrifice to the imperial gods represented a fundamental betrayal of Christ, removing oneself from the community of the faithful. But controversy soon broke out over the conditions for readmitting to the fellowship of the church those who sought it, even though they had either offered the sacrifices or obtained false certificates through bribery. North Africa and Rome were the focus of the controversy. The persecution had been intense there, and others in the Roman world were looking for pastoral guidance from them. In Carthage some of the confessors (those who suffered for the faith without being martyred) were acting on their own to grant readmission to lapsed members. Cyprian moved to stop them until he could call a council of neighboring bishops to consider the affair. When the council did meet, it established a graduated system of readmission, ranging from immediate reinstatement to lengthy penance, depending on the particular circumstances of each situation. In no case were lapsed presbyters or bishops to be reinstated as clergy, and any who accepted them as such were to be considered outside the communion of the church.

Meanwhile the question of readmission of the lapsed was being debated in Rome as well. There a majority of the church selected a new bishop named Cornelius in 251. Cornelius supported the more moderate position that eventually prevailed in Carthage. Members who had lapsed could be readmitted to communion following a period of suitable penance. Dissenting from this position was a group led by the presbyter Novatian. They insisted that no one who had failed to confess Jesus as Lord could be readmitted to church, for they had committed an unpardonable sin. Novatian was elected as an alternative bishop, and the church of Rome divided. Cornelius made appeals to the bishops of Alexandria, Antioch, and Carthage, who eventually supported him. Undeterred, Novatian's followers proceeded to establish new congregations elsewhere. The new communion was almost identical in both its theology and practice to the Catholic community from which it had now separated. The only issue over which the Novatianists disagreed with Catholics was the status of those who had lapsed.

The Novatian congregations continued to gain new converts. It was not long, however, before some who were baptized in them sought admission into Catholic congregations in Rome or elsewhere. Now the question confronting the Catholic leadership was not the status of lapsed individuals in the church, but the status of baptism performed outside the communion of the Catholic churches. The issue was a pressing one, for baptism was understood to be the means by which the Holy Spirit was conferred upon an individual, sealing the person for salvation. Cyprian argued that the Holy Spirit had been passed on from the apostles through the laying on of hands, and as such it was only conferred within the Catholic church, whose bishops were the apostles' successors. The unity of the church was an essential aspect of its spiritual life that guaranteed the validity of its various sacraments, he asserted. This unity in turn was secured through the unity of the bishops. The bishops were equal in authority, just as the apostles had been. Symbolically, their unity was expressed through the person of Peter, whom Christ had made the foundation of the church and whose successor was the bishop of Rome. The whole church was thus one, and outside the church there was no salvation.

This meant for Cyprian that anyone who was baptized outside a Catholic church, by a clergy not in good standing with the Catholic bishops, had to submit to the rite again in order to receive the mark of the Holy Spirit. In Rome one of Cornelius's successors, Stephen, followed a different line of argument. Baptism performed in the threefold name of the Trinity was valid, even if administered by one who was not in communion with the Catholic churches. Those who had been baptized by the Novatian clergy could become members of the Catholic church through a process of laying on of hands that conferred the Holy Spirit upon them, even though they had been baptized outside the Catholic church.

Cyprian responded to Stephen's decision by convening again a conference in Carthage of the bishops of Numidia to consider the matter. By unanimous vote the council decided to follow Cyprian's theological lead and refuse to recognize the validity of baptism outside the Catholic church. Those who sought admission in a congregation under the bishops that were in communion with Cyprian were required to submit again to baptism, the previous rite being regarded as invalid. Despite having asserted in his treatise *The Unity of the Church* the unity of mind of all Catholic bishops, and the symbolic role of the bishop of Rome as the successor to Peter, Cyprian now vented his anger and openly opposed Stephen.

The issue for Cyprian was left unresolved. Renewed imperial persecution led to his imprisonment in 256 and execution in 258. His successors in North Africa, however, continued to struggle with the question of the validity of sacraments performed outside the church. As they did so, Cyprian's legacy was invoked by those on both sides. Indeed, his influence upon the churches in North Africa and elsewhere was enormous. Long after his death Cyprian's theological arguments continued to shape the thinking of church leaders in numerous locations. His adamant defense of the unity of the church, his championing of the authority of bishops, and his assertion that outside the church there is no salvation continue to be heard in theological discussions today.

As for the Novatianists, they continued to spread their congregations across the Mediterranean world. A hundred years later Novatianist congregations were reported to be still gathering in Rome. Constantinople, the city that became in the fourth century the eastern capital of the Roman empire, was likewise reported to have several of their churches as late as the fifth century. Although the original attraction of Novatianism was its advocacy of a more rigorous disciplinary standard in church life, it should be pointed out that the later reports make no mention of whether the levels of sin and immorality were any lower among them than they were in Catholic congregations.

One of the places Novatianists were found in the third century was in Carthage. They were not alone in pressing for a stricter church discipline there. The position had wide support even among the Catholic churches in Roman North Africa. Christianity, martyrdom, and rigorous enforcement of church discipline in spite of persecution were always closely intertwined in the life of churches in the region. "From the days of the Scillitan martyrs (*ca.* 188) and Perpetua and Felicity (203) to the era of Cyprian (mid-third century), fidelity under trying circumstances provided a point of self-definition for North African Christians," writes historian Maureen A. Tilley. "The result was an identification of martyrdom with Christianity and a diminished tolerance for lapsed Christians seeking to return to the Church."[17]

The way of asceticism and self-denial

One of the North African writers who was a contemporary of Perpetua and Felicity, and who, as we have noted, believed martyrdom to be the best argument

---

[17] Maureen A. Tilley, trans., *Donatist Martyr Stories: The Church in Conflict in Roman North Africa* (Liverpool: Liverpool University Press, 1996), xiii.

for the Christian faith, was Tertullian of Carthage. Prior to becoming a Christian he had been an adherent of Stoicism, a philosophical school characterized among other things by a rigorous morality. Although as a Christian he expressed doubts about the benefits philosophy could offer the faith ("What indeed has Athens to do with Jerusalem?" he once wrote),[18] he could still employ his formidable skills as a rhetorician in defense of the faith, as is seen in the pages of his *Apology*. Perhaps due in part to his Stoic background, Tertullian advocated a rigorous code of morality that many have called puritanical in character. Christians ought not be too involved in affairs of the wider society, he believed. They should not serve in the military or attend entertainment events. Christian women who had taken vows of virginity were to wear veils in public to protect them from the lustful gaze of men. The tone of his work suggests that, at least from his perspective, the churches of his day had begun to relax the disciplinary requirements of membership. Tertullian opposed any such compromise in what he regarded to be the demands of Christian life.

His rigorous moral stance in part led the theologian to become associated with a group known as the New Prophecy (or Montanists) in North Africa after 200. We will consider this movement in further detail below, but here we should point out that in some places Catholics considered them heretical in the third century (although apparently not in North Africa in Tertullian's lifetime). Several generations after his death we find reports that Tertullian even started his own church, but recent scholarship has shown that there is no evidence from his own lifetime to support this. There is no evidence that he ever withdrew from communion with the larger Catholic church or was considered by others to be out of communion with it, only that he opposed those factions whom he thought to be compromising or relaxing the moral standards of the church.

Hippolytus of Rome in the first years of the third century shared many of these concerns. Ordained a presbyter by the bishop Victor, Hippolytus was a vigorous opponent of various errors he perceived were being advanced by teachers in the city. His bitterest disputes came with the Catholic bishop of the city, Callistus. Callistus had been a slave and had spent time at hard labor in the mines on account of his faith. After being released, he had risen through the ranks of the clergy in Rome to be elected bishop in 217, a position to which Hippolytus apparently also aspired. Personal animosity between the two men played a significant role in the disputes that divided them. But the overt reason Hippolytus gave was that the bishop was intent on relaxing church discipline. Callistus allowed free women to marry slave men, a practice that was not recognized as legal matrimony under Roman law. Hippolytus regarded such a practice as connivance at sin and opposed what he considered a breach of moral standards.

The fact was that the church of Rome was attracting more and more members from the wealthier classes, and most of them were women. Some even donated land that by the early part of the third century was being used for underground burial sites called catacombs. The increases in both the numbers and the overall social status of the church's members are often cited as reasons for the relaxation

---

[18] Tertullian, "The Prescripton against Heretics," in *The Ante-Nicene Fathers*, 3:246.

in church discipline that can be seen during this period. Callistus acknowledged that there were wheat and tares alike in the church. For Hippolytus, who allowed himself to be elected as a rival bishop by a minority group in the city, such laxness threatened the gospel. He was reconciled with the larger church of Rome before his death, but the controversy over the issue of readmission of lapsed believers following times of persecution was to erupt again in the middle of the century.

Even in periods when martyrdom was not an immediate threat and questions about dealing with the lapsed were thus not immediately confronting church leaders, concerns about the degree of discipline and self-denial required by Christian faith abounded. Practices of self-denial that focused on moral control of bodily desires are generally called asceticism, and were the most prominent expression of such discipline in Christian life. Asceticism has often been depicted in a negative light as being only a denial of the material body of flesh. For the early Christian movement it was understood instead as a practice of self-discipline that freed the body from excessive attachment to the social and material world, and thus the pathway of holiness that enabled one to approach God. Common ascetic behaviors included fasting, wearing of rough clothing, and various other means of self-imposed suffering. These were accompanied by long periods of solitude given over for prayer and contemplation, as well as works of service for the church community. Christians were called to present themselves as a living sacrifice, to give up the passing pleasures of the world in exchange for something more enduring and eternal.

Chief among the pursuits that ascetics gave up were the physical pleasures associated with sexual relations and marriage. Celibacy was a means for women and men to free themselves from the social demands of marriage and family life, thereby freeing them for greater love and service of God. In a world where women's lives where otherwise defined by the men to whom they were related, celibacy challenged narrow definitions of gender roles and enabled women to experience social and spiritual empowerment. It is important to point out, however, that women and men alike took on a life of celibacy in order to devote themselves entirely to God, not to pursue self-fulfillment.

Among the ministers we encounter in churches throughout the early Christian movement are young women who had either dedicated themselves, or been dedicated by their families, to a life of virginity. Other women added their names to the ranks of the ascetics after having been married, some on the death of their husbands but others while their husbands were still alive. These "widows of the church," as they were called, joined the "consecrated virgins," or younger women who had foresworn marriage, in carrying out such visible public ministries as prayer, visitation, and good works for the community. Such women were no longer regarded—by church leaders at least—as being under the authority of a father, husband, or other male member of their family. Thus they were able to exercise a degree of freedom that other women did not always have. Early in the history of the Christian movement these women sometimes appear to be living together in houses one of them owned. From the second century we also find evidence that at least some of them veiled their heads when they went into public as a sign that they did not wish to be the object of lustful male gazes.

There were some among the early churches who believed that asceticism ought to be a universal lifestyle for all Christians. Eusebius reports an exchange of letters between Dionysius, bishop of Corinth, and Pinytus, bishop of Gnossus, around the year 170. Dionysius, he said, had urged Pinytus not to impose upon all Christians in his care the discipline of continence as a requirement of holiness. He should accept the fact that the majority were too weak to keep this rule. Pinytus replied that he respected Dionysius's position but hoped for some stronger food with which to eventually feed his people so that they might not remain fed only "on a diet of milky words and treated like babes till they grow old without knowing it."[19] These were pressing questions for the churches: Does abstaining from all physical pleasures of the flesh better fit one for a life of holiness? Must one abstain from such in order to be a true Christian?

The most notable group to answer these questions in the affirmative was the Encratites, whom we have already met in the Syrian deserts in the second century. We noted that the name of Tatian was often associated with those who believed a high degree of asceticism to be an essential requirement of the gospel. Tatian is best remembered as the composer of the *Diatessaron*. His only other work to survive is an apology written to the Greeks. The work opens with a critique of Hellenistic philosophy more blistering than the ones we encountered in Justin and Clement. The Greeks plagiarized their learning from others; they learned the art of astronomy from Babylon, magic from the Persians, geometry from the Egyptians, the alphabet itself from the Phoenicians. "Cease, then, to miscall these imitations inventions of your own."[20]

Tatian's defense of Christian doctrines revolved around themes that we have likewise found in others: that the God whom Christians worship is creator of all that exists, that God is not found in time and space and is not a material being, that God created humanity with a free will, and that humanity sinned or fell away from God. With others Tatian argued that the Logos was sent from God to illuminate the pathway back. He went on: "But further, it becomes us now to seek for what we once had, but have lost, to unite the soul with the Holy Spirit, and to strive after union with God."[21] So strong was his sense of this union of the soul with the immaterial Spirit of God, or with God, that any activity which kept one bound up in the cares of bodily, fleshly existence could only be regarded as sin. His denial of the body and its pleasures at this point was strong enough to earn him the condemnation of others of his age as being docetic, that is, denying that Christ had a real human body of flesh.

The other peculiar doctrine that earned Tatian the scorn of other Catholic writers was what appears to be his belief that Adam could not have been saved. How could he? Tatian asked. Adam and Eve lived in marriage after being expelled from the garden. Tatian believed that engaging in any sexual activity was participation in corruption, even when in marriage. Marriage, he believed, was but a form of fornication. For the record, he was also opposed to drinking wine

---

[19] Eusebius, *The History of the Church* 4.23, in Williamson, 184.

[20] *Address of Tatian to the Greeks*, 1, in *The Ante-Nicene Fathers*, 2:65.

[21] Ibid., 15, in *The Ante-Nicene Fathers*, 2:71.

(Encratites partook of the eucharist using bread and water) and eating meat (the latter possibly on grounds of its associations with sacrifice to other gods). The case can be made that on some of these points Tatian's doctrine was only radicalizing what others had said, including his teacher, Justin Martyr. On the other hand, it was similar enough to the doctrines of Marcion and the Gnostics to cause Tatian to be identified as one of them by his opponents. (Marcion and many Gnostics did indeed advocate various degrees of asceticism.) But Tatian's reasoning was different from theirs. He did not regard creation as evil, only its pleasures. Continence was in imitation of Christ, whose flesh was always under self-control.

In the Syrian churches even the more extreme ascetic doctrines were acceptable to most. They appeared throughout the region and were regularly referred to in early Syrian tradition. The third-century *Acts of Thomas* (written in Syriac, most likely near Edessa) describes the apostle as eating only bread and salt, drinking only water, and wearing one rough garment. On his way east to India he is said to have visited a wedding where he converted the bride and groom to his ascetic doctrine on their wedding night, leaving the couple consecrated to perpetual virginity. Some Syrian teachers in the third and fourth centuries baptized only those who had pledged themselves to lives of celibacy. Baptism and thus salvation were restricted to those who renounced all ways of the flesh.

Such teachings were being challenged elsewhere in the Syrian churches by the fourth century. The *Didascalia*, a book that was largely Catholic in orientation, criticized a group known as the Covenanters for their extreme views on this point. Yet the strong ascetic emphasis was felt even within the Catholic party in the East, and it provided the major missionary force for the advance of Christian churches in the Persian empire. A group of Syrian ascetics called Wanderers were among these missionaries. Their freedom from attachments of the flesh translated into freedom to move across great geographical distances with the message of the gospel.

Ascetics, like martyrs, were accorded a place of authority within the church that did not fall immediately under the oversight of bishops. Women and men who exercised rigorous self-control were considered living demonstrations of holiness and hence became emblems of the holiness to which the entire community of Christians was called. Christian women who took a vow of virginity and were consecrated to church service were still subject to the patriarchal social mores of their day. Nevertheless, we would do well to pay attention to the manner in which asceticism was a means of empowerment by which women could exercise a degree of control over their own lives and begin to challenge the limited opportunity for ministry they were otherwise allowed in their day.

The work of the Spirit and the New Prophecy

Closely related to the practices of martyrdom and asceticism in the early churches were often practices associated with prophecy and reception of visionary revelations. The link between these and the tradition of resistance can be seen in the story of Perpetua, who received her visions in prison after being baptized and while awaiting execution. Prophecy continued to be exercised in Carthage and North Africa long after it appears to have died down—or been suppressed—elsewhere in the western Roman world. Perpetua's contemporary in the northern region in Gaul, Irenaeus, for instance, knew of the practice of prophecy in the church but certainly did not emphasize it. To the east in the countryside of Syria the practice was known as well. The early- to mid-second-century pastoral handbook, the *Didache*, provided rules for determining when a traveling prophet was legitimate and when not. Throughout the Christian world by the end of the second century, however, there was a growing tendency for churches and bishops to regularize and even institutionalize prophetic inspiration.

The Spirit, according to Cyprian, was passed on to new believers in the sacrament of baptism. Pope Stephen in Rome added that the Spirit could also be given through the laying of hands upon those who had been baptized in the name of the Trinity but outside the Catholic church. The Spirit was believed to be passed on in a similar manner through the laying on of hands in the rite of ordination of other clergy and bishops. In each of these cases it was the church that administered the act, dispensing the Spirit and its gifts through its institutional means. Increasingly for many in the Catholic churches, bishops were perceived to be the ones through whom such gifts were passed on. Nevertheless, experiences of a more direct or supernatural occurrence of the Spirit's presence and gifts continued to occur outside these institutionalized means. In at least one case, that of a group known as the New Prophecy from Asia Minor that was led by Montanus, Priscilla, and Maximilla (a man and two women), we have evidence of a full-fledged charismatic group in the latter part of the second century.

The New Prophecy first appeared in Phrygia in Asia Minor, a district well known for its heritage of Christian prophets. The letters to the seven churches by the seer, John of Patmos, in the Apocalypse were addressed to congregations to the immediate west of Phrygia, and the Apocalypse figured significantly in New Prophecy teachings. The apostle Philip's two daughters were remembered as prophets in the region as well. From the letters of Ignatius of Antioch, it appears that tensions between prophets and bishops had already arisen in the area by the beginning of the century. Against this background the New Prophecy arose as a renewal movement within Catholic churches after the middle of the century.

The name most often associated with the New Prophecy leadership is Montanus. Little is known about him other than he was a native of Phrygia; a convert to Christianity; an excellent organizer; and a prophet who experienced ecstatic possessions and spoke in a stranger manner of speech under the inspiration of the Spirit. Equally prominent in the leadership of the movement were two women, Priscilla and Maximilla, about whom we unfortunately know even less. Some historians recently have argued that they were the more prominent leaders of the New Prophecy, but from the existing sources we have, the claim is difficult to sustain. Montanus was the first to appear in reports on the group. He was the organizer and administrator who collected funds from the churches supporting them. According to later sources it was Montanus who pronounced the annulment of the marriages of Priscilla and Maximilla, thereby freeing them from the authority of their husbands. The two women in turn became known for their prophetic utterances throughout the churches and as equals in leadership with Montanus.

The prophets foretold the end of the age that was at hand. A new age of the Spirit was about to be inaugurated, for Christ was about to return to establish his millennial kingdom on earth. Christians were thus called to a more rigorous discipline of fasting and even celibacy in preparation. Montanus believed that the New Jerusalem that John of Patmos had foreseen in the Apocalypse would be located in Phrygia, where the group had its headquarters. Living with such a heightened sense of the in-breaking of the new age brought with it a greater openness to the in-breaking of the Paraclete. One of the features of the group that drew the attention of immediate observers was the ecstatic behavior the New Prophecy's followers experienced in worship. Women and men alike were possessed by the Spirit and received manifestations in the form of visions or utterances that were received as revelations from God. Those associated with the group accepted the sayings of Priscilla as genuine utterances of the Spirit.

According to the New Prophecy teachers the Spirit ordained individuals to be ministers through its immediate anointing. They thus did not confine ordination to those on whom bishops had laid hands. This in turn allowed for the ministry of women in a manner that was institutionally closed to them in most other Catholic churches by the later decades of the second century. There is still evidence in Catholic sources for women's ministry as widows and prophets of the church in the second century, but only in the New Prophecy do we have evidence of women being directly called *presbytera* (women priests). Priscilla, Maximilla, and later a third woman named Quintilla all functioned as bishops within the group. In time it became one of the major issues that other Catholic writers seized upon to label the group heretical.

The opposition at first was strongest in their home region of Asia Minor and in Rome. In North Africa the New Prophecy seems to have been accepted with relatively little opposition. Perpetua, the young woman who received visions while in prison awaiting her martyrdom, is often cited as having at least been influenced by their teachings. Tertullian associated as well with the group toward the end of his career, without being immediately considered as outside the Catholic church (only later did some commentators come to regard him as having departed from the Catholic faith). By the fourth century, however, opposition to the group had hardened across the Catholic churches. The movement became derided as the Montanist heresy, its few remaining churches subject to constant opposition. Montanus's claims to direct inspiration of the Spirit were twisted to be claims that he had identified himself as the Spirit, the third member of the Trinity. Montanists were even accused of eating the flesh of children.

The New Prophecy or Montanists as a group eventually declined, but the gift of prophecy that they celebrated did not disappear from the churches. Others continued to recognize and practice the extraordinary gifts of the Spirit through the third century. Some of those demonstrated by the New Prophecy, such as speaking in unintelligible or unknown tongues (glossolalia), which was cited by observers as a prominent feature, all but disappeared. Irenaeus acknowledged the practice in other churches of his day, but by the fifth century most writers assumed this particular gift had died out entirely. Prophecy, intelligible revelations of the Spirit, and visions declined as well, at least to the degree that they were regarded as marginal occurrences within the Catholic churches. This did not mean that charismatic phenomena were entirely lost to the Catholic community or that fresh expressions of the Spirit's anointing did not take place.

Chief among these latter phenomena were ongoing signs and wonders reportedly performed by individuals within the Christian movement. One of the most widely known of these was a missionary in the third century known as Gregory the Wonderworker, who evangelized the region of Cappadocia in Asia Minor. A student of Origen's in Caesarea, Gregory the Wonderworker returned around 245 to Neocaesarea, the city of his birth. There he was made a bishop and began to preach to unbelievers. According to legend Gregory's success as a missionary was due in part to the miracles he performed, such as vanquishing demons or causing a mountain to move. On a more mundane level of pastoral work, however, he distinguished himself by maintaining church discipline during an invasion by the Goths, a Germanic tribe from the north, in 253-254. By the time of his death it is said that the entire city had become Christian.

Later centuries witnessed revivals of prophecy in movements for renewal among the churches. Some of these remained within the Catholic communion, while others moved to the margins as separate groups or parties. By the fourth century direct revelations through prophecy and visions were considered suspect by most church leaders; such experiences might well have been more common but simply not reported. What we find are reports of charismatic phenomena, mainly healings and exorcisms, associated with missionary outreach of the movement in new regions. Several individuals who were examples of this will be examined in following chapters.

Household and city

Whether they were in Rome, Carthage, Edessa, or Nisibis, most persons who became Christian in the second and third centuries did so for local reasons. The theological debates of the day were often connected with the day-to-day concerns with which people lived. The meaning of salvation for most was focused around questions of sickness, moral life, diverse gods, or the afterlife. Adult conversions were still the major avenue by which people entered the churches in the third century, although the number of persons who were being raised in Christian families and baptized as children was increasing. The process through which adult converts went before becoming baptized members of a local church was still a lengthy one, although we see evidence of some attempting to shorten the preparation in order to accommodate the growing numbers. As far as we can tell, churches admitted to their eucharistic table only those who had been baptized. Once baptized, members were expected to maintain certain standards of Christian discipline. Since it was not uncommon for churches to teach that one could not receive forgiveness for sins committed after baptism, many still put off the water rite until they were close to death. Those who did undertake baptism usually did so on Easter as they passed through death with Jesus into his resurrection.

Throughout the Christian movement, as we have noted, bishops and presbyters came to exercise many of the functions carried out by priests of other religions. They led worship, oversaw the instruction of new converts, held money for people under their care, and watched over the moral behavior of members in their churches. A growing practice was for Christians to ask their bishops or presbyters to bless their weddings, much as followers of other religions did of their respective priests. Churches took up collections and distributed food to those in need. They cared for the sick and diseased as well, no small incentive for growth in an age of recurring plagues. Christians visited the burial sites of their members, communicating a sense of community that transcended even death. Justin Martyr asserted that one compelling argument for Christians having the truth was found within the quality of virtue Christians demonstrated in their collective lives. While his argument failed to convince the emperor, it did express the sense of community that was attracting so many into the churches.

One of the pervasive themes of early Christian community was that of being of the household of God. The household or family in most places of the ancient world was the basic social unit upon which the rest of society was built. Families organized economic production, social interaction, and even spiritual life. An extended family in Italy, Egypt, or Iran typically included the male head, a wife or wives, unmarried sons and daughters, other older members (usually widows), and if the family had any wealth, servants and slaves. Most families lived in small houses or, in cities like Antioch, together with several other families in buildings as high as four stories. Wealthier households might actually include several houses located together. Across the ancient urban world from China to Spain, households or families were typically defined by a single patriarch or male figure who headed the entire extended community. In most cultures marriages were arranged by the male heads of households, and women had little or no say in the matter. A marriage was generally considered legal if it was agreed to by the heads of the households and witnessed by the families.

By the first century CE Roman law and custom had come to recognize monogamy as normative, while in most other places in the world polygyny was commonly accepted. Roman society, however, accepted concubinage and men having sexual relations with prostitutes quite readily. Fathers were legally allowed to decide whether to claim as their own any children who resulted from such non-marital relationships. Sexual relations between persons of the same gender were not considered a matter of "family" in most cultures, in part because they were not open to the possibility of reproduction. This does not mean that they did not occur, for they did, although various cultures accorded them varying degrees of moral acceptability.

Against this social background the Christian movement emerged with a sense of being part of a new household of God. From North Africa in the year 304 comes a story that illustrates well the effect of this Christian understanding. The *Acts of the Abitinian Martyrs* narrates the tale of one twelve-year-old girl named Victoria who was charged with the crime of being a Christian. Although she was of age according to Roman law (twelve was considered the legal age of majority for girls, fourteen for boys), the governor hearing the case offered to release the young woman into the custody of her older brother if she would denounce her Christian allegiance. Victoria refused, asserting instead, "My brothers are those who keep the commands of God."[22] She soon joined the ranks of Christian martyrs.

.In these new Christian families bishops soon became identified as patriarchs or heads of household. The city of Alexandria in the third century had some twenty bishops, along with numerous presbyters and deacons. To distinguish the senior bishop of the city from the rest, the churches began calling him "papa," a practice that was soon known in Carthage, Antioch, and Rome as well. The designation was intended to express the familiar relationship a senior bishop had to all the churches under his administrative jurisdiction, but the relationship was not his alone. All bishops were expected to be related to their churches as heads of families. Bishops were usually elected by the members of the churches they served (the process was by collective voice) and then consecrated by others holding episcopal office. The relationship between bishop and church was considered to be that of a marriage. In the fourth century it was made a rule in the Roman world that the connection between a bishop and a particular church was one made for life, so that bishops were forbidden to change locations.

By the third century one finds judgments and decisions being made in the form of church laws. But the bonds that held churches together were not so much judicial as they were organic in nature. They rested on the recognition and love that members expressed for one another. Authority in the churches was considered to be derived from the Spirit and required mutual recognition to be effective. Certain members were permitted to exercise it over others, but the only recourse churches had to enforce it was exclusion from the community. Through their spreading network of mutual relatedness, a new extended family of peoples was emerging in Christian self-understanding.

The metaphor of the church as the household of God places before us two vexing historical questions that are often raised by contemporary interpreters of the Christian movement. What did the early Christians say about slavery? And what about the status of women within the overall Christian community? First, in the ancient world slavery in one form or another was a nearly universal phenomenon. Although the common factor remained extracted labor, the institution varied enough from place to place to make it difficult to offer blanket observations. Slaves performed a variety of functions with varying degrees of personal control and exercise of freedom in the ancient world. Some were educated and held administrative posts within governments. One such former slave was Clement of Rome, who, although favoring manumission, regarded slavery as a viable system of tutelage. Clement's argument in favor of slavery is especially important for us to see, for it rested on the need for social order. In the ancient world social roles of all types were usually narrowly defined. Except for those at the very top of a society, few human beings exercised what could be called personal freedom in their social lives. Looking at the institution in context, a slave in the ancient

---

[22] *Acts of the Abitinian Martyrs*, 17, in Tilley, *Donatist Martyr Stories*, 42-43.

world was generally better off than someone who was outside any defined social role and thus without social protection.

Early Christian comfort with slavery can be found as early as in the apostolic writings in the use of the term as a metaphor for service to God. Paul often described himself as one who was a slave of Christ. The apostles seem to have accepted such social arrangements not because they were just, but because in their view all social life was destined to be shortly displaced by the coming reign of Jesus Christ. Given the relatively short period of time they expected the present social order to endure, the issue of manumission of slaves appears to have been minimized during the first two centuries of Christian life. Ignatius of Antioch, writing to Polycarp of Smyrna a generation after the close of the apostolic era, advised against the church using its resources to redeem those held in slavery. His stated reason was that in their desire for freedom slaves might become self-centered in their thinking, although it is possible Ignatius was also trying to avoid arousing any further the suspicions of the Roman authorities that Christians were seditious. The fact that Ignatius even addressed the issue of redemption indicates that this was an option being considered or practiced by some.

Callistus and Hippolytus, we noted above, had quarreled in Rome early in the third century over the former's decision that a woman of the senatorial class could marry a man who was a slave. Such marriages were formally illegal under Roman law, the probable reason Hippolytus opposed them. Callistus's ruling that the church would recognize them has been seen by some as a reflection of the bishop's own past experience as a slave. Whether or not this is so, the ruling points toward a widening egalitarian impulse at work in the life of the church for Christians in Rome.

The ambiguity that greets us in early Christian literature regarding slavery is matched by the Christian movement's response to social inequalities between women and men. In the ancient world the plight of women was often worse than that of men who were slaves. After the first generation or two, the Christian movement in many places appears to have accommodated itself to these patterns of social inequality and oppression. Women in the Christian movement still exercised a greater degree of leadership in the church than in the religious and cultural worlds around them. Even after the movement had begun to back away from some of the radically egalitarian practices of Jesus, the stories that Christians read in scriptures of women who were influential in the ministry of Jesus continued to inspire them. In the Roman world upper-class women made use of the opportunities Roman law granted them over the control of wealth and property to become patrons of churches. In North Africa, Syria, and Persia, women often embraced the radical ascetic option of declaring themselves virgins for life and foregoing marriage and family, thereby freeing them from oppressive social roles and enabling them to pursue lives devoted to service in the churches.

Few women exercised political or military leadership in the ancient world. Most cultures defined women through their relations to men and limited their opportunities for social interaction. Any woman who was not under the authority or ownership of a man was socially exposed to personal violation. It was especially dangerous for a woman to travel on her own. A woman who did so, whether as a merchant or an evangelist, faced far greater dangers than a single man. This is one important reason we do not find single women numbered among the first missionaries of the movement. Women did exercise leadership in worship and in church life in the early days of the movement, as we have seen. Historical interpreters disagree on the extent of such leadership, but few deny it altogether. Women led prayer and practiced prophecy, for instance. The latter role continued to be practiced in the New Prophecy, which arose toward the end of the second century, where women were explicitly called presbyters or priests.

Among women in leadership, the most common roles were those of widows and virgins. As late as the fourth century the Syriac *Testament of Our Lord* allowed widows to serve as teachers and carry on pastoral functions of the clergy, including standing at the altar with priests at the eucharist. Widows might have been considered capable of spending their time in the churches on account of their being free from other distractions of household life. They were also regarded as repositories of community wisdom and insight. The ancient world generally lacked public institutions for social welfare. A woman who was widowed and without a supporting family often had no choice but to remarry for economic support. Early Christians regarded perpetual monogamy as the norm of marriage, and thus remarriage was generally discouraged. Church support for widows freed them from the necessity of remarrying. Widows were cared for by the churches' diaconal programs and in some situations could have been considered workers in the churches on this account. Ascetic women who renounced married life or practiced continence within marriage continued this tradition of widows and celibate women who, because they were free from the defining social roles of sexual reproduction, were capable of achieving a greater degree of social equality with men in the churches.

Were women ever priests in the Catholic churches? Some have argued that there was a time when women were ordained to the offices of presbyter, and exercised leadership as priests. Others deny that such was ever allowed within the churches that were part of the Catholic wing of the movement. Even those who claim women were indeed originally priests in Catholic churches have not argued that their numbers were great or that any woman in the ancient church was ever consecrated a Catholic bishop, as far as we know. Ironically, one of the reasons why the Catholic party might have backed away from women exercising eucharistic leadership (assuming that they did indeed do so among the earliest communities) was the role that women exercised among Gnostic groups in the second and third centuries. But even among the Gnostics, it should be pointed out, women were never fully equal to men in leadership or authority.

The success of the Christian movement drew churches deeper into the cultural worlds around them. Indeed, the very pattern of incarnational adaption that compelled the movement to translate itself into new cultural forms at times could work against exercise of critical judgments. Many today look back upon the early Christians' responses to the issues of slavery and women's subordination and rightly decry the lack of greater justice. At the same time the reason Christians often reflected more of their surrounding culture than we might have wished has to do with the same principle of incarnation that called them to translate the gospel into new situations. The identity of the risen Christ was certainly seeping into new cultures and locations, but this does not mean that Christians were immediately abandoning aspects one might today regard as unjust. Cultural transformations came slowly, and not without great deliberation and struggle. In the end, churches were able to transform cultures and political environments only because they had at least in certain aspects become a part of them. Co-optation was an ever-present danger, but the risk is inherent in the practice of incarnation. The ongoing process of becoming incarnate within a culture and of transforming a culture is one that continues down through the ages in all Christian traditions.

Recommended readings

Much of what we know of the Christian movement from the first centuries still comes to us from a historian of the ancient church named Eusebius of Caesarea, whose work is readily available in numerous translations, such as that by G. A. Williamson, *The History of the Church from Christ to Constantine* (New York: Barnes and Noble, 1965). More than a century ago Alexander Roberts and James Donaldson edited a series of early Christian works that continues to be printed and widely used today, *The Ante-Nicene Fathers: Translations of the Fathers down to A.D. 325* (Grand Rapids, Mich.: Wm. B. Eerdmans Publishing Co., 1981). Among recent historians of the period, Ramsay MacMullen's works, including *Christianizing the Roman Empire (A.D. 100-400)* (New Haven, Conn.: Yale University Press, 1984), provide important insights into the historical growth of Christianity in the Mediterranean world. MacMullen and Eugene N. Lane have teamed up to edit *Paganism and Christianity 100-424 C.E.: A Sourcebook* (Minneapolis, Minn.: Fortress Press, 1992).

One of the greatest finds of ancient texts in the past century was also a boon for understanding Gnosticism. *The Nag Hammadi Library* has been translated into English and brought into print by general editor James M. Robinson (San Francisco: Harper & Row, 1988). For the background of Gnosticism, see Pheme Perkins, *Gnosticism and the New Testament* (Minneapolis, Minn.: Fortress Press, 1993). The history of Manichaeism has until recently been hardly told, but a work helping to change that situation is Samuel N. C. Lieu, *Manicheism in Mesopotamia and the Roman East* (New York: E. J. Brill, 1994). A great deal of light on the tangled history of Jews and Christians through the first centuries is cast by Stephen G. Wilson, *Related Strangers: Jews and Christians 70-170 C.E.* (Minneapolis: Fortress Press, 1995).

Asceticism, charismatic experience, and the issue of women in ministry all intersect in Christian Trevett, *Montanism: Gender, Authority, and the New Prophecy* (Cambridge, Mass.: Cambridge University Press, 1996). Bonnie Bowman Thurston, *The Widows: A Women's Ministry in the Early Church* (Philadelphia: Fortress Press, 1989), examines the place of women in the context of emerging Catholic Christianity. On the issue of slavery in the early Christian movement, James Albert Harrill, *The Manumission of Slaves in Early Christianity* (Tübingen:

Mohr Siebeck, 1998), is helpful. Hugh Wybrew, *The Orthodox Liturgy: The Development of the Eucharistic Liturgy in the Byzantine Rite* (London: SPCK, 1989), explores from a contemporary ecumenical perspective the liturgical practices of Christians in both Greek and Latin contexts during these first years. Peter D. Day, *Eastern Christian Liturgies: The Armenian, Coptic, Ethiopian, and Syrian Rites* (Shannon: Irish University Press, 1972), has looked more closely at non-Greek liturgical traditions in the East.

Part IV

THE AGE OF THE IMPERIAL CHURCH

Affirmations and Dissent (c.300 to c.600)

The fourth century witnessed a radical change in the political status of Christian churches in the Roman empire. For more than two centuries, churches in the Mediterranean world had been steadily growing. Despite the encumbrance of imperial opposition marked by short but intense bouts of persecution, the political and cultural influence of churches had likewise increased. Significant numbers of converts were beginning to join from the upper classes. More than half the population of some cities were identifying themselves with this illicit religion. Members of the clergy had become well-known and respected community figures in some places. Emboldened in their witness, Christians had even begun to meet for public worship in buildings dedicated to this purpose.

Given the increasing numbers and influence of Christians in the Roman world, the turn of events in which the emperor Constantine extended legal recognition and then imperial support to the religion can seem in hindsight to have been almost inevitable. To many who were living in the Roman empire in the first quarter of the fourth century, however, the course of events appeared to be nothing short of miraculous. Little in their experience had prepared the churches for the rapid institutional transformations that took place as clergy began to receive funds from the imperial treasury, or bishops began to be invited to hear local cases as civil judges. In a few short years Christianity in the Mediterranean world went from being an illegal religion to the official creed of the Roman emperor. Historical reverberations from those events still can be felt today.

Constantine's embrace of Christianity in the fourth century was the first step toward a great synthesis of religion, state, and culture in the Roman world. At the same time, it set in motion forces that led to even greater institutional diversity in the churches of the world. By the end of the sixth century, the Christian movement had fractured into several diverging theological traditions, despite the best efforts of bishops and emperors alike to achieve unity among the churches.

Two of these theological traditions that emerged in the fourth century (Donatism and Arianism) failed to survive much beyond the seventh. In Roman North Africa (the provinces of Byzacena, Africa Proconsularis, Numidia, and Mauretania),

155

a dispute that started over the status of clergy who were suspected of having collaborated with imperial authorities during the persecution erupted into a full-fledged schism after 315. Two parties, known as Donatists and Catholics, emerged in separate communions. Their churches lived side by side for several centuries in North Africa until Islam effectively put an end to organized Christianity in the region.

The other major dispute that erupted in the first quarter of the century was known as the Arian controversy. Primarily theological in nature, it concerned the proper Christian understanding of the nature of the Logos in relation to God. This debate was the main occasion for the convening of the Council of Nicaea, whose theological decisions became the standard of orthodox faith for the majority of churches in the world. Arians and Nicenes struggled against one another throughout most of the fourth century in the Roman world, until imperial support finally decided in favor of Nicaea. In the meantime, Arianism became the national religion of a number of the Germanic tribes who were immigrating into Roman territories, beginning with the Goths in the fourth century. Arianism survived in Spain until the end of the sixth century, when the Gothic nobility converted to the Catholic form of Christian faith.

Both Donatism and Arianism effectively ceased to exist as living expressions of Christian tradition by the end of the seventh century. Faring better were the several theological streams that emerged from a series of christological debates in the fifth century. The controversy that gave rise to them focused on the relationship between the divine and human natures in the person of Jesus Christ. On the one side were teachers and bishops who believed the mystery of salvation was best represented by speaking of the one incarnate person, Jesus Christ, in whom the divine nature took on human flesh. Identified with the Alexandrian school of theology, these theologians and the churches who followed them came to speak of Jesus Christ as being of one nature after his incarnation. By the sixth century the one-nature formulation had become the standard of orthodoxy for several national churches both inside and beyond the boundaries of the Roman empire. Egyptian (Coptic), Ethiopian, Nubian, Armenian, and Jacobite (West Syrian) communions shared a common understanding of Jesus Christ and recognized one another as carrying on the orthodox Christian faith.

On the other side of the increasingly hostile theological debates of the fifth century were those who found in the language of one nature an impious mixing of human and divine characteristics. The transcendence of God required a more careful articulation of the two natures, divine and human, that were conjoined in Jesus Christ, they believed. Those who shared this perspective gathered around a group of teachers who identified themselves historically with the theological school at Antioch. They were not afraid to use the terminology of two natures to describe Jesus Christ, a formula that brought them into direct conflict with their Alexandrian opponents. Over the course of the fifth century those who adhered to the two-nature teaching were suppressed by a combination of political and theological efforts that deprived them of their foothold in the eastern Roman world. Forced into exile by the emperor, they found a hearing for their doctrine further east among the Persian churches. After the fifth century the two-nature

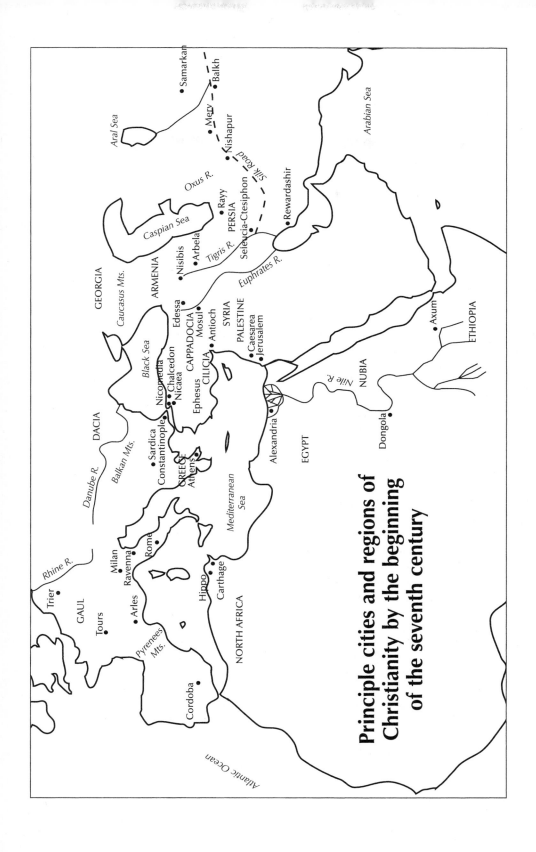

Principle cities and regions of Christianity by the beginning of the seventh century

doctrine came to be identified as the confession of the dominant churches of Persia, India, central Asia, and China. In the Mediterranean world they were usually called Nestorians, after Bishop Nestorius of Constantinople, whose teachings were ruled heretical at the Council of Chalcedon in 451. Here we will simply call the churches Persian, or East Syrian, to distinguish them from other ecclesiastical communions of the period.

Both theological positions had much to recommend them to those who were not adamant supporters of one side or the other. Most bishops in the Latin-speaking western Mediterranean found themselves in a middle ground between the two schools of thought, a position that the bishop of Rome usually occupied. In Constantinople the imperial household's perennial concern for the unity of the churches under Roman rule put it likewise on the side of compromise. The Council of Chalcedon in 451 formulated a definition of Jesus Christ in terms of two natures united in one person, thereby setting forth a middle way that combined insights from both sides. After much theological debate and political intrigue, the majority of bishops and their churches in the Roman world came to agree to this definition that remains today a standard of doctrine for most Christians throughout the world. Sizable parties on both sides of the issue dissented, on the other hand, resulting in separations and eventually even new church formations.

Most of the Latin- and Greek-speaking churches accepted the definition of Chalcedon. On a number of other issues, however, these two communities were growing apart by the fifth century. Two streams of church tradition were emerging, each claiming the inheritance of the first three hundred years of Christian history. Increasingly their representatives were unable, and sometimes unwilling, to communicate with one another as members of a common faith. Fueling the tensions between them was the antipathy between Rome and Constantinople as the latter displaced the former as the reigning imperial city. Formal separation was many centuries away, but by the year 600 the distance between Rome and Constantinople was obvious.

One of the institutions that continued to cut across the frontiers of the various churches was asceticism. Early in the fourth century a new organized form emerged from the deserts of Egypt to become a major vehicle of mission and renewal for churches throughout the world. The key element in the success of this new form of asceticism (or monasticism, as it was now called) was a community rule that was written by an Egyptian named Pachomius. A number of influential leaders from across the Christian world visited the monasteries of Egypt and adapted the community rule in versions of their own. Monasticism carried on the spiritual heritage of self-sacrifice and extreme conviction that the martyrs had often exemplified. It was also the major vehicle for the missionary expansion of Christianity beyond the borders of its existing churches. With the help of such rules, a new form of Christian life in community opened up.

Women during the centuries covered in this section found in monasticism a degree of social freedom that allowed them to exercise gifts of ministry and spirituality which might otherwise have gone unexpressed. Most of the women whose names are known to us from the Christian movement of the fourth through the sixth centuries, such as Melania the Younger, Eustochium, Olympias, or

Macrina, had taken vows of asceticism. They ranged from peasants living in Syria and Egypt to members of the upper classes of Rome and Constantinople. Their number included young girls on the verge of marriage at the age of twelve or thirteen, as well as widows and grandmothers who had already raised families. More than a few were married when they felt the call to monastic life and together with their husbands decided to embrace a life of continence. Historian Gillian Cloke calls the women ascetics of this period practitioners of "high-profile piety" and "the stars of their contemporary Christian stage no less than the men."[1] More will be said in the pages that follow concerning the women and men who populated the ranks of the monastics.

---

[1] Gillian Cloke, *This Female Man of God: Women and Spiritual Power in the Patristic Age, AD 350-450* (London: Routledge, 1995), 4.

14

The Conversion of Constantine and the Making of an Imperial Church

The last decade of the third century found the Roman empire facing a series of external and internal crises. Constant warfare with Persia to the east was costly and kept the border region in turmoil. At the same time the Germanic tribes to the north occupied an increasing amount of the Roman emperor's military resources and attention. Forced to migrate under the pressure of tribes even further to their east and drawn by reports of the wealth of Roman civilization, groups of these Germanic peoples were now regularly settling within Roman territorial lands and raiding the cities to their south. Faced with a dwindling number of citizens willing to enter the military, Roman emperors had turned to these same Germanic peoples to hire the troops that were needed to fight Rome's wars. Internally, the growing administrative complexity of the imperial government added to the increasingly heavy burden of taxation made for a combustible social mixture. Wave after wave of new faiths, including Manichaeism, Mithraism, and Christianity, were sweeping the Roman world, an indication that the older order of gods in the empire was no longer able to inspire widespread trust or devotion.

Among these new faiths strong organizational structure along with extensive outreach and relief programs gave Christian churches a distinct advantage in winning new converts. Following each wave of persecution through the third century, membership roles in the churches took a dramatic leap forward. Educated members of the Roman upper classes, especially women, were becoming Christians in greater numbers, bringing with them their wealth and a new attitude of social respectability. By the beginning of the fourth century, churches were poised to provide the most extensive social network available across the Roman empire.

This was the situation into which Diocletian stepped as emperor at the end of the third century. In response to the military, administrative, and religious problems that he faced, he decided in 286 to divide the rule of the empire by appointing Maximian to be the emperor (augustus) in the West. Several years later each emperor appointed a subordinate who was expected to succeed to the office of emperor. The entire empire was divided into four governing regions, ruled by a tetrarchy ("rule of four"). Initially Diocletian and his three imperial associates

Constantine the Great, bust from Constantinople, 4th century. Now in Naridni Muzej, Belgrade. Reproduced with permission of Giaraudon/Art Resource, New York City.

paid little attention to the growing Christian presence throughout the empire. But as reorganization progressed, the danger Christians posed in refusing to honor the Roman gods could not be overlooked. The first wave of a new persecution was launched in 303. The reasons were the same as before: Christians disrupted the unity of the empire by refusing to participate in its imperial religion; they posed a threat to the empire by refusing devotion to the gods who supposedly looked after Rome's well-being. At first only the destruction of churches and burning of scriptures were ordered. Then in 304 all citizens were ordered to sacrifice to the Roman gods on pain of death. It was a final attempt to force Christians to renounce their belief, and at least to impede, if not stamp out, the growth of their insidious atheism. In Gaul, Constantius who had ruled as one of the four, died in 306. His army immediately made his son, Constantine, emperor in the West.

By 306 the tetrarchy had proven to be an unstable arrangement, yet for six more years Constantine shared power within it as caesar over Spain, Britain, and Gaul. Persecution of Christians had again failed to curtail the growth of the movement, leading three of the members of the tetrarchy (Constantine among them) in 311 to agree to relax restrictions against the religion. The following year Constantine marched against Maxentius, who was ruler of Italy and North Africa. In October of 312, on the verge of what was undoubtedly to be the decisive battle of his campaign, the advancing emperor received a vision outside the city of Rome. According to later reports, Constantine saw a sign in the sky, the first two letters of the name Christ *(chi-rho)*. Accompanying the sign was a voice that said, "In this, conquer." Emboldened by this omen, and with the *chi-rho* symbol emblazoned on the shields of his soldiers, Constantine and his army swept away the stronger forces of his imperial rival. They took the city of Rome, and Constantine was left sole ruler of the western region of the empire.

Constantine's vision before the battle in 312 was portrayed by his biographer, the church historian Eusebius, as if it were a conversion. Most likely it was not, at least if by conversion one means a change in allegiance from belief in other gods to Christian belief in God. There is little evidence Constantine worshiped other gods prior to 312, but there is equally little evidence that he worshiped Christ publicly. By his own account he came over the course of many years to grow in his understanding of both Christian morality and truth. Decisive in this regard seems to have been his encounter with Christians a decade earlier during the time of the persecution and not his vision on the eve of the battle of 312. What was most significant in the latter was the identification of the Almighty God whom Christians worshiped with support of an imperial army.

A year later Constantine joined forces with Licinius, the emperor in the east, to form an alliance that was to last for more than a decade. Together they issued in 313 a proclamation known as the Edict of Milan, guaranteeing freedom of religious practice in lands under their rule. The edict even restored to Christians their confiscated properties and places of worship, providing compensation for those that had been sold. A transition from being an illegal faith to a national religion was under way. Christian clergy in the western regions under Constantine's rule began to receive special benefits from the imperial treasury. Constantine himself spoke of being a servant of God. Yet publicly he continued to mix Christian piety with devotion to the high solar deity, the Invincible Sun, which had become popular with the emperors of the previous century. When he declared in 321 that Sunday be set apart as a special day of worship, it is not clear whether it was the Invincible Sun or Jesus Christ whom he intended to honor.

Civil war erupted in 324 between the two emperors. The defeat and execution of Licinius left Constantine as sole inhabitant of the imperial throne. That same year he declared his unreserved allegiance to Christ and Christianity. Determining the authenticity of his conversion—or whether his embrace of Christian faith was merely a pragmatic ploy to use the unifying forces the Christian churches offered him throughout the Roman empire—continues to be a matter of historical debate today. On the one hand, there is no doubt that the emperor had come to believe that the Christian God was the one who granted him military victory and that this God ought to be worshiped throughout the world. On the other hand, the same emperor had to accommodate the devotion of the Roman gods, if only for political purposes.

A mixture of authentic belief and pragmatic consideration can be seen at work in the emperor's decision to move the capital of the empire to the East in 330. In 326 he made his last trip to Rome to participate in the traditional imperial sacrifices. The city's senatorial class was resistant to his Christian sympathies and determined to assert its devotion to the ancient gods. In response, Constantine turned his attention toward building a new capital, one that would reflect the glories of the Christian faith, free from the hold of the older Roman aristocracy and its religion. He also sought a site that could be easily defended and was closer to the eastern border of the empire to facilitate administrative control. The place he selected was the town of Byzantium, strategically located on the isthmus between the Black Sea and the Aegean Sea.

Within a few years this small town on the Bosporus was being transformed into one of the richest and most powerful cities on earth. Constantinople (its new name) was dedicated as the eastern capital in 330. Imbued with Christian symbols, it was equally a lasting tribute to its founder's imperial splendor. Members of the senatorial class, along with artisans and merchants, were invited to join him in the new Christian capital in the East. Large amounts of wealth began to pour into the city. The older temples dedicated to traditional gods were allowed for a time to remain, but new Christian churches were rapidly constructed throughout its neighborhoods. A great cathedral, later called Hagia Sophia, was begun (the edifice was destroyed and rebuilt in the sixth century). In every way the New Rome, complete with its new mint for coins, a new Senate, and even a new Roman population, was to be a new Christian city.

The effects of the emperor's tolerance and then support of Christianity were far-ranging. Christians who had for more than two centuries been a people without a homeland were suddenly a landed race. Their religion was identified as the favored imperial faith, their clergy for the first time exempt from imperial taxes. The army incorporated the emperor's Christian symbol on their shields, and the emperor's coins bore the name of Christ. The day that Christians regularly gathered for the eucharist to celebrate the resurrection, previously a regular workday in the Roman world, became a legal day of rest throughout the empire.

Church properties were no longer subject to imperial seizure without warning; instead, new churches were built with imperial monies. For at least a generation Christians had been meeting for worship in separate buildings, usually houses adapted to their purposes. Now they began taking over temples that had previously been used for worship of other gods. In Constantinople not only the churches but other public buildings and monuments were decorated with Christian symbols, reflecting the religion's new status in the empire. New building projects were undertaken in other cities of the empire, many under the patronage of Helena, Constantine's mother. Her pilgrimage to Jerusalem and Bethlehem in 326 opened the door for others to follow in this new form of popular piety. Helena oversaw the construction of churches and pilgrim stations throughout the Holy Land. Her supposed discovery of the wood of the true cross of Jesus provided Christians with one of their most important relics of antiquity.

As churches became more visible and accepted in the civil arena, they absorbed more influences from the world around them. Periodic persecution and martyrdom had played a significant role in attracting many to the Christian faith, but they had also helped maintain a distinctive Christian identity that set Christians apart from those around them. Now Christian identity seemed to require less of a break with previous lifestyles and even religious practices than it had once demanded. We begin to see church leaders addressing questions about Christians consulting soothsayers and local healers for problems they were facing, for instance. Amulets that were sold by local magicians to ward off evil spirits were noted as being popular among some of the Christians in various cities. Prior to the year 300 there had been no consensus among Christians concerning the date on which to celebrate the birth of Jesus Christ. Some argued for a spring date, but others suggested December 25. That latter date was the day celebrated in honor of the Invincible Sun, who had grown in imperial favor through the third century. Through the course of the fourth century most Christians came to accept December 25 as the celebration of the birth of Jesus, integrating elements of this solar monotheism with Christianity.

Imperial embrace brought with it new forms of imperial domination. Episcopal appointments in major sees now came under the emperor's scrutiny. Bishops who found themselves recipients of imperial funds were also burdened with new political responsibilities. One of their number, Hosius of Cordova, from Spain, was among the emperor's closest advisors. For the first time a Christian bishop was called upon to advise an emperor whose primary vocation involved waging war, drawing both bishop and the wider community of church leadership more deeply into the ambiguities of political life in the empire. The trend toward integration of church and state, and with it the pattern of imperial domination of church affairs, continued after Constantine's death in 337 with his sons who succeeded him on the throne.

Chief among Constantine's concerns was the unity of the Christian churches in his realm. Christians at the beginning of the fourth century were liturgically and theologically a relatively diverse lot. If their faith was to serve as the unifying religion of the empire, Constantine realized, Christianity had to be a unified system. The emperor himself did not appear to be strongly committed to any particular theological side regarding the various doctrinal disputes of his day. He was eager that united prayers be said to God on his behalf, believing that God would not crown him with victories if the churches were rent by schism. His concerns had a realistic political edge to them as well. Constantine recognized the structural strength provided by the leadership of bishops throughout his realm and the unifying potential of Christian belief among the disparate subjects of his empire. He sought to strengthen these aspects by securing among the churches a unified statement of doctrine and a unified practice of worship.

For better or worse, this unity eluded Constantine in his own day. Two major controversies in particular, which will be explored in detail in the following chapters, rent the Christian fabric in churches of the Roman world. The fact that in both of them the churches in Africa figured prominently suggests they had as much to do with growing cultural and political tensions around the Mediterranean as they did with theological differences. They also point toward the ambiguities experienced in Christianity's newly found imperial identity. The first of these struggles, usually referred to as the Donatist controversy, dragged on for several centuries until the coming of Islam, which put an end to an effective Christian presence in Roman North Africa. The second, known as the Arian controversy, led directly to the convening of the Council of Nicaea in 325, a gathering that easily numbers among the most important events in Christian history.

Looking back on events toward the end of the emperor's life, Constantine's contemporary, the church historian Eusebius, called the emperor the representative of the divine Word of God on earth. Other Christians from the period, such as the Donatists in North Africa, whom we shall see in the next chapter experienced the brunt of imperial power, perceived things otherwise. As a person, Constantine was capable of great acts of devotion, but he was also capable of arranging the execution of his son, Crispa, and his wife, Fausta, on questionable charges. The emperor delayed his own baptism until he was on his deathbed in 337, a practice still common in the fourth century to avoid the consequences of post-baptismal sins. He was buried in Constantinople in the church of the Twelve Apostles, reportedly joining them as the thirteenth. Yet after his death the Roman Senate deified him, an indication of the surviving power of the older imperial cult in which he still figured. There is no doubt that Constantine was increasingly committed in his own lifetime to bringing about a Christian revolution within the Roman empire. Whether such a revolution could ever be realized in history remains debatable.

15

Donatists and Catholics

A Struggle over Holiness and Unity in Roman North Africa

The changes in imperial policies toward the Christian religion looked to many in the churches in the Mediterranean to have God's hand at work in them. The emperor's new appreciation for their faith represented nothing short of the triumph of the message of Jesus Christ. Yet not all Christians saw it this way. In Roman North Africa a major fault line opened up in the fourth century. Believers were separated into two parties that were violently opposed. At the heart of the controversy lay two competing fundamental commitments. Both had long been characteristic of Christianity in the region, but in the changed context of the fourth century they became mutually exclusive.

On the one side were those who welcomed the change in status of Christianity in the Roman world. Belonging to a legalized religion required a certain amount of pastoral and theological adjustment, but they were willing to make it. Previously persecution and martyrdom had played a prominent role in shaping Christian identity in Roman North Africa. Becoming a Christian and opposing the imperial authorities had, from the earliest recorded days of the movement there, been virtually synonymous. Now church leaders were being invited to cooperate with the same authorities who only a few brief years before had been sending them off to the arenas to die. At the same time members of the clergy found themselves dealing with the question of how to respond to those whose Christian commitment during the former persecution had proven to be weak. For some, a new pastoral approach was needed, one that was not shaped exclusively by the memory of martyrdom. The church was now able to move beyond the divisiveness past persecutions had introduced. A new day had come, and with it the opportunity to build a unified Christian church throughout the Roman world.

On the other side were members of a dissenting faction who were uneasy over any arrangement with the authorities, who had only recently been persecuting the movement. Church leaders on this side were not willing to abandon their memories of martyrdom and the rigorous Christian identity that it fostered. Nor

166

were they willing to forget the deeds of other Christians who, in their eyes, had betrayed the gospel by cooperating with government authorities during the persecution. They were intent upon vigorously searching out and uncovering incidents of such betrayal, especially on the part of clergy and bishops, to the point of accepting allegations regarding such deeds. For them, the holiness of the church was at stake, for the Holy Spirit could not be passed on through the ministry of those who had committed the sin of betraying Jesus Christ.

The conflict between these two parties in North Africa broke into open separation early in the fourth century. Two different churches were formed, Catholic and Donatist. Over the course of several centuries they lived side by side, sometimes fought in open riots against one another, and eventually came to accept one another's presence to the point of limited mutual accommodation. The conflict between them was never resolved, however; only the coming of Islam at the end of the seventh century and the eventual eclipse of Christian churches in the region brought an end to the controversy.

The churches in Roman North Africa at the beginning of the fourth century were numerically strong. With some seven hundred bishops and numerous presbyters and deacons, they were clearly a political presence no matter what their legal status might have been. These churches had also suffered greatly during previous periods of persecution and had a well-preserved memory of martyrdom. For many, the martyrs ranked even higher than bishops in their spiritual authority within the church. Martyrs were believed to be able to intercede with God in a special way on behalf of those still on earth. The places of their deaths were carefully remembered, and the dates of their deaths were commemorated in the church. The sufferings of martyrs and confessors (those who suffered for the faith without dying) were embraced as a cleansing fire in the rigorous pursuit of Christian discipleship. From this perspective it is easy to see why the legalization of the Christian religion in the Roman empire, and the accompanying influx of new members who did not necessarily share such commitments to suffering through persecution, did not appear to all as a positive development.

Diocletian's persecution had begun in 303. At first it was directed mainly against the clergy, who were ordered to hand over scriptures and liturgical books from their church libraries. Only later were Christians ordered to offer sacrifices to the imperial gods or face dire consequences. The actual number of martyrs was still relatively small. More disruptive for the churches was the destruction of Christian books. In North Africa, turning over scriptures to imperial authorities was regarded by many as being a heinous offense, as bad as offering sacrifice or pouring libation to the imperial gods. Christian scriptures were considered extremely holy. To many they were literally another form of the incarnation of the Word. Those who handed them over to be burned were *traditores* (ones "handing over," traitors) who betrayed Christ by their deeds. Even those who turned in liturgical books other than scriptures or handed over texts regarded as heretical were saddled by rigorists with the label of traitors. Allegations continued to circulate even after the persecution had ended, as churches sought to deal with charges of *traditor* being leveled against members of the clergy.

The controversy became a crisis in 311 in Carthage with the election of a new bishop named Caecilian. It had long been the tradition in North Africa for the bishops of Numidia to participate in the consecration of the senior bishop of Carthage, but Caecilian was consecrated without them being present. Furthermore, in the eyes of many he had a questionable past. Seven years before, during the Great Persecution, when he was still a deacon, Caecilian had prevented members of the family of a group of imprisoned Christians from bringing food to their relatives (Roman jails did not include meals, so without an outside source for meals prisoners starved to death). The last straw for some was that one of the bishops who participated in Caecilian's ordination, Felix of Aptunga, was rumored to be a *traditor*.

The Numidian bishops took action. In a council of their own in 312 they condemned Caecilian on grounds of his actions seven years before, during the Great Persecution. Furthermore, they declared, his ordination was invalid because a bishop who was known (to them at least) to be a *traditor* had participated. They elected one of their own named Majorinus to the office of senior bishop of Carthage instead. Majorinus was succeeded shortly thereafter by Donatus, a popular presbyter whose name came to be associated with the movement he led. Carthage now had two senior bishops, and churches throughout the region were quickly called upon to identify themselves with one or the other. Before long all of Roman North Africa was embroiled in the conflict.

The Donatists rested their case on the question of the validity of an ordination in which a *traditor* was involved. They claimed to be following Cyprian on this point, arguing that the Holy Spirit was only passed on within the One Holy Church, and that there was no salvation for Christians who wandered outside it. Since bishops who were *traditores* were no longer part of this true church, they could not pass on the Holy Spirit through laying on of hands. Those in whose ordination such bishops had participated could not have received the Holy Spirit, for the presence of a *traditor* rendered the ordination invalid. Any sacraments performed by a bishop or clergy whose ordination included a *traditor* were likewise regarded as invalid. The presence of a single *traditor* in the line of episcopal succession invalidated the entire line of ordinations that followed. Any sacrament performed by clergy whose ordination was thus invalidated was itself also invalid. Since the one performing the sacrament did not have the Holy Spirit, the sacraments he performed were without spiritual validity. For the Donatists, the spiritual holiness of the church thus required the removal of all *traditores* and those whom they had ordained. There could be no compromise on this point.

In 313, a short six months after the emperor had legalized Christianity, the Donatists brought their case against Caecilian before Constantine for judgment. Constantine, in turn, handed the matter over to Miltiades, bishop of Rome, for a decision. Miltiades did what bishops had long been accustomed to doing to settle disputes among their churches: he convened a local council of bishops. That gathering decided in favor of Caecilian, but the Donatists objected that one of the bishops who had ordained Miltiades was suspected of being a *traditor* and thus the bishop of Rome himself was suspect. A second council with a larger number of participants was ordered by the emperor to convene a year later, this time at Arles in Gaul. It was the first such event to have imperial representatives.

Once again the decision was in favor of Caecilian. Those churches and bishops who were in communion with him were granted official recognition, bringing with it political benefits and substantial financial support from the imperial treasury. At the same time those churches that followed Donatus were allowed to continue to ordain bishops and presbyters and to operate churches outside official imperial sanction. The de facto compromise was in part a result of the popular support the Donatist party had throughout North Africa. Yet the emperor was not about to acknowledge the validity of their case. A year later Felix of Aptunga was found innocent of the charges against him, although many Donatists continued to believe otherwise.

Constantine's primary concern throughout the course of these events was for the unity of the religion that he hoped would bind the subjects of his empire together. This, plus the political need for maintaining peace in the region, led him directly into the ecclesiastical fray. The unity and peace of the church were also concerns for the majority of bishops throughout the Mediterranean world. Previously they had carried on their deliberations and settled disputes through local and regional conciliar meetings. From the network of their communications a consensus of at least a majority among the church leaders had usually emerged. The only means bishops had to enforce church discipline or maintain church teaching prior to 315 was excommunication. To this traditional instrument Constantine now added a new one: imperial edicts backed by troops. In 317 the emperor ordered the Donatists to be suppressed for disturbing the peace. Their properties were to be confiscated and their leaders arrested and sent into exile. It was a decisive moment: for the first time in the history of the Christian movement, a Christian government used violent force to try to quell a dissenting Christian party.

Several years of confiscations, harassment, and violence ensued, to little avail. Facing the entrenched determination and growing numbers of Donatist believers (by now there were some 250 Donatist bishops in North Africa), the emperor abandoned his policy of use of force in 321. An uneasy state of coexistence between the two sides set in. Neither party gave up its polemic against the other. Donatists were judged schismatics for breaking the unity of the church, while Catholics were regarded as practicing invalid sacraments because of the presence of *traditores* in their episcopal succession. For a time both sides simply adjusted to living next door to a hostile Christian neighbor.

One of the provisions agreed to in the compromise of 314 and accepted after 321 was that when the office of the senior bishop in any city in the region became vacant, the bishop next in line in episcopal seniority would assume the post, whether he was a Donatist or Catholic. In 346 Donatus himself came up for the post of senior bishop in Carthage, as he was next in line in seniority. But Constans, Constantine's son, who was now emperor in the West, refused to recognize Donatus. He sent a delegation to North Africa instead to review the situation. The following year Constans ordered the churches to unify under the newly consecrated Catholic

Crescentia, a 5th century child from Tabarka, North Africa, died shortly after baptism. Note that she appears to be wearing the vestments of a lector or deacon. Bardo Museum, Tunis. Photo by Robin M. Jensen. Reproduced with her permission.

bishop, Gratus, threatening the followers of Donatus with torture and exile if they refused. They did, and once again persecution broke out. More martyrdoms followed, and this time Donatus himself was exiled.

After several years it was clear that the emperor's policy had once again failed to extinguish the resistance, leaving him no choice but to relax the persecution. The two churches returned to their uneasy truce. Persecution had only succeeded in solidifying the Donatist resolve to resist the Catholics, who identified themselves with a persecuting state, while the Catholic party repeatedly condemned the schismatics who had separated themselves from the church. Despite the hostility, however, the two parties remained relatively close in a number of ways. Both parties used Latin as their ecclesiastical language, although the Donatists were more strongly represented in the countryside, where Punic was still spoken in everyday life. The two parties ordained clergy who presided over nearly identical liturgies and performed nearly identical sacraments. Their church buildings and vestments were the same; archeologists and scholars still cannot distinguish the ruins of their churches from one another in the region. Both parties looked back to the heritage of Cyprian, Tertullian, and Felicitas and Perpetua. Only one issue clearly separated them, the validity of ordinations (and therefore of sacraments) performed by clergy who were ordained by *traditores*.

Institutionally this led to two separate churches after 311. Theologically it translated into differing positions regarding the sacraments. Donatists rejected the validity of the baptism of anyone who received the sacrament in a church that had *traditores* in its line of bishops and required that an individual undergo rebaptism upon entering what they claimed was the one true church. They believed that a bishop whose ordination was invalid could not celebrate a valid eucharist in which the Holy Spirit was truly imparted. Catholics, on the other hand, rejected those who would separate themselves from the universal church. Catholics did not reject the validity of the Donatist sacraments, only their effectiveness. This was why a former Donatist joining a Catholic group was not required to undergo rebaptism, only a penitential ritual.

From time to time throughout the rest of the fourth century the Donatist controversy flared up into full-fledged conflict, with both sides periodically resorting to violence. During the second half of the century a radical group called the Circumcellions, who often sympathized with Donatists, emerged. They were mainly drawn from among rural workers and operated in the countryside, carrying out assaults against prominent landowners and wealthy members of the clergy (usually Catholic clergy but sometimes wealthy Donatist clergy as well). The Circumcellions were fanatical in their devotion to the North African martyrs, to the point of living in or around their local shrines. On the other side, Catholic theologians such as Augustine of Hippo (to whom we will return below) also justified the use of force against heretics and schismatics for the sake of the gospel. Government decrees against Donatists allowed Catholics to confiscate property or disrupt Donatist gatherings for worship. The struggle colored daily life for people in cities and towns across North Africa. In one city in North Africa, Donatist bakers at times refused to sell bread to Catholics.

Early in the fifth century another period of intense persecution opened against the Donatists. But in 429 an army of Germanic invaders known as Vandals entered North Africa from Spain. Over the course of the next decade, they overran the entire region, taking Hippo in 431 and Carthage in 439. The Vandals, who were followers of Arian Christianity (which will be explored in the following chapter), established an independent kingdom that lasted for more than a century before the eastern Roman emperor regained control of the region in 534. Under Vandal rule Donatist and Catholic churches alike were destroyed. Members of the clergy of both parties were sent into exile to work at forced labor, and the ministry of both churches was severely impaired. In the wake of the havoc the Vandals created, Donatists and Catholics moderated their attitude toward one another; they now had a common enemy in the Arian Christian Vandals. Following the restoration of Constantinople's control of the region, Catholics began allowing Donatist priests to serve in their churches, while Donatists allowed Catholic bishops to participate in their ordinations.

Political and economic conditions in Roman North Africa deteriorated even further under Constantinople's rule in the last decades of the sixth century. The years following the Vandal rule witnessed an increase in the military raids launched by non-Christian tribes living to the south, a situation similar to the waves of tribal invasion that were continuing in the Roman provinces to the north during this period. Significant sections of the North African countryside had passed into local tribal rule by the middle of the seventh century. Where Constantinople's hold was secure, the imperial government was often seen as being both remote and oppressive. A sizable number of Roman North Africans looked upon the Greek emperor and his mercenaries as a foreign occupation force.

By the time a Muslim army captured Carthage in 698, there were many in the region who were ready to accept the new rulers as liberators. Not only were these new Muslim rulers the enemy of the Roman government in Constantinople, but the moral rigor of their Islamic faith resonated with many of the traditional values of the Donatist party. To the non-Christian tribes (whom the Muslims called *Berbers*, or Barbarians) the new rulers offered full equality and participation in government as the reward for conversion to Islam. The departure of many Catholic members of the upper classes as refugees across the Mediterranean further drained the region of its Christian members. In North Africa, Christianity experienced a rapid decline under Islam, more severe perhaps than in any other place in the world. Within a century Christian churches had all but disappeared from this region where for nearly five hundred years they had flourished. Occasional references to bishops or churches linger in Roman Christian literature as late as the eleventh century, but for the most part Christianity had disappeared.

The Donatist-Catholic controversy of the fourth through sixth centuries offered competing perspectives on the relationship between Christian faith and political reality. In part it was an expression of the region's diverse cultural values, and in part it reflected the social-political conditions in Roman North Africa. Since Christianity's earliest days Christians had embraced an ethic of resistance and imperial opposition. The Donatists were merely continuing this tradition. As historian Maureen A. Tilley notes, "The attitude of the Catholic Church to the Roman Empire was modified after 312, while the Donatists retained the antithesis preached by Tertullian and Cyprian."[2]

Catholics in Roman North Africa did not abandon the tradition of martyrdom, but they accepted that the church is a community of wheat and tares. Both parties acknowledged that there were sinners in the church, but the Donatists maintained a strong eschatological expectation of impending divine judgment that required an immediate purification of the church. The Catholic party, on the other hand, embraced a more gradual eschatology that deferred such judgment until the end of time in an unspecified future. Catholic leaders believed the presence of the tares did not diminish the grace present in the church and its sacraments. Sacraments administered by unworthy priests retained their validity, argued Augustine. His was the point of view that came to be embraced by the majority of Christians throughout the world.

---

[2] Maureen A. Tilley, trans., *Donatist Martyr Stories: The Church in Conflict in Roman North Africa* (Liverpool: Liverpool University Press, 1996), xiii.

16

The Arian-Nicene Controversy and the Making of Orthodoxy

Few events in the history of Christianity have had the lasting impact of the council that gathered in Nicaea, Asia Minor, in 325. The Nicene Creed that is commonly associated with the council continues to be recited by hundreds of millions of Christians today. Its words are considered by many to be the touchstone of the orthodox Christian doctrine of God. To someone who was living in the fourth century, however, the triumph of Nicaea was anything but certain. For much of the century the position taken by the majority of bishops at the council remained out of favor with the imperial household. Only in the last decades of the century did the faith of Nicaea gain imperial support, although by then it had come to be embraced by the majority of churches throughout the world. The Nicene Creed remains today the closest thing the Christian movement has to offer in the way of a universal confession of its faith.

The Council of Nicaea and the Nicene faith

The immediate road to Nicaea began in Alexandria early in the fourth century. By 300 Egypt had been registering significant growth in its Christian population, both in the cities and among the rural population. Its churches were drawing from all levels of society. A major reason for the attraction was no doubt the inherent power of the Christian message of salvation. By the end of the third century the Christian movement had also taken on nationalist overtones in Egypt as well. Egypt was a country under Roman domination, and Christianity was a religion opposed to the imperial cult. There was a Christian element associated with resistance to the Roman emperor Diocletian in the early days of the fourth century similar to the resistance among Christians in Roman North Africa. Like Roman North Africa, Egypt also boasted a party who opposed readmitting the lapsed.

In Egypt the rigorists were known as the Melitians, named after their leader, Melitius, bishop of Lycopolis. Melitius and his followers directed their verbal attacks against Peter, the senior bishop of Alexandria, whom they accused of

173

excessive leniency toward those who had fallen away during the persecution. Peter called a synod of the Egyptian bishops in 306, which deposed Melitius and the clergy who supported him. This did not prevent Melitius from continuing to ordain bishops and clergy, thus giving rise to a schism within the churches in Egypt. One of Melitius's earlier supporters, a layman by the name of Arius (c.260-336), switched sides during the controversy and joined the Catholic party. The year after Peter's martyrdom in 311, Arius was ordained a presbyter by Peter's successor in Alexandria.

Fresh controversy broke out in Alexandria in 318, this time with Arius at its center. Opposing him was Alexander, who was senior bishop of Alexandria from 313 to 328. The dispute started as a local one, but it was soon apparent that the issues at stake were far greater than simply a disagreement between a priest and his bishop. Theologically, the questions that were at the heart of the problem went back to Origen in the third century. That first great theologian of the Christian movement had spoken of the Son as being of the same essence or substance *(ousia)* as the Father, but he had also said that the Son was eternally begotten. For Origen, the cosmos itself could also be said to be eternal insofar as it was fashioned by God's eternal Word, the Logos. Few theologians after Origen spoke so readily of an eternal cosmos, although most continued to speak of the eternally begotten Son.

Emphasizing the distinction between Jesus Christ, the eternally begotten Son, and the Father seemed to some to run the risk of asserting the subordination of Jesus the Son to his Father. Toward the end of the third century Paul of Samosata, whose tenure as bishop of Antioch was marked by ethical scandals, went precisely in this direction in his teaching. Paul rejected the preexistence of Jesus as the Son of God, arguing instead that Jesus was adopted by God through the Logos. The Logos was the mode by which God was encountered in human history, but Jesus was only a human being. On the other side of the debate were those like Dionysius of Alexandria (d. c.265), a student of Origen and later senior bishop of Alexandria. Dionysius spoke about the distinctiveness of Father, Son, and Spirit in such a way that some suspected him of tritheism, a charge of which he was satisfactorily able to clear himself. Following his teacher, Origen, he held that in Jesus Christ the eternally begotten Son, God and humanity became one.

Such theological reflections were more than intellectual curiosities, for they cut to the very heart of Christian faith and practice. Christians worshiped Jesus Christ as God. They called upon him as Lord and Savior and in all respects entreated him as a divine figure. At the same time they affirmed in strongest terms the fundamental tenet of monotheism that was the inheritance of Israel and shared with Judaism. Was Jesus Christ, the Son of God and Logos, the same God who made heaven and earth? Some said yes and held that the one who was known as the Father became incarnate in the flesh and died on the cross, a position that was accused of violating the doctrine of divine transcendence. Others said yes but held that the eternal Logos who was divine needed to be distinguished from the human person named Jesus, a position that was accused of impiety toward Jesus Christ. Alternatively, was the Logos another divine person alongside God?

Some said yes but were accused of asserting two divine subjects (three when one took into account the Holy Spirit) and hence of being ditheists (or tritheists).

An alternative option to these various positions appears to have been suggested by a bishop from Antioch named Lucian, who was executed on account of his faith in the last wave of persecution in 312. Little is known to us of Lucian's teachings, other than that he sought to synthesize these lines of thought by regarding the Logos as subordinate to God. The position was made even more emphatically by his most famous student, Arius, who was ordained a presbyter in Alexandria the year Lucian was martyred. The position that Arius staked out resolved the intellectual problem by conceptualizing the Logos as a secondary god, or what the Platonists called a demiurge. The Logos was still conceived to be the divine agent of creation but was itself a created being. In this theological model the Logos stood as an intermediary between the divine nature and the created world, thereby providing a bridge between the two. Arius expressed these ideas in Alexandria early in the fourth century in sermons that even his detractors admitted were eloquent.

By the time Alexander became bishop of the city in 313, Arius was already teaching that the Logos was not eternal but was the firstborn of creation. God the Father alone was unbegotten and eternal, he said, and thus there was a time when the Son was not. This in turn meant that the Logos was capable of change, even if only in theory. For some five years there was little overt opposition to Arius's teaching; then there was an episode resulting in public confrontation with his bishop. Alexander had called together members of the clergy in the city in what appears to have been a regular session of continuing education. The topic of this particular session was the unity of the Trinity. In the course of the discussion, Arius took issue with Alexander's position as being modalist, arguing his own view that there was a time when the Son was not. Unfortunately for Arius, some from among his former colleagues, the Melitians, caught wind of the episode and publicly demanded that Alexander discipline him. Within a year the senior bishop called a synod that considered the matter and voted to condemn Arius, banishing him from the city.

Before the sentence could be executed, the popular presbyter took off for the city of Nicomedia, where the emperor Licinius had located his capital. Not coincidentally the bishop of Nicomedia, Eusebius (d. 342), was a fellow former student of Lucian who had only come to Nicomedia a year or so earlier and was proving to be an influential church leader. Eusebius took up Arius's cause against the Alexandrian bishops, and soon the entire eastern portion of the empire was embroiled in the controversy. Support for Arius's position came from church leaders in a number of cities, especially in Asia Minor and Palestine. Others sided with the synod of Alexandria in opposing what they considered to be Arius's heretical views.

News of the controversy reached the ears of Constantine shortly after he had assumed control of the entire Roman empire. As in the previous case concerning the Donatists, the emperor's first concern was for the unity of the churches whose beliefs he had recently legalized and was now promoting throughout the empire.

Constantine took the dispute among the bishops to be a serious political affair. The area where the controversy raged the fiercest was the region formerly under Licinius, whom he had defeated and executed in 324. Already the emperor had seen controversy divide the churches in North Africa. A united religion was especially important in his former rival's territories as Constantine attempted to consolidate his control over the region and to assure that united prayers would be offered to God on his behalf. To resolve the matter the emperor decided to convene a more general council.

That council opened late in the spring of 325 in Nicaea, a summer resort near the emperor's court in Nicomedia. Eusebius of Caesarea later reported that some 250 bishops attended, while others gave the number as 318. Arius, who was still a presbyter, was there to represent his own position. Also attending was a deacon from Alexandria named Athanasius (c.300-373), who was to become an important defender of the council's decisions. Sylvester, bishop of Rome, was not present but was represented by two presbyters. Other bishops came from Gaul, Spain, Africa, and Syria. Jacob of Nisibis was a participant, as well as one who was listed simply as John, bishop of India and Persia. The great majority of participants were from the Greek-speaking churches of Palestine, Asia Minor, and Greece, regions formerly under Licinius's rule. Constantine presided over the council's entire proceedings, supported by his personal advisor, bishop Hosius of Cordova from Spain.

From the beginning Arius's support at Nicaea was weak. Western churches had already embraced Tertullian's formulation of one God subsisting in three persons. Among the Greek-speaking churches there was a general tendency to regard the Logos as divine, without pushing for a more exact definition of what exactly this entailed. Antiochene theologians were used to distinguishing between the Logos and the humanity of Jesus in such a way that the question did not present itself as a direct problem to them. The Logos was not changed in the incarnation, nor did it suffer on the cross, they said. The belief that the Logos had joined itself to the flesh of Jesus in such a way that Jesus was God incarnate, the position taken by Bishop Alexander, had popular support among the Egyptian churches. Sensing perhaps the tenor of the gathering, Eusebius of Caesarea, one of Arius's moderate supporters, presented his own church's baptismal creed for review as an indication of his own orthodoxy, which was affirmed.

The council then turned its attention to formulating a standard that clearly rejected Arius's view while being acceptable to many of his episcopal supporters. A new statement of faith was introduced, apparently based upon another Palestinian baptismal creed. Constantine himself is credited with introducing into the discussion the word *homoousios* ("same substance") to define the relationship of the Son to the Father. Although it was not a biblical term, the word had been used in theological discussions as early as half a century before to describe the relationship among the Father, Son, and Spirit. At Nicaea it was accepted into the final version of the creed as being a faithful explication of apostolic teaching. The council affirmed the revised creed and condemned the Arian position. Arius and a handful of his supporters, including Eusebius of Nicomedia, the bishop of Constantine's eastern capital at the time, were sent into exile. Several further actions were taken to help unify the churches. Disciplinary procedures for dealing with the Melitians in Egypt were set out. The canon of New Testament books was affirmed, as was the common dating for Easter. Episcopal jurisdictions were decreed to coincide with imperial administrative boundaries throughout the empire, and uniform rules for the exercise of episcopal authority were established.

Almost immediately after the Council of Nicaea adjourned, Constantine began to have doubts about the exclusive position it had taken on the Son being *homoousios* with the Father. Within two years several who had been condemned and sent into exile, including Eusebius of Nicomedia, were invited to return to their ecclesiastical posts. The emperor pressed for reconciliation and restoration even of Arius. Support for a compromise on the Arian position was strong among the eastern churches and included such influential bishops as Eusebius of Nicomedia and Eusebius of Caesarea.

Meanwhile, in Alexandria episcopal leadership passed from Alexander upon his death in 328 to a younger associate who had been at Nicaea as a deacon. The name of Athanasius was soon to be known throughout the Christian world, due to his gifted theological mind as well as his several sojourns overseas while in exile from his office in Alexandria. Early in his administration Athanasius ran into difficulties with his dealings with the Melitians. Real trouble broke out, however, over his stance against Arianism. Athanasius adamantly opposed any compromise on the Arian position, leading an imperial synod called to hear the case to depose him and send him into exile in Gaul in 335. The following year, after further controversy and consideration, Constantine ordered the bishop of Constantinople to extend communion to Arius. The fateful day on which the event was to take place, Arius died on his way to the service.

For several decades the theological pendulum continued in the East to swing toward a moderate Arian position. Eusebius of Nicomedia, Arius's early defender, not only returned from exile to his episcopal see but became a close imperial advisor, replacing Hosius of Cordova in that role. It was Eusebius of Nicomedia who administered the rite of baptism to Constantine in 337 on the emperor's deathbed. Soon after his death, Constantine's three sons were proclaimed coemperors by the army, creating a political climate that once again was extremely unstable. Three years later their number was reduced to two. Constans, who favored the Nicene position, ruled in the West, while Constantius, who favored the Arian position, ruled in the East. The churches of the empire followed this division. Rome and most of the western bishops were decidedly pro-Nicene, while a majority of eastern bishops leaned toward some form of Arianism. Athanasius of Alexandria was the major eastern exception, and he was repeatedly sent into exile for his stubborn refusal to compromise his Nicene commitments.

The division was dramatically revealed in 342 when Constans attempted to call a council at Sardica, south of the Danube River. The western bishops, who included the aged Hosius of Cordova, outnumbered their eastern counterparts. Athanasius of Alexandria, although formally from the East, sided with the western bishops. Seeing the makeup of the council, the eastern bishops withdrew on the pretext of having to attend an imperial affair. The remaining pro-Nicene bishops went on to hold the council without their eastern counterparts, condemning in no uncertain terms the Arian position. The Council of Sardica also passed several administrative acts, one of which had a lasting impact upon the West. It ruled that a bishop deposed by an ecclesiastical council in the western Roman empire could appeal directly to the bishop of Rome, who could authorize a new hearing with additional judges. The decision was but one indication of the growing administrative authority of the bishop of Rome in the western region.

The western bishops lost their imperial support in 350 when Constans was overthrown by one of his officers. Three years later Constantius was the sole ruler of the Roman empire. He actively sought to impose his Arian views on all the churches of his realm. Athanasius was forced into hiding once again, this time to the south, where he lived with monks in the Egyptian desert. Hosius of Cordova at the age of 101 was forced to sign an Arian creed. Upon his return to Spain, where he ended his years, the aged bishop who had been Constantine's first ecclesiastical advisor was disowned and excommunicated by his colleagues for signing the emperor's creed.

The dominant position of the eastern bishops is best described as moderately Arian during these years. Arius's original assertion that there was a time when the Logos was not, appealed to those who were concerned to protect the integrity of the divine nature. Many of his supporters found the assertion that the Logos was the same substance as God both unscriptural and philosophically insupportable. If the Son was begotten and of the same nature as the Father, then the Father's nature had to have undergone change in the act of begetting. Yet God's nature was unchanging. Those who were considered modalists—or denied there were eternal trinitarian distinctions within God—could support the *homoousios* doctrine, thus rendering it even more suspect among many in the East. By the 350s many were willing to affirm the more moderate assertion that the Logos was of a similar substance *(homoiousios)* with the Father and fully united with the flesh of Jesus. Such a term allowed them to praise the exalted position of Jesus Christ in relation to the rest of creation and maintain the unchanging nature of the Father without explicitly affirming the subordination of the Son.

Athanasius, on the other hand, provided an articulate defense of the cause of Nicene orthodoxy. In defense of the *homoousios*, he noted that he would have preferred to use biblical terms alone to denote his position, but that such terms lacked the necessary precision to defend what appeared to him to be the biblical truth that the Son and the Father were one. *Homoousios*, he explained, meant there was a sharing of attributes among the Father, Son and Spirit. For Athanasius, the salvation of humankind was possible only if God was immediately involved in the historical person of Jesus Christ. The logic was simple and compelling: any mediator of salvation who was part of creation would itself require a mediator between creator and creation. Ultimately salvation could be won, said Athanasius, only if God were the direct mediator of salvation, which is the heart of the Christian proclamation that the Logos is God and became incarnate in Jesus, son of Mary.

The dispute between these two Christian parties did little to slow the advance of Christianization in the Roman empire. In 341 the last local shrines were closed in Italy and the traditional sacrifices to other gods offered in Rome brought to an end. Constantius increased the pressure on Christianity's rivals by closing several schools of philosophy and sponsoring the building of more churches. Even traditional forms of magic or divination were outlawed, although they continued to be practiced in secret. At the beginning of the century fewer than one in twenty persons in the Roman world was a Christian, but by the end of Constantius's reign almost one in two was a member of a church. The transformation had been rapid, although the cost of imperial domination of the churches would often prove to be high.

The conversion of the Goths

Around the year 340, Eusebius of Nicomedia performed an ordination that was to have lasting impact upon the development of Christianity among the Germanic people in the north. That year the Arian bishop of Nicomedia consecrated Ulfilas (or Wulfila) (c.311–c.383), a native of the former Roman province of Dacia to the north of the Danube River, to serve as bishop to Christians in the Gothic lands. The Goths were a Germanic people who had originally migrated from the East. A century earlier they had invaded Asia Minor, ransacking cities all the way to the Mediterranean coast and carrying off a number of Christian captives as slaves before ending their incursion and settling in the region of Dacia. There they established an independent kingdom in land that had formerly been a Roman province. A combination of diplomatic negotiations and intermarriage had by the fourth century begun to ease the Goths into the circle of Roman cultural life. One of the participants identified at the Council of Nicaea was Theophilus of Gothia, which suggests there was a formed Christian community among at least some of the Goths by 325.

Ulfilas was most likely of mixed Gothic and Greek descent. He had been sent to Constantinople as an emissary from the Goths, but he returned as a pastor to the Christians. For the next seven years he served in Dacia, until a hostile ruler forced him with a small band of other Christians to cross back south of the Danube onto Roman soil, in what is modern Bulgaria. Seeking to provide for the pastoral needs of the Gothic people, he then undertook the project that became his most important and lasting contribution to Christian mission: a translation of the scriptures into the Gothic tongue. To do so Ulfilas first had to render the Gothic language into written form, literally creating the script. Using this he then translated the entire Christian Bible into Gothic (except the Old Testament books of Kings, which he judged to be too militaristic and thus liable to incite the warring Goths to further violence). Not only did this translation give the Gothic people access to the gospel, but it affirmed their entry into the literate world of Mediterranean civilization. With the translation of the scriptures, Christianity quickly spread among the Goths, and from them to other Germanic tribes.

Within a matter of several decades the Goths had converted en masse to Christianity. Unfortunately, little is known of the process through which this happened. We know that the Christian faith also spread quickly to other Germanic tribes on the northern Roman frontier, for within a matter of decades they too were expressing their commitments to Christian faith. By the year 400 the Vandals, Lombards, and others had all adopted Christianity as their tribal religion, abandoning the worship of their older ancestral deities and joining the ranks of Arian believers. The process remains almost entirely invisible to us historically. Other than Ulfilas, we know the names of virtually none of the bishops or missionaries who spread the gospel among them. Yet when these tribes show up in the Roman historical records, they are Christians.

Among the Goths, Vandals, and other Germanic peoples, mass conversion was facilitated by their sense of tribal solidarity and identity. The tribe was one people with one religion. In the urban contexts of the Mediterranean and Persian worlds, converts had generally entered the church as individuals and families who broke with their existing religious communities. There was precedent for the adoption of Christianity as a national religion, first in Armenia and then in the Roman empire, although in the case of the latter, official recognition came only after the church had attained a sizable number of followers. In the fourth and fifth centuries we encounter for the first time an entire cultural-linguistic community unit, a tribe, converting as a whole.

The form of Christianity that Ulfilas introduced among the Goths, and which thus spread to other tribes, was Arian. The uniformly Arian character of Gothic and Vandal Christianity was no doubt a reflection of the tribal solidarity that discouraged parties and divisions. Yet there is also evidence that the Arian orientation of the Goths, Vandals, and others was not entirely arbitrary or accidental. For one thing, the Arian identification of Jesus Christ as the firstborn of creation and an intermediary between God the Father and the rest of the human family appears to have fit comfortably within the traditional tribal framework of an exalted warrior-king. Some have argued that the Arians' conception of the Logos allowed them to accommodate other cultural forms of religion more easily. In addition, many of those who were converting to the Arian form of the Christian faith were doing so at the same time that they were moving into the western Roman provinces, sacking Roman cities, and eventually establishing new independent kingdoms within the domains of the older Roman empire. In the western provinces of the empire in particular their Arianism carried a counter-imperial Christian identity over against the dominant Catholic orientation of the Latin-speaking churches.

This is not to say that the Goths were noticeably less Christian than their Catholic neighbors, for they were not. In prayer and worship little separated Arian Goths from Nicene Catholics. The Arian eucharist was virtually identical to that of Catholics, save for their doxology. Arians prayed "to the Father, through the Son, in the Holy Spirit" rather than "to the Father, and the Son, and the Holy Spirit." We will return to the history of the Arian Goths in the West in later chapters. Eventually they settled in Spain, where they established an independent kingdom and gained significant control over much of the western empire. Several centuries were to pass before the particularities of their distinct tribal identity began to dissipate. With it went their commitment to a separate form of Christianity as well.

Julian and the last gasp of the old order

In the eastern Mediterranean world in 361 both Arians and Nicenes found themselves confronted with a new challenge. That year saw Constantine's nephew, Julian, assume the throne as sole Roman emperor. Julian had been raised as a Christian and educated by some of the best philosophical minds of his day. By the time he became emperor, however, he had become deeply antagonistic toward Christianity. He found it to be little more than superstition and a religion that glorified a failed rebel. Although he despised their errors, Julian appreciated the Christians' social concerns and the strength of their organizational structures. Upon becoming emperor he immediately set about to restore the Greco-Roman religions, recasting them as an alternative church.

Julian's own personal faith extolled a supreme Being whom he identified with the Sun. His love for the rituals of animal sacrifice took him regularly to the temples of various gods. He also drew upon classical Hellenistic philosophy, free from Christian overtones of course, for religious inspiration. The emperor did not wish so much to reestablish the older imperial religions as he did to develop a new universal religious order modeled after the organizational life of the Christian churches. Local priests were appointed to restored temples of Zeus and the other Greco-Roman gods. Others resembling bishops were appointed over them. Scholars were encouraged to return to teaching the classics free from Christian interpretation. Non-Christians were appointed to key positions throughout the imperial bureaucracy. Religious freedom was granted to all faiths, encouraging alternatives to Christianity to flourish. Julian even attempted to rebuild the Temple in Jerusalem to help strengthen the Jewish religion.

One of the emperor's first acts was to grant permission for all Christian exiles to return to their homelands, a move designed to encourage Christian divisions to flourish. Athanasius was among the first to return, but his organizing among the churches in Alexandria earned him another trip into exile in 362. In North Africa, Julian ordered officials to allow Donatists to reclaim their churches, a measure repeated for other minority Christian parties in other cities as well. Christian clergy were stripped of their official support and forced to begin paying taxes.

Julian did not resort to open persecution as his predecessors had done before 312. Thus he avoided adding to the ranks of Christian martyrs (although some stories of martyrdom under him eventually circulated). Nevertheless, his reign sent shock waves through the Christian communities in the empire. Many Christians had come to accept their new situation as secure. The possibility that they could lose the support of the government shook them profoundly. Julian's reign was viewed as a major theological crisis by his Christian contemporaries. It did more to prepare future generations to accept a more rigidly Christian state than any previous experience in the Mediterranean world. In at least one instance Julian's measures might have had a role in encouraging supporters of Nicaea to accept the *homoiousios* in a statement of faith at a council called by Athanasius in Alexandria.

For several months in 362 Julian took up residence in Antioch while he made preparations for a new invasion of Persia. Amassing the largest Roman army ever to march against its traditional eastern foe, he set off in 363 with over fifty thousand troops. At first the campaign was successful. The Romans reached the very gates of the Persian capital of Seleucia-Ctesiphon. But they had extended themselves deeply into Persian territory and cut themselves off from retreat by burning their ships on the Tigris River. Julian himself was struck down in battle and died, leaving a new Roman emperor no choice but to sue for peace. The Persians were able to extract control of the city of Nisibis and several Roman provinces as concessions.

Securing the faith of Nicaea

The years immediately following Julian the Apostate, as he came to be known, were marked by a return of Christian emperors. Debates between the supporters of Nicaea and supporters of Arianism continued, although their positions had shifted considerably closer to one another. In the West the emperor Valentinian supported the Nicene position, while in the East his younger brother Valens favored that of the Arians. Valens was the last Roman emperor to do so. Disaster struck his army in 378 when it was defeated by the Visigoths (Western Goths) and the emperor killed. A retired Spanish officer named Theodosius was called back into service and elevated to the supreme rank of emperor in 379. With the reign of Theodosius, we can mark not only the triumph of Nicene orthodoxy but the final stage of Christianity becoming the religion of the empire.

Theodosius was not on the throne a year before he ordered all the churches of his realm to conform to the faith of Nicaea as held by the bishop of Rome. The following year, in 381, he summoned a new council to Constantinople to ratify the Nicene position, securing its official status as the orthodox faith of the Roman empire. Pockets of Arian resistance remained. Several decades later a bishop in Constantinople was still complaining of Arian strongholds in the city. Nevertheless, after 381 orthodoxy in the Roman world was synonymous with the faith of Nicaea. Outside the Roman world as well, in Ethiopia and Persia by the fifth century, Nicaea was widely accepted as being synonymous with orthodox Christian belief. In the sixth century even the Arian Goths converted to the Nicene form of Christian faith.

The other great legacy of the age of Theodosius was the final transition to Christianity becoming the official state religion throughout the Roman empire and not just a legal religion or even the preferred religion of the imperial household. Over the course of a decade the emperor placed increasing restrictions on other religions. A number of temples dedicated to other gods were ordered closed, and animal sacrifices throughout the empire were outlawed entirely. Although he did not succeed entirely in prohibiting the practices of other traditional religions (as many as half the people in the empire still held to them in some form), he succeeded in making them illegal. Legal restrictions against Jews were also stiffened under Theodosius. Conversion to Judaism was outlawed, and new restrictions on property inheritance were introduced.

Among the practices Theodosius revived from the days of Constantine was that of naming a woman as empress. Traditionally the title had been bestowed by a Roman emperor upon his wife to honor her as royal childbearer. The last to hold it had been Helena, the mother of the first Christian emperor. Theodosius resumed the practice by elevating his wife, Flaccilla, to the rank of augusta, a woman who soon proved to be a worthy bearer of the royal crown in her own right. Her portrait appears along with imperial insignia on coins from the period, an indication of the considerable power she came to exercise in the court of Constantinople.

We opened this chapter by referring to the Nicene Creed, a standard that was reaffirmed at Constantinople in 381. Although Nicaea intended it to serve as a standard of belief, there is little evidence that it meant the creed be used for preparing candidates for baptism, the primary purpose of creeds at that time. During most of the fourth century the words of the Nicene Creed remained relatively unknown to most Christians, although its effect began to be seen as other local creeds had the word *homoousios* added to them. Toward the end of the fourth century we begin to find evidence that the Nicene Creed was being said by candidates in the baptismal services in Constantinople. Eventually this creed, technically known as the Nicene-Constantinopolitan symbol, came to be accepted as a nearly universal standard of Christian faith. Countless Christians still confess today that the Son was "eternally begotten of the Father, God from God, Light from Light, true God from true God, begotten, not made, of one substance with the Father."

17

The Road to Chalcedon and Christological Diversity

The eventual triumph of Nicene orthodoxy provided the basis for a broad consensus regarding the trinitarian conception of God. The questions that Nicaea left unanswered, on the other hand, laid the foundation for further controversy and division among the churches in the fifth century. Foremost among them was how the Logos, whom the Orthodox agreed was fully divine, was related to the humanity of Jesus Christ. During the fifth century this christological debate became entangled in court politics and the political struggles among several major cities in the Mediterranean world. At the center of the controversy were two major theological schools of thought, each with its distinctive methods and emphases. Most of the members of both schools were regarded as orthodox at the time. Yet their theological differences, supplemented by a mutual animosity and increasing political rivalry, resulted in violence and disunity.

The first round of controversy broke out among the supporters of Athanasius in the last half of the fourth century. It focused on the teachings of Apollinaris (c.315-392), bishop of Laodicea in Syria, who was a friend of Athanasius. Apollinaris was an ardent supporter of the Nicene position during the 350s, when Arianism was dominant in his part of the world. Following the tradition of Alexandrian theology, he emphasized the manner in which the Logos had been united with the flesh of Jesus in the incarnation. By the late 370s he was also teaching that in the incarnation the Logos took the place of a human mind in Jesus, which was why Jesus could be in perfect obedience to the Father and remain free from sin. According to his critics, most of whom were also supporters of the Nicene position, Apollinaris in effect denied that Jesus was fully human. A series of regional councils reviewed and condemned his position.

The Cappadocians

Chief among the opponents of Apollinaris was a group of theologians known as the Cappadocians. Basil of Caesarea (330-379) was born into a well-to-do Christian family. A classmate of the emperor Julian, Basil was educated in

Caesarea, Constantinople, and Athens. He was baptized in 355 after a tour of Syria, Palestine, and Egypt, and he committed himself to a life of asceticism as a monk. Over the next fifteen years he served in a variety of capacities, finally assuming the title of bishop of Caesarea in 370. There he took up the cause of defending the Nicene faith as well as to extending the ministry of the church. Basil was among the first to integrate monasticism into the fuller life of the community, a topic to which we will return below. The hospital the monastery ran near his church was an extensive health-care facility as well.

One of Basil's close friends from his days as a student was Gregory of Nazianzus (329-390). Gregory was also from a wealthy background and had taken monastic vows. For several years Gregory combined teaching with his life of contemplation. He appears to have accepted ordination only reluctantly in 361 at the hands of his father, who was bishop of Nazianzus. For several years father and son served the church together. A decade later Gregory found himself drawn further into ecclesiastical politics by his old friend Basil, who was now bishop of Caesarea. Against Gregory's will Basil appointed his friend to the episcopacy of a small town near Caesarea. Basil's purpose was to strengthen his influence on the churches of the region, but the incident left a lasting scar on their relationship. It does not appear that Gregory assumed the position. For several more years he continued to pursue a life of contemplation and study until accepting a call as a preacher in a Nicene church in Constantinople in 379.

That was the year Theodosius became emperor. Two years later Theodosius ordered all churches in Constantinople to conform to the Nicene faith and summoned a council to gather there. Gregory was appointed bishop of Constantinople and given a presiding role at the council. Within a few weeks he had resigned due to the political pressures of the position, however, making his one of the shorter patriarchal reigns in the history of the city. He returned to Nazianzus, where he served as bishop for a time before stepping down for good in 384. Through it all Gregory maintained an active writing schedule that resulted in one of the most significant bodies of theological literature the Christian movement has ever seen. It is not without cause that Gregory of Nazianzus became known as "the theologian."

A third member of their circle was Basil's younger brother, Gregory of Nyssa (c. 340-395). Although he was not formally educated like his brother, Gregory joined Basil and his other friends in the theological disputes of his day. Gregory of Nyssa was married, which did not prevent him from being ordained a bishop in 372. His writings tended to be concerned with the process of spiritual growth to perfection. Indeed, if his friend from Nazianzus was the theologian, then Gregory of Nyssa was the spiritual director among the Cappadocian circle.

The fourth member of this theological circle was Basil's elder sister Macrina (327-380). When she was only twelve, the man to whom she had been promised in marriage died. Freed from the engagement made in her name, Macrina opted for a life of celibacy that allowed her to devote both time and money to furthering the cause of the gospel. With her mother, she founded a monastic community for women in their home. Gregory describes his older sister several times as being his teacher, and Gregory of Nazianzus indicates as much as well. Although she did not write any works of her own, apparently her influence within the circle touched upon issues of both spirituality and doctrine.

Collectively the Cappadocians made a considerable contribution to a number of theological issues. By the 380s the Nicene party's position regarding Jesus Christ being of the same substance as the Father had become generally accepted. Up through this period two Greek terms—*ousia* and *hupostasis*—that were similar in meaning had been used interchangeably to name what is usually termed the substance of God. In Alexandria a theologian by the name of Didymus the Blind (313-398) had earlier proposed that a distinction be made between *ousia* and *hupostasis* in Greek. Didymus was the head of the catechetical school in Alexandria during the time when Gregory of Nazianzus had traveled there, and it is a strong possibility that the Cappadocian had studied with him. Thus Gregory of Nazianzus was not introducing a novelty when he suggested a clarification in the Nicene terminology. The proposal was to reserve the term *ousia* to name what was common to the members of the Trinity and use the term *hupostasis* to name their distinctiveness as separate persons. Trinity, said Gregory, was three *hupostases* or persons in one *ousia* or manner of subsisting, an understanding that correlated with the Latin formula offered more than a century before by Tertullian.

Following Athanasius, the Cappadocians affirmed the full sharing of attributes among Father, Son, and Spirit. The analogy they drew was that of different human persons sharing the same human nature, doing so with a caution that the manner of divine subsisting was strictly one. Both Son and Spirit derived their divine nature from the Father, for there is no divine substance apart from the Father from whom they both proceed. At the same time the Cappadocians affirmed the full humanity of the Son, rejecting the argument of Apollinaris that the Logos took the place of a human mind in the person of Jesus. On this point the Council of Constantinople in 381 followed them.

Among the questions the Cappadocians addressed was that of the full divinity of the Holy Spirit. In the 370s a group had appeared in the region who accepted the full divinity of the Son but not of the Holy Spirit. Known by their opponents as Pneumatomachians because they "fought against the Spirit," they had criticized Basil for having prayed in worship to the Father, Son, and Holy Spirit as equals. In response the bishop of Caesarea wrote an eloquent defense of his liturgical practice, extending the argument of Nicaea to embrace the third person of the Trinity. Basil refrained from addressing the Holy Spirit directly as God, although his friend Gregory of Nazianzus was not reluctant to do so. According to Basil the work of the Spirit not only extends to us the fellowship enjoyed between the Father and the Son, but the Spirit perfects us by bringing humanity into the circle of trinitarian life.

Through all of their works the Cappadocians emphasized the personal character of God and allowed for no abstract qualities of divinity apart from the Father. From eternity and not in time the Son was begotten and the Spirit proceeded from the Father, they argued, thereby establishing unity and diversity within the divine life. For them, salvation was no mere abstraction conceived along the lines of being merely a change in God's attitude toward humanity as expressed in the life, death, and resurrection of Jesus Christ. Salvation also entailed a transformation in the life of the Christian, and indeed in the whole of creation. The end of salvation was a life that was fully divine or Spirit-filled *(theosis)*, in which one could dwell with God and contemplate the fullness of divine glory. Gregory of Nyssa's treatise *On the Resurrection* purportedly described a conversation he had with Macrina, his sister, just prior to her death. Macrina instructed Basil that the final end of life was one in which the soul would exist in perfect contemplation of God. Free from its material constraints and desires, including those of sexuality and gender, the soul would become like God in eternity. The community of the divine life of the Trinity was meanwhile to be reflected in the community of life on earth. The Cappadocians found the model for this to be represented above all in the community life of monasticism.

The schools of Antioch and Alexandria

The spiritual and theological views of the Cappadocians received official sanction in 381 at the Council of Constantinople. That same council called upon other churches of the world to recognize the bishop of Constantinople as having "prerogatives of honor after the bishop of Rome, seeing that this city is the new Rome."[3] Even though Theodosius was from Spain and spent a great deal of time in the West, the eastern capital was becoming more secure as the seat of imperial rule under him. The effect was to bring the bishop of Constantinople further into the circle of imperial politics. By the end of the fourth century the senior bishop of the city was often functioning as chaplain and advisor to the imperial household. One of the canons of 381 had called for bishops to refrain from interfering in the administrative affairs of one another's regions, but the head of a church in a city as powerful as Constantinople was clearly not going to be limited by such a rule. Conflicts were inevitable as bishops sought to exercise a prophetic voice or became ensnared within the machinations of imperial politics.

Political tensions between Constantinople and Rome had become pronounced by the beginning of the fifth century. Rome could no longer boast an effective imperial presence, but it was the city that had given the empire its identity and its glory. Theodosius indicated that the bishop of Rome occupied a place of special authority within the churches of the empire as a whole. Yet after 381 the bishop of Constantinople could claim a similar place of honor in the life of the churches in the Mediterranean world.

Two other cities played a significant role in this political drama that was shaping up early in the fifth century. Both of them claimed administrative prominence among churches in the empire, and both could boast long traditions of episcopal and theological leadership. Both were named in the canons of Nicaea and Constantinople as being important for their regions of the world. Alexandria and Antioch were in fact rivals in setting the theological coordinates of the post-Nicene

---

[3] Canon 3 from the Council of Constantinople, in Archbishop Peter L'Huillier, *The Church of the Ancient Councils: The Disciplinary Work of the First Four Ecumenical Councils* (Crestwood, N.Y.: St. Vladimir's Seminary Press, 1996), 119.

debates. In the course of the fifth century, both witnessed a decline in actual power in ecclesiastical politics, and both reacted by becoming engaged in a protracted struggle. Yet it was these two cities that had supported the greatest theological schools of the early Christian centuries, and hence they shaped much of the theological debate of the day. While Antioch and Alexandria were both firmly within the Roman political domain in the fifth century and were deeply influenced by Hellenistic intellectual traditions of thought, both also harbored strong nationalist sentiments and diverse cultural traditions.

The roots of the Alexandrian school reached back to the end of the second century and the catechetical school under Pantaenus, Clement, and then Origen. Clement was the person most responsible for giving the school its theological identity. Some of those who studied under him were new converts preparing for Christian baptism, but others were advanced scholars interested in his philosophical teaching. Origen extended Clement's work, developing more fully its methods of biblical exegesis and theology. Together their writings helped give lasting shape to a tradition of spiritual theology that spoke of the mystery of the Logos that was made incarnate in the flesh of Jesus. This theological tradition was continued in the fourth century in the work of Athanasius. It received its most able articulation in the fifth in the person of Cyril of Alexandria (c.375-444).

Meanwhile, in Antioch a distinct theological tradition had also emerged by the end of the second century, as is evidenced in the writings of Theophilus. It received a more extreme (many said heretical) formulation by Paul of Samosata late in the third century. By the fourth century Antioch could claim a coherent intellectual tradition or school of exegesis and theology, one that stood in contrast to the Alexandrian school to its south. The theologians associated with Antioch preferred more literal readings of the Bible. They sought to affirm both the humanity and divinity of Jesus Christ, but to do so in a way that did not mix or confuse the categories so as to lose sight especially of his humanity. Diodore of Tarsus (d. 390) and Theodore of Mopsuestia (350-428) were among the greatest names of the Antiochene tradition.

Theodore of Mopsuestia in particular deserves special notice not only for his influence in articulating the Antiochene themes, but also because of his influence upon Syrian and Persian church traditions. Although (or perhaps because) he had been trained in Hellenistic philosophy prior to becoming a Christian, Theodore emphasized biblical exegesis as the basis for all theological work. In the Old Testament he found a clear and definite distinction being made between divine and human natures, a distinction that he couldn't help but see carried over into the New Testament and thus into the church's christological reflection. Thus in Jesus Christ one can distinguish two historical subjects at work, the divine Logos and the assumed man.

The ethical and historical dimensions of the life of Jesus dominated in Theodore's theology. In his human nature Jesus could have repudiated his messianic vocation at any time up until his death on the cross when he said, "It is finished." This also meant for Theodore that Jesus could have sinned while he was on earth, a position that was one of the more controversial that he took. It was through his obedience, therefore, performed in the power of his humanity, that Jesus won our salvation. Only in this way can we be assured that our humanity experiences salvation through him. The emphasis for Theodore and the rest of the Antiochenes fell consistently on the historical work of the human person Jesus in the flesh, which he fully shares with us.

Those in both the Alexandrian and the Antiochene traditions of thought considered themselves to be fully Catholic, although their biblical and theological methods of reflection, and often the conclusions that they drew, diverged. The Antiochenes showed a noticeable preference for historical and grammatical details of biblical interpretation, while the Alexandrians preferred to employ allegorical methods for understanding scriptures. The latter were also more prone to employ the tools of philosophical reflection, especially those of neo-Platonism, which was flourishing in the third and fourth centuries in their home city. The Antiochenes were not averse to using categories of Platonic thought but were equally influenced by Aristotle's thought as well as by Jewish theological traditions. The Antiochenes were firmly committed to the doctrine of Jesus Christ having two natures, maintaining that he had a complete human nature, which changed, and a complete divine nature (the Logos), which did not. On the other hand, the Alexandrians were just as strongly committed to the doctrine that the Logos was joined to the flesh of Jesus Christ in a complete union in one divine-human person. Where Antiochene theology emphasized the relationship between the Logos and humanity in Jesus Christ, the Alexandrians emphasized that of the Logos to the flesh *(sarx)*.

Added to these theological differences were the changing political and economic factors of the day. When a regional council in Antioch sought to condemn Paul of Samosata in 268, it appealed to the bishops of Rome and Alexandria for support. These two episcopal sees were generally recognized as the highest rank of ecclesiastical authority by the Catholic majority among churches in the Mediterranean world. The emergence of Constantinople in the fourth century had the effect of investing the bishop of that city with authority by virtue of his proximity to the imperial court. Rome continued to hold symbolic priority because of its more ancient imperial status. But supporters of Roman primacy, especially in the West, were unhappy with the decision to name Constantinople so close to Rome among episcopal sees. The rise of Constantinople was also seen as a demotion in episcopal rank for the Alexandrian church. Alexandria was no longer the wealthiest and most powerful city in the East, and many feared its power was in decline. Constantinople tended to look to Antioch for its bishops in the early part of the fifth century, further aggravating the situation.

Alexandrian concerns were raised in 398 when a Syrian named John Chrysostom (347-407) was appointed bishop of Constantinople, reportedly against his will. John was a fellow-student of Theodore of Mopsuestia from Antioch and had gained fame as an eloquent preacher (*chrysostom* meant "golden-mouthed"). He was also possessed of a fiery penchant for justice. It wasn't long before John was condemning the extravagances he witnessed among the upper class of the city. He preached that the earth was common property and that inequalities in wealth were tantamount to theft from God, who intended all to have access to the resources of creation.

The range of those in the city whom John offended was quite wide. He attacked Christians who attended Jewish religious festivals and kept Jewish laws, for instance (an indication, perhaps, that some Christians were at least considering conversion to Judaism). He also spoke against the use of amulets and other traditional practices of magic that were becoming popular. His undoing came with an unguarded reference to the empress Eudoxia as "Jezebel." John did not approve of women exercising political power, and he saw them as being by nature disobedient like Eve. It was only a matter of time before his enemies in the city, urged on by the bishop of Alexandria, were able with help from the imperial household to have the bishop banished. In 404 he was deposed and sent into exile, where he died several years later.

Two decades later, in 428, the year of Theodore of Mopsuestia's death, another Antiochene named Nestorius (381-451) was elevated to bishop of Constantinople. Nestorius shared Theodore's concern to speak of the incarnation as an indwelling of the divine Logos in the human person, Jesus. Hence one can properly speak of two natures or subjects in Jesus Christ, in a manner that does not allow the divine to become subject to human passions and changes. Concerning Jesus' external appearance, Nestorius affirmed with the other Antiochenes that he was one person. The bishop preferred the Greek term *prosopon,* meaning "face" or "appearance," and referring to the concrete individual, Jesus, over the term *hupostasis,* which was used to name the essential, or abstract, principle of individual or personal nature. The school of Antioch had long maintained the need to make a distinction between the divine and human natures in Christ, or between his being Son of God and Son of humanity. The stronger emphasis on this distinction in natures generally led the Antiochenes to avoid Athanasius's doctrine that each of the two natures shared its attributes with the other.

Nestorius went even further in this direction than others in his school. In a provocative sermon preached in 428 in Constantinople, he asserted that it was wrong to call Mary the mother of Jesus *Theotokos* ("Mother of God" or "God-bearer"). The most one could say, he argued, was that she was *Christotokos.* The term that he attacked was one steeped in the piety of the Alexandrian theologians and Constantinople alike. Alexander and Athanasius had both made use of it, as had the Cappadocians. By rejecting it he was rejecting a central tenet of the spiritual and theological inheritance of the Alexandrians, and of most Orthodox believers in Constantinople.

There was another dimension to Nestorius's theological concern. His sermon was no doubt also directed against the empress Pulcheria (399-453). Like John Chrysostom before him, Nestorius was unable to accept the political role women in Constantinople were playing. Pulcheria was such a woman. The older sister of the emperor Theodosius II (408-450), and an avowed virgin (although stories alleging adulterous affairs were continuously circulating throughout the city), she had been made empress in 414 by the Senate of Constantinople and ruled as the guardian of her younger brother.

On Easter Sunday in 428, Pulcheria attempted to enter the sanctuary as she usually did to take communion with the priests and her brother, the emperor. Nestorius barred her at the door, explaining that only males could do so. "Have I not given birth to God?" Pulcheria asked. "You have given birth to Satan," the bishop responded.[4] She claimed the dignity of Mary, but Nestorius, like John Chrysostom before him, could only grant her the ignominy of Eve.

Nestorius's public sermon attacking the Theotokos provoked an outcry in Constantinople that was almost immediately heard in Alexandria, where Cyril (375-444) reigned as bishop. As a theologian Cyril was among the greatest minds of the Alexandrian school. As a bishop he had a reputation for being hotheaded and tyrannical, and not above allowing for the use of violence to achieve the ends of the gospel. When word came of Nestorius's sermon, Cyril took up the Alexandrian cause against the Antiochene extremes he heard being voiced in Constantinople, firing off a letter and calling upon Nestorius to acknowledge the term *Theotokos*. A second letter was sent to Nestorius, this time with a copy to Celestine, bishop of Rome, who supported Cyril's position on the matter. Jesus Christ had one incarnate nature in which the Logos took on the fullness of humanity in the flesh, Cyril wrote. He called this a hypostatic union, and in a third letter added a series of condemnations against Nestorius.

It wasn't long before the emperor felt compelled to wade in on the dispute. The natural response by this time was to call a council, which met in Ephesus in 431 in what is now generally regarded as the third ecumenical council of the ancient church (after Nicaea and Constantinople). The council opened, however, without John of Antioch and his party being present, as they were delayed in arriving in Ephesus. The absence of the Antiochenes allowed Cyril to dominate the proceedings, presiding as the Alexandrian pope. He quickly secured not only the condemnation of Nestorius but of John of Antioch for supporting Nestorius. By the time John of Antioch arrived, Cyril's work was done.

Such a state of affairs could hardly resolve the dispute between two such influential schools of theology, however. Almost immediately following the council the emperor set about to work out a compromise between John of Antioch and Cyril of Alexandria. Nestorius was sacrificed, banished into exile in the Egyptian desert where he spent the rest of his life, his name ever after associated in the Greek and Latin churches with heresy. A Formula of Reunion was hammered out that affirmed Mary being called Theotokos and spoke of Jesus Christ as having two natures united in one person. John was reinstated, while Cyril's original anathemas were allowed to stand.

The Council of Chalcedon

For more than a decade relative peace reigned among the various parties involved in the dispute. But then in 444 Cyril of Alexandria died and a new bishop named Dioscorus (d. 454) assumed the office. The chief theologians representing the Antiochene school were Theodoret, bishop of Cyrrhus (393–c.460), and Hiba (Ibas), bishop of Edessa (d.457). The dispute started when a monk named

---

[4] Kenneth G. Holum, *Theodosian Empresses: Women and Imperial Domination in Late Antiquity* (Berkeley and Los Angeles: University of California Press, 1982), 153.

Eutyches, who was head of a monastery near Constantinople and had well-placed connections in the imperial court, began to teach that the flesh of Jesus came from a source other than Mary. Eutyches taught that Christ's flesh was divine flesh sent from above and hence was different from ours. His views were condemned by Flavian, bishop of Constantinople. Eutyches appealed the decision in letters sent to major sees elsewhere, including Rome, where Leo (400-474) was the pope.

Emperor Theodosius II, seeking to settle the dispute, called for a council to meet at Ephesus to hear the case in 449. Dioscorus was appointed to preside, while Theodoret of Cyrrhus was forbidden to leave his home to attend the event. Invited to attend but unable to do so in person, Leo sent a delegation along with a letter or *Tome* he had composed, setting forth the Latin position on the debate. The letter was never read before the council, however. Instead, proceedings almost immediately got out of hand. Flavian of Constantinople was assaulted after being condemned (he later died of his injuries). The views of Theodoret and Hiba were also condemned and the Alexandrian position asserted as supreme. When word reached Rome of the proceedings, Leo denounced it as a "robber synod."

The triumph for Dioscorus was short-lived. The following year Theodosius was thrown from his horse and died of his injuries. His sister, Pulcheria, whom Nestorius had kept from communion two decades before, quickly assumed control of the government. Deferring to those who believed a woman could not rule alone, she agreed to be married to an officer named Marcian. But she did so only on the condition that he respect her vow of virginity, to which he agreed. The couple were wed, and Pulcheria then crowned her new husband as emperor.

A year later, in 451, empress and emperor called a new council to meet in the city of Chalcedon. Leo of Rome was again unable to come, although he was in active communication with the empress through letters. Over five hundred other bishops attended, with Pulcheria the presiding imperial officer in place of her husband, Marcian. The council opened by deposing Dioscorus, not on grounds of his theology but on account of his actions at the council of 449. The record of Chalcedon indicates that the creed of Nicaea was ordered to be retrieved from the city's archive and read into the minutes. It is this version of the Nicene Creed that churches continue to use today.

The council next turned to the various theological positions set before it. Cyril's writings were examined and found sound, as was the position of John of Antioch from the 430s. Leo's *Tome* was also read, and it too was accepted as orthodox. Leo had stated the Latin church's belief that Jesus Christ had two natures, each of whose characteristics were distinct. "A humanity interior to the Father comes to him from us, and a divinity equal to the Father's comes to him from the Father," the letter stated.[5] Each nature communicates or shares in the properties of the other in such a way that Jesus Christ is properly called one person, it concluded.

---

[5] Richard A. Norris Jr., ed., *The Christological Controversy* (Philadelphia: Fortress Press, 1980), 151.

The council then took up the task of formulating a theological definition that joined the insights of both Antiochene and Alexandrian schools of thought. Both sides agreed that Jesus Christ was both human and divine. While the Alexandrians emphasized the divine nature that was incarnate in his humanity, the Antiochenes emphasized the possibility of his humanity suffering without denying the impassible nature of his divinity. The result was a concluding theological statement, commonly known as the "Definition of Chalcedon." It explicitly called Mary Theotokos and affirmed Jesus Christ to be one person in a union of two natures. He was without confusion and change (answering the concerns that the Antiochenes raised about the Alexandrians' theology) and without division or separation (answering the concerns that the Alexandrians raised about the Antiochenes' theology).

One of the last acts of the Council of Chalcedon was to vote in favor of extending the authority of the bishop of Constantinople over several regional metropolitan sees. Canon 28 (as this decision came to be known) caused an outcry among the western delegates by calling Constantinople the "New Rome" and assigning its patriarch a rank second only to that of the bishop of "Old Rome" among the churches of the world. The terminology had already been used by previous councils, such as the one that met in 381 in Constantinople, but had been protested by Rome. The effect of canon 28 was to confirm the bishop of Constantinople as equal in rank to the bishop of Rome in the empire. Although it was not accepted in the West, there was little that Leo or his successors could do to prevent its administrative enactment.

Chalcedon was an attempt at theological compromise. Many churches in the Roman world accepted it as such and accepted its definition as the new standard of christological orthodoxy. The Arians, of course, did not, for they never accepted the doctrine that the Logos was of the same substance as the Father, although in more moderate forms they might affirm the equality of his nature (not the sameness of his nature). To some, the final word from Chalcedon seemed to lean in the direction of the Antiochenes. Nestorius himself was condemned again as a heretic, and the doctrine of Mary as Theotokos that he rejected was affirmed. Nevertheless, the council defined Christ as one person in two natures, language that the Antiochene tradition had long maintained as orthodox.

On the other hand, the council maintained there was a distinction in natures without separation, employing the concept of the *communicatio idiomatum* (the sharing of attributes) to explain the relationship between them. The echoes of Athanasius at this point might have swayed more of the Alexandrian supporters had not the council's decision to depose Dioscorus, bishop of Alexandria, turned many in that city and the rest of Egypt against it. Significant political considerations were separating Alexandria from Constantinople, and these began to show up in the churches as parties for or against the council took shape. In Egypt and Syria those who supported Constantinople's bishop and the imperial line become derogatorily called *Melkites*, a Syrian term meaning "imperial."

The more radical wings in both the Antiochene and Alexandrian camps continued to regard the council's attempt at compromise as a capitulation to the views of their opponents. Those who continued to consider Cyril of Alexandria to be the touchstone of orthodoxy held that although there were two natures before the incarnation, Christ was one person with one united nature after the incarnation. Before long they were being derogatorily called *Monophysites* ("one-nature") by their opponents, a name that many still use today. On the other side were those who continued to follow Theodore of Mopsuestia and argued for two natures, thus two persons, in a voluntary union. Theodore believed that it was possible for Jesus to have sinned, so that by his willing obedience salvation was achieved. His followers emphasized Christ's two natures after the incarnation, leading many to label it *Dyophysite* ("two-nature"). Between them stood the Chalcedonians, who held to the formula of two natures in one hypostatic union. In the end there were three post-Chalcedonian theological options.

Over the course of another century in the eastern Roman world, imperial opinion remained generally committed to the Chalcedonian compromise. Further east, defenders of the views of Theodore, Nestorius, and Hiba found a theological home first in the regions of Edessa and then across the border in the Persian empire and the great theological school of Nisibis. Eventually Cyril's formulation regarding one nature prevailed in western Syria, Armenia, Egypt, Nubia, and Ethiopia. Most churches in the Latin-speaking world accepted the Chalcedonian perspective, although the bishop of Rome refused to accept the canon that asserted the equal authority to the bishop of Constantinople. The stresses caused by the political implications of Constantinople's rising star in the imperial church began to show tears in the fabric of orthodoxy these two communions shared.

18

The Christian Movement in the East

Syria and the Emergence of a Persian National Church

It was quite a distance from the Roman imperial city of Constantinople to the capital of the shah of shahs in Persia. While the Greek and Latin theologians were gathered in Chalcedon, Dadyeshu, the Persian patriarch in Seleucia-Ctesiphon, was facing a hostile society that suspected Christians of being sympathetic with the Romans. The story of events from Nicaea to Chalcedon, we have seen, was one that primarily occupied churches in the eastern provinces of the Roman empire. Through the unfolding of the councils and events there, what is generally called the Orthodox Christian tradition emerged. In the West, Latin-speaking Roman Catholics continued to look upon the Greek-speaking Orthodox Christians as being of the same communion, or part of the same great Church, even though they were growing apart in liturgy and theology. To the east of Constantinople, however, the political and cultural divide appeared much earlier. There, in the years after Chalcedon, the doctrines of Nestorius that had been condemned in that council were embraced by the emerging national church of Persia.

The story of tensions between these two church traditions goes back to the fourth century in the age of Constantine. One of the responsibilities that the first Roman Christian emperor took upon himself was to be the defender of the Christian faith throughout the world. The notion clearly reflected Constantine's own sense of a universal imperial mission. There was also, no doubt, a sincere desire on his part to assist the Christians beyond his own political domains. Both Eusebius and Sozomen record a letter sent by the Roman emperor to Shapur II, the shah of shahs in Persia, asking him to extend his protection to the Christians. Constantine had heard that the districts of Persia were filling with Christians, and he felt it his duty to encourage Shapur II to recognize the religion. As Sozomen noted, "The emperor extended his watchful care over all the Christians of every region, whether Roman or foreign."[6]

The impact of Constantine's letter, if indeed it was read by the shah of shahs, was quite different than the Roman emperor intended. Christians in Persia in the fourth century began to face for the first time not only the opposition of the Zoroastrian magi who officiated over the state religion but also questions about their political loyalty to the Persian emperor. Christians were now suspected of being friends of the shah's enemy, which made them enemies of the Persian state. The situation soon proved deadly when Shapur II, to whom Constantine had written, launched a major persecution in 339.

The persecution opened with the levying of a double tax against Christians. Destruction of churches and forced worship of the sun, the central Zoroastrian rite, soon followed. Many who refused were executed. The violence was directed in particular against those who had converted from the Zoroastrian faith to Christian belief. So severe was the persecution that Christians in the capital city of Seleucia-Ctesiphon went for several decades without a senior bishop, because each election brought immediate execution. Estimates of those who lost their lives for their Christian faith during the middle decades of the fourth century in Persia range into the tens of thousands and higher.

Numbers alone can hardly convey the degree of suffering endured by these Christians. Among them was a young woman named Martha who was a "daughter of the covenant," a term used by those in the Syriac-speaking churches for one who took a vow of celibacy on behalf of Christ. Martha's father had been a Christian craftsman taken captive by Shapur I from Roman territory many years before, her mother a Persian who had converted to the Christian faith. According to the story of her martyrdom, a day after her father's execution in 341 Martha herself was arrested during Sunday worship. She was interrogated by the mobed, who demanded that she renounce her Christian faith and obey the will of Shapur, shah of shahs. Martha prayed for the well-being of the Persian emperor but proclaimed her trust in Jesus Christ as the true king of kings who would soon return for her, one of his betrothed. The mobed was enraged, both for her impudence in asserting Christ as king of kings and for proclaiming her betrothal to him and thus her celibacy in preparation in this life (Zoroastrian teaching abhorred celibacy). She was taken outside the city and executed by immolation. In her dying prayer, according to the tradition of her martyrdom, she offered her life to God like the sacrifice of a lamb and the sacrifice of Isaac.

Distinctive characteristics of Persian Christianity

Not all was bleak for the Christians living in Persian territories in the fourth century. Although the number of martyrdoms was high, the movement was gaining

---

[6] Sozomen, *Ecclesiastical History* 2.15, in *Nicene and Post-Nicene Fathers of the Christian Church* (2nd series), vol. 2, *Socrates, Sozomenus: Church Histories*, ed. Philip Schaff and Henry Wace (Grand Rapids, Mich.: Wm. B. Eerdmans Publishing Co., 1983), 268.

new converts. Monastic communities proved to be important in this regard for Christianity east of the Euphrates River, for they provided safe havens where worship and prayer could be carried on, texts could be protected, and theological ideas could be debated. One of these was the early community of Mar Mattai, located outside the city of Mosul on the Tigris River. The reported head of that community during the early years of the fourth century was a skilled theologian named Aphraates (or Aphrahat) (dates unknown).

Aphraates was nicknamed the Persian Sage, an indication of both his cultural identity and theological orientation. Among his regular theological dialogue partners were several rabbis from the region. Aphraates debated with them such matters as the interpretation of Torah, the meaning of Messiah, and the place of Gentiles in the history of salvation. His theological writings suggest a great deal of Jewish influence, both in the methods of his arguments and the content of his thought. At the same time his treatises, entitled *Demonstrations*, show no anti-Jewish sentiments. Aphraates was a Christian, with a trinitarian theological frame of thought sharing much with the faith of Nicaea. Although he appears to have been familiar with at least some of the theological conversations taking place to the west, his own work remained relatively free of Hellenistic philosophical influences. He drew heavily upon the apostle Paul in developing these ideas, supporting them with copious references to other biblical texts.

Aphraates is considered one of the most important exponents of Orthodox Christian faith in the East. Among his more striking theological insights were those regarding the feminine nature of the Holy Spirit. This was more than an accidental use of gender in the language of the Spirit in the Syriac language in which he wrote. The Holy Spirit was depicted as a Mother brooding over her creation and a female dove descending upon Jesus at his baptism. Along with other Syrian writers, he described the work of the Spirit in the church in terms closely related to those used of Mary, the mother of Jesus, and Mary Magdalene.

The middle years of the fourth century witnessed a new wave of warfare between Roman and Persian military forces in the regions of Mesopotamia. In 363 the Roman emperor, Julian, conducted a disastrous campaign to the outskirts of the Persian capital of Seleucia-Ctesiphon that resulted in his death. In the settlement that followed, Shapur II retook Nisibis and the surrounding provinces of Mesopotamia, ending sixty years of Roman control there. The border between the Roman and Persian empires was once again pushed back beyond the Tigris River. Many Christians left Nisibis with the retreating Romans to escape persecution, among them another of the greatest theologians of the first Christian centuries from the East, Ephraem the Syrian (306-373), who spent the remaining ten years of his life resettled in Edessa.

Born and raised in a Christian family in Nisibis, Ephraem was baptized as a youth and later ordained to the office of a deacon. His gifts as a teacher were recognized by the bishop of Nisibis, who supported his work. Ephraem wrote a number of homilies, commentaries, and theological treatises. Several of his polemical works were directed against the doctrines of those he considered heretics, including Marcion and Mani. Also, among the targets of his writing was Bardaisan, whom Ephraem considered the teacher of Mani, a charge others have questioned. Ephraem is best known for his hymns, a body of work rich in spiritual insight and inspiration. Many of his hymns were translated into Greek and Latin in his own lifetime, spreading his reputation as a theologian beyond his own Syriac language community.

With others in the Syrian tradition Ephraem could speak of the Holy Spirit in feminine terms. The Spirit was the wind within the sails of Mary's womb, as well as the wind and fire in the bread and wine of the eucharist. The most exalted language he reserved for Jesus, whose cross formed the bridge across sheol. The hymns celebrated all aspects of the life of Christ from his nativity to his ascension on high. At the center stood the great mystery of God's self-abasement in the incarnation and God's self-giving through the Holy Spirit. In Ephraem's hymns creation itself took on revelatory meaning. Nature, humanity, and especially Mary all shared in the incarnational mystery, which was also at the heart of the sacramental practices of the church. Mary in particular he extolled as the "Second Eve," and "Mother of the Church." As the First Eve had been born from the First Adam's side, so the Church was born from the Second Adam's wounded side as he lay asleep on the cross. In a rich mixture of biblical personages, Ephraem combined Eve, Mary the mother of Christ, and Mary Magdalene to form a positive composite picture of divine/feminine nature at work in redemption.

This theologian and spiritual teacher was actively concerned with the daily matters of life in his city. In Edessa he organized a food drive when famine struck particularly hard among the poor, and he is credited with having founded a hospital in the city. Some of his hymns were intended to be used as a popular alternative to amulets and magical formulas found among the people of the city. His death was reported to have come while he was assisting victims of a plague. In many ways he embodies the complex spirituality of fourth-century Christian Syria, which was known for "the beauty of her hymns and the jarring translucence of her ascetic practices."[7] In the end his most important legacy might well be found in the manner in which he was able to translate these ideas across cultural boundaries of his day. A westward-leaning theologian from the East, Ephraem communicated the early Syriac tradition of spirituality and faith to a wide range of hearers. His works were eventually translated into Greek, Coptic, Armenian, Latin, and even Slavonic, a testimony to his importance for churches of the Christian movement throughout the world.

Formation of the Persian (East Syrian) national church

The years following Aphraates and Ephraem down to the end of the fourth century and into the fifth were a period of relative peace between Romans and Persians, and for Christians in the Persian world. New waves of invading tribes from the north, such as the Huns and the Goths, were sacking cities in the western regions of the Roman empire and threatening even eastern regions. In Persia,

---

[7] Sebastian P. Brock and Susan Ashbrook Harvey, trans. and eds., *Holy Women of the Syrian Orient* (Berkeley and Los Angeles: University of California Press, 1986), 12.

Shah Yazdegerd I issued an edict of toleration for Christians in 409, after Marutha, a bishop from Mesopotamia who was in Persia as an ambassador from Constantinople, successfully interceded with him. Marutha then proceeded to help organize a national council in 410 under Isaac, bishop of Seleucia-Ctesiphon.

The record of the Synod of Isaac, as the gathering came to be called, lists bishops attending from as far away as Samarkand, north of the Oxus River in central Asia, and other cities located along the Oxus River in Persian territory. The gathering received a letter from the patriarch of Antioch and bishop of Edessa, conveyed by the hand of Marutha. It affirmed the letter's recommendations that the churches of Persia adopt the faith of Nicaea as well as the diocesan structure and dating of Christian holy days that were agreed upon in 325. The synod then established several major bishoprics over which the bishop of Seleucia-Ctesiphon ruled as *catholicos* or supreme head over all churches of Persia.

This last decision was asserted more forcefully in 424 by the Synod of Dadyeshu. Again there were bishops from cities as distant as Rayy, Nishapur, Merv, and Herat in northwest Iran and modern Afghanistan. The catholicos of Seleucia-Ctesiphon was confirmed to be equal in authority to other patriarchs, such as the bishops of Rome and Alexandria (the two Nicaea had recognized as supreme) and Constantinople (whose authority was recognized at the Council of Constantinople in 381).

The churches of Persia were again suffering tremendously under new waves of imperial persecution even more severe than those of the fourth century. Across the Persian empire the dominance of the Zoroastrian religion created a harsh religious climate in which the churches carried on their life. Christians were part of a minority religion that was associated with the lower classes. They lived in segregated neighborhoods under a Persian system known as *melet*. Conversion was forbidden by law to members of Zoroastrian religion, but Christians actively evangelized nonetheless. In northeastern Iran in the region of the Oxus River, Christians lived alongside Zoroastrian, Manichaean, and Buddhist neighbors. Each religious community conducted an active form of missionary outreach. Syriac-speaking churches in this region, as elsewhere throughout the Persian empire, demonstrated stronger Semitic cultural influences than their counterparts in the Mediterranean. There were no images in church buildings, for instance. Empty wooden crosses were the only adornments in most Syriac churches.

Political and cultural differences were given sharper theological focus by the christological controversies that were enveloping the churches in the fifth century. The struggle between the Antiochenes and the Alexandrians spilled beyond the borders of the Roman world and into the Persian East, providing the grounds for a distinct theological separation between Roman and Persian churches. The story of this theological division takes us necessarily back into Roman-controlled territory and the cities of Edessa, Antioch, Alexandria, and Constantinople.

The school of Edessa

Prior to 431, Edessa and Constantinople had both leaned toward the theological tradition of Antioch and the christological language of two natures. The bishop of Edessa during these years, Rabbula, had been appointed by the patriarch of Antioch and supported the Antiochene position. But in 431 the political fortunes of the major theological traditions began to shift. At the Council of Ephesus, Cyril clearly had the upper hand, signaling Alexandria's ascendancy in both matters of theology and politics within the eastern Mediterranean world. Many who were sympathetic with the Antiochene school of theology after 431 took refuge further east.

By this time the dominant theological institution for learning in the East was the famed school of Edessa, which was populated by Persians and Syrian students alike. Some have argued that the school of Edessa reached as far back as the time of Bardaisan, but it is more likely that it became an organized center of learning only in the early fifth century. Its campus was located in several buildings in the city, and it included residences where students, mostly from across the Persian border, could stay while they studied. The curriculum centered on exegesis of scriptures but included philosophical and theological studies as well. To the latter end, numerous Greek texts, including the philosophical works of Aristotle and more recent work of theology such as those of Diodore of Tarsus, were translated into Syriac by scholars associated with the school. The main texts students read, after the Bible, of course, were the commentaries of Theodore of Mopsuestia. Already in his lifetime the works of this biblical scholar were almost entirely available in Syriac, a translation project that was overseen by Hiba of Edessa.

The theological situation in Edessa began to destabilize in 431 when Bishop Rabbula decided to throw in his lot with Cyril and the Alexandrian party. The change in alliance caught many in the school of Edessa by surprise. Now it was Cyril's works that were to be translated, and Rabbula went so far as to try to destroy the existing translations of Theodore. Hiba was deposed and exiled from the city, encouraging the supporters of Cyril's theological positions. In 435 Rabbula was succeeded as bishop by Hiba, whom the former had exiled, but the situation had changed and opponents of Theodore's position were strong enough to force Hiba's imprisonment in 449. After 451, it was clear that the Antiochene tradition of the school of Edessa was no longer welcomed in a city that now leaned toward Cyril's theological formulation of doctrine.

From the perspective of an observer looking at these events fifteen hundred years later, it might seem incredible that so much weight was given to such theological subtleties. But to those who were involved in the events of the mid-fifth century, the various theological positions were far from indistinguishable, nor were theological debates confined to the arenas of the scholarly elite. The finer points of the various theological arguments might have escaped the common people, but they knew what to listen for in the liturgy or in a sermon by the bishop. They lined up behind one party or another in the politics of the city.

Adding to the theological complexity of these fifth-century controversies in the East was the fact that much of what was being argued was in translation. There was bound to be slippage in meaning when Greek terms such as *physis* ("nature"), *hupostasis* and *prosopon* (the latter two both translated as "person" in

English) were translated into Syriac *(keyane, qenuma,* and *parsopa)* and debated in various locations far from Chalcedon. These Syriac terms did not carry the precise meaning the Greek terms had come to bear. While the process of translation could add depth to the meaning of various biblical terms or extend insights from the Bible into new theological directions, it could also set communities at odds with one another as they no longer found common words to carry similar cultural meanings.

The political pressures against the party of Hiba worsened considerably after 450. Students and teachers alike in the school of Edessa had no choice but to begin to immigrate across the border into Persia. Among those who departed were Barsauma (d. 496), later archbishop of Nisibis, and Narsai (c.399-503), the last director of the school of Edessa prior to its final closing in 489. On the other side of the border, in the Persian-held city of Nisibis the refugees gathered to refound their theological school. They located in a cluster of buildings near the main church in the city, with Narsai again assuming the role of director and primary lecturer. Eventually the student body at Nisibis grew to over one thousand, making it one of the most influential centers for theological education in the ancient Christian world. Its curriculum was built upon scripture, drawing from the exegetical and theological work of Theodore of Mopsuestia and others. Here the two-nature position received its clearest theological articulation in the fifth century.

Building on the theological foundation of Theodore of Mopsuestia and guided by the work of able thinkers such as Narsai and Barsauma, the Persian churches were able to steer a theological course that was independent of the West. Through several synods in the late fifth century, they condemned both the one-nature doctrine of Cyril and the position of Chalcedon, at the same time remaining firm in their adherence to the trinitarian faith of Nicaea. As late as the sixth century we still find an occasional report of a bishop from the East traveling to Constantinople and receiving communion from the church there. We even find occasional reports of individual theologians expressing their acceptance of the Council of Chalcedon, interpreting it through the theological lens of Theodore of Mopsuestia, of course. Yet it was institutionally an independent national Persian church that emerged in the fifth century. Appointments to the office of patriarch were subject to confirmation by the shah, not the Roman emperor. Successive synods through the end of the sixth century made it clear that they were Persian Christians, not Romans living in exile.

Christians were generally found on the margins of Persian life. Lacking the social support churches received from the government in the Mediterranean world, Persian Christians had to forge their own system apart from the state. By the fourth and fifth centuries, monasteries had become the most important centers for preserving Christian life and thought. Many of these had grown into full-fledged educational institutions that provided churches with important resources beyond what might be considered strictly spiritual or theological concerns. Christian educational institutions in the East provided theological and pastoral training, but they also taught other subjects; chief among these was medicine. Historical contacts with the West had given Persian Christians access to Greek medical texts, which were arguably the most advanced in the ancient world. Copies of these texts were carried across the Persian frontier by refugees from persecution and were kept closely guarded secrets in the Christian schools in Persia. By the fifth century many had been translated into Syriac. Students had access to them only through teachers in the Christian schools, which is why Christians were disproportionately represented among the medical profession in the Persian empire. Indeed, we find in numerous instances the personal physicians of shahs and other high officials in the Persian world identified as Christians, trained in these Persian schools.

Although some Christians advanced within government, especially in times of relative peace, persecution was an ever-present reality. Patriarch Mar Aba in the sixth century was a living example of the precarious existence of Christians in Persia. Mar Aba occupied the office during the reign of Chosroes I (ruled 531-579), one of the most powerful emperors in the long history of Persia. Since the patriarch was a convert from the Zoroastrian faith, he lived with the constant threat of death, the penalty for Zoroastrian converts in Persia. In 544 persecution launched by the Zoroastrian priesthood resulted in Mar Aba being arrested and brought before the shah for trial. He admitted that he was a Christian and that he was actively evangelizing others of the Zoroastrian faith. Nevertheless, he was only exiled and soon was able to return of his own accord to the capital of Seleucia-Ctesiphon. Several years later he was imprisoned and tortured, but he was also sent on a diplomatic mission on behalf of the shah to the Turks before dying in 552.

On a day-to-day basis, Christians were often at odds with their Zoroastrian neighbors in a number of ways. Christian burial was one example. Zoroastrians considered it polluting to place a body in the earth. Water that washed over the earth in which the dead were buried and then flowed into a stream polluted the entire stream, making it unfit for Zoroastrians to drink. Zoroastrians maintained sacred fires and engaged in rites directed toward the sun, the highest symbol of fire, but Christians refused to participate in these sacred rites and criticized them as idolatry. Among the most contentious issues that separated Persian Christians from their neighbors were the Christian practices involving celibacy and marriage. Zoroastrians considered celibacy abhorrent, and they allowed for polygamy as well as degrees of blood relations that Christians considered incestuous. Persian churches continued to nurture radical strands of ascetic spirituality that had long been part of the Syriac tradition but were at odds with Zoroastrian teaching.

In this regard one of the most surprising innovations of the late-fifth-century Persian church occurred when the theologian Barsauma, who was also a monk and a bishop, decided to marry a nun, thereby establishing a precedent for others. Several synods confirmed Barsauma's practice and ruled that clergy could even remarry if their spouses died, a practice many early churches had rejected. Christians were still forbidden to marry more than one person at a time, however, or to marry a first cousin, both practices regarded as acceptable among their Persian neighbors. In the sixth century a major movement under the leadership of Abraham of Kaskar (491-586) reintroduced some of the earlier rigor that had characterized the movement from the days of the Syrian deserts, reaffirming the strong ascetic impulse over against the dominant Persian cultural attitudes toward marriage.

Christianity in India

From the middle of the fourth century comes our first solid historical evidence of a Christian community in India. We have already noted the earlier evidence of mission to India, beginning with traditions concerning the apostle Thomas himself. It is entirely possible that if Thomas did indeed reach India he was successful in making converts there. Yet even those who support the tradition of Thomas in India find it difficult to argue for continuous Christian presence. Any church Thomas started most likely dwindled in number, possibly down to nothing. A later Syriac source reports that a Persian Christian doctor who was also a bishop, David of Basra, prior to the year 300 left his see to travel to India as a missionary. Again we hear nothing more of him or any church he might have started, leaving us with no evidence of an enduring community of faith being formed in the land.

Our first evidence for a sustained Christian church in India comes from around the year 350. Thomas of Cana was a Persian Christian merchant who had settled in the area of Cranganore in India. From the various streams of both Syrian and Indian historical traditions, he is said to have come with a community of settlers. Possibly this was an extended Christian family of merchants, perhaps seeking to escape the persecutions breaking out in Persia. Some reports cite Thomas of Cana as being an Armenian by descent, which is certainly possible as well. The traditions surrounding Thomas of Cana say that he was able to purchase land on which to build a church. His wealth provided political entry with a local king who granted the group freedom to establish its community. By some accounts Thomas sponsored a bishop with several priests and deacons who were sent by the catholicos of the Persian national church.

A decade or so later, according to the Greek historian Sozomen, the Roman emperor Constantius sent an Indian named Theophilus to southern Arabia as a missionary. Originally from the island of Divus in the Indian Ocean, Theophilus had apparently come to the West as a captive or slave. He returned as a Christian, although most likely holding Arian theological views. His visit is first reported by the Christian historian Philostorgius, his contemporary from the fourth century. According to the account, Theophilus journeyed to his home island in the Indian Ocean as well. There he visited indigenous churches whose practice of sitting during the reading of the gospel, though in line with Indian cultural practices, struck him as improper (Christians in the West stood for the reading of the gospel in worship). With these two accounts we have some solid historical evidence of Christian communities on Indian soil.

Thomas of Cana might well have seen that a bishop was part of his entourage that settled on the mainland of India. If so, it was no doubt one from the Persian church. By the early fifth century the bishop of Rewardashir near the Persian Gulf had been made a metropolitan see with authority over the churches of India.

This is further evidence that the church in India was composed primarily of expatriated Persians, although perhaps a permanent merchant community. The language of their liturgy was Syriac, and their bishops and priests were appointed from Persia. There are few indications that Christian belief had begun to spread beyond the Persian members of the community to others who were Indian. Intermarriage and slaves becoming converts to the religion of their masters are two significant ways by which Christianity might have spread beyond a strictly Persian identity. One also cannot discount direct evangelism, as resident merchants shared the gospel with business associates and neighbors. Some of the first evidence we have for Christianity spreading among Indians before the sixth century comes in the form of reports regarding their specific caste status. Being assigned a caste indicates Christianity was slowly becoming a part of the Indian cultural world.

An important historical witness to this development was a sixth-century Egyptian monk named Cosmas Indicopleustes (or Cosmas the Indian Navigator). Cosmas was from Alexandria, and he had traveled widely as a merchant. He considered himself something of a philosopher as well, writing a treatise on cosmology that set forth a theory regarding the relation of heavenly bodies to the earth. In the course of this work, *Christian Topography*, he provided details of his observations regarding various regions of Africa and India that he had visited on business. He had been to Ethiopia and India, he said, and had knowledge of the island of Sri Lanka. There, he tells us, was "a church of Persian Christians who have settled there, and a Presbyter who is appointed from Persia, and a Deacon and a complete ecclesiastical ritual"—but no report of a bishop.[8] Along the coast of Malabar he reports a predominantly Persian Christian community, with a bishop who was appointed from Persia. Cosmas reported finding Persian churches in a number of other ports that he visited along the trade routes around India.

At one point the Alexandrian merchant wrote that he saw a particular kind of ox in India being used for transporting pepper (a clear indication that he did indeed mean India, and not Arabia or elsewhere). The same animal was also eaten for meat. Cosmas described how Christians slaughtered the animal by cutting its throat, which was different than their non-Christian neighbors, who slaughtered by felling the ox with a blow. The passage indicates not only the existence of a Christian community (however small) in a particular region of India, but that it was recognized as a distinctive community, distinguished even by its manner of slaughtering meat. That particular method was, of course, not just Christian but Jewish. It represents further evidence that Christians in the East were still more closely related to Judaism on matters of culture and faith.

The West Syrian churches

Further to the west, Edessa and the entire region of Syria were becoming more firmly locked in Constantinople's theological grip during the fifth century.

---

[8] Cosmas Indicopleustes, *Christian Topography*, trans. J. W. McCrindle (London: Hakluyt Society, 1907), 365. See also 118-119.

Crucifixion and the Women at the Tomb, illustration from the Rabula Syriac Gospels, from Zagba on the Euphrates, ca. 586. Ms. Plut. 1,56F.13r. Biblioteca Laurenziana, Florence. Used with permission of Scala/Art Resource, New York City.

Most Syrians shared the faith of Constantinople but not the culture of Greek Christianity, which was now finding its center in the capital of Byzantium. Increasingly the Syrian bishops found common theological cause with Egypt and the Alexandrians, this despite the fact that Syria was originally the home of the Antiochene school of theology. After 451 most of the major Antiochene voices were forced to migrate across the Persian border to the East, leaving the churches of Syria dominated by western-leaning bishops and teachers.

Syrian spirituality continued to echo the jarring extremes that had for so long characterized its people. In the towns and villages the authority of ascetics often surpassed that even of the bishops. Something of the flavor of this Syrian ascetic spirituality can be found in the story of a compelling figure from the middle of the fifth century, Simeon the Stylite, who dwelt in the city of Telanissos.

In the temple of Atargatis, the Syrian Mother God, in the eastern city of Hierapolis, were two wooden columns some sixty meters high (about 180 feet). Twice a year a man would climb these like a palm tree, hoisting up wood and clothing in order to remain for up to seven days to pray. Simeon the Stylite engaged in a similar spiritual practice (and he was not alone; others performed such feats as well). He constructed a pillar that was between fifteen to twenty meters high, on top of which he then lived. He is reported to have remained there day and night for forty years, doing so as a living reminder of Christ's extreme self-sacrifice. This holy man gained a wide reputation for being both a teacher and healer from atop his pillar. He arbitrated local disputes and spoke against mistreated workers. But mostly he just stood in silent prayer, arms outstretched in the form of the cross.

Theologically during this period the western Syrian churches, especially in the major urban areas, were moving significantly into the orbit of Constantinople. As we have seen in the story of Edessa, the theological position associated with Cyril of Alexandria was receiving increasing support by the end of the fifth century. By the sixth century those who confessed Jesus Christ as having one nature after the incarnation represented the majority of Christians from Edessa to Antioch. The story of their faith will be picked up in chapter 21.

Armenia between the Greeks and Persians

The last quarter of the fourth century was a time of political turmoil for Armenia, a nation caught in the grips of competing Greek and Persian interests. Julian's death and the Roman retreat had opened the door for renewed Persian influences in Armenia. Just how volatile things had become was made evident in 373 when the Armenian patriarch Nerses (353-373) was murdered by the Armenian king because of his Hellenistic leanings. A descendent of Gregory the Illuminator, Nerses had recognized the need for Armenians to develop their own indigenous ecclesiastical institutions. Up to that time they had to read the scriptures in either Greek or Syriac versions. The same was true for the liturgies of their churches, for Armenian was not yet a written language.

It was in light of this national need that the patriarch Sahak (d. 439), assisted by a scribe named Mashtots (or Mesrop) (362-440), set to work to create a new alphabet for the language. Having done so, they then gathered a team of scholars whom they trained to translate both the Bible and a large body of liturgical and theological books into their native tongue. The result was a body of literature that helped preserve a distinctive national church. Over the course of the centuries it also preserved many texts in translation where the original works were lost.

Sahak and Mashtots had sought assistance from the school of the Persians in Edessa for developing the Armenia script. This brought the Armenian church into contact with the works of Theodore of Mopsuestia and the two-nature theology that was favored by his followers. At the same time Sahak sought to develop theological contacts with the Greek church in Constantinople. This led to his ouster as patriarch in 428 by the pro-Persian faction in Armenia. For the next decade the Armenian church was under the leadership of a patriarch approved by the Persian throne and theologically sympathetic to the school in Edessa. In the late 440s the shah of shahs annexed Armenia and attempted to force the Zoroastrian faith upon its people. The Armenian princes with their soldiers were ordered into battle in the Caucasus Mountains, thereby removing them from their homeland, where they might have joined the resistance. The stage was set for Zoroastrian priests to enter the country in 451, backed by a Persian army. When they did so, however, they were met by a mass uprising of the people led by Armenian priests.

The battle that ensued resulted in thousands of Armenian deaths that were regarded as martyrdoms. The patriarch Hovsep was arrested and taken to the Persian capital, where he was executed in 454. Violence continued to plague the nation for several more decades until the shah finally relented and allowed the Armenians to maintain their religious liberty. The Armenian church by this time had begun looking toward Constantinople to its west in its theological allegiance, partly out of respect for the tradition of Gregory the Illuminator and partly as an expression of anti-Persian resistance. The Persian national church had moved more emphatically into the camp of the Antiochene school and the two-nature theology. Politically Armenia was now effectively divided between Persian and Roman zones of influence, making its need for theological unity even more pressing.

An important theological connection with Constantinople had been forged several decades before by Patriarch Sahak, who had succeeded in sending an Armenian delegation to the Roman capital around 435. The Armenians had brought back news of the Council of Ephesus and a letter to their churches from the patriarch of Constantinople. After 450 the western orientation of many in the Armenian churches was aided by the growing acceptance of the one-nature doctrine in Edessa. Under the Roman emperor Zeno (d. 491) a theological treatise known as the *Henoticon* appeared in 482 in an effort to unite the Chalcedonian and non-Chalcedonian churches of the eastern empire. The Armenian church readily embraced Zeno's position, partly out of theological influences from Edessa and partly on anti-Persian grounds. The stage was set for the Synod of Dvin, held between 506 and 508 (the precise date is disputed).

The Synod of Dvin stands among the most important events in Armenia's long Christian history. Representatives came from churches throughout Armenia as well as from Georgia on the coast of the Black Sea. The synod moved forcefully against the two-nature doctrine. Not only was Nestorius denounced, but Leo's *Tome* from Chalcedon was rejected as well. The *Henoticon*, on the other hand, was embraced as a standard of orthodoxy. Within a few years the patriarch of Constantinople had turned away from the position set out in this document, and the non-Chalcedonian churches once again found themselves at odds with Constantinople's theological position. Churches in Georgia, which lived under an independent king, followed their patriarch in embracing the Chalcedonian doctrine and remaining in communion with Constantinople. In Armenia, however, the doctrine on Christ's one-nature remained part of the national church's confession of faith, keeping the Armenian church after that in the non-Chalcedonian family of communions.

Thus, by the early years of the sixth century, we find the national church of Armenia along with many in western Syria committed to the one-nature formulation of faith that is known by those in the churches today simply as the non-Chalcedonian tradition. Further east in the Persian empire, a majority of the churches had come to embrace the two-nature theology of Theodore of Mopsuestia and bishop Nestorius. The Persian national church had extended its mission into India and was found as far north as the Oxus River and Samarkand. A pilgrim traveling among the churches of these regions of the world might well have wondered what Chalcedon had accomplished after all.

19

Christianity in Egypt and Ethiopia

Athanasius had been bishop of Alexandria for less than a decade in 335 when his staunch defense of Nicaea's *homoousious* landed him in exile in Gaul. The death of Constantine opened the door to the bishop's return to Alexandria in 337, but two years later he was sent into exile again. This time he found safe haven in Rome, where his Nicene convictions were readily received, and where he was able to make important political connections with the bishop of Rome. Again he was allowed to return to his episcopal see in Alexandria, were he remained for a decade. One of his acts during this period was to ordain a Syrian youth named Frumentius to be missionary bishop to the city of Axum, capital of the kingdom of Ethiopia. A third period of exile in 356 took Athanasius to the Egyptian desert, where he was given refuge by the monks who lived in the wilderness of southern Egypt. He had visited these monks during his first years as bishop, when he was extending Alexandria's spiritual influence and administrative jurisdiction throughout the region. By the time Athanasius returned home from his fifth and final exile in 366, he had become a living symbol of Egypt's national Christianity and Alexandria's ecclesiastical influence throughout the Christian world.

Egypt

The tension between Athanasius and the successive emperors who sent him into exile was generated in part by clashing theological commitments and in part by political concerns. Athanasius was a popular figure in Alexandria, at a time when anti-imperial sentiments in the city were on the rise. Egypt was the breadbasket of the eastern Roman empire, its grainfields exploited for the benefit of those who lived elsewhere. Little of Alexandria's great wealth made its way into the hands of the city's working classes. Christianity among the Egyptians was taking on nationalistic overtones in this situation, and the bishop of Alexandria played a key political role. On at least one occasion Athanasius was rumored in Constantinople to be planning to block the massive grain shipments that departed Alexandria's harbor for the capital, a possibility that caused great alarm in Constantinople.

209

When Athanasius fled south to avoid arrest at the hands of the emperor's troops, he found refuge among the monks and nuns who lived in the Egyptian desert. He was even able to administer the affairs of the churches under his jurisdiction while in hiding. By the middle of the fourth century a vast network of communities in the desert had emerged, populated by monks and nuns who had renounced their worldly connections in order to pursue lives of holiness. Rapid church growth had led to increased social acceptance and greater accommodation in the practice of church discipline. At the same time legalization and imperial establishment in the fourth century had all but ended Christian martyrdom within the Roman empire. In both cases there was a growing sentiment among many that the Christian movement had lost something of its spiritual edge, something of it dynamic power. The desire for greater discipline and self-sacrifice, for the opportunity to give all for Christ, sent many into the wilderness in search of a life of holiness.

The first Egyptian desert dwellers in the third century had been *anchorites*, or ascetics who lived entirely alone. They foraged for what little food they ate, found water in isolated places, and spent most of their days in prayer and contemplation of God. Yet precisely because they had renounced the material ways of the world in order to pursue a deeper spiritual life, they proved to be attractive to the large numbers of people who traveled out into the wilderness areas who went to seek out their blessings. Finding themselves besieged, the ascetics had little choice but to respond by sharing their spiritual insights and directions.

A highly popular account of a desert hermit was *The Life of Anthony*, written by Athanasius around 357. Anthony (c.251-356) had been a relatively well-to-do Egyptian youth who at the age of twenty abandoned life in society to pursue God alone in the wilderness. He gained a reputation as having spiritual prowess, especially against demons, gaining him a rather large following. Anthony would spend time with these followers, counseling them in spiritual affairs, but he would then take off for long periods of time on his own deep in the wilderness. Although it was reported that he could only speak Egyptian, his reputation grew beyond the national boundaries of his homeland by means of Athanasius's book, which was written in Greek. By the end of the century copies of it were being read in places as far away as Germany.

Recognizing the need to provide a better structure for those seeking the deeper spiritual life of monasticism, an Egyptian ascetic named Pachomius (292-346) early in the fourth century drew up a new rule of community order. This was not the first experiment in *cenobitic* (communal) monasticism. At the time of Anthony, small communities of monks or nuns could already be found living together on the outskirts of towns and villages, but there was no general organized system among them. Pachomius provided just this. He had become a Christian while serving in the military under Constantine and after leaving the army had returned to the region near Tabennisis on the Nile. There he established his first community, which lived according to a rule of order he drew up. Members included both men and women who lived in separate quarters, often three to a room. All property was held in common, and the monks and nuns supported themselves by weaving cloth, making baskets, or engaging in other forms of

Ansate Cross, from Coptic Acts of the Apostles, Middle Egypt, 5th century. Reproduced by permission of the Pierpont Morgan Library/Art Resource, New York City.

Christ Enthroned with Madonna and Child and Saints. Fresco from church in Baduit, Egypt, 6th century. Coptic Museum, Cairo. Reproduced with permission of Vanni/Art Resource, New York City.

production. A three-year probationary period was required for new members, after which one was admitted with full standing.

Monks and nuns who lived according to Pachomius's rule ate regular meals together, abstaining only from meat and wine. Meals were conducted in silence, however, and twice a week everyone fasted. Members of the community were required to gather several times each day for prayer and the reading of the Psalms. Saturdays and Sundays they joined together for eucharistic worship led by a priest. Each person was expected to study and meditate on scriptures. Those who could not read upon entering the community were taught by others how to do so, leading to the establishment of programs for education. All were expected to wear simple clothing that resembled the dress of peasants, including a hood.

At the head of each community Pachomius's rule called for an *archimandrite* (ruler) who was referred to as *abba* (father) or *amma* (mother) by its members, indicating that those who joined were part of a new form of household in Christ. Members were in turn organized into small groups or classes, each one identified by a letter of the Greek alphabet. To various groups were assigned different tasks in the community during the week. They were also expected to study together and look after one another's spiritual well-being. Leaders of each small group could be called upon by the abba or amma to report on each member, thus facilitating the overall organization and spiritual direction of the community.

Pachomius's rule caught on, and within several decades of his death the number of ascetics who were living by it in community had swelled to the tens of thousands. A steady stream of visitors from other parts of the Christian world began to make its way into the Egyptian desert. The names of those who came read like a "who's who" of early Christian monasticism; Etherea of Spain, Melania of Rome, Jerome, Rufinus, John Cassian, and Basil the Great all spent time in monasteries along the Nile. Many, like Basil, took the basic Rule of Pachomius and adapted it to fit their own particular situation. Basil integrated the Egyptian's model into the life of his local congregation. The new rule that he wrote emphasized more the monastic community's relationship to the wider church. Basil's rule called for monks and nuns to be under the pastoral authority of a bishop, for instance. Monks and nuns were expected to serve the church by providing relief for the poor or care for the sick. His influence in developing the monastic principle for the church was great enough to earn for him the title of father of Eastern Orthodox monasticism.

The influence of Egyptian monasticism also spread rapidly in the Latin-speaking West in the fourth and fifth centuries. Athanasius is credited with having given the movement a major boost in Rome by introducing it during his exile from 339 to 346. *The Life of Anthony* was widely read in cities throughout the region. By the last decades of the fourth century, as we will see below, every major Latin theologian had become converted to the ideals of monasticism. Many made the obligatory pilgrimage up the Nile to visit the seedbed of the movement there. Martin of Tours, Jerome, Paula, Eustochium, and Melania the Younger in the fourth century; Patrick in the fifth; and Benedict of Nursia and Radegunde of Gaul in the sixth all added their names to the list of those who embraced not only the discipline but helped to found new monastic communities in the West.

Monasticism became one of the most important vehicles for cross-cultural spiritual fertilization among churches in the world. As Sebastian Brock and Susan Ashbrook Harvey point out, "For the Christendom of Late Antiquity it was holy lives that most often transcended differences of language, culture, and time."[9] In light of this international influence, it is all the more ironic that one of the characteristics of Egyptian monasticism in its own context was its nationalist orientation. Where many of the theologians of Alexandria were of Greek ethnic descent (Athanasius being perhaps the most important exception), many of the desert fathers and mothers were ethnically Egyptian. According to Athanasius, Anthony did not write or speak Greek (a claim which some have questioned). Shenoute of Atripe (d. 450), whose community numbered about four thousand, wrote entirely in Egyptian (later called Coptic).

Nationalist sentiments often found expression in the form of an attack upon the lifestyles of the wealthier classes of Alexandria and the major cities of Egypt, for members of the wealthier classes were often also persons of foreign ethnic descent. The general tenor of Egyptian monasticism reflected the culture of peasants and the countryside in the south rather than the cosmopolitanism of Alexandria in the north. Still, it would be a mistake to reduce Egyptian monasticism to a nationalistic expression, for it was more than this. The desert communities harbored a broader vision of spirituality and ministry.

One of the better-known names of the Egyptian desert tradition was Macarius the Great (c.300–c.390). Although many of the works later attributed to him appear to have been written by others, the monastery he founded at Scete was known to be an important center of teaching. Another of the rich resources left by the fourth- and fifth-century Egyptian teachers is a body of sayings preserved from the desert fathers and mothers who collected much smaller groups of disciples than those found in Pachomian communities. The sayings of the desert fathers and mothers are mostly wisdom sayings and insights gathered orally from these revered teachers. They touch upon such elements as self-discipline, prayer, love, community service, and dealing with demons. At the center is a vision of life with God that combines simplicity and eloquence.

Egyptian monasticism shared at times with its Syrian counterpart traditions of spirituality and practice that were elsewhere in the fourth century being rejected as heretical. One of the major literary discoveries of the twentieth century was a collection of thirteen ancient texts buried in the sands of Upper Egypt near the village of Nag Hammadi. They were mostly Gnostic books, many previously unknown. Dates on accompanying scraps of papyri indicate a mid-fourth-century burial for the collection. A reference to "Father Pachom" and the proximity of a known Pachomian monastery near where the jar of manuscripts was unearthed suggests that they were buried by monks of one of the communities. The best theory we have to date is that members of the community were responding to a pastoral letter Athanasius had written in 367 in which he condemned the reading of what he considered to be heretical texts. One suspects that rather than burn these treasured books, the monks hid them in the desert sands,

---

[9] Brock and Ashbrook Harvey, *Holy Women of the Syrian Orient*, 13.

perhaps forgetting later where they had secreted away their books of higher spiritual knowledge.

Chief among the virtues articulated by the desert fathers and mothers is that of service to one's neighbors. Time and again in the pages of monastic biographies we read of wealthy individuals selling all that they have to give to the poor in order to follow Christ. Among the sayings of the desert fathers and mothers are stories of monks who even sold scriptures in order to give money to the poor. Basil the Great, we have already noted, built his monastery adjacent to the church, where it served as a health-care facility, among other things. In the West, as we will see below, hospitality to strangers was a central component of the rule of Benedict's communities in Italy. In Egypt the White Monastery of Shenoute of Atripe fed thousands of refugees from the raids of hostile tribes further south.

Emergence of the non-Chalcedonian churches

By the end of the fifth century, the controversies that were dividing churches in the Mediterranean world had made their way into the Egyptian desert regions as well. Egyptian Christianity was strongly committed to the one-nature expression of christological faith, due in part to the heritage of Cyril and in part to Chalcedon being identified with Constantinople's imperial domination. One of the first acts of the Council of Chalcedon in 451 had been to depose Alexandria's spiritual leader, Bishop Dioscorus, because of his actions at the previous imperial synod in 449. The wealth of the city of Alexandria made it a major force in the empire, and by extension in the Christian movement as well. Yet we have already seen that in the fourth and fifth centuries the patriarch of Constantinople was becoming invested with greater authority and status. For many in Egypt the rising influence of Constantinople was seen as being at the cost of Alexandria's place in political and ecclesiastical life. These shifting political fortunes in the fifth century could only strengthen the nationalist sentiments that were finding their theological voice in the heritage of the Alexandrian tradition.

No one illustrates this situation better than Cyril of Alexandria (375-444), Dioscorus's predecessor and one of the most influential theologians of the ancient Christian movement. As bishop, Cyril was wont to support questionable and even brutal political tactics. One of the most notorious incidents occurred in 415, when a band of lay monks under his command viciously stripped, beat, and murdered (inside a church no less) Alexandria's last great renowned Platonist philosopher, a woman named Hypatia. As a theologian, however, Cyril provided the language that animated much of the later christological reflection of Chalcedonians and their opponents alike. Cyril argued that after the incarnation there was one incarnate nature of God the Logos. Doing so, he tied the concept of nature close to that of person *(hupostasis)*. The unified person Jesus Christ could not, for Cyril and those who followed his doctrine, be separated into divine and human components.

For a period in the fifth century it looked to many as if Alexandria's distinctive christological expression would win the day over its Antiochene theological rival. The Council of Ephesus was Cyril's triumph. It is emblematic that he was reported to have been accompanied by Shenoute of Atripe, an ardent Egyptian nationalist who opposed Hellenism and whose Coptic writings did much to strengthen the independent identity of the church of Egypt. Yet after Cyril's death his successor, Dioscorus, did not fare so well. Although he triumphed at the Council of Ephesus of 449 (what Pope Leo called the "robber synod"), Chalcedon deposed him. Immediately following Chalcedon the emperor installed by military force a new bishop of Alexandria. Proterius was opposed by a sizable number of the population of Alexandria, who elected their own candidate, Timothy Aelurus, and secured his consecration as a rival patriarch by the hands of other episcopal leaders. Alexandria now had two bishops claiming to represent the authentic line of apostolic succession, a situation analogous to that of both Carthage and Antioch more than a century before. The incendiary nature of the situation resulted in the assassination of Proterius in 457.

In 482 the emperor Zeno, in an effort to win back the non-Chalcedonian churches, issued a formula of union called the *Henoticon*. Drafted by the patriarch Acacius, it suggested a compromise that took the theological position of Cyril as the standard for orthodoxy, condemned Nestorianism, and avoided any mention of Chalcedon or Leo's *Tome*. Because of the last point the pope condemned the *Henoticon* and pronounced the patriarch of Constantinople excommunicated. Meanwhile, in the eastern regions of the empire the non-Chalcedonian churches failed to endorse the formula, leaving Zeno's political agenda unfulfilled.

Following Zeno, both patriarch and emperor returned to supporting the Chalcedonian faith. In Egypt, meanwhile, two ecclesiastical networks had emerged, similar to the situation with the Donatists in Roman North Africa. One of the churches (the Chalcedonian or Melkite) was headed by a bishop of Alexandria who embraced the definition of Chalcedon and was in communion with the patriarch of Constantinople. The other (the non-Chalcedonian or Monophysite) was headed by a bishop of Alexandria who did not accept the definition of Chalcedon and who was looked upon as the legitimate head (or pope) of the true Orthodox churches of the world. In Alexandria the liturgies of the two communions were similar, as were their sacramental vestments, their orders of leadership, their church buildings, and even their spiritual practices. Indeed, a visitor to churches of both communions in Alexandria in the sixth century would have been hard-pressed to distinguish between them. Yet those who were involved in the controversy seemed to know exactly which side they were on and who was for or against them.

Ethiopia

The Chalcedonian churches in Egypt often represented those who supported Constantinople's rule. Roman imperial influence ended around the area of Aswan. South of that lay the land that had in ancient times been known as Kush. By the first century CE the city of Meroë had risen to dominance, but it had fallen by 325 to invading tribes known from Roman historians as the Blemmyes and Nobatae.

The Blemmyes in particular opposed their newly Christian neighbors to the north, because the latter had sought to close the ancient Temple of Isis in Philae. At one point Nestorius, the former bishop of Constantinople who was sent by the emperor into exile as a heretic, was taken captive by the Blemmyes in one of the many raids they carried out upon the towns and monasteries across the Egyptian border. (Ironically it was Shenoute of Atripe, one of Nestorius's most bitter opponents, who provided refuge for many other victims of the Blemmyes' raids.)

During the fourth century several other tribes, about whom little is known, moved into the region as well. Several independent kingdoms were formed along the Nile in what was now collectively known as Nubia. Christian influences were minimal prior to 500, although there is archeological evidence that Christian practices were beginning to seep into the region. It is further south along the Nile that we must look to see the Christian movement spreading before 500 south of Egypt. There we find the city of Axum, capital of a kingdom better known as Abyssinia or Ethiopia. From the middle of the fourth century the king of Axum began to follow the Christian faith. The perspective of the Abyssinian church was catholic, for it looked beyond its own borders to the bishop of Alexandria as its pope (or father) in the faith. At the same time Christianity in Ethiopia was from its beginnings grounded in national cultural life and thus an example of a distinctive African church. Beyond the boundaries of both Roman and Persian imperial rule, the Ethiopian church has for centuries served as a symbol of independent African Christian faith.

Reports of the Christian gospel being preached in Ethiopia can be found early in the Christian movement. The *Apocryphal Acts of the Apostles* tells a story of Matthew going to Ethiopia and meeting the eunuch whom Philip had baptized. Matthew supposedly converted the king of Ethiopia and baptized him. But when the king's brother took the throne, he had Matthew executed because the apostle refused to sanction his marriage to his niece. Although the story appears to have no historical basis, the fact that it locates Matthew south of Egypt is significant in terms of early Christian self-understanding. Since the term *Ethiopia* was often used in Greco-Roman literature to refer to the entire region of Africa south of Egypt, it is not always clear what exactly is meant by it. Our knowledge of Christian expansion in the region is plagued by a persistent lack of adequate historical records. We can only assume (and it is a safe historical assumption) that Christians were traveling most places where there were traders from the Mediterranean world in the first several centuries of the movement. This included the African cities of Meroë (in Nubia) and later Axum (in Ethiopia).

One early Christian tradition that is important for the churches of Africa south of Egypt concerns an unnamed visitor to Jerusalem identified in Acts 8. Luke tells of the baptism of "an Ethiopian eunuch, a court official of the Candace, queen of the Ethiopians, in charge of her entire treasury" (8:27, NRSV). The court Luke was referring to was that of the city of Meroë, whose queen was called Candace. During the time of Augustus, that African nation had reached a treaty with the Romans that opened up diplomatic relations between them and allowed for travel and exchange. The eunuch represents an independent nation beyond the borders of the Roman empire; he works for a queen who does not pay tribute to Caesar, yet he can travel freely through a Roman-controlled territory. His conversion and baptism represent in Acts the passage of Christianity beyond the boundaries of the Roman empire, several chapters before the conversion of the Roman centurion of the Italian cohort Cornelius in chapter 10.

The historical basis of this story continues to be debated by biblical scholars today. Even if it is historically accurate, however, the story of the conversion of the government eunuch from Meroë does not necessarily mean that there was the beginnings of a Christian history in that city, nor in Ethiopia in general. He might have been baptized, but there is neither archeological nor written evidence that there was a Christian community in Meroë before the kingdom declined late in the third century.

The decline of Meroë left a political power vacuum in the region of Africa south of Egypt. Into this void stepped the kingdom of Axum, or Ethiopia, in the fourth century. The Axumites appear to have originally been colonists from southern Arabia who crossed over the Red Sea and established an independent kingdom along the Nile. Ethnically they were related to the Saracens in southern Arabia. They worshiped Arabian gods and spoke a Semitic language. Other than the occasional reference or apocryphal report, we have little historical evidence of an active Christian community in Axum before the middle of the fourth century. It is then that our evidence becomes more dependable.

The story is one that is revered in the memory of Ethiopian ecclesiastical tradition. According to several ancient versions, early in the fourth century a Christian teacher by the name of Meropius from Tyre (in Syria) had taken two youths in his charge, Frumentius and Aedesius, on a journey into the southern region of the Red Sea. Meropius was the tutor of the two youths, and the trip was an educational venture. Disaster struck on their return voyage when they stopped at a port to replenish supplies. Unbeknown to the travelers, the inhabitants of that port city had recently broken their commercial treaty with the Romans, which meant the travelers could not count upon Roman protection. All the adults aboard the ship were massacred, the ship and its contents seized, and the two youths sold into slavery to the king of Axum.

Although they were captives in a foreign land, the two youths quickly advanced in the king's household. So valuable was their service that upon the king's death they were entrusted with raising his young son, Ezana (or Aezanas). Eventually freed by the queen and her son, Aedesius returned to his native city of Tyre, but Frumentius traveled to Alexandria. There around the year 347 he sought out Athanasius, bishop of Alexandria, reporting to him on the situation in Axum and requesting a bishop be sent to ordain priests and instruct the people in the way of Christianity. Athanasius decided to consecrate Frumentius himself to this position. Frumentius, also known in Ethiopian history as Bishop Salama, returned as a missionary to Axum. He is credited by Ethiopian tradition not only with bringing about the conversion of the royal household but also with planting churches, ordaining priests, opening a school, and translating portions of scripture into the ancient Ethiopian language, Ge'ez.

Ezana's conversion can be historically confirmed indirectly from around this time from both royal inscriptions and coins that he minted. An inscription from the same king on a stele from Ethiopia, dated around the year 350, details a military excursion he carried out against Noba (Nobatae) and others to his north. The inscription begins and ends with a Christian invocation to the name of the Lord of all, by whose might the king now sought to extend the rule of his kingdom northward. A letter from the Roman emperor Constantius II to Ezana and preserved by Athanasius confirms the importance of Frumentius's role in the growth of Christianity in the Axumite kingdom. It was written in 357 after Constantius had deposed Athanasius because of the latter's uncompromising anti-Arian stance. Constantius requested that the king of Ethiopia force Frumentius to return to Alexandria to be examined on his beliefs and warned the Ethiopians against Athanasius's teachings. The Roman emperor's effort appears to have been without avail, however, for Frumentius remained in Axum and Ethiopia remained firmly committed to the Nicene doctrine of Jesus Christ being of the same substance as the Father.

Under Frumentius, Christianity did not spread far beyond the royal family and the capital of Axum. The major task of evangelizing the Ethiopian countryside fell to a group of missionary monks more than a century later. Known as the Nine Saints *(Teseatu Keddusan)*, they arrived in Ethiopia in 480, fleeing the Byzantine empire on account of their anti-Chalcedonian stance. The Nine Saints were from Syria, and at least some of them appear to have lived in monasteries in Egypt founded by Pachomius prior to moving further south. They introduced monasteries to Ethiopia following Pachomius's rule, providing the foundations for what remains today among the most distinctive monastic traditions of the Christian movement. Not long after the arrival of these original Nine Saints, other refugees fleeing Byzantine persecution followed them to make Ethiopia their home. Through their combined efforts over several decades, Christianity was extended deep into countryside of Ethiopia, including the regions of Tigre and Eritrea.

Since the days of Frumentius the influence of Alexandria and Egyptian Christian tradition in Ethiopia has remained strong. Until the twentieth century the Ethiopian church recognized the authority of the pope of Alexandria to appoint the patriarch of Ethiopia, for instance. Even today the Ethiopian Orthodox Church remains in communion with the Coptic church of Egypt, whose bishop in Alexandria it still recognizes as pope. Many of the administrative decisions of the Coptic church are shared by the Ethiopian Orthodox Church. Frumentius began the project of translating the scriptures from the Septuagint into Ge'ez, a task that took several centuries to complete. The Ethiopian canon includes several books that were not accepted by the churches of either Rome or Constantinople but are found in the Coptic canon, including the *Infancy Gospel of James* and the *Week of Enoch*. All told, the Ethiopian scriptures include eighty-one books, a number of which are regarded as apocryphal in western Protestant and Roman Catholic churches.

The influence of Egyptian monasticism strengthened the connections between the two lands, for many of the early Ethiopian communities show evidence of following the Pachomian rule. Syrian influences were also seen in the Ethiopian churches, however, for instance in the architecture and liturgy. The fact that the

Nine Saints in the fifth century were regarded as Syrian is significant in this connection. Monasticism is still strong in Ethiopia today and continues to reflect much of the ancient tradition of austerity and remoteness. Even today it is not uncommon to find monks remaining in solitude for prayer for many years.

One of the best indications we have of the spread of Christianity in Ethiopia by the sixth century comes from the Egyptian monk Cosmas Indicopleustes, whose *Christian Topography* has been referred to above. In 525 Indicopleustes was in the Ethiopian port of Adulis, he tells us, as the king of Ethiopia was preparing an expedition against Arabia (see Part V below). As he traveled throughout the kingdom, he found churches everywhere he went. The churches of Ethiopia that he saw, as far as we can tell, after the fifth century were firm adherents of the non-Chalcedonian doctrine. Administratively they were closely linked with the pope in Alexandria. Spiritually they shared with both Egyptian and Syrian Christian traditions a strong monastic heritage. Politically they were part of a kingdom that remained independent of Roman or Persian imperial control, although economic trade linked the city of Axum with both empires and with India. Historically they have served as an important symbol of African independent Christianity's connection to the earliest churches of the apostles by way of Alexandria. With the churches of Egypt, Ethiopia, and later Nubia we find a continuous historical tradition of Christian faith that is very much at home in this continent. In the fourth and fifth centuries the northern regions of Africa were in fact among the most Christian of the world.

20

Rome and the Latin Churches in the West

In the fall of 343 Constantine's sons, Constans and Constantius II, summoned a synod of bishops from their respective realms to meet in Sardica. The brothers were joint rulers at the time, the dividing line between them falling roughly along the line that Diocletian had drawn half a century before. It followed the cultural divide that cut through the Mediterranean world; the Roman West spoke Latin, while in the Roman East, Greek was the dominant language, although there were places where Egyptian or Syriac was preferred. Although the imperial court was moved to Milan in 354 to better defend the northern borders, Rome was still the dominant city in the western Mediterranean world, and the bishop of Rome was regarded as the highest ecclesiastical position among the churches. In the East, Constantinople had become the dominant political presence, although both Antioch and Alexandria continued to command substantial economic strength and ecclesiastical authority.

It was symbolic that the Council of Sardica divided even before it began. Seeing themselves outnumbered, the eastern delegates withdrew, leaving their western counterparts joined by Athanasius to go ahead with the event. Had it taken place as planned, the two bishops who had successively served as Constantine's primary advisors, Hosius of Cordova and Eusebius of Nicomedia, would have been together again. Hosius of Cordova was originally from Spain, where he had taken part in the first recorded Spanish council, held in Elvira in 306. From around the year 312 until 326 he had been Constantine's chief councilor for ecclesiastical affairs. With Eusebius of Nicomedia he had played an active role in the gathering at Nicaea, shortly after which Hosius had returned to Spain.

Eusebius, on the other hand, had been forced into exile by Constantine after Nicaea because of the bishop's refusal to condemn Arius. Within two years he was called back by the emperor, however, and took Hosius's place among Constantine's closest advisors. It was Eusebius of Nicomedia who administered baptism to Constantine on his deathbed in 337 and who now was the primary theological voice supporting a moderate Arian confession of faith in the East. Hosius presided over the gathering of western bishops that went ahead with the council at Sardica and condemned the Arian position (although not Eusebius of Nicomedia by name). The bishops then affirmed the jurisdictional role of the bishop of Rome in church affairs and sent a letter to the emperor in the East requesting that he refrain from interfering in the same.

The Council of Sardica provides us with a glimpse at the growing divide between the Greek and Roman halves of the Mediterranean world. Two distinct church traditions were emerging, although in the fourth and much of the fifth centuries they still recognized one another in full communion. There were signs of conflict on the horizon, exacerbated by the changing cultural and political climate of the Roman empire. On the surface the most important issues around which conflict occurred centered on questions of authority and leadership. The role of the bishop of Rome in relation to the rest of the episcopal collegium ranked high on the list of western concerns. At a deeper level a growing divide in both theology and spirituality was separating these two church communions in new and subtle ways as the Roman empire entered that period historians often call Late Antiquity.

The political transformation of the West

The western Mediterranean was still dominated by the older Roman ruling class in the fourth century. Spain, Italy, and parts of Gaul were entirely Latin in language and culture, while in Roman North Africa, the rest of Gaul, the western Balkans, and Britain various other languages were still spoken among the rural populations. Christians still numbered less than half the total population around the year 400, although they were the majority in many cities (including Rome). Most western Christians belonged to churches of the Catholic party, whose bishops looked to Rome for administrative leadership. A scattering of other churches were found throughout the region, such as Novatianists. The Manichaeans were attracting a following as well, although they were severely restricted by imperial policy. Adding to the mix was a sizable number of Jewish communities scattered across the western Mediterranean.

A third-century treatise by Cyprian of Carthage, *On the Unity of the Church*, had strongly defended the spiritual authority of bishops in the church. Jesus had invested all of the apostles with equal authority and power, Cyprian had argued. This authority and power was in turn passed along to the successors of the apostles, or bishops. All those who had been ordained to episcopal office were thus equal in authority and power. However, Cyprian went on, Jesus had first given authority to Peter. His temporal priority among the apostles was a symbol of the unity of the episcopacy of the entire church. It was a short step to transfer this argument for the priority of Peter to the authority of the bishop of Rome, who was considered by many to have inherited the authority of Peter much as a son inherits that of his father. In the fourth century this authority was taking on administrative and judicial characteristics in the West.

The argument for the preeminence of the bishop of Rome grew among Catholic Christians in the West while it diminished among the Catholic Christians in the East. Bishops and emperors alike in the Greek-speaking churches acknowledged the important position that the bishop of Rome held in the Christian scheme of things. Yet the actual power of Rome began to shift away after Constantine decided to move his capital to the East. The social effects of Constantine's move were dramatic. Economically it set in motion Rome's decline as the most significant commercial center of the Mediterranean region, if not the entire world. A political power vacuum was created as well, at precisely the time when increased migrations of tribes from beyond the borders of the empire were beginning to unsettle the situation in the West. The western capital was moved from Rome to Milan, at the foot of the Alps, in order to be closer to the northern frontier that was now in a constant state of military activity. Early in the fifth century the western capital was again moved, this time to Ravenna on the Adriatic seacoast. Surrounded by marshes, it was perceived to offer more protection from the invaders who by now were a regular feature of western political life. By the year 400 emperors rarely even visited the ancient city that had lent to the empire its glorious name.

Others began to visit, however, with increasing regularity. During the 390s an army of the Visigoths (Western Goths) under a general named Alaric had been carrying out military campaigns in the eastern Balkan region and Greece. Arian Christian in their faith, many Visigoths had served as soldiers under Roman command. They were now in search of land on which they could dwell. In 401 they entered the north of Italy, followed by their families with belongings in tow. They returned in 408, this time reaching the walls of Rome itself before being turned away by a payment of ransom. The amount said to have been raised by the citizens of the city was in the thousands of kilos of gold and silver. Still it was not enough. Two years later the Visigoths were back at the gates of Rome again, only now there was no viable military defense to oppose them. Most of the members of the Roman upper classes had abandoned the city in advance of the impending threat, leaving church leaders alone to deal with the crisis of invasion. The Visigoth army entered the city to plunder, rape, and burn. Their leaders had ordered, however, that no one who took refuge in a church was to be harmed, since the Visigoths were Christians. The sudden death of the Visigoth leader, Alaric, several days later ended the sack of Rome, but the Visigoths were in Italy to stay.

Some forty years later Rome was again under siege, this time by an army of Huns whose leader, Attila, had become known as the Scourge of the World. The Huns had come from the region of central Asia decades before and were conducting military campaigns along the northern Roman border. Unlike the Germanic tribes that they had pushed before them, the Huns were not Christians. Their warriors were feared as much for their ferocity as for their skill on horseback. Huns were said to eat and even sleep on their mounts, accounting for their ability to move swiftly across great stretches of terrain. For more than a decade Attila had exploited the Romans' fears to draw annual payments of tribute from the imperial treasury. Then, in 451, he launched a new series of raids through Gaul and northern Italy. The Huns returned in 452, this time reaching central Italy before being turned away by the skilled negotiations of Pope Leo. Only Attila's death the following year brought an end to the threat of his army.

While the Visigoths had been carrying out their excursions through Italy in 408 through 410, an army of another Germanic tribe known as Vandals had moved into Spain. Two decades later they had crossed into North Africa, landing in 429. Over the course of the next decade they systematically advanced from city to city until they had control of the entire region. Like the Visigoths, the Vandals were Arian in their religion. Unlike the Visigoths, however, they showed little interest in recognizing any common Christian heritage they might have shared with others. They ransacked the cities, sold off inhabitants into slavery, and destroyed many churches, Donatist and Catholic alike. By 440 they had established an independent kingdom in North Africa that survived for nearly a century. In 455 they crossed back over into Italy and advanced upon the city of Rome. Once again it fell to Leo to negotiate with a hostile army seeking to sack the great city. The Vandals were convinced to enter the city and take whatever remaining wealth they could find, leaving its people unmolested this time.

By now the numbers of immigrants pouring into the western Roman lands had become a flood. The Vandals who crossed into North Africa were said to number more than 150,000, while the total number of new settlers in Gaul is estimated to have been over 100,000. Sueves and Alani pushed into Spain. Burgundians, Lombards, and others entered the north of Italy. Facing a deteriorating political situation, successive Roman emperors sought to buy off these new invaders, incorporate their young men into the army as mercenaries, or grant sections of Roman territories for them to resettle (the last option little more than conceding the inevitable). This was why an army of the Visigoths was invited to help the empire defend its territories by resettling in Spain, which they did. In 466 they assumed political control of the entire Iberian Peninsula and established an independent Visigoth kingdom.

By the latter part of the fifth century the Visigoths were speaking the same Latin language as their Catholic neighbors, having abandoned for the most part their own original Gothic tongue. The liturgies of the two churches (Roman Catholic and Visigoth Arian) were virtually the same, save for their doxologies: Arians only gave glory to the Father through the Son in the Holy Spirit, while Catholics could also give glory to the Father and the Son and the Holy Spirit. That was enough to sustain the theological divide between the ruling Visigoth kings and the majority of their subjects in Spain for more than a century.

Further north a third wave of invasions into former Roman territory was taking place in the wake of the empire's administrative withdrawal from Britain early in the fifth century. Angles, Saxons, and Jutes poured across the North Sea and into the island in search of both land and wealth. The kingdoms they established under local military leaders did little more than wage war and collect tribute. The new residents of Britain were not Christians of any persuasion, and their arrival disrupted ministry among the peoples of Britain for more than a century. Church buildings were abandoned, and the numbers of clergy diminished among the Britons or Romans who stayed.

By 475 the northern border of the western empire had collapsed for all intents and purposes. The new inhabitants soon settled down to become farmers or to take on administrative details of running their new kingdoms. The older landowners and Latin-speaking aristocracy now had little choice but to deal with the region's new rulers. Spain, North Africa, and parts of Italy had all passed out of the tax rolls of the imperial treasury, limiting whatever dreams the nominal western Roman rulers might have had of raising an army to retake their domains. By the last decades of the fifth century the entire political, social, and cultural landscape of the western Roman world was in the midst of a profound transformation.

In northern Italy various Germanic kings continued for a time to rule along-side the western emperors, whose court was in Ravenna. By 476 Constantinople's political grip on the region had become negligible. That year a Germanic soldier named Odoacer (434-493) from one of the smaller tribes forced a young western emperor to resign. Odoacer returned the imperial insignia to Zeno in Constantinople and took for himself the title of king. Although he continued to give nominal allegiance to the emperor, with his reign historians of antiquity often date the fall of the western Roman empire.

Odoacer in turn was overthrown by an Ostrogoth (Eastern Goth) named Theodoric in 493. Theodoric (455-526) was the son of an Arian father and a Catholic mother. As a boy he had been raised in Constantinople, sent there as a guarantee that his Ostrogoth father would keep his peace treaty with the emperor. Upon the death of his father, Theodoric returned to his people to become king. With the encouragement of the emperor, he moved the entire tribe west-ward into Italy, seizing power from Odoacer and establishing himself in Ravenna in 493. Theodoric, like most Ostrogoths, was an Arian Christian, but he proved to be rather tolerant of the Catholic faith of the majority of his subjects. In name he remained a subject of the emperor in Constantinople, but in fact he exercised an independent, and sometimes tyrannical rule. Late in his reign Theodoric executed one of the ablest minds of his day, the Catholic theologian Boethius, on the suspicion that the latter had collaborated with the emperor against him.

The sixth century opened with Germanic kings ruling over the entire western Empire, including the ancient imperial city of Rome itself. Among Catholic believers the position of the pope as both spiritual and administrative head of their churches was more important than ever. There were no western Catholic kings or emperors to enforce the decisions of church councils, punish dissident believers, or help fund salaries. Churches and monasteries had to look to new avenues for financial support, mainly from among the private donations of the wealthy. Churches, which in most places were still Catholic, grew in importance in the eyes of the Latin-speaking majorities as carriers of the older culture, if not of civilization itself.

Theological developments in the West

Ambrose of Milan

The changing situation created a political vacuum in the West that called forth new resources from church leaders. Bishops were often the only officials left to carry on many of the administrative tasks in the cities. They saw that foods were distributed and looked after many of the day-to-day details of civic affairs. The authority of bishops began to supplant even that of emperors in the West, this despite the not-so-insignificant power the latter could muster. One of the best examples of this was the case of Ambrose of Milan (339-397), a former governor of northern Italy who was consecrated bishop by popular demand in 374. Ambrose had been raised in a Christian family and educated in Rome. But he was still only a catechumen at age 35 when as governor of northern Italy he was elected to the bishopric. Baptized and consecrated within a matter of days, he threw himself into his new pastoral responsibilities with enthusiasm. Like his near-contemporary in Constantinople, John Chrysostom, Ambrose condemned the excessive greed and wealth of the upper classes in his region. His sermons were full of biblical references and imagery. One of the enduring contributions he made to the churches of the world was the hymnody that he composed. Christians still sing in various translations compositions that Ambrose penned for his congregation in Milan.

For more than two decades Ambrose exercised considerable influence upon the Spanish-born emperor Theodosius. An active supporter of the Nicene cause and convener of the Council of Constantinople in 381, Theodosius was frequently in residence at court in Milan. He regularly attended the main church in the city, where he heard Ambrose preach. One of the most telling incidents in his relationship to the bishop occurred in 390. The emperor had ordered the massacre of the inhabitants of Thessalonica following the killing of one of his imperial representatives in the city. Shocked by the barbarity of the act, Ambrose ordered Theodosius to undergo public penance for the deed, forbidding him access to the eucharistic table until he did so. Theodosius submitted, providing a precedent for church-state relations that would later be drawn upon by other church leaders in the Catholic West.

Martin of Tours

Ambrose's context was an imperial urban one, and most of his congregation represented the urban ruling class. Elsewhere in the fourth century, bishops in the West were also involved in day-to-day forms of ministry and evangelism that were reaching to the rural workers and common people. No one embodies this particular form of ministry better than Martin of Tours (316-397). As a child, Martin had moved to Italy, where his father served in the army. Martin himself served as a soldier for several years, during which time he converted to Christianity. In 354 he was baptized and took up the life of a hermit. But his life was not to remain one of solitude. After spending time in Milan, he was ordained to the episcopacy in Gaul in 371 and appointed to Tours. He did not assume the trappings that were coming to characterize the episcopacy elsewhere in the Roman world in his day. Martin dressed more like a peasant than a landowner or aristocrat, and he lived in the monastery that he founded outside the city rather than in the house set aside for the bishop.

Martin's evangelistic campaign in the countryside was carried out in part by opposing the traditional gods and their rituals directly. He demolished local shrines in some places and on at least one occasion set fire to a temple that was in the service of another deity. The fire nearly destroyed an adjacent dwelling of an innocent party, until, the narrative of Martin's life assures us, the bishop commanded the fire to turn away. Such acts of destruction became standard fare in the program of western missionaries in later centuries as overzealous preachers tried to win converts from among traditional religions. Eventually the attitude that Martin exemplified toward other gods and rituals was supplemented by more accommodating forms of missionary outreach that sought to transfer people's allegiances from their traditional local deities to Jesus Christ.

Martin's acts of destruction in the fifth century were dramatic, but they do not appear to have been what most endeared him to his followers. The most effective evangelistic practices, in his own time and in centuries following, were his miracles. In them we catch a glimpse of the positive reasons why common people turned to the Christian God about whom Martin spoke. This holy man often saw visions, and he exorcised evil spirits from people who were possessed. Among the numerous miracles he is reported to have worked, many involved healing, often brought about at a distance through contact with articles he touched. Nor did these miracles cease with Martin's death. Nearly two centuries later Gregory of Tours collected an impressive body of stories that were a testimony to the healing power of the shrine associated with Martin of Tours. Simply visiting the site of this holy man's remains was enough in many cases to bring about a miraculous healing. The phenomenon reminds us of the devotion to martyrs that we previously encountered in the Mediterranean world. The spiritual power of the martyrs gave way in the Roman world to that of monks and nuns who continued to practice forms of self-sacrifice. A different form of spiritual leader, that of a holy person who exercised healing with attendant signs and wonders, found a new form of expression in the life of Martin of Tours.

Priscillian

Martin and Ambrose both are known for having opposed the imperial household on one of the more infamous cases of their day, that of a native of Spain named Priscillian (340-387). Priscillian was a convert to Christianity who had adopted a strict ascetic lifestyle. He and several associates were the target of condemnation by a council in Spain held in 380. They were accused of reading apocryphal texts and of engaging in ascetic practices that had become associated with Manichaeans in the West. Priscillian did indeed advocate the study of apocryphal texts, but he advocated even more the study of the Bible. The charges of Manichaean teaching seem to have derived not only from his strict asceticism but from his apocalyptic sense of the growing demonic power at work in the world and the highly dualistic view of the cosmic struggle that he espoused. These last points put him at odds with the direction church life was taking in the fourth century.

The situation worsened when Priscillian was ordained a bishop by several other bishops. His opponents quickly secured an order from the emperor banning him from assuming the office. Priscillian decided to travel to Milan and

Rome to make his case before emperor and pope alike. On the way he gained the support of several influential women from Bordeaux who joined his small community of supporters. The pope refused to hear the case, but a sympathetic emperor ordered him reinstated in Spain. Several months later a new emperor was on the throne, and again his opponents in Spain sought to have him removed. This time Priscillian was ordered to stand trial before an ecclesiastical court, but he appealed to the emperor himself. By now the charges against him had grown to include sorcery, conducting illicit meetings with women, and praying naked. Chief among the concerns of his opponents was his relationship with women, for Priscillian consider men and women equal. He had even developed a reputation for allowing men and women to study and pray together in private meetings. A trial was finally held at Trier. After being questioned (most likely under torture), Priscillian was found guilty of sexual immorality (the charges were fueled by rumors of pregnancies and abortions), sorcery, and Manichaeism. In 385 he and four other men and women were executed, an act to which both Ambrose and Martin objected strenuously.

The case of Priscillian reflects a number of the anxieties of his age, including questions concerning the new public role of the church and its bishops, the exercise of power in the Roman empire, and relationships between women and men in the church. Priscillian refused to recognize such sharply defined distinctions between the genders, at least among those who had committed themselves to an ascetic life in Christ. The use of capital punishment to control church teaching was also a major step down a long road of heresy trials and the use of violence in the name of orthodox Christian faith. Not all agreed with this direction, however. Martin of Tours, for one, saw the executions as a profound distortion of Christian faith.

Jerome, Marcella, Paula, and Eustochium

The last decades of the fourth century witnessed another unusual group of women and men ascetics who at times were also able to stir controversy in the western churches, but whose contributions had a more enduring effect upon the Latin theological tradition. One of their number was a man named Jerome (347-420). Born to Christian parents, he was educated in the classics of Latin philosophy at Rome before being baptized at the age of nineteen. A trip to Trier introduced him to Athanasius's *The Life of Saint Anthony* and the joys of ascetic spirituality. Several years later he traveled to Antioch to study Greek and Hebrew (the latter from Jewish teachers) and was ordained there as a presbyter. By 382 he was back in Rome where he became the secretary to Pope Damasus.

In Rome, Jerome made the acquaintance of a circle of upper-class women who had embraced the ascetic life. One of them, Marcella (325-410), as a child had met Athanasius when he was in Rome. Whether it was from the famed Alexandrian bishop himself or from others that she first encountered the ascetic teaching we do not know. In any case, upon the early death of her husband she took a vow of celibacy and opened her home to other women who were pursuing more spiritual lives as well. From Jerome's correspondence with her we learn that she and Jerome spent time together studying the Bible in private. From several of his other letters, it is clear that Jerome had a high regard for her biblical and theological insights. Marcella was sought out by other church leaders in the city on account of her ability to interpret the scriptures. Jerome said that she learned how to make her own insights appear to be those of a male teacher, thereby not seeming to violate the apostle's injunction that women not teach or to offend the pride of the male priests who came to her for assistance. She died shortly after the invasion of the Visigoths in 410, reportedly from injuries sustained during the attack.

Another woman with whom Jerome developed a close friendship in Rome was a wealthy widow named Paula (347-404). Paula had been one of the Christian women who gathered at Marcella's home. The mother of five, she became a full member of the ascetic circle following the death of her husband around the year 380. Paula quickly became one of the most visible Christian women in the city. At one point she even housed Epiphanius, bishop of Salamis, while he was at Rome for an ecclesiastical synod. Like Marcella, Paula was regarded by others in the city as a skilled interpreter of the Bible. She too carried on active study of the text in private with Jerome. So close was their relationship, in fact, that they were accused on at least one occasion of being sexually involved. There is no evidence, however, that Paula or any of the other women from her circle in Rome broke her vow of sexual abstinence. Several of Paula's daughters joined her in pursuit of a life of piety through the renunciation of the desires of the flesh. One of them, Eustochium (c. 370-419), was also a frequent recipient of Jerome's letters.

After Pope Damasus died it looked for a time as if Jerome might succeed him; when that did not happen, Jerome left for Palestine. Opinion was turning against the ascetic circle of Marcella, Paula, Eustochium, and Jerome, due in no small part to their persistent criticisms of the excessive pursuit of pleasure they witnessed among the citizens of Rome. Paula and her daughter Eustochium departed the city soon after Jerome and joined him in Antioch in 385. For the next year the three friends and spiritual colleagues traveled together through Palestine and Egypt, calling upon various church leaders and visiting monasteries, especially in the Egyptian desert. By the summer of 386 they were back in Bethlehem, where the three founded a joint monastic community for men and women, funded by Paula's wealth (at one point she owned property on three continents).

The three set to work in Bethlehem pursuing biblical study and translation. Earlier Jerome had been asked by Pope Damasus to produce a new Latin version of the Bible, a project that occupied him for many years. Eventually he and his colleagues succeeded in producing what is arguably one of the most important translations of scripture in Christian history, the Latin Vulgate. One of the major assets of the work was that the translation of the Old Testament was made from the Hebrew scriptures. It is reported that in Bethlehem, Jerome studied with rabbis in order to gain a fuller knowledge of the biblical texts he was translating. We can also gather from his letters that he had passed on to Paula and Eustochium much of what he was learning, for they continued to work alongside him in both studying and translating the scriptures.

One of the questions their relationship raises concerns the contribution such women made to theological scholarship in their day. Most history texts identify Paula and Eustochium simply as women for whom Jerome served as spiritual counselor. Little is said of what counsel they might have provided for him. This is in part due to the lack of evidence of such counsel, which comes to us mainly in the form of Jerome's letters. The problem is that women in the fourth century generally did not write letters and other literary documents, or if they did, their letters were not preserved as were the works of men. We have only one letter written by Paula and Eustochium to Jerome, and it is preserved among the collection of his epistles. We know that women of the upper classes could be highly educated. Some wrote poetry and engaged in other such literary pursuits. Certainly the letters of Jerome attest to the ability of the women who were their recipients to read them and to comprehend the various biblical and theological arguments. His letters suggest that they wrote back to him from time to time to preserve ideas or the memory of certain events. He certainly attests to their theological ideas being worthwhile.

Jerome has been credited almost universally with the translation of the Vulgate. Yet by his own account he was often prompted by Paula to consider particular insights or ideas regarding the texts on which he was working. He claims to have been primarily responsible for teaching both women Hebrew. Yet he admired Paula's fluency in the language, which came to surpass his own:

> While I myself, beginning as a young man, have with much toil and effort partially acquired the Hebrew tongue . . . Paula, making up her mind that she too would learn it, succeeded so well that she could chant the Psalms in Hebrew and could speak the language without a trace of the pronunciation peculiar to Latin.[10]

How much of a contribution Paula, Eustochium, and others made to his project we cannot tell. Ignoring them entirely in relation to the project, however, as well as to the biblical commentaries that Jerome produced, would be a mistake.

The body of commentaries is considerable. It includes works on the Psalms, the prophets, several other Old Testament books, and Paul. Jerome is also credited with translating into Latin the works of a number of other theologians, including Didymus the Blind's *On the Holy Spirit*, Pachomius's *Rule*, and Origen's *On First Principles*. That last-mentioned work he issued in response to another translation of Origen's book that had been completed by one of Jerome's contemporaries named Rufinus. Earlier in his life Jerome had shown an appreciation for many of Origen's insights. By the year 400, however, he had come to oppose what he considered to be the early Alexandrian's erroneous teachings regarding the nature of the body that would be resurrected.

---

[10] Jerome, *Letter 108 (to Eustochium)*, trans S. L. Greenslade, in *Handmaids of the Lord: Contemporary Descriptions of Feminine Asceticism in the First Six Christian Centuries*, ed. Joan M. Petersen (Kalamazoo, Mich.: Cistercian Publications, 1996), 155.

Origen, in Jerome's eyes, disregarded the value of the body by denying its sexual organs would be part of the resurrection. For Jerome, the integrity of the physical body, and by extension of the goodness of the material world of creation, required an affirmation of the resurrection of the physical body that included its sexual nature. However, Jerome was quick to affirm, all human beings in eternity would be sexually celibate. This is why he placed such an emphasis upon asceticism and the type of friendships between women and men that it permitted to develop. Asceticism on earth was a foretaste of that community of men and women to which all Christians were destined in eternity.

This ascetic eschatological prefiguring was very much at the heart of the monasteries Paula founded with Jerome and Eustochium in Bethlehem after 386. Men and women dwelled in separate quarters, where they spent much of their day studying the scriptures. All were required to learn to read and expected to memorize large portions of scripture. All property apart from food and clothing was owned collectively. Although they came from different classes, no distinctions were made among them in the monastery. No one was allowed to have servants, for instance, and all participated in the physical labor of producing the goods the community needed. Paula had by the end of her life given away all of her wealth, to the point, according to Jerome, of having left her daughter with sizable debts to pay off. Six times each day from dawn until midnight men and women gathered together for prayer and reciting the Psalms. No one was allowed to skip these daily hours of worship. On Sunday the entire community attended the eucharist at the neighboring church.

Melania the Younger

Yet another woman who founded a community of men and women monastics during this period was Melania the Younger (c. 383-439). Melania's grandmother (after whom she was named) had been a well-known figure among the Roman ascetics. The younger Melania was forced by her parents to marry around the age of fourteen. Following the birth of her second child, however, she convinced her husband to join her in taking vows of celibacy. Melania liquidated a sizable amount of her property (shortly before the Visigoths took them over), gave away most of her wealth, and moved with her husband to North Africa. Several years later they traveled again, this time to Jerusalem in order to visit the sacred places of the Bible. Sale of further properties funded this voyage and an extended visit to the Egyptian desert monasteries.

In 420 Melania and her husband returned to Palestine, where she established a new community for women, of which she was the head. Not only did she serve as its spiritual director (personally awakening the others for midnight prayer, for instance), but Melania was also a counselor to those who lived around them. Her reputation as a holy woman was enhanced by stories of healings and exorcisms performed in her presence. Melania participated in eucharistic service on a daily basis, although the others in the community were required to attend only on Saturdays and Sundays. Eventually she traveled to Constantinople where, according to the monk who wrote her story, she expounded to other women on the theological significance of Nestorius's deviations. Melania returned to her community in Palestine where she died in 439.

In Constantinople, Alexandria, and Jerusalem, Melania's message of monasticism met with a willing audience among men and women alike. Its attraction lay in the manner in which its disciplines opened one up to experience a higher degree of spirituality. Renunciation of all sexual relationships, and of the social system of marriage that regulated them, allowed women to enter into social community on a spiritual plane that was equal (in theory at least) to men. Virtually all segments of the Christian movement in the fourth and fifth century agreed that the priesthood was reserved entirely to males. But as we can see from the lives of these holy women, monasticism was a spiritual pathway men and women alike could follow.

Jerome's letters are just one of the sources to indicate that for many at the end of the fourth century, the spiritual state of the clergy was being increasingly deplored. Official establishment had brought with it a class of church leaders who were more concerned with pursuing wealth and power than they were in caring for souls. Most clergy were still married, which meant they often had families, properties, and inheritances to be concerned about. In this situation asceticism began to be seen by some in the western churches as an effective and necessary means of correction of the clergy. The message was not met with universal acceptance. Jerome, Paula, and Eustochium, as we have already seen, were forced to leave Rome in part because of their advocacy of ascetic spirituality. By the end of the fourth century, however, the monastic movement was growing rapidly enough among Christians throughout the world that it could even overcome the resistance it faced in Rome.

The Spanish Council of Elvira, held sometime before 310, had been the first on record to rule that all priests and bishops were to be celibate. It is not entirely clear if the ruling was rigidly enforced in Spain at the time, or if married men who became priests were always expected to practice sexual continence after their ordination. Pope Damasus in Jerome's time tried to make celibacy the norm for the Roman clergy, although it did not yet become an administrative rule. In 390 a church council in Carthage supported that decision, advising clergy who were already married to abstain from having any further sexual relations with their wives. By the end of the fourth century in the West the idea of a celibate clergy was catching on, although in the East the practice was required only of bishops.

Augustine of Hippo

The fourth and early fifth centuries were a time of spiritual and theological ferment in the West. Of all the Latin minds at work during this period, none was greater or had a more lasting influence upon later generations than that of Augustine of Hippo (354-430). Born in Numidia to a Libyan Christian mother named Monica and a Roman father who was not Christian, Augustine embodied many of the cultural and intellectual currents that were flowing together in this period in the Latin church. His academic preparation led him first to Carthage, where he threw himself into philosophical studies. For most of the decade of his twenties he was also a follower of a Christian form of Manichaeism that was growing in North Africa. Augustine was attracted to both its dualism and its denial of the value of the material body. During these years he began to live with a woman as his concubine in a legal relationship that lasted fourteen years and produced one son.

In 384, after a brief time in Rome, Augustine assumed a position teaching rhetoric and philosophy in Milan. It was there that he made the acquaintance of Ambrose. Ambrose addressed Augustine's religious questions on an intellectual level and provided him with a foundation for understanding Christian faith. Meanwhile, a more respectable engagement to another woman had been arranged, forcing him to send his concubine back to North Africa. For two more years in Milan, Augustine struggled with both the philosophical questions and the personal desires of the flesh before coming to the point of a decisive Christian commitment. The full story of his conversion is found in his *Confessions*, a book that is still widely read. In 387 Augustine underwent baptism by Ambrose. He accepted as well the ascetic discipline of monastic life and shortly afterward returned to North Africa, where he was ordained a priest and then consecrated bishop of the city of Hippo in his home province of Numidia.

Before long the bishop of Hippo was embroiled in several of the controversies of the region. The first was with the Manichaeans, some of them his former friends. Over against the Manichaean belief in the inherent evilness of the material world, Augustine argued the doctrine of original sin and the fall. Creation was inherently good, and evil entered into it only through the agency of the human will that had sinned. The effects of that act extended to the entire human race, he argued, but this did not mean that the creation was evil. Sin and evil had no substance, he insisted, but were rather an absence, a defection, a falling away. Salvation then meant the redirection of the will back toward its original goal or objective, which was the contemplation of God.

A second controversy that occupied Augustine's intellectual efforts during these years was the one he carried on with the Donatists. Augustine threw himself into the task of being an apologist for the Catholic tradition, not an easy task for a Catholic bishop in the Donatist stronghold of Hippo. He defended the use of imperial force and coercion on behalf of the church against heretics as a way to teach them the proper way to behave. Most of the time, however, he sought to win them back by arguing with them. Following Cyprian, Augustine asserted that for baptized Christians who left the true church (which he understood to be the Catholic church), there was no salvation. Grace was effective through the sacraments of the church not because of the purity of its ministers, but because the sacraments were given by Christ. Here the unity of the church was more important than its purity for Augustine. Even an impure minister performed an efficacious sacrament if it was performed within the Catholic church.

Augustine's doctrine upon the effectiveness of grace in the sacraments was cut from the same cloth as his other theological positions regarding predestination and free will. These themes were focused in turn through his theological debates with a movement that was known as Pelagianism. Pelagius (c.350-c.425) was a British monk and contemporary of Augustine's who had defended the human capacity for exercising free will. He thereby assigned to human beings a degree of responsibility for participating in their salvation. Most agreed with Pelagius and his followers insofar as they were referring to spiritual growth after baptism, in which one was aided by the work of the Spirit. Several of Pelagius's followers also argued that even prior to their baptism human beings were capable of exercising free will and that they were therefore only held accountable for their own actual sins in life.

Most of the Christian churches regarded baptism as an act that removed the stain of original sin with which human beings are born. For the most part baptism continued through the sixth century in the West to follow a period of catechism, which meant the baptismal candidates were normally in their teen-age years. Yet as early as the time of Cyprian, Catholic priests in the West baptized infants who appeared to be in danger of death. Girls more than boys appear to have been baptized prior to the age in which they could be expected to learn the basics of Christian belief. No matter at what age it occurred, however, baptism was regarded as the rite that removed sin. Pelagianism seemed to Augustine to entail a denial of the need for infant baptism, and indeed of the very notion of original sin as he understood it to be formulated by the apostle Paul. Over against this moderate doctrine of human responsibility and capacity to choose God, Augustine asserted a radical conception of original sin. After the fall, in the absence of baptism the human will is only free to choose evil, he argued. Salvation is entirely a work of divine grace.

Pelagius's position was far more acceptable to the Greek-speaking East, where such a sharp distinction between human and divine activities was alien. Eastern theologians such as the Cappadocians had recognized a legitimate role for human beings to participate in salvation through the power of the Spirit. For these eastern theologians, the illumination of the Spirit sanctified the inner life and led to glorification or divinization. Human beings, who had never entirely lost the image of God in the fall, were thus capable through the gift of the Holy Spirit to be co-workers with God in salvation. Where Augustine emphasized the fall and its debilitating effect upon human free will, the eastern theologians emphasized the illumination of the Holy Spirit upon humanity, which was made in the image and likeness of God.

Augustine's thinking was being formulated in the midst of the historical crisis afflicting North African society in the early fifth century. It was colored by his hostile confrontations with the Donatists, who he believed had shattered the unity of the church, and by the invasions of Visigoths who had shattered (for him at least) the order of social life. His notion of a permanent and pervasive effect of original sin was part of a wider theology of history that was worked out in greater detail in the *City of God*. Augustine started work on the book following the sack of Rome in 410 to answer the charge that the city was destroyed because it had abandoned its traditional gods. As the project unfolded over several decades, the book grew into a full-fledged theology of history. There are two cities operative in human history, the *City of God* argued. These are the earthly and the heavenly, allegorically represented as Babylon and Jerusalem. The two cities are also correlated with empire and church, the former as Egypt, Babylon, and Rome and the latter as Israel, Jerusalem, and the Church. Augustine argued that the line between the two cities in human history was never firmly drawn. Furthermore, he never totally identified the city of God with the church. Yet through the providence of God, he believed, divine judgment and redemption would one day be fully manifest in human history.

In addition to his contributions to anthropology, soteriology, and ecclesiology in the West, Augustine also played a major role in shaping the Latin theological tradition's doctrine of the Trinity. Where the Cappadocians in the East had articulated what is often called a social model of the Trinity, emphasizing the Three that are One, Augustine developed what is often called a psychological model of the Trinity that emphasized the One who is Three. As one person is revealed to be lover, loved, and the loving, Augustine argued, God is Father, Son, and Spirit. In this way the Spirit is the bond of love that joins the loving Father and the loved one, the Son, in communion. Likewise, as the human mind is memory, intellect, and will while still remaining one, so God is Three while remaining One. In order to protect the unity of the Godhead, the Cappadocians had emphasized the role of the Father as the source of the divinity of the Son who is eternally begotten and the Spirit who proceeds from the Father. Augustine, on the other hand, emphasized the common divine nature that all three share in their trinitarian relations and the inner unity of God as One. There were vestiges of the Trinity to be found throughout creation, he argued, serving not as proofs but rather as reflections of God's nature as One-in-Three.

Augustine served as bishop in North Africa during a period of social crisis. The year of his death witnessed the Vandals overrunning the city of Hippo and the destruction of much of the church there. Forged in the experience of historical crisis, his theology offered the hope of divine grace and redemption in history. His *Confessions* have often been cited as the fountainhead for a long western intellectual tradition of devotional self-reflection upon the inner life. His influence upon virtually every aspect of the subsequent Latin theological tradition remains enormous. He is arguably the single most important theological influence within the entire western Christian movement, a weighty claim indeed for one who only desired to be a faithful pastor of his battered flock living along the seacoast of North Africa.

Benedict of Nursia

If Augustine's name proved to be the most important in western theology for centuries to come, that of Benedict of Nursia (480-540) was the most important for spirituality and monasticism. Early in his life Benedict gained a reputation as a spiritual leader. At Monte Cassino he organized a new community, providing it with a rule that was modeled after those of Pachomius, Basil, and others. Central to the Rule of Benedict were three virtues: obedience, silence, and humility. Every monastery was to have an elected superior to whom absolute obedience was given. Monks and nuns were not to leave their monasteries for another community. Silence was kept at meals and other times, except the hours of prayer.

Finally, monks were to show humility in all things. The rule also called for monasteries to practice hospitality to strangers and for the monks to be involved in practical labor as part of their spiritual endeavors. In Benedict's own lifetime, communities following his rule did not grow, but a century after his death the rule had begun to find a following in Gaul and elsewhere. Eventually it became the standard for all western monastic communities, but that story must await the next section.

Changing patterns of worship

During these years churches in the West were still gaining new members by way of conversion, but most were now children of second- or third-generation Christian families. Children brought up in Christian homes still generally underwent baptism as young adults (Jerome was nineteen), but it was becoming more common for families to baptize young children. This was especially the case when it seemed that a child might die. Even if they had been baptized as infants, such children did not participate in the mystery of the eucharist but left the worship service after the sermon with those who were undergoing catechetical instruction prior to their baptism.

Such catechetical instruction was most often given in a room apart from the place where the priest or bishop was celebrating the eucharist, by teachers who followed the outline of the baptismal creed used by that particular church. It is interesting to note in this regard that the Nicene Creed remained relatively unknown in most churches in the West through the fifth century. One of the creeds that had been used in Rome since the second century that became known as the Apostles' Creed (so named on account of a legend that each of the original apostles had written a single line of the creed) was more important. Rufinus wrote a commentary early in the fifth century on this so-called Apostles' Creed, providing valuable insights into the content of catechetical instruction of churches in and around Rome.

Following baptism, the new Christian was usually confirmed in the faith by a ceremony that from the earliest days of the movement had involved the use of oil. While baptism could be performed by priests and in some cases even by laypersons when a child was in danger of immediate death, confirmation was administered by a bishop. Around the year 400 we find the first references to new members undergoing confirmation of their faith some time after their baptism. The main reason appears to have been the relative lack of bishops among churches in northern regions such as Gaul. Over time the practice of baptizing infants and young children who were then later confirmed became the dominant pattern of Christian initiation for churches in the West.

The years during which Jerome and Augustine lived and worked were more than an age filled with crises. They were a turning point in the history of the West, a time of far-reaching transformations taking place in the social and political life of what had been the western Roman empire. The effects of these changes were reaching beyond the Roman borders, and Christianity too began to spread beyond them. Over the next several centuries the center of the western churches moved northward and westward. In the fourth and fifth we see the first stirrings of that effort taking place in the form of missionary outreach and conversion. Two episodes in the life of the Christian movement in the West proved crucial. One was the story of a missionary to Ireland; the other was the story of the conversion of a Frankish king.

Patrick and the mission to Ireland

West of Britain, beyond both Roman administrative reach and the Germanic tribal invasion, lay Ireland, a land that was populated by Celts. A new method of missionary expansion and subsequently a new era in Christian history in the West opened in Ireland in 432 under the ministry of a bishop and monastic leader named Patrick (d. 460). Originally from Britain, Patrick was raised a Christian. As a youth he was taken captive, sold into slavery, and for six years forced to work as a shepherd in Ireland. Upon his escape, he joined the monastic movement and then sought ordination as a bishop in order to return to Ireland as a missionary. In 431 another Latin-speaking bishop, Palladius, had been sent to serve the small Christian community that had formed in a town in the south of the island. Most likely they were members of a small merchant community rather than Irish people who had converted to the Christian faith. Upon returning to Ireland, however, Patrick did not go to the south but instead headed to the north where, as far as we can tell, there were not yet any believing Christians. He did so out of a concern for the land of his former captivity and, according to his *Confessions*, explicitly in response to the imperative of Matthew 28:19.

By his own account Patrick succeeded in converting thousands, teaching them the Christian faith and ordaining priests for ministry. There is no evidence that he attempted to translate the scriptures into the Celtic language of Ireland. Instead, his method was to encourage Irish converts to learn to read Latin. To this end he sought to establish monasteries in the regions of his missionary labors. While we have no way of knowing how successful he was in this endeavor, the rapid growth of monasticism in Ireland over the course of the following century was a testament to Patrick's endeavors. The development of Latin learning in Ireland is doubly significant insofar as Ireland was never administratively part of the Roman empire.

One of the earliest figures of Irish monasticism following Patrick was Brigid of Kildare (c.450-523). She was born toward the end of Patrick's life, her mother a Christian slave to a non-Christian chieftain who was also her father. Brigid was raised Christian by her mother. At the age of twenty, she cut her hair and took a vow of celibacy before a local bishop rather than submit to a marriage arranged by her father. With seven other women she then organized what is believed to be the first women's monastic community in Ireland. Brigid was the head or abbess of the community, whose reputation for hospitality and compassion was soon spreading throughout Ireland. Men as well as women began to join, making it the first double community in Ireland as well. Men and women lived in separate houses but worked and prayed under one rule. A local bishop provided for the sacramental needs of those in the monastery, but Brigid's authority as abbess extended over all other areas of life.

Within the western Roman world, churches had become organized along administrative lines following towns and cities. In Ireland there were no towns and
cities as such but only villages and rural communities ruled by local chieftains. In
this context monasteries grew in importance in contrast to the parish church.
Wealthier families would sponsor a monastery in order to gain from both its spiritual and its material benefits. Travelers would stay in them as they were the inns in
the land. They became centers of learning and the crafts, becoming what one historian has described as "the closest thing to towns in early medieval Ireland."[11]

Patrick's mission to Ireland marked an important turning point in the history
of missions in the Roman empire. Catholic churches had since the second century no longer been sending bishops or other clergy into regions where no Christian presence was thought to exist. The general practice had become for bishops
to wait until they received a request from a community of believers living outside
a known episcopal domain and then to send a bishop who could provide ordained
leadership. In almost all cases the request came from a community of merchants
or former captives who had become permanent residents in the new location.
Patrick's story marks a change, for he did not go to the town in the south where a
Christian community existed. Instead, he went to the north and preached the
Christian message to people who had never heard it. He then organized monasteries among the new believers and set them to work on learning before moving
on to another site. The end result was a network of missionary monasteries under
Patrick's direction, where students were learning Latin, studying the scriptures,
and working among the local population.

The growth of the Christian movement in Ireland marked another important
milestone in the West. Here was one of the first times that the Latin Christian
tradition moved beyond the former geographical boundaries of Roman imperial
life. Ireland became part of the Catholic church without being first a part of the
Roman empire. It was a pattern that was soon to be replicated elsewhere in northern regions of Europe as more peoples entered the Christian movement in the
West. Ireland would play an important role in that wider process by sending
numerous missionary monks across the Irish Sea into Scotland, western England,
and even the continent of Europe. In later centuries there would even be traditions of Irish monks traveling all the way across the Atlantic to preach the gospel
in unknown lands to the west. While they have never been historically substanti-
ated, these legends and traditions provide us with a tantalizing piece of possible
missionary history.

Clovis and the conversion of the Franks

One of the Germanic tribal groups that had long been settled along the Rhine
River were a people collectively known by the Romans as Franks. During the
third and fourth centuries, a number of them had migrated into eastern Gaul,
where they had become partially Romanized. Many of them had served in the

---

[11] Richard Fletcher, *The Barbarian Conversion: From Paganism to Christianity* (New
York: Henry Holt and Co., 1997), 92.

Roman army as paid soldiers. In the middle of the fifth century, amid the disruptions of western Roman life, a Frankish king named Childeric in the region that is modern Belgium emerged to forge a new alliance with Rome. Childeric's son, Clovis (c.466-511), succeeded him as king in 481, the second to rule in what came to be called the Merovingian dynasty.

Clovis was only about fifteen years of age when he inherited the throne of his father, but the most significant event of his life as far as the history of the Christian movement is concerned took place around the year 500. Under the influence of his wife, Queen Clotilde (c. 470-545), a Burgundian who had already become a Christian, Clovis abandoned the practice of his ancestral religion and was baptized. He was shortly followed into the waters by some three thousand members of his army. The story is paradigmatic for later Germanic kings whose baptism owed much to the influence of Christian wives. Usually the next generation who were the offspring of these Christian wives and queens were not only baptized in the Christian faith but were raised in the church.

Although Clotilde was most likely an Arian Christian, Clovis was baptized a Catholic, indicating a new alliance with the Roman form of the faith. The decision was significant not only for the Franks but for other Germanic peoples as well. One of the places where the effect was felt was south of the Pyrenees, where Arian Visigoth kings ruled over Spain. The Visigoths did not share the faith of the majority of their Catholic subjects, and thus they could not depend upon the cooperation or support of the Catholic bishops of their land. The fact that a powerful political neighbor to the north was now Catholic could only further aggravate relations between Spanish Catholic subjects and Arian kings. Add to this new internal conflicts within the Visigoth kingdom, and one sees why the regions of Visigoth Gaul soon passed into Frankish hands.

Following the baptism of Clovis, a new alliance emerged among the older Roman classes, who were still the primary landowners, and the Frankish aristocracy. Arles grew in importance as an episcopal center, and bishops joined ranks with the nobility in forging new political alliances. Women continued to play an important role in bringing Christian values to bear upon the society, particularly women who were monastic. One of the better known women from among the Franks in the sixth century was Radegunde (c. 520-587). A Burgundian by birth, she was forced into marriage with Chlothar, king of the Franks, in 538. After twelve agonizing years that produced no children, she escaped to the town of Noyon, where she sought refuge in the church. The bishop consecrated her as a deacon, an office to which fewer women were being ordained in the sixth century.

Radegunde eventually founded a convent in Poitiers, endowed by wealth she had gained from her marriage. The community grew rapidly, numbering as many as two hundred nuns living together at one point. Radegunde was known for her hospitality and her gifts as a teacher, and clergymen from nearby dioceses came to visit her convent and listen to her. Radegunde was particularly committed to the devotional use of relics, or objects associated with saints from previous ages. She sent word to the eastern Roman emperor requesting that he provide her with a portion of the true cross, which he agreed to do, reportedly sending it to Poitiers in 568. The story of Radegunde's life, like that of many other holy men and women during this period, is filled with miraculous healings and other manifestations of holiness. Such stories helped maintain both her memory and her Christianizing influence among the common people.

By the end of the sixth century, the Germanic people were on their way toward the Catholic faith. The Franks took the lead in this regard, forging a new alliance with the older Roman classes. These were times of tremendous change in the West. Invading armies had severely disrupted and in some cases brought an end to church life. Cities and towns throughout the western Roman provinces were often devastated by the invasions. Many from the upper ruling classes abandoned the cities under siege, leaving bishops and their clergy alone to deal with the human suffering and need. Two centuries of political establishment had left the churches ill-prepared to deal with the catastrophes that were now falling upon them. This was particularly apparent in the evangelistic practices of churches in the Roman world during this period, at least until Patrick. Where ordained leadership had previously chosen only to follow church expansion, we see in Patrick an example of it leading the mission. In the process a new way of engaging the changing cultural situation of the West was being forged.

The cultural transformation of the western Roman empire by the year 600 was pronounced. Italy, Spain, and Gaul were all ruled by Germanic kings. The bishop of Rome was by far the most important ecclesiastical authority in the entire region and a political force to be reckoned with. The secular administrative features of urban Roman society were replaced by churches and monasteries carrying on basic civic tasks. A sizable number of new languages were being spoken, and there were gods and rituals that had previously been unknown in the West. Across the region a radical cultural encounter was taking place "between Roman and barbarian, Christian and pagan, Latin and Germanic, literate and oral, wine and beer, oil and lard, south and north."[12] The consequences of this encounter would reverberate for centuries to come.

---

[12] Fletcher, *The Barbarian Conversion*, 13. He is writing here specifically of the encounter between King Edwin of Northumbria in Britain, who was baptized in 627, and the missionary monk Paulinus, who was his instructor in the faith. The description fits the wider encounter happening throughout the western regions of what is now Europe.

21

The Age of Justinian and Theodora in the Eastern Roman Empire

As Christians in Gaul, Spain, Italy, and North Africa adjusted to the changing political reality brought about by the waves of invasions, Christians in the East were facing their own changing situation. The Council of Chalcedon had not succeeded in resolving the dogmatic differences that divided the churches. Few teachers who held to a strict two-nature interpretation of Jesus Christ remained within Roman territories after the fifth century, as the doctrine's main proponents were now located across the border in Persian territory. Within the regions under Constantinople's control, doctrinal differences ranged along a continuum from those who supported Chalcedon's definition of Jesus Christ as having two natures united in one *hupostasis* or person, to those who held passionately to the formula that he was one nature after the incarnation. Rather than speak of Jesus Christ being "in two natures," the latter asserted that he was "out of two natures," the different between the letters "n" and "k" in Greek (in the words *en* and *ek*).

Thus it was that in the last years of the fifth century, eastern Roman emperors found themselves still contending with a doctrinally divided Christian religion. In 482 Emperor Zeno sought the help of Bishop Acacius of Constantinople to build a bridge between the parties. The result was a brief document known as the *Henoticon* that tried to formulate the basis for reunion. It condemned several positions judged to be extreme on either side, avoided any mention of Leo's *Tome*, accepted the final definition of Chalcedon, and proposed that the writings of Cyril of Alexandria be accepted as the basis for unity. Acacius's efforts were not well received in Rome, where a synod excommunicated him in 484 on the grounds of his perceived compromise with the non-Chalcedonians. The excommunication was sent by a monk to Constantinople, who pinned it on Acacius's vestments while the patriarch was celebrating the eucharist.

The first decades of the sixth century found three main positions being staked out among the eastern Roman bishops. The first was held by those who supported the language of Chalcedon and the doctrine of Jesus Christ having two natures united in one person. A second position was occupied by those who refused to endorse Chalcedon's definition of faith because they feared that it left too much room for interpretations they considered Nestorian. The third, a minority position, belonged to those who embraced the teachings associated with Eutyches that Jesus had divine flesh that was not like our own. One of their number, a bishop named Julian of Halicarnassus, around 520 taught that the physical body of Jesus before his resurrection was already incorruptible.

The presence of this third party led those who still favored Cyril's earlier language of "one incarnate nature" over the definition of Chalcedon, but not the conclusion that Christ did not possess flesh like our own, to develop their own non-Chalcedonian perspective more fully. A leading advocate of this position was Severus of Antioch (c.465-538). Following Cyril, Severus considered the terms *hupostasis* and *phusis* (person and nature) to be virtually synonymous. This meant that the definition of Chalcedon and Leo's *Tome* were both irredeemably flawed, if not unintelligible. Severus taught that before the resurrection Jesus had corruptible flesh, but that it was the flesh of the one divine Word made incarnate.

The year 518 marked a decisive change in the fortunes of Severus and his supporters in Syria. The elevation of a palace officer named Justin to the rank of emperor brought a strong supporter of Chalcedon to the throne. One of Justin's first acts was to send word to Rome that he intended to end the schism between Rome and Constantinople that had opened up over the *Henoticon*. In 519 a papal delegation in Constantinople joined with the patriarch to declare the division healed, thus ending the rift between the two major leaders of the Roman Christian world that had gone on for more than three decades.

The same year he came to power Justin also moved against Severus of Antioch, whom he forced into exile in Alexandria. Although in exile, Severus continued to maintain contact with supporters in Syria and to write in defense of the non-Chalcedonian position. A decade or so later Severus came reluctantly to agree that in order for the Orthodox faith to survive in places such as Syria, priests would have to be ordained to serve separate churches. Such a decision was not easy, for it violated the fundamental principle that Severus also held that the churches in each town and city were to be under the authority of a single bishop. He was in effect agreeing to found a new non-territorial form of church, forced to do so of course because Chalcedonians now controlled the bishoprics. Another bishop, John of Tella, a town east of Edessa, began ordaining priests, and then bishops, who would take on the task of spreading the churches. Some came from across the Persian border, others from Armenia, and still others from Asia Minor to receive ordination from John. Nearly a thousand were consecrated to this mission from his own monastery in Tella.

Justinian and Theodora

Things changed little for Severus and his supporters with the coming of a new emperor in 527. For the most part Justin's religious policies were continued by his nephew and successor to the throne, Justinian (482-565). Originally from the Balkans, Justinian grew up in an area where Latin was the imperial language. Even after spending years in Constantinople, it was said that his Greek was rather poor. Yet as a young man he had come to the city to study and had later landed a job as an officer of the palace. After his uncle became emperor, he rose quickly through the ranks in power. Upon Justin's death in 527, Justinian succeeded to the throne of Constantinople.

Justinian did not ascend to the imperial throne alone in 527. He was joined by his wife, Theodora (500-548), who was crowned co-emperor in the ceremony. Theodora was from a family whose background had been in the circus. She herself was for some years an actor, which in that society was a profession closely associated with prostitution. Indeed, some of her contemporaries delighted in writing in lurid detail of the rumored accounts of her sordid sexual past. At some point after 518 she and Justinian had became lovers, according to some accounts after she had a religious experience. Their marriage in 525 actually required a change in the law to allow a person from the imperial household to marry an actor. Two years later they assumed the throne together.

For the next two decades Theodora exercised considerable power, doing so often when her husband's hands were tied by competing political considerations. Her main concerns were with the religion of the empire, advancing the cause of the non-Chalcedonian party. It was never clear just how much Justinian's sympathies were with the Chalcedonian party in Constantinople, and how much he simply had to accede to their demands. Certainly the position of church leaders in the West loomed large in his thinking. While Theodora often appeared to be operating behind his back in matters of religion, it is possible that he knew what she was doing and agreed with the strategy as a means to support the one-nature position. Working in tandem they were often able to support competing

Mosaics of Justinian and Theodora, early 6ᵗʰ century. San Vitale Church, Ravenna, Italy. Photograph from Faith Cimok, Hagia Sophia *(Istanbul: A Turizm Yayinlari, 1998), pp. 12–13. Reproduced with permission.*

ecclesiastical positions that were threatening to divide the land. In any case, for two decades Theodora played a significant role in helping to advance those who delighted in proclaiming that "God the Word had suffered in the flesh" in the liturgy of the church, while Justinian sought to construct a "Neo-Chalcedonian" position that distinguished more clearly the meaning of *hupostasis* from *phusis*.

The political legacy of Justinian and Theodora

Several years after he had assumed the imperial office, Justinian found himself confronted in 532 by a crisis in Constantinople. A riot, precipitated in part by his enemies in the city and in part by popular unrest over taxes, had started in the Hippodrome, where the chariot races were held. It soon spilled out into the streets, where rioters burned several buildings, including Hagia Sophia, the main cathedral in the city. After several days of uncontrolled chaos, Justinian was ready to resign. But Theodora intervened: Better to die as the emperor than as a fugitive, she counseled him. Justinian was persuaded, and with the young commander of his army, Belisarius, mapped out a strategy to end the riots. The result was a reported thirty thousand people killed by the emperor's troops in the city, bringing about a rapid and bloody end to the disturbance.

Justinian's response demonstrated the ruthlessness with which he could act as emperor. But it is not usually the achievement for which he is most remembered by history. His most lasting accomplishment was the complete codification of the existing body of Roman law by which the empire was governed. Roman emperors ruled by conducting wars and issuing edicts. The latter has often been cited as the more important of Rome's contribution to world history. Successive emperors over the centuries had simply added to the existing legal corpus by promulgating new laws. Thus a massive number of precepts had accumulated over the years, many of them contradictory. In the fifth century Theodosius II had tried to codify the existing body of Roman laws, but after a hundred years it needed revision once again. To this task Justinian appointed a commission, headed by a trusted legal mind.

For several years the commission worked to compile the entire corpus of Roman laws, resolving contradictions as they found them and removing anything that seemed to be unfavorable to the Christian religion. The result was the *Codex Justinianus*, completed in 529—by coincidence the same year Justinian forced the closing of the last non-Christian school of philosophy in the East, the famed Academy in Athens. The *Codex* was written in Latin, an indication that Justinian and his age still understood themselves to be Romans. (It would be another century before the emperor Heraclius finally proclaimed Greek the official language of the Roman empire.) Its pages covered all aspects of family and social life, providing a comprehensive legal code that guided the empire for almost another millennium. The *Codex* was influential in shaping the political life of western Europe as well, long after Greek and Latin civilizations had grown apart.

In addition to overseeing the codification of the existing body of Roman law, Justinian undertook the promulgation of new legal rulings in the form of *Novellae* (new laws). In these he brought about a greater synthesis of church and state than had been achieved by any of his predecessors on the throne. Imperial legislation now began to cover issues of church life that had previously been the province of synods and bishops. A remarkable cultural fusion of Greco-Roman and Christian ideals and values was the result, so much so that Orthodox theologian Alexander Schmemann calls Justinian "the first ideologist of the Christian empire, who brought the union of Constantine to its logical conclusion."[13]

Along with codifying the body of law that governed the empire and extending the integration of church and state, Justinian sought to restore the old imperial boundaries. During his first years in office the perennial struggle against the Persians to the east occupied the major part of his military resources. A truce reached with the shah of shahs in 532 allowed Justinian to turn his attention toward the west. In 533 General Belisarius was sent with an army of mostly mercenary soldiers against the Vandals in North Africa. Within a year they succeeded in destroying the Vandal kingdom and re-establishing Constantinople's rule over most of the region. From there Belisarius turned his attention toward Sicily, which he occupied in 535, before moving on to Italy. In 538 his army occupied Rome and in 539 took Ravenna from the Ostrogoths. Lingering resistance occupied the Greeks for another two decades, but the Ostrogoths never fully recovered. Within a generation they were gone and a new Germanic tribe, the Lombards, moved in to occupy northern Italy, establishing a kingdom of their own.

One of the precedents of previous emperors Justinian did not follow was to appoint a co-emperor in the West. Instead, he appointed officials known as *exarches* to rule as Constantinople's agents in Carthage and Ravenna. For almost half a century Italy had been under Ostrogoth rule. In the process Romans learned to live alongside Goths. Now both had to live with their new Greek rulers. Constantinople was perceived by most to be a foreign power, the ranks of its military stocked with mercenaries drawn from different peoples. The bishop of Rome continued to pay nominal allegiance to Constantinople's emperor, who, by tradition and canon law, had to approve his appointment as pope. But there was a great deal of uneasiness and distrust, exacerbated by the growing linguistic divide. By the year 550 few in Rome could read, write, or speak Greek, while in Constantinople Latin was falling into disuse.

Constantinople's armies sought to take Spain as well during these years, although they managed only to establish a Greek-ruled zone around several cities on the seacoast. In the East, Justinian managed through negotiations to maintain an uneasy peace with the Persians, although not without paying a considerable sum of gold and silver that in effect amounted to tribute. At one point Justinian suffered the loss of a sizable force that he had sent against the Persians in Armenia, allowing that small nation to be drawn further into the Persian orbit of influence. Elsewhere in the East the emperor succeeded in maintaining his borders but not in healing the divisions that separated churches. Thus by the middle of

---

[13] Alexander Schmemann, *The Historical Road of Eastern Orthodoxy*, trans. Lydia W. Kesich (Crestwood, N.Y.: St. Vladimir's Seminary Press, 1992), 144.

the sixth century Justinian nominally ruled over much of what had once been the great Roman empire, west and east. Yet within his borders, increasing religious, cultural, and political tensions were pulling the empire apart.

A new wave of invasions close to Constantinople in the 540s and 550s tore even further at the fabric of Justinian's empire. The new immigrants were known as Slavs, and their armies took up the familiar routine of plundering cities and suburbs in the region as far as the Aegean seacoast. Several times they even reached the outskirts of Constantinople itself. Numerous Greek citizens were killed or taken captive, causing further stress on Constantinople's economy. Eventually Justinian resorted to the technique he had used successfully against the Persians: he offered the Slavs payments of money if they would agree to live peaceably with their Greek neighbors. The result was the permanent establishment of Slavic people who were not Christians in the backyard of Constantinople.

Theological legacy of Justinian and Theodora

Throughout his long reign Justinian left no doubt that he was to be considered by his people the sole ruler of the empire. He forced the general who had won his battles to play a minor role in the victory parade in Constantinople afterward, while he as emperor took full glory for the triumph. Likewise in matters of theology and the church, Justinian left no doubt that he considered his to be the reigning voice over the spiritual life of the empire. He was the first Roman emperor to engage in theological disputations or render theological decisions on matters of faith and practice apart from councils or bishops. Other emperors had presided over synods and consulted with their patriarchs in attempting to influence the spiritual direction of the land. Justinian actually wrote and published his own treatises, which he sought to enforce as church doctrine.

Despite these appearances, Justinian was not alone in exercising imperial authority over the churches. His wife, Theodora, had been proclaimed augusta alongside him; although she was not as actively involved in political intrigues as other women of that rank had been in the past, she more than made up for it by her involvement in theology and church life in the eastern Roman world. Theodora's influence even reached significantly beyond the borders of the empire in at least one case, that of a mission to Nubia. Closer to home she was an effective agent of imperial support for those who shared her non-Chalcedonian commitment, often counteracting the efforts of her husband.

Theodora was already committed to the non-Chalcedonian position when she was raised to the imperial throne with her husband in 527. Within four years she had taken over one of the palaces in Constantinople and converted it into a monastery supporting more than five hundred monks and nuns in the city who shared her theological position. Most of the people of Constantinople were Chalcedonians in their persuasion, but Theodora's monastery supported a lively minority. They attended most regular worship services in the capital but distinguished themselves by adding the words, "the immortal God who was crucified for us" to the words of a doxology in the liturgy.

Justinian pursued a compromise. In 533 he hosted a synod of bishops representing Chalcedonian and non-Chalcedonian positions. It resulted in an edict he published supporting the statement, "one of the Trinity has suffered in the flesh." Still the two sides did not reconcile. To make matters worse, Chalcedonian bishops had ordered local troops to hunt down and execute several non-Chalcedonian priests. Justinian found himself not only facing dissension and violence within the churches, but he was now in need of the support of the pope in Rome for his armies, which were marching on the West. In 537 the emperor ordered Patriarch Theodosius of Alexandria be deposed and a Chalcedonian installed in his see. Theodosius was offered safe haven by Theodora in her monastery in Constantinople, where he lived the rest of his years, long after her death.

In 542 Theodora received a request from the king of Ghassanid, a small Arab nation on the border between Syria and Arabia, that she send missionaries to help convert his people. Theodora responded by having Theodosius, who in the eyes of the non-Chalcedonian supporters was still patriarch of Alexandria, ordain several bishops who would travel to that part of the world to spread their Orthodox belief. One of the two Theodosius ordained was a Syrian monk named Jacob Baradeus (500-578). Originally from the region east of Edessa, Jacob had come to Constantinople many years before; he resided there as one of the monks in Theodora's monastery. Theodosius ordained him as missionary bishop of Edessa and sent him back to his home region, where he began to work. Within a generation he had ordained twenty-seven other bishops and some hundred thousand priests, all committed to the non-Chalcedonian form of Orthodoxy and to building up churches in the East. We will return to the story of Jacob below.

That same year Justinian decided to send an official mission to the nation of Nubia, whose royal household sought entrance into the Christian faith. Three years before he had ordered without controversy the closing of the famed Temple of Isis on the Egyptian-Nubia border at Philae, a temple where the Nobataens of Nubia had traditionally come to worship. Nubian trade with Constantinople had increased, which most likely had prompted in part the interest in the mission. Theodora acted as well to dispatch a missionary named Julian, again a monk from the non-Chalcedonian monastery in the capital, to the south. Further political intrigue on her part ensured that he arrived before the party that Justinian had sent. Julian was joined at the Nubian court by the Egyptian bishop of Philae, and together they succeeded within a few short years in bringing the northern Nubian royal household into the ranks of their Orthodox faith. We will return to the story of Nubia as well later in this chapter.

While Theodora was advancing the cause of foreign missions, her husband was still trying to win some common agreement between the two parties in his empire. Debate again broke out around the heritage of Origen. There were two points now where the early Alexandrian's ideas caused controversy, in addition to the perennial concern that he had subordinated the Son to the Father. First, Origen had at one point suggested a way to think of Christ's humanity as preexisting his incarnation. Second, Origen had argued that because Christ redeemed all human flesh, all would be saved in eternity. The second point in particular, that of Origen's doctrine of universalism, drew the most heated attacks from his opponents. Justinian issued an edict in 543 condemning the ancient Alexandrian's books and ordering them destroyed, leading to the loss of a vast body of work by one of the greatest minds the Christian movement has ever known.

Not content with condemning Origen as a heretic, Justinian a short time later issued another edict, this one known as the *Three Chapters*. The three chapters (or heads) that occupied the emperor's attention this time were Theodore of Mopsuestia, Theodoret of Cyrrhus, and Hiba of Edessa, the leading representatives of the historical school of Antioch. Justinian condemned Theodore's entire body of work as heretical and ordered all his books burned, while selected works of the other two were condemned. Once again a Christian who had died in full communion with his contemporaries in the Catholic church had been ruled a heretic after his death. Such rulings were unprecedented. These were grounds enough for Pope Vigilius in Rome to refuse to recognize the condemnations, never mind the fact that Leo's *Tome* had expressed ideas regarding the two natures that were sympathetic to some of those expressed by the Antiochenes. In response, Justinian had his troops, who at the time were occupying Rome, seize Vigilius and bring him to Constantinople where the pope was forced under pressure to agree to the condemnations.

The *Three Chapters* did not end the debates between Chalcedonians and non-Chalcedonians in the East. The death of Theodora in 548 removed one of the chief actors from the scene but did not end non-Chalcedonian organizing activities. Their churches were now flourishing in Egypt and Syria. Justinian had one last move. In 553 he called for a general council to meet in Constantinople, a gathering that eventually became known as the Fifth Ecumenical Council. Its main purpose was to confirm the condemnation of Origen and the *Three Chapters,* which it proceeded to do. Justinian himself did not attend, although he set the agenda for the council. Although he was in the city, Pope Vigilius did not attend either. He was being held under imperial arrest until he agreed to the council's decisions. He finally did so, paving the way for the condemnations of Origen, Theodore, and the others to be regarded as authoritative. Only a handful of other western bishops attended. It was again an overwhelmingly eastern synod.

The Fifth Ecumenical Council accomplished little in the end. Justinian died in 565 and was followed on the throne by his nephew Justin. A decade later Justin was still seeking to close non-Chalcedonian monasteries throughout the East and to stop the work of Jacob Baradeus. Only the coming of the Arabs and the imposition of an Islamic government in the regions of Syria and Egypt in the seventh century finally put an end to the political—although not the theological—struggles between the two parties in those lands.

Looking back at the age of Justinian and Theodora, it would be a mistake to see only the conflicts that so dominated their religious lives. Justinian added to the city's architectural riches. After the main church, Hagia Sophia, was destroyed by riots in 532, he rebuilt it as a great cathedral. (Much of this original building still stands today as a museum in Istanbul, Turkey). His policy of appeasing foreign powers with gifts of wealth greatly strained the resources of his treasury and led to even more burdensome taxes, yet for a time it served the purposes of peace. Justinian considered himself a theologian and took his task as imperial overseer of the church seriously. He also wrote at least one hymn for the church that is still sung in the Orthodox liturgies of the East.

Dogmatic disputes were not the only heritage of the age. During these years an enduring tradition of mystical practices came of age in the East. Monasteries provided a home where contemplative prayer and devotional pursuits could flourish. Neo-Platonic philosophy offered a great deal to Christian mystical reflection on this count, as ultimate union with the divine became the goal of Christian mysticism, East and West. Sometime early in the sixth century an unknown teacher believed by many to have been Syrian provided the first systematic articulation of Christian mystical doctrines. Writing under the pseudonym of Dionysius the Areopagite (a follower of the apostle Paul identified in Acts 17:34), Pseudo-Dionysius (as this author is usually known) argued that God cannot be known directly but only through the indirect emanations of creation. Pseudo-Dionysius organized these into various hierarchies of heaven (the nine orders of angels) and earth (three orders of the priestly hierarchy, three sacraments, and three orders of the laity in the church). God can be known only through those things that God is not, argued this mystical author, an approach that became known in the West as the *via negativa,* or negative way. The goal of the mystical life is an assent through levels of knowing to a full union with God, an experience that is best described as being a darkness that is found beyond even the divine light.

The works of Pseudo-Dionysius were to have an influence far beyond his original home in the East. Centuries later teachers and mystics in the West drew upon his insights and devotional practices. In the same way Justinian's *Codex* was for centuries after him drawn upon in the West as the foundation of government and the Christian state. In both cases, as well as in the acceptance of the decrees of the Fifth Ecumenical Council, we see that the East Roman tradition continued to have an impact on western theology, social life, and culture long after the two civilizations had gone their separate political ways.

Just as important in many ways, the influences of Constantinople in its missions sponsored by Empress Theodora were influential to the east and beyond the Roman borders to the south. These two missions, that of Jacob Baradeus in Syria and that of Julian to the Nubian royal household, mark important milestones in the ongoing expansion of the Christian movement.

Jacob Baradeus and the Jacobite church

The tireless evangelistic efforts of the Syrian bishop Jacob Baradeus deserve far more attention than they have received in the textbooks of Christian history. Jacob, as noted above, was originally from the town of Tella, a major center of non-Chalcedonian activities. His father was a priest there, and Jacob himself entered the monastic order near Nisibis. Around 527 he made his way to Constantinople, where he joined Theodora's community. When the request came for bishops who could assist the non-Chalcedonian mission in the East, he responded, undergoing ordination at the hands of the deposed patriarch Theodosius of Alexandria. Soon Jacob was traveling throughout Syria, stopping in towns and villages to preach the "one nature" Orthodox doctrine, establishing new churches, and ordaining priests to lead them. Recognizing the danger Jacob's activities posed to the imperial government, Justinian ordered Jacob arrested, but to no avail. Disguising himself as a beggar (hence his title Baradeus or Burd'ono in Syriac, meaning "ragged coat") the indefatigable bishop labored for the next thirty-five years without being arrested.

As noted earlier, by the time he died, Jacob Baradeus had ordained twenty-seven other bishops under his episcopal authority and by some reports as many as a hundred thousand priests to carry on the work. These bishops and priests did not seek to challenge the established territorial hierarchy that was in communion with the patriarch of Constantinople. Instead, they formed their own congregations and built their own houses of worship. The clergy of Jacob's churches maintained their own separate ecclesiastical structure. One of the characteristics of their churches was the lower number of bishops in relation to clergy, giving the Jacobites (as they soon came to be called) the image of being less hierarchical and often closer to the common people. The fact that they did not have Constantinople's stamp of approval also helped their cause in areas where Greek political domination was encountering resistance.

Jacobite churches spread quickly, winning over a large number of other Christian congregations. By 600 the Jacobite churches were found from the Aegean Sea to Armenia and across the border into Persian territory. They did not gain as great a following in Persia, where the two-nature doctrine was officially embraced by the patriarch and councils recognized by the shah of shahs. The area of their strongest concentration remained in Syria and Mesopotamia, the region that was Jacob's own home base.

One of the features of the Jacobites that helped them survive without state recognition East or West was their monasteries, which were extensive. By far the most important of these was Kenneshre, located in Mesopotamia along the banks of the Tigris River. Kenneshre was an international center of Jacobite learning and organizing activity. Called the Eagle's Nest because of its protected location, it had originally been founded by refugees from Justin's persecution of the non-Chalcedonians in the 570s. By the 600s it was a flourishing center not only for theological studies but also for philosophy and medicine. One of the features that monks at Kenneshre developed as a way to distinguish themselves from others in either Chalcedonian or East Syrian churches was to cut their hair leaving a cross on top, a distinctive tonsure that immediately identified their ecclesiastical affiliation. Jacobite Christians also learned to cross themselves in worship with one finger only (not two, as did other Christians at the time) as a sign of their one-nature theology.

We have no way to know the actual number of Jacobite churches in the sixth and seventh centuries, but by the time the Arabs appeared on the scene in the 640s, the Jacobite (or West Syrian, as they came to be known) Orthodox churches might easily have represented the majority of Christians in Syria and Mesopotamia. Under both Greek and then Arab rule, their churches were without state support, and their clergy perpetually harassed by government policy. Nevertheless, they grew, aided by a committed clergy and an extensive network of supporting monasteries. To this day the West Syrian Orthodox Churches continue to exist in various parts of the world, a witness to the legacy of a missionary bishop whose untiring commitment to the mystery of the one incarnate nature of Jesus Christ was so great.

Nubia

The other major missionary expansion that Theodora helped support was that of the church in Nubia. Archeological evidence suggests Christians were living to the immediate south of Egypt as early as the fifth century. During this period the entire region had undergone a radical political transition as various migrating tribes settled and resettled along the lower Nile. Documentation for the increase in Christian presence remains sketchy, but several factors provide us with historical markers. In the fifth century rioting worshipers from Nubia prevented a Roman emperor from closing the Temple of Isis located in Philae, along the Nubian border with Egypt. In 539 the emperor Justinian again ordered the temple closed, this time without incident. By then a Christian church had been built nearby at Philae; its bishop was soon to play a role in the Christian movement in Nubia. From the indications that we have, Christianity appears to have been spreading into the Nubian countryside mainly as a result of efforts by monks from Egyptian monasteries, although the ruling family of Nubia was not yet Christian.

The story of that conversion is told in the pages of the *Ecclesiastical History* written by John of Ephesus, a non-Chalcedonian bishop who chronicled many of these events in the sixth century. According to John of Ephesus, one of the non-Chalcedonian priests in Constantinople, Julian, felt he had been called to Nobatia (northern Nubia) as a missionary of the gospel. He approached Theodora, who gave him her support and sent him on his way. Justinian meanwhile was also preparing to send a mission to Nubia, which he did. According to our chronicler, Theodora got the imperial officers in upper Egypt to detain her husband's mission and allow Julian to pass through. Julian thus entered the Nubian capital ahead of his rival and was received as an official envoy of the church of Constantinople. He was quickly able to win the allegiance of the royal family to Christ, convincing them of the dangers of the doctrines of Chalcedon in the process. When the mission sponsored by Justinian finally arrived, it was turned away by the Nobataens.

The bishop of Philae, named Theodore, joined Julian in Nubia and remained after Julian returned to Constantinople. After several years Theodore also returned to Egypt, and a third missionary, Longinus (d. c. 585), was ordained by Theodosius (who was still living in Constantinople) to serve the Nubian church. Longinus was the first to be called the bishop of Nubia, indicating perhaps that he intended to stay. Like his predecessors, he was also non-Chalcedonian in his faith. The northern Nubian kingdom was brought under the theological jurisdiction of Alexandria's non-Chalcedonian pope, a relationship that lasted for nearly a thousand years.

According to the *Ecclesiastical History*, around the year 580 Longinus was invited by the ruler of Alwa, the southernmost of the three Nubian kingdoms, to work in that country as well. A decade or so before, the middle of the three Nubian kingdoms, Makouria, had become Christian under the influence of a Chalcedonian mission from Constantinople. One suspects that the invitation from Alwa might have had political motivations behind it, at least in part, for by bringing his country into the non-Chalcedonian camp the king would have been counteracting his immediate neighbor to the north. Whatever the reasons, the mission was successful. So, by the end of the sixth century all three of Nubia's small kingdoms had become Christian.

Archeological evidence supports the report of rapid religious change in the royal household. William Y. Adams points out that in Nubia's three kingdoms,

> the royal tomb, for 2,500 years the climactic expression of human and divine authority, ceased overnight to be a meaningful symbol. While we have tombs enough to account for every Nubian king from Kashta to Silko, we have not found the burial place of a single ruler of the Christian and Moslem periods.[14]

The reason, says Adams, is that with the coming of Christianity, the cult of the divine king came to an abrupt end. No longer were earthly kings celebrated in Nubia, for now the people celebrated a heavenly king instead.

The kingdoms of Nubia, like Ethiopia, lay beyond the boundaries of the Roman empire. The luster of Greek civilization was certainly a factor in the conversion of Nubia's kings. The attraction of Constantinople was strong among those from the African kingdoms who had visited the city, heard stories of its splendor, or traded for its goods. Nubian records show Greek titles were often used after the sixth century for various political offices. Yet Nubia's form of Christianity soon proved to be more resonant with that of Egypt to its immediate north and not with the imperial faith of Constantinople. The non-Chalcedonian churches were well represented throughout Egypt, but they were especially strong in the south among the vast monasteries and the peasants who lived near them. Cultural evidence and church records alike point toward Nubia's close relationship with Egypt. By the seventh century the two southern kingdoms of Makouria and Alwa had been absorbed or conquered by Nobatia, and a single Nubian kingdom with its capital at Dongola was united in its Orthodox non-Chalcedonian faith.

World Christianity at the end of the sixth century

The majority of African Christians were divided at the end of the sixth century between Chalcedonian and non-Chalcedonian churches. The patriarchate of

---

[14] William Y. Adams, *Nubia: Corridor to Africa* (Princeton, N.J.: Princeton University Press, 1977), 435-436.

Alexandria passed back and forth between these two parties for nearly a century after Chalcedon. After Theodosius in the 530s, there were two claimants to the see of St. Mark. One was head of the Melkite churches and had the support of Constantinople; the other, who became known as the Coptic pope, was recognized as head of Orthodox churches by the non-Chalcedonians in Africa. To the south of Egypt the non-Chalcedonian faith dominated in the monasteries and among the peasants who worked the land. Further up the Nile River the kingdoms of Nubia and Ethiopia were likewise non-Chalcedonians in their faith. When churches in Ethiopia sought the appointment of a new *abuna* (or "father" of their church), after the sixth century they looked to the non-Chalcedonian patriarch in Alexandria for the appointment. The non-Chalcedonian doctrine had become the standard of African Orthodoxy along the upper Nile.

To the west, North Africa had been brought back under Constantinople's political rule, but a Greek exarche now administered a region whose churches were still predominantly Latin and still divided between Donatists and Catholics. Similarly, Constantinople's representative tried to administer an imperial government in Italy, at times at odds with the theological tenor of Rome and the bishops who supported the pope. In Italy, Spain, and Gaul a variety of Germanic kingdoms (some Arian, others Catholic) ruled over Latin-speaking Catholics with whom they had come to learn to live. Britain was now mostly in the hands of Angles, Saxons, and Jutes, who worshiped traditional Germanic gods. The Irish, who were Celtic in culture and never under Roman imperial law, were becoming Christian through the efforts of Patrick's monks.

The majority of Catholics in the West regarded the pope in Rome as occupying the highest administrative office in their churches by the sixth century. The significance of his position was acknowledged even among the Spanish bishops over whom Rome's jurisdiction did not extend. Popes in Rome had begun to send a *pallium*—a white, woolen vestment worn over the shoulder and associated with St. Peter—to other bishops in the West. At first it might have been only a gift, but by the end of the sixth century the pallium was being used as a sign of Rome's authority that the pope was thereby extending to other bishops in the West in his name.

Rome expected the bishop of Constantinople to acknowledge at least the spiritual (if not the administrative) primacy of Peter among the churches of the world. Constantinople was declared in a controversial canon from the Council of Chalcedon in 451 to be the second Rome and equal in spiritual authority to the first. By 520 the bishop of Constantinople was being called "ecumenical patriarch" by some in the East, a title that suggested he was head of the churches of the world. Western church leaders protested the title, but to no avail. After 600 the title was used without hesitation.

Churches in the eastern Roman empire had seen theological controversies divide them as long as anyone could remember. Two major factions, known as Chalcedonians and non-Chalcedonians, dominated the situation in the sixth century. In Syria and Mesopotamia an aggressive church growth campaign carried out by Jacob Baradeus laid the foundations for a permanent non-Chalcedonian church. A major church synod in Armenia, meeting amid Persian-East Roman political tensions, embraced the non-Chalcedonian doctrine as well, leading the Armenian churches into that communion. Meanwhile, in the region of the Balkans, a new round of migration had brought Slavic peoples virtually into Constantinople's backyard.

Across the border of Mesopotamia to the Persian east, the majority of churches had embraced the two-nature theology associated with the names of Nestorius and Theodore of Mopsuestia. The strength of their teaching in the East was due in part to the influence of the theological school that moved permanently across the border from Edessa after 489. The Persian church had undertaken an active mission to India by the fifth century, which had resulted in a more permanent Christian presence under the jurisdiction of a Persian metropolitan. To the north of Persia the Christian movement had spread to the city of Samarkand and along the Oxus River, reaching areas that were populated by both Turks and Huns. The head of the Persian church, the catholicos, was the patriarch of Seleucia-Ctesiphon and was regarded by the congregations there as equal in authority to the head of Old and New Rome. His administration was severely hampered by the disruptions and persecutions Persian churches suffered at the hands of their government. The catholicos never exercised the power his counterparts in Rome, Constantinople, or Alexandria did. Yet for the Persian churches he was invested with a spiritual authority equal to his counterparts in those great cities to the west.

Early in the seventh century Catholicos Yeshuyab II shared communion with the East Roman emperor when the former was sent on a diplomatic mission on behalf of the shah, but this was by then an exception. By the time Arab armies took control of Persia, the East Syrian churches were for all intents and purposes no longer in communion with those of the Roman world. The patriarch of Seleucia-Ctesiphon had effectively become the head of a separate church, one that continues to exist to this day.

The other church leader who was known as catholicos, and who since the fifth century was at the head of an independent national church, was the patriarch of Armenia. Although Gregory the Illuminator is usually cited as being the first catholicos of the Armenian church, only in the fourth century did the Roman-Persian political tensions lead the Armenian bishops to begin electing their patriarch apart from the involvement of either imperial power. The cathedral of the catholicos to this day is in Etchmiadzin, a name that means "the only begotten came down" in Armenian.

From the monasteries in Ireland where monks were diligently studying their Latin, to the towns of Nubia where newly baptized Christians were busy building new compounds, to the regions of Madras where Persians and Indians were jointly attending worship in Syriac, the Christian movement was a diverse and expanding force. Yet despite its divisions, and the refusal of many Christians to regard others as fellow believers, we see a remarkable degree of commonality among the churches of the world in the fourth through sixth centuries. Though differing in languages, the liturgies of the various communions were still quite similar in style and content. In their training of leaders, their ethical teachings, their hierarchical structures, and their monastic communities, churches shared far more than they disagreed on. Moreover, Christians from various parts of the world still visited one another, influenced one another, and shaped one another's futures. Despite its internal differences, the world Christian movement was still recognizably one.

Recommended readings

The primary writings of many Christian teachers from this period can be found in *The Select Library of Nicene and Post-Nicene Fathers,* edited by Philip Schaff (Grand Rapids, Mich.: Eerdmans, 1978). Specific attention to writings regarding women can be found in Elizabeth A. Clark, *Women in the Early Church: Message of the Fathers of the Church*, vol. 13 in *Message of the Fathers of the Church* (Collegeville, Minn.: The Liturgical Press, 1983); and Joan M. Petersen, ed., *Handmaids of the Lord: Contemporary Descriptions of Feminine Asceticism in the First Six Christian Centuries* (Kalamazoo, Mich.: Cistercian Publications, 1996). Regarding Constantine, one might wish to consult Michael Grant, *Constantine the Great: The Man and His Times* (New York: Charles Scribner's Sons, 1994). A more critical perspective is provided by Harold Allen Drake, *Constantine and the Bishops: The Politics of Intolerance* (Baltimore, Md.: Johns Hopkins University Press, 2000). Background into the social and cultural characteristics of Christianity in late antiquity can be found in Peter Robert Lamont Brown, *The Making of Late Antiquity* (Cambridge, Mass.: Harvard University Press, 1978); and Averil Cameron, *Christianity and the Rhetoric of Empire: The Development of Christian Discourse* (Berkeley and Los Angeles: University of California Press, 1991).

Two works stand out as exceptional in regard to the Donatist struggle and the history of Christianity in Roman North Africa: W. H. C. Frend, *The Donatist Church: A Movement of Protest in Roman North Africa* (Oxford: Clarendon Press, 1952); and more recently, Maureen A. Tilley, *The Bible in Christian North Africa: The Donatist World* (Minneapolis, Minn.: Fortress Press, 1997). As for the Arian controversy, one might wish to consult R. P. C. Hanson, *The Search for the Christian Doctrine of God: The Arian Controversy 318-381* (Edinburgh: T. & T. Clark, 1988), or Michael R. Barnes and Daniel H. Williams, eds., *Arianism after Arius: Essays on the Development of the Fourth Century Trinitarian Conflicts* (Edinburgh: T. & T. Clark, 1993). A guide to the development of the doctrine of the Trinity is provided by William G. Rusch, ed., *The Trinitarian Controversy*, Sources of Early Christian Thought Series (Philadelphia: Fortress Press, 1980).

Another book by William G. Rusch, *The Later Latin Fathers* (London: Duckworth Press, 1977), will guide a reader through the works of the authors who effectively shaped the Latin theological tradition in the West. Anthony Meredith, *The Cappadocians* (Crestwood, N.Y.: St. Vladimir's Seminary Press, 1995), introduces the rich heritage of these eastern theologians. The common theological heritage of Latin Catholic and Greek Orthodox Christianity during the years covered in this section was articulated by the ecumenical councils, the subject of Archbishop Peter L'Huiller's *The Church of the Ancient Councils: The*

Disciplinary Work of the First Four Ecumenical Councils (Crestwood, N.Y.: St. Vladimir's Seminary Press, 1996). The basic texts that paved the way to Chalcedon have been edited and translated by Richard A. Norris Jr. in *The Christological Controversy* (Philadelphia: Fortress Press, 1980). A focused study in the theological issues at stake in the controversy is found in R. V. Sellers, *Two Ancient Christologies: A Study in the Christological Thought of the Schools of Alexandria and Antioch in the Early History of Christian Doctrine* (London: SPCK, 1954). The reader would be introduced to the cultural diversity of Christian life in this period by consulting works such as James P. Mackey, ed., *An Introduction to Celtic Christianity* (Edinburgh: T. & T. Clark, 1989); Edward Ullendorff, *Ethiopia and the Bible* (London: Oxford University Press, 1968); and A. Vööbus, *A History of the School of Nisibis* (Louvain: CSCO, 1965). The historical formation of Byzantium, which ends Part IV of our book, is told in the first part of Joan Mervyn Hussey, *The Orthodox Church in the Byzantine Empire* (Oxford: Clarendon Press, 1986).

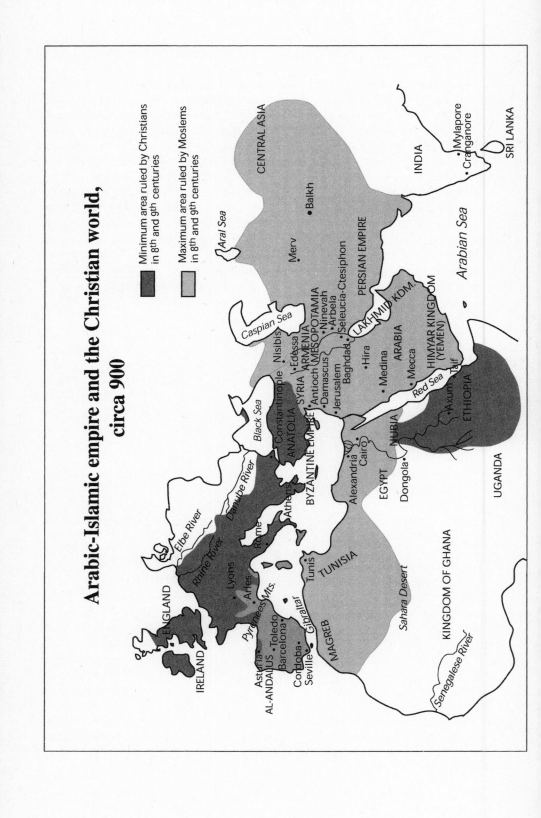

Arabic-Islamic empire and the Christian world, circa 900

Minimum area ruled by Christians in 8th and 9th centuries

Maximum area ruled by Moslems in 8th and 9th centuries

Part V

NEW CHALLENGES, NEW BEGINNINGS

600 to 1000

The conversion of the Roman imperial order over the course of the fourth century brought about dramatic changes in Christianity in the Mediterranean world. A new era in the life of the churches opened up, one that was marked by the insignia of imperial power. Other religions continued to find their adherents, and dissident groups of Christians outside the Catholic majority survived, but orthodox expressions of Christian faith came to dominate religious and cultural life around the Mediterranean Sea. The repercussions of this were felt, as we have seen, by Christians who lived beyond the borders of the Roman empire as well.

The seventh century witnessed an equally far-reaching transformation in Christian life, this time brought about by a new religious movement that erupted from Arabia. Guided by the message received through the Prophet Muhammad, Islam burst upon the ancient world with a combination of religious fervor and military strength unparalleled in human history. Within a few short decades, Arab forces united by the Islamic faith toppled the Persian empire and shook the East Roman empire to its core.

The Arab advances in the seventh century took place at a time when a new Chinese dynasty was turning its attention toward the West. The Chinese had already shown an interest in Buddhism, which had entered their land from across the Persian frontier. In the seventh century they began to show an interest in other Persian and Syrian religions as well. The flow of Persian merchants into the Chinese capital city by way of the Silk Road and to the Chinese seacoast cities by way of trade routes around South India brought Christians along with Buddhist, Manichaeans, Zoroastrians, and even Muslims into the Middle Kingdom (as China was known). One result was the first sustained encounter between Christian faith and Chinese culture. Changes in the Chinese imperial attitude toward the western religions and growth in Islam in the Persian and central Asian regions combined to bring about an end to this first Christian mission to China by the tenth century.

While Christian monks in the East were actively translating their Syriac tradition into the Chinese religious context, in the West their counterparts were busy evangelizing among the new peoples who had settled in northern Europe. These western monks and nuns were also translating Christianity, this time from its urban, Mediterranean context to a mostly rural, Germanic one. By the time the Arab armies appeared in the eastern end of the Roman empire, the political center of the western region was already shifting toward the north. The Arab advance across the southern Mediterranean helped accelerate that transformation. A new civilization was in the process of being born, one that has come to be known as Europe.

Across the world Christians in the seventh through tenth centuries continued to encounter an array of other religions. Worship of the ancient gods of Greece and Rome had become mostly a thing of the past, but in the northern regions of Europe a new encounter with the traditional Germanic gods was taking place. There were still living communities of Judaism in many of the cities scattered around the Mediterranean. Now, in the course of the seventh century, over one half of the world's Christians came to live under the rule of another monotheistic faith: Islam. Further to the east Christians along the Silk Road continued to encounter and interact with Manichaeans, Zoroastrians, and Buddhists. To a certain extent Christians who were living along the coast of southern India engaged the dominant religious culture of their neighbors. In China in the seventh century they also began to engage the religious traditions of that eastern nation.

The following section will narrate these encounters by tracing first the history of the Christian movement from 600 CE to 1000 CE along the lines of the religious and geographical expansion of Islam. Beginning in Arabia, we will move eastward into Persia, then westward into Syria, Egypt, North Africa, and Spain. The Islamic expansion reached as far as the Iberian peninsula in the West, although its effects were felt elsewhere across northern Europe.

Beyond the Islamic empire in the East, we will follow the trade routes that Christian merchants and monks traveled to reach India, central Asia, and China. In India, the Christian community grew mostly along the southern coastal region where there had been a Christian presence for several centuries. In central Asia, Christians expanded their monasteries and churches northward primarily, although not exclusively, in the cities that thrived along the Silk Road to China. The first attempt to develop an indigenous Chinese Christian church began in the seventh century but came to an end in the tenth.

From China we will turn back toward the West and follow the history of the expansion of Christianity into modern Europe. Rome was still the most important center for theology and church life in the West, but it began to look north for its new political base. The Franks were the dominant political power in the West during these years, and their most important king, Charlemagne, was crowned Holy Roman Emperor in the year 800. Yet the story of the conversion of the West belongs not so much to the Franks and their bishops as it does to the countless monks and nuns, many of them Irish and Anglo-Saxon, who were the true evangelizing agents among the peoples of Europe.

Charlemagne's coronation was not well received in Constantinople, where a Christian Roman emperor (and sometimes empress) continued to occupy the imperial throne. The East Roman (or Byzantine) empire within a single generation lost more than half its territories to the Arabs. Gone from its political control, and thus from its economic base, were Syria, Palestine, Egypt, and Roman North Africa (soon to be known as al Maghrib, Arabic for "the place of sunset"). Despite the losses it suffered, the Byzantine empire continued to sustain a vibrant Christian religious and cultural life. Drawing upon the spiritual inheritance of the first six centuries, its churches addressed the new challenges of their day by building upon the doctrinal foundations laid by the ancient teachers and the great ecumenical councils of Christian tradition.

Constantinople opened up a new mission in the ninth century to the Bulgars and the Slavs who had established kingdoms to its north. This was followed in the tenth century by the conversion of the ruling household among the Russian people. Meanwhile, in the West, the ninth and tenth centuries witnessed the advance of Christianity among the inhabitants of Scandinavia, who were brought into the family of churches that looked toward Rome as the bearer of tradition. This new wave of expansion reached as far as Iceland in the year 1000. Thus at the end of the first millennium, the movement that began in Galilee and Jerusalem reached from China and India in the east; to Ethiopia in the south; to Russia and Sweden in the north; and to Iceland in the west.

22

The Land of Arabia, the Prophet Muhammad, and the Rise of Islam

By any measure of historical significance, the Prophet Muhammad stands among the most important persons who have ever lived. Through him was received the revelation that Muslims believe to be the most sacred of books, the Holy Qur'an. Yet Muslims do not believe that their religion, known as Islam, began with Muhammad. He is the last in a line of prophetic tradition that runs from Adam through Abraham, Moses, and Jesus. According to the Qur'an, the revelation Muhammad received was given to correct the distortions that both Jews and Christians had allowed to enter their books of Torah and gospel. From its inception Islam presented its message as a corrective more than the successor of Christianity.

The religion of Islam emerged from the land of Arabia in the seventh century to reach from India to Spain by the eighth. In the process it established political dominance under a new Arab regime that ruled nearly half of the Christian world by the year 750. Over the course of several centuries, an enormous number of Christians left the church to join the Islamic community. They did so for a variety of reasons: political, economic, social, and philosophical, as well as spiritual. In the long history of Christian and Muslim relations, few have converted from Islam to Christianity. Islam brought about the first great historical decline of the Christian movement. One cannot tell the history of the world Christian movement, therefore, without telling the history of the emergence of Islam, the creation of a new Islamic empire, and its effect upon churches that lived under its domain. That history takes us first to Arabia, the home of Muhammad.

The Arabian context

Arabia had long been a land on the margins of two world empires. For centuries its people had lived on the borders of the Roman and Persian states without having been absorbed into either one. A number had migrated to live in the cities of Syria and Mesopotamia, where Arab merchants carried on extensive commercial trade. By the late 500s, several small Arab kingdoms had been formed along the borders where they had become client-states of either Persia or Rome. The majority of Arab people still lived outside the domains of either empire, however. Mostly they were organized according to traditional tribal patterns. One notable exception was an independent kingdom known as Himyar, located in the southwestern corner of the peninsula. Rains from the monsoon that blew across the Indian Ocean provided enough water for agriculture to flourish in the south of Arabia. Trees from this region were a major source of frankincense and myrrh, the fragrances brought by the magi to honor the Christ child, according to Matthew 2:11. Such products, along with the sea trade that passed through its ports from Egypt and Ethiopia to India, brought the Himyarite kingdom significant wealth.

Organized into tribes, the Arabs were a people on the move (*Arab* means "nomad" or "wanderer"). The majority were herders or Beduins (*bidwan* is Arabic for "desert dwellers") who raised sheep, goats, and camels in the arid desert lands. Dotting the peninsula were small urban centers whose life revolved around the trade generated by caravans crossing the desert. Arab merchants had long played a significant role in moving goods to the markets in Ethiopia, Syria, Mesopotamia, Armenia, and elsewhere. Some of the goods they transported were products of Arabia itself, such as camels, goatskins, or the fragrances from the south. Most were products that Arabic traders bought and then sold at a profit, making them important intermediaries in the international commercial economy.

Culturally the Arabic people belonged to the Semitic family. Their language was closely related to Hebrew, Syriac, Aramaic, and Ge'ez. Little is known about the written form of Arabic prior to the seventh century. Some have argued that the script was derived from Syriac and might have emerged from trading cities where Arab merchants needed to keep their own records. Others have suggested the script might have had Christian influences, perhaps having been devised by unknown Syriac monks who were intending to translate Christian literature. In any case, prior to the seventh century there was virtually no Arabic literary production apart from a few works of Arabic poetry. Arabic culture had known a tradition of indigenous religious prophets who engaged in ecstatic utterances, but there were no written records left of such revelations. Significantly, there does not appear to have been any translation of Christian scriptures or other Christian books into Arabic prior to the seventh century. It is likely that the Qur'an, the sacred revelation of the Islamic faith that was delivered to Muhammad through a series of divine inspirations, was the first complete book ever written in Arabic.

As a culture, the Arabs shared much in common with Judaism. Several Arab tribes traced their lineage back to a common ancestry in the patriarchs of the Jewish scriptures. Some, such as the Qurayzah in and around the city of Yathrib (latter called Medina), were practicing Jews. Belief that the Arabic people were descendants of Abraham and Ishmael was strong, a tradition that would later prove to be important for the monotheism proclaimed by Islamic faith. Nevertheless, in the sixth century the dominant religious situation of Arabia is best characterized as polytheistic. A host of local tribal deities were worshiped across the peninsula, often reflecting tribal divisions and conflicts.

The Christian movement could only claim a scattering of followers in Arabia during these years. A number of individual ascetics had immigrated into the deserts in the north. Some were refugees from East Roman persecution directed toward non-Chalcedonians, while others were escaping Persian persecution. Few appear to have had much contact with the local Arab population. Nevertheless, in the sixth century both Christian and Jewish numbers were on the increase in Arabia. Arabic Christian churches are known to have existed along the northern border and in the far south.

Aiding the process of Christian expansions were merchants, slaves, and monastics from Syria, Ethiopia, and Persia. A story recorded in the eleventh-century Syriac *Chronicle of Se'ert*, but derived from a now-lost portion of an earlier work entitled *The Book of the Himyarites*, tells of a fifth-century merchant named Hayyan from the southern Arabic kingdom of Himyar. Hayyan had traveled to Constantinople and then to Persia on business. On his way home he had passed through the northeast Arabic city of Hira where he had become a Christian and had been baptized. After returning home, he was instrumental in converting other family members and neighbors to Christ. The story is emblematic of how Christianity continued to spread through these ancient mercantile contacts.

Hira was the capital of Lakhmid, a northeast Arabic border state dominated by Persia. By the sixth century it was reported to have had Christians among the women of the ruling family, including several queens named Mawiyya, Mariyah, and Hind. In the northwest the entire tribe of the Ghassanids, who had settled along the Syrian border and had become an East Roman client-state, were Christian. (The king of the Ghassanids, it will be recalled, had sent an envoy to Theodora in Constantinople requesting missionaries to his land, prompting the ordination of Jacob Baradeus.) The Christians of Hira appear to have aligned themselves mostly with the national Persian church and the two-nature christology of the East Syrian tradition, whereas the Ghassanids embraced the non-Chalcedonian doctrine of the West Syrian churches. Among the Christians of Himyar, whose major city, Najran, was home to a bishop and several church buildings, both East and West Syrian perspectives appear to have been represented.

Muslim tradition recalls the bishops of Najran being involved in the sixth century in evangelizing work among other tribes of Arabia. Each year, according to the Muslim sources, the bishops of Najran used to journey to the great fairs of Arabia held in Mina (several miles outside Mecca) and Ukaz (further south, near the city of Taif). Lasting up to several weeks in length, and drawing people from all over the peninsula, these festivals provided Arabic poets an opportunity to recite their verses. The bishops of Najran are said to have preached at these fairs, using their camels as pulpits.

According to both Greek and Syriac historical sources, around the year 520 violence erupted in the Himyarite kingdom between the king, variously named Dhu Nuwas, Dunaas, or Musruq, and the Christians of Najran. Dhu Nuwas was either the son of a Jewish mother or a recent convert to Judaism. Conflicts between Jews and Christians in the region appear to have been going on for some time. According to *The Book of the Himyarites* a woman named Habsa, whose grandfather was Hayyan (the Christian merchant who had been among the first evangelists to the region), told the Jewish king prior to her execution that her father had once burned synagogues. The troubles of 520-525 appear to have been precipitated by an invasion in 519 of Ethiopian forces from across the Red Sea. The invasion failed to unseat the king, and upon the withdrawal of the major portion of the Ethiopian army, Dhu Nuwas attacked and destroyed the remaining Ethiopian garrison. He then launched a persecution against the Christians of Najran, reportedly in retaliation for earlier atrocities committed against both Jews and Arab traditional religionists.

The number of Christian martyrdoms now ran high and included men, women, and children. A reference to the persecution of the Christians of Najran is said to be found even in the Qur'an, in Surah 85:4-8, which tells of martyrs being thrown into pits of fire. A fuller listing of their names is recorded in *The Book of the Himyarites*. One of the women was Habsa, who has already been mentioned. Another was Ruhm, a wealthy woman from the city of Najran, who was executed with her daughter and granddaughter. Both Habsa and Ruhm are said in the text to have stood before the king and addressed him directly, Ruhm with an uncovered face and head. The latter reference indicated the relative independence, and perhaps even equality, that the Christian women claimed, in meeting face to face with the king. The courage of their martyrdom was reported to have stirred other Christians to faith.

Word of the severe persecution reached both the East Roman and Ethiopian governments, leading the *negus* (king) of Ethiopia in 525 to launch a new campaign across the Red Sea. This time Dhu Nuwas was defeated and killed, and much of Yemen was brought for the first time under Ethiopian domination. A Himyarite client-king was installed, but several decades later he was deposed by an Ethiopian general named Abrahah Ashram, who ruled as a viceroy of the negus. Abrahah appears to have been an aggressive polemicist for a Christian state. One of his accomplishments was the construction of a new cathedral in his capital city, San'a', which was intended to be a site for pilgrimage.

This in turn led to conflict with another Arabic city to the north: Mecca. Mecca was home to the Ka'bah, a popular temple and commercial rival to the church in San'a'. The Ka'bah housed some 360 representative deities, both Arabic and non-Arabic. One of the deities represented in it was the Arabic high God named Allah, while others were said to be representations of his daughters. According to tradition, the Ka'bah housed icons of Jesus and Mary as well, suggesting that Christians were also being encouraged to visit. The people of Mecca received considerable financial benefits from the merchants and pilgrims who journeyed to their city to worship in the temple. It is easy to see that the conflict with San'a' had economic as well as religious overtones.

Around the year 570, Abrahah launched a military campaign against the rival city to the north. Reportedly it was in retaliation for an act of defilement committed against the cathedral in San'a'. Although the rivalry over the pilgrimage traffic was certainly at stake, we also cannot rule out the possibility that the action was taken against the idolatry Christians would have perceived to be represented in the Ka'bah. Later Muslim history identified the incursion as having taken place in the year of the elephant, because of the elephants that the Ethiopians rode into battle. According to the Qur'an (in Surah 105), the Ethiopian forces were driven off outside the city of Mecca through divine intervention. Other historical sources indicate that the Africans were driven off by an outbreak of smallpox or some other rapidly spreading plague. Abrahah himself succumbed to disease and died before reaching home.

Word of the campaign soon reached the shah of shahs in Persia, who perceived it to be an aggression launched by an ally of the Romans. In 575 Persia invaded in retaliation, perhaps at the invitation of Arabs in the region. The Persians quickly seized control of the entire region, extending for the first time their direct rule over southern Arabia.

Muhammad, the Qur'an, and Islam

The year of the elephant, or 570, according to Muslim history, was the year of the birth of Muhammad in Mecca. He was a member of the ruling Quraysh, a tribe that claimed to trace its lineage back to Ishmael, son of Abraham. Muhammad's grandfather is remembered as having rediscovered the site of the Well of Zamzam in Mecca, the place where Hagar found water for her son, Ishmael, according to ancient Arabic tradition. Arabic tradition before Muhammad also held that Abraham and Ishmael had built the Ka'bah, which contained within it a mysterious and large black stone. By the time of Muhammad this shrine had come to house many religious deities, among them one who was called Allah, Arabic for "the God."

Muhammad's father had died before his child was born. No word has come down to us concerning his mother, but it appears she died early in his life as well. After being raised by a Beduin foster mother for several years, Muhammad returned to Mecca to live with his grandfather. At the death of the elder man, the eight-year-old boy came under the protection of his uncle, Abu Talib. During the years of his youth, he went several times on caravans with Abu Talib. Muslim tradition tells of one such journey to Syria when Muhammad was twelve. The travelers were staying at a monastery when a Christian monk saw a bright light over the young boy's head, leading the monk to prophesy that Muhammad would one day become a great prophet. Other Muslim sources tell of Christians who influenced the Prophet in Mecca, including an Ethiopian Christian slave named Jabr. From the pages of the Qu'ran it is clear that Muhammad had firsthand knowledge of Christianity, although we have no indication in Arabic, Syriac, or Greek sources of there being an organized church with bishops or clergy in Mecca or Medina.

Muhammad's business career prospered. At the age of twenty-five he married a wealthy widow named Khadijah, who was fifteen years his senior and whose caravans he had been managing for some time. Soon another side to his character began to manifest itself. For several years Muhammad had been experiencing spiritual visions. On a spiritual retreat in a mountaintop cave outside of Mecca in 610 he began to receive direct revelations that he credited with being from the angel Gabriel. The angel told him to recite the words he heard (hence the name Qur'an, which means "to recite"). The message called upon the people of Mecca to turn away from their idolatry and begin to worship the one true God of Abraham, who was Allah.

Muhammad began to preach his message of devotion or submission to God (the word *Islam* means "to submit"), gathering a small following. But the effort soon drew the opposition of the leaders of the Quraysh as well. The financial benefits Mecca reaped from those who came to worship the various deities housed in the Ka'bah were significant. Muhammad's activities were seen to pose a threat to the city.

Opposition increased. At some point before 620 approximately eighty of the Prophet's followers journeyed from Mecca to Ethiopia to seek refuge. Among them was one of the Prophet's daughters, Ruqayyah, and Hafsah, the daughter of the Prophet's companion 'Umar and a future wife of the Prophet himself. The Quraysh sent envoys to the negus of Ethiopia to persuade him that the band were outlaws and ought to be returned to Mecca. The king refused to turn them over, however. According to tradition the Muslims convinced the Ethiopian king that their beliefs were similar to his by reciting to him portions of the revelations that the Prophet had received. The sanctuary that the Ethiopians extended to the refugees has continued through the centuries to be symbolically important for Islam. It was an early Christian affirmation of the Prophet's message and by extension, of the Muslim movement.

Back in Mecca the Muslim community continued to grow. Muhammad's reputation as a leader grew with it, attracting the attention of the people of the city of Yathrib (whose name would soon be changed to Medina), who sent word inviting the Prophet to come and be their ruler. By 622 persecution in Mecca was severe enough to cause Muhammad to fear for his life. He decided to accept the invitation from Yathrib, sending the majority of his followers on ahead to the city to wait for him. Then one evening under the cover of darkness the Prophet and his closest associates fled Mecca. They were pursued by their opponents in the city but managed to escape by hiding out in the caves nearby. The year of the flight of the Prophet, or the *Hijrah* ("Migration"), is year one in the Islamic calendar.

The Muslims' numbers rapidly increased in Yathrib. Muhammad's reputation as a political leader began to spread to other cities and among the tribes in the countryside. A military force was organized from among the people of Medina to extend and defend the Muslim religion, laying the initial foundations of a new monotheistic political state. The revelations the Prophet continued to receive instructed the Muslims to exterminate polytheism and idolatry. The choice they were called to offer idolaters was simple: worship the one true God or face death.

In the case of Jews, Christians, Zoroastrians, and Sabeans, the Prophet was told not to seek to exterminate their religion and communities. These four faiths were monotheistic and were founded upon earlier revelations of divine scriptures. Despite the distortions that had been introduced into each religion, according to Surah 5:69, their members will be spared on judgment day. Believers from among the other monotheistic religions were invited to convert to Islam, but Muslims were not to compel them in the same way as the idolaters. Christians and Jews who chose not to join the Muslim movement were eventually granted limited legal status within the Islamic state as *dhimmi* ("protected people"). Their members continued to be encouraged to convert to Islam, while being strictly forbidden to proselytize among Muslims.

Concerning Christianity, Muhammad taught that Jesus (called Isa in the Qur'an) had been a great prophet who was especially chosen by God (3:45-60). The Qur'an accords a great deal of honor to his mother, Mary (3:40-47; 19). When Mary's family challenged her for having a child out of wedlock, the baby Jesus spoke in her defense (19:30-33), a miracle that substantiates for Islam both the virginal birth and the prophetic office of Jesus. According to Surah 19:3, Jesus' birth took place under a palm tree whose fruit nourished his mother, a story that reflects a tradition also found in the apocryphal *Gospel of Pseudo-Matthew*. Echoing a tradition found in the *Infancy Gospel of Thomas,* another early Christian book considered apocryphal by most orthodox believers, the Qur'an says that as a child Jesus made clay birds and breathed life into them to make them fly (5:110).

Jesus is called the Messiah in the Qur'an (4:171), a title no other prophet receives. The Qur'an assigns to Jesus a special role as well in the final resurrection of the dead on the day of judgment. These are strong themes that pervade all of Islamic teaching. Jesus is called the Word *(kalimah)* (4:171) and had the Holy Spirit from God in a special way (5:110). His spiritual empowerment was witnessed to in his miracles and healings, which included raising some from the dead (3:49). One of the miracles he performed was to call down from heaven a table for his disciples that was set with food, a reference to the Christian eucharist (5:111-115). By way of contrast, Muhammad is said to have performed no miracle other than that of delivering the Qur'an. For this last reason alone, Muhammad (and not Jesus) is the final prophet and the seal of the prophets.

At two specific points the Qur'an, and with it the entire Islamic faith, breaks sharply with orthodox Christian belief regarding Jesus. First, according to the Qur'an, Jesus was not crucified; God only made it appear thus to his enemies (4:157). Although the Qur'an speaks of an eventual ascension of Jesus (echoing in Surah 4:158 the New Testament phrase that God raised him up), the Qur'an is otherwise silent regarding the death Jesus suffered. The second, and by far the more important challenge, is to the orthodox Christian doctrine of the Trinity, which Islam believes to be in error. The Qur'an categorically rejects the notion that God has a Son, along with what considers to be the Christian practice of saying that Jesus and his mother, Mary, are equal to God. "Believe in God and His apostles, and do not call Him 'Trinity,'" it strictly enjoins (4:171). Jesus was a man through whom God chose to reveal the gospel. He never called upon others to worship him, according to Surah 5. Muslims believe the statement that God is three is a blasphemy that Jesus' followers, the Christians, later introduced.

Had the revelations Muhammad received pertained only to such doctrines concerning the nature of Jesus and his relation to God, Islam might have been perceived to be simply a new Christian party. Through the ages many Christian theologians have in fact regarded Islam in this way, seeing it essentially as a Christian heresy. From the Qur'an itself, however, it is clear that Muhammad and the Muslim community understood themselves to be institutionally distinct from

Christianity. The basic tenets of Islamic practice, often called the five pillars of Islam, were instituted early in Medina. Although they resembled Christian practices (especially those of monasticism) on a number of points, the differences were enough to make clear to the followers that they were not simply a branch of Christianity.

To this day Muslims observe these five fundamental exercises of their faith. They recite the *shahada,* or witness that there is no God but God and that Muhammad is his messenger. Second, prayer is offered five times a day (similar to the monastic Christian tradition of prayer being offered seven times each day). Third, Muslims give alms to the poor, amounting to around 3 percent of their annual income. The fourth pillar entails fasting from sunup to sundown during the month of Ramadan each year, an exercise that again is similar to the Christian fast of Lent. Fifth, if possible every Muslim is to make a pilgrimage to Mecca at least once in his or her lifetime.

Muslim prayer each day is offered mainly in a mosque, although it can be said outside if a mosque is not nearby. Men and women in the mosque pray separately, men in the front and women at the back (rather than men on one side and women on the other, as in most ancient Christian churches). In the second year of the Hijrah, Muhammad changed the direction Muslims were to turn in prayer, called *qiblah*, away from the Temple in Jerusalem and toward the city of Mecca. On Fridays the midday prayer in the mosque is followed by a sermon that is usually delivered by an elected leader of the mosque known as the *imam*. Muhammad himself began the practice in Medina by delivering his sermons from a pulpit. One sharp contrast between Islam and Christianity concerns its religious leadership in worship. Muhammad established no hierarchical priesthood and no sacramental life. Entry into the Muslim community requires no counterpart to baptism. One simply believes in one God, confesses the faith, practices the five pillars of Islam, and lives a moral life according to the will of God as revealed in the Qur'an.

During the years in Medina the revelations that Muhammad received became directed more specifically toward the day-to-day matters of social and community life. Merchants were instructed not to cheat on their scales or in other business transactions. The people of Medina were instructed not to bother the Prophet with insignificant demands on his time. Followers of the Prophet attended not only to the words that he received in his revelations but to the details of the day-to-day life of the Prophet and his companions. The latter provided material that would later be collected in the form of oral traditions that are called *Hadith* ("reports") and have authority in Islam second only to the Qur'an. Together the Qur'an and Hadith formed the basis for the eventual development of the body of Islamic law known as *Shari'ah*.

Women in particular were affected by many of these new revelations and their development in Islamic traditions. The overwhelming testimony of Islamic women is that Muhammad's revelations brought about improved conditions for them in Arabia. According to the Qur'an, women and men are equal before God insofar as their salvation is concerned, for they were both created from a single soul (4:1). Women were granted specific rights and protections that they did not previously have in Arabic culture. On the other hand, the Qur'an reaffirmed certain aspects of the traditional patriarchal social ordering of life for the Muslims. Women were regarded (as they often were in Christian societies of that day) as being under the legal authority of fathers or husbands. The Qur'an permitted a man to marry several wives but did not permit a woman to have multiple husbands. Traditional teaching allowed a Muslim man up to four wives but required that all receive equal treatment. Although he termed it a hateful occurrence, Muhammad allowed a husband to divorce his wife merely by repudiating the marriage. No reciprocal right was granted to wives by the Prophet. Both parties, however, were allowed to remarry after divorce.

The Qur'an instructed the Prophet's wives to wear a covering veil when they were outside the home, and advised all women to cover themselves adequately for the sake of modesty when they appeared in public. It will be recalled that veiling was a common practice among Christian ascetic women; the reason for the veil in Islam, namely, removing the woman's face from being the object of the lustful gaze of men, was similar. Within two centuries some Islamic religious schools were requiring all Muslim women to veil their faces in public, a practice that continues in many places today.

The Muslim community in Medina increased rapidly in the years after the Hijrah. The confidence of the Prophet and his followers increased with each victory. The first skirmish with Mecca came in the second year of the Hijrah, or 624 CE. A year later they fought again, this time the Muslims fielding a much larger army. Three years later, in 627, a combined army of several tribes led by Mecca launched an attack against Medina. During the battle the last remaining Jews in Medina, the tribe of Qurayzah, conspired against Muhammad's forces on behalf of his enemies. Unable to succeed, however, Mecca abandoned the attack, and the Muslims turned their forces upon the Qurayzah. Religious differences had taken on deadly political ramifications in Medina. The beleaguered tribe of Jews held out in their defensive towers inside the city for twenty-five days, but finally they had no choice but to surrender. As punishment Muhammad had all the adult men put to death and the women and children sold into slavery, an episode reported in the Qur'an in Surah 33:25-27.

The next year, in 628, Muhammad's forces were strong enough to negotiate a treaty with Mecca. The Muslims were allowed to enter the city for pilgrimage for three days while the Quraysh evacuated it. Two years later Muhammad entered the city of Mecca again, this time at the head of an army of ten thousand. They met no resistance, and all of Mecca shortly thereafter became Muslim. Most of Arabia was by this time united under the Prophet's rule, with Mecca and Medina, the two cities of the Prophet, forming its symbolic center. In 631 Muhammad ruled that no unbelievers could henceforth enter Mecca. Pilgrimage to that city continued to be a central Muslim practice, but now to a Ka'bah cleansed of all idols.

In the course of the next two years most of the remaining Arab tribes joined the new Islamic movement, and an initial military excursion had even been carried out against several cities in southern Mesopotamia. Among those over whom the Prophet's political control now reached was the Christian community in the south that was centered in the city of Najran. According to a Muslim historical tradition found in an eighth-century biography of the Prophet by ibn Ishaq, *The Life of Muhammad*, a deputation of these Christians led by their bishop, Abu Haritha, came to Medina to negotiate a treaty with the Prophet. The delegation arrived in Medina and found the Prophet and his companions in the mosque in Medina engaged in the afternoon prayer. Upon completion of the Muslim prayers, it was then the hour for Christian prayer. The bishop and his delegation were said to have requested and received from Muhammad his permission to pray in the Mosque of the Prophet in Medina. Muhammad and his companions are said to have left the Christians to do so. After that, several days of theological dialogue ensued. Muslim tradition cites their conversation as being the occasion for a significant revelation Muhammad received concerning the nature of Jesus Christ and the Christian understanding of the Trinity. The visit ended with the Christians successfully negotiating the extension of political rights and the appointment of a Muslim official to oversee financial affairs for their community.

The *dar al Islam* (house of Islam)

A short ten years after the Hijrah (632 CE), the Prophet died. Although he had sixteen wives (most of them representing political alliances that the Prophet had forged), he left no male successor. There had been a son born of his one Christian wife, an Egyptian named Mariya, but the child had died before the age of two. The leadership of the Muslims passed on to Muhammad's close associate Abu Bakr, who took the title of *caliph* ("deputy" or "successor"). Under Abu Bakr the military campaigns that Muhammad had ordered were continued, with a new expedition launched into southern Mesopotamia. Two years after the Prophet's death Abu Bakr died and was succeeded by another companion of the Prophet named 'Umar. A decade later 'Umar was assassinated, and the third caliph, 'Uthman, was elected as his successor. 'Uthman was also assassinated and succeeded by Ali, the only one of the first four caliphs who could claim a direct family connection to the Prophet; he was both his nephew and his son-in-law (by marriage to the Prophet's daughter Fatima).

Under the caliph 'Uthman, an authorized recension of the Qur'an was collected and edited. All other copies were then ordered to be gathered and destroyed. The version that emerged remains to this day the authorized and unchanging Book that Muslims consider the source of revelation and truth. The Qur'an that was delivered in Arabic, according to subsequent Islamic orthodox thought, is the perfect reproduction of an eternal and uncreated Qur'an that is eternally with Allah in heaven. In this sense the Qur'an is the Islamic counterpart to the orthodox Christian concept of the Logos that is with God from all eternity. According to Islam, the eternal Word of God was made manifest most clearly in the pages of the Qur'an, a manifestation most Christians believe has been given in the person and work of Jesus Christ. Moreover, for Islam it is important that this revelation was given in Arabic, a fact that leads Muslims to believe that the Qur'an cannot be translated adequately into any other language. The faithful are expected to learn Arabic instead in order to read and study its words. The Qur'an for Islam has a mystical meaning that transcends all other books. The unifying effect of the Qur'an, of the Arabic culture inscribed within it, and eventually of the Arabic language itself, joined people in many different regions and cultures into a common civilization.

In his own lifetime, as we have seen above, Muhammad had extended recognition to the Arabic Christian community in the city of Najran. In 634, however, when Muslim armies took Damascus, 'Umar began the expulsion of both Christians and Jews from Arabia. The entire peninsula was henceforth to be an exclusively Islamic land, it was decreed. By this point it appears that many, if not most, of those who had been Christian in Arabia had joined the Muslim movement. The Christians in Najran with whom the treaty of 632 had been made were the major exceptions, but after 634 they were forcibly deported to southern Mesopotamia. Elsewhere there were Arabs among some of the tribes in the north who were allowed by the first caliphs to maintain their Christian identity, but by the end of the seventh century they too appear to have become Muslim. Although there are reports from later centuries of both Jews and Christians living in the far south of Arabia, for the most part by the year 650 both of these religious movements had disappeared from Arabia. To this day there is no other religious presence legally allowed in the land of the Prophet.

Thus in a few short years a new religious faith had emerged from central Arabia. This new faith at once embraced the memory of Jesus and challenged the continuing existence of the Christian movement. At its heart was a series of revelations received by the Prophet Muhammad, and delivered to his followers who accepted them as being from God. The message of Islam was said to have been given to correct the distortions of both Jews and Christians. Christians especially were implored to cease their blasphemy of calling God "Three." Muhammad was more than a religious visionary. In Medina he proved himself to be a skilled political leader, although this too he credited to the divine revelations that continued to guide his endeavors. By the time of his death in 632, the Prophet Muhammad had laid the foundations not only of a new religion but of a new political structure, the *dar al Islam* ("house of Islam"). Continued under his successors (the caliphs), that political entity was soon to become a world empire that rivaled in size and power any that history has seen before or since.

23

The Christian Movement and the Islamic Caliphate

Syria and Persia

The rise of the Arab empire

Within a century of the death of Muhammad, as many as half of the world's Christians were under Muslim political rule. The rapid spread of the new faith was due in part to the declining political situation of both the East Roman and Persian situations, and in part to the compelling universal vision that the Prophet communicated to his followers. Muslims were also quick to add that their political success was due to the judgments of Allah upon history, a question with which more than a few Christians had to wrestle.

During the years that the Islamic community was being organized by Muhammad, Persian and East Roman armies were engaged in what would prove to be their final round of debilitating warfare. As we saw in the previous section, a century earlier the Roman emperor Justinian had purchased peace with Persia, allowing him to turn his attention to the former Roman territories in the West and to religious dissension within the boundaries of the Greek-speaking East. The period of Persian–East Roman detente had allowed the shah of shahs to focus his military attention on his eastern frontier. The Persians finally defeated their enemies, the Huns, in 571. The following year Shah Khusru (or Chosroes) I renewed the war with the Romans.

Upon the death of Khusru I, his son, Hormizd IV, assumed the throne. Although he exercised a greater degree of religious toleration, this next shah of shahs proved to be a weak military strategist, and after only a decade of rule was deposed. In the civil war that followed, Hormizd IV's son, Khusru II, sought and received from the emperor Maurice refuge in East Roman territory. A year later Khusru II returned to power in Seleucia-Ctesiphon, aided by both Greek and Armenian forces.

The status of Christians within the Persian domains was still legally restricted. For over two decades (605-628) there was not even a patriarch of the church because the government would not approve any of the church's choices. Yet under Khusru II, their visibility and access to power increased. Among the Christians, for instance, was a woman named Sirin, who of the shah of shah's thousands of wives and concubines was said to have been his favorite. Khusru II's personal physician, Gabriel, was another Christian who was highly visible in the court. Unfortunately, Christian influence was increasing at a time when the Persian government was heading toward its final collapse.

A revolt by the army in Constantinople in 602 led to the execution of the East Roman emperor who had befriended Khusru II. The shah of shahs took this as a reason to launch a new war against the Greeks. This time the Persian gains were extensive. Edessa fell to them in 607, Antioch in 611, and Jerusalem in 614. Khusru II sent home to Sirin, his wife, the wooden relic that was believed to be the true cross of Jesus, which had supposedly been discovered in Jerusalem by Helena, mother of Constantine. Egypt and Asia Minor fell next to the Persians, and by 617 they were within sight of Constantinople itself. But then, almost as quickly, the East Roman emperor reorganized his army and reversed the course of the war. In 622 he launched a counterattack by sea, which caught the Persians by surprise. Within five years they were driven back, and the Greek army was deep in Persian territory.

Khusru II, now utterly disgraced, was overthrown in his capital by his own son. That son lasted less than a year as the new shah, but that was long enough for him to kill all his brothers so as to remove any immediate claimant to the throne. Several more tumultuous years ensued. The Persian court turned to the newly elected Christian patriarch in Seleucia-Ctesiphon, Yeshuyab II, to negotiate for them a peace with the Roman emperor, which he did. A grandson of the shah was finally located and was installed in 632 on the Persian throne, taking the name Yazdegerd III. The last of the Sassanid emperors to rule, he was destined to be defeated by the new Islamic military power and replaced by the rule of the Islamic caliphate.

This new Islamic power advanced quickly from Arabia across much of the East Roman and the entire Persian empires. In 634 an army under Khalid ibn Walid defeated the Byzantine force stationed near Damascus and extended the rule of 'Umar throughout all of Syria. Damascus surrendered without a major struggle, leaving the city relatively unscathed by the conquest. Two years later the Muslims defeated a Greek army again, this time at the Yarmuk River. The caliph 'Umar entered Jerusalem for the first time. Meanwhile, Islamic forces from Medina had in 636 defeated a Persian army that was led by the shah of shahs, Yazdegerd III. Six years later, in 642, the Muslim forces completed their conquest of Persia, sending the last Sassanid ruler into hiding in the northwest region of his land, where he was assassinated in 651 by one of his own former subjects. Meanwhile, to the west Islamic forces entered Egypt in 640 and began their conquest. Two years and several major battles later they captured Alexandria, putting an end to Byzantine rule in Egypt forever.

Within a generation the Muslims had reached across the Oxus River and into central Asia to the east. To the west they reached to the gates of Constantinople (669), and across North Africa to the Atlantic Ocean (670). The Islamic military conquest had succeeded in uniting all of Persia, Mesopotamia, Syria, Palestine, Egypt, and the Maghrib (formerly Roman North Africa) under one political ruler, a feat no Persian or Roman army had been able to accomplish. Although within a century the original political unity of the caliphate broke apart, the unifying forces of Islamic religion, language, and culture continued to bind together these regions in a new historic civilization.

The swiftness of the Muslim advance and the decisiveness of their military victories were stunning. Repeatedly Muslims went up against armies that seem to have been superior—and won. We can attribute these victories in part to the superior horsemanship of the Arabs, in part to the military tactics they employed, and in part to the lack of local support for Constantinople's policies. Yet something more was at work. The Arabs were motivated by a compelling religious vision that called upon them to establish the conditions for universal devotion to the one God who rules over all the earth. They were able to communicate that vision quickly and effectively to enough of those whom they now ruled to enable their project to succeed.

Apart from the inspirational force of this universal religious vision, it is impossible to understand the Arab conquest. With extraordinary vigor they took on the project of reshaping the political, religious, and cultural geography of the ancient world. Time after time when Muslim generals came up against opposing military forces they offered three alternatives: immediate conversion to Islam, surrender and acceptance of a subjugated minority status paying taxes, or full-fledged battle with Allah entrusted to determine the outcome. Often one of the first two options was quickly accepted. When the third option was chosen, the ensuing Arab victory was interpreted to be a clear confirmation of divine support for their cause.

The rapid military expansion of Islam was all the more stunning given the internal upheavals and civil war the Arabs experienced. Revolts among various factions occupied a good portion of their energies during the early years. Of the first four caliphs who were successors of the Prophet (Abu Bakr, 'Umar, 'Uthman, and Ali), all but Abu Bakr were assassinated. A degree of internal Islamic political stability was not realized until 661, when after the brief rule of Ali's son, Hasan, relatives of 'Uthman from Mecca established the Umayyad dynasty.

In 661 the Umayyad rulers moved their capital to the city of Damascus in Syria. From there they ruled for a nearly a century, continuing their westward expansion as far as Spain. The Umayyad dynasty was then overthrown in 750, when descendants of another family from Mecca, the Abbasids, took power. The Abbasids moved the capital of the empire to Baghdad in 762, setting in motion what eventually became a major shift eastward in Islamic political and cultural life.

Christians within the *dar al Islam*

The Arabs recognized that there were significant differences among the Christians whose communities they now ruled. They knew that some had received support from the imperial treasury in Constantinople, while others had not. In Egypt they quickly discovered that many ethnic Egyptian Christians were hostile toward the Chalcedonian Greek Church. The non-Chalcedonian or Coptic patriarch Benjamin was willing to cooperate with them, at least for a time. ("Coptic" is from the Arabic word for Egypt.) The tenth-century *History of the Patriarchs of the Coptic Church of Alexandria*, a compilation written in Arabic, states that the Muslim conquest of Egypt was a divine punishment meted out against the East Roman empire because of the Council of Chalcedon.

Whether the new Muslim rulers grasped the theological subtleties that divided the churches is doubtful. For most Christians theological positions from previous centuries had hardened into formulas that were asserted more often than debated or understood. For the most part the Muslims simply ignored the theological issues that separated Christians, although they were able to exploit the animosities for their own political gain. Jacobites, East Syrians, Melkites, and Coptics were all treated as members of the same minority community. As far as the Qur'an was concerned, all who called God "Trinity" were in error. Christians of every party were regarded as unbelievers and encouraged to convert to Islam. Politically they were defined as a single community under the category of *dhimmi*. Arab rulers expected a single patriarch in each region to collect taxes and speak for the collective Christian community, achieving a degree of institutional unity that centuries of Christian debate had been unable to realize.

The Qur'an guided the treatment of Christians under Islam by providing the initial guidelines that evolved into a fuller body of law over the course of several centuries. Christians were a legal minority. They were allowed to practice their religion and maintain their communities, unlike those who were considered idolaters. As a rule (and there were exceptions), Christians were not compelled to convert to Islam, although they were encouraged to do so. On the other hand, Christians were strictly forbidden to evangelize among the Muslim population. Any Muslim who converted to Christianity could be punished by death. Christians and other *dhimmi* communities were forbidden to show any disrespect for either the Prophet or the Qur'an, both acts also punishable by death.

Christians were permitted to keep their existing houses of worship but were forbidden to build new ones. Whenever a church was taken over for use as a mosque, furthermore, the building was not allowed to revert to its former religious use. One of the traditions concerning 'Umar tells of his first visit to the Church of the Holy Sepulcher in Jerusalem. As the hour for Muslim prayer approached, the Christian bishop invited the caliph to offer prayer inside the church. The caliph is said to have declined, and instead to have stepped outside to do so. Were he to offer prayer inside the church, he said, the zealous among his followers would have claimed the building as a mosque. By praying outside the church, 'Umar preserved it as a Christian house of worship.

On the level of daily life, church bells were not permitted to be rung in Muslim lands. Christians were also not permitted to display crosses in public. They continued to use wine in their eucharistic worship, although Muslims were forbidden to drink it. Christians and other minority peoples were not permitted to

Mar Saba monastery in the Kidron Valley east of Bethlehem, as it appears today. Photograph from the Ministry of Tourism and Antiquities of the Government of Jordan. Reproduced with permission.

serve in the military, carry weapons, or ride horses. Only mules and donkeys were allowed them for their transportation needs. Christians and Jews were also required to wear special identifying articles of clothing, although it appears this rule was unevenly enforced. Muslim law forbade Christian men to marry Muslim women but allowed Muslim men to marry Christian wives. Children of such unions were to be raised Muslim, a regulation that again seems to have been unevenly enforced. Finally, Christians were required by the Muslim rulers to pay a head tax that was levied on all adult males (monks and priests being exempt). The amount varied from place to place over time, but it was always steep. At times this tax was enough of an incentive itself to lead Christians to convert.

The Arabs did not move immediately into the cities they conquered in the seventh century but lived in semi-military camps outside them. Under 'Umar, Arabs were even prohibited from owning land, a measure intended to ensure that they remained a mobile military force. The prohibition also helped limit the contact between Muslims and Christians on a day-to-day basis. Eventually the restriction was relaxed, however, allowing Arabs to move into the cities. Bolstered by conversions from among the local populations, the numbers of Muslims began to swell. By the end of the seventh century Muslims had assumed complete control of the urban landscape. Christians and other minorities in Persia had already been confined to segregated quarters under the *melet* system of the Persians, a system that was now being instituted in Syria and Egypt as well. Such arrangements tended to limit the amount of freedom Christians or Jews had on a

day-to-day level, but it allowed them to preserve their neighborhoods and communities in Muslim cities.

Despite the restrictions imposed upon them, Christian communities managed
to survive and sometimes even to grow in number during the first centuries of
Islamic rule. In both Syria and Persia churches were already familiar with political hostility or persecution. Coptic, Jacobite, and East Syrian churches had learned
to support themselves with the contributions of members rather than with imperial funds. The Chalcedonian churches under Islam soon learned to do the same.
The Arabs expected patriarchs to be both spokespersons for their communities
and administrators of Muslim rule, a somewhat new role for them. Often the
situation of the patriarchs was a delicate one, as they learned to negotiate their
way between the competing expectations of rulers and the ruled.

As monasteries were generally self-sufficient, their residents required few
material resources, and there was plenty of semi-arid terrain available for them
to build without opposition, they continued to grow for several more centuries
without significant disruptions. This was important for the well-being of churches
because the monasteries provided many of the resources for the pastoral, medical, and educational needs of the Christian communities. They also provided
Christians with relatively safe places to store their wealth and valuable goods.

In Syria and Egypt a sizable portion of the population belonged to churches
that no longer recognized the authority of the patriarch in Constantinople. For
them, the passing of Greek rule was greeted with a certain amount of indifference, even if the new Arab rulers were not always welcomed. Churches in the
former Persian empire had long contended with their minority religious status.
The inauguration of Islamic rule there brought with it a rapid end to the dominance of the Zoroastrian magi, and a short period of relaxation in official persecution. Persian Christians, Jacobite and East Syrian alike, actually fared better in
the first years under the Umayyad caliphate than they had under the Sassanids.

The Muslims were hardly prepared to handle the administrative infrastructure
required for running an empire such as theirs, stretching as it did from the Maghrib
to the border of India. For the most part they retained the administrative boundaries that they found already in place, and only made adjustments to them later.
Little changed in the relationships between cities and surrounding countryside
during the first years of Muslim rule. After the Abbasids came to power in the
eighth century, they built a new capital in Baghdad. The Muslim rulers took over
much of the traditional social and cultural trappings of Persian royal life and
incorporated them into their new city. The political religious ideology changed
in the first centuries under Arab rule, but little changed in the way of material
life, either economic or cultural.

The Arabs lacked schools of their own. There were no significant Arabic educational institutions in the seventh century to provide them with the educated
class necessary for running an empire. Muslim governors still needed scribes
and accountants to handle the details of collecting taxes, administering laws, and
conducting foreign affairs. The people that they ruled spoke many different languages, and few understood Arabic at first. For fifty years the Muslims continued
to use the imperial languages of those they had conquered for governing their

new empire, until the caliph finally ordered that Arabic be made the official language of the *dar al Islam* early in the eighth century. Both situations required extensive use of translators, a role few Arabs were prepared to assume. In this situation the Muslim rulers turned most frequently to the Christians for help. The latter had a long tradition of education and a host of existing institutions in Syria, Egypt, and Persia to prepare them for these tasks.

The curriculum of these schools was for the most part shaped by elements of classical Greek learning that had been carried over into a new Christian form. In the Persian context, where Christian schools had long carried on their educational mission of preparing leadership for churches in a minority religious context, Christians continued to teach classical Greek texts in Syriac translation. Christians in Syria and Persia were still at work translating many of these Greek works into Syriac when the Arab armies showed up in the seventh century, and Muslim intellectuals first gained access to this heritage through them. It took most of another century for the process of Arabic translation to begin, and only then did the Christians begin to see their Syriac literary tradition start to diminish in importance within the Muslim world.

It took the Arabs nearly two centuries to finally establish educational institutions of their own. When they did, they still found themselves working with Christians in the educational venture. The first truly Arab academy was the "house of wisdom" (*bayt al-hikmah* in Arabic) founded in Baghdad by the Abbasid caliph in 830. The school was something of a university whose purpose was to prepare Muslims in science and philosophy. Christians were involved in the curriculum during the early years of the school, but one of its major tasks was to translate the classical texts of the Greek intellectual tradition into Arabic, thereby giving future generations of Muslims access to this heritage. Islamic education thus developed along much the same lines as the Syriac Christian tradition had, appropriating elements of classical Greek learning but doing so with new interests. Arab schools of higher education taught the basics of grammar, rhetoric, and logic, as well as the formal disciplines of law, mathematics, science, medicine, and history. Muslim educators also taught subjects that specifically supported Islamic life, such as Qur'anic exegesis or calculating hours for prayer. Muslim and Christian education hence proceeded side by side, related through the classical Hellenistic heritage both appropriated but shaped by distinctive exegetical and theological concerns.

During the eighth century, a significant body of Syriac religious literature was being translated into new languages as the Persian church expanded into new areas. Not only were there new Arabic translations of this religious literature (some of these in Garshuni, which was Arabic written with Syriac script), but Sogdian and even Chinese versions of these works began to appear. Syriac lives of saints, catechetical teaching, and even scriptures thus were passed on into new linguistic contexts. This was happening while Syriac itself began to diminish in importance as a literary language. With the imposition of Arabic as the official language within the Islamic world and the rise of Arabic institutions of learning, Syriac began to decline even among Christians. Soon it was no longer spoken in everyday use and had ceased to be the primary language of eastern Christian theology. Syriac continued to be used as the language of the liturgy, however, even after it ceased being used in other arenas of life.

Despite the restrictions Christians faced, they were able to sustain their community life during the first centuries of Arabic rule. Here and there one occasionally encounters reports of high-ranking government officials being appointed from among the ranks of Christians. For the most part they appear to have occupied the middle levels of social class strata. Christians were often more educated than their neighbors. Their numbers included a relatively high percentage who were merchants, administrators, scribes, accountants, physicians, and artisans. Across the first several centuries one often finds reports of Christian bishops paying sizable bribes to various officials and sometimes even to other church leaders. Patriarchs were often forced to collect taxes in excess of what the Qur'an appeared to prescribe for this protected minority. Excessive bribes and taxes are indications that the community had access to considerable wealth. Indeed, from what can be gleaned from other various surviving historical sources, in the eighth through tenth centuries a number of individual Christians under Islamic rule managed to amass sizable private fortunes.

The activities of merchants accounted for most of this wealth. For centuries Christians had been well represented among the Persian merchants. Along with Jews and Manichaeans, Christians continued to play an important role in the Islamic world's foreign trade, especially with China and India. Persian, Armenian, and Syrian Christian merchants show up in numerous historical reports across the centuries. For Christians within the Islamic empire, such business activities earned them not only sizable personal fortunes but an important role as a source of wealth for the government that taxed them.

A second profession that boasted a significant Christian presence and brought both social power and wealth to the community was that of medicine. Christian schools in Persia had been for more than a century centers of medical teaching. Medical knowledge and practices were handed down with great secrecy from teacher to student. Their method of transmission, along with the primary access Christians had to classical Greek medical texts through translations, gave Christians an inordinate representation in the field during the first centuries of the Islamic era. Christian doctors were particularly skilled in diagnosing and curing diseases, which translated into financial wealth as well as increased social status. So great was the reputation they earned that Christian physicians were often retained by the caliphs even when the latter were involved in restricting the wider Christian community.

Syria

The Umayyads chose Damascus as their capital in 661 because of its location within the area of their military power base and its proximity to the East Roman capital. Christians still constituted a majority of the population in the region and would do so for several more centuries. The Umayyad caliphs could not have ruled without a measure of accommodation to their Christian subjects. Internal dissent within the Muslim community continued to occupy their attention, as did the ever-present threat of Constantinople's army. Implementing the fuller body of Islamic law, social customs, and cultural institutions still lay in the future. Consequently, daily life for most Christians continued in Syria as it had before. The one major exception was the loss of power among bishops in the Melkite churches, and even they were able to remain in communication with the patriarch of Constantinople.

The former East Roman provinces of Syria and Palestine were home to churches of two major eastern Christian traditions and a host of smaller parties. Among the two major traditions, the West Syrian or Jacobite churches appear to have been strongly represented in the region around Antioch, where their patriarch resided. Their congregations were found in Asia Minor, Palestine, and increasingly in Persia as well. Leadership for the churches east of the Tigris was provided by one known as the *maphrian*. Essentially a missionary bishop for the Jacobite churches east of Syria, the maphrian was appointed by the patriarch and resided at Tekrit in Mesopotamia. Marutha of Persia (d. 649) held this office during the first generation of Arab rule, a period which saw the rapid expansion of Jacobite churches into the former Persian empire.

The intellectual strength of the Jacobite churches was in their monasteries, such as the one at Kenneshre on the Euphrates River. Like their East Syrian counterparts, the Jacobite monasteries played a major role in transmitting classical Greek learning to their new Arab neighbors. The eighth-century Jacobite patriarch John was reported to be the first to attempt to translate portions of Christian scriptures into Arabic, doing so at the request of the Muslim governor of Syria.

Bishops and churches that recognized the authority of the patriarch of Constantinople constituted the other major Christian party in Syria and Palestine. Historically these were the churches that recognized the authority of the East Roman emperor as well. The Arab conquest did little to dissuade them on both counts (at least as far as those who did not opt to become Muslim were concerned). Not everyone was content with the change in political fortunes, of course; a sizable number went into exile in the West, some of whom (as we will see in coming chapters) figure prominently in the histories of both Greek and Latin churches. But Muslim rule also did not bring their church life to an end. Public displays of crosses were ordered torn down by the caliph, and a number of church buildings were confiscated. But bishops were permitted to lead their churches, and schools were permitted to teach theological subjects. The border between the Arabs and Greeks was never entirely sealed to trade and diplomacy. Ecclesiastical affairs were conducted along the same routes. Metropolitans and bishops from cities under Muslim control were often able to attend synods held in East Roman territory. Warfare along the shifting border between Arabs and Greeks in Asia Minor created severe difficulties for those who lived in the immediate battle zones, but elsewhere life for the churches was relatively stable.

Instances where Christians had converted from Islam or where Christians were accused of publicly denouncing the Prophet Muhammad were exceptions to this stability. In both cases the punishment was often death, opening up a new era of martyrdom among the churches in Syria and Palestine. A number of martyrdom stories remain from the era, written in Greek, Arabic, and later Georgian. One such narrative concerns a young Muslim from the eighth century named Rawh al-Qurashi, who was from Damascus. A series of visions of Christ as the lamb of God led him to desire to become a Christian. On a pilgrimage to Jerusalem, the new convert sought baptism at the hand of the patriarch of the city, who refused for fear of the authorities. He subsequently received it at the hands of two monks outside the city, taking the name Anthony and putting on the clothes of a monk. Back home in Damascus, Anthony's family turned him in to the authorities. Anthony was finally ordered beheaded by the caliph Harun ar-Rashid in 799, entering him among the ranks of a new order of Christian martyrs in the Islamic East.

John of Damascus

Among the Orthodox Chalcedonian Christians in eighth-century Damascus was a man named Mansur ibn-Sarjun, a member of a prosperous family, who was appointed to a ministerial position by the caliph in the new government in Damascus. His son, Yanah ibn Mansur ibn-Sarjun, was similarly appointed by Caliph 'Abd al-Malik to a high government post around the year 695. But then, sometime before 726 (the exact year is unsure), Yanah, or John of Damascus (c. 650-749) as he is better known in the West, resigned his position and entered the monastery of Mar Saba outside Jerusalem, where he was soon ordained to the priesthood. At Mar Saba, John took up a life of scholarship, producing an enormous literature covering philosophy, theology, liturgical studies, and interreligious polemics. His best-known work was a systematic presentation of the Greek theological tradition entitled *Fount of Knowledge*.

Part II of the *Fount of Knowledge* addressed what John considered to be the major heresies of his day. Among them he included Islam, which he called the "Ishmaelite heresy." According to John of Damascus, although Muhammad correctly combated idolatry, his teachings continued to keep people in error. The Prophet had taught that God has no Son, thus the God that Muhammad referred to was not the same as the God whom Christians knew to be the Father of Jesus Christ. John defended a number of other Christian beliefs, such as the inseparability of Word and Spirit from God, and criticized particular Muslim practices, such as polygamy. The central argument, however, remained focused on the relationship of Jesus Christ to God.

The last portion of the *Fount of Knowledge*, "An Exact Exposition of the Orthodox Faith," is the work for which John is best known in theological textbooks today. His comprehensive knowledge of orthodox tradition and skillful analysis of theological questions combined to create a work of lasting importance. John drew heavily upon Gregory of Nazianzus in particular to defend the Christian doctrine of the Trinity, this in an age of emerging Islamic anti-trinitarian polemics. Islam accused orthodox Christians of being "associationists" in that the doctrine of the Trinity associated a human person with God. John affirmed this in radically incarnational terms, pressing on to explain that the association of the three divine persons with one another was through a movement of mutual indwelling, or *perichoreses*, of one with the other. In the context of Islam, John's trinitarian theological reflection addressed fundamental questions of the divine three-in-oneness in a way that sought to preserve the orthodox faith of Christians. We will encounter his work again in chapter 28; his insights regarding the incarnation were a major contribution to an eighth-century controversy within the Byzantine church over the use of icons in worship. Because of his lasting contribution in these debates John is still regarded as being among the most important theologians of the ancient Christian movement.

Armenia

To the north of Syria the country of Armenia in the seventh and eighth centuries was able to preserve a degree of political independence unknown among the other eastern Christian regions. Armenia had long been a border state between the Persian and Roman empires. Vulnerable to the political machinations of both, it had never been absorbed by either. Since the beginning of the fourth century, Christianity had been the national religion of the land, although both indigenous religions and Zoroastrianism were practiced by significant minorities. We have already seen that the controversies of the fifth century that divided other churches in the East were felt in Armenia as well. Through these struggles the Armenian church remained institutionally independent. Its bishops selected a patriarch of their own, the catholicos, who resided in Etchmiadzin. Theologically the Armenian churches were part of the non-Chalcedonian family that included the Jacobite, Coptic, Nubian, and Ethiopian communions. These churches recognized one another's hierarchies and church practices.

The Arabs first invaded Armenia in the seventh century, securing political control over portions of the country without entirely conquering it. Armenian resistance was strong, for one thing. For another, the mountainous terrain was difficult for the Arabs to secure militarily, dependent as they were on their horsemen. The Arabs also saw value in having a semi-independent Armenian state to serve as a buffer with the Greeks to the west. Thus, rather than continue to attempt to conquer the country outright, the caliph instead helped install a national government that was amenable to Arab interests. Armenia paid tribute to the caliph but was free of direct Arab rule.

Arab influence within the country was exercised through the Armenian princes the Arabs were able to dominate. The caliph was asked to ratify the establishment of a new Armenian dynasty in the middle of the ninth century under Ashot I, for instance, a dynasty that extended Armenian rule as far as Georgia and the Caucasian region to the north. On the other hand, most of the stipulations of the Covenant of 'Umar, such as the one forbidding the building of new churches, were not imposed. Until a Muslim army finally sacked their capital early in the tenth century, forcing the catholicos into exile, the Armenian churches experienced few of the disruptions encountered in other areas where Arab rule dominated. For its part, an Armenia paying tribute to a Muslim government was free to maintain its theological independence from Constantinople. Armenian merchants also continued to be free to engage in trade and soon proved to be invaluable agents of international exchange for the Muslims.

Persia

When the dust had settled from the fifth-century christological controversy, the followers of the Antiochene school had been forced entirely out of Roman-held territories and into Persian areas. Over the course of the century their theological perspective became more firmly anchored within the Persian churches. Among these East Syrian Christians, the authority of Theodore of Mopsuestia reigned supreme. It was his method of biblical exegesis, however, more than the formulations of his christology that was taken to be decisive for his contributions to orthodoxy. The exact meaning of the two-nature formula was never as important to the theologians of the East Syrian churches as was Theodore's role as an exegete of scripture. The acceptance of the teachings of Theodore's student, Nestorius, the fifth-century bishop of Constantinople whose rejection of the doctrine of Theotokos earned him lasting reproach as a heretic in the West, led to the Persian church being labeled Nestorian. Yet Nestorius himself was hardly ever cited as an authority by eastern writers. It was theologians such as Theodore of Mopsuestia, Ibas of Edessa, and Theodoret, all of whom had been anathematized by Justinian in the sixth century, that the eastern tradition looked to for guidance in matters of doctrine.

The theological perspective of the national Persian church leaned toward a stronger two-nature formulation of faith than was accepted in the West. The Persian churches thus shared with Islam much of the latter's misgivings about identifying human and divine natures in Jesus in an indiscriminate manner. Indeed, from a strictly christological point of view, some have argued that the Islamic understanding of Jesus can be seen as a radical expression of the two-nature position. Muslims shared with East Syrian Christians an aversion to calling Mary the mother of God. They both rejected expressions of faith that would appear to confuse the humanity of Jesus with the divine nature, while each nevertheless affirmed in its own way that in the person of Jesus the Word of God was to be found in a specially redemptive way. Yet despite such similarities, Muslims rejected the East Syrian tradition because it was Christian. The East Syrian churches were trinitarian and accepted fully the authority of Nicaea. They practiced baptism, the eucharist, and ordination into the priestly ministry. As far as Islam was concerned, the East Syrian Christians had equally distorted the truth about God by calling God Trinity and were thus to be circumscribed by the same political encumbrances that were directed against Christians and Jews elsewhere within the household of Islam.

Christians in Persia in turn soon came to relate to the caliph much as they earlier had related to the shah. Following the Abbasid establishment of their new capital in Baghdad, the East Syrian patriarch was allowed to move his residence to that city from Seleucia-Ctesiphon. The Persian churches soon began to submit the name of newly elected patriarchs to the caliph for his approval, often a perfunctory procedure that nevertheless carried symbolic significance. In the cities the lives of Christians were severely restricted under Islam, much as they had been under the Sassanid system of *melet*. The Umayyad caliphate in Damascus had been more tolerant of Christian practices, if for no other reason than it had been more concerned with securing political control than in enforcing Muslim faith and conversion. The Abbasids, on the other hand, were more concerned with securing Muslim faith and thus with tightening restrictions on the Christian community. It was under the Abbasids that the final form of the Covenant of 'Umar came into being, for instance, and that a far greater expansion of Islam through conversion was undertaken. In this situation Christian monasteries, as centers of Christian life and worship set apart from regular urban locations, increased even more in importance among Christians in the East.

Monasteries had long been important centers of education and evangelism, as we have seen. Monastic communities such as that at Kenneshre on the Euphrates for the Jacobites, Mar Saba outside Jerusalem for the Chalcedonian Orthodox (which was home to both a men's and a sizable women's community), and Gundishapur in modern Iran had exercised considerable influence within the various church communions. East Syrian monasticism was similar to that of other branches of the Christian community. The hours of prayer were often similar (seven times a day), and the combination of education and spiritual practice fairly consistent across the Christian world. The form of tonsure men employed in the East Syrian churches since at least the sixth century was that associated with the tradition of St. Peter and Rome, in which the top of the head was shaved to leave a crown. Monks in the East wore black robes, distinguishing them from other priests, who wore white.

Through the first centuries of Islamic rule, there continued to be wandering Christian mendicants who lived apart from monastic community, usually alone in the wilderness. One such movement, known as Messalians, eschewed institutional church life in pursuit of mystical spirituality and sought an immediate filling of the Holy Spirit, which they believed freed one from the demonic power of sin. By the ninth century even the solitaries tended to gather in communities in remote areas in the East, however, due as much to the need for protection as a desire for community.

The impact of Christian monasticism in the East was felt among Muslims in the development of a distinctive form of Islamic mystical and ecstatic experience known as Sufism. The exact origin of the Sufis in Islam remains obscure, but they appear to have been influenced by the tradition of Christian monasticism in the East. The term *sufi* is derived from the Syriac word meaning "wool," a reference to the rough wool clothing worn by Christian monks and nuns. In the eighth and ninth centuries the Sufis grew in the form of fellowship groups seeking deeper spiritual experience in Muslim communities. Although they were usually married, Sufis adapted other aspects of ascetic life that were characteristic of Christian monasticism. Over the centuries they became known for their mystical teachings, many of which bordered on the more mystical Christian understanding of salvation as union with God.

Isaac of Nineveh

One of the more renowned Christian ascetic teachers from the seventh century was Isaac of Nineveh from Mesopotamia. Little is known of his life other than that he was consecrated a bishop by Patriarch George sometime around the year 670. Shortly after that he took up a solitary life of prayer and reflection in the monastery at Rabban Shabur, located in modern Iran. Isaac was a member of the East Syrian tradition, but in one of his writings he warned others against accentuating differences in confession that separated Christians from one another. He was a mystic for whom the immediate experience of God was more important than intellectual formulations of the faith. His spiritual writings emphasized the mercy of God and the work of the Holy Spirit in one's life, which, from time to time, said Isaac, brings one into a state of ecstasy. The spiritual life for him was one of progression moving through stages from bodily passions to spiritual wonder. Here he stood in the tradition of Basil of Caesarea, Ephraem of Syria, and Theodore of Mopsuestia. "Thirst for Jesus, that He may intoxicate you with his love. Close your eyes to the precious things of the world that you may deserve to have the peace of God reign in your heart. Abstain from the attractions which glitter before the eyes, that you may be worthy of joy in the Spirit," advised this venerated teacher from the East in his treatise *On Ascetical Life*.[1]

As important as monasticism was, it did not encompass the entire practice of Christianity in the East. There remained throughout the first centuries of Islamic rule a sizable number of Christians living in cities, towns, and villages throughout Mesopotamia and Persia. Priests and bishops practiced the various sacraments of the church, including baptism and eucharist. The liturgy was conducted in Syriac, the most common being the Liturgy of St. James, which tradition credits with first being celebrated by the brother of Christ himself. Its antiquity, apostolic authority, and historical associations with the Holy City of the East combined to give this particular service an enduring place in the life of the churches through the modern era.

Patriarch Timothy

Standing at the head of these churches throughout the entire period was a patriarch who after the eighth century resided in Baghdad. By the tenth century the patriarch in Baghdad was being appointed by the caliph directly, as head of all Christians under Abbasid rule. (Prior to that he was elected by other bishops and then ratified by the caliph.) The patriarchs of the East were not always remembered as figures of stellar spiritual leadership. By the ninth century stories of bribery and greed had become all too common among them. Nevertheless, the patriarch was an important figure, both as the administrative head who appointed other major metropolitans and as a symbol of the unity of the churches scattered throughout the East.

---

[1] St. Isaac of Nineveh, *On Ascetical Life*, trans. Mary Hansbury (Crestwood, N.Y.: St. Vladimir's Seminary Press, 1989), 55.

Among the greatest of the East Syrian patriarchs during this period was Timothy, who served in this capacity from 780 until his death in 823. Born in Adiabene and educated in the monastery of Beit 'Abhe there, Timothy became head of the church at a time when bribery and corruption were already rife in ecclesiastical affairs. He is reported to have had heavy sacks delivered to the other bishops who were going to select the next patriarch, with instructions to open them after his election. Expecting to find the sacks filled with gold, the others elected Timothy, and then opened their sacks only to find them filled with stones. The event was a precursor of the reforms he was to institute.

More than two hundred letters from this illustrious leader survive. They show him to be engaged in administrative ecclesiastical affairs not only throughout the Persian realm but far beyond its borders to the east. Timothy appears to have been one of the most missionary-minded church leaders of the first one thousand years of the Christian movement. Under his tenure the East Syrian church expanded significantly beyond the borders of Persia. In one letter Timothy reports that he has appointed a metropolitan for the church in Tibet; in another he says that he has received a letter from a king among the Turks who has become a Christian and requests of Timothy a bishop and priests. A third appointment was made to San'a', the former capital of Yemen in southern Arabia, despite the expulsion of Christians from the peninsula (we do not know if the bishop was actually allowed to assume the post or instead served the community in exile). Finally, it was Timothy who appointed a metropolitan of India, freeing the Christian community there from being under the authority of the bishop of Rewardashir in Persia, which it had been for several centuries.

This same patriarch took part in 781 in a two-day dialogue in Baghdad with the third Abbasid caliph, Mahdi. Timothy described his encounter in a letter written to a fellow bishop that was subsequently circulated as an apology for Christianity in the East. The courts of caliphs were the scene of a number of such interreligious intellectual conversations during this period, often involving Jews as well as Christians and Muslims. Timothy's account, composed in Syriac but later translated into Arabic, was one of the more popular. The patriarch had appeared before the caliph for a regular audience and was finished with various affairs when the caliph suddenly asked him how a man of such obvious knowledge as he could say that God had married a woman from whom he begat a son. Timothy answered that as a Christian he had learned from the gospel, Torah, and Prophets of one known as the Son of God, born not first from flesh but before all time and in an inexplicable way as the Word of God. This very same Word of God was born of the Virgin Mary, continued Timothy. With that the dialogue was engaged.

The caliph questioned how Timothy could say that the Eternal One was born in time. Timothy's answer followed the tradition of the Antiochene school that there were two distinct natures, one created and the other uncreated, but that these two constitute one Christ and son. It is like a soul and body joined in one person, or the tongue and word joined in one voice. Again the caliph, whom Timothy refers to reverently as "God-loving," questioned how he could believe that God was Three. Timothy responded that as the sun with its light and heat is one, so God and Word and Spirit are one. God cannot be separated from Word and Spirit, yet they both proceed from God.

The discussion next turned to questions of interpretation of scripture and events in the life of Jesus. The caliph pressed the patriarch to show his beliefs were found in the Torah and gospel, which Timothy did. If Jesus was circumcised, why was not the patriarch also? If Jesus worshiped in the Temple in Jerusalem, why did Christians turn to the east to worship? Finally, why did the patriarch accept the testimony of the Torah to Christ, but not of the gospel to Muhammad? The last point was one that Muslims asserted regarding the New Testament's reference to a coming Paraclete. Was this not a reference to the coming of Muhammad? Timothy answered by pointing out that the Paraclete according to the New Testament knew all things and thus was unconfined in presence or knowledge. Muhammad did not know what would befall him, nor was he unconfined as only a spirit could be. The Paraclete was the Spirit of God, not Muhammad. The first day's conversation concluded with a lengthy discussion of the scandal of Jesus dying on the cross, which Timothy argued had been answered by God raising Jesus up.

The second day's conversation opened with the caliph asking if the patriarch had brought a copy of the gospels, as he had said he would. From whom did he receive this book, Mahdi asked, intending to press the point that they were the work of apostles of Jesus. "It is the Word of God that gave us the Gospel, O our God-loving King." The apostles simply wrote what they had heard from the Word-God, who was Jesus. The caliph then asked bluntly, "What do you say about Muhammad." The patriarch's answer was forthcoming: Muhammad is worthy of all praise, for he walked in the pathways of the prophets. He brought his people away from idolatry and to the worship of one God. Muhammad also taught about God, his Word, and his Spirit, the mark of true prophets.[2] Again the conversation turned to questions of Three and One, and of the two natures of Jesus. This time the patriarch made his point against Melkites and Jacobites, that God did not suffer in the flesh in Jesus Christ as (he claimed) these others said.

Throughout the conversation Timothy showed high regard for the caliph's faith. The patriarch showed himself to possess at least a basic knowledge of the Qur'an, as likewise the caliph had of the Christian Bible. Timothy at times appeared to be scornful of the East Romans in a way intended to demonstrate his loyalty to the caliph. He was equally scornful of Jacobites and Melkites, the two expressions of western faith identified with the Greek theological world. At the same time the patriarch clearly identified as his own the common tradition of Cyprian, Basil, Gregory of Nazianzus, Theodore of Mopsuestia, and Nicene Orthodoxy.

Unlike John of Damascus, who a century before in Palestine had called the Prophet a forerunner to the anti-Christ, Timothy was willing to grant on Christian terms a degree of legitimacy to Muhammad, even if he and the caliph did not agree on precisely what that meant. On the other hand, both caliph and patriarch seemed to agree that Jews were to be despised and rejected by all. Muslim and

---

[2] "Timothy's Apology for Christianity," in *Woodbrooke Studies,* vol. 2: *Christian Documents in Syriac, Arabic, and Garshuni,* ed. and trans. A. Mingana (Cambridge: W. Heffer and Sons Ltd., 1928), 60.

Christian could find common ground by turning on the third, and politically weakest, member of their monotheistic family, the Jews. The conversation ended with the caliph lamenting ("If only the patriarch accepted Muhammad . . . "), and the patriarch comparing the gospel to a precious pearl entrusted to the faithful in the world. Timothy then offered a prayer for the caliph.

Decline of the Abbasids

The period of Mahdi's caliphate marked in many ways the high point of Christian-Muslim relations under the Abbasids. Under Mahdi's successors, Islamic civilization reached its most brilliant heights. But continuous political intrigue and resurgent regional loyalties took their toll. After 850 the Abbasids began to decline in their political power. Turkish mercenaries in the caliphate's army gained substantial power within the palace, reaching a point where the Abbasid rulers became little more than figureheads. Turkish military leaders exercised actual rule in the East during most of the tenth century, laying the groundwork for the political emergence of one of their tribes, known as the Seljuk (or Saljuq) Turks in the eleventh.

The situation among the church leadership mirrored the decline of the Abbasids in Persia in many ways. Corruption and abuse of office became common among patriarchs, bishops, and monastics alike. A major outbreak of official persecution began around 850, but more common were episodes of local persecution of Christians, who from time to time became targets of riots and violence. Much of the time it was their wealth (real or perceived) that the Christians' enemies were after. Continuous warfare with the Romans brought disruptions to church life in the border regions. After the ninth century the political stability of the Islamic world itself began to crumble as the ruling caliphate found itself divided into a host of new regional kingdoms, making Christian existence even more precarious in the East.

Thus the first years of Muslim rule in Syria brought relatively few changes to the majority of Christian churches, while in Persia the climate actually improved. Christians found themselves thrown together in a common political situation as *melet*. They played a significant role in the first years of the new Arab empire in administration, education, and business. Islamic proscriptions of Christian practice were felt from the beginning in areas of evangelism, social life, and personal piety, but even these were not strictly enforced in the cities during the first years of Muslim rule. Christian monasteries grew in their importance as centers of learning and pastoral resources for Christian communities. As the decades and centuries passed, life grew more restrictive, and the overall situation of Christians deteriorated as a result.

Christian teachers responded in a number of ways to the challenges posed by Islam. Chief among the challenges was the Muslim insistence that God had no Son. Jesus was not to be worshiped as God, nor were Christians to call God Three, said the Qur'an. According to some Christian teachers, such as John of Damascus, Islam was little more than a new Christian heresy and Muhammad a forerunner of the anti-Christ. But others, such as the eighth-century East Syrian patriarch Timothy, recognized Muhammad as a prophet and were willing to acknowledge a degree of truth that they found to be revealed in the Qur'an. The writings of these and other teachers of the period suggest Christian life and thought continued in new ways to express the ancient faith inherited from the days of the apostles of Jesus.

24

The Christian Movement
in Africa and Spain

The Arab advance across northern Africa was as rapid and unexpected as it was to the east. Barely a decade had passed following the death of Muhammad when all of Egypt was under Arab rule. Two decades later an Arabic army was pressing into Nubia, where it met with sufficient resistance to turn it back. No such resistance withstood the Muslims' advance toward the west along the African coast. Within sixty years of the Prophet's death, the Arabs controlled all of North Africa along the Mediterranean Sea to the Atlantic. Another generation and they had taken control of most of the Iberian peninsula (modern Spain and Portugal). The Muslim military advance across the Pyrenees was only halted in 732 at the battle of Tours, when an army of Franks under a king named Charles Martel turned back the invading force. Within a century of the Prophet's death, Arab rulers controlled much of Christian Africa and Spain, permanently changing the complexion of Christian life in these lands.

Egypt

Alexandria was still among the largest and wealthiest cities in the world in the sixth century. Despite the declining fortunes of its patriarchal see in the shifting world of ecclesiastical politics, and despite the loss of many of its great intellectual resources (including much of the ancient library, which had fallen victim to vermin and disuse), the city could still command the world's respect. Merchants came from far and wide to trade their goods in its marketplaces. The city's port was one of the busiest in the Mediterranean, while caravans departing for the East had only a short distance to go to reach the Red Sea. From there ships regularly sailed down the coast of Africa, around Arabia, and all the way to India. The trade route that passed through the Sinai peninsula from Egypt and Arabia was one of the busier roadways in the southeastern Mediterranean region. A merchant traveling along this route in the year 639 might have met up with the Muslim army under General Amr ibn al-As as it was advancing into Egypt.

The invasion was over quickly. The city of Alexandria held out the longest, falling three years after the initial battle. The Arabs had taken the East Roman garrisons stationed in Egypt almost entirely by surprise. In some places the Arabs had actually been aided by local Egyptians who were dissatisfied with Greek rule. No stories of significant Egyptian resistance in the countryside come down to us from the seventh century, no stories of national Egyptian leaders trying to raise a new army to respond to the invaders. For too many years Egypt's grains, its goods produced by cottage industries, and its wealth in the form of taxes had drained from the country like the mighty Nile itself. For too many years Constantinople's interference in Alexandria's ecclesiastical affairs had left many disgruntled. Harassment of churches that celebrated non-Chalcedonian beliefs, and especially of their patriarch, Benjamin, did not help the imperial cause among the people in Egypt. Many who lived in its towns and villages believed the new Arab rulers might even be easier to live with. This is why Arab historians are not far from the truth when they describe the conquest of Egypt as a liberation movement.

At first the Coptic Christians adopted a mostly neutral stance toward their new Muslim rulers. In the villages and towns there was little adjustment needed to the new Arab rulers, for they did little to interrupt people's daily lives. A number of cities had reached quick settlements with the advancing Arab army through treaties, thereby averting being sacked and having their populations enslaved. Even Alexandria was not entirely destroyed, although a number of churches were burned. One of the stories that circulated after the conquest of Alexandria claimed that a Christian captain in the Greek fleet had saved the bones of St. Mark from the fire that had been set in the cathedral. After the battle had subsided and order had been restored, he supposedly returned them to St. Mark's, which the new Arab rulers allowed the Christians to rebuild. Like so many other legends of this kind, the story is of dubious veracity, but it speaks volumes to the sense of restoration and continuity that Egyptian Christians were experiencing.

The Muslim general who took the city sent word throughout Egypt welcoming back to Alexandria the patriarch Benjamin, who had been banished by the emperor, an offer the patriarch soon accepted. With the support of the Arab rulers, Benjamin was able to extend his influence through Egypt. The Arabs also allowed a Chalcedonian bishop to remain in Alexandria unmolested, and the churches that were in communion with him remained open as well. The other smaller Christian communities that had continued to make their home in Alexandria found the restrictions they had lived with under Greek rule greatly relaxed. During the first decades of the Umayyad caliphate, Arab rulers were far too busy trying to administer the infrastructure of their empire to bother themselves too much with church affairs.

Thus the first decades of Arab rule in Egypt were similar to those in Syria and Persia. By the end of the seventh century, however, warning signs had begun to appear on the Egyptian horizon, much as they had in Syria and Persia. New edicts were passed ordering the destruction of gold and silver crosses and requiring churches to place on their doorways the inscription, "God is not begotten and does not beget." Taxes upon the Christian community were increased. The Coptic patriarch's relationship to the Nubian and Ethiopian churches, both of which continued to look to him as their pope, was disrupted. At one point the Arab governor of Egypt prevented the patriarch of Alexandria from sending to the Nubian and Ethiopian kings a pastoral letter encouraging them to settle a dispute between them.

Another incident recounted in the Coptic *History of the Patriarchs* involved a priest from India who arrived in Alexandria with a request for a bishop for the churches in need of pastoral services in his homeland. The Coptic patriarch hesitated to send a bishop without the governor's permission, but the Chalcedonian bishop of the city readily consented, ordaining three Egyptians to the episcopate for the task. The three never made it to India according to the *History of the Patriarchs*, but were arrested en route and were executed by the caliph in Damascus.

The eighth century brought increasing restrictions and difficulties upon the Christians in Egypt. One governor ruled that no Christian man could be buried before the annual head tax levied on him was paid, leaving destitute families with his corpse while they sought to raise the necessary funds. In several places Christians rioted in vain attempts to throw off Muslim rule, leading to even more repressive measures. The Umayyad caliphs had appointed the governor of Egypt and exercised a relatively close watch over Egyptian life. With the rise of the Abbasids in the middle of the eighth century, however, the rule of the caliphate became more removed. Egypt soon came under non-Arabic Islamic rulers who wrested control away from Baghdad. A semi-independent Muslim kingdom emerged, further isolating the Coptic churches from other Christian communities in Syria, Palestine, and even the Greek churches to the north.

Even more drastic changes in Egyptian political life were in store after 969, when an invasion of a Fatimid Muslim army from Tunisia successfully took over the country. The Fatimids were followers of the Shi'ite branch of Islam, which believed that the caliphate belonged to the family line of Ali and Fatima, the Prophet's daughter. Adamantly opposed to the claims of the Abbasids to be the legitimate inheritors of the Islamic political mantle, the Fatimids succeeded in the ninth century in wresting Syria from Baghdad's control. From their new capital in Cairo they exercised a relative degree of tolerance toward their Christian subjects at first. Many of the restrictions that had come to be placed on the churches were relaxed. At one point in the tenth century a Fatimid ruler even appointed a Coptic Christian by the name of al-Muizz as governor of Syria.

Across the first four centuries of Islamic rule, Coptic Christians under the Umayyad, Abbasid, and then Fatimid dynasties faced a situation of political marginality that was radically different from what they had known before. Even in the years after the Council of Chalcedon, when tensions between the various camps had led to imperial intervention, Christians could still count on a considerable amount of freedom in the country. Although they still constituted the majority of Egypt's population after 645, Christians had become marginal in the country's political life. There were periods when Muslim rulers relaxed their restrictions somewhat, and in the first days of the Fatimid dynasty Christians even experienced relative advancement. Nevertheless, for the most part life grew increasingly difficult. The number of reports of destitute Christians unable to pay their taxes suggests a situation that was different from that of either Persia or Syria. Coptic Christians worked as administrators and artisans, and in general they were never as wealthy as the East Syrian Christians. Many Coptic Christians were rural dwellers, and relatively few were merchants. One finds few reports of them among the Armenian, Persian, and even Greek Christian merchants who traveled the major trade routes of the ancient world.

The Umayyad decision early in the eighth century to make Arabic the official language of Islamic lands had the same effect upon Coptic as it did upon Syriac. It was only a matter of time before the Egyptian language was abandoned in day-to-day use. Soon it was not being regularly learned even by Christians in the country. Christian theological texts began to be written in the language of the rulers, and many older Coptic theological works had to be translated into Arabic to make them available to a new generation. Only the liturgy continued to be said in the ancient Egyptian language, having the unfortunate effect of isolating it from the daily lives of most people. On the other hand, maintaining the liturgy in Coptic ensured a measure of continuity with the past that would otherwise have been lost. Coptic Christians continued to celebrate in the ancient language the great liturgies associated with the names of Basil, Gregory, and Cyril of Alexandria. In doing so they found a living connection with the ancient tradition amid changing historical circumstances.

Coptic Christians, like others under Muslim rule, were prohibited by law from building new churches. The degree to which this law was enforced is not always clear; there is some evidence of churches at least being restored through these years, if not actually built new. Christians were allowed to continue to endow and build monasteries, which many did in desert regions that were removed from the larger Islamic presence around the cities. A number of the new monasteries that were built in Egypt after 700 were houses for women, indicating that monasticism continued to be a vibrant movement for women, as it had always been in Egypt.

Bishops in the towns and cities were usually able to maintain their residences near their churches in what became designated Christian quarters. The Coptic patriarch was even allowed to move from Alexandria and build a new residence in the capital of Cairo. Despite the evidence of official toleration of their buildings and even some indication of new construction, the condition of the churches in Egypt over several centuries was one of gradual deterioration. It could hardly have been otherwise, given the continuous financial burden, the decline of educational resources even for training clergy, and the political restrictions the Coptic churches had to endure.

It was during this initial period under Muslim rule that many of the distinctive traits of Coptic Christianity took on the shape they still have today. The modern Coptic liturgy remains little changed from the eighth or ninth century. Patriarchs are still elected by lot from among three names placed on the altar of the cathedral church. Most important is the Coptic language itself, a language that continues to be used only in Christian liturgy and identified with national church history. Within Egypt, the Coptic Christians became an invisible minority, but one harboring a rich tradition of faith that reached back in unbroken continuity with the earliest Christian movement.

Nubia

Soon after the Arab general Amr ibn al-As had completed his conquest of Alexandria, he turned his attention to the south. Nubia, we have seen, had been evangelized in the sixth century by missionaries from Constantinople, notably those who had been sent by the empress Theodora. A strong adherence to the non-Chalcedon christology gave the churches of this kingdom a close connection to Egyptian Christianity and the patriarch of Alexandria. Nubia was never a province of Constantinople, and its people had never been under foreign imperial rule. The seventh century had brought a united kingdom stretching from Aswan to the ancient city of Meroë. When an Arab force said to have numbered twenty thousand rode against Dongola, the capital city of Nubia, it was met by the fierce resistance of superior archers and turned back. It was the first defeat the Arabs suffered in their expansion in the seventh century.

A second Arab attack was launched in 650. Again it reached the capital of Dongola on the Nile, and again it was unable to take the city. This time, however, the Nubian king decided it was more prudent to negotiate a treaty. The result was a unique document signed by the Umayyad governor of Egypt and king of Nubia. Known as the *Baqt* (the word is believed to have been derived from a Greek term for "agreement"), it is without parallel in early Muslim history. According to the terms of the treaty as far as we can tell (no original copies survive), the Arabs promised not to wage war against Nubia and did not attempt to force the Nubians to become Muslim. Residents of each nation were guaranteed free passage through the others' territories, and the Nubians were bound to return any Muslim fugitives (mainly slaves) to Egypt. Finally, an annual payment from Nubia was to be extracted, and it was of the most severe form: according to the terms of the Baqt, each year the Nubians were to deliver some three hundred male and female slaves of sound health (neither aged nor children) to the Arab governor at Aswan. The treaty invoked the name of Allah and his Prophet Muhammad, and the Messiah and his Disciples, as its witnesses.

The earliest record of the Baqt comes from a ninth-century Muslim source. One later version reports that the treaty required that the mosque in Dongola be maintained and kept lit, an obvious reference to a later situation when Muslim merchants and possibly diplomats had established a permanent presence in Christian Nubia. An eighth-century letter from the Abbasid government complains that the Nubians had fallen far behind in the payment of their slaves. Arab sources report that in the ninth century Nubia had again suspended its annual payment of slaves, and this time the caliph demanded full back payment—fourteen years worth. This was the occasion for a diplomatic visit by the Nubian prince and future King George to Baghdad in 835. So successful was the Nubian prince in his mission that he not only returned with gifts from the caliph but succeeded in reducing the terms of payment to three hundred slaves every three years, with inclusion of commodities in exchange from Egypt. The Fatimids sent an embassy to Dongola again in the tenth century to seek to restore the payments once more. This time the king of Dongola took the opportunity to witness to the Muslim diplomatic mission on behalf of the Christian faith. There is no mention of whether the slave payment was resumed.

The kingdom of Nubia during the seventh through tenth centuries encompassed the lands along either side of the upper Nile in what is modern Sudan. Aswan remained its historic border to the north. To the south of Nubia lay the city of Axum, the capital of the kingdom of Ethiopia. When it was meeting its payment of slaves to its Muslim neighbor to the north, Nubia appears to have done so by conducting raids on the nomadic tribes living to its southeast. While it was certainly not the first time such raids were conducted on African soil, it was one of the first experiences of slaves being exchanged as part of the economy between Muslims and Christians in Africa. In succeeding centuries we will watch the numbers of people being enslaved and sold and permanently removed far beyond their homelands grow as the trade in African human flesh continued.

Archeologists examining the towns along the Nile in Nubia have found the remains of more than one hundred churches, some of them quite large and ornate, as well as numerous monasteries that date from this period. From the archeological record Nubia appears to have been a thoroughly Christianized land. Every town had one or more churches, while no evidence of other widespread religious practices during this period remain. Many tombstones included inscriptions that stated the deceased person's Christian faith. Monasteries were not as extensive as they were either to the north in Egypt or to the south in Ethiopia but were found just the same in Nubia.

Kings of Nubia were regarded as priests within the church, but they did not appoint the bishops. Rather, episcopal authority lay with the patriarch of Alexandria. Both Nubian and Ethiopian churches looked to the Alexandrian patriarch as their pope. Thus disruptions in the patriarch's office that were caused by Muslim rulers were also felt in Nubia and Ethiopia and often resulted in a lack of adequate pastoral leadership. Few records of patriarchal appointments now exist, but we can assume from the various sources that some form of regular communication was maintained across the Egyptian border. In Ethiopia, as we have seen, only the patriarch of the church was appointed by the pope in Alexandria; the Ethiopian abuna oversaw ordinations and appointments of other bishops throughout the land. The evidence from Nubia suggests a somewhat different relationship. Episcopal appointments appear still in the tenth century to have been made by the Alexandrian pope directly. Along with Nubian, which was written with Coptic letters, both Greek and Coptic languages were used in liturgy and theology. One explanation for the high incidence of Coptic in use among the clergy is that many were immigrants or refugees from Muslim Egypt.

Many of the churches in Nubia were lost after the tenth century to the increase in sands blowing from the desert into its towns and cities. The drifts simply could not be held back, piling up against outside walls and sifting into the buildings through windows and doors. These churches were often decorated with highly colorful murals on their walls, depicting biblical scenes from both Old and New

Testaments. National figures such as bishops and kings, portrayed with dark features, are included along with the biblical figures, who are most often painted with lighter features in these murals. The Madonna and Child figure prominently in paintings throughout all the churches. One of them included names for the shepherds who came to worship the Christ child at his nativity. Another of the frescoes from the cathedral in the city of Faras is reproduced on the cover of this book. The painting dates from the tenth or eleventh century. Its accompanying inscription identifies it as Bishop Marianos under the protection of the Madonna and Child.

From the evidence of both written sources and archeological discoveries, Christian churches were abundant and thriving in Nubia during the seventh through tenth centuries. Despite the presence of Islamic governors to their north, the Nubian kings were able to maintain political and religious independence through the unique treaty that their ancestors first negotiated with the Arab rulers. The paintings on the walls of the churches that were eventually filled in with desert sands suggest an active appropriation of biblical stories and themes in the people's daily lives. Indeed, the Nubian artists, like so many others in Christian history, actively painted their own people and culture into the biblical scene in order to bring the biblical story into their own world.

Ethiopia

The sixth-century Alexandrian traveler Cosmas Indicopleustes listed Ethiopia as one of the places that he had visited in his journeys. He reported seeing churches everywhere in the land. A vibrant monastic tradition was also thriving there by the seventh century. A large number of Greek, Syrian, and Egyptian texts had been translated into Ge'ez, the traditional national language of Ethiopia, by monks in the monasteries who were at work preserving books that were being destroyed elsewhere in the Christian world. Ethiopia, or the kingdom of Axum, as it was then known, became an important archive for expressions of Christian faith that were not being permitted to survive or flourish in the lands to the north under Greek imperial rule.

Ethiopian political expansion in the sixth century, as we have seen, had reached across the Red Sea into southern Arabia before being turned back. The Ethiopian expedition against the Himyarite kingdom and later the city of Mecca eventuated in the Ethiopians' expulsion at the hands of a Persian force early in the seventh century. With the rise of the powerful Islamic empire and its expansion across Arabia and into Egypt, Ethiopia's own political fortunes became severely curtailed. Whatever imperial designs its negus might have had in the sixth century, his kingdom became relatively isolated as a Christian nation in the seventh. The Red Sea became an Arabian lake, and the trade routes to India were entirely controlled by Muslims after the seventh century. Elsewhere in Africa south of the Sahara, the only other major organized kingdom prior to the ninth century was that of Ghana. Although the origins of the Ghanaian kingdom have sometimes been traced to immigrants from East Africa, by the seventh century there was little, if any, contact or communication between these two regions. The routes of commerce and communication from Ghana led northward instead to the Maghrib, bringing Islamic traders to West Africa.

The Arabs launched no direct military attack against the kingdom of Axum in the seventh century. One of the reasons cited for this is that Islam recalled the Ethiopian negus had provided refuge to the first Muslim refugees during the days of Muhammad, a memory that the Arabs honored by not launching a campaign against Axum such as that launched against Dongola. The Islamic faith spread gradually along the coastal regions of the Horn of Africa nevertheless, forcing Ethiopia to look further south for both political domains and trade.

During his trip to Ethiopia in the first decades of the sixth century, Cosmas Indicopleustes had an opportunity to journey with a group of merchants several days further south to the African kingdom's frontier. There he witnessed the silent trade that was carried on with people from across the border, a practice that was practiced by the Ghanaians as well. At a particular place, traders would lay out their goods along a fence and then withdraw. Their counterparts from across the border would then approach the fence and place alongside certain desired articles other goods that they proposed to offer in exchange. The second group would then withdraw, allowing the first group of traders to approach the fence a second time. They could then either accept the offer by taking the goods placed alongside in exchange, or reject it by leaving them where they lay. The second party could then approach again and either add to the offer or remove its goods, thereby signaling an end to the transaction. In this way goods exchanged hands without any formal communication between the two communities. The account unwittingly tells us something as well about why the Christian movement failed to spread beyond the borders of Ethiopia to the south, for without formal communication, the message of the gospel could not be passed on.

In the ninth century an Ethiopian king named Digna Jan is reported to have begun expanding the Axumite kingdom southward by extending his military control over the region of Amhara. Christian settlement and evangelization followed. A later source tells of missionary priests sent by the king performing mass baptisms, but the gains for the most part were short lived. Before long, churches were being destroyed and Christians losing their lives in a rebellion that broke out against the Ethiopian negus. One reads of occasional attempts to expand the Ethiopian kingdom southward again in later centuries, but without much effect.

The head of the Ethiopian church had since the days of Athanasius and Frumentius been historically appointed by the patriarch of Alexandria. The arrangement continued under the watchful eye of the new Arab rulers in the seventh century. After the sixth century the Ethiopian church looked to the non-Chalcedonian patriarchs for the appointment of their abuna, in line with their non-Chalcedonian theological commitments. The practice of having its abuna appointed from Alexandria helped the church in Ethiopia to maintain a degree of independence from ruling monarchs who might otherwise have sought to make the church an extension of their own personal interests. As Ethiopia's kings grew in power, there was increased pressure upon the church to appoint its own abuna.

The fact that it did not do so indicates the authority that tradition held even for the royal household.

The Alexandrian patriarch's ability to engage in international relations was greatly restricted by his Muslim rulers, imposing new difficulties for the Ethiopian church in turn. The disruptions brought about as a result of the Muslim rule in Egypt left the Coptic patriarch with his hands full just dealing with the life of his own churches after the seventh century. At times the Coptic church was even unable to secure its own patriarch's appointment, much less attend to the needs of the churches to the south in Ethiopia. From both Egyptian and Ethiopian sources, it appears that there were periods of up to fifty years when no one was appointed to the position of abuna. Lack of adequate historical records makes it difficult to hazard a judgment regarding the situation, but it appears that the churches simply went without filling the office rather than make an appointment themselves. This in turn meant that for long stretches of time, ordinations of other bishops, and thus in turn of lesser clergy, also diminished, leaving churches without adequate priestly leadership.

This did not mean that Ethiopian Christians were entirely without pastoral resources during these periods, however. While the appointment of an abuna originated in Alexandria, Ethiopia's monastic movement had since the fifth century been entirely indigenous. The vibrant tradition of holy men and women in Ethiopia reached back to the time of the Nine Saints and before. Monastic communities provided an array of spiritual and educational resources for Christians in the land, even when the church was experiencing disruptions in its hierarchical life. They were depositories of the rich Ethiopian tradition of literature that had been gathered from a variety of sources: Greek, Egyptian, Syriac, and indigenous. Monastic communities continued to thrive in Ethiopia during these years, even though after the seventh century they appear here, as in other parts of the world, to begin to move to more remote locations. Some have suggested that Ethiopian monasticism ceased being as active a missionary force as it had been in earlier years, but it is possible that this too was related to the difficulties both church and nation faced with the dominant Islamic power to its east.

The Maghrib

The Muslim military advance to the south along the Nile was stopped in the mid-seventh century by a Nubian army. No such army met the Muslims to the west of Egypt in what was formerly Roman North Africa. The Arab victory at Alexandria in 642 was quickly followed by an excursion to the west to Cyrenaica and Tunisia. East Roman naval power and the combined resistance of Numidia and the tribes who dwelled along the northern border of the Sahara desert halted the expansion for a time. Greek governance by this time had been reduced to the coastal section of the former Roman provinces. Most of the land was in the hands of the tribes the Arabs called *Berbers* (Barbarians). An Arab expedition further west in 683 ended in defeat, but another was launched in 695. This time the

African defense was a coalition force led by Damia al-Kahena (the Prophetess), queen of the Aures from the hill country near Tunis. Her army included exiles from Visigoth Spain, remnants of Greek Christians, Latins, and indigenous peoples gathered in common cause against the Arab army.

Al-Kahena defeated the Arabs after they had taken Carthage, sending the invaders back to Cyrenaica. But then, anticipating another attack, she instituted a scorched-earth policy, destroying the crops and cutting down the trees. Her purpose was to render the land undesirable to the Arab invaders, who knew of its immense agricultural productivity. The effect was to turn the local populations against her. Many crossed over to the Arab side when they returned several years later. The final, bloody battle in 702 between the armies of the Arabs and the African queen is shrouded in legend. What we know is that she was eventually defeated, dying in battle according to some accounts in the Roman amphitheater in El Djem.

Victory for the Arabs brought a swelling of their ranks through Berber conversions. The Arab-Berber coalition was ruled from a new city of Tunis, near Carthage. Meanwhile, a mass exodus of Latin Christians across the Mediterranean began, depleting the urban Christian numbers. As in other places where Arabs established their rule, Christian churches were not immediately closed, although their numbers, already reduced from the period of the Vandals and the continuous unrest of the seventh century, were depleted even more by emigration or conversion to Islam. Several major educational institutions were kept open, and after 702 several restoration projects were even undertaken. Latin continued to be used even in official transactions of the government in the Maghrib until the tenth century, with many Latin words making their way into the Arabic language of the new rulers. Nevertheless, the Arabs introduced a new dominant religion in the region, changing centuries-old patterns of worship, building mosques where churches once had stood, and transforming the culture of the region. By the tenth century Christian churches had all but disappeared from the Maghrib, with only a few scattered congregations along the seacoast remaining.

The Arab-Berber coalition opened up new commerical routes to the south across the Sahara that took them farther than the Romans had ever gone. The Arabs' experience with crossing deserts proved to be particularly valuable in this regard. From ninth-century Arab sources we know that regular trade contact with the court of the king of Ghana had been established. In some places Arabs also conducted silent trade similar to that described above between Ethiopia and its neighbors. The most lucrative product the Arabs sought was gold which came from the Senegalese River basin; gold was exchanged primarily for salt from the north.

Where Muslims traveled, they also took their faith. For several centuries Islam expanded into West Africa as it had along the eastern seacoast of Africa, through commerce more than through military expansion. Conversions came more slowly, but by the tenth century there were a number of Africans reportedly from the court in Ghana who had become Muslims. This is one of the first regions of the world into which Islam spread where there were not already established Christian communities of faith in some form. This means that West Africa first encountered the story of Jesus and the Christian movement through the Qur'an and the teachings of Islam. The message of Jesus was first heard in its Islamic form, along with Islam's criticisms of the Christian religion.

The Arab-Berber coalition looked north from the Maghrib as well, not for trade but for military expansion. Arab forces had already engaged in skirmishes against Sicily and other Mediterranean posts in the 680s and 690s, as they increased their military presence at sea. In 710 a small force crossed the narrow mouth at the western end of the Mediterranean from the Maghrib into the Iberian peninsula. The Arab governor, Musa, had authorized a Berber general named Tariq to undertake the expedition to give him a scouting report. The party met with little resistance, and the following year a Muslim army of several thousand returned under Tariq (his name was lent to Gibraltar, *gibal tariq* or "the rock of Tarik"). Within a matter of months the Muslims had taken control of almost the entire Iberian peninsula.

Spain

The Muslim conquest of Spain brought an abrupt end to several centuries of Visigoth rule there. The Goths, it will be recalled, had in the fourth century converted as a tribe to Arian Christianity. In the fifth century an army of their people, along with their families, had moved into Spain and established a new independent kingdom. For more than a century an Arian Visigoth minority had ruled over a Spanish Catholic majority. Catholics and Arians alike had worshiped in Latin, with similar liturgies. The most substantial differences were variations in their doxologies to the Trinity. These alone were enough to maintain a divide between bishops and aristocracy in Spain.

The conversion of the Franks to Catholic Christianity in the sixth century had begun to put pressure on the Arian Visigoth kings in Spain, whose subjects were still mostly Catholic. Spain's rulers finally joined the western Christian family in 587 when the Visigoth king, Reccared, converted and was baptized into the Catholic faith. Two years later he summoned the Catholic bishops of Spain to gather at his capital city in what became the Third Council of Toledo. Working together, the bishops and king passed a series of rulings intended to eliminate Arianism in the land. A number of anathemas were pronounced, and the decisions of the four earlier councils of Nicaea, Constantinople, Ephesus, and Chalcedon reaffirmed. At the suggestion of Reccared, the council ruled that the creed that had come down from Nicaea and Constantinople be recited before the Lord's Prayer each time the eucharist was celebrated in order to help strengthen the Catholic faith of the people.

The wording of the creed that the Third Council of Toledo passed along to the churches contained an addition that was not in the creed that had been read at Chalcedon. At the end of the sentence stating that the Holy Spirit proceeds from the Father, the theologians at Toledo inserted *filioque* ("and the Son"). It did so ostensibly to bolster the creed's affirmation of the equality of the Son with the Father. Certainly the phrase appeared to resonate with the theologies of Ambrose and Augustine, who exercised such great authority in the West. Hardly could the bishops have imagined that centuries later their addition would become a divisive issue between eastern Orthodox and western Catholic churches.

Turning toward matters of administration, the Catholic bishops at Toledo, in alliance now with the Visigoth king, set about to reorganize their national church structure. The Spanish episcopate had already come to regard the bishop of Seville as their highest ecclesiastical authority. In the sixth century Justinian's attempt to restore the western boundaries of the Roman empire by bringing Spain under Constantinople's rule had not been successful, and the endeavor had only further solidified the Spanish Catholic churches' sense of national identity. Although the Roman papacy was being reorganized and infused with new vitality from within toward the end of the sixth century, the Spanish bishops continued to chart a course of their own. Eventually the primacy among their churches passed from the bishop of Seville to the bishop of Toledo, the city where the Spanish kings held court, but it remained within the Spanish national church.

Isidore of Seville

The name Isidore of Seville (d. 636) dominates the theological landscape of seventh-century Spain. A contemporary of Muhammad, he was a bishop, pastor, political advisor, historian, and theologian all rolled into one. Isidore's book *Etymologies* was a compendium of knowledge written in the form of an encyclopedia and intended to provide the necessary content for a sound, general education. Its contents covered areas of grammar, logic, astronomy, medicine, religion, nature, history, social life, and more. The very scope of the work suggests something of the state of intellectual life in Spain during the seventh century. Another of Isidore's books was a *History of the Goths,* which is as far as we know the first text to attempt to chart the national history of Spain. In addition to these literary endeavors, Isidore was also an advisor to other bishops and pastors. His letters to fellow clergy reveal a detailed administrative mind concerned with liturgical order and clerical functions in the church.

One of Isidore's most lasting contributions to Christian history concerns the western form of the Nicene Creed. The fourth-century Arian-Nicene controversies had centered for the most part on the question of whether the Son was of the same substance or a similar substance with the Father. Virtually all of the defenders of Nicene orthodoxy had also affirmed that the Holy Spirit was the same substance as the Father. On the question of the relation of the Spirit to the Father and Son, a number of theological options emerged. Specifically, the issue concerned the nature of the procession of the Spirit. Did the Spirit proceed from the Father in all eternity, to be sent by the Father into the world at creation and then again sent by the Son after the resurrection in time? Or did the Spirit proceed from both the Father and the Son eternally, thereby differentiating the nature of the Spirit's relation to the Father from that of the Son?

The wording of the Nicene Creed as it was reported at Chalcedon stated that the Spirit proceeded from the Father, and that together with the Father and the Son the Spirit was worshiped. The Greek theologians of the ancient church generally kept to that wording. In the Latin world, however, Augustine and other writers had suggested that the Spirit proceeds from the Father through the Son, or from the Father and the Son. That last phrasing, filioque in Latin, we saw above was added to the form of the Nicene Creed ordered to be recited in churches in Spain in 589 at the Third Council of Toledo. The phrase quickly became a part of the Spanish church's theological confession of faith. The Fourth Council of Toledo in 633 reaffirmed its use, with Isidore's strong consent. In *Etymologies* Isidore explained that the Father is unbegotten, the Son is alone called begotten, and the Spirit alone proceeds from them both.

Life in the churches of Spain prior to the Islamic invasion

The councils in Spain did more than introduce changes in worship in the churches. Since the time of Constantine, life for Jews in the Roman world had become increasingly difficult. Judaism was the target of numerous canons and imperial edicts which made its practice a criminal offense and sought to hinder its growth through conversion. Spanish Christianity had been among the most violent in its relation to Judaism. These tendencies became even more pronounced over the course of the seventh century. Council after council passed vehemently anti-Jewish canons intended to eradicate the faith from the land. Eventually Jewish children were forbidden by law to be circumcised, and Jewish parents could not leave their property to children. The last of these anti-Jewish canons came in 694 when a council of Toledo ordered that all Jews dwelling in Spain be sold into slavery and their property confiscated by the state. It is difficult to tell the extent of the canon's enforcement, for twenty years later there were still Jews in Spain when the Muslims arrived and took control of the country. In any case, life had become much harsher for Jews living in Spain under Christian kings.

Another characteristic of Spanish Christianity was its rigorous stance on celibacy among the clergy. We have seen that throughout the churches of the world there had been since at least the fourth century a widespread appreciation for the discipline and spirituality of asceticism in Christian life. In the Latin churches there was a movement to bring that discipline to bear upon all sacerdotal life. The earliest attempts to mandate celibacy for all ordained clergy in Spain can be found in the fourth century, but again in the seventh we find fresh canons concerning the practice. The fact that Spanish councils in the seventh century were still passing such canons indicates the difficulty bishops must have faced in putting the decrees into effect. A council in 590 ordered local bishops to seize the wives of clergy and to send them off to convents as a last resort. There is no word on how many bishops did so, but the canon itself was indicative of the bishops' commitment to a celibate male priesthood.

Islamic conquest

Early in the eighth century the Visigoth nobility found themselves engaged in civil war following the death of their king. The ruler who emerged from the struggle in 710 to hold the throne, Roderick, was still dealing with an uprising in the north when the Muslims crossed Gibraltar in 711. The Visigoth king marched his soldiers south to meet the invaders, but by the time they arrived they were exhausted, and no match for their foe. In a single decisive battle the Muslims defeated the Visigoth army. Tariq soon found there was no significant resistance anywhere else in Spain except in the far north, where several small Christian Spanish kingdoms managed to survive the Arab conquest. In 712 Musa became governor of almost the entire Iberian peninsula, which was now called in Arabic *al-Andalus*. The Muslims continued to push north across the Pyrenees for several more decades, controlling much of southern Gaul by the 720s. Following their defeat by an army of Franks under Charles Martel at Tours in 732, they retreated back over the Pyrenees to establish firm control over most of Spain.

The Maghrib was already a long distance from Damascus, but Spain was even further. Although the Muslim governors in Spain and the Maghrib nominally acknowledged the authority of the caliph, in reality they exercised a semi-independent rule of their own. Wealth and tribute did not flow into the coffers of Damascus as much as the caliphs would have liked, but they had no effective way of extracting it from so far away. Civil war in the middle of the eighth century brought about a change of Muslim dynasties as the Abbasids came to power. One of the Umayyad royal family escaped to Spain, where he established an Umayyad line of rule that continued the older dynasty. Thus by 755 most of Spain had effectively become an independent Islamic kingdom, not entirely unlike the situation of the independent Visigoth kings that preceded it. Only the regions around Astoria and Barcelona, which would eventually become the Christian kingdoms of Castille and Aragon, remained under Christian rule throughout this period in Iberian history.

The Umayyad rulers of Spain might have been a long way from Damascus, and even farther from Baghdad, but they were still Muslims. The army that had conquered Spain included North Africans as well as Arabs, and the North African presence continued to be represented among the Muslims who immigrated across the Mediterranean (Christians in Spain called Muslims *moros*, a word derived from the Latin term *maurus,* "dark-skinned"). But the dominant cultural influences were Arabic, and they soon were evident in all aspects of Iberian life. Spanish Christians, who came to be called by others in the West *Mozarab*, or "Arabized," absorbed many aspects of the culture into their lives. They could hardly have helped doing so. Arabic music was introduced in the cities. Homes and other buildings began to reflect Arabic architectural influences. The marketplaces, government administrative practices, and even the products of artisans began to have more in common with the eastern Mediterranean than with the cultures north of the Pyrenees.

Although they began to reflect the culture of their Muslim rulers, Mozarabic Christians were marginalized by the new Islamic regime. Christians were faced with restrictions much like those applied elsewhere in the Islamic world. At first there was little real persecution of Christians, apart from the efforts necessary to enforce the regulations and collect taxes. As the Muslims' numbers grew, mainly through conversions, tensions began to increase between the two religious communities. Added to this was a deeper memory Spanish Catholicism had preserved of a tradition of martyrdom from the earliest days of the Christian movement. Crisis erupted in 850 when a group of Christians in Cordoba decided to challenge the Muslim blasphemy laws. The result was a series of executions that gave the Spanish church a new generation of martyrs.

One of those executed was Flora of Cordoba. Her father had been a Muslim, making her conversion to the Christian faith a capital offense. After being turned in to the Muslim governor by her brother, she decided to denounce the Prophet in public, thereby ensuring her martyrdom. Flora and another Christian woman named Maria were both beheaded in November of 851 for their crimes of conversion and blaspheming the Prophet. Their names were among a dozen or more of Christians from Cordoba who were executed between 850 and 860.

Muslim rule brought new restrictions and eventually new martyrdoms for Catholic Christians but radical improvement in the situation for Jews in Iberia. For the first time since the fourth century Jews were given legal equality with Christians, allowing them much more political freedom than they had previously known. Spain became an attractive place for many Jews to immigrate to, from Christian and Muslim lands alike. By the ninth century a lively Jewish intellectual and cultural life was thriving in several cities of Spain, in sharp contrast to the severe persecution Jews had suffered there under the previous religious regime.

One of the places where Jews, Muslims, and Christians cooperated was in the academic arena. Spain became one of the great intellectual centers of the world during its years under Muslim rule, a tradition that was to have an impact not only throughout the Muslim world but upon later European history as well. The great Arabic library at Cordoba was said to have contained four hundred thousand volumes by the tenth century. Spanish scholars worked in Arabic, Latin, Hebrew, and Greek. Christians were allowed to attend the Muslim university in Cordoba, and enough did so to bring a vital Christian intellectual tradition to fruition. By the middle of the ninth century they had translated the entire Bible into Arabic in Spain, giving those who only spoke the new language access to the Christian scriptures.

Among the theological developments from this period, two deserve to be noted for their wider impact upon the Christian world. The first was a theological controversy in the eighth century regarding the manner in which Jesus Christ is to be understood as the Son of God. Called Adoptionism by those who came to oppose the doctrine, its chief exponent was a bishop named Felix of Urgel. Adoptionists held that Jesus was the Son of God by adoption, an act that was manifested at his baptism. In some ways the position resembled aspects of the Antiochene theological tradition, which sought to distinguish more clearly between the two natures of Jesus Christ. The Adoptionist position was also directed toward the Muslim charge that Christians falsely state that God had a Son. The concept of Jesus' adoption preserved divine transcendence without abandoning Christ's unique claim to being the Son of God, or so they thought. The position gained little following outside of Spain, although it was known among the Franks and to later generations of European theology.

The second, and by far more influential, theological development that emerged from this period was the cult of St. James. Spanish Christians had for several centuries believed the legend that St. James, the brother of Christ, had visited Spain and established a church prior to his return to Jerusalem, where he was martyred. The city he was often associated with was Compostela in the far northwest, hence giving it the name Santiago de Compostela, which it has to this day. According to the legend the body of St. James was returned to Compostela after his martyrdom, and his grave was supposedly found, making the city a major site for Christian pilgrimages from across the West. In the ninth century St. James became adopted as the protector of the small Christian kingdom in the northwest where Compostela was located. Eventually the brother of Christ came to be known in Spanish Christianity by the title Muslim Slayer, the patron saint of military efforts against Islam. The cult of St. James had little effect in the ninth and tenth centuries, when the Christian kingdoms were too weak to pose a serious threat against the rulers of al-Andalus to their south. It only became a major ideological weapon later as Spanish Christian armies began the long process of reconquest of the peninsula.

By the tenth century the life of Christians in Spain, as in most other places where Islamic governments ruled, had become burdened with restrictions that for many were becoming intolerable. Christians in Spain exercised little political power; their faith was severely restricted in its public expressions. The situation was similar to that of Christians in other parts of the Muslim world. In Africa churches had all but disappeared in the Maghrib and were feeling the constant pressures of taxes and restrictions in Egypt. Only in Nubia and Ethiopia did independent Christian kingdoms continue to exist on the African continent in the tenth century. Elsewhere along the southern Mediterranean and in Spain, Christians had again become aliens in their own homelands in ways they had not experienced since the first days of their movement.

25

Expansion of the Christian Movement in India, Central Asia, and China

The expansion of the Christian movement east of Persia after the year 600 was primarily the work of East Syrian monks, priests, and merchants who traveled the trade routes across Asia. The institutional advance of the movement was marked mainly by monastaries built in or near the cities that lay along these routes. Typically, one or more monks (and sometimes nuns) would establish a community in a new city, securing property and local support. Before long the monastery would have gathered a small group of local workers along with others who were interested in the religion. Through these contacts new converts would be made, and sometimes new members of the monastic community recruited. Other members would join from previously established monasteries in other cities. It this way the community would grow.

By the tenth century Christian monasteries could be found scattered across central Asia from Persia to China. Not only did they serve as centers of worship and evangelism but also as inns for Christian merchants, centers of medical care, and even schools. There were Syriac texts to be copied and translated, including Christian scriptures, liturgical books, and stories of saints and martyrs. There were guests to be served, and work to be done for the local community. Most of all, there were hours of prayer to keep, both individual and corporate.

Local residents of cities across Asia made much of their living by providing goods and services for the merchants who were passing through. Local goods were sold at the markets, along with provisions for the long trip to the next city along the way. Fresh animals were needed to carry these goods and provisions across deserts or over rugged mountain ranges. News concerning conditions further ahead needed to be ascertained. Through these contacts in the marketplace Christianity also began to seep into the local life of central Asia and western China before the tenth century.

The agents of this often inconspicuous evangelism were Persian and Armenian merchants who took great risks to move large caravans of goods back and forth across the thousands of miles of dangerous roads. One didn't have to make the trip often to attain a sizable fortune, so profitable was the trade. But it was also perilous. Distances between cities were vast. Roads passed through dangerous

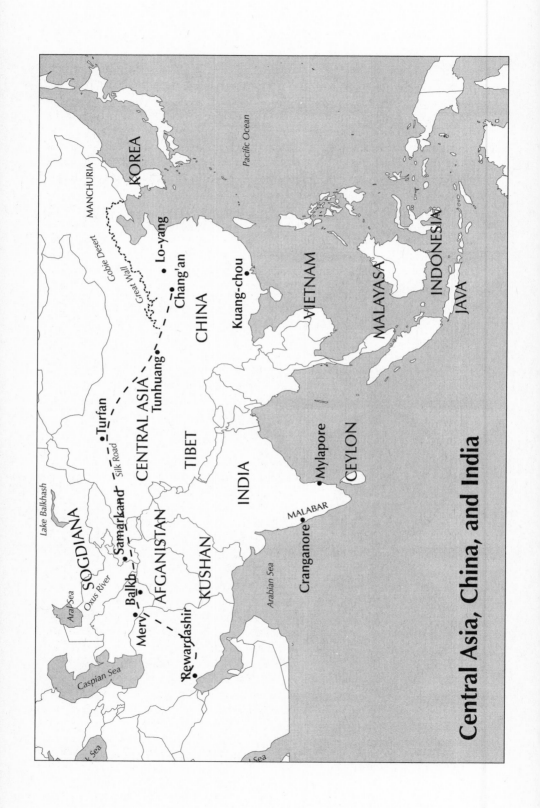

Central Asia, China, and India

MANCHURIA

KOREA

Pacific Ocean

Gobie Desert

Great Wall

• Lo-yang
• Chang'an

CHINA

Kuang-chou

INDONESIA

VIETNAM

MALAYSA

JAVA

Silk Road

Tunhuang •

CENTRAL ASIA

• Turfan

TIBET

INDIA

• Mylapore

CEYLON

Samarkand

Lake Balkhash

SOGDIANA

AFGANISTAN

KUSHAN

MALABAR

Oxus River

Aral Sea

Balkh •

Merv •

Arabian Sea

Cranganore •

• Rewardashir

Caspian Sea

Sea

mountain passes and across arid deserts. Where they did not face rugged terrain, travelers had to chance bandits or local kings who threatened merchants and mendicants alike. Still they persevered, planting small Christian communities from Sogdiana to China. Monasteries were almost always at the heart of this endeavor, establishing the most enduring Christian presence in the East.

Unlike those spurred on by the promises of wealth, monks found little material reward for their endeavors. They traveled without supplies, with only their cloaks, walking sticks, and copies of sacred books. Letters sent back and forth by way of members of the community or merchants on their business trips kept the leadership in touch. Eventually the patriarch in Baghdad decided that minimally once in every six years the metropolitans under his appointment across Asia were to communicate with him, an indication of the distance and difficulties these churches faced.

In the seventh century the East Syrian patriarch was the single most important church leader in the East. Much of his time was spent dealing with the demands of ministry in a hostile political climate. It should not surprise us that church leaders in the East paid far less attention to the theological differences that separated them from one other than they did to practical and political concerns. This is not to say that there were no divisions among the churches, for there were. There were also the usual disputes, jealousies, and intrigues found among all human associations. Some of the things eastern churches shared set them apart from Christians in the western world. East Syrian Christians typically did not allow images in their churches, for instance. Their eucharistic liturgies were in the Syriac language rather than Greek, Latin, Egyptian, or Ge'ez, and followed a different tradition. Yet they shared much more with other Christians than has often been acknowledged, such as their ecclesiastical structures, their confession of the Nicene faith, and their understanding of the role of Jesus Christ in the salvation of the world.

Among the patriarchs who served the churches of the East during the first centuries of Islam in Persia, none was to exercise as much influence as Timothy I. We have already referred to his famous defense of Christianity before the Abbasid caliph at Baghdad. As an administrator he was a tireless organizer, writing letters, making appointments, and overseeing affairs of churches spread thousands of miles apart. He personally sent more than one hundred missionaries into new regions where churches were not yet in existence, ranking him among the most important missionary leaders of the Christian movement in the East in the first millennium of its history. Yet for all of this, were there not monks and families ready to move, Timothy's efforts would have been for naught. Much of the history of these churches that were scattered across the landscape of east Asia in India, Persia, China, Tibet, Afghanistan, Sri Lanka, and even Indonesia is still waiting to be uncovered.

India

Concrete historical information on the Christian movement in India is sparse prior to the sixteenth century. What we have are occasional references in Persian records, fragmentary bits of evidence from India itself, and a rich (if not always historically reliable) body of oral tradition handed down through generations of Indian Christian families. Cosmas Indicopleustes, we noted above, reported in his *Christian Topography* that he knew of an island (which most take to be Sri Lanka) where there was a Christian community. He had visited Christian communities along the southern coast of India as well. At the time of his visit, the churches of India were still under the episcopal jurisdiction of the metropolitan of Rewardashir, in southern Persia. Their priests were from Persian theological schools and most likely spoke Syriac and Persian as their first (or only) languages.

They were still a mostly foreign community of merchants and perhaps refugees from Persian persecution who had settled in India. From the meager historical descriptions that have come down to us over the centuries, it is clear that these churches nevertheless considered themselves a continuous established community in India, joining themselves to a venerable tradition that originated with the ministry of the apostle Thomas. By the sixth century these Christians living in India had become integrated enough with the surrounding society to have become a separate local caste. Either through marriage or conversion, indigenous Indians were becoming a part of these churches under Persian ecclesiastical authority.

The next historical word we have of these churches from Persia comes from the middle of the seventh century. Ishoyahb III, patriarch of the East Syrian communion, reported in several of his letters that the metropolitan in Rewardashir had broken his relationship with the patriarch. One guess is that it was for financial reasons. Whatever the case, the schism had interrupted ecclesiastical appointments to India. The metropolitan of Rewardashir's ordinations were now in

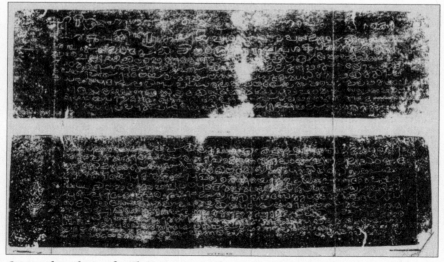

Copper plate charter for Christians in Kerala, South India, taken from Ian Gillman and Hans-Joachim Klimkeit, Christians in Asia before 1500 *(Ann Arbor, Mich.: University of Michigan Press, 1999). Reproduced with permission of Curzon Press.*

Scene from mural of church at Kocho, near Turfan oasis. A Sogdian (Persian) priest with chalice in hand addresses two Turkish men and a Chinese woman. Taken from Ian Gillman and Hans-Joachim Klimkeit, Christians in Asia before 1500 *(Ann Arbor, Mich.: University of Michigan Press, 1999). Reproduced with permission of Curzon Press.*

question, and the church in India was rightly concerned for its own spiritual well-being. The patriarch reported that the Indian churches had continued to support his office financially, an indication of their communion with him as well as their relative financial health.

When we find mention of the Indian churches in the Persian records again, in the eighth century, they have a metropolitan of their own, elected from among their community in the presence of the other bishops. According to the Persian tradition, metropolitans were normally established with at least six bishoprics under them, and we have no good reason to doubt this would have applied to India. The letter referred to here came from Timothy I. In it he instructed the church to send him the name of the metropolitan for confirmation before they submitted it to the local king, a further indication of the established nature of churches there.

Other letters of Timothy provide information about the churches in India at the end of the eighth century. One addresses a monk named Thomas who was traveling with a group of immigrants to India. Another provides instructions regarding ministerial irregularities the patriarch was concerned to correct. From later Indian sources we find reports of two Armenian brothers who came in the ninth century as missionaries.

The earliest historical evidence that comes from India itself comprises several copper plates with inscriptions that date from around the same period, 850 CE. The plates recorded land grants given by local kings to the Christians to build their communities. Together with several stone crosses that date from the ninth century (if not earlier), they provide bits of physical evidence pointing to small, established churches surrounded by Christian homes in a handful of locations in the south of India.

Who were these Christians? They were still mostly immigrants of Persian descent who had settled in Malabar over several centuries. Some no doubt came as merchants, some as refugees from Persian or Islamic persecution, and some as missionaries. A number of times the Persian travelers are also called pilgrims. These were Christians who had come to reside near the spiritual home of St. Thomas, to Cranganore, for instance, the traditional site of the landing of St. Thomas, or even to Mylapore, near Madras in the east, the traditional site of St. Thomas's tomb in India. Eventually they became a separate caste, which means they were granted social and political recognition by the Indian rulers according to traditional Hindu religious custom. Like members of other castes in India, they lived in houses near their religious center, in this case their churches, forming distinct Christian neighborhoods, which visitors such as Cosmas Indicopleustes could easily have found.

After several centuries even Christians of Persian descent would have come to speak the language of their Indian neighbors for everyday use. But the Indian Christians for many centuries continued to use Syriac in their liturgy. The reasons for the retention were complex. Syriac was the language of the churches in the East, even after Arabic displaced both it and Aramaic as the most common language of the Persian region. But Syriac was also identified as being close to the language that Jesus and his apostles had spoken, and hence it carried a connection with the land of Israel and Semitic culture that otherwise might have been lost. This in turn helped to keep them from being absorbed in the Indian religious world, thereby maintaining a distinctive Christian identity. In their worship services the Indian churches celebrated liturgies that carried symbolic connections with Jerusalem. Yet in reference to their own immediate surroundings, in their eucharist they utilized rice cakes and palm wine, indigenous elements available where bread from wheat and wine from grapes were not.

We know very little of any distinctive ethical teachings the community may have upheld, although in one of Timothy's letters he states that marriage between Persian and Indian Christians is permissible, another indication that there were Christians whose cultural identity was fully Indian. We do have indications that they were attempting to carry out further missionary expansion by sea to Sri Lanka, and perhaps to Java, the Malay peninsula, and even up the coast to China. Persian and sometimes Armenian merchants are recorded in these various locations carrying on trade during the seventh through tenth centuries. It is highly unlikely that among their number some would not have been Christian. While there is little evidence yet of permanent Christian communities formed in southeast Asia by the tenth century, the possibility remains.

Central Asia

Reports from fifth-century Persian synods consistently list churches for several cities along the Oxus River to the north of Iran (the modern Amu Darya River). A half dozen or so bishops provided leadership for these Christian communities along the northeastern frontier of Persia. Their cities were a gateway though which the traffic of the Silk Road passed on its way to the Mediterranean world. To the north of the Oxus River was Samarkand, capital of the province of Sogdiana and the last city in Persian territory. Beyond it were the vast expanses of central Asia, inhabited by nomadic tribes of Huns and Turks. Further north and east lived the Mongols. To the immediate east of the Oxus River region lay the mountainous terrain of Kushan (modern Afghanistan, Tajikistan, and Pakistan), and then the high plateau of Tibet. To the west were the desert plains in what are now the nations of Uzbekistan and Turkmenistan.

The cities of northeastern Persia were not only a gateway but a crossroads. The international trade that passed along the Silk Road brought through them goods from as far away as China, Rome, and Alexandria. It brought people and ideas from the distant lands as well, making these cities a meeting place for cultures and religions. Influences from distant cultures could be found mixed with local. Samarkand marked the northernmost extent of Alexander the Great's conquests three hundred years before Christ, and after Alexander's death the region around the Oxus River had become a Greek kingdom known as Bactria. A thousand years later, even after the region had passed into Sassanid and then Islamic hands, Persian and Turkish inhabitants were still telling stories of Alexander and his Greek companions. The capital of Bactria, the city of Balkh, was also the place where the prophet Zoroaster was reported to have died. From him had come one of the great prophetic faiths of world history and a tradition that had influenced both Islamic and Christian religions.

In the seventh century one could still find Zoroastrian believers and priests in Balkh, Merv, Samarkand, and other cities in northeast Persia. One could also find a growing Buddhist presence spreading to the region from India. As many as one hundred Buddhist monasteries and convents may have dotted the landscape of northwestern Persia and central Asia in the seventh century. A number of the Buddhist missionaries who brought the faith to China actually came originally from Persia. Among their number, for instance, was Kumarajiva, the fifth-century Buddhist missionary of Indian and Tocherian descent who oversaw one of the most popular Chinese translations of the Buddhist *Lotus Sutra* scripture from its original Sanskrit. A third religious presence in the north of Persia and central Asia was the Manichaeans, followers of the Persian prophet Mani who had been executed by the Sassanids in 277. Manichaeism incorporated into its teachings elements of Buddhism, Zoroastrianism, and Christianity. So close did Manichaeans and Christians become in central Asia that it is often hard to tell whether a particular text belongs to one faith tradition or the other.

The fifth major missionary faith that joined in the movement along the Silk Road from Persia to China in the seventh century was Islam. Much like the other traditions, the Muslim faith also eventually made its way from the cities into the surrounding countryside. In central Asia the Islamic faith advanced ahead of Islamic armies, forming communities of believers beyond the political domain of the caliphate and Islamic law. Muslims did not have monasteries such as the Christians and Buddhists had, although to some extent the development of the Sufis eventually provided Islam with comparable spiritual resources. The Muslims did have a strong literary tradition, coupled with the material resources of an emerging civilization to their south to draw from. Over the centuries Islam eventually gained a larger following among the population than the other missionary religious traditions, becoming the dominant religion of central Asia.

In addition to these missionary religious traditions were the many local tribal traditions of spirits and gods. Among the Turks, Huns, and Mongols across central Asia shamanism was a major religious force. Quite often the people of the region learned to mix various components of religious traditions with which they had come into contact for local needs. A Christian cross might be used by some to try to keep away evil spirits, while a Buddhist chant might be addressed to a local spirit in order to take away a fever.

This then is the pluralistic missionary context in which the Christian movement spread into central Asia. The first Christian presence was strongly dependent on the monasteries located in or near cities. Their main purpose was closely connected with the trade of Christian merchants. Thus they provided shelter and religious services to other monks and travelers alike. Local inhabitants often came to view Christian and Mahayana Buddhist monks and nuns as holy people, even those who did not share either religion. The East Syrian Christian churches were known for their physicians, many of whom were also priests and monks, and Christian monasteries in the East often were identified as places for local medical care. Cemeteries with Christian burial inscriptions for women and men and evidence of both elementary and advanced education in these cities of central Asia indicate permanent Christian communities along the Silk Road from Persia to western China.

Nor did the Christian faith remain entirely bound within the cities. Historical accounts are far too sketchy, and the very nature of their nomadic existence makes what would count as documentary evidence hard to come by, but from what we can surmise, by the sixth century Huns and Turks had begun to be identified as Christian. At one point in mid-sixth century the East Syrian patriarch in Seleucia-Ctesiphon received a request from a king among the Huns, asking that a Christian bishop be sent among them. In another case, in the 580s, a group of Turkish prisoners taken during a rare joint Byzantine-Persian military campaign in the East were brought back to Constantinople to be sold as slaves. Some of them had Christian crosses tattooed on their foreheads, according to Byzantine accounts. When questioned, the Turkish prisoners responded that the tatoos were to protect them, a practice they had learned from Christians in their homeland. Both of these cases indicate that the Christian movement had begun to spread among at least some of the peoples who inhabited the central Asia mountains and plains apart from any well-organized effort on the part of church leaders.

From time to time there were also more organized efforts to send missionary priests, bishops, and monks beyond the urban centers. As is most often the case, it is from Timothy I that we have the best information from the eighth or ninth century regarding such missions. Timothy reported in one of his letters in 781 that he had recently received a request from a king among the Turks. The Turkish king had reported that he and his people had become Christians. They requested that a bishop be ordained and sent to them, which Timothy did, along with a cadre of missionary monks. By this time the episcopal see of Samarkand had been elevated to metropolitan status, and thus its bishop would most likely have been the one who exercised authority over this mission. We do not know what role the bishop of Samarkand was asked to play in this case. Timothy, as was his style, took the initiative on his own.

Elsewhere in his many letters this missionary-minded patriarch indicated an interest in assisting the growing number of churches, monasteries, and episcopal sees across what are now the nations of Uzbekistan, Kazakstan, and Tajikistan. In one of his letters Timothy reported that the metropolitan of China had died and that he was appointing a new one. In another he wrote that he was preparing to consecrate a bishop for the Tibetans. We have no evidence for how the Christian movement found its way to Tibet. One would assume that once again it was merchants who came for business who founded the first communities. A few Christian texts written in the Tibetan language before the tenth century suggest there was an interest, if not a need, for Christian literature in the Tibetan tongue. Timothy's decision to consecrate a bishop for Tibet indicates there was more than a handful of Christians, or at least the hopes for such in the near future.

By the end of the seventh century the Christian message had reached what is now western China. The ancient cities of Tunhuang and Turfan both have provided evidence of established Christian communities. At Tunhuang, a city near the western end of the Great Wall of China, Buddhist monks had since the fourth century been carving caves into the steep cliffs outside the city. An entire monastic community was built in the soft stone of the mountain cliffs, including sleeping cells, worship halls, and libraries. The caves at Tunhuang were sealed shut by their occupants early in the eleventh century to protect their contents from invading armies. They were not discovered again until 1908, when they were opened to reveal an extraordinary find of Buddhist, Christian, and Manichaean writings. A similar discovery of long-lost documents from the ancient western Chinese city of Turfan, north of Tunhuang, has provided further evidence of at least some Christian presence in this region prior to the tenth century.

The Christians who lived near Tunhuang and Turfan were Persian, Turkish, Mongol, and Chinese, with a scattering of Armenian and Greek influences found among their writings. Besides scriptures, the libraries included worship books, homilies, biblical commentaries, lives of saints and martyrs, medical treatises, and philosophical works. In the case of several of the texts, it is not clear if they should be classified as Christian or Manichaean. Even those that are clearly identifiable as Christian sometimes show Buddhist influences. Buddhist concepts were borrowed to interpret Christian teachings in the community. In several instances Christ is represented as a bodhisattva, a messianic Buddhist savior figure who has attained Buddhahood but who forgoes passage into Nirvana in order to return to the world and work to save others.

A letter from 'Abdisho, bishop of the city of Merv, written to the patriarch in Baghdad around the year 1000 and cited in a work by a thirteenth-century eastern church scholar named Bar Hebreus, provides us with evidence of the northernmost extent of Christian missionary influence during this period. 'Abdisho reported that the king of the Kerait Turks who lived around the region of Lake Baikal in north Mongolia had been in contact with him. The king had been converted to the Christian faith through an apparition of a Christian saint who had showed him the way through a snow storm and identified himself as a follower of Christ. As a result the ruler had sought out Christian merchants who were traveling through the region, and they had instructed him in the basic tenets of the faith. They had even left him with a copy of the gospel. According to 'Abdisho, some two hundred thousand members of the king's tribe had now embraced the Christian faith.

The king was reportedly serious about adhering to his new faith and was requesting baptism as well as guidance in its practice. Of particular concern were the requirements of fasting for extended periods of time during the year. The Turks understood that they were now to refrain from eating meat or dairy products during such fasts, but they had no other food. The patriarch answered that 'Abdisho was to send a priest and deacon to baptize them and minister to them. As for fasting, he continued, given the absence of the usual lenten foods found in other parts of the world, they were simply to refrain from eating meat but were free to consume milk products.

China

The eastern end of the Silk Road along which these Christian merchants and monks traveled began at the Great Wall of China. After the fall of the Han dynasty in 220 CE, China experienced several centuries of political turmoil as successive regional rulers competed for power. The instability had opened the door in the fourth century to invasions from tribal groups from the north who succeeded in establishing a series of non-Chinese kingdoms in that part of the country. In the south a series of Chinese-ruled kingdoms came and went with no single potentate emerging. Toward the end of the sixth century a local Chinese military leader seized power in the north, conquered the south, and established a new imperial dynasty. Although it succeeded in reuniting the country and extending Chinese influence into other areas of southeast Asia, the Sui dynasty was not destined to last long. A military leader named Li Yüan (known after his death as Kao-tsu) overthrew the Sui emperor and established a new dynasty known as the T'ang.

By most historical accounts the T'ang dynasty ranks among the greatest in China's long history of civilization and culture. Estimates of the population of the capital city, Ch'ang-an, suggest there were two million people or more in its vicinity, making it the largest urban center on earth at the time. From that capital, near the modern city of Xi'an, the T'ang rulers undertook extensive reorganization of the centralized administrative structures of the empire. Land reforms were instituted, and the military greatly enhanced. The new policies helped in turn to secure internal political stability across China and to extend Chinese influence beyond its borders into Vietnam, Korea, Manchuria, and central Asia. All of this added up to conditions that were highly favorable for international trade, which had been hampered by the instability of the warring years. The seaport city of Kuang-chou (or Canton) alone is estimated to have had as many as one hundred thousand foreign merchants a year coming through its port at the height of the T'ang dynasty. Ships loaded with goods plied the waters off the Chinese coasts as never before, while merchants traveled back and forth across central Asia in unprecedented numbers.

Like other dynasties before them in China since the second century BCE, the T'ang dynasty made Confucianism the ruling political ideology of the state. Entry into the administrative bureaucracy was by way of the competitive exams in Confucian learning that were given each year in the capital. A Confucian university in Ch'ang-an provided the necessary training for scholars seeking employment within the imperial bureaucracy. But the T'ang dynasty began to recognize other religious ideologies in China as well, the most important being the indigenous teachings of the Taoist school. Under the T'ang, Chinese political interests had been extended in the West and there was a growing interest in the religions of Persia. Buddhism had first come to China from India during the Han dynasty by way of this western route, and Buddhist priests had supported the T'ang emperor in his rise to power. Now Chinese interests in western religions was beginning to extend even further. Manichaean and Zoroastrian missionaries had made their way across central Asia into western China and had been granted admission to the capital by the second T'ang emperor, T'ai-tsung, after 631. By 635 they had been joined by monks representing a faith that had originated in the westernmost Asian region of Syria and was soon known in Chinese as *Jing Jiao* (Illustrious Religion or Luminous Religion).

These missionaries from the East Syrian Christian churches in 635 are the first documented evidence we have of Christians in the Chinese imperial capital. While there could have been Persian and even Armenian Christian merchants in China prior to that, perhaps as early as the fifth century, we have no evidence of Christian communities inside the imperial boundaries of China itself prior to the year 635. By way of comparison, by that time there had been several centuries of active Indo-Persian Buddhist missionary work and a number of translations of Buddhist scriptures into Chinese. Not until the T'ang dynasty in the seventh century do we find what appears to be the first full-fledged attempt to translate Christian texts into Chinese, or to compose Christian works in the Chinese language; when we do, the effort is minuscule compared with the translation of Buddhist scriptures that had already been undertaken.

Stone monument at Xi'an with inscription recording Christianity in T'ang dynasty, China. Taken from Ian Gillman and Hans-Joachim Klimkeit, Christians in Asia before 1500 *(Ann Arbor, Mich.: University of Michigan Press, 1999). Reproduced with permission of Curzon Press.*

The name associated with what appears to be the first active Christian mission into China is that of Alopen. A monk most likely originally from the region of Balkh, he arrived in the city of Ch'ang-an, the imperial capital of the T'ang dynasty, around 635. Much of what we know today of the history of this mission comes from a monument discovered in the early seventeenth century in China. Workers digging near the modern city of Xi'an (the site of the ancient imperial capital of Ch'ang-an) uncovered a large black stone stele that measures approximately 3 meters tall by 1 meter wide. At the top is a large cross that is set above what appears to be a cloud and a lotus flower, symbols of Chinese Taoist and Buddhist schools, respectively. Inscribed in Chinese at the top is a title that identifies it as a monument commemorating the teaching of the *Ta-ch'in* (Chinese for "Rome") Illustrious Religion in the Middle Kingdom.

The text of the inscription opens with a brief statement of the basic tenets of Christian belief. There is one true being who is the invisible origin and mysterious creator of the universe, the confession begins. This is "*Aloha* [a Chinese transliteration of the Syriac word for God] the Triune, mysterious Person, the unbegotten and true Lord."[3] An account of the East Syrian Christian mission to China over the course of the previous 150 years follows, closing with a list of the

---

[3] P. Y. Saeki, *The Nestorian Documents and Relics in China* (Tokyo: The Academy of Oriental Culture Tokyo Institute, 1937), 53.

names of the monks in the community at the time the stone was completed. Most of the inscription is in Chinese, save for the names of the monks and a scattering of other terms, which are in Syriac. The text on the stone says it was erected in 1092 in the year of the Greeks (781 CE).

According to the inscription, in the year 635 Alopen arrived in one of the western suburbs of the capital, carrying sutras and images. We are left to speculate what these might have included: copies of Christian scriptures no doubt, and perhaps liturgical texts, catechetical literature, and a cross. Upon hearing of his mission, the emperor T'ai-tsung had Alopen officially conducted to the palace and authorized him to translate his texts into Chinese in the imperial library. We have no indication whether Alopen knew much Chinese; if the texts that are often associated with his name are any indication, he must not have known the language well. We can assume, on the other hand, that he had assistance from Chinese scholars in the city. The imperial library in which he worked is reported to have had as many as two hundred thousand volumes in it and a full contingent of resident scholars. There would have been ample resources for handling the work of translation.

Three years later, in 638, the emperor, having personally investigated the doctrines contained in the translated sutras, gave his approval to the teachings. The inscription on the monument indicates that the sage and the emperor had to work together, for the support of the emperor was essential for the mission in his land. The emperor ordered a monastery to be built within the capital, funded by the imperial treasury and with a faithful portrait of himself copied on its walls. Twenty-one priests, we are told, were ordained and attached to the community. The inscription does not tell us if they were Syrian or Chinese, but one would assume they were other members of Alopen's mission.

Several Chinese Christian treatises that were discovered in the caves of Tunhuang and Turfan appear to date from this original mission in the seventh century. One, called the *Jesus-Messiah Sutra,* has been dated as early as 638. The other three, which are grouped together under the title *Discourses on Monotheism,* appear to have been composed around 641. They have often been labeled Alopen's documents in the belief that they date from the translation project undertaken under his direction in Ch'ang-an. Indeed, the *Jesus-Messiah Sutra* could well be, in the words of one historian, the first Christian document "ever composed in Chinese."[4] While all four could be works translated in whole or in part from earlier Syriac texts, we cannot rule out that one or more were composed specifically to address questions raised by imperial scholars regarding Christian teachings.

Stylistically all four are similar to Buddhist sutras. The *Jesus-Messiah Sutra* actually uses the term "Buddha" for the divine person, while the other three use the Chinese term *I-shen* ("One God"). The *Jesus-Messiah Sutra* uses the Chinese term *Liang-feng* or "Cool Wind" for the Holy Spirit, while the *Discourses on Monotheism* use the term *Ching-feng* or "Pure Wind." In places the sutras employ the Buddhist term *Shih-tsun* or "Lord of the Universe" as a christological

---

[4] Ibid., 121.

title. In Buddhism this is the name of the bodhisattva Avalokitesvara, who in China is identified as the female goddess figure Kwan Yin, the bodhisattva of compassion. In addition all four also use Chinese phonetic characters to transliterate the term "Messiah," resulting sometimes in awkward literal meanings. P. Y. Saeki points out, for instance, that the combination of Chinese characters used in one place to transliterate the title for Jesus, I-shu-Messiah, literally mean "remove-rat-confusing-teacher."[5]

The *Jesus-Messiah Sutra* opens by speaking of the unseen Lord of Heaven, who lives in peace and calls upon all people to lead virtuous lives. The sutra decries the making of any images to represent this unseen "Buddha." The Lord of Heaven has given precepts by which all are to live, the three highest being obedience to God, to the Sacred Superior, and to one's father and mother. These three cardinal virtues, which clearly echo the official Confucian teachings of the Chinese imperial ideology, are followed by a summary account of the ethical teachings of the Christian faith. The Ten Commandments and the teachings of Jesus provide the substance of this section. Then comes a synoptic account of the gospel narrative. Because of humanity's sins, the Lord of Heaven took pity on them and caused a Cool Wind (the Holy Spirit) to enter Mo-yen (Mary), who suddenly became pregnant. The virginal conception was intended to show the whole world the dignity and power of the one who was born of Mo-yen. His name was I-shu (Jesus), whose birth in the land of Fu-lin (Ephraim) was announced by the sign of a star. The narrative continues with Jesus's visit to the Temple at age twelve, his baptism by John, his calling of the disciples, his teaching, and his miracles. These aroused the opposition of the literary scholars who were wicked people and who persuaded the ruling king to have him put to death. At the end of the passion narrative the text breaks off, its end unfortunately lost.

The other three texts follow in much the same vein. One provides a metaphysical discussion of the unseen nature of God, and of human nature being visible and invisible. A second makes a case for a particular understanding of creation and human nature. The sutra argues for "five attributes" of existence reflective of the "five aggregates" of Buddhist philosophy, and a threefold anthropology of body, soul, and spirit. The third text offers a fuller presentation of the ethical teachings of Jesus, followed by the narrative of his death and resurrection, the spread of the Christian movement, and the sanctifying transformation that the gospel brings about. This third sutra, entitled *The Lord of the Universe's Discourse on Almsgiving,* provides an illustration of the Syrian Christian emphasis upon the important role women played in the event of salvation. Women were the first witnesses to the resurrection, the text explains, and reported the fact back to the men who were Jesus' disciples. It was their predecessor, a woman, who first conveyed to the original man, Adam, a lie, thus bringing sin into the world, the sutra states. So it is fitting that women reverse the process by bringing the truth of the Messiah's resurrection, thereby introducing salvation into the same world.

It is easy to see from these texts how the Christian movement was regarded by the Chinese authorities as a sect that was similar to Buddhism. This identification

---

[5] Ibid.

no doubt facilitated the Christians' entry into China during the reign of T'ai-tsung. According to the monument discovered at Xi'an, a measure of imperial favor continued into the reign of his son, Kao-tsung, who assumed the throne in 650. The inscription says that monasteries were built in cities throughout the country, although historically the number appears to have been no more than a dozen, most of them in the proximity of the western capital. It also states that the emperor bestowed a prestigious title upon Bishop Alopen, although again there is no confirmation of such an act apart from this inscription.

The tides turned for a time against the Christian community after Kao-tsung died in 683. Several years earlier he had taken one of his deceased father's con-cubines, named Wu Chou, into his own palace. She had been only a young girl when taken as a concubine by the elder emperor and on his death had been sent to a Buddhist monastery. Shortly after her return to the palace, she engineered the death of the new emperor's first wife and assumed the position for herself. After Kao-tsung's death in 683, she was able to depose her two sons and rule as empress of China until 705. Wu Chou was vigorous in her support for the Bud-dhist faith. In 691 she declared it the official religion of the empire for the first time. This in turn appears to have directly led to persecution of the small Chris-tian community. Around 698 Buddhist mobs began attacking the monastery in the city of Lo-yang, which served as Wu Chou's eastern capital. By the time Hsüan-tsung assumed the throne in 712, Taoists had joined in the assault upon the Christian communities and violence had reached the monastery in the impe-rial capital.

The rise of a new emperor in 712 helped stem the anti-Christian persecution for a time. The monasteries were repaired by imperial order, their altars restored for worship, and new portraits of emperors delivered to be displayed in them. According to the inscription, the arrival of a new contingent of priests from the West further strengthened the Christian community. Among them was one named Lo-han; another was Bishop Chi-lieh from Persia. The latter arrived in 713 as part of an official embassy from the caliph. The Chinese imperial history records his presence as well in 732 as part of another embassy from the Arabs. Other missions included a monk named Chi-ho, who was reported to have come by sea in 744; he, along with Lo-han and others, led a service of Christian worship inside the palace itself.

The first century of Arab rule brought little direct conflict between Muslims and Chinese. The two empires were separated by an enormous expanse of land. During the seventh century the T'ang rulers had been successfully extending their influence over much of the region inhabited by the Turkish tribes to China's west. By the middle of the eighth century, Arab expansion toward the east, nota-bly Tibet, brought them for the first time into military conflict with forces under Chinese command. During the last quarter of the century Islam was expanding into central Asia while the Chinese empire had become more and more depen-dent on the foreign mercenaries in its army. Among the most important figures in Chinese national history during these years was Duke Kuo Tzu-i. As general of the northern armies, the duke had successfully put down an internal revolt, sup-pressed a mutiny of foreign troops, and defeated an invasion from Tibet. The monument from Xi'an says that one of the commanders appointed by the emperor to accompany the duke was a Christian priest by the name of I-ssu. I-ssu was listed on the monument as being its donor.

I-ssu, whose name in Syriac was Yazdbozid, hailed from the city of Balkh. A convert to Christianity, he had immigrated to China many years earlier and through faithful service had become a subject of the emperor. Among the positions he had held, according to the monument, were lieutenant governor over the northern region and Assistant Overseer of the Examination Hall. Not only was he a government official and scholar but also an ordained Christian priest. The inscription records him being one of the "white-robed scholars of the Illustrious Religion"[6] who was also married and had children. As a wealthy member of the Christian community, I-ssu played a prominent role through his donations to the monasteries and to the poor in Ch'ang-an, where he lived.

The author of the inscription was another priest named Ching-ching (Adam, in Syriac) who was associated with the monastery. The monument identifies him as a bishop. From other sources we know him to have been a prolific scholar as well. One of the later manuscripts found in the Tunhuang cave reports that Ching-ching translated more than thirty books into Chinese, several of them portions of scripture. One of the surviving works ascribed to him is a translation of the hymn of adoration of the Holy Trinity that is sung in the Syriac liturgy. The find indicates that at least some in the churches were worshiping in Chinese by the eighth century, and not only in Syriac. We have an indication here that by the end of the eighth century, at least, Chinese was beginning to be used in worship, and at that the Christian community was not exclusively populated by Persian exiles in China.

Ching-ching did not confine his scholarship to translating Christian texts. A catalogue of Chinese Buddhist works from the ninth century records his name as having collaborated with the northern Indian Buddhist scholar Prajna. Prajna had traveled to the Chinese capital by sea in 782. Upon arriving in the Buddhist monastery in Ch'ang-an he had begun to work on translating the scriptures into Chinese. One of these, according to the catalogue, was a translation of the *Satparamitra Sutra* in Uighur, a language Prajna could neither read nor understand. To help him he sought the aid of Ching-ching, who according to the Chinese text could neither read nor speak Sanskrit. The bishop nevertheless joined this eminent Buddhist scholar in his project, perhaps carried out inside the walls of the Buddhist monastery in Ch'ang-an. In this same Buddhist monastery in Ch'ang-an early in the ninth century were two of the most important figures in Japanese Buddhist history: Kobo Daishi, founder of the Shingon school in Japan, and Dengyo Daishi, founder of the Tendai school that was the source of a number of Japanese Buddhist schools.

Ironically it was this close identification with Buddhism that appears to have brought about the rapid decline of the Christians in the middle of the ninth century. During the 840s the emperor Wu-tsung, aided by many of the leading Confucian scholars, presided over a nationalistic revival of religious ideologies. Persecution began against the Manichaeans in 843 but soon spread to Buddhists,

---

[6] Ibid., 64.

who were again identified as adherents of a foreign religion. Christians and Zo-roastrians were caught up in the persecution as well. An imperial decree in 845 commanded the government Board of Worship to reduce drastically the total number of monasteries throughout all of China. The Christian and Zoroastrian religions were banned entirely, and all foreign religionists were ordered expelled. Over 250,000 Chinese Buddhist nuns and monks were forcibly returned to secu-lar life. The number of Christian and Zoroastrian monks and priests forced to abandon their vocations is listed as more than three thousand.

The Christian movement appears to have been unable to recover from this severe wave of persecution. Although an edict of toleration was issued within fifteen years, the dozen or so Christian churches and monasteries that had been built were never restored. While it is likely that there were still Christians among the numerous foreign merchants who came to trade in China after 860, there is little evidence that they established any permanent churches or monasteries. The last years of the T'ang dynasty continued to be marked by an increasingly domi-nant Confucian ideology with nationalistic overtones. The dynasty fell in 907 and was followed by a new period of internal conflict among the various Chinese states. Added to this was a steady increase in the numbers of Muslims in the central Asian region to the west. All of these factors seem to have combined to keep the mission to China from being refounded. The last word we hear from this period comes from an Arab chronicler who reports having had a conversation with a Christian monk in Baghdad in 987. Seven years earlier the monk had been part of a mission sent by the patriarch to set in order the affairs of the churches in China. They could not find one Christian left in China, the monk reported.

Looking back at the first three centuries of the Christian movement in China, we find a community that never numbered more than a dozen established monas-teries and several thousand Christian believers. The number of Christians pales in light of the strength of the Buddhist and Taoist schools at the time. The large number of religious schools that could be found in Ch'ang-an during the peak of the T'ang dynasty is remarkable. Nowhere else in the world in the seventh and eighth centuries could one find Christians engaged in active study and dialogue with Buddhist, Taoist, Zoroastrian, Manichaean, and even Confucian neighbors. The monument from Xi'an shows that the Christians were criticizing the doc-trines that they were encountering. Among the errors it identifies as being a con-sequence of original sin, for instance, are the ideas of emptiness and existence. It is a not so veiled reference to a particular school of Buddhist teaching. At the same time, as we have seen in the texts from Tunhuang, Christians borrowed from the Buddhist and Taoist archive of ideas to find ways to articulate their own messianic faith. There was a great deal of mixing of ideas among these various traditions in China. Perhaps, as some have suggested, this was in part responsible for the downfall of these first Christian communities in the end. The partial eclipse of a distinct Christian identity left Chinese Christians with little reason to main-tain their own separate existence amid the schools of T'ang era China.

A more likely historical argument is that despite the remarkable work in trans-lation and even composition of new theological works in Chinese, for the most part the Christian church in China from the seventh through tenth centuries remained a community of resident foreigners. Although sometime in the eighth century Ch'ang-an was made a metropolitan city by the patriarch in Baghdad, the churches for the most part remained dependent on foreign clergy from the region of Balkh for their leadership. Communication was difficult across the Silk Road after the rise of the Arabs or by sea from India. Often it took years for messages to make their way between Seleucia-Ctesiphon or Baghdad and Ch'ang-an. While there was at least the beginnings of an attempt to translate Christian scriptures and liturgy into Chinese during this period, it did not come close to the level of translation being actively carried out by Buddhist missionaries before and after the East Syrian Christian mission.

The decree of 845 calls for foreign religionists to be deported but then refers to some three thousand Christian monks, nuns, and priests who were forcibly secularized. If we were to assume that the three thousand returned to secular life in 845 were Chinese in nationality, we would have some indication that the movement was beginning to take hold among indigenous peoples. This would explain as well why both the Bible and the liturgy were beginning to be translated into Chinese. Here we might see the beginnings of a Chinese indigenous church tradition. Nevertheless, we are left with the enormous difference in numbers of Buddhists during the same period. The same document from 845 puts the number of Buddhist monks and nuns at 260,000. It is often said that Buddhism never fully recovered its strength and numbers in China after the T'ang dynasty. The same was even more true for the Christian movement.

Looking back upon this period in Asian Christian history, one is struck by the degree of interreligious dialogue and sometimes even cooperation in which Christians were involved. Christians joined missionaries from other religions who were journeying across central Asia into China, and by all appearances learned much from them. In India the Christian community accepted a place within the caste system, which was fundamentally an Indian religious construction; they accepted being integrated into the Indian religious cosmos without abandoning their own identity as different. In this regard, as we have seen in other places of the world, the use of the Syriac language in religious worship helped the Indian Christians preserve a distinct identity. Indian Christians could not become swallowed up in the unbounded cosmic sea of Indian religiosity so long as they floated on a Syriac ecclesiastical vessel.

Among the Chinese Christians of the East Syrian mission we find the opposite tendency at work as well. Christians there were actively translating their Syriac texts into Chinese, drawing upon the attraction the Chinese imperial household at the time was expressing for things western. Christians made use of this interest to extol the greatness of their doctrine, which had originated in the most western part of Asia, in Syria. But to explain it they turned to the concepts of Buddhism. One longs to know what lively dialogues might have been conducted as East Syrian Christians and Mahayana Buddhists presented their two religions in the imperial halls of China in the seventh century. It would be several more centuries before such an encounter again occurred.

26

The Making of Christendom
in the West

The continent known today as Europe had long been populated by various tribal peoples when a Roman army first crossed the Alps under Julius Caesar in 58 BCE. From modern Turkey to Spain, France, and Britain lived people who were collectively known as Celts. The name of the region of Galatia in Asia Minor, where the apostle Paul evangelized and whose inhabitants received an epistle from him that is now part of the New Testament, is derived from the term *Celt,* as is Gaul, or the modern nation of France. Irish, Welsh, Gaelic, and Briton were all members of the larger Celtic family. East of the Rhine River lived another family of peoples that Caesar called Germans. Historical and archeological evidence indicates their settlements stretched as far north as Scandinavia in the first century BCE.

Caesar's campaign into Gaul was followed by others that eventually extended Roman control from the Rhine River to Britain. In the wake of Rome's armies came governors, administrators, and members of the upper class who took over ownership of the land. Small urban centers sprang up as outposts of Roman culture, introducing Roman laws and Roman ways into what remained a mostly rural landscape. Those who lived in what is now Spain, France, Italy, and Britain soon spoke Latin as their common language.

Christian baptisms rose sharply in number among the towns and administrative cities of the Roman empire in the fourth century, as well as among members of the ruling Roman classes in the countryside. Things were otherwise for the lower classes in the rural areas, however, where the traditional gods held on to the allegiance of the people a century or so longer. The town and country religious division eventually made its way into several modern European languages, where a form of the Latin word *paganus,* or "country dweller," is still used by many today as a collective name for non-Christian religions and religious practices.

By the third century CE Germanic immigrants had begun to trickle across the Rhine River into Roman-controlled lands. Soon that trickle became a flood that shifted the ethnic composition of Europe forever. The names of these newcomers are familiar to students of western history: Franks, Goths, Vandals, Lombards,

Angles, Jutes, Saxons, Suevi, and others. They came, entire families or tribes at a time, drawn by the prosperity of the Roman empire. At first they inhabited relatively empty lands outside settled Roman territory. Soon their armies were roaming throughout the Roman empire, warriors often leading assaults upon cities and villages with their families following close behind. Most eventually settled into lives of farming or were employed by the Romans as mercenaries in the imperial army. Some even mastered the administrative and legal systems that made Roman civilization work.

These new immigrants were tribal peoples, organized according to clans and ruled by an aristocracy of warriors. Kings were simply the most powerful among the warriors, their authority resting strictly on their use of might. As we have seen, the first of their numbers who joined the Christian movement were converted to the Arian Christian faith following the mission of Ulfila in the fourth century. In true tribal fashion, when the aristocracy converted, the entire tribe converted, for there was little room for divergence in beliefs. The conversion of the Franks to the Catholic form of Christianity was an important marker in the turn of the entire Germanic people toward the Catholic faith. The formal conversion of the Visigoth king of Spain in 589 was another such marker. By 600 only the Lombards who ruled northern Italy were a significant force for Arian belief, and by the end of the century even they had joined the ranks of the Catholics.

The closing decades of the sixth century found the former western regions of the Roman empire in political and social chaos. A bewildering family of languages was now spoken, and innumerable separate kingdoms lay scattered across the landscape. For a brief period in the sixth century under Justinian, Constantinople had managed to regain administrative control over portions of Italy, North Africa, and Spain. By the end of the seventh century all that remained of Constantinople's territories in the West were southern Italy and Sicily. In the north of Italy the Greeks had managed to destroy Visigoth power, but the Lombards had quickly moved across the Alps and established a new kingdom. They in turn were soon swallowed up by the Franks.

Limited commercial activities had continued to link Spain, Italy, Gaul, and Britain during this period. Marriages arranged among various members of the ruling aristocracies also helped forge alliances across the region. Daughters of royal families were given away as wives to kings and sons of kings in other parts of the West in order to create new blood alliances among rulers and widen the circle of each family's political influence. The single most important factor linking the peoples of these regions together around the year 600 was the Catholic religion; its bishops provided an administrative network of a moral and spiritual nature. Churches owned land, sponsored education, and supported regional gatherings of their leaders. Within this network in the West the single most powerful bishop was the one who occupied the historical see of Peter in Rome, the pope. No one understood the importance of this office better or did more to define the role of the pope in the West for the next four centuries than Gregory the Great (540-604).

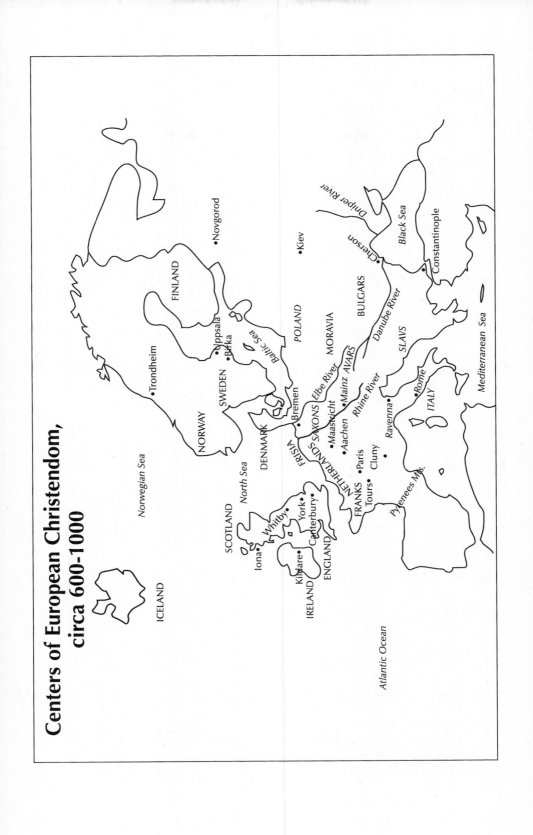

Centers of European Christendom, circa 600-1000

ICELAND

Norwegian Sea

Atlantic Ocean

North Sea

SCOTLAND

Iona

Whitby

York

Canterbury

Kildare

IRELAND

ENGLAND

Tours

FRANKS

Pyrenees Mts.

Paris

Cluny

Aachen

Maastricht

NETHERLANDS

FRISIA

SAXONS

Mainz

Rhine River

Bremen

Elbe River

DENMARK

NORWAY

Trondheim

SWEDEN

Uppsala

Birka

Baltic Sea

FINLAND

Novgorod

POLAND

MORAVIA

AVARS

Kiev

Dnieper River

Cherson

BULGARS

Danube River

SLAVS

Ravenna

Rome

ITALY

Black Sea

Constantinople

Mediterranean Sea

Gregory the Great

Gregory was born into the old Roman aristocracy. After his formal education and a brief stint in civil government, he took up monastic life. The death of his father, and his mother's entry into the ranks of the ascetics as a widow, afforded him the opportunity to use his inherited family wealth to endow a series of monasteries. For several years Gregory lived in one of these communities outside of Rome. A call to serve as envoy for Pope Pelagius II to Constantinople in 579 took him to the East for a time. After returning to Italy, he was elected by the people of Rome to the episcopal see of Peter in 590. Gregory assumed the position without waiting for the emperor Maurice in Constantinople to confirm his appointment (still a canonical requirement of the Roman church in the sixth century). By the time of his death in 604 he had done much to redefine the office.

A competent administrator, theologian, pastor, biblical exegete, and political leader, Gregory did as much by dent of personality as by actual institutional power. Since at least the fourth century the pope had been recognized as having a judicial role among other churches in the West, but otherwise the authority he exercised was spiritual and theological. Churches in Spain had held their own national councils without any involvement from Rome. Several popes had sought to extend their administrative authority over churches in Gaul without much result. Gregory marks a turning point in this history.

The bishop of Rome controlled a significant number of estates in Italy that had passed into the ownership of the church, making him in effect one of the major landowners in the West. Among the first tasks Gregory undertook was to reorganize the administration of these papal estates, thereby providing a model for other bishops in the West who were also becoming landowners and administrators of large estates. Cities and countryside alike had been devastated by years of warfare in northern Italy. Gregory organized a new system of food distribution, housed refugees, collected taxes, and maintained legal records to help restore political order. Faced with plagues, he organized public days of prayer to end the epidemics. Invasions and political turmoil had also disrupted life for several generations in Italy, but Gregory was able to negotiate a political settlement with the Lombards, securing an uneasy peace for a time.

While carrying on these civic and administrative tasks at home, Gregory kept up a lively engagement with others abroad. He corresponded widely with bishops and clergy in other regions and didn't hesitate to express his pastoral opinion regarding matters in their churches. He also contributed to the theological development of various doctrines in the Latin West, expanding on Augustine's teaching about the manner in which sins committed after baptism and without adequate penance will be addressed in the afterlife through purgatory, for instance. In spiritual and theological matters Gregory exercised his influence as much by the sheer power of his personality as by the authority that had accrued to his office as pope. At the same time he consistently demonstrated a sense of his own humility, often signing his letters "your servant" and by all indications meaning it. Future popes would look back to his tenure as a model for both authority and service within the church.

Britain and Ireland

One of Pope Gregory's lasting contributions to the spread of the Catholic faith was in the role he played in missionizing England. According to a story preserved in an eighth-century work known as *The Ecclesiastical History of the English Nation,* by the Venerable Bede, prior to becoming pope Gregory was in the marketplace in Rome one day when he came across a group of merchants who had recently arrived in the city. Among the merchandise they were offering were two boys of fair complexion being sold as slaves. Gregory inquired about their origin and religion. He was told that they were Angles from Britain, and thus *pagani.* So moved was he by their plight that he went to the pope and asked him to send a mission to the Angles to convert them to Christ. Gregory volunteered to go, says Bede, but the request was turned down due to the pressing need for him at that time in Rome. The mission had to wait until Gregory himself became pope.

The opportunity came in 595. Gregory appointed a fellow monk from Rome named Augustine to head up a missionary delegation to England. Some forty monks were chosen and equipped with vestments, relics, and books. They did not know the language of the people to whom they were being sent and according to Bede's account were stricken by fear as they approached England. Augustine was sent back to Rome to beg Gregory's permission to abandon the project. Gregory convinced them instead to continue with the mission. With Frankish interpreters whom they secured en route, the group landed in England in the region of Kent.

England during these years was little more than a land of local kings, their warring bands, and the villages that supported them. Centuries of invasions and warfare had taken their toll on what was left of the Roman structures. There were no major urban centers, only what can at best be called towns. Most of the people lived in villages scattered throughout the countryside. Houses were simple stone and wooden structures, palaces and temples little more than rustic cabins.

Upon their arrival the missionaries from Rome sent word of their purpose to the local king, Ethelbert. Ethelbert happened to be married to a Frankish woman named Bertha, the daughter of a former king from the western region of the Franks. She was a Christian who had been given in marriage to Ethelbert to cement an alliance between Franks and Anglo-Saxons on either side of the channel. Bede says that Ethelbert "had received her from her parents on condition that she should be allowed to practice her faith and religion unhindered, with a bishop named Liudhard whom they had provided for her to support her faith."[7]

---

[7] Bede, *Ecclesiastical History of the English People*, ed. Bertram Colgrave and R. A. B. Mynors (Oxford: Oxford University Press, 1969), 74.

Thus when Augustine arrived in Kent there was already a Christian queen, her bishop, and most likely a worshiping Christian community at the town of Canterbury. It has even been suggested that a request for missionary assistance might have come from Bertha by way of her relatives among the Franks to Gregory in Rome. Augustine secured the conversion of Ethelbert by bringing not just the Christian message but also the authority and prestige of Rome. This latter message was not so subtly communicated in the letters Gregory wrote to the king. In one such epistle preserved by Bede, Augustine tells Ethelbert that his role is like that of Constantine himself. The lure of the Roman imperial past was an effective tool to help bring a local English king into the Christian fold.

Ethelbert was baptized around Christmas time in 597. Earlier that year Augustine had returned to Arles where, again at Gregory's instruction, the archbishop there, who held a pallium from Rome, ordained Augustine to be archbishop of the English people. Back in England the king gave Augustine as his episcopal see an ancient church in Canterbury that dated from Roman times. Although Ethelbert did not require that his subjects be baptized immediately into his new faith, he granted Augustine and the other Roman missionaries permission to preach the Christian message throughout his kingdom. We can safely assume that many of the king's subjects followed the royal lead.

A similar development took place to the north of Kent in the kingdom of Northumbria some three decades later. Edwin of Northumbria underwent Christian baptism on Easter Sunday in 627. Again, it was primarily through the intervention of his Christian wife, Ethelburga, who was the daughter of Ethelbert of Kent. Ethelburga had been sent north to be married to Edwin in 619 in a political arrangement designed to cement relations between the two ruling families. She took with her as her chaplain Paulinus, a member of the missionary team from Rome who was ordained a bishop specifically for this task. As far as one can tell from Bede's narrative, there was at that time no existing Christian community in Northumbria. Ethelburga and Paulinus thus formed something of a pioneer missionary team. Following Edwin's baptism the bishop (soon to be made archbishop of York by the pope in Rome) continued to work among the king's subjects. Bede writes:

> So great is said to have been the fervour of the faith of the Northumbrians and their longing for the washing of salvation, that once when Paulinus came to the king and queen in their royal palace at Yeavering, he spent thirty-six days there occupied in the task of catechizing and baptizing.[8]

Of particular interest in the history of Augustine, Gregory, Paulinus, and the spread of Christianity among the Angles and Saxons in England is the method of evangelization that was pursued. During this period in the West, evangelistic work almost always occurred under some form of royal sponsorship and protection. It was directed not so much to individuals as it was to entire communities and districts. Each adult or child entering the Christian faith had to undergo individual

---

[8] Ibid., 189.

baptism, but the decision to do so was usually made by people responding in groups. Elsewhere in the West the general practice had been for bishops or monks to attack the traditional beliefs and practices of the people whom they sought to convert. Sharp opposition to local gods and practices was deemed necessary to win the people of the countryside to the Christian faith.

Augustine appears initially to have been instructed by Gregory to pursue such a method. But a second set of instructions from Gregory followed, suggesting a different approach to mission; in this letter the pope advised them not to try to destroy the local religious shrines. They should only seek to remove the idols that were housed in them, replacing them with Christian relics of saints they had brought with them to England. The shrines and temples themselves they were to adapt to Christian worship. Gregory wrote:

> When this people see that their shrines are not destroyed they will be able to banish error from their hearts and be more ready to come to the places they are familiar with, but now recognizing and worshiping the true God.[9]

The pope in effect was calling for a more open attitude toward the indigenous religiosity. Modified accommodation was to replace immediate eradication. To this end Gregory sought to distinguish indigenous religious practices that could be appropriated legitimately for Christian worship from those that could not. For their part, the missionaries were to seek to turn various indigenous practices in the direction of Christian worship as part of this overall strategy of gradual Christianization.

> It is doubtless impossible to cut out everything at once from their stubborn minds; just as a man who is attempting to climb to the highest place, rises by steps and degrees and not by leaps.[10]

For the most part the method appears to have been successful. Bede reports on one particular case involving a certain Redwald, king of the East Angles. Redwald had accepted the Christian faith but housed within the same building one altar for the Christian sacrament and another, smaller one for the indigenous gods. There were others no doubt like Redwald who similarly kept two altars for a time, in their hearts if not in their actual places of worship. Yet in the long run, Christianity won.

The policy of gradual displacement was effective in part because Gregory and his missionaries offered an alternative to the local deities in the form of Christian relics of saints. The cultivation of devotion through holy relics was by no means unique to England or even to the western Christian world. Relics were among the most common Christian artifacts throughout the world. They could be a bit of a martyr's clothing or a bone believed to have come from a particularly holy person from long ago. Teeth, personal effects, even the dirt from the grave site of

---

[9] Ibid., 107.
[10] Ibid., 109.

saints and martyrs were believed to have special power. Because it was such a widely practiced phenomenon, devotion to relics lent itself to being an effective means of bringing people into the fold of Catholic faith. People in new locations could be connected to people from older Christian traditions and places in materially symbolic ways.

The use of relics in places such as England helped people at a popular level make the change from traditional religions to a new Christian identity. Devotion to traditional goddesses among these northern peoples was gradually transferred to the cult of holy women from the Christian past, for instance, so that these holy women and martyrs became a part of the living cosmology of people who had previously sought the interventions of a grain goddess for their fields. Across the social spectrum, in place of tribal deities and spirits, the relics of saints and apostles now connected people—aristocracy and commoners alike—with those who had lived far to the south in the Christian Mediterranean world. They connected them especially with Rome, the center of apostolic authority in the West. The relics that came from the older Roman world were a part of a wider strategy that tied the English not only to the Roman ecclesiastical world but allowed Anglo-Saxons to gain fuller access to the glories of the Roman cultural heritage.

The Anglo-Saxon connection to Rome stood somewhat in contrast to Christian experience among the Irish and other Celtic peoples during these years. We saw earlier that Christianity had spread to Ireland by the fifth century, and that it found its organizing genius in Patrick. Irish Christianity was dominated by the influences of monasticism from its inception. Abbots and abbesses were considered to possess greater spiritual authority than bishops. Monasteries were the closest thing to towns that Ireland knew in the sixth and seventh centuries. They were not only centers of learning (no Irish translation of scriptures and liturgy were attempted; local inhabitants were instead taught to read Latin), but of economic and cultural life as well.

Irish, Gaelic, Welsh, and Britons were all part of the wider Celtic cultural family. Their traditional way of life had known fierce warriors and human sacrifice, yet it was a way that celebrated the mystery of life and nature with a playful lyricism that can be heard in its poetry and prose down through the ages. To the rhythms of traditional Celtic life Irish monasticism added a great love of Latin and Greek learning and a hunger for their classical texts. Roman literature and Christian scriptures were studied with equal fervor in the monasteries founded by the early Irish Christians. Nobility and commoners alike were welcomed into their company.

One of the best-known names in Irish monasticism from the sixth century is that of Columba (520-597). His most important contribution was a series of monasteries he founded in Ireland and Scotland. One of these was the monastery at Iona, which became a leading center of learning and training for later generations of monks in both England and continental Europe. Another important Irish monk from this period was Columbanus (d. 615), who first entered the monastery of Bangor in Ireland in 565. In the late 580s Columbanus traveled to Gaul, where he began founding monasteries among the Franks. Finding himself at odds with local rulers, he made his way into northern Italy, where he continued his mission of organizing new monastic communities. Like so many other spiritual leaders from this period, he is remembered for the miracles and wonders he performed; these helped turn the common people from their traditional gods to Christ.

By the middle of the seventh century, conflict was apparent between the Irish monastic leaders, on the one hand, and the Anglo-Saxons on the other. The conflict involved a number of factors, such as differences in monastic disciplines, the authority of bishops as opposed to abbots and abbesses, and at times the Irish monks' support of the Britons and Welsh in their clashes with the Anglo-Saxons. The most visible point of controversy between the two communities was the dating of Easter. The Irish dated Easter on the Sunday falling between the fourteenth and twentieth day of the first moon of spring, while the English church followed Rome and Constantinople in observing Easter on the Sunday falling from the fifteenth to twenty-first day of the same moon. The Irish claimed to be following the tradition of St. John, while the Anglo-Saxons claimed theirs was the practice of the Catholic churches everywhere.

Central to the Anglo-Saxon argument was their determination to adhere to the traditions of Rome, which provided their connection with the apostolic past. The Celtic Christians did not reject either the Roman or apostolic dimensions of faith. Irish monasteries from their inception had been centers for learning Latin, and the Irish both read the scriptures and conducted their worship in that language. Prior to the mid-seventh century, however, the Irish did not link the religious and cultural aspects of their Latinized Christian identity with the institutional authority of Rome. The form of Latin that they used had begun to take on a distinctive Irish form; as for the pope, he was regarded as having ecclesiastical authority only insofar as his life exhibited Christ's gospel. Anglo-Saxon churches were far more closely connected institutionally to Rome and gave greater weight to the authority of the pope.

England was simply too small. The conflicts were bound to produce a crisis as the two traditions grew closer in physical proximity to one another. The differences in the dating of Easter meant some Christians could be fasting while others were feasting, a crisis which involved different members of the same royal household in Northumbria at one point. Representatives from both sides of the debate finally gathered at a synod in Whitby in 663 to determine which tradition the Anglo-Saxons would follow. What swayed the debate for the Anglo-Saxon royal party was the argument made from scripture that Jesus had given Peter authority over the church, and that this authority resided in Rome. The specific merits of the question of dating notwithstanding, it was Peter's authority at the gates of heaven that finally persuaded the Anglo-Saxon kings to follow Roman rule.

A major contribution to deepening the Anglo-Saxon churches' sense of connection with the wider Catholic church came through the ministry of its seventh archbishop of Canterbury, Theodore of Tarsus. Theodore was living in Rome as a refugee from the Islamic East when he was consecrated by Pope Vitalian in 668. Rome fully accepted the standards of orthodoxy issued by the ecumenical councils of the East, but by the late seventh century there was a significant cultural distance between Greek and Latin church traditions. Concerned that Theodore might introduce into the English church Greek customs that were alien to the true faith, the pope sent along a trusted Roman theological advisor with the new archbishop.

He hardly needed to have worried. Theodore set about immediately to bring a new sense of vitality to the churches in England. He founded schools for the teaching of both Greek and Latin, and he worked diligently to improve the pastoral leadership and overall spiritual life of the land. A significant number of other scholars and artisans followed him to England, contributing to expanding the country's religious and cultural horizons as well. From the multifaceted inheritance of Irish spiritual discipline, Roman ecclesiastical connection, and classical theological learning, a distinctive form of Christianity emerged in seventh-century England. The eighth and ninth centuries would witness the fruits of these labors elsewhere in western lands as Anglo-Saxon missionaries traveled across the channel to help evangelize the continent.

The Christian movement among the Franks

Western Europe was dominated by the Franks from the sixth through the tenth centuries. Several other smaller Germanic kingdoms had emerged in the wake of the collapse of Roman rule in the West, but many from their aristocracy were being integrated into the ruling order of the Franks through marriage. Even more important for unifying the peoples of western Europe during this period was the Catholic faith. Since the end of the fifth century the Franks had been ruled by a Merovingian dynasty that was Catholic in its Christian faith. Due in part to this influence, Catholic Christianity had been embraced by all of the other Germanic peoples in the West. As we saw in the case of the Anglo-Saxons, Catholic faith was often tied to the heritage of the ancient Roman empire in the perceptions of the new ruling households of Europe, an inheritance many hoped could be absorbed through Christian baptism. That heritage was now being carried into a new cultural context, however, as the Franks, Burgundians, and others brought their own languages and laws to the table of Christian life.

Like the Visigoths in Spain, the Franks, Burgundians, and others did not simply abandon all former ways of life. Much that was part of their culture was carried on in a new Christian form. Kings who were once considered to be of divine descent were now demoted to the ranks of human nobility, but the role they played in assuring the salvation of their subjects continued. Heroic warriors became standard-bearers of a new form of social virtue that was emerging in codes of chivalry, but it was still essentially a warrior culture. There was no tradition of philosophers among the Franks, but there were prophets or seers, a role women as well as men had played in traditional Germanic tribal life. After the sixth century, monks and nuns assumed many of these functions as the holy men and women within the culture.

Germanic society had generally regarded men and women who worked the land for subsistence as more equal to each other than their counterparts in the Roman cities of the Mediterranean world. This was due as much to the lower level of material development in the culture, which usually translated into less social stratification among the rural workers, as it was to an inherent sense of gender equality among Germanic peoples. Traditional Germanic culture had recognized only men as having social rights and power. For the most part women were considered to have access to social power only through the men to whom they were related by blood or marriage, namely, fathers, brothers, and husbands. The only arenas where women in Germanic society exercised social power apart from men were in their roles as healers and midwives, and in certain situations as recipients of mysterious religious visions or experiences. This last tradition of women visionaries continued in Christian form through many who had given themselves in spiritual marriage to Christ and had entered the ranks of monasticism.

All of the Germanic tribes, including the Franks, were polygynous in their normal practice of marriage, although it was mainly the men of the upper classes who took more than one wife. Merovingian kings continued to have several wives even after their conversion to Catholic Christianity, despite the teachings of the church to the contrary. Traditional Roman law before the Christian era had embraced monogamy while accepting concubinage. Catholic teaching was likewise strictly monogamous but was also officially against concubinage. The Visigoths had followed Catholic practice regarding monogamy but accepted concubinage if both parties were unmarried. It was not until the rise of the Carolingian dynasty among the Franks, however, at least three centuries after their official conversion to Catholic faith, that the practice of polygyny was finally ended among them.

One of the reasons Catholic teaching on marriage was so slow to be implemented among the Franks was that the bishops themselves were often less than whole-hearted in their commitment to changing the dominant culture. After the Franks had converted in the fifth century, they had instituted control of the churches by their own nobility, a system known as the *Adelskirche*. The way to this had already been paved in the Roman empire, where after the fourth century bishops had largely ceased to be selected by their congregations. The emperor played a role in choosing episcopal leadership in the major cities of the eastern Mediterranean, while in the provinces metropolitans or archbishops made appointments. In Rome the people of the city in theory still selected the pope, although in actuality it was the most powerful members of the upper class who made the decision. The pope in turn exercised jurisdiction over much of Italy, but in other places in the West authority for church appointments was mostly in the hands of local rulers.

The Frankish nobility selected their bishops from among their own class. Although such appointments had to be confirmed by other bishops to be regarded as valid, the fact that the entire episcopal leadership was from the aristocratic class meant there was little active resistance to nobility's control of the church. The hierarchy of the church itself was fully integrated into the land-based economy of the Frankish realm. Bishops were landlords who owned large tracts of farmlands and thus the rural workers who were essentially tied to them. The secular nobility in turn supported the churches, and often even the monasteries, through sizable grants of land and endowments. The entire situation was one that was often ripe for abuse.

The one mitigating factor in this situation under the Franks remained the symbolic authority commanded by the bishop of Rome. The pope was still perceived to be the most important spiritual leader in the West. Frankish nobility expected Rome to recognize the bishops they appointed, but this in turn opened the door for popes to exert some influence within the hierarchy of the church in Frankish lands. As he had for the Anglo-Saxon kings, the pope embodied for the Franks their political connection to a Roman imperial past. In 751, when the weakened Merovingian king was deposed by the mayor of the palace named Pippin the Short, who then assumed the royal title for himself, it was the pope who extended legitimacy by recognizing the new ruler.

The reign of Charlemagne

The Merovingian rulers had for more than a century been undergoing a decline in both the power and effectiveness of their rule. Increasingly among the royal household it was the palace mayors, whose position was akin to that of a chief of state, who were making decisions and governing the military affairs of the kingdom. Pippin the Short (the third Pippin in his family line) was such a palace mayor, and in 751 he acted to depose the last Merovingian king, who was sent into retirement in a monastery. Pippin's father, Charles Martel, was the military commander who had led the army that defeated the Muslim invaders from Spain at the battle of Tours in 732. Pippin's son, Charles the Great or Charlemagne (ruled 768-814), would become known to history as the first in a line of new Roman emperors in the West.

Shortly after deposing the Merovingian king, Pippin sought the blessings of the pope for his action, which the pope granted. In return, Pippin invaded northern Italy and the kingdom of the Lombards who had continued to pressure Rome. The newly recognized king of the Franks defeated the Lombards and then turned over to the bishop of Rome possession of several major cities, including Ravenna, the residence of Constantinople's titular representative in the West. The alliance between Rome and the Franks had assumed a new dimension.

That alliance reached its fruition under Charlemagne, the king who succeeded more than anyone before him in reviving the Roman imperial past in its new Germanic garb. With Charlemagne we can speak for the first time of a distinct political and cultural entity called Europe. Through a combination of military campaigns against the Lombards and marriage to the daughter of one of their nobility (whom he shortly thereafter divorced), he brought an end to the independent Lombard kingdom in Italy. His expeditions against the Avars destroyed that independent kingdom and brought much of what is now Austria under his control. An attempted invasion of Muslim Spain ended in defeat, but he effectively extended Frankish control over the south to the Pyrenees. At the peak of his power Charlemagne's rule extended over most of modern France, Germany, Austria, and Hungary all the way to the Balkans.

Beginning in 772 Charlemagne undertook a series of brutal military campaigns against the Saxons to the northeast, whose lands bordered those of the Franks. For

Crowning of Charlemagne, illumination from the manuscript "History of the Emperor."
Biblioteque de l'Arsenal, Paris. Reproduced with permission of Scala/Art Resource, New
York City.

decades the Saxons had been harassing the Franks by carrying out raids on their
towns and farms. The Saxons were organized in a loose confederacy of clans that
lacked any unified political center that the Franks could attack and conquer. The
Saxons had no king to speak of, but for each campaign would select one of their
warriors as leader. Most of the time they operated as semi-independent raiding
parties. Time after time the Franks inflicted military defeat on the Saxons and
extracted from them agreement to end the raids. Young Saxon warriors would be
taken off as hostages to ensure their peoples' adherence to the agreements, only
to have them broken and new raids launched against the Frankish territories.

This was the background to Charlemagne's decision to end Saxon autonomy
once and for all. The campaign he launched was excessively brutal. At one point
Charlemagne himself oversaw the mass execution of more than four thousand
Saxon prisoners of war, a move many historians have interpreted as being intended to break the Saxon will for resistance. Although a number of Saxon leaders did submit, others continued to hold out, resulting finally in Charlemagne
ordering their forced resettlement inside Frankish territory to the west. Frankish
rule was finally extended over all of Saxony and a code of law put into effect that
was extraordinarily severe. Saxons were forced to undergo Christian baptism or
face execution. Capital punishment was also prescribed for worship of the traditional gods, failing to have one's children baptized, eating meat during Lent, or
cremating the dead. In a few short years many of the more oppressive aspects of
these laws were relaxed or rescinded, in part due to pressure exerted on
Charlemagne by his religious advisors. Nevertheless, the legacy of this brutal
conquest continued to be felt for years.

The fact that a Christian ruler could act with such savagery confronts us with fundamental questions about the degree of Christianization that had taken place among the Franks. With the baptism of the Saxons, we see the first full-scale use of military force and violence to compel a people to convert to Christianity. Roman law had increasingly hardened over the course of several centuries of Christian religious dominance to proscribe heresy, restrict the rights of Jews and other religions, and favor the institutional advancement of Catholic churches. Christian emperors had forcibly closed traditional temples and centers of learning. But they had not forced people into baptism under pain of death. Even in Visigoth Spain, where Jews were severely persecuted, their children were not forced to convert or face execution. Charlemagne set a precedent, one that Christian rulers all too often came to follow.

The pinnacle of Charlemagne's power, and the symbolic beginning of a new era in western history, took place in the year 800. The king had come to Rome late in the year to preside at a synod called to hear charges being brought against Pope Leo II by opponents in the city. Leo was judged innocent and his accusers guilty of treason. Then on Christmas day, while Charlemagne was kneeling in prayer in the midst of worship in St. Peter's, Pope Leo took a crown he had previously placed on the high altar and fitted it on to the Frankish king's head, declaring the king to be *Imperator Romanorum*.

The act was unprecedented. Nowhere previously in Roman church history had the bishop of Rome presumed to have the authority to elevate someone to the imperial throne. Historically the title of emperor was bestowed by the army. Popes themselves were traditionally expected to seek ratification of their election from the emperor in the East. As late as the 770s popes still nominally acknowledged the authority of Constantinople, although there was little the emperor could do to enforce this authority. At the time of Charlemagne's elevation, the imperial throne in Constantinople was occupied by Empress Irene, who had deposed her son and continued to rule alone as augusta. Disdain for a woman being on the throne in the East might well have played a part in the pope's decision to act independently in the West, although the evidence for this remains weak. There had been other occasions on which Rome had questioned the authority of an emperor in the East, and they had not resulted in the elevation of a new imperial presence in the West.

Charlemagne was later reported by his chronicler to have said that had he known such an event was to take place, he would not have entered the church that Christmas day. Fourteen years later, when Charlemagne decided to elevate his own son, Louis, to the rank of co-emperor, he conducted the coronation ceremony and crowned the younger king himself. No representative of the church was even invited to participate in Louis's coronation, leading some historians to suggest that it was not so much the title as the fact that it was conferred by the pope that Charlemagne regretted. Yet Charlemagne himself avoided any direct use of the imperial title for the fourteen remaining years of his life. He never referred to himself as emperor but preferred to be known as "king of the Franks, governing the Roman empire."

Reluctance notwithstanding, the king of the Franks took on many of the trappings of Roman imperial identity. Several years before 800 he had flirted with the prospects of one of his daughters marrying the son of Empress Irene in Constantinople, but unfortunately the empress had deposed this son. After 800, when Charlemagne had again become a widower, Frankish envoys journeyed to Constantinople to explore the possibility of marriage, this time between Empress Irene herself and Charlemagne—a proposal the Greeks rejected immediately. Aachen, Charlemagne's capital in modern Belgium, was no Rome or Constantinople, but the symbolism of those two great southern metropolises guided the architects and builders who constructed the Frankish city. Nothing like the administrative bureaucracy, the great architectural structures, and the immense populations of Rome or Constantinople ever came to characterize the northern capital. But that did not mean that the Franks did not see themselves as the rightful heirs to the imperial legacy of both cities and Charlemagne in some sense as a rightful bearer of the Roman imperial insignia.

If one is to bear even in symbolic form the Roman imperial insignia, one must carry on at least in rudimentary form the duties of an imperial court. Emperors have to have envoys and ambassadors to send on missions to other courts in the world, and Charlemagne was not without his diplomatic corps. He sent ambassadors to Constantinople to negotiate imperial business from time to time, although there was no major permanent Frankish presence maintained in the eastern emperor's court. Most in Constantinople considered his coronation as Roman emperor an affront and continued to see him as little more than a barbarian king.

Another world ruler of the time proved to be more receptive to Charlemagne's ambassadors. The king of the Franks appointed a Jewish merchant named Isaac to serve as his ambassador to Baghdad, a mission that was successful in earning the Muslim ruler's respect for the Frankish king. In 802 the caliph Harun al-Rashid, who was known as a friend of the East Syrian patriarch Timothy I but is better remembered by history as the famed ruler in "1001 Arabian Nights," responded to the news of Charlemagne's enthronement by sending a gift. The Jewish merchant Isaac was entrusted with bringing to the Frankish king the gift of an elephant, which the caliph had obtained from India. Accompanied by several Abbasid envoys, Isaac returned to Aachen with word of the caliph's recognition. The elephant had to wait until the following summer to be led across the Alps, but it survived to be a curiosity for several years at the court in Aachen.

The legacy of their Roman past resided above all for the Franks in their use of the Latin language. Latin was not the first language for these Germanic people. Although it had been commonly spoken throughout Gaul and Britain under Roman rule before the period of Germanic settlement, it had remained in use after this period only as the language of theology and law in the West. Few of the new Germanic settlers spoke Latin or encountered it in a regular manner in their everyday lives. It was used by the Merovingian kings at court for formal purposes but without any extended educational system promoting it beyond that. Under Charlemagne that was to change. The eighth century ushered in a period that many historians have referred to as the Carolingian Renaissance in the West. At the heart of this renaissance was literacy in Latin, encouraged by a king who could barely read and could not write his own name without the help of a stencil.

Foremost among the factors contributing to the Carolingian Renaissance was the king's encouragement of schools. A new Latin script was developed in the West, called the Caroline minuscule, which was designed to help those unfamiliar with Latin grammar and syntax to read it more easily. Copyists were set to work as never before, reproducing books that could be easily read and understood. Historian Peter Brown estimates that as many as fifty thousand books were copied in the scriptoriums of monasteries in the West during the ninth century, an enormous production given the limitations of technology for writing at the time.[11]

Charlemagne encouraged a steady flow of these Latin texts into his capital in Aachen. With his bishops the king concurred that not only was Latin the language of theology but also of the liturgy and sacraments and of the administration of the church. The decision reaffirmed the role Latin had come to play in unifying churches throughout a region where a number of different dialects and languages were regularly spoken. Preaching was still to be conducted in the vernacular languages of the people, the bishops ruled, but this was little more than a concession to their illiteracy and lack of education. The proper language of the church and learning in the West was Latin.

Along with sponsoring schools and the production of Latin texts, Charlemagne encouraged the best theological minds in the West to come to his capital, where they took on the role of imperial advisors. Two of those who did so were Alcuin (735-804), an Anglo-Saxon from England, and Theodulf of Spain (760-821). Both names became closely identified with the ninth-century Carolingian theological legacy. As an advisor to the king, Alcuin played a particularly important role in supporting the monks, many of them fellow Anglo-Saxons, who were working as missionaries along the frontier to the east. We will look at these missionary endeavors in the following chapter when we explore in more depth the role of monasticism in the conversion of Europe during these centuries; here it is important only to point out that their endeavors were greatly facilitated by having a sympathetic voice at the Frankish court. Theodulf played a similar role for those within the Frankish churches by supporting education. Every priest was required to establish a school for boys to be educated, and every priest was expected to encourage fathers to send their sons.

Over the course of several years Charlemagne issued a series of *General Directives* intended to address a number of issues of social reform. One of these concerned the legal status of marriage. The reforms regarding marriage were introduced slowly but eventually, due to the persistence of bishops and synods, became the general law of the Franks. Chief among them was an end to polygyny, even among the aristocracy. Marriage was made monogamous for the first time among the Germanic people. It was also made binding for life, this despite the fact that Charlemagne himself had earlier in his reign divorced his

---

[11] Peter Brown, *The Rise of Western Christendom: Triumph and Diversity AD 200-1000* (Cambridge, Mass.: Blackwell Publishers, 1996), 184.

Lombardian wife. Previous generations of Christian clergy had often been asked to bless marriages, but in general they were considered civil contracts. Under Charlemagne marriages became a matter for the church as well, for they were made legally valid only after being blessed by a member of the clergy. The bishops were also able to impose a more restricted degree of consanguinity for marriage among the Franks.

The bishops were not as successful in extending their teaching against the practice of concubinage. While the Frankish nobility accepted the reforms of marriage and divorce, concubinage continued to be practiced by both men and women in their realm. In his later years, and after the death of several wives, Charlemagne himself decided to live with several women rather than to marry again. He accepted his own daughters having similar relationships, and he accepted the children that they bore as single parents. Nor were the king's daughters alone in this regard, for among the Franks there were other women from the nobility who chose to maintain their legal freedom (that is, to remain unmarried) while having male sexual partners and bearing children.

Another area of reform undertaken during the time of Charlemagne and involving sexual practices was that of marriage among the clergy. Although celibacy had long been valued as a spiritual exercise among Christians, priests in most places were still permitted to be married. The majority of ancient churches allowed clergy who had married prior to their ordination to remain in these relationships without requiring continence but forbade priests to marry after they had been ordained. The Franks added to this tradition the expectation that those priests and bishops who were married prior to ordination were to abstain from sexual relations after their ordination. Couples were even supposed to live in separate quarters to avoid the appearance of sexual relations, although there is little evidence that such arrangements were regularly observed. Bishops, priests, and deacons were all forbidden to remarry if their spouse died, as were the widows of clerics.

One of the topics addressed in the *General Directives* was monasticism. Charlemagne was concerned with unifying the various communities within his territories. To this end the Rule of Benedict was made mandatory, and no other rules were supposed to be in use. Of course there was virtually no way for bishops or the king to check on the rules being followed in all the monastic communities. In many cases other rules were adapted or combined with the Benedictine program to conform to the law. Nevertheless, the overall result was a large degree of conformity in monastic practices throughout the West. The spread of Benedictine influences beyond the Frankish borders was also encouraged by Charlemagne. Following his coronation as emperor in 800 and the successful mission of Isaac to Baghdad, he was able to secure the caliph's permission to open a Benedictine monastery in Jerusalem, a move that was less than enthusiastically welcomed by the Byzantine monks already in and around that Holy City.

Charlemagne's legacy included a number of lasting influences, but none was to have a longer-term impact than his decision concerning the inclusion of the filioque in the Latin version of the Nicene Creed. Earlier it was noted that this clause stating that the Holy Spirit proceeded from the Father and the Son had first been used in the creed in Spain. The Council of Toledo in 589 had adopted it as an anti-Arian measure. Spanish churches had introduced the practice of reciting the creed in regular worship on Sundays as a way of combating residual Arianism in the land. This particular wording of the creed had begun to make its way across the Pyrenees and into Frankish churches by the eighth century.

Support for the clause was strong among the churches of the Franks for some of the same reasons that had first been advanced in Spain. In the eighth century two Spanish theologians, Felix of Urgel and Elipand of Toledo, had argued that in his humanity Jesus had been adopted as the Son of God at his baptism. There were two forms of sonship in Jesus Christ, they argued. In his divine nature Jesus was the eternal Son, but in his human nature he was adopted Son. Their position reflected christological currents flowing through the Mozarabic church in Spain, which was contending with the dominant Muslim intellectual context. It was perceived by the pope and other western bishops, however, as being a dangerous heresy. Inclusion of the filioque in the Nicene Creed was seen to be a means of strengthening its teaching concerning the full divinity of the Son in relation to both the Father and the Spirit.

Charlemagne was also concerned by an argument he understood was being advanced by Tarasios, then patriarch of Constantinople, to the effect that the Holy Spirit proceeded from the Father "through the Son" *(per filium)*. This seemed to the king and his theologians among the Franks to amount to an Arian-style reduction of the full divinity of the Spirit. Responding to these concerns, a synod of the Frankish bishops with Charlemagne at its head in 809 declared the filioque orthodox and ordered it included when the creed was recited among their churches. Theodulf prepared the document that defended its use on the basis of earlier church teachings, foremost of which was that of Augustine.

The following year Leo III acknowledged to Charlemagne that he found the phrase to be essentially orthodox but thought that it ought not to be used. He urged the Frankish bishops not to recite the creed with the phrase at mass and refused to include it in the creed that was recited in Rome. The pope even went so far as to have two silver plaques inscribed with the words of the Nicene Creed, one in Greek and the other in Latin, to be hung in St. Peter's Church in Rome. Conspicuously missing from both plaques was the filioque. Not until the eleventh century did a bishop of Rome finally allow the use of the phrase in the recitation of the Nicene Creed in Rome, only after it had been in use for several centuries in other places in the West.

Charlemagne's theological legacy lived on long after the king's death, much longer than his political empire survived. The empire Charlemagne ruled was built almost entirely on his personal authority and power. There was little in the way of institutional or administrative structure that could survive him. Politically, Europe was still little more than a collection of local estates united through networks of oaths of fealty and organized around individuals on a personal basis. Charlemagne tried to pass this system on to his son Louis, but the empire soon dissolved into a series of smaller and more fragmented kingdoms, dukedoms, and ecclesiastical lands. One of the major partitions that took place shortly after Charlemagne's death was the division of his domains between two sons. The east-west divide among the Franks can still be seen after many centuries as roughly the border between modern Germany and France.

At a popular level Charlemagne's attempt to inculcate classical Latin learning had far less effect than he might have hoped. Among the common people Christianity was becoming translated into a Germanic cultural idiom that made more sense to them in their own world. One of the best examples of this popular form of Germanic Christianity comes to us from an anonymous poem from the late ninth century known as the *Heiland*, or *The Saxon Gospel*. The Saxons, it will be recalled, had been brutally conquered and forced to undergo baptism by Charlemagne's army late in the eighth century. Under such conditions one can hardly speak of an authentic conversion. Evangelization came instead through other means, mainly from the work of Anglo-Saxons and Frankish missionary monks who began working among the Saxons. Saxon Christianity developed as the conquered people appropriated the stories of the gospel at a popular cultural level.

Such cultural translation is well illustrated in the lines of *The Saxon Gospel*, a long, narrative poem that retold the gospel story in Saxon idioms. The poem was intentionally patterned after Tatian's *Diatessaron*, that harmony of the four gospels originally composed in the second century and popular among the early Syriac-speaking churches. A Latin translation of the *Diatessaron* had been made in the fifth century, and copies were brought north by monks who found in its simple narrative form a way to communicate the gospel to illiterate peoples. *The Saxon Gospel* followed a similar pattern of narrative harmonization, having a similar effect in communicating the message to a new people.

Composed in Old Saxon, it presented Jesus as a Saxon warrior leader who was accompanied by his thanes or earls. Towns became forts or palisades on hilltops *(burgs)*, the closest thing Saxons had to cities. The desert became the forest, Mary a woman of noble birth, Jesus the Lord of the land, and the disciples his retainers. The Lord's Prayer was depicted as a spell in secret runes, similar to those wizards and soothsayers used in their incantations. In one of the most colorful songs of the narrative, Jesus and his band attended a wedding feast in a guest hall at Fort Cana. The warriors who had gathered were all drinking merrily when the apple wine ran out. Like a magician working his magic spells over the water vats, with words and signs (specifically of the cross), Jesus used his hands to work the water into wine. The result was much pleasure and merriment among the warriors who had gathered for the feast in that great meadhall. In its pages *The Saxon Gospel* shows us how Germanic people were making sense literally of the "God-spell" (source of the English word "gospel") of Jesus Christ at a popular cultural level in the countryside.

The post-Carolingian West

Back among the courts of the ruling nobility, the Carolingian line of kings finally came to an end in the year 911. By then western Europe was well along the road of the political economic system known as feudalism. In the European feudal system peasants lived and worked on estates, or manors held by the nobility.

In return for the goods that the land produced, the lords of the manors provided protection and served as courts of law. These lords in turn were related to other members of the nobility through oaths of fealty given in return for the lands over which they ruled. Overlords invested their vassals with the lands or fiefdoms through ceremonies involving symbols of political power. In return vassals swore solemn oaths of loyalty to their suzerains with promises to provide military service in the form of mounted knights, the basic unit of soldiering after the Carolingians. The complex network of fealty oaths was organized hierarchically. At the top of the pyramid resided kings, whose power lay in securing the loyalty of other high-ranking members of the nobility through various means of persuasion or threats of violence. These nobles in turn provided military resources in the form of mounted knights for whom service was a part of their fealty.

Early in the tenth century a new family of kings emerged with Saxon roots among the aristocracy in Germany. The first in this new line was Henry, who was elected by the higher members of the nobility and was able to secure peace among the various warring lords of the region. His son, Otto I, followed him in 962 in establishing an even wider circle of rule. One of Otto's most important legacies was the use he made of appointments of bishops to extend his control. Although bishops were forbidden by church law to carry arms, they were otherwise fully part of the feudal land system. They took oaths of fealty to the nobility on whose lands their churches lay and in turn acted as lords of the manor over those who lived on them and worked them. By appointing bishops who supported him and establishing new episcopal centers, Otto extended his power significantly while bringing bishops more fully into the political ranks of his realm.

Otto's influences reached northward into Denmark and as far south as Italy. To the east he succeeded in extending Saxon dominance over the region of Poland, a land inhabited by people of Slavic descent. Otto was not responsible for bringing Christianity to the people of Poland during this period, however; that honor belongs to Dobrava, the wife of a Polish king, who was herself originally from Bohemia. In a pattern that is now quite familiar to us, she brought with her a priest as a chaplain and before long had converted her husband to the Christian faith. King Mieszko was baptized in 966. Soon there were churches being built with bishops appointed from Germany, reflecting the Polish king's subordinate relationship to the Saxons at the time. In time the kings of Poland sought to gain their independence from German rulers, but by then Christianity had taken hold among the people and was on its way to becoming their national faith.

Following 900, the political life of western Europe fragmented again into a number of kingdoms and centers of power. The religious life of its Christian people, on the other hand, remained surprisingly united. This was in part due to the effects of the early Frankish clergy, who had insisted on a unifying Latin tongue for Christian worship and intellectual life throughout their lands. Far more important both for extending the boundaries of the Christian movement and for maintaining the unity of the western churches, however, was the work of missionary monks and nuns. For several centuries they crisscrossed the countryside, becoming not only the major missionizing factor but in many cases the major civilizing force among western European people.

27

Monasticism in the West

People in western Europe did not abandon traditional religious beliefs simply because members of the aristocracy were now baptized. The various ancient gods, along with traditional ways of worship, did not end when bishops were appointed to various districts. Many continued to make use of the incantations and potions that had served them for so long. Through the Merovingian and Carolingian periods, church councils repeatedly condemned witchcraft and magic. It is the surest evidence that such practices continued, and sometimes thrived, in the countryside. In the eighth century under the Carolingians we have evidence for the first time of a woman being executed for being a witch. Gerberga was her name, and she was a nun. Political considerations might have played a part in her demise (she was the sister of a lover of one of the German queens), but the fact that her opponents could make the charge of witchcraft against her suggests that such traditional practices were still known, if not flourishing.

Germanic kings converted to Christianity, we have seen, not only because they came to believe in the superior power of the Christian God (although that played no small part in their decision), and not just because their wives had become Christian (an equally important consideration at times). Becoming Christian was for the royalty among the Franks, the Anglo-Saxons, and others a means of joining themselves to the Roman imperial legacy of the past. Bishops among the Anglo-Saxons and the Franks shared the perception of a historical legacy, as much as they were concerned with inculcating a Christian mindset among the people. The presence of traditional religions could not simply be ignored, of course, if the goal was to enter the world of Christian civilization. But the task of evangelizing the people fell beyond the hierarchy of the church. The work of bringing Christianity to the common people in a meaningful way fell instead to the monks and nuns who established their communities throughout western Europe. It is to them that this chapter turns.

A peculiar tradition of monastic spirituality had emerged in the West by the seventh century that suited its practitioners for the task of evangelizing the countryside. The tradition was born in the practice of monks and nuns journeying as pilgrims to shrines of holy women and men in various locations throughout the West. Often after having visited such shrines, these pilgrims continued to wander across the countryside with no apparent goal. The practice was called *peregrinatio* or "wandering." It was essentially a form of self-imposed exile, of monks and nuns making themselves strangers to their homelands. Itinerancy itself was the purpose and goal of these *peregrini* ("wanderers"), not any particular place or activity. They did not always have evangelism or mission as their purpose, although certainly a number of them did. Yet this is precisely the heritage these itinerant monks and nuns left; in their wandering and exile, these strangers throughout the land laid the foundations for the fuller evangelization of the people.

They did so by founding new monastic communities wherever they went. Typically an individual would travel with several companions to a new region where there was not much of a Christian presence, often doing so under an inner spiritual urging or call as much as through explicit planning. There the group would secure land (possibly a donation from a local lord) on which to build a new monastic house. This in turn would became a new center for spreading Christian influence among the common people. Local members of the community would be recruited, and then the founder and several others would move on.

A large percentage of the *peregrini* were Irish and Anglo-Saxon and thus of a culture somewhat different from those among whom they were establishing new houses on the continent. Most did not have connections with the Frankish aristocracy that ruled much of Europe during the sixth through ninth centuries. Although they received the protection of the bishops and nobility, they were not always supporters of the policies and decisions of the Frankish rulers.

Monasticism in the West had since its development in the fifth century been relatively flexible in its structures, especially when compared with the institutional organization of parish churches. The boundaries of dioceses in the Roman world had since the Council of Nicaea in 325 been firmly established along administrative lines. The practice had been carried over among the Franks and Anglo-Saxons as well. Bishops generally did not move beyond the boundaries of the church to which they were ordained, and very few priests who served under these bishops did so far from their hometowns. Monks and nuns, on the other hand, were not confined to the region where they were raised or ordained. They were often able to travel great distances to establish new monasteries or join existing communities.

We have already noted above the names of the Irish monks Columba and Columbanus. Columbanus in particular was an important figure among the *peregrini* on the continent of Europe, having labored in southern France and northern Italy. One of the most revered names of the seventh century came from the old aristocratic Roman class in Gaul. Amand (590-675) was an itinerant monk who was also eventually ordained a bishop. The story of his life was told in a popular account written by one of his contemporaries, Baudemond of Elnone. Like most narratives of the lives of saints from this period, the *Life of Amand* freely mixed the wondrous with the everyday. He was reported to have performed numerous healings and even to have raised people from the dead. On the more mundane side, the author included a copy of Amand's last will and testament in the book.

Early in his life Amand (or Amandus as he is also known) visited the shrine of Martin of Tours. So moved was he by the saint that he made a vow to become a pilgrim monk and wander the countryside, spreading the gospel. He underwent tonsure, entered the ranks of the clergy, and began his wandering service. Several years later he journeyed to Rome, where he went to St. Peter's, intending to pray in an all-night vigil. Instead, he was thrown out by a guard. St. Peter then appeared to Amand in a vision and instructed him to return to Gaul to preach.

After returning to the north, he was ordained a bishop. He continued his life as a traveling evangelist, winning converts by the time-honored method of performing signs and wonders. It was in the region near Ghent that he was said by his hagiographer to have raised a man from the dead, causing the local inhabitants to abandon their traditional gods and temples in favor of the Christian religion. Amand even traveled to the land of the Slavs to preach before finally settling in the region of the Netherlands and becoming the first bishop of Maastricht. After his death in 675, his remains became relics for generations of successive believers after him.

The first decades of the eighth century witnessed an increase in the traffic of monastic teachers beyond the eastern frontiers of the Franks. One of the first in this new generation of wandering missionaries was Willibrord (658-739), an Anglo-Saxon monk originally from Northumbria, in England, who had been educated in a monastery in Ireland. During the last decade of the seventh century Willibrord made his way to the court of the Franks to seek their support for a mission to the people of Frisia, east of the Rhine along the coast of the North Sea. After founding several new houses he eventually established the center of his work in Utrecht.

Boniface

The name that is most often identified with the eighth-century mission to the peoples east of the Rhine is that of Winfrid (or Wynfrith), who is better known to history by his Latin name, Boniface (680-754). An Anglo-Saxon like Willibrord, Boniface was educated in the monasteries in his native land. In 716 the monk who would soon be known as the apostle to the Germans made his first visit there. After returning home to England, he then journeyed to Rome, where he met with Pope Gregory II. It was Gregory who gave him the name Boniface, commissioning him to serve as a missionary among the people east of the Rhine River. Boniface then returned to Frisia and worked with Willibrord for several years. He journeyed to Rome again in 722 and this time was ordained as a missionary bishop by the pope himself. A brief visit to the court of Charles Martel secured both the protection and the financial backing of the ruler. Boniface then returned to the region of Hesse, where he established the base of his work.

There were already churches in Hesse in 723 under the jurisdiction of the bishop of Mainz. Christian influences did not reach far beyond the nobility of the Franks to whom the clergy mostly related, however. Traditional religious beliefs were still prevalent even among those who had undergone baptism. One of Boniface's main concerns was to increase Christian beliefs and practices among the people. He did so by establishing monasteries and attracting monks and nuns who in turn exerted a Christianizing influence upon the countryside. Much of his story fits the well-worn pattern of missionary activity we have already seen develop in the West. So we find Boniface at one point taking up an axe and felling a sacred oak tree, Frankish troops standing close by in the background just in case he encountered any resistance. The tree had been a place of sacred worship for the traditional Germanic gods. Felling it was designed to show the superior power of the Christian God. But Boniface then provided a measure of continuity with the old ways by using the wood of the tree to build a chapel for a new monastery at Fritzlar.

Just as critical to Boniface's ministry was the effect he had upon the hierarchy among the Franks. Having been ordained by the pope himself, Boniface was able to operate with a degree of independence from other local church leaders. He was often at odds with the Frankish bishops who claimed to have authority over the region in which he was laboring. Boniface was critical of both the laxity of discipline exercised by the church leaders and their lack of enthusiasm for evangelism. He ordained his own clergy, many of them fellow monks from England, to assist him in his missionary endeavors. This alone was enough to generate resistance from the bishop of Mainz, for he feared the Anglo-Saxon interloper was seeking to establish a separate church. Nevertheless, Boniface's reforming influences eventually were felt across the region. He was almost single-handedly responsible for the resumption of church councils among the Franks, for instance. Boniface was elevated in 745 to the bishopric of Mainz, thereby resolving once and for all the issue of a separate missionary church.

The spirit of *peregrini* and the call of missions in the end proved to be too strong for Boniface. In 753 the Anglo-Saxon bishop, now in his seventies, once again set off. This missionary venture took him to Frisia, a region that was still beyond the frontiers of the Franks militarily. The following year Boniface and a small group of faithful were preparing for worship along the coast when they were set upon by a group of pirates. Boniface was killed along with the rest of the members of his party. To his reputation as teacher, missionary, and reformer, Boniface now added the final crown of martyrdom.

Women in monasticism

During the years of his missionary activities Boniface never labored alone. He always had others with whom he worked as the head of a team. Both monks and nuns labored with him in this regard. Two of the Anglo-Saxon women who joined him in Germany, for instance, were Teckla and Lioba, who established monastic houses specifically for nuns.

One of the most prominent names of women monastics from the seventh century was that of Burgundofara, a noblewoman of Burgundian descent. While still a young girl, she resisted her parents' attempt to force her to marry and instead took a spiritual vow of celibacy. Several years later, in 617, with the support of an endowment from Balthild, the Merovingian queen who was wife of Clovis II, Burgundofara founded a community of her own, south of Paris. This new monastery soon grew to become a joint community of men and women. As the abbess, Burgundofara served as the head over men and women alike, making her one of the few women in seventh-century Europe to exercise either spiritual or institutional authority over men.

Another incident of a woman from among the nobility taking vows of virginity and entering monastic life in the seventh century was that of Queen Etheldreda in England. Bede reports that she had been married to an Anglo-Saxon nobleman who had died and had then been given in marriage by her family a second time, to King Egfried, in 660. Soon after this second wedding, however, Etheldreda informed her new husband that she had taken a vow of virginity and thus would not consummate the relationship. The king sought the local bishop's help in convincing his wife to have sexual relations, but the bishop supported Etheldreda instead. For twelve years the couple lived under this arrangement, until Etheldreda finally prevailed upon her husband to allow her to enter a convent, which he did. Several years later she became its abbess, and according to Bede was recognized locally as one who exercised a gift of prophecy.

Monasticism had long been the major vehicle for Christian women's spiritual development. It also was the major institutional means by which women in the West could exercise social control over their own lives. Convents provided women a way of partially escaping the confinements of their male-dominated society. Frankish law, for instance, provided little in the way of punishment for the crime of rape, other than what a woman's male family members could extract by way of payment or other form of retribution. The law, on the other hand, severely punished men who raped or even sought to seduce nuns. These protections extended even to women who had taken vows of celibacy but continued to live outside convents (a practice that Charlemagne effectively ended by ordering all nuns to be cloistered). For young girls, a convent could offer an alternative to life within a patriarchal marriage. For older women who were widows, they were an alternative to being forced by male family members to remarry and a form of social support in old age.

Among the Franks, women were legally allowed to inherit and own property. Many of them donated lands to monasteries and convents, in a number of cases allowing the women to assume much more control over estates than if they were to remain within the secular order of feudalism. As we saw in the story of Burgundofara, in some places women actually ruled over the joint monastic communities of men and women. They not only heard confession from women and men alike but gave absolution to persons of both genders, a degree of spiritual authority not exercised elsewhere. In some places nuns learned to read and might even have worked to copy scriptures or other sacred books. Spiritual biographies of saints appear most frequently among the list of works nuns composed, an important contribution they made to the literature of the Christian movement among the Franks.

In the ninth century these women's monastic communities were greatly curtailed. The Carolingian church leadership did not appreciate women's contributions to the degree the earlier Merovingian dynasty had. No longer were there Christian queens seeking to convert their non-Christian husbands, engendering the support of the bishops for their endeavors. The power of many of the wealthier women who could endow convents and monasteries also declined during the ninth century. Although their total numbers underwent a decline, convents continued to play an important role in the life of women, as monasteries did overall in the life of the West.

Changing patterns of spirituality

Whether they were women or men, monastics were the most common agents of evangelization among the peoples of the West in the seventh through tenth centuries. Monasteries were mission stations attracting men and women who sought to give their lives to Christ in service. Monks and nuns brought prayer close to people's daily lives. All who lived nearby, who worked inside the compounds, or who studied in their libraries could hear the community's prayers said several times each day. Monastery chapels were often the place people went to worship and receive the sacraments. Monks and nuns provided education along with Christian teaching to the people of the countryside, modeling Christian moral life for the rest of the community. As holy people, they were in effect called upon to replace the soothsayers and healers of the traditional religions. Monasteries handled day-to-day problems in people's lives, serving as safe houses for those who were in danger or as places for care-giving when travelers were sick. In the West they were virtually the only places common people had for storing any valuables that they might possess, not so incidentally making monastic houses targets for robbers and pirates as well.

One of the major changes in the lives of individual Christians and churches that took place in the West was in the dominant pattern of baptismal practices. Earlier generations of Christians had undergone baptism only after a period of catechization, and only at the hands of bishops. Even as late as the fifth century in the Latin West, baptism normally took place after the age of twelve. Infants or children could be baptized in case of need, as Cyprian in North Africa in the third century had allowed. But this was only in the context of Christian families, and usually if the child's life appeared threatened. In these cases the children, usually girls, were expected to be included later with the others who were preparing for baptism.

The baptism of infants born into Christian families had become a common practice in most churches of the world by the sixth century. Adults who converted from other religions, however, were still expected to undergo some form of instruction in the faith. In the case of Clovis and his three thousand warriors, there is no evidence that they underwent anything like a formal catechetical process. The pattern was repeated not only in the experience of other kings and warriors in the West, but soon became the common practice. Baptism began being regularly administered to infants by other members of the clergy in addition to the bishops and no longer only during the Easter season. One of the outcomes of infant baptism becoming the normal practice was the final dissolution of the office of the deaconess, whose primary ministry had for centuries been to assist in the baptism of adult women.

Another consequence of making infant baptism the normal practice for Christian families was the increase in importance of confirmation. According to Bede, bishops in England had to visit each of the churches under their care and administer the rite through laying on of hands. Confirmation was expected to take place following a suitable program of instruction in the faith and only applied to persons who had been baptized earlier. While there was no unified program of instruction among the churches, it was expected that the basic teachings of the Christian faith, both doctrine and practice, be presented prior to the rite.

Confirmation was not the only means by which churches in the West sought to inculcate Christian faith among the people. Even more important for most Christians in the West was the developing body of ethical teachings that addressed the concrete, day-to-day issues of people's lives. Much of these teachings were collected by the monasteries in books called "Penitentials." These anthologies identified various individual sins that people practiced and then provided pastoral direction by prescribing appropriate forms of repentance. This aided greatly in the development of a fuller system of spiritual penance, one of the most important theological occurrences in the West during this period. Previous centuries had known penance primarily as a public event, usually conducted by a bishop. As such, it tended to bring with it a measure of ostracism from the community. After the seventh century in the West penance increasingly became a private practice, guided even for laypeople by a monastic spiritual director. This allowed it to be accomplished without public humiliation. A full penitential system emerged in the West to guide believers through all of life's ups and downs. It addressed both major and minor ethical infractions and led to a fuller realization of spiritual discipline among Christians.

Traditional ethical codes of the Germanic culture had emphasized honor and solidarity. Revenge was demanded for infractions against one's tribe, and absolute devotion to one's leader was expected. Salvation was understood to be a collective reality, for it was identified with the well-being of the tribe as a whole. The system of penance that monasticism introduced into people's lives reoriented that conception of salvation away from the collective level of the political well-being of the people to securing a place in the afterlife for one's individual soul. The result was no small matter, given the later development of western individualistic concepts of salvation in the modern period. But in the seventh century this new emphasis upon individual responsibility and personal spiritual development through penance was considered a significant advance over the earlier tribal religious identity of the people.

It was at the level of day-to-day life among laypeople of all social classes that monasticism had its greatest and most lasting impact in the West. Monks and nuns were holy people, identified with the tradition of saints of the Christian past. Saints were believed to be capable of interceding before God in heaven. Chief among them was Mary, the mother of Christ, but others were important as well. St. Peter, St. Jude, and St. James could all be called upon to give guidance or protection for an endeavor one was undertaking. In the West the saints of the Christian past quickly appropriated the place in popular life that had been earlier occupied by local gods and spirits. St. Brigid, for instance, assumed many of the attributes of the Celtic goddess of fire in Ireland. Living monks and nuns likewise took the place of soothsayers and wizards in religious life. They did so in continuity with the ancient Christian missionary practice of employing signs and wonders to demonstrate the superior spiritual power of the gospel. Monks and nuns also used miracle stories, pictures, and relics of saints to help communicate and strengthen belief among the people.

Of these aids to the faith, relics were by far the most preferred for inculcating Christian identity. Pieces of clothing, fragments of bones, and even the ground dug up from around the burial site of a saint—all were considered powerful sources of spiritual energy by the faithful. During the time of Charlemagne oaths were taken on relics, so great was their authority. Relics created sacred Christian spaces in people's lives and brought the great memory of saints and holy events into the everyday world where people lived. Small containers for them, called reliquaries, were worn around the neck for protection. Relics were believed to have curative power, a tradition supported by an abundance of stories of persons being healed after touching them or even strapping them to their bodies. Dust that came from the burial sites of saints was commonly mixed with water and drunk in the belief that it could cure. Nor was this tradition of relics confined to popular religion outside the realm of the clergy. By the end of the ninth century nearly every church altar in the West had a relic associated with it.

As a result of the great demand for relics, a lively trade sprang up across the countryside, much of it unscrupulous. Often people's willingness to believe resulted in extravagant claims for relics that found their way into churches, monasteries, and people's homes across Europe. Wood from the true cross, fingers or bits of clothing from an apostle, dirt from the grave of a well-known saint abounded. One only needed a story of a miracle to verify the claims that were often made for a particular relic, which could then be sold to a local bishop for his church or even to a local member of the nobility who might give it as a gift.

Trafficking in relics was one area of abuse in spiritual life. Another was the fact that many monasteries amassed sizable wealth and their occupants became absorbed with matters of material increase. Similar problems were affecting the churches as a whole during this period. Bishops and priests easily lost sight of their ministerial calling when they were so closely aligned with the ruling class of the society and so much a part of the new feudal order. Even Rome did not escape the stigma of scandal during these centuries. Such scandals were often magnified by being coupled with the growing institutional power of the papacy during these years.

Pope Nicholas I

Sometime during the middle of the eighth century in Rome a forged document known as *The Donation of Constantine* first appeared in the archives of the city. The document might well be one of the most important forgeries in human history. After being baptized by Pope Sylvester, the document stated, the first Roman Christian emperor himself had given to the pope the extensive papal lands around the city of Rome. Hence the political authority of popes in Italy was not a new innovation but had begun with the reign of Constantine.

After the eighth century *The Donation of Constantine* was used to justify the pope's claims to be the rightful ruler of central Italy. But not until the middle of the ninth century would there be a pope who could put those claims into effect beyond the estates of central Italy. Nicholas I (d. 867) extended the power of his ecclesiastical office beyond any of his predecessors since Gregory the Great. One of the claims he made, for instance, was the right to judge all bishops and other patriarchs of the church throughout the world, a stance that was bound to bring him into conflict with the ecumenical patriarch in Constantinople, as we will see in the following chapter. The papacy was the final court of authority within the entire Christian church, Nicholas asserted, its power higher than that even of a council.

Nicholas rested much of his claims on a collection of forged documents known today as the *Pseudo-Isidorian Decretals*. Like *The Donation of Constantine*, these documents purported to be official letters and legal decisions of church leaders from across the centuries. In fact, they were written in the north of France, most likely in the period just before Nicholas's ascent to the papal throne. Although we have no way of knowing for sure, of course, we can assume that he took them to be legitimate parts of the church's historical canonical tradition. Not only did they support his contention that Rome rightly exercised authority over every bishop in the church, but also they asserted the rights of bishop and pope over political rulers in matters of ecclesiastical life, a contention that would continue to grow in the West.

Nicholas was by most accounts an able leader. Following him, however, the papal office came under the control of various rival families in Italy. For almost one hundred years a succession of popes had tenures marked by scandal, intrigue, corruption, and even murder. By the beginning of the tenth century corruption was not only common among the papacy and the wider hierarchy of the church, but among monasteries as well. The time was ripe for reform.

Two forms of abuse in particular began to be identified by those concerned to reform the church during these years. The first was the practice known as *simony*, the purchasing of ecclesiastical appointments. The term is derived from the story of Simon in Acts 8, who sought to purchase spiritual power from the apostles. Under the Franks, appointments to church office were made essentially by members of the nobility. As the social system known as feudalism emerged, such appointments were accompanied by exchanges of gifts that symbolized the oaths of fealty bishops, abbots, and clerics made to the feudal lords on whose lands their churches and monasteries were founded. Increasingly members of the clergy were expected, or offered, to pay for their ecclesiastical appointments in the form of gifts or money. By all accounts the practice was widespread throughout the West by the tenth century.

The other target of reformers' efforts was that of clerical marriages or concubinage, known as *nicolaitism*. Celibacy among the clergy had long been an issue for churches in the West. Synods in Spain had been among the first to require it for all priests, and not just for bishops, as it was in the East. Pope Gregory the Great endorsed the rule in the sixth century, as did Charlemagne in the eighth. By the year 1000, however, many clergy and even bishops in the West were living with women in marriage or out of wedlock. Clergy often sought to secure an inheritance from church lands for their children, an indication that the practice was not simply going on in secret. Having families often further entangled the clergy within the complex social web of feudalism in the West.

Cluny

The beginning of a new wave of reform is often traced to the founding of Cluny in southern France in 910. Cluny was established by a local nobleman named William the Pious with a healthy endowment of land. It was placed by its founders under the direct authority of the pope, thus insulating it from the control of local nobility. The monastery was governed by a series of abbots who proved to be able administrators. The full Rule of Benedict was restored, and strict ascetic discipline was reestablished. Word of Cluny's spiritual revival soon spread to other communities. Some existing monasteries associated themselves with Cluny and followed its design for reform. Others were founded as new communities, and their members sought from the abbot of Cluny the appointment of their own abbots or abbesses. This was the first time such an organizational structure had

Abbey of Cluny monastery and tower as they appear today. Photograph by Lionel Chocat, Office de Tourisme, Cluny. Reproduced with permission.

been employed, and it placed these other monasteries virtually under the authority of Cluny. The idea eventually became the norm among communities in the West.

Guided by both abbots and abbesses, more than a thousand new monasteries and convents were eventually founded under or associated with Cluny. The movement had a major impact both on monastic life and in the churches of the West. The two practices discussed above emerged in the tenth century as the particular focus for reforms among those who were identified with Cluny: simony and nicolaitism. As we will see in the following section, both of these practices were related to the church's place in western feudal society. The reformers pressed their case especially in Rome, opening up an important new chapter not only in western spiritual life but in the institutional understanding of the papacy, as we will also see in following chapters.

In the four hundred years from Gregory to Cluny, monasticism in the West had proven itself to be the single most important factor in evangelizing the European countryside. Often it was in the monastic communities that the spiritual lights shown brightest across the land. Monks and nuns were holy people who performed spiritual gifts of healing, sometimes prophecy, and always education and pastoral care. They brought their spiritual authority to bear on moral practices of the day-to-day world where they mattered most. People came to monasteries to hear monks pray, have a sickness cured, or receive the sacraments from a priest. From the time of Charlemagne it was Benedict's rule that reigned supreme in the West. All monastic reform movements after 800, including that of Cluny, which began in 910, were essentially based in revisions and revivals of Benedictine spirituality.

28

Christianity in the East Roman Empire

There is no year, no decade, no century when one can say with precision that Greco-Roman civilization ended, and the great historical enterprise often called Byzantium began. Historians might speak of something called the Byzantine empire emerging in the period of Late Antiquity, but it is more an interpretive convenience than it is an actual historical event. In the eyes of most of those who occupied the so-called Byzantine world, there was no such break in the passage of civilizations. There was only a time of intense readjustment as Greek-speaking Christians in the eastern Roman empire came to grips with new configurations of power and culture. From within the circle of this Christian community, there was an experience of considerable shrinkage, both in terms of land and political identity. Politically, Constantinople was cut off from the Latin-speaking West by the rise of independent Germanic states; and from the Syriac-speaking East and Coptic-speaking South by the rise of Islam. What remained was a Greek-speaking state that still perceived itself to be a transnational empire. The emergence of Byzantium had more to do with its relationships to those who lived outside its political and cultural boundaries than it did with the community within them.

What did the women and men who lived and spoke its history say about themselves? Historian Alexander Kazhdan says that they perceived themselves to be citizens of Constantinople, and Romans.[12] The latter is also how the Arabs perceived them. *Rum* was the political entity whose capital city, Constantinople, they sought for nearly eight hundred years to capture. Throughout the pages of this text they have been called East Romans or Greeks, terms that invoke a longer memory that predates a Christian identity. Yet the city of Constantinople and the empire over which its foremost citizen ruled (however small that empire had become by the period we are exploring) were nothing if not Christian. The Council of Chalcedon affirmed to all who cared to listen that they were neither Hellenists nor Jews but something else, a third people called Christians. The seemingly endless rounds of theological debates were, from one perspective, a result of Christian leaders seeking to articulate more precisely this identity.

---

[12] Alexander Kazhdan, "Byzantium: The Emperor's New Clothes?" in *History Today* 39 (September 1989): 26.

Many historical surveys of the East Roman civilization cite its beginnings in the time of Diocletian, who moved his capital to Nicomedia and divided the empire between two equal emperors. Constantine's decision to build a new city (actually to build upon the site of what was an existing town known as Byzantium) was another marker in the emergence of a separate state. By the time of Theodosius, Greek and Latin halves were clearly drifting apart administratively, culturally, and even spiritually, if not yet theologically. Soon new Germanic rulers established independent kingdoms in the former western territories. Justinian was the last to rule over a unified Roman imperial world. He was one of the last to speak Latin as his governing language in the East as well. By 620 the official language in which Constantinople conducted politics, not just the language its citizens spoke on the street, was Greek.

Justinian no longer needed Rome the way other emperors had before him, both symbolically and materially. It was during his period (or just before) that the bishop of Constantinople began to be called the ecumenical patriarch. Ecumenicity had long been identified with the councils that had gathered since Nicaea, the first, had been called by Constantine himself. Pope Gregory of Rome wrote letters to everyone he could think of—the emperor, the empress, the patriarch of Constantinople, the patriarchs of Antioch and Alexandria—to ask them to stop the bishop of the eastern capital from making use of the title. They all pretty much ignored him

The rise of Islam less than a century after Justinian was a far more serious challenge than the complaints of the spiritual leader from Rome. With the arrival of the Arabs on its eastern frontier, the East Roman empire could no longer claim to be the sole heir in the East to the Greco-Roman heritage. The Arabs, like the Germanic peoples in the West, laid claim in their own way to both the spiritual and philosophical inheritance of the Greeks. Furthermore, the new Islamic empire sought to take over the lands and territories that Constantinople ruled and sought to destroy the emperor and his armies. The rapid victories that the Arab armies achieved in their first years on the field took the East Roman empire completely by surprise. The Arabs, of course, credited their military victories with being a divine sign of approval upon their historical mission that was no less universal and "ecumenical" than that of the patriarch of Constantinople. The possibility that divine judgment was indeed being sent upon Christian churches and Christian lands was not new, just the possibility that such judgment was being sent upon Constantinople. The Greeks struggled to find theological categories that would enable them to reconcile historical events with their self-understanding as being the inheritors of the splendor and glory of Christ's triumphant kingdom as it had come to reign on earth. Such categories were not readily forthcoming.

Within a century much of the East Roman territories were under Muslim rule. Under the domain of the Muslim caliph were the cities of Antioch and Alexandria, along with all the wealth they produced. Muslim armies continued to whittle away slowly at East Roman territories in Asia Minor, North Africa, and Sicily. Periodic reverses in the Greek armies' fortunes merely served to heighten another year's losses. Each spring the Muslim armies would return to take up the debilitating warfare along the border between the two empires that ran through Asia Minor. Each winter they withdrew once more, halted by the snows that impeded their troops in the mountains. Muslim ships launched numerous naval attacks along coastal towns and preyed upon any Greek or Latin ship that ventured out into the Mediterranean Sea. St. Nicholas became the patron saint of eastern Christians who were forced to travel by sea in the Mediterranean world, invoked for his protection against the feared Muslim "pirates."

By the 800s the East Roman empire was reduced to the territories of Asia Minor and Greece on either side of the Bosporus, the southern end of Italy, and a scattering of islands in the Mediterranean Sea. The only true city left was Constantinople, and it was a shadow of its once-glorious self. Far fewer people now lived within its walls and immediate suburbs. Much of the administrative bureaucracy was gone, as was a good deal of its former wealth. The city could still raise a sizable amount of gold when it was needed to buy off a passing army, but it was cut off from most of its traditional source of income to the east. Compared with the level of urban development to its north and west, Constantinople could still impress its visitors. Its libraries still contained the canonical texts of the Roman Christian past, and its theologians were still versed in the intricacies of Orthodox dogma. The people of Constantinople continued to look upon themselves as citizens of a glorious city and inheritors of its glorious heritage. To a significant degree so did their Muslim opponents, which is why Islamic rulers sought so adamantly to conquer Constantinople. Likewise in the West, kings and popes alike still looked toward Constantinople as the standard-bearer of the imperial past, if not always in their eyes of orthodox Christian faith. Despite having seen better days, Constantinople was still for many the capital of the Christian world.

This is why in the seventh century Rome still looked to Constantinople not only as a spiritual partner but as the historical source of political legitimacy. Although Rome was the city from which the empire drew its name, Constantinople was the capital built by the first Christian Roman emperor. Already in the era in which it was built, the cultural distance between western and eastern ends of the empire was apparent. The ecumenical councils called by emperors in the East were overwhelmingly Greek-speaking affairs. The bishop of Rome never played a significant role in any of them, beginning with Nicaea, although representatives from Rome were always present to speak on behalf of the western apostolic office. Popes sometimes sent letters to be read before such gatherings. Theologians in Rome carefully sifted the canons and doctrinal formulations of the councils after the fact, weighing in on questions they considered crucial to the orthodox faith. But any contribution Latin theologians had to make greatly diminished after the fifth century. The absence is indicative as much of Constantinople's inward turn as it is of Rome's decline as a center of theological acumen.

In 663 Constans II visited Rome, the last time a Roman emperor from the East was to do so. Ten years before that troops from Constantinople had entered the city of Rome to take the pope as a prisoner to Constantinople, where he was forced to stand trial. By the end of the century, no eastern imperial presence was left in the vicinity of Rome or northern Italy to enforce Constantinople's will. As late as the beginning of the seventh century, popes still felt compelled to ask the emperor in Constantinople to ratify their appointments in Rome. By the end of the century that was no longer the case. Bishops and theologians in Constantinople had traditionally recognized in name at least the ecumenical significance of the apostolic office of Rome. Admittedly Rome's importance in this regard often served more as a political device to be exploited by the emperor than as an effective source of theological counsel. By the seventh century even this political support was no longer needed in the East. Communication between the two cities had so declined that few bothered to learn to read or speak the other's language. The relationship between the two churches had become characterized more by hostility and conflict than by mutual love and recognition. This was especially the case along the borders where the two Christian worlds met, as in southern Italy and central Europe.

The problems the East Roman empire had in the seventh century with Rome to its West, as we have said, were small in comparison to the pressures generated by the Arabs from the East. The Roman emperor Heraclius had just won a great victory over the Persians in 629. Not only had he defeated the shah, but he had recovered the true cross of Jesus, which had been taken by the Persians from Jerusalem but was now returned by him to Jerusalem. Nothing prepared him for what was to come next in his imperial career, however. In 634 an Arab army took Damascus. Two years later, the Greeks brought an enormous army to the field against them—some reports say there were eighty thousand troops. For several weeks the two sides faced each other along the Yarmuk River in Syria. Then one day a sandstorm suddenly blew up from the south. Muslim historians to this day credit it to being an act of God. The Arab general, Khalid, gave the command, and the Arabs attacked. The Greeks were blinded by the sand blowing into their eyes and thrown into sudden confusion. None made it home; the Arabs destroyed the entire Greek army, leaving no East Roman military presence of any significance in the region. Swiftly, decisively, and permanently the cities and lands of the East were removed from the Roman empire's historical domains.

The monothelite or "one will" controversy

On the eve of the Arab conquest of Syria and Egypt, Patriarch Sergius of Constantinople had been at work once again trying to resolve the perennial problem of how to speak about Jesus Christ's relationship to God and to humanity in a manner on which all in the East Roman empire could agree. The patriarch had proposed a formula that he believed both sides could affirm, a proposal Emperor Heraclius subsequently embraced. The rift between the two parties (Chalcedonian and non-Chalcedonian) was taking on new dangerous political overtones. Theological reconciliation could help ameliorate the political climate of the region.

The proposal the patriarch offered was to conceive of the unity of Christ being in the area of his activity or energy. Although he had two natures, Jesus Christ acted in a singular manner. The new formulation was called *monoenergism* ("one energy") or more commonly *monothelitism* ("one will"), and it soon gained the support of a number of other bishops. In Alexandria the Melkite patriarch Cyrus (not to be confused with Benjamin, the Coptic patriarch) agreed that the definition of Chalcedon could be interpreted in this way. Not everyone rushed to endorse Sergius's new position, but enough did to lead some to think for a brief moment at least that the theological divisions of the eastern Roman world might be resolvable after all.

The illusion was soon shattered. A Palestinian monk named Sophronius was among the opponents of the new proposal from the Chalcedonian side. His election to the patriarchate of Jerusalem in 634 gave him a platform from which to launch his theological offensive. Soon he had convinced other supporters from the Chalcedonian side to reject the one-energy doctrine. Meanwhile, word of Sergius's theological proposal reached Rome, where Honorius I (d. 638) was pope. Honorius was sympathetic to the idea. He suggested in his response that following Chalcedon we can conceive of Christ as having had two natures (divine and human), and that these two came together in him in one will (a will need not be defined strictly as belonging to one or the other nature). Back in Constantinople the emperor Heraclius issued an edict in favor of the monothelite doctrine in 638. Further discussion of the issue was officially banned

Honorius died in Rome that same year. His successor, Pope John IV, took up examination of the controversy and in 641 resolutely condemned the one-will doctrine that his predecessor had supported, without condemning Honorius himself. A council to examine the matter was called by John IV's successor, Pope Martin I, in 649, the year he assumed office. It reaffirmed the condemnation, drawing upon Leo's *Tome* of 451 for theological guidance. Just as Christ had two natures, he had two wills, each perfect and complete, the western bishops asserted. The report did not sit well with the emperor in Constantinople, who had the exarche in Ravenna dispatch a contingent of troops to Rome to arrest the pope and bring him in chains to Constantinople. Pope Martin was tried, tortured, and sent into exile where he died in 655, a martyr in the eyes of those who shared his convictions.

The monothelite doctrine that Jesus had one will was originally proposed as a means of bridging the Chalcedonian and non-Chalcedonian divide in Syria and Egypt. For the most part non-Chalcedonian bishops did not rally around the new position as its supporters in Constantinople hoped they would. One group that apparently did affirm the monothelite doctrine was an obscure community of churches in western Syria. Little is known of the group other than that it was centered around a monastery founded several centuries earlier at the grave site of an ascetic teacher named Maron (or Maro). The Maronites, as they were called, were reportedly non-Chalcedonian by the beginning of the seventh century and were organized under a separate episcopal structure. Their location in the mountains of what is now Lebanon provided a degree of isolation that allowed them to maintain a separate identity for many centuries.

Maximus the Confessor

One of the victims of the monothelite controversy of the seventh century was a Greek theologian named Maximus the Confessor (580-662). Born and educated in Constantinople, he worked for a short time in the bureaucracy of the empire before leaving to join a monastic community. Around 628 he moved to North Africa, where he resided for almost two decades. The year 649 found him at the synod in Rome that condemned the one-will doctrine, a decision with which he concurred. His opposition cost him his freedom, for, like Pope Martin, he was arrested in Italy in 662 and taken to Constantinople to stand trial. There he was condemned and sent into exile in 655 to a village on the southeastern shore of the Black Sea. Still he refused to remain silent regarding his opposition to the new teaching. In 661 Maximus was brought back to Constantinople where he had his tongue cut out and his right hand cut off, the punishment for refusing to keep silent or to sign the emperor's statement of faith. He died the following year in exile, having never fully recovered from his mutilation. His death won him the title of confessor in the eyes of those who shared his theological commitments.

As a teacher, Maximus had sought to demonstrate the unity of theology and spirituality for the Christian life. In this he followed the lead of the Cappadocians, developing a fuller mystical understanding of the incarnation. The importance of the doctrine of the two wills in Jesus Christ was closely related to the doctrine of his two natures. According to Maximus, humanity was deified, not lost, in the event of the incarnation, thereby opening the pathway to our own deification through grace. Maximus emphasized the apophatic (or negative) approach to spiritual life. The mystery of love leads to unutterable peace in the end, a peace that transcends our comprehension.

By 680 much of the Greek Christian East was weary of theological controversy and longing for the peace that so eluded them. The break with the Latin West had not been without great symbolic theological cost. On the other hand, reconciliation with the Egyptian, Syrian, and Armenian churches had not been forthcoming. The Arabs had been defeated in their attempt to take Constantinople and had been forced to sign a treaty of peace. But elsewhere in the former Roman East they were consolidating their rule, removing any political incentive Constantinople might have for a formula of doctrine that met with the approval of non-Chalcedonians. In this climate a new emperor called an ecumenical council that met over the course of nearly a year in the capital. Eventually it came to be recognized as the Sixth Ecumenical Council, or Constantinople III. Its major decision was the rejection of monothelitism and the extension of the Chalcedonian paradigm to confess "two wills" along with "two natures" in Jesus Christ.

A decade later a new emperor summoned the eastern bishops to return to Constantinople for the purpose of appending to the decisions of the council a series of governing canons. Because this subsequent gathering had only representatives of the East, and many of the canons it passed appeared directed against practices accepted in the West, it was not recognized by Rome at the time.

Indeed, a number of the canons have a local flavor that suggests they were directed specifically toward conditions in and around Constantinople. One permitted deacons and priests who were married prior to their ordination to remain married, a practice that in the West was discouraged. Another forbade Christian priests from consulting Jewish physicians, suggesting there were Jews in Constantinople and other cities who held professional positions. Still others forbade playing dice, consulting fortunetellers, or selling protective charms—an indication of some of the pursuits people carried on in their everyday lives. Some addressed issues of dress, others observances of festivals, and still others proper practices of religious fasting. For the Greek church in the East, the canons of 692 were considered a legitimate part of the Sixth Ecumenical Council, while in the West, Rome eventually accepted some without recognizing them all as having universal authority.

The iconoclast controversy

Even a successful ecumenical council could not forestall the next wave of trouble that lay just over Constantinople's horizon. In the first decades of the eighth century, Muslim armies were again marching toward the Christian capital. Help came in the form of a new emperor named Leo. Originally from Asia Minor near the Syrian border and Arab-controlled territory, Leo had risen through the ranks in the army to become a governor. At one point he had been successful in turning back a Muslim army through negotiations, some say due in part to the fact that he spoke fluent Arabic. In 717 he had become emperor just in time for a new major Arab assault on Constantinople. Through a combination of strategic defenses, negotiation, and a Bulgar army that arrived just in time to assist the Greeks, Leo turned back the Arabs once again. For several decades after that, under Leo and then his son, the Greeks were able to push back the Islamic forces to their east.

By the time Leo became emperor, new theological storm clouds were ready to break on the Greek churches. This new controversy concerned the devotional use of images or icons. Throughout the churches of the Greek East, icons had long been a prominent part of the devotional life of the people. Icons were venerated not because of any inherent material value, but rather for the spiritual truths that they made manifest. In the mind of many they served as a reminder of spiritual truths and thus a means of spiritual insight or grace. Icons also signified the spiritual completion or glorification (theosis) of other mortal beings alongside Christ. These artistic representations of Christ, other biblical personalities, and the saints and martyrs of Christian history were everywhere in the Greek East. People often used them in personal devotion to help focus their prayer or meditation. Some even treated the icons as if they were the persons they represented, having them present at baptisms, for instance, to stand in the place of godparents. An icon of the Virgin Mary had been carried through the streets of Constantinople during the Arab siege to rally the populace around her.

To some, however, including the emperor Leo, the veneration of icons appeared to be a practice that was forbidden by the Ten Commandments. They soon came to be known as *iconoclasts*, or "icon-breakers." Those who came from the East, such as Leo, knew well the Muslim prohibition of representational art in worship; Muslims consider it a form of idolatry. Some historians have noted that the cult of the emperor was growing as an alternative center of power in the Greek world during these years, and that this was also a cause for opposition to icons; those who opposed the religious images did not also oppose the emperor's depiction in art with the same fervor, it is pointed out. Among the most devoted to icons were monks and nuns, whose communities were exempt from paying imperial taxes. Members of monastic communities did not reproduce children to provide soldiers and workers for the empire, yet they engaged in criticism of imperial excesses. Added to all of this was the fact that for many common people icons did indeed function as objects of worship in and of themselves. One writer expressed concern that the people's devotion to the icons was supplanting their attention to the divine liturgy.

The storm clouds of the iconoclast controversy broke in 730 when Leo published an edict against the icons. The patriarch of Constantinople, who opposed the emperor on this, was removed and replaced by a candidate who shared the emperor's point of view. Riots broke out when soldiers tried to remove icons from public locations and people, notably groups of women in the city, tried to stop them. Leo's son, Constantine V, continued his father's policies with even greater fervor after he became emperor in 743. A council summoned in 753 condemned icons, and martyrdoms soon followed. Persecution fell primarily upon monks and nuns in the monastic communities, for they were the major supporters of icons. Imperial troops raided monastic houses, destroying the images and arresting resisters. So deep were their convictions that many members of the "pro-icon" party, now known as *iconodules,* or "icon-devotees," were willing to give their lives.

In 775 Constantine's son, another Leo, assumed the throne. Although he continued to hold iconoclastic views, the persecution began to be relaxed. Not least among the reasons for the moderation in policy was the influence of Leo's wife, Irene. An Athenian by birth, Empress Irene had come from a region that was well known for its devotion to the cause of the icons. She made no secret of her own iconodule position and worked openly to support its cause. When her husband died in 780, leaving only a son who was not yet of age, Irene took over the reins of government, acting as the young boy's regent. Quickly she set to work reversing the iconoclastic policy of her late husband and his predecessors. When her son, Constantine VI, finally came of age, Irene had herself formally declared co-emperor with him.

Mother and son proceeded in 787 to call a new ecumenical council to meet in Nicaea and formally settle the question of the icons. Like the previous gatherings that had come to be designated as ecumenical, the council in 787 was composed almost entirely of bishops from the eastern Mediterranean churches. A letter was sent to Pope Hadrian in Rome inviting him to attend, but like his predecessors he appointed representatives in his stead. The heads of the churches from Antioch, Alexandria, and Jerusalem who were still in communion with Constantinople attended as well. Patriarch Tarasius, whom Irene had appointed to office in Constantinople, guided the gathering. The council wasted no time in affirming the veneration of icons to be an orthodox practice. The bishops were careful in their deliberations to point out that veneration of the icons of saints was different in nature from worship, which is properly offered only to God. Moreover, such acts were not directed toward the images themselves but toward the reality of the person that transcended its image. The honor paid to the image passes on to what the image represents; it is the subject of the icon who is revered, not the icon in and of itself. Icons of Christ, the saints, and especially the Virgin Mary were then ordered to be placed in churches, on liturgical vessels, in private homes, and even along the roadsides.

The Seventh Ecumenical Council did not put an end to turmoil in the Roman East. Before long, Constantine VI and his mother Irene were locked in a power struggle. The immediate issue was Constantine's divorce and subsequent remarriage to his mistress, although questions of theological commitments also played a role. Irene moved against her son and soon proved able to muster greater political support. Outmaneuvering her son, she had him arrested and mutilated by having his eyes gouged out, wounds that soon led to his death. The year 797 found Irene in sole possession of the East Roman throne, the first woman to reign as empress without a husband or son along with her. Her rule lasted only five more years. In 802 a group of Constantinople's leading men finally were able to depose her. The following year Irene died in exile.

After the empress Irene's death, supporters of the iconoclast position attempted one last time to press their case. A new round of restrictions were imposed by imperial edict on icons in churches. In 815 an army of the Bulgars, a newly settled people from the north, reached Constantinople's walls in yet another wave of invasions. The parallel between the political misfortunes of the Christian empire of the Roman East and those of the nation of Israel in the Old Testament seemed all too obvious to the iconoclasts to be ignored. Didn't the Old Testament constantly warn that Israel's political decline was the consequence of practicing idolatry? Events seemed to be supporting their conviction that the veneration of images was idolatrous. That same year, on Palm Sunday in 815, thousands of monks paraded through the streets of Constantinople in support of veneration, openly carrying their icons in defiance of their opponents. Persecution again broke out, this time more severe than before. Monks and bishops alike were tortured for their support of iconodulism.

Finally, in 840, the persecution wound down. Many were simply exhausted by the controversy. Opposition to the icons had come primarily from the emperors and the military, yet for all the violence, the practice of venerating them was as popular among the people as ever. With the death of the last iconoclastic emperor, Theophilus, his wife, Empress Theodora, who was a supporter of the iconodules, ordered an end to the persecution. On the first Sunday of Lent in 843 the patriarch of Constantinople preached a sermon in Hagia Sophia proclaiming that icons were to be reinstated in the church. It is a date that the Orthodox still celebrate as the end to the controversy.

In the West, where the iconoclast controversy had never been entirely understood, the decisions of the Seventh Ecumenical Council were eventually recognized as orthodox, this despite their initial rejection by Charlemagne, who had access to them only through a poor Latin translation. The western churches had witnessed from time to time their own iconoclastic movements, but in general they had regarded both iconoclasm and iconodulism as extremes to be avoided. The pattern of christological thinking found historically in Leo's *Tome* from the fifth century continued to shape their responses to these questions. Western theologians sought to distinguish between the divine and material natures while affirming some mode of communication by which each shared its properties with the other. The result was a tendency to try to find a middle place between the two sides of the controversy in the Roman East. More important than the resolution of iconoclasm for the Latin West was the symbolism it eventually found in the Seventh Ecumenical Council of 787. Centuries later theologians could point to the unity of the Greek and Latin churches to which the council witnessed.

The theological gains from the iconoclast controversy were much more significant for churches in the East Roman world. In addition to securing the orthodoxy of spiritual practices involving icons, the Greek church found its reflection on the mystery of the incarnation being deepened. The most important theological name attached to this reflection is that of John of Damascus, the administrator who had left the caliph's government to become a monk outside of Jerusalem. Although he had died some two decades before the Seventh Ecumenical Council met, a significant portion of the council's theological thinking reflected John's earlier response to the iconoclasts' position. Living in Palestine under the Muslim caliphate as he did, John of Damascus was relatively free from the political reach of the Christian emperor in Constantinople. Had he lived in East Roman territory, it is likely that his *Defense of Holy Images* would never have seen the light of day outside his own monastic community. As it was, John's treatise has come down to us not only as an affirmation of the practice, but as one of the most important theological statements of the principles at stake in the controversy as well.

In his treatise John located the theological foundation for the practice of venerating icons in the event of the incarnation. The Christian doctrine of the incarnation proclaimed that material reality could be a vehicle for divine presence and reality. For John of Damascus, the meaning of the term *nature* extended to more than just the specific historical body or flesh of Jesus, although it certainly was not less than that. To speak of a union of two natures (as Chalcedon had done) was to speak of a union of two levels of reality, the material and the divine. Material images made of wood and paint could represent the divine in the same way that the liturgy did, John argued. Icons had the capacity to make the divine present in the same way as the eucharist did. Wood, paint, bread, wine—all were a part of the creation God had made, and all creation was capable of sacralization. Was not the cosmos itself an icon of the divine? Furthermore, according to the doctrine of the incarnation, our access to the divine life is only through the material nature that belongs to the order of creation. Thus icons in some form were essential for leading people into the divine presence. They provided visions of glorified humanity and thus were invitations to one's own spiritual perfection. Representations of the Christian past through icons provided access to the living tradition of Christian faith.

Paulicians

There was little persecution of iconoclasts in the churches following the final restoration of icons in the 840s. Unfortunately, persecution fell upon another group that was only marginally connected with the struggle. For nearly two centuries a Christian group called Paulicians had been gaining adherents, primarily in Armenia. The Paulicians can be described as radical adherents of the one-nature doctrine, who shared much with the Manichaean faith. In terms that harked back to the Marcionites and the Gnostics of the second century, they believed that the material world was fundamentally evil and that Christ therefore had a nature that was entirely spiritual. He had come into this world through Mary but had received nothing of a human nature from her.

In a similar manner the Paulicians rejected everything associated with the institutional or historical nature of the church regarding salvation: the sacraments, the hierarchy, icons, and even most of the Christian scriptures. Members where expected to lead righteous lives, and from what can be discerned they represented no military threat to the empire. Nevertheless, their growing numbers and rejection of the church made them targets of imperial persecution. Sporadic activities were directed against them at the beginning of the ninth century, until an imperial edict in 852 called for direct military action. The results were reportedly massacres and dispersion. Many Paulicians fled to Bulgaria as refugees, where they continued to spread their beliefs.

Monasticism in the Greek church

Support for the icons during the years of controversy, we have seen, was strongest in the monasteries in the East. So much was this so that "the victory of icon-veneration, therefore, was also a victory for monasticism," writes Alexander Schmemann.[13] The consequences of this victory for the East Roman world are important, for they point in the direction of the long-term victory of asceticism over imperialism as the more significant factor in extending Orthodox Christian faith and practice. Spirituality in the Greek East, as in the Latin West, was virtually synonymous with monastic asceticism and celibate community life.

[13] Alexander Schmemann, *The Historical Road of Eastern Orthodoxy*, trans. Lydia W. Kesich (Crestwood, N.Y.: St. Vladimir's Seminary Press, 1992), 212.

Throughout the Christian movement, as we have seen, monasticism had for centuries connected renunciation of worldly pleasures and wealth with the experience of salvation. Those who followed its path were free to be agents of ministry and spiritual direction. In both the East Syrian and Latin traditions, monks and nuns were often missionaries (even if unintentionally so). In the Byzantine world, on the other hand, monasticism was less characterized by its missionary agenda (most members of the Byzantine empire were baptized Christians from infancy). Monasteries in the West often served as educational and sometimes even administrative centers. In the East Roman world the imperial government supported education among the elite, while others who could afford it paid for private teachers. Hence among the Greek-speaking churches in the eighth and ninth centuries, the monastics were left to focus more on the devotional life and spiritual contemplation. Monastic teachers paid a great deal of attention to the stages of ever-increasing spiritual light through which one moved on the way toward the divine presence. Monks and nuns in the Greek world tended to emphasize even more than their western counterparts the austere dimensions of spiritual life. They placed a greater emphasis upon the spiritual gifts or *charismata* as well.

Monastic communities in the West depended on their endowments from the upper classes, and in many of the frontier regions depended for protection on Frankish troops. In the Byzantine East there was little such dependence upon state or nobility; hence monasteries were less identified with the nobility. Monasteries there had long been exempted by law from paying imperial taxes and experienced much more political autonomy. Most of the time, as we have seen, during the iconoclast controversy of the eighth and ninth centuries the relationship between the emperor's troops and monasteries was one of hostility and violence. Christian emperors had even ordered Christian soldiers to execute Christian monks. One unintended result was that the monks and nuns who had suffered came to be seen as symbols of political opposition and an alternative to imperial power in the churches.

The dominant organizing rule for Greek monastic communities was that of Basil from the fourth century. Basil, it will be recalled, had sought to integrate monastic communities into the life and ministry of the local churches. This integration had begun to come apart, however, after the sixth century. In the East Roman empire bishops felt an increasing degree of imperial control in the years after Justinian. Monastic communities, on the other hand, remained relatively free of imperial interference. Most monasteries functioned as independent communities. Many had little or no institutional connections with the local bishops in whose diocese they sat. Monastic communities were moving into more remote areas in the East during this period, seeking to be freer from the dangers of worldly associations as much as from the constant warfare that the East Roman society was experiencing.

As monastic communities grew in numbers and spiritual influence, they also increased in wealth in the Greek East. This in turn caused no small amount of difficulty for a spiritual tradition whose heritage was one of renunciation of worldly pleasures. The number of monks and nuns in Greek communities is estimated to have been around a hundred thousand in the eighth century, indicating the attraction the practice had for many throughout the society. Such numbers also suggest ample opportunities for abuses and corruption, which, as in the West, were no strangers to these eastern communities. Nevertheless, the spiritual contribution monasticism made overall to the Greek church and cultural life was an important one, comparable to the contribution monasticism made in other parts of the Christian movement.

The tenth century brought a renewal of monastic spirituality in the Greek East that many consider to be its highest achievement. The monastery on Mount Athos is often cited as being the center of this monastic renewal, which was also associated with a growing degree of hermitism or solitary monastic practice. St. Simeon, known as the New Theologian (949-1022), was the most influential ascetic teacher of the period. Simeon developed a fuller understanding of the spiritual process of deification (theosis) by which the Holy Spirit filled the contemplative believer with divine light. From him the spiritual practice known as *hesychia* (quietude of mind) is often traced, although it most likely had a longer history among the monks and nuns prior to the tenth century at Mount Athos. Simeon taught that sin had blinded humanity, keeping us from seeing the uncreated light of God. The gift of salvation had removed the condition that blinded us, but a higher degree of spiritual discipline was subsequently needed in order to enable one to see that divine light. Hesychasm embodied the practice of such discipline, stilling and focusing the mind in order to behold that inner light. Through Simeon's influence such practice became firmly established as a part of Eastern Orthodox spiritual life.

The spread of the Orthodox church to the Slavs and Bulgars

The East Roman empire absorbed the initial shock waves of Arabic expansion to its east and settled into a long period of political stalemate. The Arabs did not abandon their initial quest to take control of the entire Roman empire, but after the seventh century they found their westward advance slowed dramatically. Meanwhile, a new series of migrations were bringing new peoples into Constantinople's northern neighborhood. Two linguistic groups in particular arrived on Constantinople's political horizon during this period: the Slavs and the Bulgars.

The pattern of migration, invasion, and resettlement was a familiar one. Waves of Goths, Vandals, Suevi, Franks, Saxons, Lombards, and others had all followed it before. The reasons were likewise mostly the same: pressures from migrating tribes from further to the east sending people westward in search of new land; the attractions of material wealth and the level of cultural life it supported in the west; and the lure of the ancient heritage of Roman civilization. All played a part in bringing new clusters of people into the eastern European arena in the sixth and seventh centuries.

Chief among the new inhabitants were a people known as Slavs. Originally from the area near Kiev, by the sixth century they were resettling into the Danube River basin region, lands once inhabited by the Goths. They brought their traditional gods with them, and a common language that as yet had no written form. The Slavs first appeared in East Roman history during the time of Justinian, when they began invading the Roman provinces along the Danube. In the seventh century the Slavs were on the spiritual horizon of a number of itinerant monks in the West, although any form of evangelistic action in Slavic lands still lay beyond the pale of political possibility. The Slavs were on the other side of the political frontier of Frankish power, and the relationship between Franks and Slavs was not always peaceful. A high number of Slavs were taken hostage or prisoner of war in the West, enough to make their name synonymous with the status of forced servitude in the English language (the word *slave* is derived from *Slav*). It was from among these captives that the first Slavic converts to Christianity came.

Within their own land Slavic national political aspirations benefited greatly, if unintentionally, from a campaign Charlemagne conducted in 795 against the small Avar kingdom in central Europe. Up to that time the Avars had dominated the Slavs, preventing any real national structure from emerging. Charlemagne's destruction of the Avar kingdom left the Slavs free to develop such a structure. By the early decades of the ninth century, they had formed an independent kingdom known as Moravia (so named from the Morava River, which runs between modern Czech Republic and Slovakia). In 846 King Rastislav came to power in Moravia. It was during his reign that the Slavs formally joined the family of Christian peoples.

South and west of Moravia was another recently emergent independent kingdom in the ninth century, populated by a people known as Bulgars. The Bulgars were of a different ethnic background from the Slavs. They were of Turkish origin, coming originally from the land east of the Black Sea. In 681 a Byzantine emperor made formal what was already a political reality by recognizing an independent government of a Bulgarian *khan* (king) on the lands west of the Black Sea and south of the Danube. The new Bulgar kingdom included many Greek Christians, although there is no evidence of Christians being persecuted. The Bulgars worshiped their own national gods and had their own language, but soon after 681 they began using Greek for official documents. Through the eighth and early ninth centuries, the Bulgar kingdom grew in strength, extending its borders into areas where both Slavs and Greeks lived. At times various khans even threatened Constantinople itself, whose imperial heritage they had begun to emulate.

In 862 King Boris of the Bulgars proposed to King Louis an alliance with the eastern Franks. The khan even agreed to undergo conversion to Christianity as a condition of the alliance. It is more than coincidental that Rastislav, king of the Slavs, soon dispatched a diplomatic mission to Constantinople with a request for Christian teachers to be sent to Moravia. The emperor complied, sending two brothers named Cyril and Methodius in 863. Cyril's résumé included earlier stints as ambassador to the caliph in Baghdad and the king of the Khazars, east of the

Black Sea. Methodius was a monk living in the community at Mount Olympus. Their mission was to have a lasting impact upon Slavic Christianity.

Meanwhile, the emperor did not sit by and let the alliance with Boris and Louis go unaddressed. Military pressure was brought to bear on the Bulgars, and in 865 Boris was baptized according to the Greek tradition. Boris and his family underwent the rite at the hand of a bishop sent from Constantinople. The emperor and his family were named as godparents, and Boris even took the emperor's name, Michael, as his own Christian name. The ecumenical patriarch, Photius, sent a letter outlining the principal points of Christian belief. Once again Constantine the Great was invoked, and a new Christian king was offered an opportunity of being wrapped in the symbolic mantle of the memory of that first Christian emperor. One of Boris's sons, Symeon, was even sent to Constantinople to be raised among the Greeks.

At home Boris continued to make overtures toward the West. A letter was sent to Pope Nicholas I in 866 with a series of questions inquiring after matters such as the proper observance of Lent, or the permissibility of traditional spells and rituals. For a time an Italian bishop was even assigned to the Bulgar court. Despite these gestures, however, the Bulgar king maintained a close ecclesiastical relationship with Constantinople and the Greek church. In the third decade of the tenth century, when the Bulgar churches finally received an archbishop, it was one appointed by the ecumenical patriarch in Constantinople.

While Boris was still preparing for his baptism, Cyril and Methodius, the two brothers sent by the emperor to Moravia, were busy laying the foundation for a lasting Slavic church. One of their first tasks was to provide a body of Christian literature in the Slavic language. Before they could do so, however, they had to create an alphabet for writing the language. Historically Cyril has received the greater share of credit for the accomplishment, by tradition having received the letters through divine inspiration. The reality most likely is that the two brothers collaborated in creating the script, known as Glagolitic, which was then used to translate Greek works into the Slavic tongue. (Several generations later the Cyrillic script was developed to replace Cyril's original work; it is this later script that is the basis for the modern Slavic languages.) The Greek missionaries soon had produced a body of vernacular Christian literature. Included were Slavic translations of books for teaching Christian faith, the four gospels, the book of Psalms, and the liturgy. The project had the full support of the Greek church and Constantinople but quickly was opposed by the Frankish bishops across the border to the west.

Frankish opposition focused on the fact that the two brothers had translated the sacred liturgy of the church into a vernacular tongue. For the Franks, Latin was considered the proper language for liturgy. Only two other languages that they were aware of could be used for liturgical purposes—Greek and Hebrew. Of course, territorial concerns also played a role in the Frankish bishops' opposition. Constantinople regarded the mission effort to be a legitimate means of extending its imperial domain. The mission of Cyril and Methodius was planned with that in mind. The Greek brothers were serving in Slavic lands close to the eastern frontier of the Franks' territory. Byzantine and Frankish political interests could not help but clash in the mission to Moravia.

In 867 Pope Nicholas I intervened, inviting Cyril and Methodius to Rome for consultation. The two brothers accepted, arriving in the ancient city with gifts of relics and an entourage of native candidates for the priesthood whom they had trained. By the time they arrived, Nicholas I was dead, but his successor, Hadrian II, received them openly. After deliberating with them for a time, the new pope not only agreed with the aims of their work but invited the two brothers to celebrate the Slavic liturgy in the Church of St. Peter. The pope himself ordained the candidates Cyril and Methodius had prepared for the priesthood and agreed to send a bishop so they could continue the work of building a native clergy. Before they could return to Moravia, however, Cyril died in Rome in 869. Methodius returned alone in 870, having himself been ordained by the pope as a missionary bishop.

The eastern Frankish bishops were not about to accept this new situation in Moravia without a struggle. After the death of Rastislav, Methodius was soon arrested and held in a monastery in Germany. He remained there for over two years until yet another pope, John VIII, was able to intervene to secure his release. The die was now cast, however, and the Frankish bishops determined to intervene among the Slavs. Soon they were sending clergy and even bishops of their own into Moravian territory. In 885, when Methodius died, his last co-workers were expelled from the country. Several took refuge in the kingdom of the Bulgars, where they continued to develop a Slavic church and liturgy. The new alphabet that is now called Cyrillic was developed, and the work of translation continued. The vernacular work begun in Moravia found its continuing home among the Bulgars, while by the end of the ninth century the Moravian church itself was becoming increasingly Latinized. That process came to an abrupt end early in the tenth century when yet another migrating people, the Magyars, invaded and overran Moravia. They virtually wiped out Christianity in the kingdom, leaving it to another generation to begin the missionary work again.

The filioque controversy

Against the background of conflict between Byzantium's northern missions and eastern Frankish territorial interests another conflict was played out, more theological in nature, and involving the bishops of Constantinople and Rome directly. Since the time of Justinian, as we have seen, eastern Roman emperors had become increasingly more involved in theological disputes. The use of imperial edicts for regulating doctrinal life had become more prominent in the Roman East, as did imperial control of the office of the ecumenical patriarch. In the middle of the ninth century, emperor, ecumenical patriarch, and pope became embroiled in a political controversy that proved to have lasting theological consequences for churches throughout the world.

The controversy began in 858 when Emperor Michael III deposed the patriarch Ignatius, for reasons having mostly to do with internal politics. In his place the emperor appointed a brilliant theologian named Photius (whom we have already met in connection with the mission of Cyril and Methodius). But Ignatius refused to accept the deposition and appealed for help from Rome. Pope Nicholas I backed Ignatius and declared Photius to be in schism. Photius responded by accusing the Latin church of heresy on several grounds. Among other things, Photius pointed out, the western church allowed the eating of milk products during Lent, kept Saturdays as a fast day, and used unleavened wafers for the eucharist, all practices which differed from the East. Most important, the western church had introduced the filioque into the Nicene Creed, thereby unilaterally changing the ecumenical symbol of faith that had come down to the churches from Chalcedon in 451.

In 868 a new emperor restored Ignatius to office and removed Photius. Ten years later Ignatius died and Photius was again appointed to the patriarchal see, this time serving from 878 to 886. Between patriarchal terms Photius had penned a treatise against the Latin filioque doctrine. Entitled *The Mystagogy of the Holy Spirit*, it summarized succinctly what Photius perceived to be the heretical implications of the western position. The western church had introduced two causes into the Trinity, doing so at the expense of the personal monarchy of the one Father. Furthermore, it appeared to the patriarch to divide the Spirit into two by assigning two separate origins. While it was true that a number of western theologians, including Ambrose, Augustine, and Jerome, appeared to support the doctrine of the Spirit's procession from the Father and the Son, they were in error and stood in need of correction by the wider Christian tradition.

Photius's treatise received little theological attention at the time. Only in later centuries as the divide between the two churches widened even further would his points be made again in opposition to the western doctrine. The conflict in Constantinople between supporters of Ignatius and Photius continued for several more decades to divide the church there, and the schism involved members of the imperial household in their struggles for power. It is always difficult to determine how much of a role political considerations play in theological debates, or how much the personal ambitions of rulers and ecclesiastics alike play in these affairs. In the complexity of ninth- and tenth-century politics between Constantinople and Rome, unfortunately, the seeds of theological divisions were sown that would continue to grow long after their immediate political contexts were gone.

Eventually relations between Rome and Constantinople were restored, but relations remained tense. Differences concerning the form of bread that was to be used in the eucharist, the days on which fasting was to be observed, and the proper theological understanding of the Trinity continued to divide the two communions. The conflict to the north in which Greek and Frankish political interests collided was also a factor in the distance that had grown between these two claimants to the Roman past. In Constantinople the succession of emperors and empresses was stained by the marks of bloody intrigues. And always there were the Muslims, whose navies controlled much of the sea and whose armies were as regular in the field as the spring itself.

The conflict with Islamic military forces occupied a great deal of Constantinople's energy and attention during these centuries. In the course of time a slow evolution in East Roman attitudes toward the Islamic religion took place. Greek Christians originally exhibited a relative degree of ignorance toward Islamic teachings, as might well be expected. Misrepresentations arose in part from poor translations of the Qur'an, as well as from the hostility generated by clashing Arab and Greek armies. Eventually the religious dispute in the Greek church came to focus on the question of whether the God to whom Muhammad had prayed was the God known to Christians through their own scriptures and traditions. On this point the Greek church as a whole refused to declare the God of Muhammad anathema. Implicit in this stance was an acknowledgment that Muslims did indeed worship the one true God, even though, according to the Christians, Muhammad had distorted God's message. The position eventually proved to have implications for Orthodox understanding of Christian relations with other, non-Christian religions in general.

The tenth century offered moments of renewed political expansion for the Greek empire. A weakened Islamic state allowed the Byzantine emperor's army to take control of Armenia for a time. To the north the Russian peoples were in the process of becoming converted to the Eastern Orthodox faith, a process that shall occupy the next chapter in greater detail. In the eleventh century Constantinople's expansion was to be cut short. A new political power from further east, a Turkish dynasty known as the Seljuks, had seized control of the mechanisms of the Islamic state after having themselves been only recently converted to Islam. Under the Seljuk Turks a new series of Islamic advances against the East Roman empire were begun, severely weakening the Christian state and setting in motion a long process that ended with the fall of Constantinople to Muslim armies four hundred years later.

When it did ultimately come to an end, it was the legacy of Constantinople's theological tradition that proved to be the gift it gave to the rest of world Christianity. One need not accept all the canons and theological subtleties of the first seven ecumenical councils that gathered in Constantinople's vicinity to appreciate the coherent theological vision they represented. The unbroken continuity Orthodox churches of the world today continue to experience with the great teachers of the first centuries is a vivid testimony to the significance of that tradition. Despite centuries of conflict, intrigue, and violence, the splendor of Orthodox faith that Constantinople preserved remains for all Christians of the world to perceive.

29

Christian Expansion Northward

During the controversy surrounding the appointment of Photius in the ninth century, there were envoys in the city of Constantinople from among the Slavs and Bulgars. Increasingly these two kingdoms were to figure in the emperors' strategic designs, if for no other reason than they often posed a greater threat than did the Muslim armies to the east. In the midst of the controversy in 860 a new group of invaders from the north, known as Russians, suddenly arrived to raid the countryside in the vicinity of Constantinople. The counterpart to the Russians in the West were peoples the Franks called the Norse or Northerners. Groups of wandering warriors from the northern lands—Vikings—were soon raiding monasteries and towns along the North Atlantic seacoast from Scotland to Spain. They set up new kingdoms and eventually found their way into the Christian movement—just as the Slavs, the Bulgars, and others did before them. The expansion of the Christian religion among them is the subject of this chapter.

Scandinavia

On his way to Rome where he was to be crowned emperor in 800, Charlemagne had traveled first to the northern coast of his territories. The region had recently begun to be raided by seafaring warriors from further north who were known as Vikings. They were the dispossessed sons of Scandinavia, members of the warrior class for whom there was no longer suitable land or employment at home; thus they took to the open seas and to raiding to make a living. The wealth that they brought home, including material booty and slaves, enhanced their status among their own people and encouraged others from Scandinavia to set off on similar raids. Soon inhabitants of coastal areas from Scotland to the Mediterranean feared the sight of Viking ships on the horizon.

The Vikings learned early to attack monasteries along the coasts, mostly because that was where most local treasures could be found. Some of the northern monasteries, such as the famed center of Irish Christianity at Iona on the coast of Scotland, were more exposed than others and subject to repeated attacks. Eventually many were forced to move inland, and to more protected locations. Sometimes the raiders wreaked havoc on entire villages or towns, but they quickly learned that this was not the most productive way to secure wealth in the long run. Raiding eventually gave way to trading as the Vikings found more could be gained through peaceful exchange than through violence. Trade in turn paved the way for permanent settlement. Bands of Viking warriors came ashore in England, Scotland, Ireland, France, and even Spain in the ninth century. Bases for military raids soon became settlements, and then towns. In many places the Norsemen established new local kingdoms under their rule as they intermingled with local populations.

Viking settlers soon adopted the language, religion, and culture of their Christian neighbors. Burial sites show early evidence of mixed religious symbols, the cross of Jesus and the hammer of Thor both being represented among burial ornaments at one location, for instance. Christianization of the Norse settlers came gradually at first, and mostly without any organized missionary effort. One of the most important settlements was that of a Viking party along the Seine River in modern France from around the year 900. The West Frankish king at that time could do little to prevent the group of northern seamen from establishing their base on his land. Soon it grew to become an independent kingdom. The settlers did not keep their own language but adopted that of the Franks. Within half a century they had begun to take on the region's dominant Christian faith. The descendants of the original Viking settlers eventually increased their control over the entire province known as Normandy, in the process becoming known themselves as Normans. In time the Normans conquered England and much of southern Italy, becoming a world power in their own right and extending their military influence far beyond northwestern France.

In Scandinavia, Viking raiders unintentionally helped introduce Christianity into their homelands. Christians taken captive and brought back as slaves quickly introduced the practice of their faith there. By the time churches to the south sent missionary bishops to Scandinavia, there was already some familiarity among the inhabitants regarding Chritianity's teachings and practices. Christianity proved attractive to the northern inhabitants on several counts, not least among them its associations with the wealth that Vikings brought back in the form of plunder. Stories of what visitors among the Frankish Christian court had seen were also a major factor in this regard, winning a hearing for the Christian religion especially among the kings of Scandinavia. The eventual conversion of the peoples of Denmark, Sweden, Norway, and Iceland owed much to the attractions the Frankish civilization exercised over the Norse, just as the conversion of the Franks owed much to the attraction of Roman civilization before it.

Charlemagne's campaigns against the Saxons in the east had brought the Franks into proximity with a people known as Danes. Earlier Anglo-Saxon missionaries had looked beyond the frontiers of Frisia toward Denmark without much success. The breakthrough for the mission came early in the ninth century. A member of the nobility by the name of Harald Klak was offered refuge among the Franks during a struggle over the throne in his homeland. Harald returned to Denmark in 819 and with the help of the Franks assumed power. Approximately seven years later the Danish king returned to the court of the Franks to undergo Christian baptism. Charlemagne's son Louis stood as his godfather. The following year Harald was overthrown, but not before he had introduced to his land a young missionary monk from Germany by the name of Anskar (800-865). By 830 Anskar had established a base in the Swedish merchant town of Birka, near Lake Mälaren to the west of modern Stockholm. In time he was ordained bishop of Denmark and Sweden, the first to carry such an appointment. It would be another century before the Christian movement spread in any sizable way across Scandinavia, but Anskar would long be remembered as the first apostle of the North.

By the middle of the tenth century, the center of political power in western Europe was shifting toward the eastern Frankish territory. A new Saxon dynasty had come to power under King Henry, who was followed by Otto I. In Denmark, King Harald Bluetooth (950-986) became a Christian, converted by a miracle performed in his court by a priest named Poppo. The new Christian king ordered all of his subjects to convert as he had. Priests and bishops from Germany were invited to enter the Danish realm and begin the process of evangelization among the people. After his conversion Harald decided to have the remains of his parents, who had ruled Denmark before him, removed from their traditional royal burial mound and reburied under the church he had built in his capital. It was symbolic of the transition taking place among the northern peoples.

A similar process of conversion took place among royal households in Norway and Sweden in the tenth century. Around 946 a Norwegian prince named Haakon left England to return to Norway and assume the throne of a local kingdom. Haakon was already a Christian when he returned to his native land, having been raised in the royal household of an Anglo-Saxon king. Under his sponsorship Christianity was spread through portions of his kingdom. Toward the end of the century another Norwegian king, Olaf Tryggvason, returned from England, having been confirmed there in 994. He too set to work spreading Christianity among his people, with the assistance of missionaries and bishops from England.

A similar story of royal sponsorship of a Christian mission is attached to Eric the Victorious of Sweden late in the tenth century. Eric was later suspected of being less than total in his conversion to the Christian faith. It was his wife, who was from Poland, who was the more avid supporter of the new religion. Their son, Olaf of Sweden, is credited with having established a new bishopric with assistance from the German church. The best-known name in the history of the Christianization of Norway and Sweden is that of another Olaf—Olaf Haraldsson—who became a king in Norway in 1015. Like his predecessors in Norway, he too invited English bishops into his land to help spread the Christian faith. Killed in a civil skirmish over the throne in 1030, his body was buried in his capital city of Trondheim and his memory elevated to that of St. Olaf in Norwegian history.

Sweden and Norway were far from being unified nations in the tenth century. In many ways they resembled Anglo-Saxon England in the seventh century: a patchwork of small kingdoms whose boundaries were rather undefined and whose cohesion rested solely on the military might of a king. The few towns that existed were little more than fortified trading centers. The people were primarily farming or fishing folk. Yet the upper class of the Scandinavian nobility, mostly descended from the warriors of old, had become familiar with ways of life in other parts of Europe. They were also in the process of becoming acquainted with the Latin form of Christianity, which was the thread by which a larger civilization was being stitched together. Entry into the western community as a participant in the tenth century meant entry into Christendom, a word that first appeared in Anglo-Saxon England around this period.

Anglo-Saxon, Norwegian, Dane, Frank, Saxon, Burgundian, or Slav—these were traditional identities people had carried as they migrated from place to place. By the tenth century intertribal mixing had reached a point where boundaries were no longer clear, in either language or geography. The traditional local histories of national warrior heroes and gods were being superseded by a longer history, that of the Roman Christian past. What was emerging was a common civilization. While a host of local cultures, economies, vernacular tongues, and political institutions covered the land, it was held together by a fairly unified ecclesiastical structure, led by a class of educated leaders and clerics who spoke a common language (Latin) in their liturgy and theology. The single most important ecclesiastical authority within the quilt of western Christendom was the pope, yet even his authority did not extend across the landscape evenly or without interruption. Individual popes could prove to be corrupt or inept without diminishing the overall role of the Catholic church throughout the West. In the end the Latin tradition carried the faith forward in western Christendom.

Russia

The history of the Christian origins in ninth- and tenth-century Russia is similar to that of Scandinavia and eastern Europe. Several centuries earlier, migrating Slavs had settled north of the Black Sea along the rivers and in the forests. Religious practices among these early inhabitants were similar to those of their Germanic neighbors. A host of gods were worshiped through sacrifices and other rituals. Strong shamanistic elements were found among these eastern Slavs as well, religious traits shared with other northern peoples from Scandinavia to Siberia. Sixth-century Greek sources speak of these inhabitants as being a hardy people who led a semi-nomadic life. Early reports give their Slavic name as Rus.

A band of Viking warriors (called Varangians in Russian sources) settled in the region to the north of Kiev in the ninth century and established their rule over the local Slavic population. Although they continued to have regular contact with their kinspeople at home, these Vikings soon began to adopt much of the language and customs of those around them, a pattern similar to that in the West. One of the elements retained from their Scandinavian past was their style of ships, which were adapted to the rivers that crossed the landscape between the Black Sea and the Baltic.

It was in such boats that Russians in 860 sailed down the Dnieper River, across the Black Sea, and into Byzantine history. The first contact was in the form of raids on Constantinople, but soon the Russian princes came back to trade. They brought furs and slaves from the north to exchange for fabrics, wine, fruit, weapons, and even luxury items such as jewelry. Some historians have claimed that several of the Russians were baptized in the 870s in Constantinople, and Patriarch Ignatius is reported to have sent a bishop back with them at one point. There is no historical evidence, however, that any Russian who might have undergone the rite of initiation into the Christian faith had any intention yet of abandoning the traditional gods or sacrifices.

A Viking king known as Ryurik (d. 879) was the founder of what is often called the first Russian national dynasty. From his home in Novgorod, along the Luga River that empties into the Baltic Sea, he was able to extend his influence as far south as the trading center of Kiev. Upon Ryurik's death in 879, the kingdom passed to a kinsman named Oleg, who was also the protector of Ryurik's young son, Igor. One of the earliest narrative accounts of the history of the conversion of the Russian kings, the twelfth-century *Russian Primary Chronicle* (also known as the *Tale of Bygone Years*), tells how Oleg seized control of Kiev from comrades of Ryurik's and extended his rule over much of the country. He was soon raiding the Greek cities to his south, burning churches and leaving a path of destruction in his wake. Once again the emperor was forced to negotiate a peace treaty that required the Greeks to pay a sizable sum in order to avert further destruction. The encounter between Christian faith and Russian power is summarized succinctly in the pages of the *Russian Primary Chronicle*:

> Emperor Leo, with Alexander, made a pact with Oleg, agreeing to tribute and swearing oaths to each other. They themselves kissed the cross, while Oleg and his men took an oath according to the religion of Russians and swore by their weapons.[14]

For several years after that the Russians returned without causing destruction. One year they were given a tour of the city that included a visit to the famed church of Hagia Sophia. Their raids resumed after Oleg died and Ryurik's son Igor became king. That continued until 945, when the Russians once again concluded a treaty with the emperor and returned to trading instead of raiding. Igor's reign was cut short the following year when he was killed while attempting to collect tribute from a local village. His wife, Olga, assumed control of his army and stepped into the center of Russian history.

Olga immediately set about to revenge her husband's killing, proving herself in doing so to be a skilled military strategist. With her young son Svyatoslav, she soon gained control of the entire kingdom. Olga was also attracted to the glories of Constantinople, and in 957 went there to receive Christian baptism. The queen was some sixty years of age when she asked the emperor himself to undertake her instruction in the Christian faith and baptize her. She returned to her people the goddaughter of the emperor with the Christian name Helena. The event did not yet prove to be decisive for the conversion of the rest of the Russian people, but it foreshadowed the shape of Christianization that was to come.

---

[14] *The Russian Chronicles: A Thousand Years That Changed the World*, ed. Joseph F. Ryan (Godalming, England: Quadrillion Publishing Ltd., 1998), 32.

Svyatoslav eventually gained control of the kingdom from his mother. Although he allowed others in his kingdom to practice the Christian faith, he himself refused to be baptized for fear of losing the support of his *boyars*, or nobility. The evidence we have of the Christian movement among the Russian people from this period remains sketchy. There was already a Christian church in Kiev by the time Olga was baptized. Most likely they worshiped using the Slavic liturgy that had been first translated by Cyril and Methodius and that had later spread among the Bulgars. Priests could also have been sent from among the Bulgars, as well as from Constantinople. The story of Olga's death in 969 indicates the presence of priests in helping usher in the new faith. She "had ordered that no funeral feast was to be held over her. For she had a priest, and he buried and blessed Olga."[15]

In 972 Svyatoslav's life was cut short, like that of his father, by violence at the hands of a subjugated minority people. A struggle ensued among his three sons and the youngest, Vladimir, was forced to take refuge in Scandinavia. Vladimir returned in 980 and with the help of an assortment of Viking warriors wrested control of the Russian kingdom away from his eldest brother. One of the first acts he undertook was to send representatives to visit other countries to investigate their religious beliefs and practices. His interests were not confined to questions of religious truth alone but were also concerned with the political role religion might play in his realm. To this end the unifying and universalizing message of Christianity, especially as it was expressed in the imperial tradition of Constantinople, proved to be especially attractive.

In 988 Vladimir made his move toward Constantinople. Holding the Byzantine city of Cherson on the Black Sea as his base, he proposed a marriage to the emperor's sister, Anna. The Greeks informed the Russian king that such a marriage was impossible even if Anna consented, for Vladimir was not a Christian. It was the invitation the Russian king needed. He offered to undergo instruction and baptism, which was quickly arranged and accomplished, *The Russian Chronicles* say, in Cherson. Anna was then persuaded (and apparently it took some convincing on the part of her brother, the emperor) to be married to the Russian king. In quick succession the Russian royal family was joined to the Christian tradition and then to the imperial throne of Constantinople.

A large number of Vladimir's subjects, including the boyars and his army, soon followed him into the Dnieper River to undergo Christian initiation in baptism themselves. Back home in Kiev, this new apostle of Russia sponsored the building of several new churches and the appointment of bishops to serve them. Sacred vessels, works of art, vestments, and other items for worship were brought from the south to furnish the Russian sanctuaries. From Constantinople came artisans, teachers, and others. A school was founded for training a Russian Christian clergy. Monasticism came as well, in the form of monks and nuns who crossed into the country and founded new communities on Russian soil—the most famous being the Monastery of the Caves founded in the eleventh century near

---

[15] Ibid., 44.

Kiev. By the time of his death in 1015 (which came at the hands of the same subjugated people that had killed his father), Vladimir had laid the foundations for a strong Russian national Christian identity.

Russian Christianity was from its earliest days closely tied to the Greek tradition and Constantinople. Almost fifty years would pass before the first Russian bishop was ordained. Even after that the Russian church leadership looked to the ecumenical patriarch as the head of the church for several more centuries. The liturgy of the Russian church was in Slavic, as were its instructional books and hymnody. But for the most part these were translations of Greek texts. To the Greek emperor, the Russian king was in something of a client or subordinate relationship, even though it was not always a perspective that was shared in Kiev. Vladimir's conversion and marriage gave official Russian Christianity a starting point within the orbit of Constantinople and the Greek tradition. Nevertheless, the Russian king and the Russian churches continued to draw from the cultural and religious resources that lay beyond the boundaries of Byzantium, shaping a new Russian Christian identity in the process. It would soon grow to become a national Christian tradition that would outlast the Byzantine empire politically and become one of the dominant expressions of Eastern Orthodox tradition in the world Christian movement.

The conversion of Iceland and the end of the millennium

The year 1000 provides a convenient marker to assess the state of the Christian movement at the end of its first millennium. Through the course of its first thousand years, it had expanded into a number of new geographical and cultural locations. In doing so it had given birth to a variety of cultural expressions of Christian faith, doing so against various traditional religious backgrounds. In several places it had also suffered setbacks and decline. This was so especially in places where the spread of the Arab empire created political conditions that encouraged conversion to the Islamic faith—Persia, Mesopotamia, Syria, Palestine, Egypt, North Africa, and Spain.

In India, Christian communities had gained official acceptance in several regions, most notably along the southwestern coast. Although they were under the Persian church hierarchy, and conducted their worship in Syriac, they had become integrated into the dominant Indian culture as a distinct caste. As far as we can tell, their evangelizing activities were relatively modest. In central Asia and China the Christian movement traveled the trade routes in the persons of monks, priests, bishops, and merchants who eventually founded monasteries and churches inside the walls of the imperial capital of the T'ang dynasty. Christians journeyed over these routes with other missionary faiths of their age; Buddhists, Zoroastrians, and Manichaeans were often the companions of Christian monks and priests in central Asia and China. In the process the Christians borrowed much from these other missionary religions. The experiment in interreligious borrowing and the nascent contextual religious dialogue in the seventh through tenth centuries in east Asia prefigured important historical trends that reappeared in later periods in the East.

The Christian movement experienced its greatest growth in the lands north and west of its birthplace in the seventh through tenth centuries. Distinctive Latin and Greek traditions moved northward from the Mediterranean basin during these centuries, meeting along a border that can still be discerned between eastern and western Europe today. At the same time, among the Franks, Anglo-Saxons, Russians, and others, new national cultural forms of Christianity were emerging, closely related to the land upon which the people had settled. Traditional gods went into decline without ever being entirely eclipsed. Partly they were brought over into a new Christian synthesis, where they were drawn upon as elements in the new Christian civilizations that were emerging.

In the western areas of this region, the unifying intellectual force of the Latin language and the unifying spiritual authority of Rome worked together closely to provide the connecting threads stitching this new civilization together. It is here that we see for the first time something we can speak of politically and culturally as Europe. Likewise, it is here that we find the basis for what will eventually be termed western Christendom, an integrated, social-religious construct that joined many little kingdoms and cultures into one more or less unified civilization. In the eastern areas the city of Constantinople served as the unifying political force, and the theological heritage of the Greek church as the unifying spiritual factor. Constantinople was attractive to far more people than the emperor's armies could control. This is why Byzantium was more a glorious city than it was an effective empire during these centuries. The result was the emergence of separate national Christian churches under kings in the East, in communion with Constantinople without always being politically congruent with its interests.

By the tenth century the term *Christendom* had been invented in the Anglo-Saxon language to describe this new cultural expression of the Christian movement in the West. Most Christians in the tenth-century West would not have said they were members of an Anglo-Saxon or a Frankish church. Asked about where they belonged, most would have said that they lived in this particular dukedom, were subjects of that particular king, or owed their loyalty to another lord or lady. Asked about their religion, they would simply say they were baptized in the Catholic church, which was the religion of their people. Their ancestors had entered the Christian movement as tribal units, as whole communities. Once within it, they found themselves connected with others in a wider western experience. It was the church that connected the lands, the peoples, and the cultures together in a unified whole. Being Catholic thus meant being a part of a social-political complex, a new tribe of sorts, known as Christendom.

One of the best illustrations of this tribal form of Christianity in the West is a conversion narrative that provides us with the northern- and western-most extent of Christian mission in the first millennium as well. It is a story that literally locates us in the North Atlantic world: the story of the conversion of Iceland. The first inhabitants of Iceland were Norse settlers who arrived around the year 875. According to later Icelandic historians, the immigrants came seeking to escape the rising power of kings in Norway. The community they established on Iceland was ruled by a non-monarchical assembly that followed a traditional code of Nordic common law.

Christianity was already beginning to seep into Iceland from Scotland and Norway by the end of the ninth century. Jesus was introduced into a community that kept traditional company with Odin and Thor. Problems emerged where the accompanying law of Christianity at places was at odds with the common law of the Icelanders. External pressures were increased in 955 when the Norwegian king, Olaf Tryggvason, sent a missionary named Thangbrand from Trondheim to the island. The possibility of a hostile king whose power was increasing was certainly a threat that could not easily be dismissed. But according to the early-twelfth-century *Book of the Icelanders*, our earliest narrative source for the history of the island's conversion to Christianity, the real problem lay with the possible division of the community into competing faiths and laws.

The issue was debated before the entire Icelandic assembly, known as the *Althing*. At the conclusion of the debate, the president of the assembly (or Law Speaker), Thorgeir of Ljósvatn, was called upon to make a decision on behalf of the entire people. The title describes well his role within the community as the living embodiment of the traditional law by which the Icelandic people lived. He was also not himself a Christian, suggesting that the process was even weighted against the new religious view. Nevertheless, both sides agreed to abide by the decision that the Law Speaker would render. Thorgeir then withdrew to a full day and night of shamanistic-style divinization that he performed in a trance under his cloak. The following day he reemerged with his decision: Iceland was to become Christian. The year was 1000.

Recommended readings

The most important single text for understanding the emergence of Islam is the Qur'an, which can be found in several English language interpretations (Muslim belief holds that the Qur'an cannot be adequately translated from Arabic). A helpful secondary source for the various aspects of Islamic faith and practice is Cyril Glassé, *The Concise Encyclopedia of Islam* (San Francisco: Harper SanFrancisco, 1991). An English translation of Severus Ibn al-Mukaffa', *History of the Patriarchs of the Coptic Church of Alexandria II: Peter I to Benjamin I (661)*, trans. B. Evetts, can be found in *Patrologia Orientalis* 1 (1948).

For a discussion of events concerning Nubia, see William Y. Adams, *Nubia: Corridor to Africa* (Princeton, N.J.: Princeton University Press, 1977). On Ethiopia in the period during the sixth through ninth centuries, see E. A. W. Budge, trans., *The Life and Miracles of Takla Haymanot* (London: 1906); and Stevan Kaplan, *The Monastic Holy Man and the Christianization of Early Solomonic Ethiopia* (Stuttgart: Franz Steiner Verlag Wiesbaden GmbH, 1984).

A new wave of scholarship has looked at the religiously pluralistic environment of the Silk Road, which stretched from Iran through central Asia to China. Among the works commonly cited is Hans Joachim Klimkeit, ed. and trans.,

Gnosis on the Silk Road: Gnostic Texts from Central Asia (San Francisco: HarperSanFrancisco, 1993). Richard C. Foltz, *Religions of the Silk Road: Overland Trade and Cultural Exchange from Antiquity to the Fifteenth Century* (New York: St. Martin's Press, 1999), is a well-written account covering nearly a millennium of history. Alphonse Mingana, *The Early Spread of Christianity in Central Asia and the Far East: A New Document* (Manchester: University Press, 1925), remains one of the best sources for information regarding central Asia, while P. Yoshio Saeki, *The Nestorian Documents and Relics in China* (Tokyo: The Academy of Oriental Culture Tokyo Institute, 1937; reprinted 1951), remains the single best source for documents and interpretation of the Christian community in T'ang dynasty China.

The story of Christian expansion on the other side of the Eurasian continent is told by Richard Fletcher in *The Barbarian Conversion: From Paganism to Christianity* (New York: Henry Holt and Co., 1997). A more technical approach to the topic is provided by James C. Russell, *The Germanization of Early Medieval Christianity: A Sociohistorical Approach to Religious Transformation* (New York: Oxford University Press, 1994). For a fuller discussion of the role of early monastics in the Christianizing of Europe see Barbara Abou-el-Haj, *The Medieval Cult of Saints: Formations and Transformations* (Cambridge: Cambridge University Press, 1994). One might wish to read the work of the Venerable Bede, *Ecclesiastical History of the English People*, ed. Bertram Colgrave and R. A. B. Mynors (Oxford: Oxford University Press, 1969), or G. Ronald Murphy, S.J., trans., *The Heliand: The Saxon Savior* (with commentary) (New York: Oxford University Press, 1992), for a taste of the life of Christians during this period. Issues affecting women are explored with exceptional clarity by Suzanne Fonay Wemple, *Women in Frankish Society: Marriage and the Cloister, 500 to 900* (Philadelphia: University of Pennsylvania Press, 1991), while Peter Munz, *Life in the Age of Charlemagne* (London: Batsford; New York: Putnam, 1969), offers an overall introduction to Carolingian life. Judith Herran, *The Formation of Christendom* (Princeton, N.J.: Princeton University Press, 1987), examines the empire of the Franks in relation to Byzantium and the empire of the Arabs, those other two inheritors of Greco-Roman civilization.

Part VI

NEW POLITICAL HORIZONS

1000 to 1453

W estern Europe was divided into a bewildering political patchwork of feudal estates and kingdoms at the beginning of the second millennium. Its people spoke an array of languages and dialects. The majority lived in villages or towns that belonged to various feudal lords and barons whose energies were often consumed by local intrigues. The only force that provided cohesion for a common civilization was the Catholic religion. Classical Latin was no longer spoken as the day-to-day language in any region of the West, but it remained the common language of liturgy and scholarship alike. Thus it was the means by which the elite from one end of the continent to the other could interact. Latin was foremost identified as the language of the church, which was in turn the carrier of classical Roman culture. The situation thus favored the emergence of a strong institutional papacy under whom western civilization could be united. The impetus for this last development came from a series of church reformers who supported the authority of the papacy over against that of secular rulers in the churches. The institutional changes they set in motion in the eleventh century had a lasting impact on the history of the West.

At the same time, a new round of conflict emerged between the Latin West and the Greek East. The conflict boiled over in 1054 when a papal delegation in Constantinople excommunicated the ecumenical patriarch, who quickly responded in kind. The excommunications did not prevent the Byzantine emperor, who was facing hostile armies on several fronts at once, from turning to the West four decades later to request military assistance from the pope. Instead, Pope Urban II at a council in southern France in 1095 issued a call for a military campaign under the sign of the cross *(crusade)* against the Muslims in the Holy Land, opening up a new era in the history of world Christianity.

The pope's call for a crusade was precipitated in part by the changing political situation of the Muslim world. A new Muslim dynasty known as the Seljuk Turks had taken control of Palestine and cut off Christian pilgrimages to the Holy City of Jerusalem. Meanwhile, in Spain the army of a Christian king had captured the city of Toledo from Muslim forces, and the era of reconquest was under way. The time had come, the pope declared, to liberate the Christian lands of Palestine and Spain from the rule of Muslim unbelievers. The first round of crusades to the Holy Land succeeded in establishing a western presence in Palestine and Syria, but the effort was soon reversed. In Spain the process of Christian reconquest continued for many years, leaving in its wake a militarized history of violence that was not soon forgotten. After further attempts to take the Holy Land failed, a fourth crusade in 1204 diverted its attention to attack Constantinople. The fourth crusade established a Latin ruler on the imperial throne of that ancient Christian city, in what can only be described as a most ignominious chapter in the history of Greek and Latin Christian relations.

The powerful religious ideology that was unleashed within western civilization by the call for the crusades had repercussions within Europe as well. Before long, holy wars were being launched against unbelievers and heretics who lived in the West. They came at a time when Europe was undergoing rapid social changes. New cities were emerging north of the Alps, fueled by expanding trade and a revived monetary economy. The older feudal economy that was based directly on the land and operated in large measure through the simple exchange of goods and services was giving way to a new commercial economy that was more urban in character. The older political system of feudalism, in which relations were shaped by the exchange of oaths of fealty and sealed through symbolic exchanges of gifts, was likewise giving way to a new urban political reality in which associations of artisans and traders played a significant role.

One of the outcomes was the emergence of new religious groups, some of whom were judged to be heretical and met with violent responses from the church hierarchy. Others gained acceptance from church authorities, however, and were able through their practices of apostolic poverty and mendicancy to spread their message throughout the West and beyond. The new order of Franciscans and Dominicans in particular became important vehicles for mission and for expanding western Christendom beyond its geographical borders. New intellectual currents were also flowing in the West during these years, sparked by contacts with Islam and nurtured by the new urban centers. One notable result of this last development was a series of new universities in the West that supported the work of thinkers such as Thomas Aquinas.

In the Byzantine East, six decades of Latin rule further weakened Constantinople. The Greek empire survived in exile mainly in the kingdom of Nicaea where the ecumenical patriarch resided. Eventually the kingdom of Nicaea retook Constantinople and a Greek emperor was restored on the throne, but Byzantium never fully recovered from the debacle of the fourth crusade in 1204. One result was greater animosity between the churches East and West. Another was the development of independent national churches within the Byzantine communion.

Further to the east, churches outside the immediate war-zone of the Holy Land were less affected by the crusades. More important for their lives were the changes taking place in the political landscape of Asia. A new empire under a Mongol ruler named Temüjin emerged in the thirteenth century. Taking the name Genghis Khan ("Great Ruler"), he aspired to universal domination over all the earth, seeking to weld together all nations and religions under one universal law. His successors came as close to achieving that goal as any human dynasty on earth has ever done. At its height the Mongol empire extended from the Pacific Ocean to Europe, and encompassed most or all of China, Manchuria, Mongolia, central Asia, northern India, Persia, Mesopotamia, and Russia.

During the first century of their rule, the Mongols allowed a significant degree of religious pluralism under their universal *yasa* or divine law. A number of the wives and mothers of the first generations of Mongol rulers were Christians, including those of several great khans, while the male members of the Mongol ruling order practiced shamanism. Kublai Khan, the grandson of Genghis Khan and fifth in the succession of great khans, departed from this pattern to embrace Buddhism. One of the sons of the khan who ruled Russia reportedly became a Christian, but others among the Mongol rulers there were becoming Muslim. In Persia, Mongol rulers supported a limited degree of religious pluralism and several even flirted with the Christian faith before the successive khans became Muslim at the beginning of the fourteenth century. After that the Mongol dynasty in Persia restored Islam as the dominant faith of the regime, opening up a new period of Christian persecution.

In Africa a new Egyptian Islamic dynasty known as the Mamelukes (or Mamluks) stopped the advance of the Mongols and gained control over all of Palestine and Syria. The Mamelukes then turned their attention to the south to bring about the end of the Christian kingdom of Nubia. Ethiopia remained the lone Christian kingdom in Africa by the fourteenth century, and its churches found themselves facing new pressures from both within and without. A new emphasis upon its continuity with Judaism, often termed the Solomonic Revival helped revitalize both religious and cultural identity among Ethiopian churches during this period.

The fourteenth century thus found almost all of Asia under Mongol rule and much of northern Africa dominated by the Mamelukes of Egypt. Western Europe, which had become the most important material base for Christianity, continued to be fragmented politically by internal wars and intrigue. Even the institution of the papacy in Rome was affected by the political infighting that divided Europeans. The papacy itself was moved in 1309 to Avignon, near the border of southern France, where it remained until 1377. The following year competing claimants were elected pope within several months of each other and by the same body of cardinals, resulting in a period known as the Great Schism in the papacy that lasted another four decades. The end of the schism in 1417 coincided with an age of renewed conciliar activity in the West that reunited the papacy and then brought the pope and the ecumenical patriarch together at the Council of Florence in 1438-39 for one last attempt at reunion. The council sought to achieve unity entirely on theological terms set by the West, however, and met with considerable opposition among the churches of the Byzantine East. Its lasting contribution was to provide an indication of the potential power of the pope and the western church as actors on the world Christian stage.

The ascendancy of the western church came at time when the Christian movement in Asia was undergoing rapid decline. The first quarter of the fourteenth century witnessed the conversion to Islam of the Mongolian rulers of Persia and a new wave of violence against churches throughout Mesopotamia in particular. Even more severe was the terror against the churches unleashed by the armies of Timur the Great (or Timurlane) in the last decades of the century. In Asia Minor a new Turkish dynasty known as the Ottomans came to power in 1300 and began once again an inexorable assault upon the dwindling domains of the empire of Constantinople. By this time the Greek Christian tradition had taken root among the Russian peoples, and the city of Moscow had become its major center. The churches of Russia elected a new metropolitan of Moscow in 1448, the first not to be consecrated by the patriarch of Constantinople. Five years later, in 1453, the Ottoman Turks mounted their successful assault on the city of Constantinople, ending a thousand-year experiment in Christian empire.

30

Controversy and Crisis in Christendom

Late in November of 1095, Pope Urban II (d. 1099) presided over a synod at Clermont, France, composed mostly of French bishops. The pope had been traveling through northern Italy and France for most of the year, dealing with a host of administrative and disciplinary problems facing the churches. Earlier that year he had presided at a synod at Piacenza, Italy, where an embassy from the East Roman emperor had appealed for help against a new Muslim power in the East. At Clermont the council passed legislation forbidding clergy from taking oaths of fealty to lay rulers or from being symbolically invested in their church offices by secular nobles. The bishops also confirmed an earlier decision to excommunicate the reigning king of France on charges of adultery, a decision that made it difficult for Urban to travel through France. At the end of the council, the pope went outside the city to deliver a public address to a crowd that had come to meet him. Before that audience he made an announcement that was eventually to affect the world from England to Egypt: he called for a crusade to liberate the Holy Land from Muslim rulers.

The Council of Clermont took place at the intersection of several crises and changes that were taking place in Christendom in the eleventh century. Developments in the relation of the office of the papacy to western political life over the previous half-century figured prominently in the background, as did events involving relations to the churches of the Byzantine East. The armies of the Seljuk Turks, which had advanced precipitously against the Byzantine empire, had also taken Jerusalem, and for the first time in centuries prevented Christian pilgrims from entering that city. On the other hand, the army of a Christian king in Spain had retaken the city of Toledo from Muslim rulers, raising hopes that the rest of the Iberian peninsula could soon be reconquered by Christian forces. All of these matters were on the mind of the pope at Clermont that November.

The Investiture Controversy

Urban II stood in a line of reforming popes in the eleventh century who left an enduring mark not only on the papal office but on the entire character of western civilization. The struggle in which they were engaged came to be known as the

Investiture Controversy, so named because of the central importance attributed to the practice of lay rulers investing clerical leaders with their symbols of authority. Clergy in western Europe took oaths of fealty to the feudal lords on whose lands the churches sat, thereby making them vassals of secular rulers. Such rulers, who were members of the laity, exercised a great deal of control over the churches by means of their power to appoint their bishops and priests. Bishops and priests in turn often paid the secular rulers for these appointments, the practice known as simony. The abuse reached all the way up the hierarchy to the top of the church and the papal office itself, which had become a prize over which competing political parties vied.

At stake was the question of the relationship between temporal and spiritual authority in a Christian society. The Investiture Controversy, says Gerd Tellenbach, "was a struggle for right order in the world."[1] Should lay rulers have authority over bishops and clergy who serve within their domains, or did the spiritual power invested in priests, bishops and ultimately the pope put them above the authority of secular rulers who were members of the laity? The reforming popes of the eleventh century stood for the latter. In doing so they articulated a clearer sacramental understanding of the hierarchy of the church, through which spiritual power flowed into the world.

Church reform in the eleventh century thus started at the institutional top with the papacy. The tenth century had witnessed competing political factions in and around Rome dominating the process of selecting the one believed to be St. Peter's successor. The situation was not unique to Rome, of course, but reflected church-state relations throughout the West at the time. Royal domination of the church was widespread. The nobility often owned the churches and monasteries on their lands, and they assumed it was their prerogative to appoint bishops, priests, and abbots. Ecclesiastical appointments could be purchased and the clergy then entitled to the income produced by the land. The clergy were expected to take binding oaths of loyalty to their secular lords, thereby becoming their vassals. This did not necessarily seem to many to conflict with the spiritual nature of the clergy's office. Kings were perceived to rule by divine right and thus were regarded as fit to judge matters of church and state alike.

Although the winds of change were already beginning to blow, royal domination was still the order of the day when Emperor Henry III of Germany arranged to place a German bishop who was also his relative in the papal office in 1049. The candidate entered Rome to the applause of the people of the city (signaling their canonical election of him as pope) and assumed the name Leo IX (d. 1054).

One of Leo's most important acts was to begin to appoint non-Roman clerical leaders to the office of cardinal in the church in Rome. The term *cardinal* had originally designated leading members of the clergy in the city, and bishops of its surrounding towns. Cardinal priests, cardinal deacons, and cardinal bishops played an important role in early church councils in Rome and over time had become a body of local advisors to the pope. When Leo assumed the office in 1049, the

---

[1] Gerd Tellenbach, *Church, State and Christian Society at the Time of the Investiture Controversy*, trans. R. F. Bennett (Oxford: Basil Blackwell, 1948), 1.

cardinalate was composed entirely of members of the various ruling political factions of Rome. He began to appoint non-Romans to these positions, thereby breaking the various political parties' hold on the office while drawing to the city other like-minded reformers. One of them was a monk from Lorraine named Humbert (d. 1061) who was to play a significant role in events in Constantinople several years later. Another was a young man from Tuscany of Jewish descent named Hildebrand (c.1020-1085) whom Leo made an archdeacon and who was later elected Pope Gregory VII.

Leo died in 1054 and was followed by another German who like his predecessor was selected by the emperor, Henry III. Henry then died in 1056, leaving a young son as his heir. When the papacy became vacant again in 1058, the Roman nobility sought to regain control of the office by pushing through the election of their own candidate. Hildebrand and Humbert, along with their supporters, maneuvered to elect a bishop who shared their position, securing his recognition from enough of the population of Rome to allow him to assume the papal office as Nicholas II (d. 1061). The following year during Easter Nicholas held a synod in Rome. This synod passed a new canon forbidding any priest or bishop from being invested in the church by a member of the laity. Furthermore, the synod decreed, hereafter cardinal bishops would deliberate first in the selection of a pope, consulting with other cardinal priests and cardinal deacons of the church before seeking the assent of the people of Rome. To this day this is the method by which a new pope is elected in the Roman Catholic Church.

A dozen years and several popes after the death of Nicholas II, Hildebrand himself was elected to the papal office, taking the name Gregory VII. Meanwhile, the young son of Henry III had come of age and was sitting on the German throne as King Henry IV. During the first years of Gregory's pontificate, civil war in Germany forced Henry to concede to Gregory in ecclesiastical matters. In 1075, however, Henry appointed a new archbishop of Milan, a move that was sternly criticized by Gregory. Henry in turn called a council that rejected Gregory's authority. A month later Gregory held a council of his own in Rome that excommunicated the king and stated that the German nobility were thereby free from any fealty oaths they had made to him, an act that was unprecedented in western history. Before long, ranking members of the German nobility made it clear that they would regard the king's excommunication as valid and would seek to depose him.

Gregory was on his way to meet with members of the German nobility the following winter when Henry decided to take the bold step of seeking absolution. The German king traveled to northern Italy where the pope was staying late in January in a castle at Canossa. Barefooted and dressed as a penitent, Henry appeared for three days in the snow outside the pope's castle, asking forgiveness. Gregory had little choice in the end but to absolve him, thereby removing his excommunication.

Despite the encounter, civil war still broke out again in Germany. Three years after lifting the first excommunication Gregory issued a second one against Henry. This time the king was able to subdue his rivals and marched against Rome itself. Gregory turned to the Normans for help, a move that only worsened the situation in the city by bringing in another foreign military power. Henry secured the election of an alternative pope who in turn granted the king the title of emperor. Gregory, on the other hand, was forced into exile in southern Italy where he died in 1085 a defeated man. Nevertheless, his name came to stand for the position that asserted the sacramental authority of the church over the whole of life, and thus of the pope over princes and kings.

Gregory and his supporters regarded the whole of society as being under the spiritual authority of the church, and the church in turn under the unifying authority of the pope. The church was the body of Christ on earth, and the clergy were his representatives. The head of the church on earth was the pope, who was the successor of the prince of the apostles, whom Christ had appointed over it. Through the sacraments that priests performed, Christ's grace was made available on earth. This understanding of the place of the clergy within the world also stood behind the reformers' opposition to simony and nicolaitism. Both of these practices allowed temporal or worldly concerns to taint the spiritual office. Priests and bishops were to be married to their churches, the bride of Christ. Simony reduced this bride of Christ to being a prostitute, while nicolaitism made clerics to be adulterers.

It is important to note that the reformers' program was never fully realized in the West. Sometimes the pronouncements of popes and synods simply went unheeded, while other times popes found it expedient to compromise. The prohibition against clergy being vassals of lay rulers that was issued by the Council of Clermont in 1095, for instance, appears to have been mostly ignored. Nevertheless, despite the difficulties of implementing the Gregorian vision of reform, popes such as Urban II exercised considerably more power in both spiritual and political realms of western Christendom than had their predecessors in previous centuries. The change in political status of the popes is important for understanding how they came to exercise the authority they did over the crusading armies from the West for several centuries to come.

As for the Investiture Controversy, over time compromise solutions were worked out in various parts of western Christendom, such as that of the Concordat of Worms in 1122 in Germany. According to this agreement, bishops were henceforth to be chosen according to canonical rules of the church but would still take oaths of loyalty to temporal rulers. In no case were church leaders required to pay secular rulers for ecclesiastical offices. Emperors and kings were permitted to attend church elections but could not dictate their outcome. The compromise recognized that there were two centers of authority within a Christian society, a situation that was to continue to bring conflict in the West in successive centuries.

The schism of 1054 between Rome and Constantinople

By appointing persons from other parts of Europe to the rank of cardinal in Rome, Leo IX began to give concrete expression to a particular institutional understanding of the papal office. Since at least the second century, the bishop of

Rome had been recognized as the successor to St. Peter, whom Christ had appointed head of the church. Rome had contested the claim first advanced in the fourth century that the bishop of Constantinople was equal in authority, though not necessarily in spiritual dignity, with Rome. Western theologians claimed that Constantinople was a Second Rome, and hence its authority was not equal to that of the First Rome. Furthermore, they asserted, the pope had the unique right to intervene in affairs of all churches of the world; for while there were bishops who exercised legitimate ecclesiastical authority derived from the other apostles, only Peter's authority extended to all churches universally. To the pope as Peter's successor was entrusted the spiritual care and administrative oversight of all churches of the world.

Rome's claims to primacy within the universal church conflicted with the ecclesiological understanding of the ecumenical patriarch and other theologians in the East. A number of other differences had come to separate Latin and Greek churches over the centuries as well. Some of these involved questions of church discipline, such as the western practice of eating meat that had been killed by strangulation and fasting on Saturdays. Some involved differences in clerical practices. Eastern clergy beneath the rank of bishop were permitted to be married whereas in the West a rule of celibacy was imposed on all clergy. Some of the differences concerned the liturgy. The western churches omitted the "alleluia" during Lent and used unleavened bread in the eucharist, where in the East the "alleluia" was retained and only leavened bread was used in the eucharist. Added to all of these was the issue of the western use of the filioque in the Nicene Creed. Pope Benedict VIII had for the first time in 1014 permitted the filioque to be included in the creed that was chanted in worship in Rome, thereby giving papal blessing to what had been a longstanding practice among other churches in the West.

The eleventh century brought a new round of political conflict between western powers and the Byzantine empire that only made these theological tensions worse. Since the seventh century a large part of southern Italy had been under Constantinople's control. Early in the eleventh century, however, the Normans (those former Vikings who several generations before had settled in northwestern France) had begun invading southern Italy and Sicily. Like other western churches, the Normans practiced the Latin rites and began forcing the Greek-speaking churches in the regions they conquered to do the same. In Constantinople the ecumenical patriarch, Michael Cerularius, who was a harsh critic of what the Greeks regarded as western errors, responded by ordering the remaining Latin-rite churches in Constantinople to conform to Greek practices. Meanwhile Pope Leo IX, who feared the growing power of the Normans to his south, sought an alliance with the Byzantine governor in the region. The Normans responded by taking Leo captive. In April of 1054 Leo sent three envoys to Constantinople, led by Cardinal Humbert, to pursue negotiations.

Upon their arrival in Constantinople the representatives were received by the emperor. Cerularius on the other hand refused to meet with them. Humbert had brought a letter to the ecumenical patriarch protesting the changes forced upon the Latin churches there, which he did not deliver in person but circulated in the city. For several weeks the western envoys engaged in theological debate with various eastern theologians, still waiting to meet with the patriarch.

The content of the discussions between the two parties during this period covered a full range of issues that divided the Greek and Latin churches. One that was especially vexatious that summer for the Greeks was the Latin practice of using unleavened bread in the eucharist. The Latins, like Armenians, who also used unleavened bread in the sacrament, were accused of Judaizing tendencies in this regard. Greek theologians regarded the leaven in the eucharistic bread to be an important symbol of the fullness of Christ's humanity, an argument they had first developed against what they considered the monophysite doctrine of the Armenians. Humbert rejected the charges and defended the Latin practice as biblical. On the other hand, he castigated the patriarch for failing to acknowledge the primacy of Rome and charged the Greeks with an assortment of heresies that he believed they were guilty of harboring in the city.

The debates had failed to produce a change in either side's position, and the Latin delegation had still not met with the patriarch when Humbert decided on a drastic course of action. Acting in his capacity as papal envoy, the cardinal drew up a bull of excommunication against Patriarch Cerularius. On the morning of July 16, 1054, while members of the Greek clergy were preparing for the celebration of the eucharist in Hagia Sophia, the three representatives entered the church and laid the document on the altar before departing the city. The patriarch convened a synod and four days later excommunicated the papal legates, who by that time were well on their way back home to Italy.

Cardinal Humbert's excommunication of the patriarch Michael Cerularius, and the patriarch's excommunication of the envoys in return in 1054 are sometimes cited in textbooks as being the final break between Christendom's East and West. The event was more symbolic of the distance that had grown between the two communions, however, than it was a permanent stage of institutional separation or schism. Humbert acted in his capacity as papal envoy in drawing up the statement of excommunication. But Leo had already been dead for three months by the time the envoys entered Hagia Sophia that morning, and no successor had yet been elected. While it is not clear whether word of Leo's death had yet reached Constantinople by July, it is certain that no pope had a hand in drawing up the bull. Furthermore, Humbert's excommunication was directed only against Cerularius and his followers, not against the Greek church in general. It explicitly stated that it regarded the citizens of Constantinople to be both Christian and orthodox. Forty years later Urban II ignored the excommunication when he received representatives from the eastern emperor at the synod in Piacenza, Italy, which has already been mentioned above.

The reality is that the Latin and Greek traditions, represented respectively by pope and patriarch, had grown apart over the seven centuries since Nicaea. The accumulated weight of institutional, cultural, and theological differences had effectively severed the living communion of these two Christian families of churches. Far more decisive in the history of division between the two traditions was the sack of Constantinople by western crusaders in 1204, which will be looked at below. Events in Constantinople in 1054 certainly did not help matters between the churches, but neither did they permanently end the dialogue between them. However unsuccessful subsequent encounters proved to be, hope for eventual restoration of communion continued to live on both sides of the controversy.

Political crisis in the Byzantine empire

Cardinal Humbert's visit to Constantinople came at a time when Byzantium was on the eve of one of the greatest crises in its history. On the surface things looked relatively stable in the middle years of the century. Constantinople's armies had been able to expand into Syria, and Armenia had even been annexed. No Muslim army had been able to muster a credible threat against the empire for almost one hundred years, lulling many into a false state of security. The result was a significant decline in the Byzantine military. The success of the Normans against Constantinople's territories in southern Italy was one indication of the condition of the Byzantine forces. The success of Hungarian excursions from the north was another. Still, no one in Constantinople seems to have foreseen the military disaster that its forces were soon to suffer to the east.

The army that was to inflict a devastating defeat on the Greeks was under the command of a new Muslim Turkish dynasty that had swept across northern Iran. For several centuries the Abbasid rulers had been filling the ranks of their military with Turkish slaves. By the beginning of the eleventh century many of these Turks had risen to positions of power in the army and had begun to take control of sections of the Abbasid empire. In the 1030s and 1040s a Turkish general named Seljuk began to amass considerable power in northern Iran. Seljuk's grandson continued his drive, taking Baghdad in 1055 and reducing the caliph to a figurehead under a Seljuk sultan. Without a great deal of fanfare a new Islamic dynasty had emerged.

In 1064 an army of the Seljuks overran several major cities in Armenia and Georgia, including the Armenian city of Ani. A large number of Armenians went into exile, many to the district of Cilicia in the southeast corner of Asia Minor where the Byzantine government had already been resettling members of their nation. In Constantinople the Turkish invasion of Armenia was cause for alarm. A new emperor was chosen from the ranks of the military, Romanus IV Diogenes (d. 1072), who set about to put together a credible force that could go up against the Turks. The army that marched with him into Armenia in 1071 was largely composed of mercenaries, including Franks and Turks who soon proved to be unreliable. Near the Armenian town of Manzikert the entire Byzantine army went into battle against the Seljuk forces. A combination of poor strategy, desertions, and outright betrayal resulted in the Byzantine force being utterly destroyed. The entire eastern frontier of the empire was suddenly without a defense.

Within a decade the Turks had seized control of most of Asia Minor, leaving only the westernmost region in Greek hands. A new state was created known as the Sultanate of Rum. A sizable amount of the land that had long provided food, wealth, and human leaders for the East Roman empire was now under Muslim Turkish control. Had the Turks continued to press toward the west in the last years of the eleventh century, it is highly likely that they could have even taken Constantinople itself. But that was not their intent. Instead, their main objective lay to the south and the Egyptian dynasty of the Fatimids, to which they proceeded to turn their attention. Turkish forces took Jerusalem in 1077 and soon after began restricting access of Christian pilgrims to the city—an action that played a significant part in Urban II's decision to call for the crusade.

In Constantinople, Alexius Comnenus (d. 1118) assumed the throne in 1081. The empire was now facing military pressure along several fronts, east and west. A Norman invasion of the Adriatic coast in the early 1080s was repelled, but not before it inflicted great damage. Serbia was in civil war, and various new tribes who were settling into Constantinople's territories to the north were launching raids that reached right to the gates of the city. Seeking military assistance for the fight against the Turks in Anatolia, Alexius sent representatives to appeal to the pope at the Synod of Piacenza in March of 1095. In November of that year Urban II called for the crusade, which was not at all what Alexius had in mind.

31

Christendom on Crusade in the Twelfth and Thirteenth Centuries

The crusade that was launched at the end of the eleventh century was an unprecedented event in the history of the world Christian movement. Wars that were judged to be justified on Christian principles had long been waged by Christian kings and emperors. Since the days of Constantine, Christian princes had invoked God's blessing on their military ventures. Popes and bishops too had long been involved in the temporal affairs of the state and were not averse to the use of arms. But the idea of a crusade gave a new theological justification to armed force that made it possible for a war to occupy a place at the very heart of the church's understanding of its task on earth.

This justification can be found in part within the conceptual framework of the Gregorian reformers of the eleventh century. Leo IX, Humbert, Gregory VII, and Urban II did not separate the secular realm from the sacred in a Christian society. They conceived of that society instead as a single whole, united under the spiritual authority of the pope. Spiritual power flowed through the church from its hierarchy because Christ had bestowed it upon Peter and the apostles. Accordingly, war waged at the pope's bidding acquired a sacred meaning that significantly transcended immediate material and political ends. Although there is no denying that many of those who went on crusade did so for material interests such as the prospect of wealth or territory, the conviction of the sacred character of the project was so profound and general that the crusade cannot be seen merely as an occasion or excuse for earthly gain.

But why launch a military crusade against Muslims, and specifically against Palestine? The reason for this lay in the western Christian understanding of the world in the eleventh century, and of the place of the Holy Land in particular. Jerusalem was still considered to be the center of the world by western Christians. Maps were still drawn depicting western lands on the periphery of the Holy Land. Jerusalem was also the center of the history of world salvation. The Holy Land was sacred because Christ had lived and died there. He had consecrated its soil with his physical blood, making all of it literally a holy relic. The Turks' act of stopping pilgrimages had closed western access to something many considered to be of sacramental significance.

395

The call to crusade was supported by the weighty spiritual resources the popes commanded regarding penance. Most western theologians believed that according to Matthew 16:19, the pope had ultimate authority to grant forgiveness for actual sins committed by Christians on earth. Popes exercised this authority to declare that anyone who undertook the arduous journey of a crusade would be released from punishment by God in the afterlife for all sins that they had committed, a concept known as *indulgence*. Crusaders were granted such indulgences, making their journey an ultimate form of penance. There were other spiritual factors at work as well. Crusading was depicted as a means of taking up the cross and following Christ, making the crusaders the contemporary counterparts to the confessors and martyrs of the Christian past. Christians were called to take a vow of crusading that was similar to the one pilgrims took before going on a journey. Such a vow, once taken, brought spiritual benefits, although if left unfulfilled it brought the risk of excommunication from the church.

Along with these spiritual factors there were political reasons for the crusade in the western mind. Most western Christians did not consider the crusade to be an unprovoked act of military aggression so much as a campaign of liberation. The eastern lands that were the initial object of the crusaders were regions that had once been under Christian political rule. The goal of the crusade was to free them from Muslim control and restore them to Christian rulers. This ideology was also applied to Spain, allowing a unified political picture to be drawn for what were otherwise separate military struggles against Muslim political powers. French, German, and English knights were expected to go on crusade in Palestine, while Spanish and Portuguese knights were expected to crusade at home.

These spiritual and political reasons for crusading combined to create one of the most powerful and effective ideologies the Christian movement has ever seen. It is estimated that the number of knights who eventually made their way east numbered in the hundreds of thousands, a military operation unprecedented in Christian history at the time. The great majority did so at their own expense and without pay. Many sold properties and went into debt in order to finance their expedition. No doubt those who went hoped to be able to bring home plundered wealth from the cities they hoped to conquer. Some of the lesser nobles who went on crusades did so in hopes of attaining new lands to rule, but most of the soldiers who went expected to return home after a short time. Most crusaders considered themselves pilgrim warriors who were on a higher spiritual quest. The material benefits to be gained were largely secondary.

The first crusade to the Holy Land

The first waves of crusaders were mostly bands of peasants led by a smattering of knights. One such rabble army, a relatively small one, formed in Speyer before marching on to Worms, Mainz, and several other German cities. The targets of its assaults were the Jews whose communities had been quietly growing for some time in the northern cities. Those who refused to undergo immediate baptism were massacred. Jewish property was confiscated and Jewish grave-yards desecrated by these crusaders, making the first crusade against the Muslims a pogrom against the Jews as well.

Another such band gathered in France around a monk known as Peter the Hermit. Reports from the period indicate that as many as twenty thousand peasants might have taken part in his "people's crusade," which was headed toward Jerusalem. In 1096 Peter the Hermit and his peasant army marched across Germany and Hungary into East Roman territory. Large numbers perished on the way, victims of hunger and exposure or at the hands of local populations. After a brief stay outside Constantinople, the remaining members were ferried across to Asia Minor, where they marched on toward the Holy Land. These untrained peasants, armed mainly with household implements, were no match for the Muslim military forces composed of foot soldiers and calvary. Before winter the entire crusade was exterminated by Muslim armies in Asia Minor. Any survivors were sold into slavery.

The first outfitted military forces began to leave Europe late in the summer of 1096. Urban II had not only continued to preach the crusade in his public appearances but had sent letters to rulers throughout western kingdoms suggesting the late summer date for their launch. Members of various noble families responded by raising armies, securing financial support, and departing for the East. For several months Constantinople served as something of an unwilling gathering place for the crusaders. Alexius Comnenus, it will be recalled, had appealed to the West for military assistance to fight the Turks who had seized Asia Minor, but he had not envisioned anything along the lines of a crusade. The appearance of these crusaders outside the gates of his capital city was a cause for alarm.

Alexius had little choice, however, other than to enter into negotiations with the hordes that had descended on his territory. He extracted from the crusading Franks (as both Byzantines and Muslims alike tended to refer to the Latin warriors) oaths of loyalty to him as emperor. They were, after all, aiming to retake territories that from Constantinople's point of view rightly belonged to the East Roman empire. Their leaders having made their oaths, in 1097 the crusaders crossed over into Asia Minor (ferried by Alexius's ships) and proceeded to take Nicaea from Turkish forces before continuing on.

At the eastern end of Asia Minor, one of the nobles, Baldwin of Boulogne, who had brought his family with him, separated his troops from the main body of the crusaders and set off through Cilicia, which since 1064 had become populated almost entirely by Armenians. Baldwin succeed in gaining the support of a number of the local Armenian princes in the region, but his main destination was the city of Edessa. There he was able not only to take the city from Muslim control but to establish a new Latin kingdom, the first tangible military success of the crusades in the East.

The main body of the crusaders marched on to Antioch which fell to them in 1098 after a lengthy siege. Later that year they took Jerusalem as well. The crusaders massacred all the Muslim inhabitants they found in the city and burned the synagogue where Jerusalem's Jews had taken refuge, deeds that have gone down in history as examples of the terror Christians have been capable of inflicting in the name of their religion. An older brother of Baldwin, Godfrey of Bouillon, who was duke of Lotharingia, was elected king of Jerusalem but chose only to be called Guardian of the Holy Sepulchre. Upon Godfrey's death two years later, his brother Baldwin readily assumed the title king of Jerusalem.

The first wave of military success brought a sense of euphoria to many of the crusaders. Latin nobles now ruled the regions of Edessa, Antioch, and Jerusalem. Muslim armies had proved at first to be incapable of stopping the Franks. The crusaders meanwhile opened the doors for western immigration. New monasteries began to be built, housing monks who came to take up residence in Syria and Palestine. Latin liturgical rites were introduced into churches in the cities the crusaders controlled. Western bishops even began to be appointed in cities, in some cases preventing bishops who were there from ministering to their people. In Antioch the Orthodox patriarch was forced from the city and his title given to a Latin bishop.

One of the outcomes of the first crusades was the development of several militarized monastic orders. More than a century before, western monks had founded a hospital order to aid Christian pilgrims traveling to the Holy Land. Known as the Hospitaller Knights of St. John, their work quickly expanded in the twelfth century as the crusading enterprise grew. Another western order of monks known as the Templars had been founded in 1019 in Jerusalem near the ancient site of the Temple. Both the Hospitaller Knights of St. John and the Templars expanded their identity to become military orders after the start of the crusade, a move that was without precedent in the West. Traditionally pilgrims to the Holy Land or elsewhere had been known to carry weapons for self-defense but not for engaging in planned warfare. In the West bishops often had troops at their disposal and were expected to provide knights and infantry from their lands to support the liege lords to whom they had sworn fealty. But prior to the eleventh century, monks had been forbidden to carry arms. The new crusading orders changed that, merging monastic and military disciplines in their members.

Crusading soldiers, monks, and nuns were not the only westerners the crusades brought to the Holy Land. Many western knights brought their wives and other members of their families with them. Local Muslims, many for the first time, began seeing women without veils walking the streets of the city. The Muslim historian Imad ad-Din even reported an account of a Frankish woman who was fully armed and clothed in a knight's mail leading troops into battle. Artisans and merchants from the West began to appear as well in the cities under the crusaders' rule. Muslim historians reported the influx of prostitutes from among the lands of the Franks with particular concern.

The indigenous inhabitants of Palestine and Syria, Muslim and Christian alike, generally looked down on the westerners. Muslims considered many of the practices of Franks barbaric. Western medical practices were considerably behind those of the East at the time. Western bathing practices, if they existed at all, were considered uncouth, and western eating habits offensive. Both Muslims and Christians in the East regarded the cultural codes of chivalry that governed western social life as strange and inferior. However much the crusaders thought of themselves as liberators, the Christians and Muslims whose lands they were invading saw them as barbarian aggressors.

Beginnings of the reconquest in Spain

During the months before the Council of Clermont, the situation in Spain was very much on the mind of Urban II. Christian forces had captured Toledo a decade before. The first part of their military drive south had begun toward the Duero River valley in the tenth century. Meanwhile unified Muslim rule in Spain had collapsed and a host of independent Muslim kingdoms had emerged in its wake. The disarray had been a factor in allowing the army of Alfonso VI of León to capture the city of Toledo in the heart of al-Andalus in May of 1085, an event many use to date the beginning of the reconquest.

Alfonso caused the great mosque in the city to be converted into a cathedral but otherwise did not inflict great damage on the Islamic community. Muslims were not forced to convert, nor were there large-scale massacres or enslavement. Nevertheless, elsewhere in Spain Muslim leaders were alarmed, leading them to turn to North Africa for assistance. For some time a rigorous Islamic regime known as the Almoravids had been in power in the region that is modern Tunisia. The Almoravids followed a conservative interpretation of the Qur'an and led a

puritanical lifestyle. It was a far cry from the lifestyle of ruling-class Muslims in Spain. Most Spanish Muslim women did not wear a veil in public, and many Muslims drank wine. Muslim rulers in Spain collected taxes that were not sanctioned by the Qur'an. The Almoravids opposed all of these practices, and after entering Spain they turned quickly against the Spanish Muslim rulers who had invited them. Seizing control of the southern half of Spain, they stopped Alfonso's push to the south.

While the forces of Alfonso consolidated their hold over Toledo, other Spanish Christian armies were advancing from the northeast. Christian nobles such as Rodrigo Díaz de Bivar, better known as El Cid (d. 1099), gained romantic reputations for their exploits against the Almoravids.

The Giralda tower in Seville was built in the 12th century by Muslim rulers as a minaret but was later made the tower of the Christian cathedral. The bell tower was added in the 15th century. Photo used by permission of Interec (http://www.hispalis.net/turismo_y_cultura/monumentos).

From across the Pyrenees came French assistance, helping the kingdom of Aragón in particular. By the end of the eleventh century, continuous warfare had opened up on several fronts, resulting finally to the collapse of the Almoravids' rule. Parts of southern Spain remained under Muslim rule for several more centuries, until 1492, when the last Muslim foothold, the kingdom of Grenada in the extreme southern end of the Iberian peninsula, was defeated. But after the twelfth century, Muslims were in decline as a ruling force in Spain.

Among the Christians, five separate kingdoms had emerged in Iberia by 1200: León, Navarre, Castile, Aragón, and Portugal. Although there were language and cultural differences among them, these Iberian Christians nevertheless had much in common. The majority of peasants in the countryside had remained Christian during the time of Muslim rule. They still spoke a form of old Latin that had evolved by the twelfth century into what is now known as old Spanish. Even among the Mozarabs (Christians who had adopted Arabic culture and were largely found in the cities), the liturgy was still said in old Spanish and continued to reflect the distinctive heritage of Spanish Christianity before the Muslim period. Reconquest in the twelfth century began to introduce changes among these Christians. In some places the Roman liturgy was imposed upon churches for the first time (it will be recalled that the older Spanish church had been relatively independent of Rome prior to the year 700). Spanish monastic communities likewise began to feel the effect of influences from across the Pyrenees that had been relatively unknown for several centuries.

At the same time the Iberian crowns gained crucial concessions from Rome that were not generally granted other rulers in the West. Iberian kings were given authority over nominations for main ecclesiastical offices and demarcation of diocesan boundaries. The crowns were also granted control over the administration of church finances, a concession that went contrary to developments happening elsewhere in Europe during this period. These powers granted the Iberian crowns by Rome became the basis for a system of royal patronage that was transferred in the sixteenth century to the Americas.

These Iberian distinctions notwithstanding, the first years of the crusades (both in the Holy Land and in Iberia) succeeded in greatly increasing and extending papal authority throughout the West. The crusaders had responded to a call to arms issued by the pope. The vows that they took were oaths made to his cause. Anyone who took such a vow of crusade and did not fulfill it was excommunicated by Rome, a frightening prospect for a twelfth-century Christian to face. Papal indulgences greatly extended the pope's influence over personal spiritual life, for he was able to grant forgiveness through institutional means at great distances. In reconquered Christian Spain a new relationship with Rome was begun that continued for centuries to come.

Second crusade

The western crusaders had caught Muslim rulers in Syria and Palestine by surprise. At first their major problems involved their complex relationship with the Byzantine empire. The western military leaders had taken oaths of fealty to the eastern emperor Alexius Comnenus as they passed through Constantinople, partly in order to secure safe passage and partly because he was considered the nominal Christian ruler of the lands to which they were going. Once they reached Syria most of them ignored their oaths, leading Alexius to take military action. Greek forces were sent against Antioch and parts of Cilicia sporadically for several decades in the early part of the twelfth century, although without any lasting effect.

The Latin crusaders faced a more effective opponent in the person of 'Imad ad-Din Zengi (d. 1146), who was appointed governor of the Muslim city of Mosul in 1127. The following year he took Aleppo and began his march toward Edessa, clearing the East Syrian region of the Latin forces. By 1144 his forces were strong enough to mount an attack on the city of Edessa, which fell to him on Christmas Eve that year. Zengi died two years later, victim of an assassination. His son Nur ad-Din continued the effort to drive out the western armies and unify Syria under Muslim control. Through political maneuvering Nur ad-Din was able to gain control over the city of Damascus by 1154, uniting the region from Damascus to Edessa under one ruler. At this point the crusaders held Antioch on the seacoast and a few remaining cities in Palestine, including Jerusalem. In some places western defenders numbered only several hundred knights.

News of the fall of Edessa reached Pope Eugenius III who issued a new call to crusade in 1146. Eugenius was joined in the effort to promote a second crusade by an abbot from a new monastic order known as the Cistercians. The Cistercians had been founded in Cîteaux, France, in 1098; they sought to pursue a more rigorous Benedictine discipline. Bernard of Clairvaux (1090-1153) was among their early and most important leaders. Many consider him to have been one of the greatest preachers of Christian history, judging from reports of his sermons as well as from the response they elicited from his contemporaries. Bernard was an advocate of monastic reforms that promoted greater discipline among the communities, and he supported further efforts toward institutional reform of the papacy. His writings are known for their mystical devotion to Christ. Along with these other concerns, he took up the task of preaching the second crusade, doing so more effectively than any other church leader of his age. King Louis VII of France and Conrad III, emperor of Germany, were both inspired by Bernard's preaching to go on this second crusade to the Holy Land.

The first crusade, as we saw above, was primarily focused on the Holy Land. Those who were engaged in warfare against Muslims in Spain were also to be considered crusaders, however, and were granted access to the same spiritual rewards. The second crusade likewise included Iberia, but then added a new dimension. In 1147 German rulers from Saxony sought permission to launch a crusade not against Muslims but against a Slavic tribe known as the Wends who lived to the east of the Elbe River. The Wends were not Christians but rather worshiped traditional Slavic tribal deities. Decades before there had been the beginnings of Christian expansion in the area under the sponsorship of a Wendish king who had been educated in a German monastery, but that had ended in a popular uprising. Yet the Wends were feeling the effects of having German Christian neighbors. Both their temples and their religious practices showed Christian influences, and Wendish cities were beginning to expand their economic activity.

No doubt the Saxons' desire for land was a major factor in their aggression against the Wends, for already Saxon immigrants were making their way into the region. The pope decided to grant the Saxon request to recognize their excursion as a crusade and even appointed a bishop from the region to lead the campaign. The Saxons were soon joined by an army of Danes, and Wendish independence was brought to an end. The temples honoring their gods were destroyed, and new churches endowed in their stead. The Wends were forced to undergo baptism and enter Christendom as subjects of German and Danish kings. The concept of crusading had been extended significantly in the West.

While Saxons were laying plans for their crusade to the north, five separate French and German armies were en route to the Holy Land in 1147. Louis and Conrad commanded the two largest forces, which were once again joined by hosts of unarmed pilgrims. The Germans departed first, traveling overland to Constantinople where they planned to cross into Asia Minor and march on to Antioch. Although they were treated by the East Roman emperor with caution, all went relatively smoothly with their plans until they were in Asia Minor. There they were ambushed by a Turkish army and defeated. Forced to retreat, the Latin crusaders found little support among the local Greek Christian population and continued to be attacked by the Turks. Only a remnant of Conrad's army made it back to Nicaea, where it regrouped.

There they met Louis and the French crusaders, who were on their way toward Antioch. Conrad and his remaining troops joined the French and started off again across Asia Minor. Once again Turkish attacks greeted them while they were still in Byzantine territories, inflicting casualties. Short on supplies and hampered by poor planning, the crusaders finally made it to Antioch in the middle of 1148. They decided that their best option was to launch an attack against Damascus and the forces of Nur ad-Din, an attack that proved to be a disaster. The Christians were outmaneuvered and forced to withdraw, retreating without a fight. Both kings and their armies ended up going home demoralized before 1148 was over.

Nur ad-Din was able over the next two decades to consolidate his power over most of Syria. New mosques were built and new Muslim Sufi monasteries endowed in Syria, counteracting the spiritual influence of Christians in the region. Newly built churches and Christian monasteries were ordered destroyed, and the legal restrictions against Christians reimposed. At the same time Nur ad-Din was extending his reach to the south. By the time of his death in 1171 he had successfully taken control of Egypt. One of Nur ad-Din's officers, Salah ad-Din (Saladin), moved to consolidate power at that point. Salah ad-Din was a Kurd who had risen from the ranks of a military slave to become vizir of Egypt. Although he continued to pay nominal allegiance to the caliph in Baghdad, he was clearly the major Muslim political power in his day.

In 1187 Salah ad-Din launched an attack against the Christian stronghold in Galilee, destroying the western forces. Later that same year he took Jerusalem as well, putting an end to almost eighty-eight years of Christian rule. Among

Christians and Muslims Salah ad-Din gained a reputation during this battle for being a humane general; although hundreds of Christian prisoners of war were beheaded, the Muslim ruler allowed Christian noncombatants from the city to be ransomed at modest costs. Jerusalem itself was restored as a Muslim city.

By the time of Nur ad-Din and Salah ad-Din, a new meaning had emerged within Islam for the traditional concept of *jihad*, one that now roughly paralleled the western Christian concept of a crusade. In Arabic the word *jihad* meant "strife." In the Qur'an it was used to describe efforts to extend the *dar al Islam* ("house of Islam"). Although this could mean through warfare or political domination, *jihad* meant more generally convincing others of the truth of Islam and strife against evil practices. Now *jihad* began to be used almost exclusively with military connotations. The term came to mean "holy war" along the lines that the term *crusade* was used in the West.

Third crusade

News of the fall of Jerusalem reached the West late in 1187. Within several weeks a new pope, Gregory VIII, had issued an appeal for a third crusade. As with previous crusades the pope promised indulgences (relief in the afterlife from penalties for sins) to any who took what was called a vow of the cross, that is, a vow to go on crusade. Once such a vow was taken, of course, one had actually to go on crusade or face excommunication.

Among the military leaders who took the vow this time was the emperor Frederick Barbarossa of Germany. Frederick assembled one of the largest armies ever to go off to the East, departing in 1189. With hardly any incident he marched across Asia Minor and into Armenian territory. But then, on the eve of entering the Holy Land, Frederick decided to go for a swim in the Goeksu River. He drowned in its current, leaving his troops demoralized. While some continued on toward Antioch, many others went home.

The third crusade also drew King Richard of England, known as Richard the Lion-Hearted, and King Philip of France. Richard sailed by way of Portugal and Sicily to arrive at the city of Acre in 1191, where he joined forces with Philip. For the next year their armies fought Salah ad-Din's forces up and down the coast of Palestine until Richard finally reached a truce with the Muslim ruler in 1192. Jerusalem remained under Muslim rule, while the coastal region of Palestine was under Latin Christian rulers. Christian pilgrimages to the Holy City were resumed.

Fourth crusade

Enthusiasm for crusading was running high in western Europe in the last decade of the twelfth century. Following Richard's truce with Salah ad-Din, another German expedition was undertaken. This time the crusaders were able to make more gains in Palestine, fueling interest in a new effort to retake Jerusalem.

That was the intention at least behind Pope Innocent III's call in 1198 for yet another crusade. The call was issued, as with the other crusades, to all the western nobility. This time it was mainly the French nobles who responded, and the outcome was far from what the pope had intended.

Facing the problem of how to outfit their massive undertaking, the French crusaders turned to the city of Venice, whose merchants were equipped with both the necessary funds and ships. Venice had been gaining in economic strength for several centuries. An independent city ruled by a *doge,* its leaders had been able to negotiate a degree of independence that was still relatively unknown in the West. Along with those of its main economic competitor, Genoa, Venice's ships controlled much of the trade passing into Christian Europe. Venetians promised to provide the necessary ships and supplies the French crusaders needed in return for French payment.

Several other factors figured into the Venetian decision to support the fourth crusade; in the end those factors helped determine the outcome of the endeavor. For many years Venice had been challenging both Hungarian and Greek control of a number of port cities along the coast of Dalmatia on the eastern Adriatic. Venetian merchants were substantially increasing their business dealings along the coastal area of the Black Sea as well, which meant Venetian ships had to pass through the Bosporus Strait at Constantinople. Constantinople meanwhile was in turmoil. Several years previous the emperor Alexius III had blinded his brother Isaac and had imprisoned Isaac's son, also named Alexius, for their part in a palace coup. The younger Alexius had escaped, however, and had come to Venice seeking western help in claiming the throne. All these factors were background to what came next.

The crusaders who finally showed up in Venice in 1202 were far fewer than their leaders had projected, leaving the Venetian merchants who had undertaken preparations with a huge debt that had to be met (it will be remembered that crusaders financed their own way). The doge suggested a compromise: Venice's navy and the crusaders would go together, and whatever plunder they took would be shared equally after paying off the debt to the Venetian merchants. The first stop the new coalition made was at the city of Zadar along the coast of Dalmatia. Upon arriving, they were met by a delegation from Rome with a letter from Innocent III explicitly forbidding them on threat of excommunication to attack the Christian city (the king of Hungary who ruled it had himself taken a vow of crusade). The crusaders went ahead and sacked the city anyway, plundering its wealth. Bishops traveling with the army granted absolution to the crusaders and appealed to Rome to remove the excommunication, arguing that if the pope did not the crusade would fail.

Now Alexius entered the picture. Through western representatives he proposed that the crusaders restore him and his father to the imperial throne of Constantinople; in return he would pay a large sum of money and also bring the Greek church under Rome's authority. In 1203 the large Venetian fleet with French troops headed for Constantinople. In July of that year they launched their first assault against the ancient city, French troops by land and the Venetian navy by sea. Alexius III fled, Isaac and the younger Alexius were made co-emperors, and the crusaders withdrew to await their payment. Wintering outside the city, they soon discovered the new emperor could not afford to pay them. The people of Constantinople, meanwhile, moved against the young Alexius and overthrew him.

In April of 1204 the crusaders launched a second attack against the city. This time they breached the walls and sent emperor and patriarch fleeing. For three days the crusaders pillaged the city, carrying off treasures, relics, and anything else of value that they could lay their hands on. Even the famed bronze horses that had stood outside the Hippodrome were removed to Venice. A new western (Latin) emperor was installed, elected from among the leaders of the armies of the crusaders. Venice was granted a dominant say in the operations of the new government. A Latin patriarch was installed over the church, and the clergy of the city forced to begin following Latin liturgical practices in worship. Across the straits in Asia Minor a new Greek imperial government formed in exile and continued to rule the new kingdom of Nicaea for nearly six decades, until the Latin rule in Constantinople came to an end in 1261.

The story of the kingdom of Nicaea and the Greek church's exile from its own capital city will be continued in the next chapter. For now it is sufficient to note that the sack of Constantinople would go down in history as one of the most ignominious episodes of a long and inglorious period in East-West relations. Not only did the fourth crusade further harden the resentments Greek-speaking Christians felt toward the Latin West, but it further weakened the empire of Constantinople, many say fatally so. After the restoration of Greek imperial rule the city survived as the capital of Byzantium for another two centuries, but it never fully recovered.

Crusading continued for several more centuries after the fall of Constantinople in 1204. Urban II's original call back in 1095 had been made against the complex background of changing historical circumstances. Little could he have imagined how much crusading itself would further accelerate those changes. In the eleventh century the material economy of the West was undergoing profound changes, and new social-religious forces were beginning to take shape. Crusading armies brought about expanded contact with cities and peoples in the East, contacts that furthered both the economic and social changes that were taking place. The enthusiasm for crusading was eventually replaced by enthusiasm for wealth, as is evident in the driving motivations behind the Venetian-financed expedition known as the fourth crusade. In western Europe crusading unleashed new violence against those who were considered to be infidels, or Christendom's outsiders. Before long the same crusading spirituality was turned with a vengeance against groups in the West who were identified as heretics by the Catholic church. The holy fires of the crusades against heresy continued to burn in western Christendom's memory long after the physical fires were extinguished. Four hundred years after Urban II made his memorable public call, Europeans who were still on a crusade landed in the Caribbean to open up a new chapter in world history.

32

Spiritual Renewal in Western Christendom 1100-1300

The twelfth and thirteenth centuries were a time of rapid social change in the West. Although the majority of people still lived in villages or on farms under the rule of feudal lords, an urban revolution was well under way. Towns and cities were on the rise everywhere from Italy to Scandinavia. With them came a new urban class made up of artisans, cottage industrialists, and merchants. Advances in engineering enabled masons to build vaulted stone arches and ceilings, opening the door to a new age in urban architecture all across Europe. The result was a number of new church buildings and cathedrals rising on the western skylines. Cities meant increased economic activity and the contacts with other parts of the world that mercantile activities produced. The growing international awareness of those in cities and towns was helped along by the contacts that the crusades created with the East.

The church was the single most powerful institution in society, and the pope arguably the single most powerful individual in the West. Despite a growing class of urban merchants and artisans, land was still the primary source of wealth. As much as one-third of the arable land was in church hands, making bishops, abbots, and priests significant economic players as well. Guided by the Gregorian conception of a monarchical papacy, Rome's administrative bureaucracy (called the *curia*) expanded rapidly. A new corps of ecclesiastical lawyers and administrators emerged, and they ran church affairs with an efficiency that was the envy of kings. England and France had both begun to take on traits of unified kingdoms by the thirteenth century, but the rest of Europe remained divided into an array of kingdoms and dukedoms. Thus there was no political development of an imperial state corresponding to the unified church.

The vision of a unified, ordered Christian society was paramount for church leaders. Christendom was conceived to be an integrated, hierarchical whole. Any person or group who pursued religious life outside the established ecclesiastical structure was by definition a heretic, and liable to the punitive discipline of secular authorities that was called for by the church. Moral failings or personal indiscretions were not considered to be major religious problems within this framework. The church had a system of absolution in place that was capable of dealing with such matters on the part of clergy and laity alike. What was reprehensible was religious life pursued outside the orders and discipline of the church.

This is not the whole of the religious story of the age, however. One of the most remarkable phenomena in the period was the surge of new religious vitality that burst upon western Christendom in the twelfth and thirteenth centuries. Across the West a number of movements for spiritual renewal took shape, led by a host of popular preachers. Usually an individual reformer or preacher was at the center of a particular movement, although some evidenced communal patterns of leadership. Women played an important role in many of them, and in some cases even exercised leadership, this in contrast to the institutional exclusion of women from the clerical ranks of the hierarchy of the Catholic church. Some of these movements had a rustic flavor to them, but most were decidedly urban. Some stood within the traditions of monastic reform, while others sought to open new options for collective spirituality. Some were opposed to the doctrines of the church, but most considered themselves to be fully consonant with the Catholic faith.

Among the most common characteristics of these movements were the practice of popular preaching and a penitential message that called for conversion to a more spiritual life. The latter was often manifested by abandoning individual wealth. So much was this a part of the message that historians have often interpreted these new movements as expressions of popular resistance against the rising wealth of the age. The message of the twelfth and thirteenth century reformers focused on the life of Jesus and the apostles, who provided the model for a wandering life of discipleship. Voluntary poverty and itinerancy seemed to be inherently linked with moral and spiritual betterment.

The notion that the apostolic life entailed poverty, itinerancy, and mendicancy (or begging) posed a serious challenge to the growing wealth of the church. The fact that so many of these movements found their inspiration through a direct engagement with scriptures posed the additional threat of bypassing the institutional order of the church as the sole established means of salvation. The hierarchy's response to most of these groups was initially one of rejection. After 1200, however, a more nuanced approach was followed. Although the Fourth Lateran Council in 1215 forbade recognition of any new orders, the papacy eventually allowed several to be organized. Two orders that received official sanction in the thirteenth century, the Franciscans and Dominicans, soon became major forces for the church's mission forward throughout the world. Other individuals or groups were judged by the church's hierarchy to be heretical, however, and continued to be persecuted and suppressed.

One of the more noticeable aspects of this period is the number of individuals and groups that were regarded by the church as heretics. Some historians have argued that the increase in heresy in the West was an expression of social differentiation that accompanied growth in urban life or the result of increased contacts with people from other parts of the world. Certainly these factors played a role. But the increase in the appearance of heresy was also in a certain sense a creation of the growing judicial and administrative bureaucracy of the hierarchy of the church. For one thing, the expanded bureaucracy detected such deviations better, and in turn encouraged the clergy to be more diligent in reporting aberrant beliefs. We have more detailed accounts of what such heretics stood for in part because of the investigations undertaken by the church bureaucracy during this period. As the institutional bureaucracy of the church grew, resistance in the form of heretical movements grew as well, a second reason for the increase that is recorded. Finally, the machinery for detecting heresy was a key means by which the power of hierarchy was being enhanced, which meant that it was necessary to find heretics in order to fulfill its function of building up the church.

To the mendicant preachers and heretics of the age we need to add a third new type of person, the scholastic theologians who appeared in the twelfth and matured in the thirteenth century. Many have argued that this was the greatest age western theology has ever known. The roster of names who greet us from the pages of the era require volumes to do them justice. We will have to be content to look at their contributions in a separate chapter that follows this one.

Social developments in West

The most effective engine of social development in the twelfth century, then as today, was the material economy of production and trade. Two cities in northern Italy, Venice and Genoa, played a particularly important role in western economic life during this period. Venice had been one of the first western political entities to recognize the value of trading with the Muslim world as an alternative to warfare. Commercial relations had been opened in the tenth century, giving Venetian merchants important access to Muslim ports. Genoa soon followed, and by the eleventh century both cities had become independent republics. The crusades proved to be an economic windfall for them, as they were the major transporters of troops going by sea to the Holy Land. Their ships returned laden with goods, which in turn spurred further demand in the West for the items they carried. The sack of Constantinople in 1204 and the installation of a Latin king over the city enabled Venice especially to extend its naval reach throughout the Mediterranean, increasing both its wealth and political dominance.

While the Venetians were extending their trade relations with Muslims in the East, Spanish and Portuguese kings were continuing their drive to expel Muslims from Iberia in the West. The city of Córdoba fell in 1236 to Ferdinand (Fernando) III (d. 1252), a king who had earlier united the two Christian states of Castile and León. In 1248 the city of Seville fell to his forces as well. By the end of his career, "he had conquered more Islamic territory than any other Christian, expelled the Muslims from most of Andalusia and turned their remaining kings into his obedient vassals."[2] In Spain he became known as San Fernando, while in England he was said to have brought more honor to the church than even the pope and the crusaders in the Holy Land.

Most Muslim inhabitants of the conquered cities were forced to leave, taking with them whatever few possessions they could carry and abandoning the rest to

---

[2] Derek W. Lomax, *The Reconquest of Spain* (London: Longman, 1978), 156.

the new Christian rulers. New settlers were invited from other parts of Spain to occupy the cities. Mosques became churches, and Arabic was replaced as the official language of government. Church law forbade the forced baptism of Muslims, who like Jews were regarded as infidels, but that did not entirely prevent it from occurring. Muslims who were captured in warfare were also permitted by church law to be sold into slavery, a condition that baptism did not reverse. Registers from the Genoese markets indicate an active trade in Muslim slaves, both women and men, taken from the border region in Andalusia during the twelfth and thirteenth centuries.

In Córdoba, Christian conquest brought an end to several centuries of Jewish and Muslim intellectual work that had been carried on in the university there. This was the city in which the famed Jewish philosopher Moses ben Maimon (1135-1204), or Moses Maimonides as he was known in the West, had resided prior to immigrating in 1148 to Cairo. Maimonides is regarded by many as one of the greatest Jewish thinkers who ever lived. One of his best-known works, *Guide for the Perplexed,* written in Arabic in 1190, took up once again the task of reconciling biblical faith with the philosophy of Aristotle and Plato. Maimonides also wrote a commentary in Hebrew on the Mishnah, a collection of Jewish Oral Law that was passed down from the rabbinic period. In addition to being a philosopher and teacher of Jewish Law, he was a physician, mathematician, and scientist.

Córdoba was also the city where the Muslim philosopher Ibn Rushd (1126-98), better known in the West as Averroës, had been born and raised. Ibn Rushd combined a brilliant career in Islamic jurisprudence and medicine with philosophy. For a time he served as a judge in Seville before returning to Córdoba and was later appointed as physician to the Muslim governor of Spain. His most lasting contributions came in the form of his philosophical work on Aristotle. Ibn Rushd defended the ancient Greek thinker's theory that the creation had no beginning in time and that God was the "unmoved mover" of the universe. Attacked by other orthodox Muslim thinkers for these views and even forced into exile for a time, Ibn Rushd's work, like that of Moses ben Maimon, was to have a major impact on Christian thought in places such as the University of Paris in the following century.

While Muslims were struggling with their new situation under Christian rulers in Spain in the thirteenth century, Jews were immigrating into Christian cities in northern Europe in sizable numbers. Jewish communities had survived under Christian rule in the Mediterranean since the fourth century, although conditions had often been highly oppressive for them. A small number of Jews had immigrated north over the centuries, mostly working as merchants or sometimes artisans. Christian kings granted Jewish communities residence because of the manufacturing skills that Jews brought and for the wealth they could generate through their international commercial connections. Official church teaching considered the Jewish religion to be odious, however, and Jews as a people were said to be responsible for the crucifixion of Christ and thus guilty of deicide. Jews were often the target of efforts to convert them. Outbursts of violence against them were common and became more frequent as their numbers grew in northern

European cities. Local Christian populations resented their wealth, feared their unfamiliar customs, and continued to consider them guilty of the death of Jesus.

Jews in the West often were stereotyped as moneylenders. Jews, we have noted, were encouraged by various Christian rulers to move north because of their skills and commercial connections. Lending money was one such activity, but Jews were certainly not the only ones to do so. Christian kings were happy to enjoy the material economic benefits that were generated by such financial activities. When times were bad, on the other hand, Jews often bore the brunt of resentment. Resident aliens in the West, Jews lived outside the integrated religious-political complex of feudal Christendom and thus did not have access to political power that was grounded in the fealty oaths and landed estates. Nevertheless, they were able to gain enough space within urban areas to create communities they could sustain. Synagogues began to appear and Jewish schools opened up, as Jewish neighborhoods grew in the various locations.

Following the sack of Constantinople in 1204 several further efforts were made to ignite anew the passion for a crusade to the Holy Land, but none of them was successful. An effort to organize a popular crusade in 1212, the so-called children's crusade, resulted in bands of peasants taking to the roads. Without military training or sanction from the church, the movement soon collapsed. The closest anyone came to establishing a western presence in Palestine was when Frederick II of Germany in 1225 married Yolande, a woman who in Western eyes was queen of Jerusalem. Two years later Frederick, in the midst of fighting the papal army for control of southern Italy, took the crusaders' vow of the cross. He delayed going to Holy Land, however, leading the pope to excommunicate him. The situation was convenient for Rome because the pope could not easily wage a war against a crusader who was under a vow of the cross. Frederick, however, opened negotiations with the sultan of Egypt, and in return for the promise of his assistance against the Turks in Syria was given title to the city of Jerusalem. The king claimed to have fulfilled his vow and returned home a victor without having engaged in a battle in Palestine. The agreement soon collapsed, however, and Jerusalem remained firmly under Muslim political control.

Across Europe the spirit of crusading was finding new expression in regional conflicts. We have already seen how the reconquest in Spain was interpreted through the lens of a crusade. Similar developments brought crusading armies against the Wends in the north and against other Slavic peoples in the East. By the thirteenth century the language and the spiritual apparatus of crusading—holy violence—was turned against heretics within western society. The consequence was the unleashing of a reign of terror that lasted for centuries directed by the hierarchy of the church.

New religious currents

Among the most remarkable aspects of western religious life during this period was the large number of religious renewal movements that emerged. Those who were involved in them shared a number of common convictions, chief among these a commitment to voluntary poverty and to the pattern of apostolic ministry in the church. The first was partially in response to the increasing wealth of western society during the period, which many saw to be detrimental to a more spiritual life. The second was in part a response to the institutional patterns of leadership that emerged in the wake of the Gregorian reforms of the eleventh century. Like other renewal movements before them, those of the twelfth and thirteenth centuries looked first to the New Testament for their models of discipleship. There they found not only an early apostolic warrant for holding all things in common but for wandering evangelistic activities through the countryside. The injunction of Jesus to take nothing with them on their journey summed up the apostolic vocation, joining mendicancy and wandering in a vision of spiritual renewal.

The first major waves of this renewal emerged from a monastery organized in 1098 at Cîteaux, in France. The Cistercians, as the new order was known, committed themselves to what they considered to be a stricter version of St. Benedict's rule. They were also concerned with reviving aspects of spiritual devotion that had long been associated with the contemplative life. The greatest impetus for their movement came in the form of one of their early leaders, Bernard of Clairvaux, whose role in promoting the second crusade we have already noted. Partly because of Bernard's popularity, the Cistercians grew at an unprecedented rate, numbering over five hundred houses throughout Europe in the first one hundred years of their existence. As other monastic communities had done before them, the Cistercians often served as the seedbed for leadership for the wider western church.

Waldensians

Outside the Cistercian order a host of popular preachers toward the end of the twelfth century began to follow in the pattern of Bernard of Clairvaux, most doing so without license from any church authority. One such case involved a well-to-do merchant in Lyons named Waldo (also spelled Waldes or Valdez). Around the year 1175, Waldo underwent a conversion experience that led him to give away a sizable portion of his money to the poor. Leaving his home and family, he took up a life of itinerant public preaching. Soon he had gathered a small group of like-minded people around him who formed a band they called the Poor in Spirit. Waldo found a local scholar who provided them with a translation of the scriptures into French, which they made the centerpiece of their preaching. The bishop of Lyons responded to all of this religious activity by issuing a ban against the group, forbidding its members to meet because they were not a part of any recognized church order. Waldo and his followers refused to heed the ban, claiming that they had to obey God rather than the church. Within a short time they were ordered expelled from the city.

In 1179 several members of the band traveled to Rome to appeal their case to Pope Alexander III. Waldo and his circle appear to have had no intention of separating from the Catholic church at this point; they were only seeking formal recognition for their endeavors. The pope refused to grant them authority to preach apart from the permission of the local church, in effect returning the issue to the jurisdiction of the bishop of Lyons. Waldo and his group refused to cease their preaching, however. Five years later Alexander's successor included them along with several other groups in a general excommunication of heretics, placing them finally outside the institutional boundaries of the church completely. Still the Waldensians, as they were known, did not give up their activities. The group continued to grow, spreading into other cities.

The Waldensians were organized into small communities that gathered for prayer, Bible study, and worship. Within a few years of their official excommunication they began to elect their own bishops and priests whom Waldo himself ordained. Both men and women were allowed to preach, which was the most prominent aspect of their public witness and worship. The leadership of their community was not entirely egalitarian, however, since only men were allowed to perform the sacraments of baptism and communion. The Waldensians believed such sacraments were not valid if they were performed by unworthy ministers. Members of the group dressed in simple clothes that resembled those of monastics, but they did not require celibacy. They were strict pacifists and continued to embrace voluntary poverty as an important part of their identity. Central to their spiritual life was reading scripture, which they believed was to be followed in every detail.

By the middle of thirteenth century, the Waldensians had communities in France, Austria, and northern Italy. Because they were not located in only one region, efforts to stamp out the movement proved difficult. The fact that they were primarily located in remote cities of the Alps helped them in this regard as well. Friends of the movement within the Catholic church also extended protection in many places. Although from time to time there were incidents of violence against the Waldensians, persecution of them was primarily polemical in form, with attempts made from time to time to entice their members back into the Catholic fold. They nevertheless survived and can be found today as a separate church located primarily in northern Italy.

Cathars and the founding of the Inquisition

The Waldensians were among several groups that raised the alarms of heresy for the hierarchy in the last decades of the twelfth century. Another movement, one that proved to be of far more concern to the hierarchy of the church, was more widespread across southern France and northern Italy. These were the Cathars (from the Greek word *katharoi*, "pure ones") or the Albigenses (so- called because of their numerical strength around the city of Albi, in southern France). Most historians believe that the roots of the Cathar movement were in the East in a group from Bulgaria known as the Bogomils. The Bogomils appear in turn to have been related to an even earlier group known as the Paulicians, who came from Armenia. Both Bogomils and Paulicians shared tenets of Manichaean teachings and have even been suspected of having had their origins in ancient Gnostic teachings. Their attraction lay in the rigorous moral code that adherents were able to follow. Some historians believe that they even had a following in Constantinople.

Itinerant missionaries from among the Bogomils had made their way across northern Italy and into southern France by the thirteenth century. The first propagators of their doctrines in the West remain obscure, but most likely they followed the same itinerant pattern of preaching that the Waldensians and others used. According to the tenets of Cathar teaching, there were two principles at work in the universe, one manifested in the spiritual realm as Good, and the other at work in the material realm as Evil. Salvation was gained by freeing one's spiritual being from material creation. The Cathars followed Manichaeaism (and resembled Buddhism) in establishing two levels of believers: those who were the perfected, and those who were only believers. The perfected were the elite who maintained a strict ascetic regimen, including celibacy and abstinence from meat or dairy products, while believers were those who looked to the perfected as spiritual teachers and priests. A large number of the perfected were women.

Only the perfected were baptized in Cathar religious life. Baptism was practiced without water but with a laying on of hands that was believed to pass on the Holy Spirit, thereby purifying its recipient and enabling the person to enter eternal life. The New Testament was accepted as revelatory, and worship focused on the reading of the scriptures. The Cathars rejected the doctrine of the Trinity because it associated the divine with material creation, and they rejected the sacraments for the same reason. They held instead a simple meal of bread and water that resembled those of other ancient ascetic communities.

Listing the Cathars' beliefs and practices in this way risks making the movement appear more unified than it actually was. In southern France a large portion of its support came from members of the nobility. Many of them were committed believers, but others appear to have extended protection to the Cathars in an effort to diminish the influence of Catholic bishops and Rome in the region. In Italy the Cathars found a following among many in the cities who were attracted to its emphasis upon voluntary poverty and a deeper spiritual life, the same things that were attractive about other renewal movements in the twelfth and thirteenth centuries. The Cathars understood their leadership to be an alternative to the Catholic hierarchy, however, putting them on a more direct course of confrontation with the Catholic hierarchy. This, along with the fact that they were winning a following among the nobility, made them of much greater concern to the pope than other groups.

The use of force to suppress Cathar teachings remained sporadic and localized until the first decade of the thirteenth century. Then, in 1208, a papal representative was assassinated in Languedoc, in southern France. Pope Innocent III suspected the local nobility, who were Cathar sympathizers, especially Raymond of Toulouse, of being behind it. Unable to get the regional nobility to respond to his demands that the perpetrators be punished, the pope declared a crusade against the Cathars and published it throughout western Europe. Military forces from across the continent were invited to invade the region. All who took up arms against the heretical Cathars were promised spiritual indulgences (a decision that was later rescinded).

The response was terrifying. By summer armed crusaders from all over Europe, although mainly northern France and Spain, and from various social classes, came pouring in to Languedoc. The most prominent ranking noble in the region, Raymond of Toulouse, quickly confessed his sins and underwent public whipping. The crusading armies then turned their attention to the cities and towns throughout the countryside, unleashing a reign of terror against Cathars and Catholics alike. Estimates of the civilians who were massacred run into the tens of thousands.

The local nobility soon found their champion again in Raymond of Toulouse, who struggled to regain his territories. For two more decades various armies fought throughout the region without either side gaining substantial control. Finally, by 1229, a new generation of political leadership worked out an agreement that ended hostilities. The arrangement was ratified by a synod that met in Toulouse. The same synod set up an investigative body charged with the systematic uncovering of heretical beliefs among the people in the region. Various means were placed at the disposal of the church authorities, who were now empowered to carry out the program of inquisition.

The church had long been able to call upon governing rulers to punish those whom ecclesiastical courts judged to be heretics. The powers of investigation and judgment were now vested in a central ecclesiastical office or bureau known as the Inquisition. This was in effect a special court system, complete with investigators, examiners, security forces, and of course the inquisitors or judges. Trials were usually not open to the public, and witnesses were often kept secret. Various methods, including torture, were used by church authorities to ferret out heresy among the people, while trials by ordeal were often used to determine innocence or guilt. Those who confessed to heresy and denounced their unbelief could receive forgiveness and be reconciled through a variety of means. Those who were found guilty and refused to renounce what the church deemed to be heretical were turned over to secular authorities to be punished. The most dramatic form of execution the authorities exercised was public burning at the stake, a fate that many met in western Christendom.

Dominic and the Order of Preachers

Crusading and inquisition were not the only ways the church was able to respond to the real and imagined threats of heresy. The alternative was disputation and preaching, methods that reflected more of the spirituality of new movements the church was seeking to counter. In the first decade of the thirteenth century, Bishop Diego of Osma from Spain was traveling through southern France accompanied by a member of the cathedral clergy named Dominic Guzmán (1170-1221). Originally from the country of Castile in Spain, Dominic had finished his studies and was serving under Diego. In southern France the two men encountered a number of Waldensians and Cathars, whom they eagerly engaged in public conversations or disputation. His experience led Dominic to realize that the most effective way to reach such heretics for the church was not just through preaching but by demonstrating a life of purity that surpassed even that of the perfected among the Cathars.

Following Diego's death in 1206, Dominic continued the work in southern France. He adopted the lifestyle of voluntary poverty and itinerancy that was attractive to those in the other movements and began to gather followers of his own. A visit to the curia in Rome failed to win him official sanction for a new order, but neither was Dominic told to cease his efforts. By 1215 he had begun to organize groups of his associates or followers into bands of preachers not unlike those of the Waldensians. The difference was that Dominic lived a generation after the condemnation of Waldo of Lyons and his community of the Poor in Spirit. A different pope, Innocent III, showed more appreciation for the contribution such a band of preachers could make to the church.

The Fourth Lateran Council gathered in Rome in 1215 to deal with a number of issues, including the new movements that were blossoming across the landscape. One of the decisions the council made was to forbid recognition of any new orders. The move is often represented as an attempt by the hierarchy to clamp down on what it perceived to be a dangerous explosion of potentially heretical impulses that were taking shape within these movements of spiritual renewal. Dominic himself visited Rome to make his case before the council, and although his request for recognition of a new order was rejected, he was permitted to continue his endeavors under the Rule of Augustine.

For several more years Dominic continued his work, organizing new houses of men and women who lived by the Rule of Augustine but whose concerns were primarily for public preaching. The Order of Preachers, as his followers were known, was organized under the authority of a single overall director. Members of various monasteries and convents were expected to follow a mendicant life, begging for their daily food as they wandered the countryside preaching in public places. One of the convents associated with his movement was at Pouilly. Its residents were mainly women who had converted from the Cathars and had taken on the task of educating girls. Dominic himself stayed at the convent in Pouilly when traveling through the region.

By the time of his death in 1221, Dominic's new order had been recognized by the pope. Since the Dominicans, as they were known, followed the Rule of Augustine, they did not violate the Fourth Lateran Council's ban on new orders. So successful was the Order of Preachers in bringing heretics back into the fold of the church that after 1229 the pope turned over to them the newly formed office of the Inquisition. Dominicans were soon heavily involved in the apparatus of the Inquisition, an unfortunate identification since not all members of the Order of Preachers participated in it. Dominic himself never endorsed the violence that had been unleashed in his lifetime against the Cathars, and he most likely would have refused to take part in the violence of the Inquisition. His own life represented an effort to give expression to the reforming impulses of his age through preaching, bringing those who were searching for a more vital spiritual life back into the communion of the church.

Francis, Clare, and the Minor Brothers and Sisters

The Fourth Lateran Council in 1215 considered the request of another popular preacher who was seeking recognition for his new order: Francis of Assisi (c.1182-1226), a spiritual reformer who was to become one of the most important figures in western church history. Born into a wealthy family whose money came from the textile industry, he entered the militia as a young man and took part in a local war with another city. After being captured and imprisoned for a brief time, he left the military. Sometime around the year 1208 Francis experienced what is usually described as a conversion to a more spiritual way of life. Much to the displeasure of his family, he began to give away the wealth they had accumulated and took up the life of a mendicant wandering preacher. Soon a group of followers joined him, and they formed a small community with a simple rule drawn up by Francis himself. Two years later Francis and a group of his followers traveled to Rome to present their case before Pope Innocent III. The pope received them and decided to permit them to continue their work as penitential preachers without granting their request for formal approval as an order.

At this point it was important that Francis and his group, who were soon being called Friars Minor (Minor Brothers), had the support of the bishop of Assisi who granted them a license to preach. Preaching for Francis was not simply a local affair, however, for in 1212 he set off for Syria as a missionary, intending to preach to the Muslims. Prevented by misfortune from completing the trip, he attempted a year or so later to go through Spain to North Africa, failing again to complete the trip. Back in Italy in 1215, he continued to lobby to secure formal recognition of his work as a new order at the Fourth Lateran Council, but like Dominic found the pope quite cautious about extending his authorization. In 1219 Francis undertook another trip to the East, and this time he preached before the Sultan of Egypt (the Sultan did not convert). In 1223 Pope Honorius III finally granted formal recognition to the Friars Minor as an order. The rule Francis had written, which was mainly a collection of scriptural sayings, was judged to be too difficult for members to follow. A modified rule was adopted instead, and by the time of Francis's death in 1226 the order was on its way to becoming a major spiritual force within western society.

Francis left a rich if small body of writings as part of his legacy. Most of his writings were songs and prayers that gave expression to his spiritual insights. The Rule of Francis was one of voluntary poverty, but it was rooted in the richness of God's gift of the incarnation. The image of the crucified Christ and the mystery of the cross occupied him in particular in his contemplation and spiritual writing. In 1224 Francis went even further in his meditation on these themes; according to the traditions of his life that year he miraculously received the stigmata of Christ in his flesh. Francis's hands, feet, and side are reported to have actually begun to bleed, so thorough was his identification with the crucified One. It is important to note in this regard that it was the humility of Jesus and not just a judicial understanding of his sacrificial death on the cross that Francis celebrated in his work. The mystery of the incarnation for him began with the lowly birth of Jesus. One of the more memorable stories associated with Francis is the tradition that recalls one Christmas day when he set up a crib scene to dramatize the birth of Christ for his followers, a practice that continues to be one of Christendom's most enduring cultural symbols of the season.

Along with emphasis upon the mystery and humility of the incarnation, the works of Francis of Assisi reflect an elevated sense of the presence and power of the Holy Spirit. The work of the Spirit for Francis was not confined to the institutional church but could be seen in and through all of life. Francis found in creation an intense sense of holiness and communion. One of his most celebrated hymns, the "Canticle of Brother Sun," gives expression to his spirituality, which celebrates God through all creation:

> Praised be You, my Lord, with all your creatures,
> especially Sir Brother Sun,
> Who is the day and through whom You give us
>   light. . . .
> Praised be You, my Lord, through Sister Moon and the
>   stars,
> in heaven You formed them clear and precious and
>   beautiful.[3]

Dominic helped organize several houses for women, but Francis had virtually no involvement in his lifetime with women followers. The one major exception was a woman who was also from his native Assisi and in many ways his spiritual and organizational equal. Clare of Assisi (c. 1193-1253) also came from a wealthy family in the city. As a young girl, the legends of her life recall, she was inclined toward a life of spiritual devotion. Promised in marriage to one of the men in the city, she instead opted to join Francis's movement and follow a life of virginity. Francis helped make arrangements for a house in San Damiano, and soon Clare had formed the Poor Ladies of Assisi.

Clare wrote the rule for the community, an original copy of which was discovered in 1893 in her habit, which had been kept for centuries in the convent. Even more than Francis, she emphasized the manner in which Christ, who was rich in things eternal, had made himself poor in order to bring the riches of eternal life to humankind. Voluntary poverty was thus the narrow pathway of salvation found in solidarity with Christ and the most perfect way to follow him. Free from the distractions of wealth in this world, Clare believed that life was open to the richness of things eternal. Her writings, which in addition to the rule include a handful of letters, give evidence of an awareness of the special insights that she and other women had into the mystery of the incarnation. One of these letters was

---

[3] *Francis and Clare: The Complete Works*, trans. Regis J. Armstrong, O.F.M. Cap., and Ignatius C. Brady, O.F.M. (New York: Paulist Press, 1982), 38.

written in the 1230s to Agnes of Prague, a noblewoman who had come into contact with the preaching of the Friars Minor in her home city. Clare wrote:

> Therefore most beloved sister, or should I say, Lady worthy of great respect: because You are *the spouse and the mother and the sister* of my Lord Jesus Christ . . . and have been adorned resplendidly with the sign of inviolable virginity and most holy poverty: Be strengthened in the holy service which You have undertaken out of an ardent desire for the Poor Crucified.[4]

Like the Dominicans, the Franciscans grew rapidly following the death of their founder. As part of a papally authorized order, members could travel from city to city preaching in public and spreading the movement. Furthermore, both orders gave evidence of being concerned to preach beyond the cities of western Christendom, especially in Muslim lands. By mid-thirteenth century some had begun to propose that Christians undertake peaceful efforts to convert Muslims and Jews through preaching, as an alternative to the military force of the crusades. Muslims and Jews were considered by western church law to be unbelievers rather than heretics, and thus were supposed to be free from forced conversions. Church law encouraged preaching to such unbelievers, however, in hopes that they would convert and undergo baptism. The notion of preaching as an alternative to crusading was not new, but no concerted effort in that direction outside the West had been made.

One of the persons who took up that task in relation to Islam, following the example of Francis himself, was a Mallorcan named Ramon Llull (or Lull) (c.1230 -1315). A Third Order Franciscan (a layperson who lived outside the order but followed the Franciscan way of life), Ramon formulated a comprehensive missionary alternative to crusading late in the thirteenth century. His plan called for schools of language that would teach Arabic, Greek, and Hebrew. Mission efforts were to be organized under the direction of a single leader and sent throughout the Muslim world. A gifted intellectual, Ramon learned Arabic, becoming fluent enough to preach and write in it. He also put his hand to writing several missionary treatises that sought to demonstrate the truth of the Christian message to unbelievers. Due to his influence, several Franciscans went to North Africa as missionaries, some traveling in the thirteenth century with Muslim traders as far south as West Africa. Ramon journeyed a number of times to North Africa to preach in person, his last trip made when he was more than eighty years of age. Ramon Llull was judged by some of his contemporaries as being emotionally unstable. His method of public preaching in Islamic countries was certainly confrontational. Yet his conception of missions as an alternative to the violence of the crusades and his advocacy of a comprehensive program that included language study and translation pointed in the direction that future generations of missionaries would follow.

During the last half of the thirteenth century the Franciscans experienced internal controversy that finally split the order. Following the death of Francis,

---

[4] Ibid., 191.

some in the community remained committed to a life of absolute poverty. The more radical members of the order rejected all use of money and believed the community as a whole ought not to own property. There were others, however, who took a more realistic stance and argued that while as individuals the Franciscans ought to follow a life of poverty, the community as a whole could hold property and, when necessary, deal with money. The latter group was willing to place community holdings in the hands of the cardinal protector, who was appointed by the pope to oversee the order on behalf of the curia. The more radical members of the community, known as Spiritual Franciscans, refused this compromise and soon began to go their own way. In time they found their efforts opposed not only by other Franciscans but by the pope as well. The fourteenth century brought eventual condemnation of the Spiritual Franciscans, who continued to insist that they were the rightful heirs of their founder's legacy.

Joachim of Fiore

One of the most intriguing figures of the twelfth century was a monk in southern Italy named Joachim of Fiore (c. 1135-1202). He spent time as a wandering preacher before joining a monastic community that was in the process of coming under the new Cistercian order. Joachim eventually left the Cistercians to start a new community with a group of fellow monks, putting himself at odds with the order's leaders. His legacy was not to be found as the head of new order, however. Rather, it was as an apocalyptic interpreter of both scriptures and his age that his reputation and influence was to spread throughout the West.

In the last decades of the twelfth century, Joachim began to experience a series of visions related to biblical themes. These visions provided him with an interpretive key to unlock new and mysterious meanings of scriptures, especially the apocalyptic passages. Over against the predominant method of biblical interpretation of his day, which read apocalyptic sections of scripture in an allegorical manner, Joachim took them to be prophecies related to actual history. One needed to have a code for unlocking the mystery, however. His visions provided precisely that, in the form of figures and images that he recorded in books of pictures.

Joachim believed several of the visions that he received were showing him that the two testaments of scripture represented two ages of revelation, that of the Jews and that of the Gentiles. In trinitarian terms these were represented as the age of the Father and the Son. Placing the two testaments alongside one another, he found that they "seem to gaze into each other's faces," providing what he called "concordances."[5] Biblical generations from Adam through Jesus seemed to fall into sequences of sevens, fourteens, and twenty-ones. Laying these alongside one another revealed overlapping ages or time periods that marked out the changes in the spiritual standing or *status* of humanity. Counting the generations

---

[5] Joachim of Fiore, *Book of Concordance*, in *Apocalyptic Spirituality*, trans. Bernard McGinn (New York: Paulist Press, 1979), 120.

from Jesus to his own day brought him to the edge of a new *status* that he prophesied was about to begin, the *status* of the Holy Spirit, which proceeded from that of the Father and the Son.

In this new age the Spirit was going to renovate not only the church but the whole world, Joachim believed. A new type of spiritual intelligence would be given to the monastics in particular, making them the vanguard of the new age. Joachim did not predict that the institutional church and the papacy would necessarily be eradicated, but he did not see much need for them in the third age or *status* of the Spirit that was about to break forth. In one of his books he laid out the plans for the new ordering of the Christian world in the third age that was about to begin. Where other reformers of his day looked back to a restoration of the apostolic age, Joachim looked forward to a spiritual renovation that took in all of history.

This new age or *status* would not come without suffering and tribulation, however. Here Joachim's apocalyptic interpretation engaged current events at a very specific level. In one of his books of figures he reproduced the seven-headed dragon depicted in Revelation 17. Each head represented one of the historical persecutors of Christianity he explained, from Herod and Nero on. The sixth head of the dragon of anti-Christ was Salah ad-Din, the Egyptian sultan who had recaptured Jerusalem in 1187. The seventh was about to come, the greatest persecutor of Christians of all time. Joachim expected he would be the final anti-Christ. He speculated that Islamic armies might even overrun Christendom, but then the spiritual effect of the new order of monks and nuns would be the successful agents through whom the Spirit would work to redeem the whole world. The final tribulation of history would then usher in the beginning of the millennial kingdom on earth, the age of the Spirit.

Such intense expectations for history provided Joachim with new insights into the nature of the Trinity, an interpretation he again developed through pictures, or *figurae*. He accepted entirely the western tradition of the double procession of the Holy Spirit from the Father and the Son. This was why there was not a third testament corresponding to the third *status* of history. Each person of the Trinity was uniquely identified with an age, nevertheless, so much so that Joachim was perceived to be saying that the divine was historical in nature. Joachim did indeed favor an economic, as opposed to ontological, view of the Trinity. On this count he criticized the views of one of his contemporaries, Peter Lombard, one of the scholastic theologians whose work will be considered in the next chapter. The Fourth Lateran Council in 1215 considered the dispute and decided in favor of Peter Lombard against Joachim of Fiore. A dozen years after his death, his views concerning the Trinity were condemned as heretical, although the rest of his teachings were left unaffected.

After his death many of the Spiritual Franciscans, those more radical followers of Francis of Assisi, claimed Joachim of Fiore as their own. Many regarded his prophecies of the coming spiritual age to be fulfilled in their radical mendicant order. New books of prophecy and figures were written in his name and circulated under the mantle of his prophetic inspiration. Through them his expectations for a coming transformation of history and the inauguration of the third age of the Spirit were translated into more popular forms of apocalyptic expectation and crisis. Joachim's influence on biblical interpretation reached beyond these immediate followers. His method of relating scripture to historical periods and specific crises continued to inspire similar attempts by others to develop their own prophetic interpretations of scripture.

Beguines

Half a continent away from southern Italy in the 1170s, an effort was under way to organize new communities of laywomen in Belgium. The project was a controversial one because the women were not actually nuns. They were not taking permanent vows and were not living in cloistered communities as part of an existing order recognized by the church hierarchy. Nevertheless, they were taking vows of chastity and living together in ways that resembled monastic life, a situation that was an anomaly as far as church order was concerned. Resistance from some of the local clergy was strong, especially to the notion of laywomen taking vows of chastity, but the communities had the support of others in the hierarchy who intervened on their behalf with the pope. Innocent III eventually granted them formal permission to live together without being a part of any existing order within the church.

These communities were soon known as Beguines, a name that appears to have come from a popular priest in Liège by the name of Lambert le Bègue (Lambert the Stutterer), who was well known for having translated portions of the Bible for popular devotional reading. The Beguines shared this commitment to devotional reading of the Bible, but they were also involved in education and service to the poor in the various towns where they formed. Some of their houses became virtual hospitals or shelters for the destitute. Many of their communities supported themselves by developing cottage industries to supplement their endowments. The Beguines had soon spread throughout the lowlands and into Germany. Similar communities of men, known as Beghards, were also soon organized.

The Beguines and Beghards were never fully able to convince church authorities of their orthodoxy. The reason was not because of any beliefs that the groups harbored so much as because of their commitment to spiritual life apart from convents and monasteries. By late in the thirteenth century many of the Beguines were being identified with the Spiritual Franciscans. The fourteenth century brought explicit charges of heresy, and some Beguines were even burned at the stake. Eventually the Beguines were forced to merge with older existing orders of women religious, bringing a sad ending to one of the more vibrant renewal movements of the period.

The desire to lead a more spiritual life outside the confines of monastic community was not exclusive to the Beguines, nor did it end with their suppression. Such groups existed throughout western Europe. The most common were the Third Orders of the Franciscans and the Dominicans. These were communities of laypersons who followed the spiritual teachings of their founder but did not take formal monastic vows. Some who were members of the Third Orders were even married. The spiritual impulses of the age simply could not be contained by the older structures of monastic order. The desire for ministry and spiritual renewal among the laity was as much a factor in the life of churches in the thirteenth century as it is today.

33

Intellectual Renewal in Western Christendom 1100-1300

The rise of scholasticism

Popular preaching and new religious movements were not the only signs of renewal in the twelfth century. New intellectual currents were flowing across the landscape of western Christendom as well. Monasteries had long been among the most important centers of learning in the West. Monastic life was structured by liturgy, and the reading of scripture was prominent. In addition to the regular hours of prayer, monks and nuns practiced a form of active devotional reading that required the words of scripture be read aloud and then meditated upon prayerfully. Hence the study of grammar was foundational for spiritual life. Monasteries were publishing houses in the West. In the scriptorium, texts of scripture and various books of theology had to be critically and carefully studied, compared, then copied to avoid errors. Many monasteries had libraries that served not just as archives for local records but as depositories for the great texts of Christian tradition as well. Many also supported individual members who wrote new works to be added to the treasury of Christian learning. Not all who took monastic vows became literate, but it was generally held that learning and spirituality were intrinsically related in Christian life.

Monastic education drew upon three major sources for learning: the Bible, the works of authorities from Christian tradition, and the classical works of the Greco-Roman past. Learning was directed toward devotional practice and never for its own sake. Faith and reason were integrated in religious experience that was directed toward the love of God or the love of truth. Community life required other, more mundane forms of learning as well, including medicine, law, finance, and administration. These need not be separated from the central practices of devotion and service, however, for the monastics considered work in the world but another means of approaching God.

The rapid growth of monastic communities that were associated with the reforms of Cluny in the tenth century, and then with the Cistercians at the end of the eleventh, naturally brought about an increase in monastic schools throughout Europe as well. A second type of educational institution was growing as well in the eleventh century: cathedral schools run by bishops. For centuries bishops had often run local schools out of their homes to provide basic theological education for members of the clergy who served under them. As cities in the West grew, and as the cathedral grew along with them, the bishops' schools likewise increased in both numbers of students and the quality of education.

Urban life fosters abstraction. Bankers and merchants engaged in the financial transactions of a monetary economy no longer equate wealth directly with land. Urban life also fosters social differentiation and specialization. Tasks become more specialized in material production, the number of people living in close proximity requires greater organization for distribution of resources, and the social rules that govern interaction increase dramatically. The cathedral schools in western European cities in the twelfth century began to reflect these basic traits of urbanization. New, abstract methods of intellectual work began to appear. Specialized studies increased, a more highly organized curriculum began to be employed, and a new elite group of students and teachers emerged. The study of logic for its own sake was undertaken as an intellectual field or discipline known as *dialectics*. Those who specialized in the discipline of study became known as *scholastics*, and their efforts collectively were known as *scholasticism*.

As the terms imply, the effort was closely identified with educational institutions, or schools. The first generations of scholastics were located either within monastery schools or cathedral schools. By the beginning of the thirteenth century, however, a new institution was taking shape in cities of the West, one which was soon to provide the most secure home for the kind of critical intellectual reflection upon language and logic that the scholastics undertook. In the Christian West that new institution was known as the university. Essentially it was an independent guild of scholars. Cities had welcomed the influx of students to cathedral schools and under independent masters because of the financial benefits that were derived from renting rooms, selling food, and providing services. At the same time students and teachers had few legal protections. Like other artisans who were immigrating to the cities and thus without the protections of citizenship, the formation of a guild provided them a means for dealing collectively with the authorities of both city and church. Thus it was that in the year 1200 the king of France recognized an independent guild of scholars and students in the major city of his realm, the University of Paris.

Along with Paris, Oxford, Montpellier, Bologna, and Salerno were soon recognized as cities hosting universities. Some developed out of older centers of learning. The University of Bologna, for instance, traced its roots back to the efforts of Matilda of Tuscany (d. 1115), a noblewoman who had endowed an independent school for the study of law in the midst of the Investiture Controversy. The new universities were not under the direct control of any bishop or cardinal, however. Independent charters from city authorities, along with letters of support from the pope, provided universities the authority to police their own ranks and, most important, to establish their own boundaries for intellectual work. Students paid a fee to come and learn from members of their faculties, who lectured and engaged in public debates, or disputations, to further knowledge. In this way the schools were thus financially self-supporting.

Universities organized higher knowledge into three major fields or disciplines that corresponded to the three major professions of western social life: medicine, law, and theology. To gain access to study in one of these areas, a student had first to complete the general course of study that covered the seven traditional areas of preparatory learning that made up the liberal arts: grammar, rhetoric, and logic (the *trivium*); and arithmetic, music, geometry, and astronomy (the *quadrivium*). The major requirement for admission to this level of study was that one knew Latin, could pay the necessary fees to the teachers, and was male. Students could begin their work around the age of twelve or thirteen, and usually completed the course of study in four years.

After completing this first level of work, a student could apply for further study that culminated in a thesis that was defended in a public forum, or disputation. Upon successful defense of the thesis the student was admitted to the ranks of master of arts, which entitled one to teach the liberal arts. One could also then go on to one of the three higher schools of medicine, law, or theology, and engage in a course of study that culminated in a doctorate. As at the master's level, the doctoral degree was awarded by the faculty after the successful defense of a thesis at a public disputation. Anyone, including a woman, could submit a thesis for public defense and be awarded a doctorate, and several thirteenth-century women whose fathers were professors did so.

Medical studies in western schools in the twelfth century were rudimentary. For a long time western schools depended heavily upon Latin translations of Arabic textbooks, which were by far the most advanced of the period. Such works as the *Canon of Medicine* by the eleventh-century Persian scholar, Ibn Sina (known in the West as Avicenna) were standard fare. A number of treatises by az-Zahrawi, a Muslim surgeon from Andalusia, provided detailed drawings of instruments and instructions on a range of new medical procedures that were translated into Latin. Where medical studies relied heavily at first upon Arabic sources, university instruction in law depended upon ancient Roman sources and church canons. Justinian's *Codex* was among the most important texts in this regard for western legal instruction, although in England traditional common law was also studied as a source. For obvious reasons the study of secular law in particular tended to draw students from local populations.

The queen of the sciences in the thirteenth century was theology. Scholastic theologians took their responsibility seriously and set out for themselves the grand task of organizing the whole of human knowledge into an intelligible system. Their main concerns were with the philosophical questions of universal principles and how these related to the revealed truths of Christian religion. Aristotle's writings, in their various Latin and Arabic transmissions, were their major resource on the philosophical side of things, while the archive of Christian scriptures as interpreted by ancient Christian orthodox authors was the source for theological reflections. Scholastic theologians combed both the scriptures and the works of accepted Christian authorities from the past, organizing their insights around various theological topics and comparing them with a precision that earlier generations of western thinkers had hardly attempted to attain. One of the problems that confronted the scholastic theologians was the fact that the

authorities of the past did not all agree on various issues, and thus various con-
flicting positions had been accepted as orthodox truth. Reconciling the contradictions they found among the authorities of Christian teaching required a more
critical approach to knowledge. To this end they applied the methods of disputation, arguing pro and con until reaching a sure conclusion through dialectics.

Anselm of Canterbury

Among the most important predecessors to the scholastics, if not exactly one
of them himself, was Anselm of Canterbury (1033-1109). Originally from northern Italy, he was educated at the monastery at Bec, in Normandy, before becoming its abbot. From there he went on to be consecrated archbishop of Canterbury
in England in 1093. Anselm represented something of a bridge between the older
tradition of monastic and cathedral schools, and the universities of learning that
still lay in the future. A devoted student of Augustine's theology, he sought to
provide rational arguments to support what the Christian faith claims about God.
To this end he employed methods of logic that were derived from the translations
of Aristotle's work circulating in northern France at the time.

One of Anselm's best-known works is a short meditation on the being of God
entitled *Proslogion (Discourse)*, written while he was the abbot of Bec. Its opening chapters develop a logical argument that God exists, doing so apart from an
appeal to special revelation. God is by definition "that than which nothing greater
can be thought." If such a being did not exist, however, the thought about that
being in the mind of the thinker would necessarily be greater, thereby implying a
logical contradiction. There must logically be a being "than which nothing greater
can be thought," a being otherwise called God, argued Anselm. The rest of the
work went on to examine the nature and attributes of God. *Proslogion* stated in
its opening sentences that the author was seeking to understand what it was that
he believed. He had originally considered issuing this along with a previous work
under the title *Fides quaerens intellectum* ("Faith Seeking Understanding").

Another of Anselm's works that had lasting influence in the West was *Cur
Deus Homo (Why God Became Human)*. Here the archbishop of Canterbury provided a reasoned argument for the substitutionary atonement of Jesus Christ.
Drawing upon a legal frame of reference, Anselm argued that human sin had
caused an affront to God's honor, an affront that God could not simply dismiss or
overlook. God's righteous nature required satisfaction; a penalty had to be paid.
Sinful humanity by definition was unable to pay this debt to God's righteousness
and honor. Here is where God's mercy prevailed, for God took upon himself, in
the form of Jesus Christ, the penalty of sin that humanity could not pay, in effect
substituting Jesus Christ for the human beings who deserved condemnation and
death. Those who accepted the penalty paid by Jesus Christ were thus freed from
the legal consequences of their sins and rewarded eternal life through Christ.

Anselm's arguments in both cases depend on methods of logical reasoning that
did not require the illumination of revelation. Nevertheless, it was not his intent to
dispel the need for revelation. On the contrary, Anselm asserted forcefully that

belief was necessary for understanding. Following Augustine, he argued that faith leads to understanding, which can then make use of philosophical reasoning to illuminate the truths of salvation. Philosophy could only be a servant of theology, albeit an important one.

Peter Abelard and Héloïse

Among the first scholastic theologians of the twelfth century was Peter Abelard (1079-1142). Born in Bretagne, he studied at the cathedral in Paris and then taught at several other schools before returning to Paris around the age of thirty-five to teach. There he fell in love with a young woman named Héloïse, the niece of another member of the cathedral staff. Abelard arranged to rent a room within the household in return for serving as Héloïse's tutor. In an autobiographical letter written many years later, he recounted, "Under the pretext of discipline, we abandoned ourselves utterly to love."[6] Héloïse soon became pregnant, and after giving birth to a son, she and Abelard were secretly married in the presence of her uncle. They continued to live apart, however. Fearing that marriage would destroy her lover's scholarly career, Héloïse had attempted first to dissuade Abelard of the step and then later publicly denied it. Her uncle was enraged when he heard of this, forcing Héloïse to take flight to a convent. Believing now that Abelard had dishonored his niece, the uncle arranged to have the teacher attacked one evening and castrated. Upon recovering, Abelard forced Héloïse against her will to take the vows of a nun and enter a convent, after which he then entered a monastery.

Their story was a tragic one of love and betrayal, set amid the dynamics of day-to-day life in the twelfth century. At one point in his reflections Abelard recalled that during the height of their affair, in order to conceal their true relationship he occasionally pretended to beat Héloïse, a punishment administered by teachers to students who failed to learn their lessons. At the same time, the letters the two exchanged later in life reveal a love that transcended the age. Héloïse was forced to leave the pleasures of Paris life and take up life in a cloistered community, where she eventually became the abbess. Her letters to Abelard are among the few examples of women's writings from the era. In them she discusses Jerome and other authorities of the church, but she also reveals much of her own personal struggle to be faithful to the one she loves. Abelard often appears arrogant and conceited, on the other hand. One wonders whether he ever understood the suffering that his wife endured because of his behavior.

Héloïse was correct in her assessment regarding Abelard's intellect. The young scholar was among the most skilled of his age in the use of the new method of dialectics. One of the theological works that he wrote was a book entitled *Sic et Non (Yes and No)*. The title captures well the essence of dialectical thinking. In its pages he catalogued views of ancient Christian authorities regarding various theological topics. He identified the contradictions that he found without trying

---

[6] Peter Abelard, "History of Calamities," *The Letters of Abelard and Heloise*, trans. C. K. Scott Moncrieff (New York: Alfred A. Knopf, 1926), 13.

to resolve them. The work served a valuable function in allowing students to engage past sources and attempt to work through their own solutions to theological issues.

Abelard's appreciation for past authors reached beyond the Christian tradition to the philosophical school of the Platonists as well. He did not hesitate to state that he found the doctrine of the Trinity among them, even though they were not Christians. Perhaps his most famous position concerns the doctrine of Christian salvation. In distinction to Anselm, Abelard did not believe that the death of Jesus was effective because it satisfied the demands of divine righteousness and justice. Rather, the death of Jesus Christ demonstrated God's excessive love for humankind. Its effectiveness lay in its capacity to move human beings to moral repentance rather than as a penalty paid for human salvation. For Abelard, sin was fundamentally a problem of the human will, leading him to focus upon the inner act of contrition rather than the external acts of the sacraments as means of forgiveness. On each of these views he faced opposition from his contemporaries, including Bernard of Clairvaux. Toward the end of his life Abelard faced censure from the pope himself.

Peter Lombard

Another early scholastic theologian, and arguably the most important of his age, was a northern Italian named Peter Lombard (c.1100-1160). A student of Abelard's work, Peter Lombard likewise taught in the cathedral school at Notre Dame in Paris before becoming bishop of the city the year before his death. Unlike Abelard, however, he enjoyed the support of Bernard of Clairvaux and others who were influential in Rome. Peter Lombard's *Four Books of Sentences* followed Abelard's method of organizing statements from early Christian sources around various themes (God; creation, humanity, and the fall; Christ, salvation, and virtue; sacraments and last things). The *Sentences* went further in trying to resolve apparent contradictions among ancient authorities, while leaving room for further development of ideas of others. These tendencies, and breadth, made it a popular textbook for students of theology.

Anselm, Abelard, Peter Lombard, and others made their theological contribution as educators within either monasteries or cathedral schools in the twelfth century. Their works bear the mark of a lively intellectual environment that included students and other scholars. The fact that many of the issues that they were debating were engaging teachers in various locations across western Europe suggests that a fuller academic culture was emerging, one that provided the necessary support but also the demand for more theological works such as these. The questions that occupied the scholastic theologians were not always ones that were of concern to church administrators, popular preachers, spiritual visionaries, or secular rulers. Sometimes they were of general interest though; debates about the nature of the divine presence in the sacraments of the church, for instance, drew a wide circle of interest. More often, however, the scholastic theologians' debates seemed to be merely matters of formal semantics.

The Cathedral of Notre Dame de Paris as it appeared in the 16th century. Anonymous, Bibliothèque National. Reproduced with permission of Art Resource, New York City.

Of course this is precisely what they were. Following several hundred years of philosophical reflection by Muslims such as ibn Rushd and ibn Sina, or Jews such as Moses Maimonides, the Christian scholastic theologians took Aristotle as their philosophical starting point. Specifically, they were interested in Aristotle's logic and the manner in which it allowed them to find answers to questions at a formal level. Anselm's proof of the existence of God is a case in point. All of the scholastic theologians agreed that concepts are less real than the things they signify. This is a necessary condition for Anselm's proof to work. At the same time they agreed that formal resolution of questions at the level of logic and semantics satisfied the requirements of a proof. Again, in Anselm's case one did not need to see or touch God to be able to prove at a formal level the extra-mental existence of God. The university provided the arena where such ideas could be formulated, disputed, and refined.

High scholasticism: Thomas Aquinas

Western Christendom did not have to wait long to realize the fruit of this endeavor. Thomas Aquinas (1225-1274) was his name, the son of nobility from central Italy. In 1243 he entered the Dominican order and was sent to study in Paris under one of the order's masters, Albert the Great. After finishing his studies he taught in Cologne before returning to the University of Paris as a faculty member. Over the remaining years of his life Thomas wrote a number of treatises, biblical commentaries, and commentaries on the work of other scholastics. A request from the friars in Spain, who were looking for apologetic literature that might help convert Muslims, resulted in a book entitled the *Summa Contra Gentiles (Summary against the Gentiles)*. The major work of his life, however, was his *Summa Theologiae (Summary of Theology)*, a massive project in systematic theology that remains to this day one of the major accomplishments of Christian theology. The *Summa Theologiae* has often been compared to an elaborate cathedral in its intricacy, complexity, formal development, and coherence.

The *Summa Theologiae* illustrates well the value of dialectical reasoning that the scholastics employed. Each section opens with a question posed in the form of "whether it is the case that . . . " Next follows a summary of points that would seem to be the case regarding the initial question, drawn from various authorities. Thomas seeks to be as inclusive as he can in these sections, often citing Muslim sources and Aristotle along with ancient Christian authors and the Bible. His purpose is to give as full an airing as possible to the various points that would seem to be the case regarding the question under consideration. These points are then followed by other, opposing points of view or arguments that can be raised against the various perspectives. Here again the scholastic theologian seeks to raise points even-handely and without distorting their authors' perspectives.

Once the pros and cons have been considered, Thomas moves toward his own constructive engagement in the form of a series of assertions that begin with, "I respond . . . " This response seeks to move beyond the apparent contradictions to a new perspective that, at least as far as he can tell, refutes specific points or resolves apparent contradictions among the various arguments while satisfying their positive insights. A series of concluding responses to each of the previous points is offered at the end of each article by way of summation. The whole process is then repeated with a new "whether it is the case that . . . ," unfolding the next round of insights in what seems a natural progression of ideas from beginning to end.

Much of the content of Thomas's *Summa Theologiae* bears evidence of a mature engagement with Aristotle and the body of Aristotle's Muslim commentators without being uncritically bound to the philosopher. With the rest of the scholastic movement, Thomas follows Aristotle in taking as a central question of philosophy the relationship between individual things and the universal concepts that the mind can abstract from them. For Thomas, all knowledge begins with sensation that provides the mind with the images from which it then abstracts ideas. The universals that the mind grasps through this process exist both within the world outside the human mind and within the human mind itself, which is why the mind can know the real world. But they also exist in the mind of God, who is the creative and sustaining source of all that exists. Such a framework provides assurance of a necessary degree of coherence among thought, the world, and God that allows the whole work to go forward.

The mind knows something by forming ideas that are gathered from sensation through images. But what of those realities that have no corporal form and thus do not give rise to sensation? How can they be known? Here Thomas argues that we form ideas about non-corporal beings by way of analogies and metaphors, reasoning from the images we have through sensation to what is beyond sensation. Once again the argument implies a degree of continuity between natural and supernatural worlds, or between what is capable of empirical sensation and what is beyond it. Thomas argues that analogical reason alone cannot arrive at a full measure of the truth. Theology requires revelation in this regard, revealed truths in theology taking the place of self-evident axioms in logic. Revelation, according to Thomas, is found first of all in the Christian scriptures, and then in the reflections upon them that theological authorities and the church have composed.

The *Summa Theologiae* opens with a discussion of the existence of God, which Thomas thought could be demonstrated through logical means apart from revelation. Several arguments are advanced in this direction, including that of the need for a supreme designer, first cause, and ultimate source of goodness in the world. God is by definition absolute substance and pure act, or one in whom essence and existence coincide. Reason teaches that God is a simple or undifferentiated being who is omniscient, omnipotent, and omnipresent. Beyond these assertions divine revelation takes over to show God to be Father, Son, and Holy Spirit. For Thomas, the persons of the Trinity are functions of their relations. Each member of the Trinity exists only in relation to the others, so that the three persons mutually define one another.

The world God created is examined next. Here again Thomas's thinking is highly relational and integrated. God is the active creator of all that is, not the unmoved mover of Aristotle's philosophy. Creation is organized hierarchically from angels at the top to basic elements of nature at the bottom. In the middle are human beings, composed of body and soul. These are not two substances, according to Thomas, but rather are related as material and form. Because the soul of a person can act to transcend the body, it is shown to have an existence beyond that of the material body. Nevertheless, for Thomas the doctrine of the resurrection means that the soul is not an immortal entity living in heaven apart from any corporal body.

Humanity was originally created free and intended to realize its end in perfect happiness in the presence of God. Human beings sinned, however, thereby corrupting both their natural and moral powers of body and soul. Salvation is thus only possible by the unmerited grace of God given through Jesus Christ. Salvation does not eradicate what God has created, however, but perfects it. Even sinful human beings are endowed with reason and conscience, faculties that can discipline the appetites and lead into virtue or the disposition toward doing good. Temperance, courage, justice, and prudence are all attainable through the natural facilities. To these are added the theological virtues of faith, hope, and love, which are attained through the sacraments as gifts of grace. As these virtues operate within persons, so there are laws that operate external to them and are likewise under the overall governance of God. Of special concern in this regard is the existence of natural law, to which human beings are morally accountable; human laws enacted to express the natural law found in creation itself; and the revealed law of God's commandments.

God alone is the sole cause of grace for Thomas. Grace is given principally by the Holy Spirit, but instrumentally through the sacraments. Human beings can do nothing to prepare themselves for grace, for grace is its own preparation. Yet human beings must respond to grace, which is the proper movement of the soul, the movement of faith. Because Thomas understands God's relationship to the creation to be so thorough, and so thoroughly one of grace, he can conceive the response of human beings to the prompting of grace to be their own responses. God does not move one to being justified apart from moving the will. Human beings who are so moved will continue to act in order to grow in grace (sanctification), availing themselves of the sacraments of the church, which are the instruments of grace.

Thomas's work was not received without resistance. His dependence on Aristotle for the ethical discussion of virtue and as a constant philosophical companion throughout the *Summa Theologiae* earned the Dominican theologian the condemnation of a synod in Paris in 1277, only two years after his death. Through the fourteenth century his reputation remained very much a matter of debate. Yet over time his work became accepted as the standard of orthodox theology among western Catholics, so much so that today many still consider him the preeminent theologian of the Catholic faith.

Bonaventure

One of Thomas's fellow students in Paris during the 1250s was a young man from Italy named Bonaventure (1221-1274). As a child he had been healed of a serious illness after meeting Francis of Assisi, and around 1238 the young Bonaventure entered the order of Francis. Bonaventure and Thomas both received their doctoral degrees on the same day from the University of Paris in 1257. Whereas Thomas went on to teach, however, Bonaventure was elected that same year to be minister general of the Franciscan order. His life and work demonstrate well the continuing integration of monastic spirituality and scholastic theology in the thirteenth century.

More than most others of his age, Bonaventure perceived that the purpose of scholastic education was to draw people into a deeper knowledge of God. Intellectual endeavors have as their end the contemplation of God, which was the goal of all monastic spirituality as well. To this end he wrote philosophical works, commentaries on scripture, mystical reflections, and sermons. Bonaventure went against the reigning Aristotelian thought of his day to argue that the Greek philosopher ought not be granted a place of authority alongside ancient Christian teachers such as Augustine. Divine revelation and not reason is the proper starting place for Christian understanding, leading him to affirm the mystical over the rational as pathway to God. One historian even went so far as to assert, "St. Bonaventure's doctrine marks for us the culminating point of Christian mysticism and constitutes the completest synthesis it has ever achieved."[7]

Later scholastics: Duns Scotus and William of Ockham

Scholasticism as a movement continued to develop after Thomas and Bonaventure in new directions as theologians continued the work of analyzing logical propositions, debated the relative merits of various concepts, and sought to use them to illuminate a Christian understanding of God, creation, and salvation. Two later scholastic theologians in particular deserve notice because of their lasting impact upon the direction of western thought. The first of these was Duns Scotus (c.1265-1308). A Franciscan who was educated at Oxford, he taught at Oxford, Cambridge, and Paris before moving on to Cologne. An original thinker, he shaped his ideas mainly in response to Thomas in order to refute the Dominican's views.

Scotus believed that Thomas had been overly committed to an Aristotelian view of the natural world, especially regarding natural law. Thomas appeared to him to bind even God to these laws, thereby impinging upon the freedom of God. To the contrary, the freedom of God transcends both natural or divine law, Scotus argued. The law is but an expression of God's will, not a rule that God must follow. God could have created a different world with different laws, if God had so chosen, he asserted. Along these lines Scotus drew a distinction between God's absolute power and God's ordained power, that is, between what God could do and what God ordains to do. Creation and the laws by which it works are therefore not necessary but contingent. For the same reason Scotus rejected Thomas's

---

[7] Etienne Gilson, *The Philosophy of St. Bonaventure*, trans. Illtyd Trethowan and F. J. Sheed (New York: Sheed and Ward, 1938), 494.

notion of natural law ethics in favor of an ethic derived from the revealed will of God. The will rather than reason is the faculty most involved in the process of salvation. Salvation entails human beings' responding to God's revealed will in an act of obedience that is the exercise of their own free will. He regarded love, not knowledge, as the primary pathway of salvation.

Another Franciscan who joined Scotus in forging a scholastic alternative to Thomas's theology was William of Ockham (c.1280-1349). Like Scotus, he was educated at Oxford, although Ockham's teaching career was interrupted by political controversy. Ockham took a stand in favor of the Franciscan notion of apostolic poverty at a time when the doctrine was not popular among many in the hierarchy of the church. He also expressed strong views regarding the limits of papal power. His positions brought him into conflict with church authorities and eventually forced him out of England and into exile in German territory.

His problems with the church hierarchy did not prevent Ockham from adding his contribution to the theological debates of his day. The question of universals had been a part of the scholastics' agenda since before Abelard. Mostly the scholastics had sided with Aristotle and against Plato by arguing that the universal categories of being do not have independent existence apart from the particular things in which they are found. Ockham went further than most of his contemporaries, however, by arguing that such universals exist only in the mind as symbols or terms. However useful they might be as concepts, they do not exist in reality apart from the mind. In support of this position he formulated a rule of logic that is known as Ockham's razor. Ockham argued that we ought to eliminate from a theory any concepts or causes that are not necessary to explain the phenomenon we are considering, thereby making our arguments as economical as possible. The notion of universals existing independent of individual things is not necessary to explain the existence or meaning of the world, he argued. Hence it is unnecessary and ought to be eliminated.

In terms that were even stronger than those of Scotus, Ockham rejected reason as a facility that was useful for theology. Only faith gives us access to theological truths. The ways of God are not open to reason, for God has freely chosen to create a world and establish a way of salvation within it apart from any necessary laws that human logic or rationality can uncover. Like Scotus, he argued for a distinction between God's absolute will and God's ordained will. God has ordained a way of salvation that includes the incarnation of Jesus Christ and the sacraments. God could have ordained things differently, coming not as a man but as some other being, for instance; the reasons why God chose this way and not another remain utterly hidden from us. What is revealed is that we are to avail ourselves of the sacraments of the church to receive forgiveness and enter eternal life.

William of Ockham and Duns Scotus helped give fuller expression to a theological school that came to be known as Nominalism (so called because its proponents argued that the universal concepts Aristotle and Thomas talked about were not real apart from individual things; rather, were merely names or terms we use to talk about such concepts). The Nominalists made a distinction between the absolute and ordained will of God and placed a great deal of emphasis upon the contingency of creation. Salvation was found by obeying the ordained will of God, and God in turn had ordained the sacraments of the church. With Thomas, they believed that grace was infused through the sacraments. Human beings could not arrive at the truth about God through reason or natural law but only through revelation that was given in the Bible, interpreted by the church, and communicated through the sacraments.

Christian life in twelfth- and thirteenth-century Europe

For most Christians in the West, the debates among scholastic theologians were at most a matter of marginal concern, if they were aware of them at all. For most, being a Christian meant participating in the sacramental life of the church where they were promised eternal life. Most people in the West attended worship services in a church or chapel on a regular basis, and almost always these were services where a priest celebrated the eucharist. But most people did not regularly take part in the communion portion of the service. One of the decrees passed by the Fourth Lateran Council in 1215 made it mandatory that every Christian was to take communion at least once a year, suggesting that many were not even participating with this frequency at the time. The same council made confession mandatory at least once a year as well; this suggests that the practice of penance was also not widely being practiced in the twelfth century.

Despite such apparent laxity in practice, most western Christians looked to the church as the mediator of salvation. Priests and bishops administered the rites that granted individuals access to eternal life. They even exercised a degree of influence over life on the other side of death. Most western Christians in the twelfth century believed in a complex afterlife. After death one might go to limbo or hell; or purgatory and then eventually paradise, as the Italian poet Dante Alighieri so masterfully depicted in the *Divine Comedy*. Corresponding to the elaborate world of the afterlife was an equally elaborate world of sacramental graces administered in this life. The Fourth Lateran Council formally defined seven sacraments: baptism, confirmation, penance, eucharist, marriage, ordination, and extreme unction (or last rites). Each of these, Peter Lombard had argued, were means of grace that Christ himself had ordained, and thus the church administers them as the institutional continuation of his salvation.

Among the sacraments the two that were practiced most often were confession (or penance) and the eucharist (or communion). For many Christians penance was the more important of the two. After confessing to a priest or monastic confessor, the individual believer would be given a list of practices to perform in order to complete the process of penance. Through such a discipline people took care of the variety of day-to-day sins they committed or the problems in their lives. Confession was also necessary before one could commune at the sacrament of the Lord's body, the eucharist.

For several hundred years theologians had been debating in the West how exactly one ought to understand the relationship between Christ's presence and the elements of bread and wine that are on the communion table. Some had argued that when Christians partake of the bread they are actually eating the flesh of Christ with their teeth, while others shied away from such a graphic description. Scholastic theologians suggested that one ought to make a distinction between the substance and the appearance of the elements in the eucharist. In the material appearances, which include their properties or accidents, the bread and wine remain the same; but in their deeper substance, what one might call their subject, they are changed by the words of the priest to become the body and blood of Jesus Christ. The Fourth Lateran Council followed this distinction and used the verb *transubstantiate* to express the change or transfiguration that takes place. Believers still taste bread and wine, the doctrine suggests, but the deeper reality, the subject of the elements, is the literal body and blood of Jesus Christ.

The Fourth Lateran Council also determined that it was permissible for priests to serve only the bread to the communing members of the congregation, while those who celebrated the mass partook of both the bread and the wine. Partly this was a decision made in response to the difficulties of serving large numbers of people in urban churches with a common cup of wine, and partly as a theological reflection of the widening gap between clergy and laity in the church. The argument offered by theologians was that Christ was fully present in both elements of bread and wine, and hence one received the full benefits of salvation even if one only partook of the bread and not the wine. The reservation of the cup reflected a changing social situation in the churches, however; priests usually said the mass alone, in a language that the majority of the people did not understand very well, with few people actually participating by receiving the elements of bread and wine.

People's participation in eucharistic liturgies might have been less than it was in ages past, but this did not mean they failed to be confronted with the message of Christianity on anything other than a regular basis. Everywhere one went in twelfth-century Europe one saw church buildings: large cathedrals, small country chapels, monasteries, and even roadside shrines. Pictures and statues representing biblical characters and events, as well as persons from church history, adorned these buildings, providing constant reminders of the faith. The figure one encountered most often in such places, after Jesus of course, was that of the Virgin Mary, reflective of the significant growth of her importance at the popular level. Public life was organized by the church seasons, and public festivals were often held celebrating religious events. Even if one did not go into a church, one could hardly help but hear popular preachers from time to time in the marketplace or see mendicant friars out begging.

One might even be a member of such an order. Here one could pursue spiritual life most fully, often experiencing various gifts of the Holy Spirit that were rare or even unknown outside the monastic community. Sometimes these gifts were ordinary benefits of the discipline of daily spiritual life, such as insights that might come through prayer and fasting. Other times they were of a more intense nature, such as a visionary experience. We end this chapter with the story of one of the most extraordinary visionaries of the twelfth century, Hildegard of Bingen (1098-1179), a woman who was an abbess, poet, mystic, and writer.

Hildegard of Bingen

Hildegard of Bingen was born near the city of Mainz in 1098. At eight years of age she was sent by her parents to live in a convent. Already she had shown evidence of having an acute spiritual awareness manifested through visionary experiences. In the convent she had the opportunity to learn enough Latin to be able to write in the language. Around the time of her thirty-eighth birthday, she was elected by the other sisters to be the head of the community. Shortly after that she heard a directive in one of her visions that she was to begin to write them down. She did so beginning in 1141, and before long a copy of her first writings had reached the pope. Church officials in the twelfth century kept a close watch over revelatory visions, for they easily lent themselves to anti-authoritarian movements. Hildegard's writings were scrutinized for any whiff of heresy but were found to be entirely orthodox by the pope himself. Hildegard was instructed to continue to write down an account of any further visions that she received, which she did. The result was a book of visions known as *Scivias* (a contraction of *Sci vias Domini*, "Know the Way of the Lord") completed a decade later.

Scivias is organized into three sections, each containing a set of visions. For each vision Hildegard first records what she saw and then presents the interpretation of the vision that she claims to have heard from heaven. The interpretive sections compose what in effect is a book of theology. The themes are familiar: the Trinity, the creation of Adam and Eve, the introduction of sin into the world, the purpose of the incarnation, and the importance of the sacraments in the church. The church figures prominently in a number of these visions as a powerful woman able to take care of her children, illuminated by the blazing light of the Holy Spirit, which destroys all corruption and kindles fiery virtues.

Hildegard's other writings included two smaller collections of visions, *Book of Life's Merits* and *Book of Divine Works*; a work on science entitled *Natural History* and a medical text entitled *Causes and Cures*; a musical play, numerous hymns, and poems; and several volumes of letters. The latter offer numerous instances of her pastoral advice sent in answer to various questions that were posed to her as well as to requests for her prayers. She was consulted by an enormous range of persons, from popes and emperors to local clerics and laypeople. Some sought her insights regarding specific theological questions, while others sought her healing prayers (according to her contemporaries they were often successful). All this she did while dealing with the politics of organizing a new house for women and maintaining it as an institution.

In the end, however, her greatest contribution was as a theologian of the church. Hildegard was one of the first women ever to be accorded formal recognition as a theologian by the pope. Hildegard always professed to be without formal education, but her writings were regarded by all as theologically instructive and sound. This in itself is remarkable for an age in which women were considered by most men to be physically, spiritually, and morally inferior. Venturing into the realm of theological mysteries in the twelfth century was considered a highly

ad exponendum ⁊ indocta ad scriben
dum ea dic ⁊ scribe illa ñ sedm os homi
nis· nec sedm intellectum humane ad
inuentionis nec sedm uoluntate huma
ne compositionis· ɧ sedm id quod ea in
celestibʔ desup in mirabilibʔ di uidet ⁊ au
dis· ea sic edisserendo pferens· quemadmo
dum ⁊ auditor uerba pceptoris sui pcipi
ens· ea sedm tenore locutionis illi· ipso uo
lente· ostendente· ⁊ pcipiente ppalat· Sic
ɋ ⁊ tu ó homo· dic ea ɋ uides ⁊ audis·⁊ se
be ea non sedm te· nec sedm aliu homi
nem ɧ secundu uoluntate scientis uiden
tis·⁊ disponentis omnia in secretis miste
riorum suorum· Et iteru audiui uoce
de celo michi dicente· Dic ɋ mirabilia
hec·⁊ scribe ea· hoc modo edocta ⁊ dic·

factum e in millesimo centesimo
quadragesimo pmo filii di ihu x
incarnationis anno· cu ɋdraguita duoɽ
annoɽ septe̅ q; misum ee̅m maxime coruisca
tionis igneu lum apto celo ueniens totu
cerebru meu trusfudit· ⁊ totu cor totuq;
pectus meu uelut flamma ñ tam ar
dens ɧ calens ita inflammauit· ut sol
rem aliquam calefacit· sup quam radi
os suos ponit· Et repente intellectum
expositionis libroɽ uidelicet· psalterii
euuangelii ⁊ alioɽ catholicoɽ tam ue
teris quam noui testamenti uolumi
num sapiebam· ti aute inpretatio
nem uerboɽ textus eoɽ nec diuisione

Ecce quadra
gesimo tercio
temporalis cur
sus mei anno
cum celesti uisi
oni magno ti
more ⁊ tremu
la intentione inhererem uidi maxi
mu splendore· in quo facta e uox
de celo ad me dicens· O homo fragi
lis ⁊ cinis cineris ⁊ putredo putredi
nis· dic ⁊ scribe ɋ uides ⁊ audis· Sed
quia timida es ad loquendu ⁊ simplex

Self-portrait of Hildegard of Bingen inspired by divine fire, from the pages of Scivias. *From the Codex Rupertsberg (which disappeared during World War II). Reproduced by permission of Eric Lessing/Art Resource, New York City.*

dangerous undertaking for anyone, man or woman, for one's eternal salvation and the salvation of others who might be led astray were at stake. Innovation was not a theological virtue, and gaining the sanction of church officials, never mind the pope, was no small matter. Usually one had to undergo years of formal educational training and testing before being granted permission to speak as a theologian. Hildegard's warrant came by an alternative means: prophetic inspiration. The fact that she was granted formal approval by the highest church office makes her all the more remarkable.

Hildegard of Bingen serves as something of a summary for the entire era that has been examined in this chapter. She was a preacher, monastic leader, theologian, and church woman. Her correspondence with the pope, and the importance of having received his approval, reflected the important role the papal office had come to play in the lives of Christians throughout western Europe. The fact that her work was so carefully scrutinized for signs of heresy reflects the anxieties of the age. Her vision of the church as a holy mother giving life to her loving children exemplifies the ecclesiastical sensitivities and sacramental spirituality of the age as well. It was a vision of the kingdom of God brought close, however incomplete or partial that remained. The vision would not last, but for the thirteenth century for many it appeared to be a glorious one.

34

Byzantium in the Thirteenth Century

Historians have often cited 1054 and the excommunications exchanged in Constantinople as the point at which the Latin and Greek traditions parted ways for good. A far better candidate for dating the separation between them is the year 1204, when the combined forces of a French army and the Venetian navy attacked and defeated what was then still one of the wealthiest cities on earth. The carnage was appalling, as unrestrained crusaders plundered the city's treasures. Constantinople never truly recovered, even after a Greek emperor was returned to the city's throne six decades later. After 1204, attempts to heal the breach that had opened up between these two branches of the Christian movement were burdened by the memory and consequences of the fall of Constantinople. It is at the beginning of the thirteenth century that we find what one Orthodox historian calls "the moment of division in the history of united Christendom."[8]

For more than a century the crusades had been bringing western soldiers, pilgrims, merchants, monks, and opportunists through the streets of Constantinople and into its surrounding countryside. Political tensions between emperors and crusaders had been especially volatile, and military confrontations had erupted several times. Added to the stresses of crusaders passing through was the ever-present threat of invasion by the Normans, who from southern Italy greedily eyed Greek territories. One might have expected a certain religious solidarity among fellow Christians to have prevailed between Constantinople and various western powers of the era, but that was not the case. Political interests and dreams of wealth proved far more compelling.

The strained relations between ecumenical patriarch and pope did not help matters. The Latin claim that the pope was the administrative ruler over all Christian churches of the world was viewed by the Greeks as violating canonical privileges and responsibilities that ancient tradition had assigned to the ecumenical patriarch and other bishops in the East. Eastern theologians did not dispute the importance of the bishop of Rome, only the claim that he exercised jurisdiction

---

[8] Aristeides Papadakis, *Crisis in Byzantium: The* Filioque *Controversy in the Patriarchate of Gregory II of Cyprus (1283-1289)* (New York: Fordham University Press, 1983), 14.

over all other bishops in the world. They looked to the decisions of the ancient ecumenical councils for support for their position, discounting many of the sources to which western supporters of the papacy appealed for their support. Meanwhile the other eastern patriarchs, after centuries of Islamic domination, had lost much of their ancient importance. In matters of liturgical practices and theology, the patriarchs of Antioch and Alexandria tended to follow Constantinople's lead. The ecumenical patriarch was left as the single most powerful ecclesiastical leader in the East. The only effective counterpart to his office in administering church affairs was the emperor in Constantinople. The offices of both patriarch and emperor were severely disrupted by the sack of their city in 1204.

Byzantium 1204 to 1261

The first thing on the western crusaders' mind that April was plunder. For several days they pillaged the churches, public buildings, and even homes, removing anything of value. Sacred vessels, relics, and countless works of art were carried off from the city along with whatever stores of wealth they could locate. Reports of rape and other forms of physical violence accompanied their desecrations. Even the papal representative who had been accompanying the crusaders all along on their trip and had already intervened on their behalf with Rome is reported to have joined in looting the city. After three days the crusaders settled down to running what remained of their newly acquired empire. Baldwin of Flanders was elected to be the emperor of the city, while an obscure Venetian monk was elected to be the patriarch of Constantinople. The doge of Venice was the real winner in the scramble for power in the city, for the Venetians made sure that their interests were well protected when Constantinople's holdings were divided up among the victors.

At first Pope Innocent III had opposed the crusaders' attempt to take the city. Even after he received word of the deed he was uneasy, fearing Venetian designs. Once the Venetians assured him that they recognized papal authority, Innocent confirmed the appointment and accepted the event. Perhaps this was the means by which the unity of Christendom was finally to be restored. Greek bishops in areas under Latin control were required to swear oaths of loyalty to the pope, which many did only reluctantly. Latin practices were forcibly introduced in churches throughout the city, while Greek practices were discouraged. Rebaptisms even became common as western clerics formed new congregations apart from the existing ecclesiastical structures. In Cyprus the Latin rulers forced many of the Greek bishops into exile and even executed several clerics who resisted.

Outside the areas under the crusaders' control, three new Greek kingdoms emerged after 1204. One of these, known as the kingdom of Epirus, was formed along the Adriatic coast and eventually included the city of Thessalonica. The second, known as the kingdom of Trebizond, was formed along the coast of the Black Sea by grandsons of a former Byzantine emperor with the assistance of the kingdom of Georgia. The third, and most important, was the kingdom of Nicaea, formed by Theodore Lascaris, who was a son-in-law of the former Greek emperor. All three kingdoms initially claimed to be the rightful successor of the Byzantine empire, but eventually the third—that of the kingdom of Nicaea—was able to establish its authority as the legitimate continuation of the imperial tradition. After the death of the former patriarch, who had gone into exile as the western crusaders sacked Constantinople, Theodore invited a number of Greek bishops and other church leaders to Nicaea to elect a successor to the ecumenical patriarchate, which they did in 1208. Among the first acts of the new patriarch was to crown Theodore emperor. There were now two emperors who had been crowned by patriarchs, one in Constantinople and one in Nicaea. Needless to say, the majority of eastern church leaders recognized the emperor and patriarch in Nicaea as being the legitimate successors to the imperial tradition of Constantinople.

For the next five decades Theodore and his successors were able to maintain a viable kingdom in western Anatolia despite the political turmoil that embroiled the region. The year 1241 brought an invading Mongol army into Asia Minor, and soon the kingdom of Trebizond, the Sultanate, and Cilician Armenia were all reduced to being vassal states of the Mongol empire. The kingdom of Nicaea remained the only independent entity in Asia Minor. Meanwhile, to the north and west of Constantinople, continuous fighting among various armies in Bulgaria and the Balkans kept that part of the region in disarray. Eventually the Latins' infighting reduced their effective hold on anything but the city of Constantinople itself.

A young general, Michael Palaeologus, came to the throne in Nicaea in 1258, being elevated to co-emperor along with an eight-year-old son of the former ruler. For several years he extended the kingdom of Nicaea's territories. Then in the summer of 1261 he sent a small army across the Bosphorus to scout out the defenses of Constantinople. Upon arriving, the scouting party discovered that most of the city's defenders were off aiding the Venetians in a campaign they had launched against the Greeks elsewhere. Michael's forces took the city with virtually no resistance. The Venetians' quarters were destroyed, leaving their navy no choice but to abandon the city when they returned. Most of the remaining Latins retreated with them. In contrast to the destruction unleashed upon the inhabitants by the invading crusaders in 1204, the recapture of Constantinople in 1261 seemed almost anticlimactic.

The city Michael Palaeologus now entered as emperor was merely a shadow of its once great self. Everywhere were the charred remains of the fires that had accompanied the destruction fifty-seven years earlier. The lead roofs of its buildings had been stripped clean. Whole neighborhoods had been abandoned. There were breaches in the defensive walls around the city. The city's administrative bureaucracy had all but disappeared entirely with the exodus of Greek leadership; there were few left who knew how to run a government. Greeks from the countryside were thus invited to move back to the city to help begin rebuilding the imperial infrastructure. In an effort to reinforce his position, Michael and his wife held a second ceremony of imperial coronation. Then, in December of 1261, Michael ordered his eleven-year-old co-emperor, who was still in Nicaea, blinded, an act of cruelty that assured Michael alone would rule.

The Council of Lyons (1274)

The western powers were not about to abandon their claim on Constantinople without a struggle. The pope called for another crusade against the city. Michael had earlier struck a financial agreement with Genoa to provide him with ships to help counter Venetian naval strength, but the Genoese were still no match for their Venetian rivals. Finding himself with few options, two years after re-entering Constantinople Michael opened negotiations with the pope for a union of the two churches. The vast majority of the Greek clergy actively opposed such a course of action, but Michael was facing the likely invasion by Charles of Anjou from southern Italy. Papal envoys met with the emperor with a statement of faith that Rome had drawn up. Michael in turn agreed to recognize papal primacy and the right of all bishops to appeal to Rome. Pope Gregory X then arranged to have the emperor's representatives meet with the western bishops at the Council of Lyons in 1274.

Only three high-ranking eastern church officers attended the council that summer, in contrast to the fifteen hundred western bishops, priests, and theologians who were there. The eastern representatives came with a signed statement of faith from the hand of the emperor himself that stated his submission to the western church. The Greek delegate agreed on behalf of the emperor to accept at all points the western position on matters of doctrine and practice, including papal primacy, use of unleavened bread in the eucharist, belief in the doctrine of purgatory, and other such matters. They then recited the Nicene Creed in Greek with the addition of the clause regarding the double procession of the Holy Spirit. The council ended with a formal declaration that the breach in communion between the two church traditions had been healed.

In Constantinople the council's decisions were met with public outrage and demonstrations against the emperor. The patriarch resigned in protest, although a pro-Latin unionist was soon found to replace him. Michael's own sister joined the opposition and took up residence in the kingdom of Bulgaria, from where she continued to plot his overthrow. The emperor responded by instituting repressive measures against the rising tide of opposition. Some among the clerics were blinded, others had their tongues cut out by his soldiers. Such actions did little to convince the majority of bishops and priests to accept the changes they were ordered to make, however. The majority of Greek bishops were opposed to any declaration of reunion in which all of the heads of eastern churches had not participated openly and freely, and before all of the doctrinal differences had been resolved in mutually agreed-upon terms

Word of the resistance reached Rome and caused the pope in turn to increase the pressure for unity. Papal approval of every episcopal appointment was demanded, and preachers were to be appointed for every church to instruct them in the western ways. The Greek rites were no longer to be practiced, and a cardinal legate was to take up residence in Constantinople to oversee the affairs of the church. The new sets of demands proved to be more than even Michael could implement. The year 1281 brought a new pope to the throne, who decided that the best course of action was to support a military invasion by Charles of Anjou from Sicily. Michael Palaeologus was accused of duplicity and excommunicated on charges of supporting schismatics in his domains. The invasion from Sicily never came. Popular revolt, engineered by Michael's diplomatic cunning, broke out against Charles and his French troops, removing them from power and thus ending the threat they posed to Constantinople. Michael died the following year, in 1282, while on a new campaign to the north.

The Council of Blachernae (1285)

One of the first acts of Michael's son and successor as emperor was to depose the unpopular patriarch John Beccus, who had supported the efforts to forcibly unite the Greek church with Rome. A new patriarch, Gregory II from Cyprus (c.1241-1290), was installed, and one of his first acts was to depose all bishops who had supported the forced union of the churches and suspend all clerics ordained by the former patriarch. The unionists were still strong enough to call for a full airing of their case. Gregory agreed, and a council was convened in 1285 in the imperial palace of Blachernae, located in the northwestern corner of the city.

From the outset the Council of Blachernae focused on the subject of the double procession of the Holy Spirit from the Father and the Son. Although this was not the only issue that separated Latins from Greeks, among the eastern theologians it was viewed as being the key provision in the Council of Lyons for or against which they now were to decide. The unionists argued that the Cappadocians and other eastern theological authorities could be called upon to support the statement that the Holy Spirit proceeds from the Father *through* the Son, a phrase they believed to be the same as the Latin formulation that was so often opposed. The result, argued the unionists' opponents, was nothing less than to assert that the Son in some sense participates in being the "cause" *(aitios)* of the Holy Spirit. This would then violate the Orthodox trinitarian doctrine that the Father alone is the single source or cause within the Godhead.

The majority of those participating in the Council of Blachernae sided with Gregory against the unionists. Their position was published in the final statement of the Council, the *Tomus*, which was penned by Gregory. In response to the filioque doctrine of the Latins, the *Tomus* articulated forcefully what has been termed an eastern church's "biblical-personalist approach."[9] This eastern tradition emphasized first the threeness of God and the distinctiveness of the hypostases of each member of the Trinity, and then the oneness of God. The essential unity of God is preserved in the personhood of the Father, the Orthodox historically argued. Yet all three persons of the Trinity are co-equal and co-eternal in glory. The Father generates the Son and projects the Spirit in such a way as not to imply any inferiority or subordination.

---

[9] Ibid., 88.

Concerning the relation of the Son to the Spirit, the *Tomus* summarized the Orthodox position that rejected the Son being in any sense understood as a cause of the Spirit. Instead, the *Tomus* asserted, the Son eternally manifests the Spirit. What is manifested through the Son is the gift of the eternal Spirit in the historical arena. Gregory's point was that more than a different phrasing of the same faith was involved in the eastern church's disputes with the West. A different understanding of God was involved, presenting a serious problem for those who made unity in the essentials of faith a condition for sharing communion with one another.

As significant as the *Tomus* was as a thirteenth-century theological statement of Orthodox trinitarian theology, the Council of Blachernae did little to end the internal disputes in Constantinople. Some conservatives in the church accused Gregory of doctrinal innovations in the *Tomus*, while others still clamored for some kind of theological accommodation with the West. The struggles led Gregory to offer his resignation in 1289, doing so only after the entire synod affirmed the orthodoxy of the *Tomus*. The emperor accepted the patriarch's resignation, hoping to find a candidate around whom all could unite. The hope proved elusive. Meanwhile, continuous battles and military intrigues kept the refounded Byzantine empire from gaining its political feet. A decade later a new Turkish commander named Othman appeared in Asia Minor to begin a new chapter in Constantinople's troubled affairs.

Serbia and Bulgaria

The shock of the fall of Constantinople in 1204 had been felt not only in the political territories under imperial control but in the kingdoms of Bulgaria and Serbia to Constantinople's west. Both kingdoms had broken free of Byzantine imperial rule late in the twelfth century under national princes. The churches in both kingdoms had remained in communion with the ecumenical patriarch, however. The northern Balkan kingdom of Croatia had come under Hungarian domination in the last part of the twelfth century, and its churches were already in the process of being drawn into the Latin tradition by 1200. Serbia's princes had flirted for several decades with the idea of accepting papal jurisdiction, but in the end its churches remained in communion with Constantinople's patriarch. This was where the shock waves of 1204 had their most serious repercussions, resulting in both churches within several decades becoming *autocephalous* ("self-heading").

A key figure in the development of Serbia's national church leadership during this period was a prince named Sava (d. 1236), who for sixteen years was a monk on Mount Athos. In 1207 he returned to his native land and was soon engaged in ecclesiastical politics. After flirting for a time with papal recognition, Sava opened negotiations with Theodore Lascaris in Nicaea. In 1219 the patriarch in Nicaea recognized the Serbian church as autocephalous, or independent. Sava stepped up his efforts throughout the eastern Mediterranean region, journeying as far as Jerusalem and Alexandria not only to advance the prestige of the archbishopric

*Icon of St. Sava, first Serbian archbishop, from the Serbian
monastery on Mount Athos. Photograph of Hans-Erik Lundin,
reproduced from the Orthodox home page* (http://www.ocf.org/
OrthodoxPage), *used by permission of Michael Vezie.*

but to gather liturgical and theological resources to strengthen the churches under him.

Bulgaria's churches followed a similar course after 1204. Prior to the tenth
century the patriarch of Bulgaria had been the head of an independent church
that had nevertheless adhered closely to Constantinople in its canons and doctrines. Toward the end of the tenth century the Byzantine emperor had been able
to extend political control over the kingdom of Bulgaria. Appointments to the
head of the Bulgarian church had been handled by Constantinople after that,
with a succession of Greeks occupying the post. The Bulgarian princes revolted
in 1185 and formed an independent kingdom. The Bulgarian archbishop was
recognized by the pope in a move to bring the church into communion with
Rome, and for a time Bulgaria too flirted with recognizing papal authority. Then
came the events of 1204. Bulgaria extended refuge to the patriarch of Constantinople, who spent his last years in a monastery on its soil. In 1206 the Bulgarians
successfully attacked the Latin forces and took captive Baldwin of Flanders,
who had been installed in the office of emperor. In 1235 the Bulgarian church

gained formal recognition from the patriarchs of the various churches of the East as an autocephalous church.

Georgia

On the eastern shores of the Black Sea immediately south of the Caucasian Mountains was the kingdom of Georgia. Since Greek traders had first introduced Christianity into the region around the middle of the fourth century, the churches had maintained a close relationship with their co-religionists across the Black Sea. The church of Georgia could also claim a historic relationship with the patriarchate of Antioch, however, along with the churches of Armenia and Edessa. For a short time in the fifth and sixth century the Georgian churches had joined with the Armenians to their immediate south in rejecting the decision of the Council of Chalcedon, but by the seventh century they had returned to communion with the Chalcedonian patriarch of Constantinople. The Georgian bishops continued to elect their own patriarch, however, and they remained an autocephalous church within the Eastern Orthodox family.

Christianity had helped shape Georgia's national identity, while the country's remote location helped preserve its independence from both Byzantine and Abbasid governments. In the eleventh century a strong united kingdom emerged under Bagrat III (975-1014) and by the twelfth had expanded its control into Armenia. Several reforming kings extended educational institutions and strengthened discipline among the clergy. Queen Tamar (reigned 1184-1212) continued to extend Georgia's political influence into the first decade of the thirteenth century, strengthening her own international reputation along the way. It was she who was ruler of Georgia when Constantinople fell in 1204; she helped two grandsons of a former emperor establish a new Greek kingdom at Trebizond. After taking control of Jerusalem the Egyptian sultan Salah ad-Din returned to her the Georgian monastery in the city that had been taken over by Latins, an indication of the high regard she commanded even beyond the borders of eastern Christendom.

Signs of the trouble that was ahead first appeared on the Georgian horizon in the 1220s with the arrival of a Mongol army in the Caucasian region. The Mongols were a new power on the world political scene, arising from northwestern Asia to transform the landscape of history across the continent. Two decades later they returned to stay, reducing Georgia to a vassal state of the great khan in Mongolia. But that is a story that must await the next chapter.

Russia

Constantinople's ecclesiastical jurisdiction still extended to the north in the thirteenth century over the churches of Russia. We have already seen something of the close historical connections between the Russian and Byzantine churches. Following the baptism of Vladimir in 988, Kiev quickly became the center of the Russian church. The patriarch of Constantinople appointed and consecrated a metropolitan for Kiev who in turn exercised jurisdiction over all other bishops in Russia. For the first several centuries the metropolitan of Kiev was always a Greek. The selection was made from among three names submitted to the patriarch by the clergy of Kiev, but not until the end of the twelfth century were any Russians appointed to the metropolitanate, and even then on an alternating basis with Greeks. Russia was not technically a vassal state of the Byzantine empire, but in both its economic and cultural ties was heavily dependent on the great city to its south.

As with the other branches of the world Christian movement in the twelfth century, monasteries dominated the spiritual life of Russia. A large number of monasteries were founded early in Russia's Christian experience, the most famous perhaps being the Cave Monastery near Kiev. Organized in the tenth century under Greek influences, monks lived in cells that were dug into the side of the mountain. Although the monastery had an abbot, its members were not organized as a community. Each monk lived in his own cell, which he technically owned, and took care of securing his own food. In addition to spiritual devotion, these monks offered assistance to the poor and provided care for the sick, making the Cave Monastery among the first institutions of public welfare in the Russian state.

Christianity was the religion of Russia's rulers after the tenth century, and indeed many would say it came to be synonymous with the Russian soul. In the cities that soon sprouted across the Russian landscape, evidence of Christian influence was everywhere. Thirteenth-century Russia still provided a home for traditional religious beliefs, however, especially among the lower classes. People still visited traditional seers or sorcerers in cities and villages alike. Priests in the service of the traditional gods still offered animal sacrifices in the Russian countryside. Bishops in the thirteenth century were still condemning the tendency of church members to mix their religious commitments.

Looking back at events in the Byzantine East, we see the thirteenth century as a time of great change. The century opened with Constantinople at the center of an empire facing trouble on several fronts. To the east in Anatolia were the Turks, the Armenians, and the crusaders. To the west were the Bulgarians and the Serbs. In southern Italy were the Normans. Constantinople itself had become a meeting place for a great diversity of cultures. Anglo-Saxons, Scandinavians, Russians, Khazars, Pechenegs, Armenians, and Turks all served as mercenaries in the Byzantine army and could be found in or around the city. Venetian and Genoese merchants were increasingly stopping at the city's port and had established a permanent residence in the city. A mosque had been built for Muslim merchants who traded in the city, while a community of some four hundred Jews inhabited an island just outside the city.

The crusaders took control of the center of the empire, but their attempt to establish a new Latin state was a failure. The only political consequence was the long-term weakening of the Byzantine empire. In the ecclesiastical arena, on the other hand, the disruption of the ecumenical patriarchate had the effect of furthering the development of autocephalous churches in Bulgaria and Serbia. Eventually the patriarchate was restored, and the city of Constantinople brought again under a Greek imperial ruler. The autocephalous character of the churches in communion with the patriarch remained a permanent feature of the churches of the East.

Political events raised again the theological question of union between Constantinople and Rome. For several centuries questions of papal authority, liturgical practices, and church discipline had separated the two communions. In the theological debate over church union at the end of the thirteenth century in the Council of Blachernae, the Greek theologians made clear that the differences between East and West reached to the very core of church doctrine, specifically the doctrine of the Trinity. Church union would be impossible as long as the two communions had what appeared to many to be incompatible understandings not just of ecclesiastical structure but of God.

35

Christianity in Asia under the Mongols

Three hundred and fifty years of living as a minority under Muslim rule had diminished the Christian community, but by no means had it eradicated the churches from Syria, Mesopotamia, Palestine, and Egypt. In Iran, where traditional Persian culture had experienced a revival under the Abbasids, Christians in the eleventh century were able to enjoy a greater degree of freedom than they had seen in previous centuries. Christian faith was also spreading among the various tribes of central Asia, and new missionary efforts were being launched from Persian churches. Many from among the Uighurs, a tribe that had for several centuries been Manichaeans, were becoming Christians by the tenth century. The bishop of Merv wrote to the patriarch of Baghdad in 1009 to inform him that an entire tribe among the Kerait Turks had become Christian along with their king. Archeological evidence in the form of graves with Christian inscriptions in Syriac and the ruins of monasteries in the region support the case for a growing Christian presence among Turkish and Mongol tribes during these years.

Many from among the Turkish tribes immediately north of the Oxus River were also converting to Islam during these years. One of the Turks who had risen to power through the Abbasid ranks in the military was named Seljuk. Early in the eleventh century he successfully mounted a campaign to assume power over the Abbasid government in Baghdad, maintaining the caliph as a figurehead. An army of the Seljuk Turks, as we have seen, moved against Armenia and in 1071 dealt the Byzantine empire one of the most devastating military defeats in its history. Within a decade the Seljuk Turks had seized control of most of Asia Minor from Constantinople, creating a new political entity they named the Sultanate of Rum. The Turks' attempt to consolidate control over Syria and Palestine had stalled by the time the crusaders arrived. For their part, the crusaders did not establish a lasting presence in the region, although they did bring changes to the lives of the churches. In some places, as already noted, they forced changes in episcopal leadership and installed Latin bishops. The West Syriac (Jacobite) churches remained relatively untouched by the crusaders, who were content with merely approving their episcopal elections. The most significant event in the Jacobite relationship to Rome was the submission of the patriarch to Roman authority in 1236, an act that did little to affect the other West Syriac churches. After his death in 1252 they continued as an independent church.

The story was different for the Maronite churches. These non-Chalcedonian congregations traced their roots back to the time of the Arab conquest in the seventh century. Located in the mountains of Lebanon, they had maintained their separate identity over the centuries. One writer from the period placed their number at forty thousand. Negotiations with the crusaders resulted in an agreement in 1181 that brought the Maronite churches under the authority of the Latin bishop of Antioch, and thus into communion with Rome. Maronite churches were allowed to maintain their own hierarchy (the Maronite patriarch, Jeremiah al-Amshiti, attended the Fourth Lateran Council in 1215), married priests, and the use of Syriac in their liturgy. They agreed in return to recognize the universal authority of the pope, use unleavened bread in the eucharist, and affirm the double procession of the Holy Spirit.

Cilician Armenia

Tucked in the southeast corner of Asia Minor along the border with Syria is a district known as Cilicia. In the tenth century it had become home to a sizable number of Armenian immigrants. Following the Seljuk Turk invasion of the Armenian homeland in 1064 and the Byzantine disaster at Manzikert in 1071, their numbers had swelled rapidly. A network of ruling Armenian nobility began building fortresses and taking over towns and seaports. Cilicia even became home to the Armenian patriarch (or catholicus, as he was known), who moved from Etchmiadzin, in Armenia, in the twelfth century. The arrival of the crusaders brought the establishment of a new Latin kingdom of Edessa under Baldwin, who ruled most of the traditional Armenian homeland (or Greater Armenia) as well as portions of Syria. An alliance through marriage brought much of Cilicia (or Lesser Armenia) into the Latin orbit, only to be reversed by renewed Greek military activity in the region. Finally, in the middle of the twelfth century an independent Armenian kingdom was established under Toros II.

The Armenians in Cilicia found themselves in a highly precarious international situation. Few doubted that some form of alliance with either Greek or Latin military forces was desirable, but church leaders were divided over which was the better option. Toward the end of the twelfth century, the Armenian catholicus entered into a series of conversations with the Greeks intended to bring the two churches into theological union. The central dogmatic issue that separated them remained the definition of Chalcedon from 451, which the Greek church accepted as normative for Orthodox christology but the Armenians rejected as being Nestorian in essence. The catholicus, Nerses IV (d. 1173), finally agreed that he could affirm the definition of Chalcedon without abandoning the historical Armenian position. A synod of the Armenian bishops meeting in Hromcla in 1179 failed to agree, however, leaving the two communions separated.

While the catholicus was holding conversations with representatives of the Greek church, other Armenian bishops were looking further west toward Rome for a dialogue partner. The Armenian nobility of Cilicia had maintained fairly cordial relations with the Latin crusaders for the most part and had managed to seal their political alliance through intermarriage. Armenian churches shared much in common with the Greek tradition, but on some matters, most notably the use of unleavened bread in the eucharist, the Armenian churches were closer to the Latin church. A council of Armenian bishops meeting in Tarsus in 1198 voted to unite with Rome, although little was done following the council to move in that direction.

The Armenian bishops assumed union meant mutual recognition, but from all accounts Rome expected union would bring Armenian acknowledgment of papal authority. Early in the thirteenth century the Armenian king Leon II sought and received from the pope formal recognition as the legitimate ruler of Cilicia. But political and ecclesiastical worlds did not necessarily coincide among the Armenians. Many in Cilicia even in the church hierarchy were pro-Latin in terms of military policy while being highly ambivalent at best about adopting Latin rites or recognizing papal authority over their church. The arrival of Franciscan and Dominican friars in Cilicia by the middle of the 1200s tended to divide the community even more. The friars actively proselytized among the population, forming separate Armenian Latin churches that were alienated from the national communion. Toward the end of the thirteenth century opposition to Rome was so great that several pro-western patriarchs of the church were assassinated.

The Mongols

Early in the 1240s a new military force appeared in Anatolia to make political matters in Cilicia much more complicated. The invaders were Mongols, and they had efficiently destroyed local resistance. The Armenian king Het'um I (1226-1269) had little choice but meet the Mongol demands that he become their vassal and pay tribute to their supreme ruler or khan. Before long an Armenian ambassador was on his way to the great khan's capital in Karakorum, Mongolia, south of Lake Baikal. About the same time another group of Christian envoys was on its way to the Mongol camp at Karakorum as envoys of the pope. An army of Mongols under a different general had swept across Russia and into eastern Europe after 1236, leaving behind a wide swath of destruction that ran through Poland, Hungary, and Austria. Alarmed by reports of the terror they had spread and the fierceness of their forces, Pope Innocent IV in 1245 commissioned several envoys to make contact with the Mongol leaders. Thus it was that a Franciscan friar named John of Plano Carpini, along with several companions, came to undertake a journey halfway around the world to the Mongol capital of Karakorum, where he arrived in time for the coronation of the third great khan in 1246.

The Mongols (also known in the West as Tatars, the name of one of the other tribes the Mongols had earlier conquered) were not entirely strangers to Christian ways. For several centuries Christianity had been spreading among many of their neighboring tribes. The Uighurs had been the first of these to adopt writing, using the Sogdian script to do so. By some reports Christian monks had played a major role in this process in order to translate scriptures and other religious works into the Uighur tongue. Christian monks were joined by Manichaeans, Buddhists, and Muslims in spreading their faith among these northern tribes. Despite such efforts, however, the majority of people among the Mongols and Turks across central Asia and north of China were followers of the ancient shamanistic religion of their ancestors. They believed in a high God known as *Tangri* (or Eternal Heaven), whose representative on earth was the great khan.

Toward the end of the twelfth century, a Mongol warrior named Temüjin (or Temurgin, c.1165-1227) overthrew his Kerait suzerain and assumed control of a sizable coalition of tribal armies. The new ruler, known to history as Genghis Khan ("Great Khan"), assimilated the Keraits by taking a number of women from among their ruling family and giving them to his sons as wives. Kidnapping and forced marriage of women from other tribes, it should be noted, was a common custom among the Mongols and Turks of central Asia. In this case the Kerait woman Genghis Khan gave to his youngest son was named Sorghaghtani (d. 1252). By some accounts Sorghaghtani (the name is spelled a number of different ways) was a Christian. Three of her sons, Möngke (d. 1259), Hülagü (d. 1265), and Khubilai (d. 1294), were among the most important Mongol rulers to follow their grandfather, Genghis Khan.

Genghis Khan took the wives and daughters of the Keraits in order to assimilate ruling families. He took over the Kerait and Uighur administrative system for governing as well, adopting most aspects with little change. According to the thirteenth-century Syrian Christian scholar Gregory Bar Hebreus, "Since the Mongols had neither literature nor writing, Genghis Khan commanded the scribes of the Uighurs, and they taught the children of the Tatars their books, and they wrote the Mongol language with Uighur letters."[10] Many of these scribes were Christian monks and priests. Genghis Khan appointed Christians as governors and administrators in some of the regions he conquered and made use of their skills as interpreters. While we can only speculate as to the extent of Christian cultural influences in the camp (the Mongol rulers were nomadic and continued to live part of each year in camps) during the first years of the Mongol empire, we know that the new rulers had contact with Christianity.

The Mongols rose to power in a religiously pluralistic environment. They exercised a considerable degree of religious tolerance toward the various faiths within their empire. Genghis Khan himself, like most Mongol men, practiced traditional shamanistic rites that were a part of the fabric of Mongol life. A shaman advisor played a key role in many of Genghis Khan's decisions. The first great khan at his death was buried with traditional shamanistic rites that included the sacrifice of both horses and young women. It was a shaman woman who delivered the Mongols' demands to the princes of Russia before the Mongols attacked them in 1237, indicating that shamans traveled with the army in their campaigns. At the same time the law of Genghis Khan, known as the *yasa* and

---

[10] *The Chronography of Gregory Abû'l Faraj, the Son of Aaron, the Hebrew Physician Commonly Known as Bar Hebreus, Being the First Part of His Political History of the World*, trans. Ernest A. Wallis Budge, vol. 1 (London: Oxford University Press, 1932), 354. Changes in the spelling of names in Budge's text have been made for the sake of conformity with present usage.

said to have been delivered from Tangri, called for all people to believe in this high God without specifying any particular creed or practice.

All religious traditions were to be respected, and all holy men and women were to be granted religious privileges under Mongol rule. When the Franciscans arrived in the camp of the great khan they found Buddhist priests, Manichaean teachers, and a handful of Muslims in residence. The Franciscans also described a church tent in the camp outside Karakorum with wooden gongs in the East Syriac tradition. These monks and priests were fully part of the camp of the great khan and were holding regular worship services. From various sources it appears that the Mongol ruler's wives and daughters were actively practicing their Christian faith.

Soon after he had consolidated his rule among the various tribes of Mongolia, Ghenghis Khan turned his forces against northern China, where a Manchurian dynasty was in power. He destroyed the capital at modern Beijing, then turned his attention back toward the west. Crushing several smaller kingdoms along the way, he marched his army across the Oxus River into eastern Persia. A separate Mongol force continued on into Azerbaijan and Georgia, while Genghis Khan turned southeast, battling his way across modern Pakistan into northwest India until he reached the Indus River. There the great khan's armies turned back to consolidate their control over the territories they had conquered. The empire was divided into four regions among the sons or grandsons of Genghis Khan, who agreed to elect from among themselves a successor as the next great khan. By the time of Genghis Khan's death in 1227, the Mongol empire extended from northern China across central Asia to India. Whole cities, armies, and kingdoms had been literally wiped off the landscape by their onslaught.

The Mongol army that had marched east into Georgia in the early 1220s had advanced as far as the Dnieper River and the Black Sea and defeated a Russian army under the prince of Kiev before turning back. Fifteen years later an army under one of the grandsons of Genghis Khan, a general named Batu, returned. This second Mongol campaign brought far more destruction than before. The forces of the Golden Horde, as the Mongols were known (so called because of the golden tent in which the khan resided in their camp at Sarai), destroyed city after city. Kiev was burned to the ground and almost its entire population annihilated. Several years later western visitors through the region reported seeing the bones of the dead still piled up along the road outside the city. In 1241 Mongol forces swept through Poland and Hungary into Austria, crushing the European armies that it met along the way. Only the death of Genghis Khan's successor back in Mongolia brought an end to the campaign of terror as the Mongol leaders withdrew to their permanent camp at Sarai, on the mouth of the Volga River, to await the election of the third great khan.

The first Franciscan envoys to Karakorum

Reports of the devastation in eastern Europe soon reached Pope Innocent IV, who greeted them with both alarm and a sense of hope. The Mongols were virtually unknown to the West, and their forces had proved to be unstoppable by European armies. But it was also known that the Mongols had attacked Muslim armies and had done so with equal ferocity. The possibility of an alliance against Islam presented a prospect too inviting to ignore. Several missions were appointed to try to make contact with the Mongol rulers. The head of the Franciscan order in Saxony and one of the original group around Francis himself, John of Plano Carpini (1180-1252), was chosen to lead one of these delegations. Two other Franciscans joined him, Lawrence of Portugal and Benedict the Pole. None of them knew the languages of the Mongols, and John of Plano Carpini was already sixty-three years of age. Nevertheless, the friars accepted their assignment and set off across the Polish frontier in the spring of 1245.

It did not take them long to make contact with a Mongol outpost, which dispatched them under guard to the camp of the Golden Horde along the Volga River. After a few days the Mongol ruler of Russia, Batu, decided to send them on to Karakorum to be a part of the gathering that witnessed the election of the third great khan in 1246. The Mongols had established a series of relay stations in camps across Asia by which they maintained communication throughout their empire. It was across this northern route that the barefoot friars were sent, outfitted with Mongol horses and accompanied by a small detachment of guides. For several weeks the band rode relentlessly, living mostly off millet and salt, with boiled snow for water. Finally they arrived in the middle of the summer in Karakorum in time to record the enthronement of one of Genghis Khan's grandsons, Güyük as the great khan.

John of Plano Carpini's account of the experience was published after his return under the title *History of the Mongols*. In it he provided a detailed account of the Mongol customs that he observed, including how they lived in camps as hunters and herders, how their political life was organized, how their polygynous families were structured, and how from a young age all males were trained for fighting. At the end of the book he even provided recommendations for those whom he expected would soon be going against the Mongol armies in battle. Concerning their religious life, shamanism was clearly the dominant practice among the people he had observed. The Franciscan described several purification rituals he had witnessed that involved someone passing between fires and women making leather dolls for exorcisms or other rites.

In Karakorum the group met a number of Russians and Hungarians who had been taken captive by the Mongols, including Yaroslav I of Vladimir, who died while the Franciscans were there. A Russian goldsmith showed them the work he had fashioned for the great khan, while other Russians served as interpreters for the western visitors, along with the Mongols' own secretaries. They also met Syriac-speaking Christians who were a permanent part of the Mongol community. According to Plano Carpini, Christians who were part of the imperial household thought that the great khan himself was about to become a Christian (a possibility that appears to have been little more than the hopeful speculation of evangelically minded believers). The brother of Het'um I of Cilicia was there representing the Armenian Christian king. Plano Carpini also reported an ambassador from the caliph in Baghdad along with other Muslim sultans, and ambassadors from China and Korea. Gifts were bestowed on the Franciscan envoys, indicating that the Mongols regarded them as representatives of heads of state along with the others; the fact that the Franciscans had brought none in return created a minor diplomatic embarrassment.

Finally the friars met the great khan, who had been given the two letters they had carried from the pope. One of these letters had outlined the basic story of the Christian faith and explained that the purpose of the friars' visit was to advance the apostolic mission of the church under him. The other called upon the Mongol rulers to end their assault on other nations or face the wrath of God. A letter from the great khan to the pope had already been composed, which the great khan's secretaries offered to translate into Russian or Arabic. The friars agreed to take back the original in the Mongol script and a Latin translation. The great khan also suggested sending a Mongol envoy back with the friars, but the westerners declined, suspecting their host wanted to send spies into Europe in preparation for a new Mongol invasion. The three Franciscans then departed for their return trip back across central Asia, making the several-thousand-mile journey over deserts and steppes late in the spring of 1247.

The letter that the great khan sent back with the Franciscans was not what the pope wanted to hear. It opened by commanding that the pope and princes of the West should come themselves before the throne of the great khan and serve him as his vassals. It was he, the great khan, who was appointed by God to make known to all people his divine law, the *yasa*, which Genghis Khan had originally propagated. The pope's invitation to Christian baptism was rejected, as were his protests over the Mongol invasion. The Mongols' victories were nothing less than a sign of the favor of God upon their mission to bring the whole world under the law of Genghis Khan. Divine sanction for world domination was a rather widespread phenomenon in the thirteenth century.

The second Franciscan envoy to Karakorum

The reign of the third great khan did not last long. In 1251 Möngke, grandson of Genghis Khan by his youngest son, Tolui, and Sorghaghtani, became the fourth great khan. During the previous decade the Mongols had not added significantly to the lands they controlled. Soon after ascending the throne Möngke changed that by sending his brother Hülagü with an invasion force against Persia and Baghdad. A second brother, Khubilai, assumed control of the eastern district of the Mongol empire in northern China and soon began extending his rule toward the southeast. Möngke's reign did not last a full decade, but it marked another period of enormous expansion of Mongol rule throughout the world.

The year after the initial Franciscan mission had returned from Mongolia, two envoys from the great khan, one a Syriac Christian, arrived in Rome to meet with the pope. Envoys on behalf of the Mongol emperor also made contact with King Louis of France while he was in Cyprus, on his way to a crusade in Palestine. From the city of Samarkand in central Asia came a letter from the brother of Het'um I, king of Cilician Armenia and brother-in-law of the king of Cyprus.

There were Christian influences everywhere in the central Asian territory of the Mongols, the envoy reported. In Russia one of the sons of Khan Batu, named Sartach, was even reported to have become a Christian. By the time Louis arrived in Acre, he had decided to send an envoy to Russia to investigate this last claim.

Once again the task fell to a Franciscan, William of Rubruck (dates unknown). William departed from Acre in 1253, traveling by merchant ships to Constantinople and then into the Black Sea. Once on land he set off with four carts full of fruit, wine, and biscuits, which he intended to bring to the Mongols as presents. His immediate destination was the camp of Sartach, to whom he bore a letter from the king of France (written in Latin, but with Arabic and Persian translations on hand). After a number of weeks the friar and his companions reached Sartach, who sent him on to the camp of Batu. From there William was ordered to go on to the camp of the great khan. There was little choice but to comply.

At the end of August he set out with his guides to the court of the great khan, a journey of several months duration. Along the way he noted evidence of Christians and Muslims alike inhabiting the countryside they passed. One village that was three days' journey from Lake Balkash, he reported, was entirely Christian. In the camp of the great khan he found an even larger Christian presence, both native Mongols and Turks who were part of the Syriac churches and a number of westerners who had been enslaved by the Mongol invaders. A German woman who had been taken captive in Hungary was now a servant of one of the Christian wives of the khan. A goldsmith named William from Paris was in the service of the great khan himself. The goldsmith had adopted a Mongol son and had taught him enough Latin for the boy to serve as interpreter for the friar. While he was there, William of Rubruck baptized six children of western Christians.

The Franciscan had ample opportunities to talk with Christians of other confessions as well, such as an Armenian monk with whom he stayed and who had come to preach to the great khan, and the East Syrian Christian priests who were under the bishop in China. From the latter he learned that there were Christians and Muslims in as many as fifteen cities of China, and that the see of their bishop was in a city he recorded as "Segin" (most likely Beijing). William was rather disparaging overall in his description of the spiritual condition of Syriac churches and priests in central Asia and in China, but he was equally prone to reciting words of the Latin liturgy every chance he had in one of their churches. He noted how pleased he was to be able to find churches and altars, one even in the camp of the great khan. As for the non-Western Christians and others in the Mongol camp, the sight of a barefooted priest walking around in Mongolia in winter struck them as a bit bizarre, and it was left to the other westerners in the capital to explain the peculiarities of a Franciscan.

When he finally was granted an audience with the great khan, William was prepared. Armenians at the court had interpreted the friar's visit to the Mongol ruler as a political mission sent to secure assistance against the Muslims. Aware of the diplomatic problems that could result from such an interpretation at the foreign court, the Franciscan explained that his purposes were entirely pastoral. He had been sent by the king of France to meet Khan Batu's son, Sartach, whom the Europeans had heard had become a Christian. The purpose was to bring words of Christian encouragement to the Mongol ruler. Möngke continued to question the friar on a number of topics, including religion. The friar was then introduced to some of the wives of the great khan, several of whom were Christians, and his son, before returning to his residence.

William stayed in the Mongol camp throughout the rest of the winter, visiting with people and noting especially the customs of his hosts. The spring of the following year finally brought permission for the Franciscan to return home. On one of the last days before he was to depart, William found himself engaged in what appears to have been an impromptu theological discussion with some of the Muslims who served in the khan's administration. Word soon reached Möngke, who decided to hold an interreligious debate in his presence. Representatives from each of the various faith communities (Western Roman Catholic, Eastern Syriac Orthodox, Muslim, and Chinese Buddhists) were told to write down in advance a basic statement of their faith to help prepare the great khan for the event. The day of the debate, three judges (a Christian, a Muslim, and a Buddhist) were selected from among the court scribes to referee the conversation. The participants were enjoined on pain of death to show respect for one another's religions.

It is a remarkable scene that the Franciscan described. Gathered before the most powerful military ruler then living on earth, inside his lavish tent, were representatives of several of the world's faith traditions, invited to engage in an interreligious debate for the benefit of the great khan. The debate opened with the questions of whether the world was created and what happens after death. William says he quickly shifted the discussion to the nature of God, arguing for the priority of the question of a creator. The Chinese disputed the notion of there being one God, uniting Muslims and Christians against them. More points followed concerning the nature of the one true God. The East Syrians then took over, making the case for the Trinity and incarnation. William reports dryly, "When this was finished the Nestorians [East Syrians] and Saracens [Muslims] alike sang loudly while the *tuins* [Buddhists] kept silence, and afterwards they all drank their fill."[11]

The following day William was summoned to meet with the great khan again, who informed the Franciscan he had granted permission for him to depart. Before the friar's departure, however, Möngke wanted to share his own religious beliefs. According to William, the great khan explained that the Mongols believed in one God who had given different ways to various peoples like different fingers on one hand. Christians had the scriptures, which few among them followed, while Mongols had prophets or shamans. The Mongol rulers perceived themselves to have been given a mission by God to unite the entire world under their laws. They also sought to extract a great amount of wealth from the people of the world whom they conquered, of course, although the great khan didn't say this. The commitment to a religious vision of pluralism and tolerance that the Mongol leader professed was not to last.

---

[11] Christopher Dawson, ed., *The Journey of William of Rubruck* in *The Mongol Mission: Narratives and Letters of the Franciscan Missionaries in Mongolia and China in the Thirteenth and Fourteenth Centuries* (New York: Sheed and Ward, 1955), 194. The term *tuin* that Rubruck used is the Chinese term *tao jenn* ("follower of the way") and was used by the Mongols for Buddhist monks.

Mongol conquest of Persia and Mesopotamia

One needs to understand the world as it looked to the Mongols in the thirteenth century. They were seated on the northern edge of the world, surrounded on three sides by great civilizations whose cities brimmed with wealth. The Mongol vision was to conquer all three and unite them—Chinese, Islamic, and Christian—around one great camp and throne. Originally Genghis Khan succeeded in extending this empire by marching his armies east against China, then south through Afghanistan into northern India. A small force was sent across the northern edge of Persia and into Georgia at that time, but the major force unleashed against the West did not come until the reign of the second great khan. After 1240 most of Russia was brutally brought under Mongol rule, while the rest of Europe lived in fear of any further attack. By the 1250s, however, the Mongols were turning their major political attention toward the south once again, and specifically Islamic civilization.

The main effort in that direction was entrusted to the brother of the great khan, Hülagü. In 1258 a Mongol army under his orders marched across the Oxus River and toward Baghdad. The Abbasid caliphate had long been in political decline, holding onto its claim to honor as the legitimate successor to the Prophet but little else. Still, no one expected that a great city such as Baghdad could so quickly fall. The Mongol general surrounded the city and demanded total surrender. When the caliph refused, the Mongols began an onslaught that ended in near-total destruction of the city. Contemporary reports put the number of dead in the hundreds of thousands. The ruling elite of the city was wiped out, including the administrative infrastructure of the Muslim government. Hülagü had the caliph brought before him in a great hall and handed him over to his troops, who rolled the caliph in a rug and trampled him to death, as it was the custom of Mongols not to spill a prince's blood.

Christians played a prominent part in the army that destroyed the city of Baghdad. Dokuz, one of Hülagü's wives, had accompanied him on the campaign and served as a close advisor. She traveled with an entourage of priests and monks, and even a portable chapel on a wagon. One of his most trusted generals, Kitbuka, was also a Christian. Priests and monks accompanying the army served as chaplains for Christians who were part of the Mongol forces. The Christian patriarch of Baghdad had participated in the failed negotiations that went on between Hülagü and the caliph prior to the destruction of the city, and during the battle itself the patriarch had gathered as many Christians in the city as he could into the church of the Third Bazaar, where the Mongol army did not harm them. After the Mongols assumed control of the city, Dokuz saw that protection was extended to Christians who lived throughout the region.

The year after he took Baghdad, Hülagü, accompanied still by Dokuz, whom Bar Hebreus called "the believing Queen and lover of Christ,"[12] and his Christian general, Kitbuka, marched his army across Mesopotamia and into Syria. The city of Damascus soon fell to the invaders. Christian princes from Cilician Armenia

---

[12] *Chronography*, 1:435.

and Antioch joined his army and prepared for an assault against the Muslim power in the region, Egypt. But then word came of the death of Hülagü's brother, the great khan, back in Mongolia, and Hülagü departed with a portion of the army to attend the election of the next great khan. The loss of the commander and a sizable number of their forces left the Mongols greatly weakened. In northern Palestine an army of the new Egyptian rulers, the Mamelukes (whom we will meet in the following chapter), destroyed the Mongol forces, thus ending their drive toward the west. The Mongols were forced to withdraw to their Persian territories, where they consolidated their rule.

Hülagü's older brother, Khubilai, was elected by the family to become the next great khan. Following his enthronement, he moved the court of the great khan to his capital in China, the city known as Khanbalik (or Cambaluc, near modern Beijing). Hülagü returned to Persia, where he assumed the title of *ilkhan* ("lesser khan"). Both he and Dokuz died a few years later, in 1265. The legacy they left behind them was an important one in the history of Persia, for it marked the beginning of a new political era.

As for the Christian churches in Persia, it was a time of greater freedom. Hülagü was certainly no Christian, and at times he could show great brutality without regard to religious grouping. A rumor that Christians were the cause of a riot brought the massacre of one entire local community, while word that some had withheld taxes brought the massacre of another. At the same time there were enough Christians close to the ilkhan to give their communities greater access to power than they had had before. Muslims still vastly outnumbered Christians in the Persian world and violence was still a constant threat, but under the Mongols a generation of Christians had greater freedom than they had experienced in Persia in almost a thousand years.

Hülagü's son, Abaka (d.1282), assumed power as the second ilkhan on the death of his father. He continued the trend of having Christian influences close to the throne. One of Abaka's wives, Mary, was the daughter of the emperor Michael Palaeologus of Constantinople, who had restored Greek rule in Constantinople. She was a Chalcedonian Christian and is known to have sponsored a church, as well as on at least one occasion intervened in a local dispute to save members of a Christian community from violence. Another wife of Abaka, Kotai, was an East Syrian Christian.

Following Abaka, his brother assumed the throne for a short period. It was an important indication of what was to come of the Mongol rule in Persia, for while Abaka's brother had been baptized as a child (his mother was a Christian), he had converted to Islam, taking the name Ahmad. Two years after Ahmad's ascent to power, Abaka's son, Arghon (d. 1291), overthrew him, and for the next seven years under Arghon's reign Christians experienced a time of relative peace. Following the death of Arghon in 1291 a period of confusion set in, as the complex politics of Mongol family rule worked themselves out across several civilizations in Asia. When the dust settled in 1295, one of Arghon's sons had come to power in Persia, a convert to Islam named Mahmud (d. 1304). Successive ilkhans after that followed in the way of Islamic faith, thereby restoring Islam's political dominance in the Persian world. By the first decades of the fourteenth century new storm clouds had formed on the horizon of Christian history in Persia, storm clouds that would bring renewed violence and eventual demise to a vast number of eastern churches.

Thus the period of Argon's ilkhanate proved to be not only one of the most sympathetic political ages for Christians under Mongol rule in Persia but one of the last such periods. Although he did not become a Christian himself, Arghon reportedly allowed one of his sons to be baptized. With the knowledge and approval of Khubilai Khan, new feelers were extended to the West to see if an alliance with the Christian kings against the Muslim rulers of Egypt could be arranged. One of the envoys was a Christian monk named Rabban Sauma. His visit to the West is as remarkable a tale as that of William of Rubruck a half-century before to the East.

Rabban Sauma and Mark (later Patriarch Yaballaha)

Around the year 1275 two monks, Rabban Sauma (c.1230-1294) and Mark (c.1245-1317), departed from the capital of the great khan at modern Beijing to go on pilgrimage to Jerusalem. Their story is told in an anonymous Syriac text from the fourteenth century known in English as *History of Yaballaha, Patriarch of the East, and Rabban Sauma*. Sauma was an Uighur who had received the tonsure of monastic discipline around 1250 in Beijing. Mark was the younger of the two and was probably a member of the Onguts, another tribe that was closely related to the Mongols. The son of a Christian leader, he had come to Beijing from one of the western provinces to study spiritual discipline under Sauma and had also become a monk. From Beijing the two friends had decided to go to Jerusalem on pilgrimage.

They set off for the Holy Land. It took them the better part of a year to cross central Asia. In areas controlled by the Mongols they passed unmolested, indicating that they traveled with safe-passage permits from Khubilai Khan. They reportedly spent time with Christians in Khotan, a city north of Tibet, where they were given fresh supplies. At other places along the route local warfare delayed their journey, as did highway bandits. Eventually they made their way across northern Persia to the city of Maragah in Azerbaijan. Upon arriving, they discovered that the patriarch was in residence at the time, and they called on him. He in turn provided a letter of introduction that they took with them to Baghdad.

War in Syria between the Mongols and Egypt kept the two monks from going to Jerusalem. For several years they had to content themselves instead with visiting monasteries and churches in the Mesopotamia area. They returned to Baghdad in 1280, where the patriarch ordained Mark to be metropolitan of northern China and gave him the name Yaballaha. War prevented the newly ordained metropolitan from departing for home, however. The following year Patriarch Denha died. The day after he was buried, the other bishops gathered at the patriarchal residence elected Yaballaha to become the next patriarch of the East, and sent him to the ilkhan Abaka to be confirmed. Although his ability to speak Syriac was limited, he was well-suited to lead the church at the time, given his cultural identity and his relations with the Mongol rulers. Abaka even offered to pay for the cost of his consecration service at Baghdad.

Abaka died a year later, and his brother assumed the throne. This was the same brother who had been baptized as a child, but upon becoming ilkhan he announced publicly his conversion to Islam. Ahmad's relationship with the Christians was stormy, but they were still guided by the Mongol policy of religious toleration. Yaballaha was imprisoned at one point by the ilkhan, but on suspicion that the patriarch was supporting a rival, Abaka's son, Arghon, for the throne. Two years after the death of his father, Arghon overthrew his Muslim uncle and the situation improved somewhat for Christians.

Several years later, in 1287, Arghon turned to Yaballaha for diplomatic help in his search for an alliance with the West against Egypt. Bishop Sauma (he was now of episcopal rank), who had still not visited Jerusalem, was chosen by his old friend for the task. Outfitted with a safe-passage permit from the great khan himself, horses, funds, letters from the East Syrian patriarch, and several companions, Sauma set off. The party traveled by way of the Black Sea to Constantinople, then on to Rome, where they arrived at a time just after a pope had died and the cardinals had assembled for a new election. Sauma requested an audience with the cardinals, which was granted.

Upon meeting him, the cardinals first inquired about his home church. Sauma explained that he came from the part of the world where Mar Thomas, Mar Addai, and Mar Mari had evangelized, and that the churches there still followed their canons. He told them that many among the Turks, Mongols, and Chinese had confessed Christ and were baptized, that the Mongol rulers had established churches in their military camps, and that the ruler in Baghdad now wished to establish an alliance with the West in order to take Jerusalem. The cardinals inquired as to the particulars of his confession of faith, asking him to recite his creed, which according to the *History* he did. Regarding the second person of the Trinity, Sauma told them he affirmed an inseparable personal union without mingling of natures in a manner that was satisfactory to the western cardinals. They debated the third article regarding the issue of the procession of the Holy Spirit without reaching agreement. Sauma then requested, and was granted, a tour of the city with its many relics of the apostles and saints.

From Italy, Rabban Sauma traveled to Paris, where he met with Philip IV and again presented his request from Arghon for an alliance against the Egyptian Muslim rulers of Palestine. In Paris the visitors from Baghdad were shown more relics and, the Syriac history notes, the "thirty thousand scholars who were engaged in the study of ecclesiastical books of instruction, that is to say of commentaries and exegesis of all the Holy Scriptures, and also of profane learning."[13]

---

[13] E. A. Wallis Budge, trans., *The Monks of Kublai Khan Emperor of China, or the History of the Life and Travels of Rabban Sawma, Envoy and Plenipotentiary of the Mongol Khans to the Kings of Europe, and Markos Who as Mar Yahbhallaha III Became Patriarch of the Nestorian Church in Asia* (London: The Religious Tract Society, 1928), 183-184.

While the numbers were an exaggeration (a more likely figure for the student population in Paris was three thousand), the report suggests how impressive the University of Paris appeared to a visitor. Sauma next went to meet Edward I of England, who was in Gascony, northern France. Edward promised assistance against Jerusalem, then requested Sauma celebrate the eucharist, which the Uighur bishop did.

Upon returning to Rome in 1288 Sauma found that one of the cardinals he had earlier met had been elected pope: Nicholas IV. The eastern bishop then requested permission to celebrate a public eucharist during Lent so that his hosts could witness the eastern liturgy. Permission was granted, and after watching it the western hosts acknowledged that although conducted in a different language, the service was nearly the same as theirs. The pope then heard Sauma's confession, and on Palm Sunday the eastern bishop received the eucharist from the hand of the pope. Sauma celebrated the eucharist one more time in the city and joined in Holy Week observations in Rome. The entire tone of the narrative is one of respectfulness and even excitement as the two ecclesiastical traditions encountered one another.

Expectations ran high in Arghon's court when Sauma returned to the East in 1288. So great was the excitement over a possible alliance that Arghon allowed one of his sons to be baptized a Christian, sponsored several new churches, and even joined personally at several ecclesiastical celebrations. His hopes for a military alliance with the West were soon to prove illusory, however, for none was forthcoming. Arghon undertook several more diplomatic missions without success. In 1291 the ilkhan died and soon a ruler who had converted to Islam was on the throne, thereby ending any hope for alliances with the Christian West. The last Latin foothold in Palestine was uprooted that same year.

Bar Hebreus and the Jacobite churches

One of Rabban Sauma's contemporaries was the Jacobite scholar Gregory Abu'l Faraj, better known in the West as Bar Hebreus (1226-1286). He was born in Melitene on the Euphrates River in Mesopotamia, where his father was a Jewish physician (hence the name Bar Hebreus). As a boy Abu'l Faraj moved with his family to Antioch where he encountered the teachings both of the Jacobites and the East Syrian theological traditions. By the age of seventeen he had become a Christian and had decided to enter the monastery. Shortly after that, at the age twenty, he was ordained a bishop (many years short of the normal canonical age, it should be pointed out) and eventually assigned to the church in Aleppo. Two decades later he was elected maphrian of the Jacobite church, which made him the missionary bishop over all churches east of the Euphrates. Gregory (the Christian name he assumed) died in Azerbaijan in 1286.

Bar Hebreus was one of the more prolific writers the Christian movement in the East has known. As a historian, exegete, grammarian, theologian, scientist, and poet, his efforts seemed to know no boundaries. Among his best-known works was *Chronography*, a history of the church that began with creation and Adam and Eve but covered mostly the previous century of eastern church history under Arab and then Mongol rule. His books covered medicine, philosophy, theology, and spirituality, in addition to translations from Arabic. All told he produced more than forty major works, while maintaining a busy life managing the affairs of the Jacobite churches of the East.

As a church leader Bar Hebreus undertook countless negotiations with various Mongol and Muslim rulers on behalf of the Christian communities he oversaw. These were difficult years for the churches in Mesopotamia, who faced not only the constant antagonism of their mostly Muslim neighbors but continuous internal strife among church leaders. Bar Hebreus showed himself to be not only a competent bishop and maphrian, but one of the more ecumenically minded ecclesiastics of his age. His elevation to the office of maphrian took place in Cilicia and was attended by the Armenian nobility and bishops, as well as the members of the Jacobite hierarchy. Once in the office of maphrian, he made contact with the East Syrian patriarch Denha and sought to resolve disputes between the two churches in order to present a united witness before the Mongol ilkhan.

The Jacobite churches that Bar Hebreus served as maphrian in the thirteenth century were divided into eighteen different episcopal regions in Persia and Mesopotamia. Altogether there were twenty archbishops, and over one hundred other bishops serving the churches. The main centers of institutional strength were always the Jacobite monasteries scattered from Cilicia to India. Monasteries provided Christians with protection in time of trouble and were remote enough to make it difficult for invading armies or hostile neighbors to attack. From *Chronography* one gains a sense of an active community facing continuous challenges as a minority religious movement in the East. Leaders such as Bar Hebreus not only provided spiritual and theological direction but handled constant struggles over money and property and dealt with the normal jealousies of human institutional life. Bar Hebreus did all this while maintaining an active life as a scholar of the Christian movement in the East.

Christians in the court of Khubilai Khan in China

Bar Hebreus wrote in his *Chronography* that the two monks Sauma and Mark had originally been sent from the court of the Mongol great khan in Beijing on the journey that brought them to Persia. That Mongol ruler was Khubilai Khan (1215-1294), who had assumed control of the eastern region of the Mongol empire after 1240. In 1260 he was elected great khan but decided to maintain his capital at Khanbalik, now modern Beijing. The Mongol rulers were vastly outnumbered by their Chinese subjects and had to accommodate themselves to many Chinese ways. Although he abolished the Confucian exams that had for centuries provided entrance into the state bureaucracy, Khubilai Khan had to make use of Chinese administrators to handle the taxes of the empire. These administrators were Confucian scholars, and they brought their ideology with them to the Mongol court. Other Chinese cultural influences were soon reshaping the Mongol culture of the rulers. Khubilai Khan himself became a follower of Buddhism under the influence of Tibetan teachers.

Under the emperor were others in the court who were Christians, including some of his court physicians. Several of the Mongol governors who were appointed over provinces under his rule were also Christians. East Syrian church history records the names of a number of bishops identified as metropolitans in the Mongol capital at Beijing. Monasteries and churches were planted in a number of cities in China where the Mongol presence had spread or where Persian traders had founded communities. Along the seacoast in particular there is evidence of East Syrian Christians having established churches and monasteries in districts where foreign merchants stayed.

A lack of Chinese literary records from this period leaves us without much information or knowledge of what the Mongol court in Beijing was like. We do have a description from an Italian merchant named Marco Polo, who journeyed all the way to the court of Khubilai Khan in northern China in the thirteenth century. Marco Polo's father and uncle first reached the court of Khubilai Khan around 1265. They returned a decade later with Marco who was seventeen years old when he left Europe, but around thirty-five when he returned. Marco Polo's account of the East was important for introducing Europeans to the urban civilization of the East. More to the point regarding our concerns, his account contained numerous references to the Christian communities he had seen scattered across central Asia and China. It is one of the best sources we have for gaining a sense of the overall condition—at least physically if not spiritually—of the churches and monasteries he saw.

The greatest concentration of Christians was still found in the cities along the Silk Road through central Asia. In this regard his account verifies reports from other travelers through the region in these centuries who report worshiping in Christian churches or staying with Christian communities. Elsewhere along the route he found evidence of monasteries that had been abandoned and of churches that were in decline. The situation was clearly one of the church in transition but still evidencing strength among the various ethnic tribes that were part of the Turkish and Mongol families in the region.

Among the surprises Marco Polo recounted were the number of Christians he encountered in southeastern China along the coastal cities. Most of these were small communities of Persian and Armenian traders who had a permanent presence. At most they numbered one or two thousand, in cities whose population could reach half a million inhabitants in and around the metropolitan centers. One small community that Marco Polo reports on that was an anomaly was in the coastal city of Fuzhou. He was directed by Muslim merchants to this small community whose members followed an ancestral tradition of Christian origin. They remembered three apostles as their founders, used the psalter in worship, but said they had been for seven hundred years without contact with teachers. We have no indication of the actual size of this community, but the description indicates it was not very large. Some have concluded its members were indeed the remnant of Christians from the T'ang dynasty period, but others have argued that the community was a remnant of Manichaeans in China. In either case the story demonstrates that fragments of memory of Christian identity were scattered along the seacoast of China in the thirteenth century.

In the years after Marco Polo's visit to the court of Khubilai Khan, several Franciscans made their way to China on a mission to the land they called Cathay. One of these was John of Monte Corvino (1247-c.1330), who had spent several years working as part of the Franciscan effort in Cilician Armenia. In 1289 he was sent to Rome as an envoy of the Armenian king, but the pope quickly sent him back in the other direction, this time as a papal envoy with letters of introduction to the Mongol rulers of the East. Two years later he departed from the ilkhan's occasional capital at Tabriz, Azerbaijan, to go to Khanbalik. War in central Asia forced him to go to China by way of India, where he stayed for thirteen months while awaiting passage. He visited as many Christian communities as he could find there, naming specifically the community at Mylapore, where he found the church of Thomas the Apostle. John said he baptized about one hundred new Christians, although it is unclear if they were children of believers or converts.

From India, John finally made his way to Khanbalik, where he began building a permanent Latin community in residence. Among the accomplishments he lists in his first decade was building a church out of wood with a tower for bells. A second church was underway, this one with a red cross on top of it, close enough to the tent of the great khan that he could hear the singing of the mass each day. To help him sing that mass John had purchased a total of forty young boys (one imagines from a local slave market) and had taught them enough Latin to handle the liturgy, thereby creating a choir for his church. Strange as it might seem to have an Italian priest building a Latin liturgical community in the court of a Mongol great khan in thirteenth-century China, this is precisely what happened. His success engendered stiff opposition from the East Syrian clergy at the court, one of the first times we find eastern and western churches engaged in such conflict in China. The opposition had gone on for five years, he said, until the great khan himself intervened to end the East Syrian complaints.

John reported in a letter that finally made its way back to Rome that he had baptized over six thousand persons by the end of his first decade, although again it is difficult to tell if he means new converts or people who were members of other Christian communities. One of the missionary successes that he trumpeted in his letter was the conversion of the Ongut king George in western China (possibly the home kingdom of Patriarch Yaballaha) to the Latin form of the Catholic faith. Marco Polo had several years before met this same king, who was related to Khubilai Khan by marriage. When John of Monte Corvino arrived, King George appears to have been receptive to the idea of joining the Roman church. The king even built a church for Latin worship and joined the Franciscan in celebrating the western liturgy in it. Although many of his people were reported to have joined him as well in confessing the western form of Christianity at first, after the king's death they again aligned themselves with the Syriac-speaking churches of the region.

The letter of this lonely friar in Khanbalik reporting on his isolated mission succeeded in securing seven more Franciscans who were sent to join him in 1307. The pope took the extraordinary step of ordaining John archbishop of Khanbalik with the authority of a patriarch over all of Asia—this despite the fact that there already was a patriarch in Khanbalik. The seven new Franciscan friars were sent to join their archbishop as the members of what amounted to a new missionary diocese. It was a momentous step, for Rome was establishing a parallel church in a region of the world where there had for many centuries been an established church that could claim apostolic origins. No permanent churches resulted from these first Franciscan efforts. By 1330 many of the priests, including John himself, appear to have died. The last word of one of their number comes from around 1360. No further efforts were made by Rome or the Franciscan order to establish a Latin church so far east for another one hundred and fifty years. Yet the pattern of parallel churches and interchurch conflict had been set. And Bar Hebreus had been right in that such conflict could only weaken the overall witness Christians in that part of the world made before their neighbors.

Approximate areas of predominant

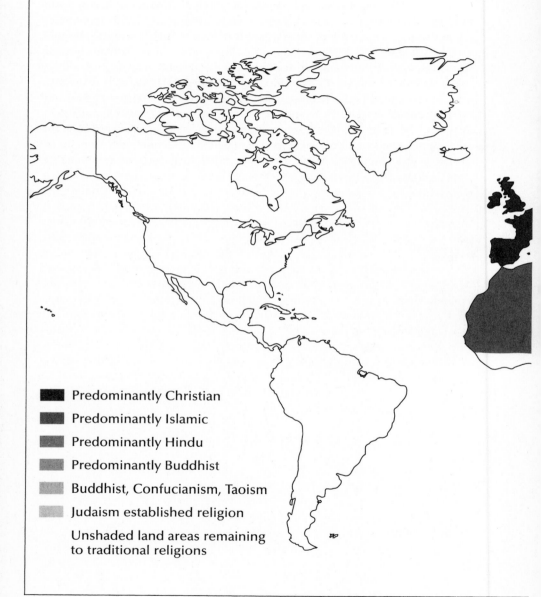

Predominantly Christian
Predominantly Islamic
Predominantly Hindu
Predominantly Buddhist
Buddhist, Confucianism, Taoism
Judaism established religion
Unshaded land areas remaining
to traditional religions

world religions, circa 1450

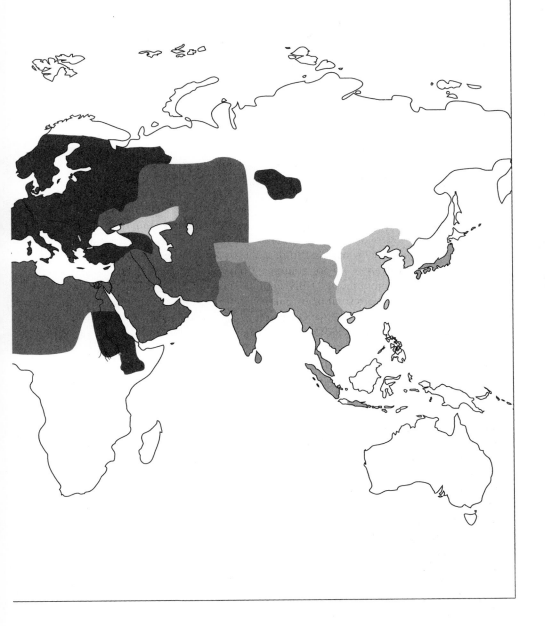

36

Egypt, Nubia, and Ethiopia

Egypt

The twelfth century found Christians in Egypt living through a period of relative calm. Elsewhere in the Middle East the crusaders had brought about significant disruptions in church life, but in Egypt churches felt little effect from the western armies. Individual Coptic Christians had been able to advance into the lower levels of government administration, and some were even prospering financially. Church repair was permitted, and some new construction allowed to take place. Christians were still exposed to persecution and violence. A story from Cairo around 1240, recounted by the Muslim historian Ghazi ben al-Wasiti, illustrates well their predicament. A Muslim man in need of the signatures of two witnesses on a legal document stopped two men on the street who were dressed as members of the Muslim nobility and asked them to oblige. Unbeknown to him, they were Christians. When he later discovered their religious identity, he reported them to the sultan, who ordered that the two Christians be given a beating and be made to wear again the distinctive belts that identified them as part of a degraded community.

The rule of the Fatimid government that had been in power since the tenth century was brought to an end by Salah ad-Din in the last quarter of the twelfth. The dynasty he in turn founded did not last long before it was overthrown by another group known as the Mamelukes. Their name means "slave" in Arabic, denoting the origin of their movement. The Mamelukes were descendants of Kipchak Turks from Russia who had been sold to Egypt. Many had become soldiers in the Egyptian army and had risen through the ranks. In 1250 a group of them overthrew Salah ad-Din's successor to establish a new sultanate that was first headed by a woman named Shajar ad-Durr, a concubine of the former sultan. The Mamelukes soon extended military control throughout Egypt and Palestine, and into Syria and parts of Armenia. In 1268 they captured Antioch, destroying the city for the last time. Twenty years later the last Latin presence at Acre was defeated. Cilician Armenia disappeared as an independent kingdom as well. All told, tens of thousands of Christians and Jews were sold into slavery from the cities in Syria and Armenia that were taken by the Mamelukes as they extended their political rule.

470

Back in Egypt the Mamelukes launched a new wave of persecution against Coptic Christians. The traditional codes of *dhimmi* were restored, and new poll taxes instituted. Churches and monasteries that had been newly built were ordered torn down, while other ancient religious sites were allowed to be raided. Christian peasants were forced off the land in many places, and the overall material wealth of the Christian community diminished. By the end of the century the Coptic church in Egypt found itself facing a new and prolonged crisis.

Nubia

The effect of Mameluke rule was soon felt to the south in the land of Nubia as well. The Fatimids had restored the traditional Red Sea trade routes and extended them to ports along the African coast. New Muslim settlements had emerged in the east of Nubia and along the coast all the way to Ethiopia by the end of the twelfth century. Apparently a permanent Muslim community had even been established in the Nubian capital city and a mosque had been built. Salah ad-Din had sent forces south in 1171 against a Nubian army that was raiding in the Aswan region. The next year he sent a military party further south into Nubia itself. The Muslim expedition took a number of Nubians captive to be sold into slavery but withdrew without further incident. The sultan turned his attention toward Palestine and Syria instead.

After 1260 the Mamelukes turned their attention again toward Nubia, only this time the effects were severe. In 1268 the Egyptian rulers demanded resumption of the traditional Baqt treaty. The Nubian king responded by raiding several towns along the Egyptian seacoast, a move he could ill afford. Within Nubia itself political strife among various ruling families was weakening social cohesion. Somewhat symbolically, drifting sands from the Sahara were slowly swallowing up the major cities of the region. Sands around buildings such as churches reached the point where they entirely covered the structures. People had to dig pathways through the dunes to enter what had became underground houses of worship. Many churches simply caved in from the weight against the walls, while others were abandoned.

In a similar manner but on a larger social scale, pressure from Muslim immigration backed by renewed military activity along the Nubian border forced Nubian Christians out of their hometowns and villages. Many had to move into more rugged regions where monastic communities had been built, away from major trade routes and behind more protective walls. In 1275 a Nubian claimant to the throne sought Mameluke help in overthrowing the king. The Egyptians eagerly obliged, but in the process effectively reduced northern Nubia to a vassal state. A long period of instability followed in which Egyptian rulers continued to intervene through assassinations and direct military action, unsettling Nubia even further. Finally in 1323 the Mamelukes installed a Muslim king in the northern region of Makouria. In Cairo they prevented the patriarch of Alexandria from sending any further priests to Nubia, thereby isolating its churches even further.

The last evidence of Christian communities in the region comes from the mid-fifteenth century. After that Nubia appears to have become entirely Muslim.

Ethiopia

The political pressure of the Mameluke state was felt further south in Africa in the Christian kingdom of Ethiopia as well in the thirteenth century. In response Ethiopia underwent a revival both of its political and its religious identity. Political Revival came in the form of a series of new dynastic regimes. Theological renewal, on the other hand, came through a stronger identification with the Ethiopian Semitic cultural past and historical ties to Judaism. What is often called the Solomonic Revival in Ethiopia strengthened not only the churches, but national Christian identity against Muslim encroachments from the north and east. To set the context of that thirteenth-century revival, we need to go back in Ethiopia's history several centuries.

The tenth century had been a time of political decline for Ethiopia's kings. A long conflict with neighboring tribes had ended in Ethiopian defeat, weakening its overall presence in the East African region. Partly as a result of the decline in Ethiopia's power and partly as a result of renewed commercial activities along

Church of St. George, one of the churches at Lalibela in Ethiopia hewn from living rock, 13ᵗʰ century. Reproduced with permission of Werner Forman Archive/Art Resource, New York City.

the Red Sea, the Islamic presence in the Horn of Africa grew. Muslim preachers were drawing new converts from the traditional religionists to the east of Ethiopia, one of the places where Islam spread apart from direct military efforts. Commercial contacts between Ethiopia and the Islamic world brought into the Christian country Muslim merchants who appear to have been permitted to practice their faith without incident.

A new ruler from among the Agwa people of the Ethiopian north rose to power in the twelfth century to found the Zagwe dynasty. The exact year of the beginning of this ruler's reign is unknown, but a bit of evidence from the Egyptian *History of the Patriarchs* provides a clue. Around the year 1150 the Coptic patriarch received a request from the king of Ethiopia to replace the Ethiopian abuna as head of the church, for he had refused to recognize the legitimacy of the king's rule. One possible scenario is that the new king was in fact the founder of the new dynasty.

In the years just prior to the emergence of the Zagwe rulers, Ethiopian kings had begun expanding their influence south and west among neighboring tribes. Only a decade before the rise of the new dynasty, according to the *History of the Patriarchs*, the Ethiopian king had requested the Coptic patriarch to send more bishops. The appeal, which does not appear to have been granted, suggests that the king needed to provide for the geographical expansion of the churches under his domains, and hence indicates a time of political expansion was under way.

The Zagwe dynasty continued this expansion. They were also more aggressive in pursuing international trade. New commercial ties with Egypt and with other Muslim countries along the Red Sea were forged and increased Ethiopian pilgrimages to the Holy Land were noted. In 1189, Salah ad-Din turned over several churches in Jerusalem to the Ethiopians to provide services for their pilgrims to that city.

One of the decisions of the Zagwe kings was to move the capital of Ethiopia from Axum to Adefa, a city further to the south. Perhaps this was in response to continuing local resistance, or perhaps they sought to move further from Islamic influence. In any case, the Zagwe dynasty reached the height of its power under King Lalibela early in the thirteenth century. It was he who was responsible for a series of eleven churches that were literally carved out of rocks in the hillside just outside the capital. The churches represented Jerusalem by re-creating pilgrimage sites (Church of Calvary, Church of the Tomb) within the Ethiopian homeland, an indication as well of the ongoing place the Holy City played in Ethiopian national faith.

The thirteenth century was a time of significant Christian growth throughout the southern region of Ethiopia. In 1248 Abba Iyesus-Mo'a (d. 1292) left his monastic community in the north to found a new monastery on the island in Lake Hayq. It quickly became a center of education and evangelism, spreading Christianity through the Amhara region. One of the students from Lake Hayq was Yekunno-Amlak, a descendant of earlier kings from the dynasty prior to the Zagwe. In the last half of the thirteenth century, he emerged as the ruler of a semi-independent kingdom in the Ethiopian south that then went up against the last Zagwe ruler in battle. In 1270 Yekunno-Amlak became king of the whole of Ethiopia.

This new (or restored) dynasty coincided with the revival of theological identity within the churches. This is also the period historians have often referred to as the Solomonic Revival, a reference to the role played by Solomon and the Queen of Sheba in Ethiopian historical memory. The most important source for the Solomonic tradition was a book known as *Kebra Nagast (Book of Kings)*. The history of the *Kebra Nagast* itself remains obscure prior to the early thirteenth century when a copy was brought to Ethiopia from Egypt and an edited version translated into the Ethiopian language. According to its pages, after her visit with Solomon, recounted in the Old Testament book of I Kings, the Queen of Sheba returned to Ethiopia carrying a child she had conceived by Solomon. The son born from their liaison was named Menelik.

After he was grown, Menelik returned to Jerusalem to meet his father, Solomon, and was embraced as the son of the king. Solomon in fact entrusted to Menelik the Ark of the Covenant, including the two stone tablets on which Moses received the Ten Commandments. Menelik returned with the Ark to Ethiopia, the *Kebra Nagast* continued. Thus the royal line that descended from Menelik is directly related to King Solomon, and through him is a member of the royal house of Israel's greatest king, David. To Ethiopia was entrusted the Ark of the Covenant, signifying that it had become the land of Israel's true faith.

The *Kebra Nagast* provided the immediate ideological basis for opposition to the Zagwe dynasty. The Ethiopian nation was the legitimate successor to Jerusalem, or Zion, a belief that significantly strengthened its historical religious identity over against Islam. Ethiopian kings were descended from King Solomon and were members of the house of David, a claim no Egyptian ruler in the thirteenth century could make regarding the Prophet Muhammad or his companions. Religious and cultural affinities with Judaism were not new. Ethiopians were a Semitic people, and their churches had historically had a strong identification with the people of the Old Testament. Dietary laws of the Old Testament were being followed long before the thirteenth century, and there is evidence that some even found polygamy acceptable on the grounds that it was allowed in the Old Testament. The practice among Ethiopian Christians of keeping both the Jewish Sabbath and Christian Sunday as holy days appears to be ancient. In the ninth century an Egyptian bishop had even been forced to return to Cairo when church leaders in Ethiopia suspected that he had not been circumcised. Earlier Ethiopian literature, including the traditions surrounding Frumentius and the Nine Saints, had not explicitly mentioned many of these practices. But the history told in *Kebra Nagast* was accepted as the source of a unique Ethiopian Christian identity.

The national revival of the tradition of Solomonic kingship brought with it renewed tensions between Ethiopia's kings and the abunas appointed from Egypt. The head of the Ethiopian church was still an Egyptian who came with his attending clergy. His appointment was for life, although this did not prevent Ethiopian monarchs and lesser clergy from sending him back to Alexandria when there were disagreements. In such cases the patriarch in Alexandria had to await the death of the abuna before making another appointment. When an abuna died in Ethiopia, the king had to send word to the Coptic pope and Egyptian sultan requesting a new appointment. All of this took time, and was often intentionally delayed by a hostile Egyptian government, leaving the Ethiopian church for long periods without a legitimate ecclesiastical head.

When the abuna was in Ethiopia he was part of the king's court and had a residence in the capital that was supported by extensive lands that were his source of income. His most important task was to ordain priests and other bishops, thereby maintaining their canonical authority. Local bishops in various parts of the country were likewise usually connected with the ruling nobility. Secular priests in most villages were poorly educated, and in most cases were rural workers themselves. Their pastoral work for the most part was confined to saying the liturgy and administering local church affairs on behalf of the bishop. The bulk of pastoral work in Ethiopia fell to the monks and nuns who lived in Ethiopia's many monasteries and convents. Monasticism was still the generating core for the spiritual life of the churches. Ethiopian monasticism in particular was traditionally nationalistic in its orientation, from the days of the Nine Saints who came seeking refuge from imperial persecution under Roman rule. This anti-imperial tradition was carried over in anti-Egyptian Islamic influences, which increased as the Coptic patriarch become increasingly pressured by the rulers of Egypt to serve their interests in Ethiopia.

By the fourteenth century these monastic influences had merged with the Solomonic tradition to extend the unique Ethiopian Christian identity throughout the countryside. Monastic spirituality in the fourteenth century also became more strongly connected with the traditions surrounding the Virgin Mary and her devotion in Ethiopia. Mary's devotion was identified with monastic resistance against corrupt Ethiopian kings and clergy alike, adding to the Old Testament Solomonic tradition a renewed emphasis upon Mary and especially her bodily assumption into heaven.

Thus by the fourteenth century Christianity in Africa was on a firm footing only in Ethiopia. Christians in Nubia had all but disappeared, while the Coptic churches of Egypt were facing the continuous pressures of a hostile Muslim regime. Further to the west in the Maghrib, a handful of Franciscan missionaries had crossed the Mediterranean from Spain to preach in North African villages or towns. There is at least one report of a Franciscan traveling with Muslim merchants into West Africa, although there is no evidence that his efforts resulted in any Christian conversions. Ethiopia was surrounded on three sides by Muslim-dominant states. Such political and economic pressures made difficult any further missionary activity of its own.

37

Western Christendom 1300-1450

Western Europe might have been a predominantly Christian civilization, but it was hardly a unified one by the fourteenth century. The growth of cities had brought new social tensions, for one thing. The new urban classes were often at odds with the old feudal order and its land-based economy. Urban commercial interests and influence reached far beyond the borders of local kingdoms and principalities. Merchants from the Italian city of Florence in particular had developed extensive networks of credit and finance across Europe, making its gold *florin* the standard for exchange throughout the West. Florence was also a major center for the production of commercial goods. It is estimated that as many as thirty thousand people were employed in the wool industry in the city, providing a commodity that was sold as far away as China.

Two other Italian cities, Venice and Genoa, were most responsible for extending western economic life beyond the borders of Latin Christendom during this period. They were responsible for extending western political interests as well. By the year 1300, merchants from these two independent cities had established a permanent presence in Cilician Armenia, around Constantinople, along the coast of the Black Sea, and in the seaports of Egypt. Western clerics, mostly from the new orders of Franciscans and Dominicans, had soon followed. At first the clerics had been concerned with providing religious services for the western inhabitants of these merchant colonies. In some locations, such as Cilician Armenia, the orders had established Latin-rite churches and were beginning to recruit members from the local Christian population. Clerics also served as emissaries of western interests. Religion and politics were never far removed from one another in the fourteenth century.

The course of the reconquest in the Iberian peninsula had brought most of it under the rule of the Christian kingdoms of Aragón, Castile, and Portugal in the fourteenth century. Only the small kingdom of Grenada in the south remained under Muslim control. This was enough to provide a common border along which the two sides could continue a low-grade level of warfare, however. Slave traders on both sides were the most significant beneficiaries of the continuous border wars in Andalusia. Records of the sale of Muslims taken into slavery from the region and sold in the markets of Genoa indicate a large number of Muslims were entering the Christian economy under conditions of forced labor.

Many major cities in the West had a neighborhood or street where a permanent Jewish community dwelt. The center of Jewish life was the synagogue, which functioned as house of worship, community center, and government hall all in one. For the most part, Jews ran their own affairs in the West, and did so under relatively democratic conditions. Christian kings imposed taxes on Jews that were similar to taxes Christians bore under Muslim governments, but left it to the community itself to collect and pay them. On an individual basis there was often a great deal of social interaction between Jews and their Christian neighbors, as might be expected in an urban setting. At the same time Jews were increasingly becoming targets of organized violence at the hands of their Christian neighbors. Ever fearful of heresy and deviant beliefs, the hierarchy of the church often condoned such violence implicitly if not explicitly.

Throughout Europe a new sense of national identity was taking shape under a host of reigning monarchs. English, French, German, and Spanish had all emerged as distinct national languages by the fourteenth century, helped along by the appearance of new genres of popular (or vernacular) literature. England and France in particular witnessed not only a growing sense of national identity but increased participation of people outside the nobility in matters of political life. Edward I of England was forced to invite commoners to join the English Parliament for the first time in 1295, while in 1302 Philip IV of France summoned the clergy, nobility, and representatives from cities to the first meeting of the Estates-General.

Europe's social fabric was regularly tested by the hardships of famine and disease during these years. Crop failures, harsh winters, and lack of adequate means of food preservation all took their toll in hunger and death. Regular outbreaks of contagious diseases added to the suffering. One of the most devastating examples of the latter was the wave of bubonic plague that swept across Europe in the middle of the fourteenth century. The disease was caused by bacteria that were spread by fleas, which in turn were carried by rats. Although it appears to have originally spread from Asia, the full wrath of the disease was saved for Europe. The first wave of the plague was reported to have reached Constantinople in 1347. A year later it had spread through Italy, and within three years had engulfed the rest of the continent all the way to Scandinavia. It is estimated that one-third of the fifty to seventy million people who lived in the West died from the epidemic in the middle years of the fourteenth century. Whole neighborhoods in urban areas succumbed to it. In the countryside labor shortages were severe; fields went unplowed and feudal estates were left without reigning lords.

Constant warfare among Europe's ruling monarchs was disruptive of city and countryside alike. Virtually every ruler was involved in some form of regional conflict, but the most debilitating was that between the French and English kings. Rival claims to the French throne in 1337 led to open warfare between England and France that continued on and off for a full century. Toward the end of the Hundred Years' War, as the conflict between the English and French kings is known, one of more memorable figures in western political history appeared, a woman named Joan of Arc (1412-1431). Born into a family of peasants, at the age of thirteen Joan began hearing celestial voices telling her that she had a mission to save France from the English. A theological inquiry was held to investigate her visions, and the bishops determined that they were authentic. Shortly afterward Joan of Arc joined the French army, where she soon was serving as a commander. Dressed in the full armor of a knight, she led the French troops into battle against English forces and to victory in 1429.

Her success on the battlefield elevated her to a place of honor alongside the king of France as a national figure. The following year, in 1430, she was again leading a campaign against the English when she was captured. The English turned her over to an ecclesiastical court in the French region of Rouen, which they controlled at the time. The court found her guilty of heresy because of her visions, and guilty of wearing the clothing of a man. She repented of the heresy, thereby avoiding for a time the condemnation of death, but was soon brought back again on charges of her masculine dress while in prison. This time the court invoked the death sentence. In 1431 Joan of Arc was burned at the stake in Rouen on the charge of being a heretic.

That is not the end of her story, however, for twenty-five years later the papal authorities in Rome reopened the case. This time she was found innocent of the charges against her. Although the pope's verdict did little good as far as her life was concerned, it opened the door to Joan of Arc becoming a popular figure in western literature and cultural life. The young woman who heard voices calling her to a mission on behalf of France became in death the patron saint of her nation.

As devastating as the effects of warfare and plague were, they did not stop urban economic advance in the West. Several cities in Italy approached a population of one hundred thousand residents during the fourteenth century. Cottage industries prospered in city and countryside alike, as did new technologies. Several innovations that were destined to play a major role in transforming the face of western civilization reached Europe from China by way of Arabic culture during this period. The first was gunpowder. The Chinese had known for centuries of the explosive effects of potassium nitrate mixed with sulfur when ignited by a spark. Early in the fourteenth century Europeans began experimenting with using the mixture to propel objects in battle. Before long the musket and cannon had transformed the nature of warfare across the world.

Equally transformative, if less dramatic, was the spread of the compass in navigational use. The Chinese again appear to have been the first to discover that small bits of magnetized iron, when floated on water, would point to the north. European sailors had learned to float an iron needle on a splinter of wood in a bowl of water, and then later attached a movable needle to a card showing the four directions to help them navigate out at sea.

A third major technological development in the age came with the invention of the printing press. By the thirteenth century the Arabs had introduced both paper making and woodblock printing into Spain. The invention of a movable metal type in the city of Mainz around 1450 built upon this earlier technology to set in motion a revolution that eventually reached around the world.

New intellectual and cultural movements began to appear as well in the West during the fourteenth century. The most important of these emerged from the same Italian city-states that were at the heart of the economic boom. Historians often refer to this intellectual and cultural movement as the Renaissance, although at the time most of those who were part of it referred to themselves simply as humanists. The humanists of the fourteenth century were in many ways able to build upon the work of the scholastics from the twelfth and thirteenth centuries. Humanists in the fourteenth century paid greater attention to classical Roman and Greek philosophy and literature, and they sought new ways to preserve the intellectual heritage of pre-Christian antiquity. Leading the movement was a Tuscan poet named Francesco Petrarca (in English, Petrarch) (1304-1374). As a boy Petrarch learned Latin from the monk who was his tutor. He later began combing monasteries and church libraries for forgotten manuscripts that opened up the world of classical Roman civilization to him. Others soon followed, seeking out old manuscripts that they then copied and studied in an effort to revive the knowledge of the past. They called themselves humanists because of their focus on Latin grammar and rhetoric, the so-called humanities, as distinct from theology. Although most, if not all, considered themselves a part of Christian civilization, they did not consider themselves bound intellectually to the authorities of the Christian faith from the past in the same way as their scholastic predecessors had.

Humanists were not the only ones stirring the spiritual waters of the fourteenth century. In Germany a Dominican named Meister Eckhart (1260-1327) made a name for himself as a teacher and preacher. Eckhart sought to foster in his listeners an inward spiritual experience with God. The inward journey took one along the metaphorical pathway from darkness to divine light. The highest goal was union with God, an experience that was by definition beyond words. One looked inward to discover the divine within the soul, Eckhart taught. His critics perceived his teaching to represent a challenge to the external mediations the church exercised in the project of human salvation. Eckhart was charged by the hierarchy with heresy, a charge the pope confirmed shortly after his death.

Half a century after Eckhart's death, a woman in England named Julian of Norwich (1342-1423) began to receive a series of revelations. The "showings," as she called them, served to help her organize a series of biblical and theological reflections that she wrote in English. For Julian, the mystery of God was experienced through the soul contemplating God's all-encompassing love. Christ manifested that love in the flesh, thus revealing the Trinity through his suffering. Christ also revealed the maternal image of God that complemented the image of divine fatherhood in the Trinity, Julian's showings revealed. The painful images of Christ's passion and the tender images of Christ's loving motherhood combine in Julian's *Showings* to make it one of the more compelling mystical texts of the age.

Petrarch, Eckhart, and Julian made exceptional intellectual and spiritual contributions to their age, but by the same token they were exceptions to their era. Most ordinary believers knew little, if anything, of classical learning. Few were receptive to the mystical insights received by Eckhart or Julian. Religion for most ordinary believers was carried out by participating in the sacraments of the church, the most common being penance. The goal of life was salvation, which for most people meant reaching paradise after death. To do so one had to navigate through the perils of the world's temptations, a world filled with demons who were seeking to cause harm. But the universe was equally full of angels and saints sent to assist humankind; they were just as real for most people as the neighbors that they engaged in daily commerce.

The one saint who stood above all others, the person closest to Jesus in all of human history was Mary, his mother. For many, she was nearly as worthy of devotion as Jesus. One of the debates among theologians concerned whether Mary was free from original sin when she gave birth to Jesus. Several influential Franciscan theologians made the case that God had by grace preserved Mary from original sin in the moment of her conception, a position that was eventually embraced as official Catholic doctrine. In the fourteenth century the role of Mary was of great practical concern, however, and not just a dogmatic matter. People would talk to the mother of Jesus directly, asking her to pray for them or sharing with her their burdens while sitting before her stone or wooden image in a church. Mary could relate to these concerns because she was a mother and was privileged above all women by God.

Pope and crown

The complicated course of the history of the papacy in the fourteenth century begins with renewed conflict with the French crown. The financial burdens of military expansion led King Philip IV to attempt to tax the clergy and the French churches in 1295. Pope Boniface VIII condemned the act the following year. In response Philip attempted to cut off the flow of money from France to Rome and arrested one of Boniface's allies in the French ecclesiastical hierarchy. In effect, the king was asserting, the churches in his realm were under his control. Boniface did not agree, and in 1302 he issued a papal bull entitled *Unam Sanctam* that was directed against Philip's position.

There is one, holy, catholic, and apostolic church, *Unam Sanctam* began. As with the ark of Noah, one must be in it to be saved, for outside the church there is no salvation. Christ appointed one head of the church, namely Peter, and the pope is his successor. Hence all human beings (including princes and kings) "by necessity for salvation are entirely subject to the Roman Pontiff." Furthermore, there are in the church "two swords, one representing spiritual authority and the other temporal authority."

> Certainly anyone who denies that the temporal sword is in the power of Peter has not paid heed to the words of the Lord when he said, "Put up thy sword into its sheath" (Matthew 26:52). . . . One sword ought to be under the other and the temporal authority subject to the spiritual power.[14]

Thus kings were to exercise their authority on behalf of the church, and under its direction. Any temporal ruler who did not do so was outside the church, therefore outside the provenance of eternal salvation.

---

[14] *Unam Sanctam*, in Denzinger, ed., *The Sources of Catholic Dogma* (New York: Herder Book Co., 1954), 187.

The following year Boniface drew up a bull of excommunication against Philip. Before he could officially promulgate it, however, a troop of soldiers under an Italian ally of the French king broke into the pope's residence and roughed Boniface up in an effort to force him to resign. Boniface died shortly thereafter, leaving the status of the excommunication uncertain. Philip's next move was to insure the election of a pope more accommodating to French interests. Clement V, who assumed the papal throne in 1305. was soon supporting the French on a number of issues.

Clement resided for several years in southern France before deciding in 1308 to locate the papal residence permanently in Avignon, a city near the Mediterranean on the Rhone River. Political instability in central Italy continued to render the situation in Rome difficult for communication and governance. At the time Avignon was still part of the papal states, so the move was not technically out of Roman jurisdiction. Nevertheless, for all intents and purposes it put the pope within the sphere of French political influence. For the next seven decades a succession of French popes continued to reside in the city.

The decision to move the papal office to Avignon was in part a result of Clement's realistic assessment of the situation in church-state relations at the time. Like Boniface before him, Clement was committed to launching a new crusade against the Muslim rulers of Palestine, but he recognized that to do so he would need the support of kings. This pope also showed an interest in the mission to the Mongols. Fifteen years earlier Pope Nicholas IV had met Rabban Sauma and sent letters to the great khan. The carrier had been John of Monte Corvino, the Franciscan we met in the last chapter, who departed Rome in 1289. It was Clement V who made John archbishop of China in 1307 and authorized the other Franciscans sent to work with him. The results of their mission were negligible in the long run for Chinese Christianity but an important indication of Rome's global concern for missions.

The passion for missions and crusading abroad did not translate into a commitment to self-denial at home. During the time of Boniface, and continuing during the years at Avignon, the papal curia expanded significantly, both in numbers and in the wealth of its members. Along with a treasury and chancery, a bureau of justice had evolved by the fourteenth century, complete with ecclesiastical courts and officials. The office of Apostolic Penitentiary handled excommunications, marriage dispensations, and lifting of sacramental suspensions. An enormous portion of the administrative burden of running the church fell to the cardinals, who also served as theological advisors to the pope. They were not mendicants. "The papal court outshone all the other courts of Europe by the extravagance of its living and the splendor of its feasts," writes one historian of the period.[15]

The need for funds increased proportionately, this at a time when political instability was disrupting the economy of the papal states. In response, successive popes expanded the taxes that were levied on various offices of the church

---

[15] G. Mollat, *The Popes at Avignon 1305-1378* (London: Thomas Nelson and Sons Ltd., 1949), 310.

throughout western Europe. Voluntary contributions were transformed over the course of the century into actual church taxes, with church tax collectors empowered to excommunicate those who refused. Resentment and opposition to papal authority were bound to increase, not least among secular rulers who were often seeking to tap into the same sources of revenue to support their courts.

By 1375 the political climate in Italy had improved enough to allow Gregory XI to consider returning to Rome. Encouragement came from an unlikely source, a woman mystic by the name of Catherine of Siena (1347-1380). From an early age Catherine had experienced mystical visions. She joined the Dominicans at the age of sixteen, and for the rest of her life practiced severe austerity. A large part of her time was devoted to work on behalf of the poor, and through her severe self-denial, she shared in the pain of their oppression. In 1375 the stigmata, or scars of the wounds suffered by Christ, appeared on her body. Meanwhile the visions continued, leading to an investigation by the church hierarchy, which pronounced her to be orthodox.

Throughout her career Catherine took part in public debates regarding the spiritual condition of the church. She dictated many letters (she never learned to write), many of which were sent to the pope. She also dictated devotional works such as *Treatise on Divine Providence*. Around 1370 she began urging the pope to return to Rome, even visiting Gregory XI in person to make the case. Her efforts appear to have been a decisive factor in Gregory's decision to move the administration of the papacy back to Rome in 1377.

Schism in the papacy

Gregory died a year after returning to Rome. Many of the cardinals who were gathered there (most of them by this time were French) preferred to move back to Avignon, but popular support in Rome prevented them from doing so. Faced with few alternatives, they proceeded to elect a new pope, who took the name Urban VI. Urban began almost immediately to alienate many of the cardinals by publicly denouncing the extravagant lifestyle and moral lapses of the members of the curia.

Four months later the cardinals regathered outside Rome and declared that their decision had been forced under the threat of mob violence. The election of Urban VI was therefore invalid, they asserted, and they proceeded to elect another pope, a Genevan who took the name Clement VII. He took up residence in Avignon. Urban VI proceeded to elevate a new group of bishops to the rank of cardinal, thereby providing himself with a new college. There were now two popes and two colleges, both duly elected and both claiming canonical authority and continuity with the past.

Political powers across Europe began lining up behind one or the other pope and supporting cardinals: the French behind Clement VII, the English and Germans behind Urban VI. Many, such as rulers in Spain and other parts of Italy, went back and forth. All agreed that the situation had to be resolved, but how?

With the death of each of the popes, their respective college of cardinals proceeded to elect a new pope so as not to be without a leader. Hence there were two
lines of succession developing. A plan was finally put forth by the faculty of the
University of Paris to have both popes abdicate and to call a general council to
elect a new, single pope. Meanwhile, various on-going negotiations between the
two parties were held by national rulers throughout Europe.

Weary of the quarter-century debate, cardinals from both sides finally issued
a joint decision to call for a general council to meet in 1409 at Pisa. Both sitting
popes rejected the council, although ruling houses of most of Europe supported
it. The Council of Pisa convened and formally declared both popes deposed. The
cardinals then elected a new bishop to the papal throne; he took the name
Alexander V. Neither of the other two popes accepted his claim, and both found
enough political support to survive. So now there were three popes, all duly
elected according to ancient canonical tradition.

Upon the death of Alexander V, the cardinals supporting him elected a successor, John XXIII. Political turmoil forced John XXIII to take up residence in Germany, where he was shortly persuaded by the German king Sigismund to call a
new general council. That council met from 1414 to 1418 in the city of Constance
on Lake Geneva and marked the end of the papal schism, although not in the way
John XXIII expected.

Conciliar activity

The Council of Constance (1414-1418) was called jointly by King Sigismund
of Germany (soon to be emperor) and Pope John XXIII. One of its main concerns was to prevent a recurrence of events at Pisa. To this end, the cardinals
organized to vote according to languages representing Western Christian "nations" (English, German, French, Italian, and by the end of the council, Spanish),
with an additional vote for the college of cardinals as a whole. Establishing a
national basis for the council assured that when all three popes were deposed, no
major European throne would refuse to accept the decision. The council then
proceeded to depose all three popes and elect a new one, an Italian who took the
name Martin V.

One of the key principles that emerged from this action was the theological
understanding of the role of a council in the western church. Faced with the
chaotic situation of several canonically elected popes, the theologians gathered
at Constance turned to conciliar ideas that had been voiced in various ways within
the churches over the centuries. Eastern theologians had long argued that a general council had authority over a pope. Now in the West such a concept seemed
appropriate in light of the condition of schism that was facing the church. The
immediate situation called for rectification and the election of a new pope who
had the consensus of western nations. To some it even seemed as if the council's
action advanced a more general conciliar principle which held that the authority
of any general council was greater than that of an individual pope. Those who

had gathered at Constance did indeed seem to lean in that direction. New general councils were ordered to be convened every five years thereafter. That decision, however, was soon abandoned.

Martin V, as directed, called a new council at Pavia within five years, in 1423. The council was poorly attended and accomplished little. Seven years later he called another council to meet at Basel (modern Switzerland). Before it could convene, however, he had died, and a new pope, Eugene IV, had been elected to succeed him. Eugene sought to move the council to Bologna, but the cardinals who had gathered already at Basel refused and went on with their work without him. Several reform measures were passed, aimed at correcting some of the more flagrant abuses of the clergy. In addition the cardinals sought to limit the administrative powers of the pope, including those of taxing the churches. Basel continued to follow the notion that a general council was canonically superior even to the pope. Eugene IV, however, expressly denied this and asserted that while he as pope embraced canonical decisions of councils such as Constance and Basel, preeminence resided in his apostolic see, whose dignity was conceded to it by Christ himself in the person of St. Peter.

Council of Ferrara-Florence

In the midst of the Council of Basel an opportunity arose that gave Eugene the ideal reason he needed for shifting the purpose of the gathering. A delegation from Constantinople arrived in Rome in 1433 to propose a council of union between Greek and Latin churches. The Byzantines once again were facing renewed pressure from the Muslim forces under the Ottoman Turks. The situation had to have reached crisis proportions for both emperor and patriarch to be willing to negotiate on the theological issues dividing Greek and Latin churches. Their hope was that reconciliation with the West would open the door for military and financial support. Eugene IV recognized that reunion with the Greeks that included a statement of Roman primacy would greatly strengthen his hand with the cardinals. All were aware of the larger ecumenical significance such a negotiated reunion might have. Messages were sent to the other ancient patriarchs in Antioch, Alexandria, and Jerusalem, inviting them to join what was perceived to be potentially a general council on the order of the first ecumenical gatherings in Christian history, although Muslim authorities in each of the cities prevented the patriarchs from attending.

Where should such a council meet? The Greek delegates initially proposed Constantinople as the site of the gathering, but the threat posed by the Ottoman Turks was too great a risk for so many heads of world Christianity. As an alternative the Greek delegation strongly preferred a site in Italy that was near the Adriatic Sea. The cardinals gathered already at Basel wanted the Greeks to come to that city. Pope Eugene IV settled on the city of Ferrara and ordered the Council of Basel to move there. A majority of the cardinals did eventually do so, but some stayed in Basel, attempting to keep that gathering in session. By 1439 only one cardinal and a handful of ecclesiastical administrators remained in Basel, but that did not prevent them from voting Eugene IV deposed. No one in the western capitals was paying any further attention to Basel, however, for Eugene had successfully transferred the council to Ferrara.

The new Council of Ferrara formally opened in January of 1438. Soon Eugene IV, the Byzantine emperor John VIII, and Patriarch Joseph II were gathered with cardinals and supporting delegations from both Latin and Greek churches to begin the process of negotiating their reunion. Isidore, a Greek who had recently been appointed metropolitan of Kiev, joined the proceedings as well. The pope bore the burden of financing the event, which was quite costly; the Greek dignitaries did not settle for inexpensive accommodations.

It soon became apparent that it would not be a short council. Preliminary conversations dragged on for four months without any substantial doctrinal conversations taking place. In January of the following year (1439) the council moved to Florence, due to local political problems and the threat posed by the plague in Ferrara. The delegates continued to work for another six months, seeking to hammer out a joint theological statement that would provide the two traditions with a basis for renewed communion.

Chief among the theological issues that were considered at the Council of Ferrara-Florence were the traditional ones that had divided the two churches for many years: the doctrine of purgatory, the use of leavened or unleavened bread in the eucharist, the procession of the Holy Spirit (the filioque), and the question of the primacy of the pope among the churches of the world. Hanging over these theological conversations was the Byzantine emperor's need for military and financial assistance against the Ottoman Turks to his east. These political considerations finally won out. On each of the points the Latin theological position was adopted. Eugene and his supporters viewed it as a victory for the papacy as an institution. On July 6, 1439, a "Decree of Union" was signed by delegates of the two churches. The decree called for the name of the pope to be included in the liturgy of Greek churches. The Greeks were also forced to acknowledge the validity of the filioque but were not required to insert it in the Greek version of the Nicene Creed they recited in worship. The decree also allowed for either leavened or unleavened bread to be used in Greek eucharistic services.

Before he could return home that summer, Patriarch Joseph II died. The rest of the Greek delegation, including the emperor, returned home to face a hostile reception. (We shall look at the subsequent history of events in Constantinople in the next chapter.) Meanwhile, in Italy, an Armenian delegation from Cilicia showed up after the council had adjourned. Its delegates were informed of the "Decree of Union" and joined with the pope in agreeing to a further set of conditions by which they would be united with Rome. The "Decree for the Armenians" *(Exultate Deo)* of November 1439 defined the seven sacraments of the Roman Church as universally binding on all Christians, going even beyond the "Decree of Union" in this regard.

After the Greek representatives had departed from Florence, Eugene IV sent a delegation of Franciscans to make contact with Coptic, Ethiopian, and Jacobite churches of the East as well. The purpose was to inform these churches of the "Decree of Union" and invite them to join the process by which there would be one Catholic church under one shepherd. In Jerusalem, the Franciscans made contact with monks in the Ethiopian monastery in the city. One of their number, an Ethiopian monk named Peter, was sent by the rest of the community to travel to Florence to meet with the pope. Peter eventually appeared before the Latin delegates who were still at Florence in 1441 and presented a letter from the abbot of his monastery. He could not speak for the Ethiopian negus, he informed them, and only brought word that the Ethiopians were hopeful for the union. Other Franciscans had attempted unsuccessfully to reach Ethiopia from Egypt. Letters from the pope did eventually reach the Ethiopian negus, Jacob, by way of the monastery in Jerusalem, addressing the pope's desire for the union of Christians throughout the world.

Franciscan envoys of the pope were also sent to Alexandria, where they met with Patriarch John of the Coptic church; the Franciscans were assisted by Venetian merchants in the city who served as their translators. John authorized Andrew, the abbot of the monastery of St. Anthony, to travel to Florence on behalf of the Coptic patriarch. Andrew did so, meeting with the pope and the rest of the Latin delegation in August, again with Venetians translating from Arabic into Italian and Latin. A letter of instruction in matters of faith and practice from the council was delivered to the Coptic church by Andrew. Both Egyptian and Ethiopian delegations then went to Rome to visit holy sites before heading back to Cairo and Jerusalem respectively.

The Council of Ferrara-Florence offered greater ecumenical promise than any Christian council since the eighth century. Unfortunately, however, the outcome of the fifteenth-century council fell far short of its intended goal. The decisions were dictated almost entirely by Latin theological interests and concerns. In the long run little was accomplished in the way of achieving the union of Christian churches across the world. The only real impact of the council was to increase the prestige and power of the pope in the West, reversing in some ways the cause of conciliarism that had emerged in the previous half-century. Even the ecumenical patriarch had acknowledged his primacy over churches throughout the world, the pope could claim, thereby diminishing significantly the claims on behalf of conciliarists in the western church.

In Constantinople, as we will see in the next chapter, anti-unionist forces greeted the returning delegation with disdain. Even though both emperor and patriarch formally supported the "Decree of Union," its conditions were never fully implemented. It took a decade for the patriarch to introduce the name of the pope into the liturgy said in Hagia Sophia. A year later the final Christian worship service was conducted in that church as the city of Constantinople fell to the Muslim forces of the Ottoman Turks.

Elsewhere among the churches of eastern Christianity, Latin proselytism was quickly displacing union as the preferred method of western ecumenical relations. Franciscans and Dominicans were both proving to be effective agents in this regard. Although they were by no means able entirely to persuade Christians in Cilicia, Syria, Persia, India, or even China to join themselves to Latin-rite congregations, they were able to bring enough into their churches to cause alarm among the indigenous bishops and patriarchs alike. Few Muslims, Hindus, Buddhists, or other religionists became Christian in the fourteenth century through the efforts of the friars. Most of the Latin church's gains were made at the expense of other Christian communions.

Challenges to the unity of the Catholic church in the West

While various popes, cardinals, and kings all struggled with the situation of papal schism and growing conciliarism in the late-thirteenth century, other religious forces within Christendom were beginning to stir again the fires of reform at a popular level. The most important of these new stirrings was a renewal movement spurred on by John Wycliffe (1330-1384) in England. Wycliffe had studied at Oxford, where he then taught for a time. He had also served for a while as a theological advisor for the crown. At one point he had served as a member of a royal commission sent by the king of England to negotiate with Gregory XI in

Photograph of 14th century edition of John Wycliffe's English translation of the Bible. Archives of the American Bible Society. Reproduced with permission.

Avignon. Eventually he was rewarded by the crown with a parish appointment at Lutterworth, where he settled into the role of reformer.

In the last years of his life Wycliffe began to call for changes in Christian life. The immediate target of his concern was the wealth and political power of the church of his day. He opposed what he saw to be excesses of papal power and wealth, and advocated clerical poverty. Wycliffe argued that the legitimate papacy had ended with Urban VI and the schism of 1378. Since that time, it could no longer be assured that the Holy Spirit was working through the papal office, he argued. Therefore the church had to return to scriptures as the only source of its authority. Like other reformers before him, Wycliffe advocated apostolic poverty as the ideal of Christian life. He opposed the monastic orders of his day, however, especially the Franciscans and Dominicans because they were under the authority of Rome. Wycliffe opposed clerical celibacy, although he supported mendicant priests. He placed strong emphasis upon the need for the spiritual development of the laity, whom he termed the "elect" of Christian salvation.

Wycliffe turned repeatedly to the Bible as the basis for his arguments. He contended that the Bible was the ultimate source of authority for spiritual life and therefore ought to be available to all Christian believers to read. To this end he and several of his supporters undertook a new translation of the Bible from the Vulgate into English, a project that was completed the year he died and revised again several years later. It was the first full translation of scripture ever accomplished in the English language and stands as a landmark in the history of vernacular translations in the West.

All members of the elect have immediate access to Christ through the Bible, Wycliffe argued. This led him in turn to challenge the notion that the sacraments are necessary for the people to receive grace. He also did not accept the doctrine that the substance of the elements is changed in the eucharist or the doctrine of transubstantiation, although he still accepted the practice of the sacraments of the church as meaningful for worship. Wycliffe also argued for the authority of temporal rulers over the material dimensions of ecclesiastical life. His opposition to the papacy suited the English court's political purposes at the time, so Wycliffe was supported. His views were first condemned in 1382 by a synod under the archbishop of Canterbury, but neither he nor his supporters were able to be touched.

The supporters went on after Wycliffe's death in 1384 to organize a movement known as the Lollards or Mumblers, supposedly so named because of their public preaching. The Lollards were a lay-led movement of reform that argued all believers were priests. Their doctrines were spread by popular lay preachers who traveled in twos throughout the English countryside, living the lifestyle of apostolic poverty. In 1395 the Lollards presented a statement of their beliefs to the English Parliament, a statement that was essentially the beliefs held by Wycliffe. They rejected the sacramentalism of the church, the discipline of clerical celibacy, the need for confession to a priest, and the validity of prayers for the dead (hence the church's ability to affect the afterlife).

The English Parliament soon proved to be less than receptive to their petition. In 1401 it passed a law authorizing Lollards to be burned at the stake as heretics.

Few actually suffered such a fate. For the most part the English rulers simply ignored their agitations, at least until 1417 when open rebellion broke out. It was soon suppressed, and the Lollards were forced to go underground with their beliefs. Their movement did not die out entirely, however, but resurfaced a century later during the time of the Reformation in England.

As for Wycliffe, his teachings were finally condemned as heretical at the Council of Constance in 1415. The council charged him with thirty different points of error, including his views regarding the nature of the sacraments, his denunciation of ecclesiastical possessions, and his opposition to recognized monastic communities. Since he was already dead, the council could not order him burned at the stake, so it settled for ordering his bones dug up and burned as those of a heretic.

Copies of Wycliffe's books were carried by his supporters to various other centers of learning in Europe, where they received a mixed reception. One place they found fertile ground was in Bohemia. John Huss (1373-1415) was the rector of the University of Prague after 1402. He agreed with Wycliffe that the true church was a spiritual fellowship made up of the elect, and that Christ, not the pope, was its head. Huss supported Wycliffe's claim that all members of the clergy ought to follow Christ in a life of simplicity or apostolic poverty, and that the laity—not just the priests—ought to receive wine in the communion service. Wycliffe's works were banned by the archbishop of Prague, who tried to restrain Huss's advocacy of these positions by restricting preaching to churches and monasteries. The intent was to deny Huss his pulpit at the university. Although specifically ordered by the archbishop to cease preaching, Huss continued, and in 1411 he was excommunicated.

Huss was not deterred. The power of excommunication in the western church was ultimately derived from the pope. Wycliffe had argued, however, that an unworthy pope need not be obeyed, and that by definition because of the papal schism, all claimants to the papal throne were unworthy. Furthermore, Huss argued, the Bible was the ultimate authority of Christian life and thus could be cited over against the decisions of a pope. His criticisms of the papal office went even further. A pope cannot grant indulgences (dispensations of grace that extend to the afterlife), for instance. The elect are chosen by Christ, and thus their fate in the afterlife is not up to a bishop of the church.

The convening of the Council of Constance provided an opportunity for the airing of these ideas before the gathered body of western church leaders. Huss was invited to come to Constance to defend his views. Emperor Sigismund of Germany issued a safe-conduct order to allow him to come and go unmolested by the bishops. Huss then agreed, but upon arriving in Constance was placed under arrest by Pope John XXIII. Sigismund ignored his own safe-conduct promise and allowed the proceedings to go forth. An ecclesiastical court was convened, and Huss was ordered to recant his heretical views. He refused on grounds that none of his actual views had been proven to be heretical by his opponents. Ironically, John XXIII was now also made a prisoner of the council, but it is unlikely that he would have acted to save the Bohemian detractor of the papal office. Along with Wycliffe (who was already dead), Huss was condemned as a heretic.

In July of 1415 he was burned at the stake in the city of Constance by official order of the council. Accompanying him into death was a colleague, Jerome of Prague, who had traveled with Huss to Constance to attend the hearing in his support. The ashes of both men were scattered around the city to prevent their followers from later arranging a Christian burial.

Back home in Bohemia, Huss's supporters refused to concede defeat. A number of intellectuals and members of the nobility in the city had been attracted to his teaching, as well as people in the surrounding countryside. Calls for more popular preaching and reforms in the lifestyle of the clergy increased. In 1420 a newly elected pope, fresh from the Council of Constance, called for a crusade against the Bohemians. Sigismund of Germany was called upon to lead the fight against the heretics, but his forces met strong resistance and suffered a series of military defeats. Several more German military excursions in 1427 and then again in 1430 were turned back. Finally the two sides turned to negotiation, and a compromise was reached. Those who wished to remain Catholic would be allowed to do so within Bohemian churches, while others who wished to form separate communities following Huss's teachings would be allowed to do so, adhering to their own practices. In 1453 a group of the latter formed a fellowship they called *Unitas Fratrum* ("United Brethren"). Thereafter Huss's followers were generally known as the Brethren.

The challenge Wycliffe and Huss posed to the church was fundamentally institutional in nature. Both sought to reform the integrated complex of western Christendom by drawing upon traditions of biblical renewal and apostolic poverty that had long echoed through corridors of western Christian life. Neither reformer shied away from making his case in public in ways that were intended to draw support from secular political rulers, and both were able to inspire others to join them in the cause. It is no wonder the conflict they stirred within Christendom eventually broke out in open civil war.

Looking back across the period, we can see western Christendom becoming institutionally torn by the struggles between popes and secular kings. The growing influence of secular rulers helped create a schism within the office of the papacy itself in the fourteenth century. This in turn led in the fifteenth to the rapid growth of a conciliar theology. For the first time in the West in centuries some within the hierarchy of the church itself were successfully arguing the authority of councils over popes. The day of the conciliarist was soon past, however, as a united papacy once again made its case for universal supremacy over the entire world Christian movement. Aiding this assertion in the middle of the fifteenth century was the "Decree of Union" from the Council of Ferrara-Florence. A document that proclaimed the universal office of the Roman pope had been signed by both the Byzantine emperor and the patriarch of Constantinople. Through Franciscan and Dominican emissaries, the extension of the western Latin church throughout the Christian world to the east was becoming a reality.

At precisely the moment the Latin church was extending its ecclesiastical influences within Christian communities to the east, at home in Europe new movements of dissent were emerging to challenge absolute papal authority. These new movements championed the local vernacular over the universal role of Latin in the church. They sought, and won, local political support for their efforts as well. From the margins of western Christendom a new reforming mission was taking shape, one that would challenge the unity of the West to its core in the next century.

38

The Christian Movement in the East until 1453

The rising tide of Europe's economy carried its merchants and goods far beyond its borders to the east. Friars and priests often traveled with them, serving as agents for the spread of western Christian beliefs. The growing strength of western Christendom stood in stark contrast to the diminishing life of eastern Christian churches in the fourteenth and fifteenth centuries. The decline of the Christian movement in the East during this period was due to a number of factors, internal as well as external in nature. The most persistent were the realities of a changing political landscape that undercut the ability of Christians to sustain a common life.

Cilician Armenia

The southeast corner of Anatolia was one of the last strongholds of an indigenous Christian community in Asia at the end of the thirteenth century. In the course of the century the Armenians had faced outside political pressure first from the Mongols and then from the Mamelukes in Egypt. Through it all they had managed to maintain at least the semblance of semi-independent political life. On the ecclesiastical front the Armenians found themselves faced with an alternative challenge. Western friars had settled in the region and were busy attempting to win Armenian converts to the Latin churches they were building in the region. The Armenian church at first sought to oppose such endeavors. The patriarch declined to send a representative to the Council of Lyons in 1274 to participate along with the Greek delegation in its deliberations. By 1300, however, growing Mameluke military pressure was changing the situation, forcing the Armenians to open a new round of discussions with the Roman church.

The Council of Sis (capital city of Cilicia) in 1307 represented a major turning point in Armenian church history. Facing the pressures of hostile Muslim armies and hoping to gain assistance from the West, leaders of the Armenian churches joined the patriarch in agreeing to bring their liturgical practice into conformity with the Latin church. The decision was met with resistance by others among the ranks of the Armenian monks and clergy after word of the agreement was published among the churches of the region. A rival party of Armenian church leaders in Jerusalem went so far as to elect an alternative catholicus, although their candidate failed to gain widespread recognition among Armenian churches.

In the West, church leaders still doubted the sincerity of the Armenian clergy and nobility who had participated in the deliberations at Sis. Furthermore, the promised military assistance was not forthcoming. The Mameluke presence in the region increased until Armenian rule in Cilicia was finally brought to an end in the last decades of the fourteenth century. Some in the church even began to advocate the return of the patriarchal office from Cilicia to the traditional homeland. In 1441 a gathering of Armenian clergy and bishops elected a new catholicus in the city of Etchmiadzin, the historical home of the patriarch in Greater Armenia. This meant there were now two recognized catholicoi of the church: Kyrakos of Virap in Etchmiadzin and Gregory IX at Sis. A new schism in Armenian church history had opened up, as patriarchs and churches straddled the political and theological divides of the region.

Christianity in Persia and central Asia

While the Armenians were struggling once again with the loss of their national homeland, this time to the Mamelukes of Egypt, Christians in Persia and central Asia were facing a different set of political pressures. From 1282 to 1295 a succession of ilkhans ruled from Baghdad under conditions that were politically unstable. The Mongol rulers in Persia were simultaneously moving away from the authority of the great khan in China and closer to their own subjects, of whom the great majority were Muslim. Several within the ruling family of the ilkhans in Persia flirted with Christian conversion, as we have seen, before Ghazan formally converted to Islam in 1295. From that point on we can mark a new era of decline in the life of the Christian movement in Persia and central Asia, reversing several decades of official toleration.

Ghazan ordered the destruction of a number of churches, synagogues, and temples throughout his domain. A new wave of violence was unleashed against Christians as Muslim mobs attacked churches and individual believers alike. At one point the patriarch Yaballaha himself was taken hostage and tortured for several days until his followers could raise a ransom, while his church and residence were looted of all their valuables. Following his release the patriarch was forced to remain on the move, staying in monasteries or Christian fortresses within the cities of Persia that he visited. A new ilkhan named Oljeitu assumed the throne in 1304. Although baptized by his Mongol Christian mother as an infant, he had converted to Islam as an adult. Attacks against Christians became more frequent. Christians in Arbela were massacred in 1310. Patriarch Yaballaha was forced into permanent residence in the fortified monastery at Maragah. By the time of his death in 1317, Christians across Persia and Mesopotamia were under constant attack. The age of tolerant Mongol regimes was all but a distant memory.

The last synod of the East Syrian church was formally allowed to meet by the ilkhan in the year 1318. After that such gatherings were banned. That same year the pope appointed the first Dominicans to head a new Latin archdiocese of Persia. The appointment was made along the lines of John of Monte Corvino and the Franciscans in China. Essentially the Dominicans were to organize new Latin-rite churches in the regions to which they were appointed, hoping to draw Persian Christians and others into them. Several Dominicans eventually made their way into various cities of Persia and India, although there is very little evidence that their efforts were successful.

Further east, in China, both the Syrian- and Latin-rite churches faced the prospect of declining Mongol rulers. The pope appointed several successors to John of Monte Corvino to guide the Latin churches, but their efforts produced few results. Even among the East Syrian Christians, the attractions of Confucianism and Buddhism in China were becoming stronger. In 1368 the Mongol dynasty was overthrown by a national rebellion that established the Ming dynasty. Christians were too strongly identified as foreigners by their liturgies to survive the wave of cultural nationalism that swept across northern China. Latin and Syrian churches that had been tolerated by the Mongol rulers appear to have withered away.

Timur Lenk

The fall of the Mongols in China left their empire without a titular head. The scattered khanates of central Asia, Persia, and Russia were already fighting among themselves, creating further instability. In the region near Samarkand a Turkish military officer in the service of a Mongol khan rose to power in the political vacuum that had been created. His name was Timur Lenk (1336-1405), better known in the West as Tamerlane. A Muslim by faith, he began to move against his Mongol sponsor in 1365. Within several years he had taken military control of the region around Samarkand. The khan was kept on as a nominal ruler in order to legitimate Timur Lenk, whose goal was to reestablish the empire of Genghis Khan.

Over the next several decades Timur Lenk led his armies into Iran, India, Mesopotamia, Syria, Anatolia, and Georgia. From Russia to India people suffered under a reign of terror as bloody as any in history. Not without cause was he called Scourge of God and Terror of the World. Christians, Muslims, and Hindus all suffered under the extreme brutality of his conquests. In northern India he is reported to have massacred one hundred thousand people rather than take them captive, which would have slowed his army's advance. In Georgia he burned hundreds of Christian villages and destroyed whatever churches he could find. The Muslim defenders of Anatolia were crushed by his forces, despite the fact that the majority of soldiers on both sides shared the same Islamic faith. At the time of his death at the age of seventy-one, he was preparing to invade China and no doubt was intending to unleash similar destruction there.

Timur Lenk does not appear to have singled out Christians in particular as victims of his reign of terror. Although tens of thousands died in the onslaught of his army, he was at times capable of bestowing favors on others. He showed a remarkable appreciation for scholarship and learning, which he sought to attract to his capital at Samarkand, and was not against Christians providing them for him. His main objective was always conquest, however, and the scorched earth that his army left behind provided little on which to rebuild. This more than any other reason accounts for the decline of the churches under Timur Lenk. He destroyed too much of their urban and commercial infrastructure for the Christians of the East to recover. Not even his own descendants could sustain the empire after he died, so great was the destruction. The Mamelukes were soon back in power in Syria, while in Persia a new national dynasty eventually arose. Both showed themselves to be harsh opponents of Christianity. By the end of the fifteenth century only a handful of churches clustered in northern Mesopotamia remained of the East Syrian tradition.

Christians in India

The army of Timur Lenk reached as far as northern India, where there might have been some Christian communities, although most Christians lived scattered along the coastal regions further south. Christians had become assigned to a caste of their own under the dominant Hindu religious culture in India. They generally referred to themselves in India as followers of St. Thomas, although they were part of the East Syrian tradition. Bishops were still being sent from Persia when possible, and worship was still mainly conducted in Syriac, as it was elsewhere across Asia. Armenian Christians had established trading communities in several Indian seaports by the fourteenth century, as had members of the West Syrian (or Jacobite) churches. As far as we can tell, there was no Christian liturgy said in a native Indian language, and no Christian works written in Indian tongues. Although these communities maintained a separate Christian identity, they clearly lacked adequate resources for leadership and pastoral care. For many, the sheer weight of their tradition as bearers of the heritage of St. Thomas in India appears to have sustained their Christian faith identity.

This was the situation in the fourteenth century when the western friars began to appear. A Dominican named Jordan Catalani reported visiting a handful of Christian communities in the area of modern Bombay, where he arrived in 1321. Several of his colleagues were executed by local Muslim officials who opposed the Dominicans' efforts to win Christian converts in the area. John of Monte Corvino several decades earlier had visited Mylapore (later Madras, since 1996, Chennai) on the southeast coast of India during the thirteen months he spent in India waiting for a ship to take him to China. One of his fellow Franciscans had died while they were there and was buried at the church of St. Thomas.

Latin priests were sometimes asked to baptize members of the indigenous churches, perhaps because of the lack of indigenous priests. Within several decades they could claim Indian converts, at least some of whom appear not to have previously been members of other Christian communities. The indication one receives from reading their accounts is that the friars were not generally antagonistic to the other Christians they encountered in India. We do not have enough evidence, on the other hand, to know if that sentiment was shared by the St. Thomas Christians as well. In any case, the small number of friars and the declining resources of the East Syrian churches overall precluded any major confrontation between the two church traditions in the fourteenth and fifteenth century.

Byzantium

All that remained of the East Roman empire was the city of Constantinople and the lands to the immediate west stretching some 250 miles. What that represented historically was much more: a rich heritage of Christian faith shared with a number of national churches in communion with the ecumenical patriarch, and a wider heritage of classical culture shared with other Christians, Muslims, and the world. Constantinople was still the repository of that twin heritage, an active center for learning and church life. Yet its economy was entirely dependent on the dwindling resources of its taxes. Gone were the secondary cities of the empire and the kingdoms that paid tribute to the emperor. Gone were the rich farmlands to the east that could provide food for the tables of Constantinople's people. The Byzantine empire had no navy of its own left to speak of by the year 1300, and the emperor depended entirely upon paid foreign mercenaries for his troops. The old aristocratic order was ill-prepared to deal with the new commercial world that was emerging. At one point the royal family was forced to pawn the crown jewels in order to pay its debts and survive.

On every side Constantinople felt political pressures. To the north was the kingdom of Bulgaria, and to the immediate west the kingdom of Serbia. Both shared the Byzantine empire's historic form of orthodox Christian faith but not its current political aspirations. The navies of the cities of Venice and Genoa controlled the waters around Constantinople. Their frequent skirmishes were often at the East Romans' expense. When the Venetians or Genoese were not creating trouble for the emperor, the Normans further west in southern Italy stepped in to fill the void. And always there was the persistent issue of failures to achieve reunion between the two great Christian traditions of Rome and Constantinople.

As if these problems were not enough, the fourteenth century brought a new political threat from the east. The Turks in Anatolia had succumbed to Mongol invasions in the middle years of the thirteenth century, as we have seen. The fall of Baghdad to the Mongols in 1258 had ended the Abbasid dynasty, leaving the Mamelukes in Egypt as the major Muslim political power. The situation did not last long, however, for in 1300 a Turkish emir named Othman emerged in Anatolia to establish a new kingdom that had soon swept up the remaining Greek territories east of Constantinople. Unlike the Seljuk Turks before them in Asia Minor, the Ottomans (as the dynasty of Othman was known) did not look eastward for further conquest. They turned their attention instead to the west, across the Dardanelles and Bosporus straits to Constantinople and eastern Europe. By the 1350s they had secured control of several cities on European soil and were advancing into territory where Muslim armies had not previously been.

Hagia Sophia as it appears today as a museum in Istanbul (formerly Constantinople), Turkey. Photograph from Fatih Cimok, Hagia Sophia (Istanbul: A Turizm Yayinlari, 1998), p. 17. Reproduced with permission.

Hesychast controversy and Gregory of Palamas

Within the city of Constantinople a new theological controversy around monastic devotional practices broke out in the 1340s. At places like Mount Athos and Mount Sinai, many of the monks had for centuries practiced a form of meditation known as *hesychasm* ("holy silence"). The spiritual practices of *hesychasts* had traditionally focused on reciting what was known as the Jesus prayer: "Lord Jesus, Son of God, have mercy on me." Gregory, a monk from Mount Sinai, began in the 1330s to teach a particular set of techniques that were to be used in meditation as well. By lowering the chin, regulating one's breathing, and reciting the Jesus prayer continuously, one could attain a vision of the uncreated light that surrounded Jesus Christ on the Mount of Transfiguration, the hesychasts explained.

Gregory spent several years traveling throughout the eastern Mediterranean world teaching these techniques to members of other Orthodox monasteries. Before long his efforts began to attract criticism. In Constantinople the theologian Barlaam, who was originally from southern Italy, led the opposition. Barlaam attacked the notion that physical practices could open the door to perception of the uncreated light that surrounds Jesus Christ. The hesychasts were not without theological defenders in the city, however. Into the fray on their behalf stepped one of the most capable Christian theologians of the century, Gregory of Palamas (1292-1359), who was eventually to become archbishop of Thessalonica. The debates reached crisis proportions in the city, forcing the patriarch to call a council in 1341 to decide the orthodoxy of the practice.

The council only lasted a day or so, making it one of the shortest on record in Christian history. Palamas made the case so persuasively for the hesychasts that Barlaam's position was declared heretical. To those who decided the case, Palamas was more clearly within the stream of Eastern Orthodox theology that reached back through the centuries to the Cappadocians of the fourth century. This tradition had always affirmed that the doctrine of the transcendence of God means God is ultimately unknowable to us. God is unknowable by human beings not just because of human sin, Palamas pointed out. Even sinless angels do not fathom the depths of the divine. God's transcendence is such that no created being can plummet the depths of divine reality. Knowledge of God must proceed by way of negation and silence (a tradition known as *apophasis*). The best one can do in terms of attaining true knowledge of God is to be able to say what God is not. Otherwise one must remain silent altogether. Yet along such a pathway of negation, paradoxically, one can attain a positive vision of the God who is beyond limitations, or an experience of mystical union with God through contemplation that is beyond knowing.

The goal of such mystical union was theosis, a life that is fully divine or Spirit-filled; on this point Palamas agreed with the long tradition of Eastern Orthodox theology. Theosis does not mean that human nature becomes the same as the divine nature, he argued. The doctrine does not imply the identity of deified ones and the deifying One. Grace overcomes the distance between the divine and human natures without confusing the two. Hence it is grace that is shared with humans in order to deify them, not the divine nature. Palamas followed the pattern of the distinction between divine grace and divine nature to draw a parallel distinction between the divine energy and the divine essence. Both are uncreated and eternal. The former in both cases (divine grace or divine energy) is the means by which humanity participates in the divine life, however, while the latter (divine nature or divine essence) remains beyond our participation. The former is associated with the procession of the Holy Spirit in the temporal economy of God, the latter with the eternal procession of the Holy Spirit by which the Spirit shares the essence of divinity, Palamas said.

With this framework in place, he could then go on to argue that believing there are practices that can prepare the senses to receive grace does not violate the doctrine of the transcendence of God. The unity one experiences through mystical contemplation is not with the divine essence but with the divine energy. As the rays of sunshine are not the same as the sun itself, so the energy of God is not the same as the essence of God. Through meditation involving the use of the senses, human beings can experience the divine energies, Palamas asserted, but not the divine essence. Opponents of the proposal charged him with separating the created and the uncreated within the Godhead, but the majority of eastern bishops and theologians did not agree. They saw that by distinguishing between the energy and essence of God, Palamas was providing a way to affirm both that we participate in God and that God infinitely transcends us. They recognized the doctrine as fully orthodox and the practice of meditation as a vital means of opening one's self up to God.

The resolution of the hesychast controversy in Palamas' favor was more than a victory for the position that held direct knowledge of God to be possible through mystical experience. Monasteries had long cut across the political and cultural borders of Greek, Serbian, Georgian, and Russian identity in the East. The spiritual practices of hesychasm likewise cut across these political and cultural borders, thus providing a degree of unity and cohesion in the Eastern Orthodox world at precisely the time that the Byzantine empire was fragmenting and the power of the ecumenical patriarch was diminishing. After the fifteenth century the unity of the Eastern Orthodox world rested on a common spirituality more than it did on imperial politics or ecclesiastical institutions.

Ottoman Turkish advance

The hesychast controversy was resolved rather quickly and in a relatively conclusive way. Not so easily resolved was Constantinople's disintegrating political life. The Ottoman Turks were soon expanding across the Balkans from the European foothold they had established in the 1350s. Commercial ties between the Turks and the Genoese further weakened Constantinople's situation. The emperor traveled once again to Italy and in a personal act submitted to the pope, hoping his action would secure some form of assistance from the West. Once again none was forthcoming. The Ottomans continued to strip away the remaining imperial lands outside the city. By 1375 the Greeks had no choice but to begin paying tribute to the sultan. The emperor of the East Roman world, a ruler who stood in unbroken political succession with the great emperors of the Roman past and who was the living embodiment of the ancient imperial Christian ideal, was now reduced to being a vassal of a Turkish sultan.

A series of engagements with Bulgar and Serbian forces left no doubt as to Ottoman intentions further west. A decisive battle took place in 1389 in Kosovo when the Serbian army under Tsar Lazar was destroyed by the Turks. Soon all of Serbia, Bulgaria, and Macedonia were effectively under Ottoman control. At the same time the Turkish rulers were securing control over all of Anatolia. The remaining parcels of the older Seljuk sultanate were incorporated into the new Ottoman state, whose ruler appropriated for himself the title Sultan of Rum. An invasion by Timur Lenk in 1402 brought a temporary halt to the Ottoman advance, but before long their military was back on its feet and on the move.

The Ottoman rulers were Sunni Muslims, but the great majority of people they had conquered were Christian. Faced with the challenge of building an army from among a mostly Christian population, toward the end of the fourteenth century they instituted a practice known as *devshirme*. Essentially it was a system of forced recruitment from among their Christian subjects. The system proved successful. Every several years, as the need arose, the Ottoman authorities would go out among the villages and cities of their lands and remove from Christian families one-fifth of the male children between the ages fourteen and twenty. These young men were enrolled in special military units called *janissaries*. A strict discipline was imposed upon them, members were tied to their units for life, and close bonding among them was encouraged. Only the officers or older members of the units were allowed to marry. Educated to become Muslims, they were granted privileges and status beyond other Christians. The practice not only served as an effective way to build the military force during the first centuries of Ottoman rule, but it also had the effect of reducing the male Christian community in Ottoman lands by 20 percent on a regular basis.

Christianity in Russia prior to 1448

While the Ottomans were increasing their hold on Anatolia and the Balkans, Mongol rule in Russia was beginning to show signs of deteriorating. The first years of the rule of the Golden Horde had been brutal. The khanate encompassed all of Russia south of the city of Novgorod. Numerous cities had been destroyed during the invasion, and the Russian nobility that survived was kept firmly under Mongol control. John of Plano Carpini reported that he had learned of a Russian prince, Michael of Chernigov, who had refused to venerate an image of Genghis Khan and was beheaded by Khan Batu in 1246. At Karakorum the Franciscan met another Russian prince, Yaroslav I of Vladimir, who died while being held as a hostage in the great khan's camp.

The ferocity of the initial conquest of Russia was soon tempered by the realities of running an effective empire. The Mongols collected tribute from the peoples that they subjugated. Even the fiercest generals among them quickly found that there was more wealth to be gained in times of peace than could be plundered through warfare. Cities such as Kiev were rebuilt and soon regained their place in the regional economy. The Mongols did not migrate into lands that they controlled, and thus they did not attempt to install their own aristocracy over the cities. They depended instead on a policy of keeping local Russian princes at odds with one another to prevent them from uniting against Mongol rule. At the same time the unified Mongol empire, stretching from China to Poland, provided a degree of stability across Asia that translated into safer passage for commercial goods. New trade routes between northern Europe and China were opened up across Asia, cutting out the Muslim intermediaries while spurring economic growth in several northern cities. All of these factors translated into ample opportunity for Russian artisans and merchants to advance.

The first generation of Mongol rulers, in Russia as elsewhere in their empire, exercised a relative degree of religious toleration toward the people under them. Like their cousins in central Asia, the first Mongol rulers in Russia were practitioners of shamanism. By the fourteenth century a number had begun to convert to Islam, but there was never any attempt to impose Islamic law on the Russian people. Christian clergy were not taxed under the Mongol rulers, and new churches and monasteries were allowed. Church officials traveled freely throughout the region and were allowed to collect funds for the ecumenical patriarch. The Mongols had good diplomatic relations with Constantinople and even treated the "metropolitan of Kiev and all of Russia," who until the fourteenth century was always a Greek, as a foreign diplomat. Despite these freedoms afforded the churches, however, the fact remained that the Russians were a politically subjugated people.

One of the cities that grew in importance during the period of Mongol rule was Moscow. By the fourteenth century it had not only become a major commercial center, but its prince had become a major factor in Russian political life. After 1310 the metropolitan of Kiev and all of Russia moved his residence permanently to Moscow, while retaining the older title. The Golden Horde had welcomed Moscow's rise in power at first, as it served their policy of playing one prince against another. By the last quarter of the century, however, the principality of Moscow was strong enough to challenge Mongol rule directly. In 1380 forces from the city under the command of Grand Prince Dimitri handed the Mongols a major military defeat at the battle of Kulikovo. Even though the Mongols returned two years later to sack the city and bring Dimitri back under their vassalage, the victory made Moscow the symbol of nationalist hopes among the Russian people.

The principality of Moscow emerged to become one of two major political entities shaping Russian life in the fourteenth century. The other was the kingdom of Lithuania. Squeezed between the Latin Christian kingdoms to the west and the Mongols to the east, Lithuania had emerged in the thirteenth century as an independent kingdom to extend its control over a sizable portion of Russian soil, including the historical city of Kiev. The king of Lithuania was not yet a Christian in the early fourteenth century, but his Russian domains included a number of Orthodox churches. Moreover, he was not a vassal of the Golden Horde, whereas the metropolitan of Kiev and all of Russia, now residing in Moscow, recognized the legitimacy of Mongol rule. Because of the difficulties Russian Orthodox churches in Lithuanian territories faced in this situation, the ecumenical patriarch in Constantinople consented to the appointment of a separate metropolitan.

For much of the fourteenth century there were thus two metropolitans among the Russian people, the metropolitan of Kiev and all of Russia, who resided in fact in Moscow, and the metropolitan of Lithuania, who in fact sometimes oversaw Kiev. The various occupants of the two metropolitan sees struggled constantly for Constantinople's blessing as first one, then the other, and sometimes both were recognized as the legitimate head of the Russian churches. The situation was only resolved after 1386 when the king of Lithuania, who had by then been baptized into the Orthodox faith, converted to Roman Catholicism and joined his kingdom to that of Poland in what is known as the Union of Krewo. Thereafter the center of Russian Christianity was located firmly in Moscow.

By the first decades of the fifteenth century, tensions between the Russian churches and Constantinople were becoming quite visible. The Mongols' grip on the Russian princes was weakening for one thing, and Russian nationalism was on the rise. Surrounded by a host of hostile forces, Constantinople was becoming increasingly isolated, for another. Earlier in the fourteenth century, the ecumenical patriarch had begun to alternate Russian with Greek appointments to the metropolitanate, and after 1380 nominations to the position were to come from Russia, but the latter stipulation was not being followed. Russian church leaders also expressed a growing disenchantment with the ecumenical patriarchate's efforts toward union with the Roman church. In 1436 the ecumenical patriarch appointed Isidore, a Bulgarian who considered himself Greek, to be metropolitan of Kiev. Isidore was a unionist. Not only did he participate in the Council of Florence and sign the "Decree of Union" in 1439, but following the council he served as a papal representative to other churches in the eastern Mediterranean.

Back in Moscow most other church leaders rejected the "Decree of Union" and the ecumenical patriarch's role in the whole affair. Isidore was expelled from the city after he tried to return in 1441, and the Grand Prince of Moscow requested another metropolitan be appointed in his place. After seven years, when none was forthcoming, the bishops of Russia took the momentous step of electing and consecrating one of their own, a cleric named Jonas (Iona) to be the new metropolitan of Russia. The year 1448 thus marks a decisive turning point in the life of the Russian church. By elevating Jonas without the involvement of the ecumenical patriarch, the Russians were in effect announcing that theirs was an autocephalous church. The act was not that of a schismatic body, nor was there a break in the continuity of their Orthodox faith. The need for a self-governing church and the difficulties facing the patriarchate in Constantinople had combined in their minds to mandate such a course of action. Three decades later, in 1480, Ivan III of Moscow put an end to the rule of the Golden Horde. An independent Russian kingdom and a national church under the primate of Moscow had emerged almost in tandem.

The last days of Constantinople and the East Roman empire

Timur Lenk's invasion of Anatolia in 1402 proved in the long run to be a minor setback to Ottoman aspirations. Soon the Turkish rulers were able to turn their attention again toward the west. Constantinople was soon under a state of perpetual siege. Surprisingly the city still stood, due to the strong defenses that its walls provided and to the sheer perseverance of its remaining inhabitants. Even so, the city's population was clearly in decline; the bureaucracy and physical infrastructure also were diminishing. The farmlands immediately outside the city were no longer under Constantinople's control, so vineyards and grains had to be grown inside the city's walls in order for the people to have food. Little commercial activity stirred within its markets, although some trade was still being carried on with the Venetians and Genoese. The imperial family sold off whatever items of value it had left in an effort to bring new income into the city. A shadow of its former self, the city was nevertheless holding on.

At the Council of Florence in 1439 the eastern delegation, which included both emperor and patriarch, agreed once again to a formula of reunion between Greek and Latin churches. The Greeks still hoped that this might pave the way for western military assistance against the Turks. As we saw above, the council served instead to bolster the position of the papacy both in the West and among other churches in the Mediterranean. In Constantinople the reception accorded the returning delegates was quite cold. Anti-unionist sentiments still ran high among clergy and laity alike. Not until the end of 1452 were the unionists able to introduce even the minor change of adding the pope's name at the head of the listing of patriarchs of the world church who were blessed in liturgy at Hagia Sophia. Perhaps they need not have bothered, for within six months the liturgy itself would fall silent within the cathedral.

The Ottoman Turks launched their final attack against Constantinople in 1453. Cannons that had been designed for them by a German engineer were dragged into place and fired against the city. These new weapons soon proved their value by destroying portions of the city's walls. There was an ominous occurrence on the eve of the battle. The icon of the Virgin that was being carried through the city, as it had so many times before when the city was under siege, fell from the shoulders of its carriers. Finally, on May 29 the Ottoman sultan, Mehmet II, mounted what would prove to be the final siege. The elite corps of janissaries, along with other troops (many of them Christian mercenaries), stormed through the broken walls. The last round of defenders went down, among them the emperor, who had discarded his imperial insignia as he waded into the fray. His body was never identified.

For several days the invaders reportedly raped and massacred many of the remaining population. Many members of the remaining Greek nobility were summarily executed. Priests in Hagia Sophia were killed at the high altar as they were celebrating a final eucharist. Within days the cathedral and most of the other churches of the city had been converted into mosques. The Ottoman sultan appointed a new patriarch, a monk named Gennadius (formerly George Scholarius). Gennadius had been at the Council of Florence, where he had supported the union agreements, but he had later turned against them to become a leader of the anti-unionist party. The new patriarch now headed a Christian community that was relegated to separate quarters in the city that Constantine had originally built for it. After more than a thousand years, New Rome had fallen.

The fall of Constantinople in 1453 brought about the end of a Christian empire in its Byzantine form. The fall of the Mongol empire in China nearly a century before brought about a strong national movement against foreign religions, and thus the second eclipse of the Christian movement there. Elsewhere in Asia the Mongol rulers underwent wide-scale conversion to the Islamic faith of the majority of their subjects in the fourteenth century. Christians were generally the losers in the aftermath of such conversions. The brief but bloody reign of Timur Lenk accelerated the rapid decline of churches throughout central Asia, Persia, and Mesopotamia. The rise of the Ottomans in Anatolia further diminished the Christian presence in west Asia.

After 1453 the ecumenical patriarch was subject to the Ottoman rulers, who were Muslims. In eastern Europe, Serbia, Bulgaria, Macedonia, and Greece were all brought under Ottoman rule as well. The effect on the churches in these regions was not only to limit their access to power but to diminish their numbers through warfare and conversion. The one exception among churches in the family of Byzantine Orthodoxy was Russia, which was soon to be heralded as a New Constantinople and even the Third Rome. Along with the kingdom of Ethiopia, Russia was the only state outside western Europe at the end of the fifteenth century where Christian kings exercised political rule.

After fifteen hundred years the Christian movement thus found itself in a rather lopsided situation. The majority of the world's Christians resided in the European West. The dominant culture of western Europe was virtually synonymous with Latin Christianity. The social and political institutions were shaped by those of the church. Western armies marched on behalf of Christian as much as national political impulses. These same armies, accompanied by friars and followed by merchants, were soon to spread across the world in a new phase of Christian expansion that accompanied European colonialism. The history of that expansion awaits us in volume II.

Recommended readings

Among the works detailing the history of the crusades, Jonathan Riley-Smith, *The Crusades: A Short History* (London and New Haven, Conn.: Yale University

Press, 1987) is a relatively straight-forward account. Francesco Gabrieli has translated a collection of Muslim accounts of the period in *Arab Historians of the Crusades*, trans. E. J. Costello (London: Routledge and Kegan Paul, 1969; reprinted New York: Barnes and Noble Books, 1993). John Edwards, *Christian Cordoba: The City and Its Regions in the Late Middle Ages* (Cambridge: Cambridge University Press, 1982), provides the reader with a glimpse into the life of this Spanish city in the wake of Reconquest.

Two excellent general introductions to European Christianity between 1000 and 1450 are R. W. Southern, *The Making of the Middle Ages* (New Haven, Conn.: Yale University Press, 1959), and Joseph H. Lynch, *The Medieval Church: A Brief History* (London and New York: Longman, 1992). A detailed look at the theological issues at the root of the Investiture Controversy can be found in Gerd Tellenbach, *Church, State, and Christian Society at the Time of the Investiture Contest*, trans. R. F. Bennett (Oxford: Basil Blackwell, 1948). William J. La Due, J.C.D., *The Chair of Saint Peter: A History of the Papacy* (Maryknoll, N.Y.: Orbis Books, 1999), covers two thousand years of papal history but is especially helpful for the period of 1000 to 1500.

Currents of wider religious renewal are the subject of Herbert Grundmann's influential work *Religious Movements in the Middle Ages: The Historical Links between Heresy, the Mendicant Orders, and the Women's Religious Movement in the Twelfth and Thirteenth Century, with the Historical Foundations of German Mysticism*, trans. Steven Rowan (Notre Dame, Ind: University of Notre Dame Press, 1995). Women's spirituality is examined as well in Caroline Walker Bynum, *Jesus as Mother: Studies in the Spirituality of the High Middle Ages* (Berkeley and Los Angeles: University of California Press, 1982). A more detailed look at issues of gender in Western society during this period can be found in E. Ann Matters and John Coakley, eds., *Creative Women in Medieval and Early Modern Italy: A Religious and Artistic Renaissance* (Philadelphia: University of Pennsylvania Press, 1994). On the intellectual roots and trajectories of Western scholasticism, one might consult Steven Ozment, *The Age of Reform 1250-1500—An Intellectual and Religious History of Late Medieval and Reformation Europe* (London and New Haven, Conn.: Yale University Press, 1980).

John Meyendorff, *The Byzantine Legacy in the Orthodox Church* (Crestwood, N.Y.: St. Vladimir's Seminary Press, 1982) draws upon the historical heritage of Byzantium as a whole, especially from the period of 1000 to 1500. Another book by the same author, *Byzantium and the Rise of Russia: A Study of Byzantino-Russian Relations in the Fourteenth Century* (Cambridge: Cambridge University Press, 1981), delineates the theological lines of connection that ran back and forth from Constantinople to Kiev and Moscow. Papadakis Aristeides, *The Christian East and the Rise of the Papacy: The Church 1071-1453 A.D.* (Crestwood, N.Y.: St. Vladimir's Seminary Press, 1994), details aspects of Byzantine Christian life and practice during the period in relation to the Latin West.

One can read primary accounts of Christian life and experiences among the Mongols in Christopher H. Dawson, ed., *The Mongol Mission: Narratives and Letters of the Franciscan Missionaries in Mongolia and China in the Thirteenth and Fourteenth Centuries* (New York: Sheed and Ward, 1955). Lawrence E. Browne, *The Eclipse of Christianity in Asia from the Time of Muhammad till the Fourteenth Century* (Cambridge: Cambridge University Press, 1933), narrates the story of slow decline, while Henry Yule, *Cathay and the Way Thither*, 4 vols. (London: Hakluyt Society, 1913-1916), tells of Christianity in China as seen through the eyes of the traveler from Italy, Marco Polo. Finally, an outstanding resource for locating and assessing the value of all Christian texts in China from this period is Nicolas Standaert, *Handbook of Christianity in China, Volume One: 635-1800* (Leiden, Boston, Köln: Brill, 2001).

Index to Names of Persons and Deities

Abaka, Ilkhan, 460-62
'Abdisho of Merv, 314
Abel, 116
Abelard, Peter, 427-28
Abgar, King, 60
Abgar VIII (the Great), 60
Abraha Ashram, 263-64
Abraham, 10, 39, 261, 264
Abraham of Kaskar, 202-3
Abu Bakr, Caliph, 269, 273
Acacius of Constantinople, 240
Adam, 116
Addai, 60
Aedesius, 217-18
Agnes of Prague, 418
Ahmad, Ilkhan, 460, 462
Ahura Mazda, 20
Alcuin, 338
Alexander III, Pope, 411-12
Alexander V, Pope, 483
Alexander of Alexandria, 174, 176
Alexander the Great, 17, 311
Alexius Comnenus, Emperor, 394, 397, 401
Alexius III, Emperor, 404
Alfonso VI, King, 399
Allah (deity), 263-69
al-Muizz, 291
Alopen, 316-19
Amand, 344-45
Ambrose of Milan, 224-25, 232, 299-300
Amr ibn al-As, General, 289, 293
Angra Mainyu, 20
Anicetus of Rome, 78-79
Anna, 52
Anna, Queen, 377
Anselm of Canterbury, 426-27
Antipater, 12
Aphraates, 197
Apollinaris, 184
Apollos, 30, 86
Aquila, 30
Aquinas, Thomas, 430-35

Aratus, 42
Ardashir, Shah, 111
Aretas IV, King, 28
Arghon, Ilkhan, 460-63
Aristotle, 20, 189, 200, 409, 425, 430-35
Arius, 174-77
Ashoka, 4
Atargatis (deity), 206
Athanasius of Alexandria, 176-78, 181, 184, 188, 209-14, 217-18, 227
Attila, 222-23
Augustine (missionary), 327-29
Augustine of Hippo: and filioque, 299-300; on heresy, 171; theology of, 231-34, 426-27
Augustus, Ceasar, 9, 22, 43-44
Avalokitesvara (deity), 317-18
Averroës, 409
Avicenna, 425
Avircius Marcellus, 106
Baal (deity), 55
Bagrat III, King, 447
Baldwin of Boulogne, 397-98
Baldwin of Flanders, 441, 446
Bardaisan, 60, 92-93, 125-26, 197-98
Bar Hebreus, Gregory, 453, 463-64, 467
Barlaaam, 498
Barnabas, 28, 29
Barsauma of Nisibis, 201, 202
Bartholomew, Apostle, 94-95, 113-14
Basil (the Great) of Caesarea, 184-86, 212, 214, 365
Basilides, 88, 116
Bathsheba, 23
Batu, Khan, 500
Baudemond of Elnone, 344-45
Bel (deity), 59
Belisarius, General, 243-44
Benedict of Nursia, 234-35
Benedict VIII, Pope, 391
Benjamin, Patrarch, 290
Bernard of Clairvaux, 401, 411, 428

Bertha, 327-28
Bivar, Roderigo Díaz de (*See*, El Cid)
Blandina, 82
Boethius, 224
Bonaventure, 432-33
Boniface (missionary), 345-46
Boniface VIII, Pope, 480-81
Boris, King, 367-68
Buddha, the, 8, 86, 127
Burgundofara, 346
Caecilian of Carthage, 168-69
Callistus, 138, 141-42, 150
Candace, Queen, 217-18
Carpocrates, 87, 116-17
Cassius, 18
Catalani, Jordan, 495
Catherine of Siena, 482
Celestine of Rome, 191
Celsus, 102, 137
Cerinthus, 67
Charlemagne, King, 258-59, 334-41, 363, 367, 372-73
Charles Martel, 289, 302, 334, 345
Charles of Anjou, 443-44
Childeric, King, 238
Chi-lieh, Bishop, 319
Ching-ching, Bishop, 320
Chosroes I, Shah (*See*, Khusru I)
Clare of Assisi, 417
Claudius, Emperor, 30
Clement of Alexandria, 86-87, 89-90, 110, 122-24, 188
Clement of Rome, 69, 78, 84, 149
Clement V, Pope, 481
Clement VII, Pope, 482-83
Clotilde, Queen, 238
Clovis, King, 237-39
Columba, 330
Columbanus, 330, 344
Confucius, 8
Conrad III, Emperor, 401-2
Constans, Emperor, 169-70, 177
Constans II, Emperor, 356
Constantine, Emperor: building of city, 162-63, 355; conversion of, 155, 160-65; as defender of Christendom, 195-96; and Donatists, 168-69; and Eusebius, 220-21; and Nicaea, 175-77
Constantine V, Emperor, 361
Constantine VI, Emperor, 361-62
Constantius, Emperor, 177, 203
Constantius II, Emperor, 218

Cornelius, 38
Cornelius of Rome, 102, 139
Cosmas Indicopluestes, 204, 219, 295, 308
Crispa, 165
Cyprian of Carthage: on eucharist, 105; execution of, 110; on unity of church, 138-40
Cyril (ambassador), 367-68
Cyril of Alexandria, 188, 191, 193-94, 200, 214-15, 240-41
Cyrus, Patriarch, 358
Dadyeshu, Patriarch, 195
Damasus, Pope, 227-28
Damia al-Kahena, Queen, 298
David, King, 10
David of Basra, 114, 203
Decius, Emperor, 110, 138
Demetrius of Alexandria, 89-90, 94
Denha, Patriarch, 461
Dhu Nuwas, King, 262-63
Didymus the Blind, 186
Diego of Osma, 414-15
Digna Jan, King, 296
Diocletian, Emperor, 110-11, 160-61, 167-68, 173, 355
Diodore of Tarsus, 188, 200
Diognetus, 95-96
Dionysius of Alexandria, 113
Dionysius of Corinth, 143-44
Dionysius the Areopagite (*See*, Psuedo-Dionysius)
Dioscorus of Alexandria, 191-94, 214
Dobrava, Queen, 342
Dokuz, 459-60
Dominic, 414-15
Domitian, Emperor, 35, 44, 61, 77
Donatus of Carthage, 168-71
Duns Scotus, 433-34
Eckhart, Meister, 479
Edward I, King, 463, 477
Edwin of Northumbria, 328
El Cid, 399-400
Elipand of Toledo, 340
Ephraem of Syria, 126, 197-98
Eric the Victorious, 374
Ethelbert, King, 327-28
Ethelburga, 328
Ethelreda, Queen, 347
Eugene IV, Pope, 484-87
Eugenius III, Pope, 401
Eudoxia, Empress, 190

Eusebius (historian), 43, 60, 67, 78-79, 133, 162
Eusebius of Nicomedia, 175-77, 179, 220-21
Eustochium, 228-30
Eutyches, 192, 241
Eve, 116
Ezana, 217-18
Fausta, 165
Felicitas, 83, 110
Felix of Urgel, 303, 340
Ferdinand III, King, 408
Flaccilla, 183
Flavia Domitilla, 35, 77
Flavian of Constantinople, 192
Flavius Josephus, 11, 14
Flora of Cordoba, 303
Francis of Assisi, 416-17, 433
Frederick Barbarossa, 403
Frederick II, King, 410
Frumentius of Axum, 209, 217-18
Galerius, Emperor, 110-11
Gallienus, Emperor, 110-11
Gamaliel II, Rabbi, 77
Genghis Khan, 384-85, 453-54
Gennadius, 504
George, King (of Nubia), 293-94
George, King (of Ongut), 466
Gerberga, 343
Ghazan, Ilkhan, 493
God: character of, 186-87; and Christ, 120-26, 134; Gnostic views of, 116-17; Holy Spirit as, 186-87; household of, 148-49; Jewish conceptions of, 131-33; love of, 39; name of, 42, 88; as Trinity, 135-36, 173-83
Gregory II, Patriarch, 444-45
Gregory II, Pope, 344-45
Gregory VII, Pope, 389-90, 395
Gregory VIII, Pope, 403
Gregory IX, Catholicoi, 493
Gregory X, Pope, 443
Gregory XI, Pope, 482, 487-88
Gregory of Nazianzus, 185, 186, 280
Gregory of Nyssa, 185-87
Gregory of Palamas, 498-99
Gregory the Great, Pope, 324-30, 355
Gregory the Illuminator, 113
Gregory the Wonderworker, 147
Gudnaphar, King, 93-94
Güyük, 455
Guzman, Dominic (See, Dominic)

Haakon, Prince, 374
Habsa, 262-63
Hadrian, Pope, 361-62
Hadrian II, Pope, 369
Harald Bluetooth, 374
Harald Klak, 373-74
Harun al-Rashid, 337
Hayyan, 262-64
Hegesippus, 106
Helena, 163, 183
Héloïse, 427-28
Henry III, King, 388-89
Henry IV, King, 389-90
Heraclius, Emperor, 357-58
Hermas, 78
Herod the Great, 10, 12-13, 22-23, 420
Het'um I, 452, 455-56
Hiba of Edessa, 191-94, 200-201, 247
Hildebrand (See, Gregory VII)
Hildegard of Bingen, 436-39
Hillel, 13, 16
Hippolytus of Rome, 115, 138, 141-42, 150
Honorius I, Pope, 358
Honorius III, Pope, 416
Hosius of Cordova, 164, 220-21
Hovsep, Patriarch, 207
Hülagü, 453, 456, 459-60
Humbert, Cardinal, 389, 391-93, 395
Huss, John, 489-90
Hypatia, 214
Hystaspes of Edessa, 125
Ialdobaoth (deity), 116
Ibas (See, Hiba)
Ibn Rushd (See, Averroës)
Ibn Sina (See, Avicenna)
Ignatius of Antioch, 41, 43, 61-63, 66, 72, 78, 145, 150
Igor, King, 376
'Imad ad-Din Zengi, 401
Innocent III, Pope, 404, 413, 415, 421, 441
Innocent IV Pope, 452, 454-55
Irenaeus of Lyon, 54, 67, 72, 74, 79, 80, 82, 88, 90, 92-93, 117-18, 121-22
Irene, Empress, 336-37, 361-62
Isaac, co-Emperor, 404-5
Isaac (ambassador), 337
Isaac of Ninevah, 284
Isaac of Seleucia-Ctesiphon, 199
Ishmael, 261, 264
Ishoyahb III, Patriarch, 308
Isidore, 123
Isidore, Metropolitan, 485, 502

Isidore of Seville, 300-301
Isis (deity), 117, 250
I-ssu, 320
Jacob, Negus, 486
Jacob Baradeus, 246-50
James, Apostle, 14, 25, 28, 40, 50-53, 88, 304
James the Just, 62
Jerome, 227-30
Jerome of Prague, 490
Jesus Christ: controversies over nature of, 72, 117, 121-26, 132-34, 156-58, 173-94, 214-15; early views of, 42-43, 55, 63-64; "law of," 39; in Trinity, 135, 173-89
Jesus of Nazareth: baptism of, 133; bodily existence of, 34, 117; celebration of birth of, 164; external appearance of, 190; family of, 22-23; and Gentiles, 38; as human being, 43, 63, 121, 132-34; Logos incarnate in, 55, 63, 120-26; as Messiah, 1, 132; ministry to women, 23, 36; as powerless, 48; in Qur'an, 266; and resistance movements, 15-16; resurrection of, 24-25, 53; risen, appearances as, 27; and Sadducees, 12-13; as Saxon warrior, 341; secret teachings of, 53, 87-88; sin of, 188-89; suffering in the flesh, 72
Joachim, 52
Joachim of Fiore, 419-20
Joan of Arc, 477-78
John, Apostle, 25, 28, 40, 41, 52, 66-67, 71, 88
John, Patriarch of Alexandria, 486
John IV, Pope, 358
John VIII, Emperor, 485
John VIII, Pope, 368
John XXIII, Pope, 483, 489
John Chrysostom, 189-90
John Hyrcanus, King, 12
John of Antioch, 191
John of Damascus, 280-81, 363-64
John of Ephesus, 250
John of Monte Corvino, 466-67, 481, 494-95
John of Patmos, 145-46
John of Plano Carpini, 452, 455-56, 500
John of Tella, 241
John the Baptist, 14, 23, 86
Jonas, Metropolitan, 502
Joseph, 22, 52

Joseph II, Patriarch, 485
Judas, 24, 50
Julian, Emperor, 181-82, 197, 206
Julian (missionary), 250
Julian of Halicarnassus, 241
Julian of Norwich, 479
Justin, Emperor, 241
Justin Martyr, 55, 58, 77-78, 80, 84, 115, 120-21, 144
Justinian, Emperor, 241-48, 324, 355
Kali (deity), 94
Kao-Tsung, Emperor, 319
Khusru I, Shah, 202, 271
Khusru II, Shah, 271-72
Kitbuka, General, 459-60
Kotai, 460
Kublai Khan (Khubilai), 385, 453, 456, 460, 461, 464-67, 481
Kumarajiva, 311
Kuo Tzu-I, Duke, 319-20
Kwan Yin (deity), 317-18
Kyrakos of Virap, Catholicoi, 493
Lalibela, King, 473-74
Lambert of Bègue, 421
Lao Tzu, 8
Lascaris, Theodore, 442, 445
Lazar, Tsar, 500
Leo, Emperor, 360-61
Leo of Rome (Pope), 192
Leo II, Pope, 336
Leo III, Pope, 340
Leo IX, Pope, 388-92, 395
Licinius, Emperor, 162, 175-76
Liu Bang, 4
Li Yüan, 314-15
Llull, Ramon, 418
Lo-han, 319
Lombard, Peter, 420, 428-30, 435
Longinus of Nubia, 250-51
Louis, co-Emperor, 336, 373-74
Louis, King, 367, 456
Louis VII, King, 401-2
Lucian of Antioch, 175
Luke, Apostle, 22-23, 51-52
Lydia, 23
Macarius the Great, 213
Macrina, 185-87
Mahdi, Caliph, 285-87
Mahmud, Ilkhan, 460
Maimonides, Moses, 409
Majorinus of Carthage, 168
Mani, 125-28, 197-98

Mar Aba, Patriarch, 202
Marcella, 227-28
Marcian, Emperor, 192
Marcion, 72, 80-82, 116, 131, 144
Marcus Aurelius, Emperor, 55, 82, 133
Marianos, Bishop, 295
Mariya, 269
Mark, Apostle, 41, 51, 87-88, 290
Martha, 48
Martha (martyr), 196
Martin I, Pope, 358
Martin V, Pope, 483-84
Martin of Tours, 225-27
Marutha, 199
Marutha of Persia, 279
Mary: devotion to, 480; intercession of, 349-50; and Logos, 133, 135; as Mother of Jesus, 22-23, 43, 48, 190-91, 193; parents of, 52; in Qur'an, 266; and the Spirit, 197-98
Mary, mother of John Mark, 23
Mary Magdalene, 23, 48, 88, 197-98
Mashtots, 206
Matthew, Apostle, 22, 41, 43, 51-52, 54, 88, 216
Maurice, Emperor, 271-72
Maximian Emperor, 160-61
Maximilla, 145-46
Maximus of Tyre, 47
Maximus the Confessor, 359-60
Mehmet II, Sultan, 503
Melania the Younger, 230-31
Melitius of Lycopolis, 173-74
Melito of Sardis, 130, 134-36
Menelik, King, 474
Methodius, 367-68
Michael, Emperor, 368
Michael III, Emperor, 369-70
Michael Cerularius, Patriarch, 391-92
Michael of Chernigov, 500
Michael Palaeologus, Emperor, 442-44
Mieszko, King, 342
Miltiades of Rome, 168-69
Möngke, 453, 458
Montanus, 145-46
Moses, 10, 11, 12, 13, 58
Moses ben Maimon (See, Maimonides)
Muhammad, Prophet, 257, 260, 264-69, 286
Narsai, 201
Nebo (deity), 59
Nero, Emperor, 44, 61, 77, 420

Nerses, Patriarch, 206
Nerses IV, Catholicus, 451-52
Nestorius of Constantinople, 157-58, 190-91, 193-95, 253, 282
Nicholas I, Pope, 350-53, 368-70
Nicholas II, Pope, 389
Nicholas IV, Pope, 463
Nicodemus, 13
Noah, 10
Noetus, 134
Novatian, 139
Nur ad-Din, 401-3
Odoacer, King, 224
Olaf Haraldsson, King, 374
Olaf Tryggvason, King, 374, 380
Oleg, 376
Olga, Queen, 376-77
Oljeitu, Ilkhan, 493
Onesimus, 34
Origen of Alexandria: in Alexandrian school, 89-90, 188; and Arian controversy, 174; on Celsus, 102; Jerome and, 229-30; orthodoxy of, debated, 107-8; persecution of, 110; as Platonist, 124-25; theology of, as foundational, 108-9; on universalism, 246-47
Otto I, King, 342, 374
Pachomius, 158, 210, 212-14
Palladius, 236
Palut of Edessa, 60
Pantaenus, 89-90, 94-95, 188
Papias of Hierapolis, 54, 67
Patrick, 236-37, 330
Paul, Apostle: on circumcision, 20; conversion of, 26-27, 57; and Corinthians, 29-30, 33; as craftsman, 5-6; execution of, 32, 41, 77; and Galatians, 66; and Gentiles, 38-40; and Gospel of Luke, 51; on marriage, 36; and Peter, 28; as Pharisee, 12-13; as pillar of church, 40, 74; and Romans, 30, 32, 44, 75; and slavery, 34-35; and Thecla, 48; on women, 37, 48
Paul of Samosata, 132-35, 174, 188, 189
Paula, 228-30
Paulinus, 328
Pelagius II, Pope, 326
Perpetua, 83, 109-10, 145, 146
Peter, Apostle: and Asia Minor, 66; and Cornelius, 38; execution of, 41, 77; Gnostics and, 88; and Paul, 28; as pillar of church, 40, 74, 139-40; primacy among apostles, 61; on Spirit, 2; suc-

cession from, 78-79, 391; and Temple, 25
Peter (monk), 486
Peter of Alexandria, 173-74
Peter the Hermit, 397
Petrarch (Francesco Petrarcha), 479
Philemon, 34
Philip, Apostle, 66-67
Philip, King, 403
Philip IV, King, 462, 477, 480-81
Philo Judeus, 18, 19, 52, 87
Phoebe, 23
Photius, Patriarch, 368, 370, 372
Pinytus of Gnossus, 143
Pippin the Short, 334
Plato, 18, 20, 58, 122-25, 131, 409, 434
Pliny the Younger, 69-70
Plotinus, 124
Polo, Marco, 465-66
Polycarp of Smyrna, 43, 67, 69-71, 79
Pompey, 18
Ponticus, 82
Pontius Pilate, 1, 24
Prajna, 320
Praxeas, 134-35
Priscilla (Prisca), 23, 30, 145-46
Priscillian, 226-27
Proterius of Alexandria, 215
Psuedo-Dionysius, 247-48
Ptolemy II, 17
Pulcheria, Empress, 190-92
Quintilla, 146
Rabbula of Edessa, 200
Radegund, Abbess, 238-39
Rahab, 23
Ratislav, King, 367
Rawh al-Quarashi, 280
Raymond of Toulouse, 414
Reccared, King, 299
Redwald, King, 328
Richard the Lion-Hearted, 403
Roderick, King, 302
Romanus IV Diogenes, Emperor, 393
Ruhm, 263
Ruth, 23
Ryurik, King, 376
Sabellius, 134-36
Sahak, Patriarch, 206-7
Salah ad-Din (Saladin), 402-3, 420, 447, 470, 473
Salome, 52, 88
Sarah, 10

Sartach, 457-58
Saturn (deity), 55
Saul of Tarsus (See, Paul)
Sauma, Rabban, 461-64
Sava, Prince, 445-46
Septimus Severus, Emperor, 83, 90, 109-11
Serapion of Antioch, 60
Sergius, Patriarch, 357-58
Seth, 116
Severus of Antioch, 241
Shajar ad-Durr, 470
Shammai, 13
Shapur I, Emperor, 110, 112
Shapur II, Emperor, 112, 195-97
Shenoute of Atripe, 213
Sigismund, Emperor, 483-84, 489-90
Simeon, St., 366
Simeon bar Kochba, 15, 129
Simeon the Stylite, 205-6
Simon Magus, 88, 115
Simon of Cyrene, 76
Sixtus II of Rome, 110
Socrates, 120
Solomon, 10
Sophia (demiurge), 116
Sophronius, 358
Sorghagtani, 453
Sozomen, 195-96
Stephen, 25
Stephen of Rome, 139-40
Sun, Invincible (deity), 162, 164
Svyatoslav, King, 376-77
T'ai-tsung, Emperor, 315, 317, 319
Tamar, 23
Tamar, Queen, 447
Tamerlane (See, Timur Link)
Tangri (deity), 453-54
Tanit (deity), 55
Tarasios, Patriarch, 340, 362
Tariq, General, 299, 302
Tatian, 58, 62, 80, 93, 143-44, 341
Teacher of Righteousness, the, 14
Temüjin (See, Genghis Khan)
Tertullian of Carthage, 55, 80, 83-84, 90, 105, 107, 134-35, 141, 146, 176
Thaddeus (See, Addai)
Thecla, 48
Theodora, Empress, 241-48, 362-63
Theodore of Mopsuestia, 134, 188-89, 194, 200, 201, 206, 247, 253, 282
Theodore of Philae, 250

Theodore of Tarsus, 331-32
Theodoret of Cyrrhus, 191-94, 247, 282
Theodoric, 224
Theodosius, Emperor, 182-83, 185, 187, 225
Theodosius, Patriarch, 246, 250
Theodosius II, Emperor, 190-92
Theodulf of Spain, 338, 340
Theophilus (missionary), 203-4
Theophilus of Antioch, 64, 65, 132, 135-36, 188
Thomas, Apostle, 41, 93-95, 113-14, 308, 310, 466
Thomas of Cana, 203-4
Thorgeir of Ljósvatn, 380
Timothy, 66
Timothy I, Patriarch, 284-88, 307-10, 313, 337
Timothy of Aelurus, 215
Timur Link (Timurlane), 386, 494-95, 500, 503
Tiridates III, King, 113
Titus, 66
Titus, Emperor, 50
Tobias, 60
Toros, II, King, 451
Trajan, Emperor, 69-70
Trismegistus (deity), 91
Ulfilas, 179-80, 324
'Umar, Caliph, 269-70, 272-74
Urban II, Pope, 383, 387-88, 390, 393-94, 399, 405
Urban VI, Pope, 482-83, 488

'Uthman, Caliph, 269-70, 273
Valens, Emperor, 181-82
Valentinian, Emperor, 182
Valentinus, 80, 88, 115-16, 123
Valerian, Emperor, 110, 112
Varahran II, Shah, 112
Venerable Bede, the, 327-32
Victor of Rome, 77, 79-80, 141
Victoria, 148-49
Vigilius, Pope, 247-48
Vitalian, Pope, 231
Vladimir, King, 377-78, 448
Waldo, 411-12
William of Ockham, 434
William of Rubruck, 457-58
Willibrord, 345
Winfrid (See, Boniface)
Wu Chou, Empress, 319
Wu Tsung, Emperor, 320-21
Wulfila (See, Ulfilas)
Wycliffe, John, 487-90
Yaballaha, Patriarch, 461-64, 493
Yanah (See, John of Damascus)
Yaroslav I, Prince, 500
Yazdegerd I, Shah, 199
Yazdegerd III, Shah, 272
Yekunno-Amlak, King, 473-74
Yeshuyab II, Catholicos, 253, 272
YHWH (deity), 80
Yolande, Queen, 410
Zeno, Emperor, 207, 215, 224
Zenobia, Queen, 132-33
Zoroaster, 8, 20, 127

Index to Subjects

Abbasid dynasty, 273, 276, 283, 287-88, 459
abuna, role of, 294, 296-97, 473-75
Acts, Book of, 2
Acts of the Abitinian Martyrs, 148-49
Acts of John, 53
Acts of Paul, 53
Acts of Peter, 53
Acts of the Martyrs, 112
Acts of Thecla, 48
Acts of Thomas, 53, 60, 93-95, 144
Adelskirche system, 333
adoptionism, 303
Against Celsus (Origen), 102
Albigenses, 412-14
Alexandrian patriarch (pope), 199, 294, 296, 471-75
Alexandrian school, 156, 173-79, 187-91, 214
Almoravids, 399-400
anchorites, 210
Angles, 223, 327-2-39
Antiochene school, 64-65, 132-36, 156, 174-79, 187-91, 205, 214, 282
Apocalypse of John, 71
Apocalypse of Peter, 82, 89
apocalypse texts, 14-15, 44, 71, 420
Apocryphal Acts of the Apostles, 216
Apostles' Creed, 235
apostolic memory, 49-56, 66-69, 72-75, 81, 108-9
Apostolic Tradition (Hippolytus), 81
Arabic language, 261-62, 276-77, 279, 310
Aramaic language, 16-17, 22, 42, 57-58, 112, 310
Arian confession, 220-21, 299-301, 324
Arian controversy, 156, 162, 173-84
Ark of the Covenant, 474
Arles, Council of, 168-69
Armenia, Christianity in, 113, 206-8, 253, 281-82, 392, 451-52, 470-71, 485, 492-93

asceticism, 100-101, 140-44, 158-59
Asclepius, 91
Augustine, Rule of, 415
Avar kingdom, 366
Avignon, papal office at, 481-82
baptism, 61-62, 103, 105, 133, 147-48
Baqt, the, 293
Basel, Council of, 484
Basil, St., Rule of, 365
Beguines and Beghards, 421-22
Benedict, St., Rule of, 234-35, 339, 353, 401, 411
Berbers, 172, 297-98
Bible: authority of, 487-91; levels of meaning in, 124-25
bishop role, 41, 50, 61-62, 64, 67-68, 80-81, 89-90, 103-9, 148-49, 164, 168-69
Blachernae, Council of, 444-45, 449
Blemmyes, 215-16
Bogomils, 412-13
Book of the Himyarites, 262-64
Brahmins, 93-94
Brethren (*Unitas Fratrum*), 490
British Isles, Christianization of, 327-32
bubonic plague, 477
Buddhism, 4, 127, 199, 257-58, 311-22, 465, 494
Bulgarian national church, 445-47, 496
Bulgars, 259, 362
Burgundians, 223
Canaanites, 23
"Canticle of Brother Sun" (Francis), 417
Cappadocians, 184-87
cardinals, role of, 388-91, 481-85
Carolingian dynasty, 333-42, 347-48
catechetical instruction, 89-90, 235, 348-49
Cathars, 412-15
cathedral schools, 424, 428
Catholicism: abuses under, 350-51, 388; challenges to, 487-91; and Donatists, 169-72; early theologians, 118-26, 227-34; in East, 466-67, 494-96; and Gnos-

tics, 117-18; and Greek church, 158, 240-48, 383-84, 390-93, 402-5, 440-49, 484-87, 496, 503-4; as "majority party," 102-3, 221; renewal in, 406-39; sacraments defined, 139-40, 435-36, 485; spread in Western Europe, 74-76, 302-4, 323-53, 372-75, 378-80, 501-2

"catholicity," 41, 67-69, 72

catholicos, role of, 199, 253, 281, 451-52, 493

celibacy, 64, 142-43, 192, 196, 227-30

Celts, 92-93, 323-24, 330-31

Chalcedon, Council of, 158, 191-94, 201, 214, 240-48, 274

Chalcedonian compromise, 194

children's crusade, 41

China, Christianity in, 257, 313-22, 457-58, 461-67, 481, 494

Chinese language, 315-22

chivalry code, 398-99

Christendom term, 379-80

"Christian," term, 28

Christian Topography (Cosmas Indicopluestes), 204, 219, 308

Chronicle of Arbela, 103

Chronicle of Seert, 114, 262

Chronography (Bar Hebreus), 464

church: as network, 160-61; structure of, centralized, 80-85, 103-9, 176-78, 199; unity of, 120-21, 138-40

Circumcellions, 171

circumcision, 19-20, 28, 32, 38

Cistercians, 401, 411, 419

City of God (Augustine), 233-34

Clermont, Council of, 387

Codex Justinianus, 243, 248, 425

confession, mandatory, 435-36

Confessions (Augustine), 232, 234

confirmation, 235, 349

Confucianism, 4, 315, 318, 320-21, 494

Constance, Council of, 483-84, 489

Constantinople: building of, 162-63, 355; fall of, 386, 486, 499-500, 503-4; crusades and, 400-405, 440-42, 445; Latin rule of, 405, 408

Constantinople, Council of, 187, 225

Coptic church, 218, 274, 276, 289-93, 470-71, 485

Coptic language, 213, 215, 292-94

courts, ecclesiastical, 414, 481

Covenant of 'Umar, 283

Crusades, 383, 387, 393-405, 410, 413, 440-42, 445, 490

Cur Deus Homo (Why God Became Human) (Anslem), 426

Curia role, 406-7, 415, 481-82

Cynics, 80

deacon role, 25, 50, 62, 80-81, 103

deaconess role, 62, 103, 349

"Decree for Armenians," 485-86

"Decree of Union," 485-86, 490, 502-3

Defense of Holy Images (John of Damascus), 363-64

"Definition of Chalcedon," 193

devshirme system, 500

dialectics, 424, 427-28, 430-31

Dialogue with Trypho (Justin Martyr), 77-78, 120

diaspora, 16-22

Diatessaron (Tatian), 58, 141, 341

Didache (Teachings) of the Twelve Apostles, 57, 61-63, 145

Didascalia Apostolorum, 57, 62-63, 144

Discourses on Monotheism, 317-18

diversity in early Christian movement, 41-56

Docetism, 43, 72, 123-24

Dominicans, 384, 407, 414-15, 421-22, 452, 486, 494-96

Donation of Constantine, The, 350-51

Donatists, 156, 162-72, 181

Dvin, Synod of, 207

Dyadeshu, Synod of, 199

Dyophysite position, 194

East Roman Empire (Byzantine Empire; Byzantium): crusades and, 400-5, 440-42, 445; fall of, 386, 486, 499-500, 503-4; decline of, 384, 393-94, 440-52; and Islam, 355-57, 360-61, 366, 370-71; monothelites in, 357-60; and Nicaea, 175-79; rise of, 160-65, 182-83, 190-94, 230-48, 354-55; and Russia, 375-77, 502

East Syrian churches, 156, 158, 199-203, 240-41, 262, 274, 282-87, 305-22, 457-58, 465-66, 493-95

Easter, dating of, 79-80, 134, 331

Eastern Orthodox (Greek) church: and Catholic church, 158, 383-84, 390-93, 402-5, 440-49, 484-87, 496, 503-4; and Chalcedon, 158, 190-94, 240-48; ecumenical councils of, 187, 355-56, 359-63, 498; ecumenical patriarch role, 187, 252, 355, 383-84, 391, 502, 504; emergence of, 158, 187, 240-48; hesychast controversy in, 498-99; and Islam, 355-57, 360-61, 366, 370-71; monothelites

in, 357-60; and Nicaea, 175-79; and Russia, 502
Ebionites, 43, 130
Ecclesiastical History (Eusebius), 43
Ecclesiastical History of the English Nation (Bede), 327-32
ecumenical councils, 187, 355-56, 359-63, 498
ecumenical patriarch, role of, 215, 252, 355, 383-84, 391, 502, 504
Edessa, school of, 199-203
Edict of Milan, 162
Egypt, Christianity in, 209-14, 289-93, 470-72
Egyptian language, 91, 103
ekklesia, 66-67
"elect," the, 488-89
Elkesaites, 126-27, 130-31
Elvira, Council of, 231
Encratites, 62-63, 143-44
English language, 488
Ephesus, Council of, 191, 200, 207, 215
Epistle of Barnabas, 87
Essenes, 14-15, 25
Ethiopia, Christianity in, 92-93, 215-19, 295-97, 472-75, 504
Ethiopian Orthodox Church, 218
Etymologies (Isidore of Seville), 300-301
eucharist, 28-29, 105-6, 147-48, 180, 485
evangelizing, 343-53, 407
excommunication, 68, 215, 392-93
Exodus, the, 10
Fatamid Muslims, 291-92, 394, 470-71
Fate, 125-26
Ferrarra-Florence, Council of, 484-87, 503
feudal system, 341-42, 351
Fifth Ecumenical Council, 247-48
filioque, 299-300, 339-40, 369-71, 391, 444-45, 485
First Apology (Justin Martyr), 78, 120
Florence, Council of, 385
Formula of Reunion, 191
Fount of Knowledge (John of Damascus), 280-81
Four Books of Sentences (Lombard), 428
Fourth Lateran Council, 407, 415, 420, 435-36
friars, mendicant, 436-37, 495-96
Franciscans, 384, 407, 416-22, 433, 452, 454-58, 474, 481
Franks, 237-39, 258-59, 289, 299, 331-41, 345-46, 366-69, 372-74
Galilee, 22-25

Ge'ez language, 218, 295
General Directives (Charlemagne), 338-39
Georgia, church in, 447
Germans, 92-93, 156, 258, 323-27, 332-34
Ghana, Kingdom of, 295-96, 298
Ghassanids, 262
Glagolitic script, 368
God-fearers, 27, 32
Golden Horde, 455, 500-503
Gnosticism, 80-82, 87-90, 100, 115-28, 213-14, 412-13
Gospel of Egyptians, 51, 87
Gospel of Hebrews, 51, 87
Gospel of John, 52, 63
Gospel of Luke, 51-52
Gospel of Mark, 51, 87-88
Gospel of Mary, 51-53
Gospel of Mary Magdalene, 53
Gospel of Matthew, 43, 51-52
Gospel of Peter, 53, 61
Gospel of Psuedo-Matthew, 266
Gospel of Thomas, 51-53, 57, 62, 117
gospels, canonical vs. apocryphal, 40-41, 47-54, 80-81, 87-88
Goths, 179-80, 182 (*See also,* Ostrogoths; Visigoths)
grace, 39, 232-33, 432, 435
"Great Church," creation of, 101-14
Greek language, 8, 9, 16-18, 54, 59, 76-77, 103, 294
Gregorian reforms, 395, 411
Guide for the Perplexed (Maimonides), 409
gunpowder, 478, 503
Hagia Sophia cathedral, 162, 247, 362-63, 392, 504
Han dynasty, 4
Hasmonean dynasty, 11-12, 18
Hebrew language, 16
Heiland, or, The Saxon Gospel, 341
Hellenistic culture, 17-20, 25, 59, 89-90, 115-26
Henoticon, the, 207, 215, 240-41
hesychast controversy, 498-99
Himyarite Kingdom, 261-64, 295
History of the Patriarchs, 473
Holy Spirit, 186-87, 197-98
homoousios, 176-78, 181, 183
Hospitaller Knights of St. John, 398
house churches, 29, 32, 54-55, 66-67, 77-78, 99
humanists, 479
Hundred Year's War, 477-78
Huns, 222-23, 253, 312

hypostatic union, 191, 194
I Clement, 77
iconoclasts, 360-64
Idumeans, 12
incarnation, 184, 363-64, 417
India, Christianity in, 93-95, 113-14, 307-11, 322, 495-96
indulgences, 396, 413-14, 489
Infancy Gospel of James, 218
Infancy Gospel of Thomas, 52-53, 266
Inquisition, 412-15
investiture controversy, 387-90
Irish: Christianization of, 330-32; as missionaries, 344; and monasticism, 236-37
Isaac, Synod of, 199
Islam: Chinese and, 319-20; Christians under, 260-64, 268-303, 312, 393-94, 450-51, 496, 499-500; and East Roman Empire, 355-57, 360-61, 366, 370-71; and Judaism, 261-63, 268, 270; and Mongols, 455-64, 493-94, 504
Israel, 9-17
Jacobite churches, 204-6, 249-50, 262, 274, 279, 450-51, 463-64
janissaries, 500, 503
Jesus-Messiah Sutra, 317-18
Judaism: conversion to, 182-83, 190; in diaspora, 16-22; early Christians and, 33-34, 63-65, 75, 77, 87, 119-20, 129-36; and Islam, 261-63, 268, 270; in Israel, 10-17; Rabbinic movement in, 100; in Roman world, 129-36
Ka'bah, 263-64
Kebra Nagast (Book of Kings), 474
Kerait Turks, 450-53
Kiev, metropolitan of, 501-2
Kipchak Turks, 470-71
Krewo, Union of, 502
Kulikovo, battle of, 501
last supper, 24, 105
Latin language, 76-77, 81-82, 103, 223, 228-30, 323, 330-31, 337-38, 400
leadership in early church, 61-63, 66-69, 80-81
Life of Amand (Baudemond), 344-45
Life of Anthony (Athanasius), 210, 212, 227
Lithuania, Christianity in, 501-2
Logos, 18, 55, 63, 120-26, 132-33, 175-76, 184, 186, 188, 193
Lollards, 488-89
Lombards, 244, 324, 334
Lord, term, 42-45

Lyons, Council of, 443-44, 492
Maccabean revolt, 11
Mameluke dynasty, 385, 460, 470-75, 492-95
Manichaeism, 100, 118, 125, 221, 226, 232, 257-58, 311-12, 412-13, 466-67
maphrian, role of, 279
Mar Mattai community, 197
Marcionites, 80-82
Maronites, 358, 451
martyrdom, 69-73, 82-85, 109-11, 119, 137-40, 167-72, 196
melet system, 199, 275-76, 283
Melitians, 173, 175, 177
Melkite churches, 193, 215, 274
Merovingian dynasty, 238, 332-34, 347-48
Messalians, 283
Messiah, 33, 42
messianic movements, 16-17
metropolitan, role of, 307
Middle-Platonism, 90
missionary identity, 92-96
Monastery of the Caves, 377-78, 448
monasticism: in China, 317-19, 321; East Syrian, 283; in Egypt, 209-14; in Ethiopia, 218-19, 297, 473-74; in Greek church, 364-66, 499; in Ireland, 236-37; Jacobite, 279; in Palestine, 230-31, 339; in Persia, 201-2; in Russia, 377-78; in Western Europe, 339, 343-53, 411-24; women in, 158-59
Mongols, 311-14, 384-86, 447, 450-51, 454-67, 493-94, 500-504
monogamy, 36, 148, 333, 338-39
Monophysites (*See,* New Chalcedonians)
monotheism, 19-20, 100, 129-36, 265-66
monothelite controversy, 357-60
Montanists (*See,* New Prophecy movement)
Mt. Athos monastery, 366, 498
Mozarabic Christians, 302-4, 340
Muratorian Canon, 81-82
Mystagogy of the Holy Spirit (Photius), 370
mystery religions, 87-88, 100
Nabateans, 27-28, 215-16
Nag Hammadi texts, 52, 118, 213-14
Nazarenes, 13, 15
neo-Platonism, 189, 248
Nestorians (*See,* East Syrian churches)
New Chalcedonians, 194, 215, 392
New Prophecy movement, 107, 141, 144-47
New Testament, 81-82, 84, 119-20
Nicaea, Council of, 79, 114, 156, 173-79, 182-83, 344

Nicaea, Kingdom of, 405, 441-42
Nicene Creed, 173, 176-77, 182-83, 192, 235, 299-301, 339-40, 443
Nine Saints, the, 218-19
Nisibis, school of, 201
Nominalism, 434-35
non-Chalcedonian churches, 207-8, 214-15, 218-19, 240-48, 250-51, 281, 296-97, 357-60
Normans, 391, 393
Novatianists, 139-40
Nubia, Christianity in, 246, 250-51, 293-94, 471-72
Ockham's Razor, 434
Odes of Solomon, 57, 63-64
On Ascetical Life (Isaac), 284
On First Principles (Origen), 108, 229-30
On the Resurrection (Gregory), 187
On the Unity of the Church (Cyprian), 140, 221-22
Oration Addressed to the Greeks (Tatian), 58
original sin, 232-33
Osrhoene kingdom, 59
Ostrogoths, 224, 244
Ottoman Turks, 386, 484, 486, 496-500
Pachomius, Rule of, 210, 212-14, 218-20, 229
Pahlavi language, 112-13
papacy: authority of, 324-27, 331-32, 350-53, 355-60; origin in Rome, 74-75, 78-82, 103, 149, 187, 220-23; power opposed, 488-91; primacy of, 389-93, 485, 503; schism in, 385, 482-83, 490; succession from Peter, 74-75, 391
papal states, 326, 481-82
Parthian dynasty, 3, 16-17, 44, 61, 137
Passover, 21, 79
patriarch, role of, 276, 292-93
patriarchal cultures, 48, 148-49
Patripassianism, 134
Paulicians, 364
Pelagianism, 232-33
penance system, 349
Pentecost, 2, 39
peregrini, 343-45
persecution: of Christians, 1, 25-26, 77, 82-85, 109-12, 114, 118-19, 137-40, 167-72, 302-3; of Jews, 28, 77, 182-83, 301
Persia: and East Asian Christians, 305-22, 459-61; as empire, 3, 16-17, 61, 109, 111-14, 137; Latin church in, 494; and Mongols, 459-61, 493-94; national church in, 195-203, 282-83

Peshitta, 54, 57-58
Pharisees, 12-15, 51, 63
Philistine cities, 10
Pisa, Council of, 483
Platonists, 115-26, 428
Pneumatomachians, 186
Poland, Christianization of, 342, 502
Poor in Spirit, 411, 415
Poor Ladies of Assisi, 417-18
poverty, voluntary, 407, 411, 413, 415-19, 488
presbyter, role of, 50, 80-81, 90, 103, 148
printing press, 478
prophecy, 38, 71, 144-47, 419-21
Proslogion (Discourse) (Anselm), 426
Proto-Gospel of James, 51-53
Psuedo-Isidorian Decretals, 351
Ptolemies, 17
Punic language, 55, 82, 84, 170
Q-hypothesis, 51-52
Qumran scrolls, 14
Qur'an, 260, 261, 263-69, 274, 277-78, 287-88, 371
Qurayzah, 261, 268
Ravenna, court at, 224, 244, 334
relics, holy, 329-30, 350, 395
Rennaissance, 479
Revelation of John, 44, 52, 74
Rig Veda, 20
Roman Empire, West: Christianization of, 99, 155-56, 160-72, 180-83, 195, 220-24, 239; decline of, 180, 182, 222-24, 244, 300, 323-24; and early movement, 22, 30-32, 34-36, 41, 43-44, 55, 61, 69-85; and Far East, 5, 8, 94-95; and Israel, 9-11, 15, 18-19; Judaism in, 129-36; persecution in, 109-11, 118-19, 137-40, 161; split from Eastern Empire, 110-11, 160-65, 182, 187, 220-24, 355
Rome, rise of church in, 74-82, 220-24
Rum, Sultanate of, 393-94
Russia, Christianity in, 375-77, 447-49, 500-503
sacraments, defined, 103, 139-40, 435-36, 485
Sadducees, 12-13
St. James, liturgy of, 284
St. Peter's Church, Rome, 340, 345, 369
St. Simeon, 366
saints, intercession of, 349-50
salvation, early interpretations of, 54-56, 122, 124
Sanhedrin, 12

Sardica, Council of, 177-78, 218-19
Sassanid dynasty, 59, 111-13, 276
Saxons, 334-35, 341-42, 374
Scandanavia, Christianity in, 259, 372-75, 378-80
schism: between Eastern and Western churches, 390-93; in papacy, 385, 482-83, 490
Scholasticism, 423-35
Scivias Domini (Hildegard), 437
Second Apology (Justin Martyr), 120
Seleucids, 17, 18, 59
Seljuk Turks, 287-88, 383, 393-94, 450-51
Semitic culture, 63-64, 84
Septuagint, 17
Serbian national church, 445-46
Seventh Ecumenical Council, 361-63
Shari'ah, Islamic law, 267-68
Shauvot festival, 2, 21
Sic et Non (Yes and No) (Abelard), 427
Silk Road, 5, 18, 58, 257-58, 311-14, 465
signs and wonders, 37-38, 147, 344, 350
simony, 351, 388
Sis, Council of, 492-93
Sixth Ecumenical Council, 359-60
slavery, 34-35, 76, 141, 149-51, 466, 470, 476
Slavs, 245, 259, 366-69, 375-78, 401-2, 410
Sogdian script, 452
Solomonic Revival, 385, 472, 474-75
Spain: under Islam, 302-4; reconquest of, 383-84, 399-400, 408-9; Visigoths in, 223, 299-302
speaking in tongues, 38, 146-47
Spiritual Franciscans, 420-21
Stoics, 20, 42, 94
Sufis, 283
Summa Theologiae (Aquinas), 430-32
Syriac language, 57-58, 103, 112-13, 199-203, 277-78, 305, 307, 310
table fellowship, 13, 24, 28-29, 105
Talmud, 13
T'ang dynasty, 314-22, 465-66
Templars, 398
Temple of Jerusalem: destruction of, 11, 13-14; Jesus in, 24
Testament of Our Lord, 151
Tetragrammaton, 42
third orders, 421-22

Three Chapters (Justinian), 247
Toledo, councils of, 299-301, 340
Tome (Leo), 207, 215, 240-41
Tomus (Gregory II), 444-45
Torah, 10, 11, 16, 24, 129-31, 285-86
Tours, Battle of, 334
traditores, 167-71
transmigration of the soul, 125
transubstantiation, 436
Trinity, Holy: controversies over definition of, 134-36, 173-94, 197-98, 201, 449; early views of, 126-34; Islamic view of, 266, 270, 274, 280-82
true cross, 163, 357
True Doctrine (Celsus), 102
Uighurs, 320, 450, 452-53, 461
Umayyad dynasty, 273, 276, 278-79, 283, 290-91, 302
Unam Sanctam (Boniface), 480-81
universities, 409, 424-31, 462-63, 483
Upanishads, 8, 20
Vandals, 171, 180, 223, 234-35, 244
Vedanta, 20
Venetians, 404-5, 408-9, 476, 478-79, 496, 503
Vikings, 372-73, 376, 379-80
Visigoths, 182-8, 222-23, 233, 298-302, 324
Vulgate, Latin, 228-29, 488
Waldensians, 411-12, 414-15
Week of Enoch, 218
Wends, 401-2
West Syrian churches (*See*, Jacobite churches)
Western Europe, spread of Christianity in, 74-85, 302-4, 323-53, 372-75, 378-80, 501-2
Wisdom of Solomon, 82
witchcraft, 343
women: early Christian, 26, 48-49; Islam and, 267-68; leadership by, 25-26, 53, 150-51, 190-91, 238-39; ministry of Jesus to, 23, 36; in monasticism, 142-43, 158-59, 346-48; Paul on, 37, 48; as witches, 343; writing by, 427, 436-39
Xi'an stele, 316-17, 319-21
Zagwe dynasty, 473
Zealots, 15
Zoroastrianism, 20, 22, 111-13, 125-27, 196, 199, 202, 257-58, 311